Blackstone's

Magistrates' Court Handbook 2026

Blackstone's

Magistrates' Court Handbook 2026

Bartholomew Dalton

Caroline Liggins

OXFORD
UNIVERSITY PRESS

OXFORD
UNIVERSITY PRESS

Great Clarendon Street, Oxford, OX2 6DP,
United Kingdom

Oxford University Press is a department of the University of Oxford.
It furthers the University's objective of excellence in research, scholarship,
and education by publishing worldwide. Oxford is a registered trade mark of
Oxford University Press in the UK and in certain other countries.

Fifth Edition published in 2017
Sixth Edition published in 2018
Seventh Edition published in 2019
Eigth Edition published in 2021
Ninth Edition published in 2023
Tenth Edition published in 2024
Eleventh Edition published in 2026

Published in the United States of America by Oxford University Press
198 Madison Avenue, New York, NY 10016, United States of America

British Library Cataloguing in Publication Data
Data available

Library of Congress Control Number is on file at the Library of Congress
ISBN 978–0–19–896394–3

DOI: 10.1093/oso/9780198963943.001.0001

Printed and bound by
CPI Group (UK) Ltd., Croydon, CR0 4YY

The manufacturer's authorised representative in the EU for product safety is
Oxford University Press España S.A. of Parque Empresarial San Fernando de Henares,
Avenida de Castilla, 2 – 28830 Madrid (www.oup.es/en or product.safety@oup.com).
OUP España S.A. also acts as importer into Spain of products made by the manufacturer.

FSC
www.fsc.org
MIX
Paper | Supporting responsible forestry
FSC® C013604

Preface to the 2026 Edition

This book aims to provide ready access to the law relevant to busy criminal lawyers seeking immediate answers to the common issues that arise in the magistrates' court. We have continued to concentrate on matters that arise without warning and to omit matters that more commonly arise on notice or where there is time for preparation. Only the most common indictable-only offences are included or those likely to affect children in the magistrates' or youth court. We actively welcome and encourage feedback in relation to any areas of the book that users feel could be strengthened.

Last year, in the 2023 edition, we included the increases to magistrates' maximum sentencing powers. This change was of course reversed a mere two days after publication. We have therefore reduced the maximum sentencing powers in this edition. Time will tell whether the government can resist tinkering yet again.

The 2023 edition also introduced a major change by removing most of the extracts from the sentencing guidelines for the offences contained within the book. This was done as the digital versions of the guidelines are now the official guidelines and changes are made often and quickly. We have sought feedback in relation to this and, whilst we acknowledge there are a vocal few who would have preferred the inclusion of the guidelines, the vast majority of the feedback has been supportive of that decision. Since the manuscript for the 2023 edition was finalized, on 31 December 2022, to 31 January 2024, the Sentencing Council introduced ten new sentencing guidelines and made amendments to a further 27 guidelines. We feel this vindicates the decision made previously and have therefore maintained the same approach this year. We have included the titles of the relevant sentencing guidelines so that users can quickly find the correct, up-to-date guideline online.

This year's edition includes new offences created by, inter alia, the Public Order Act 2023 and the Online Safety Act 2023 and the case law we feel most important to busy magistrates' court lawyers.

We have attempted to state the law as at 31 January 2024, although we have shown as being in force statutory provisions which it was known, on that date, would be in force by the date of publication.

Sections *in italics* relate to matters not yet in force and for which there is no known implementation date by 31 January 2024.

Sentencing

Where there is a reference merely to a fine, it is reference to an unlimited fine. Unless otherwise stated, guidelines apply to those aged 18 and over.

Supplement to Handbook of Youths in the Criminal Courts

As the companion handbook for youths in the criminal courts is not updated annually, a supplement is provided in Appendix 4.

Bartholomew Dalton
Caroline Liggins
London

Contents

Part B Youths in the Adult Court

Part C Offences

Part D Sentencing

Appendices

Icons List

The following icons are used throughout this book:

DO Dangerous Offender

EW Either Way

Sentence

SCG SCG Sentencing Council guideline reference

SO Summary Only

SON Sexual Offence Notification: registration required under s 80 and Sch 3 Sexual Offences Act 2003. The periods for notification are set out at **D22**

Cross-reference to Blackstone's Criminal Practice

GC Grave Crimes

IO Indictable Only

Key points Key Points

Key points: General defence Key Points: General Defence

Key points: Sentencing Key Points: Sentencing

Key points on conviction Key Points on Conviction

Key points on acquittal Key Points on Acquittal

Driving Penalties

Table of Cases

United Kingdom Cases

European Union

European Court of Human Rights

Table of Practice Directions

Table of Statutes

Table of Statutory Instruments

Table of Treaties and Conventions

Abbreviations

ABH	actual bodily harm
CJA	Criminal Justice Act
CJIA	Criminal Justice and Immigration Act
CPD	Criminal Practice Direction
CPIA	Criminal Procedure and Investigations Act
CPS	Crown Prosecution Service
Crim PR	Criminal Procedure Rules
CTL	custody time limit
DCP	Director of Public Prosecutions
ECHR	European Convention on Human Rights
EU	European Union
MCA	Magistrates' Courts Act
PACE	Police and Criminal Evidence Act
PCCSA	Powers of Criminal Courts (Sentencing) Act
PCSCA	Police Crime Sentencing and Courts Act
PET	preparation for effective trial
RTA	Road Traffic Act
RTOA	Road Traffic Offenders Act
SA	Sentencing Act
YOT	Youth Offending Team
YRO	youth rehabilitation order

Part A
Procedure and Evidence

A1 **Abuse of Process**

A1.1 **Introduction**

Abuse of process is something so unfair and wrong with the prosecution that the court should not allow a prosecutor to proceed with what is, in all other respects, a regular proceeding: *Hui-chi Ming v R* [1992] 1 AC 34.

A stay on these grounds falls into two main categories:

- where a fair trial of the particular defendant is impossible (eg due to loss of evidence);
- where there is a misuse of court process (where it offends the court's sense of justice and propriety to be asked to try the accused in the circumstances of the particular case). Abuse of process remains available in principle to all human trafficking cases, regardless of whether or not they are included in schedule 4 of the Modern Slavery Act 2015 (*R v AAD and others* [2022] EWCA Crim 106 (see **A1.2.9**)).

In both cases the magistrates' court has jurisdiction to determine the issue, subject to the very limited exception envisaged in *R v Horseferry Road Magistrates Court Ex p. Bennett (No. 1)* [1994] 1 AC 42, HL. That exception, in relation to which the issue of abuse can be determined solely by the High Court, would seem to be limited to executive misconduct in relation to extradition (*Mansfield v DPP* [2021] EWHC 2938 (Admin) (see **A1.2.7**)).

A stay of proceedings based on an abuse of process will be rare and should be allowed only in exceptional circumstances (see *Attorney General's Reference No 1 of 1990* (1992) 95 Cr App R 296); and if the court process can compensate for any unfairness or wrongs, so as to allow for a fair trial, that is the way in which it should proceed.

On an application to stay for abuse of process, it is for the defendant to satisfy the court on a balance of probabilities that no fair trial is possible. The application should be decided on material adduced by the prosecution and defence, with both parties having the right (subject to usual judicial discretion) to call evidence (*R v Clerkenwell Magistrates' Court, ex p Bell* [1991] Crim LR 468).

A1.2 **Relevant grounds**

A1.2.1 ***Alternative remedy***

The exclusion of evidence under s 78 PACE 1984 to secure a fair trial is to be preferred to using the abuse jurisdiction (see **A2.2.8**). In *R v DS and TS* [2015] EWCA Crim 662 the court held that whether the breach by the Crown is of a general or specific nature the consequences should be the same, and whether the failure related to evidence (*R v Boardman*, see **A2.2.8**) or disclosure (in this case), all such breaches affect the fairness of the trial and undermine public confidence in the criminal justice system. Whether a breach is dealt

Blackstone's Magistrates' Court Handbook 2026. Bartholomew Dalton and Caroline Liggins, Oxford University Press. © Oxford University Press 2026.
DOI: 10.1093/oso/9780198963943.003.0001

with by a stay or by exclusion of evidence under s 78 PACE 1984 the same considerations apply. They include:

- the gravity of the charges;
- the denial of justice to the complainants;
- the importance of disclosure in sexual offences;
- the necessity for proper attention to be paid to disclosure;
- the nature and materiality of the failures;
- any failures by the defence;
- the waste of court resources and the effect on the court;
- the availability of other sanctions.

A1.2.2 *Missing evidence or disclosure*

The issues identified in *R v Dobson* [2001] EWCA Crim 1606 are as follows:

- What was the duty of the police?
- Did the police fail in their duty by not obtaining or retaining the appropriate material?
- If so, was there serious prejudice which rendered a fair trial impossible in the light of such failure?
- Alternatively, did the police failure result from such bad behaviour, in the sense of bad faith or serious fault, as to render it unfair that the accused should be tried at all? The requirement for bad faith was doubted in *Clay v South Cambridgeshire Justices* [2014] EWHC 321 (Admin) which held that the issue was whether or not there could be a fair trial.

There is a duty on the police to contact identified witnesses (*Morris v DPP* [2014] EWHC 105 (Admin)). There is no *general* duty on the prosecution to retain CCTV evidence that might have given insight into whether a warning was given to a detainee during a breath test procedure (*Morris v DPP* [2008] EWHC 2788 (Admin)). This decision follows the leading case of *R v Feltham Magistrates' Court and another, ex p Ebrahim* [2001] EWHC Admin 130.

That case emphasises that the early identification of the significance of the relevant material is a key factor to ensure that the prosecution are under a duty, not least under the code of practice made under the Criminal Procedure and Investigations Act 1996. The case confirms the possibility of using s 78 PACE to exclude some or all of the prosecution evidence if the failure to produce the material sought or to comply with disclosure obligations may render the trial unfair.

The duties of the prosecution are set out in the Attorney General's guidelines on the disclosure of unused material.

A1.2.3 *Failure to supply initial details of the prosecution case*

There is no jurisdiction to stay proceedings for failures in service of initial details of the prosecution case under Part 8 of the Criminal Procedure Rules; the appropriate remedy is to adjourn (*R v Leeds Youth Court, ex p P (A)* [2001]

EWHC 215 (Admin)), although repeated failure to comply with the rules may provide for a stay in truly exceptional circumstances (*R v Willesden Magistrates' Court, ex p Clemmings* [1988] 152 JPN 46). A threat to stay a prosecution if there were further disclosure breaches did not give rise to any legitimate expectation on the part of the defendant so as to require the court to carry through its threat on the next occasion (*R v Leeds Youth Court, ex p AP and others* [2001] EWHC 215 (Admin)).

A1.2.4 *Improper motive*

The fact that there was a mixed motive for launching a private prosecution will justify a stay only if the conduct of the prosecutor is truly oppressive, as it is obvious that many private prosecutions would be brought with mixed motives (*Dacre v City of Westminster Magistrates' Court* [2009] 1 Cr App R 6).

In *Asif v Dutta* [2021] EWCA Crim 1091 the court found that the private prosecution had been pursued because it was a more tactically advantageous form of litigation than civil proceeding in attempting to recover money from the defendant. The court, in finding there was an abuse of process, noted that while a dominant public interest is not required, the absence of any expression of a public interest rationale, taken together with the clear expression of an oblique motive, is telling.

In *Morjaria v Westminster Magistrates' Court* [2023] EWHC 2936 (Admin), the private prosecutor's primary motivation in issuing criminal proceedings was to use those proceedings as a threat to force the defendant to settle a civil claim. That was an improper motive for prosecution. Whilst restitution for the victim may be a proper objective of the criminal justice system, it may not be used as a means to an end. The criminal process is not to serve the private interests of any individual. The fact that there was *prima facie* evidence of fraud on the part of the defendant and others could not legitimise criminal proceedings when their purpose was to threaten.

Parallel civil proceedings do not mean that a private prosecution is improperly brought, and the fact that the police have not supported further investigation is unlikely ever to be determinative (*R (Smith-Allison) v Westminster Magistrates' Court (No. 2)* [2021] EWHC 2361 (Admin)).

A1.2.5 *Misuse of executive power*

In *Warren* [2011] UKPC 10 it was emphasised that where officers of the state act unlawfully, a balancing exercise must be carried out between the need to protect the integrity of the criminal justice process and the public interest in ensuring that those charged with grave crimes should be tried.

A1.2.6 *Delay*

In the absence of other compelling reasons, a lengthy delay, in itself, does not justify a stay of criminal proceedings (*Spiers v Ruddy* [2008] 1 AC 873, PC).

In *Ali v CPS* [2007] EWCA Crim 691, proceedings brought seven years after the incident should have been stayed, as important documentary evidence, relevant to assessing the victim's credibility, had been lost. The court emphasised that:

> this is a rare case where prejudice following from the delay was not alleviated and probably could never have been cured during the course of the trial.

In *Halahan* [2014] EWCA Crim 2079, the court held that in a case where prejudice by delay, resulting in the loss of documents, was alleged, it is necessary to show more than speculation that the document would assist the defence. It was necessary that the missing evidence represented a significant and demonstrable chance of the disclosure of strongly supportive evidence emerging on a specific issue in the case.

However, in *Brown v DPP* [2019] EWHC 798 (Admin) the court indicated that an undue delay in serving a requisition, issued within 6 months for a summary only matter, may give rise to the abuse jurisdiction. It was also said as *obiter* in *Candlish v DPP* [2022] EWHC 842 (Admin) that an egregious delay in charging low-value theft from a shop may be an abuse of process, especially if there had been any unfair manipulation of the process by the police.

A1.2.7 *Legitimate expectation*

The prosecution of a person who has received a promise, an undertaking, or a representation from the police that he will not be prosecuted is capable of being an abuse of process (*Croydon Justices, ex p Dean* [1993] QB 769). So too will be the prosecution of a person denied a caution by the failure of the police to make appropriate disclosure to enable legal advice to be given (*DPP v Ara* [2001] EWHC 493 (Admin)).

In finding an abuse of process, the court in *Mansfield v DPP* (see **A1.1**) found that the seriousness of the offence, possession of a bladed article, and the fact that the assurance was given by mistake and rectified later the same day, but crucially after the defendant had admitted the offence in interview, did not outweigh the public interest in holding a state official to their promise that the case would be dealt with by way of a caution. The defendant's age, 18, and his previous good character were also relevant factors in the appellant's favour.

Abu Hamza [2006] EWCA Crim 2918 suggests that there must be both an unequivocal representation and, as a result, an action by the defendant to their detriment. New facts coming to light may also justify further proceedings. The administration of a caution may make it an abuse for there to be a later prosecution (*Jones v Whalley* [2007] 1 AC 63) but the Crown may in appropriate cases, where there is a proper basis, change its mind as to how to proceed. Much will turn on what was said to the suspect at the time the caution was imposed and what the complainant knew and said about the caution being imposed (*R (Lowden) v Gateshead Magistrates Court* [2016] EWHC 3536 (Admin)).

The Crown is required, absent a change of circumstances, to proceed in a single prosecution with all the charges it proposes to bring arising out of the same incident (*Connelly v DPP* [1964] AC 1254; *R v Beedie* [1997] EWCA Crim 714). The abuse jurisdiction may be used to stay an appropriate case when the strict *autrefois* doctrine does not apply (*J* [2013] EWCA Crim 569).

A1.2.8 *Autrefois acquit*

This bar is confined to cases that are the same in fact and law. The rule will be construed narrowly and if this causes injustice amounting to oppression the remedy is to stay the proceedings. Although on an allegation of common assault the Crown offered no evidence, it could proceed with an allegation of occasioning ABH if the defendant had never been in peril of trial on the lesser offence (*R v JFJ* [2013] EWCA Crim 569). Where a case is dismissed for the failure of the prosecution to appear (s 15 MCA 1980) it is not an abuse to commence again as the defendant was not in jeopardy (*DPP v Jarman* [2013] EWHC 4391 (Admin)). *DPP v Bird* [2015] EWHC 4077 (Admin) confirms that the doctrine of *autrefois acquit* only applies if the defendant was put at risk of conviction and the case was heard on the merits; that is, the court could have convicted but did not do so.

A1.2.9 *Decisions to prosecute*

A decision to prosecute is susceptible to review, as an abuse of process, if it is one that no reasonable prosecutor would make, or which misapplies a policy, or is based on a policy which is unlawful (*Campaign against Anti-Semitism v DPP* [2019] EWHC 9 (Admin)).

R v AAD and others (see **A1.1**) confirms that mere disagreement with a decision to prosecute, following due regard given by the prosecution to the CPS guidance and to any conclusive-grounds decision in relation to trafficking, gives no basis whatsoever for an application for a stay. If, in exceptional cases, there has been a failure to have due regard to CPS guidance or if there has been a lack of rational basis for departure from a conclusive grounds decision then a stay application may be available.

The case of *AFU* [2023] EWCA Crim 23 A is recent overview of the relevant legal principles relating to modern slavery: decisions of the Competent Authority are not admissible at trial, but are admissible on appeal when it is contended that a person's trafficking status has been overlooked or inadequately considered (see *R v Brecani* [2021] EWCA Crim 731; [2021] 1 WLR 5851 at [40] and [41] and *AAD* at [79]–[89], [88]. The extent to which expert evidence can be of assistance when assessing an account of trafficking will likely depend on the extent to which it relies on the accuracy of an individual's untested account of events. [90] The relevant enquiry is whether, had the prosecution known the true facts, the prosecution would not have (or might well not have) been maintained in the public interest. [106] 'It is clear that the police failed to discharge their duty as first responders and that the prosecution failed to comply with the Guidance. We emphasise the following: i) There were clear indicators of trafficking from the outset, given the circumstances of the applicant's arrival as an unaccompanied Vietnamese child/very young adult, his involvement in the cultivation of cannabis and the express reference in his first prepared statement to having been exploited; ii) No proper enquiries were made upon his arrest, nor was there any referral to the National Referral Mechanism; iii) There being good reason to believe that the applicant was a victim of trafficking, there was no review on evidential grounds as to whether there was clear evidence of a credible s 45 defence; iv) There was no consideration in any event of whether or not the public interest lay in proceeding to prosecute/continuing a prosecution or not.'

R v AJW [2023] EWCA Crim 803: Abuse of process cases may succeed even where a defendant has entered a not guilty plea and given evidence in their defence at trial, if the appeal court determines that it was unfair to try them altogether.

See *Blackstone's Criminal Practice 2026* **D3.66**

A2 Adjournments

A2.1 Criminal Practice Directions

CPD 5.4 deals with trial adjournments in magistrates' courts. The directions restate procedural principles established in a long line of judgments of the senior courts and supersede those judgments. It is to these directions that magistrates' courts refer in the first instance and may be summarised:

Trial adjournment in magistrates' court

5.4.1 Parties and other participants must further the overriding objective and prepare cases so that they can proceed on the date set. Any change that may affect the listing of a case must be communicated between the parties and to the court as soon as reasonably practicable. Any communication must clearly identify the issue and any direction sought and should be referred to a legal adviser or case progression officer.

Trial adjournment

5.4.4 Section 10 of the Magistrates' Courts Act 1980 confers a discretionary power to adjourn. The starting point is that the trial should proceed. The court must not be deterred from a prompt and robust determination. As an exercise of discretion, the High Court will only interfere with a decision on adjournment if there are compelling reasons so to do.

5.4.5 A court may be justified in refusing an adjournment even if that means the prosecutor is unable to prove the prosecution case or a part of it, or that the defendant is unable to prove the prosecution case or a part of it, or that the defendant is unable to explore an issue. Even in the absence of fault on the part of either party it may not be in the interests of justice to adjourn, notwithstanding that an imperfect trial may be the result.

5.4.6 The court must ensure that any adjournment is for as short a period as possible, for example by using time vacated by another trial or by conducting the hearing at another court or court centre. A just outcome may be achieved by a short adjournment to later on the same day. The shorter the time the more favourably the court may consider an application for an adjournment, but even a short adjournment must be justified.

5.4.10 In reaching a decision whether to adjourn the court must consider the following matters:

a. That the court's duty is to deal justly with the case, which includes doing justice between the parties.
b. The need for expedition and that delay is generally inimical to the interests of justice—it has the potential to bring the criminal justice system into disrepute.
c. That proceedings in a magistrates' court should be simple and speedy.
d. That applications for adjournments must be rigorously scrutinised and the court must have cogent reasons for adjourning.
e. The need to review the history of the case.
f. The need to examine the nature of the evidence and whether memories of relevant evidence are liable to fade.
g. The interests of any co-defendant(s).
h. The interests of any witness(es) who have attended, with particular emphasis on their age and/or vulnerability.

Blackstone's Magistrates' Court Handbook 2026. Bartholomew Dalton and Caroline Liggins, Oxford University Press. © Oxford University Press 2026.
DOI: 10.1093/oso/9780198963943.003.0002

i. The interest of the defendant(s) in resolving the matter without undue delay but also the public interest in ensuring that criminal charges are adjudicated upon thoroughly, with the guilty convicted as well as the innocent acquitted.
j. The fact that the more serious the charge the greater the public interest in the trial proceeding and the greater the responsibility of the parties to have engaged in effective preparation.
k. Where a defendant asks for an adjournment whether they will be able to present the defence fully without one and the extent to which the ability to do so may be compromised by an immediate trial.
l. The court must consider the consequences of an adjournment on:
   i. the ability of witnesses and defendants accurately to recall events;
   ii. the impact of adjournment on other cases;
   iii. the length of time it may take to list the case for trial.
m. The court must also consider the nature and gravity of fault on the part of the applicant for the adjournment and who is responsible for it.

Absence of defendant (see A2.2.6)

5.4.11 Where the reason for which the adjournment is sought relates to the absence of the defendant some particular issues arise.

5.4.12 **If a defendant is aged 18 or over:**
a. the court shall proceed in the defendant's absence unless it appears to the court to be contrary to the interests of justice to do so;
b. proceeding in the absence of a defendant is the default position where the defendant is aware of the date of trial and no acceptable reason is offered for that absence;
c. the court is not obliged to investigate if no reason is offered;
d. the court will take into account all factors, including:
   i. such reasons for absence as may be offered;
   ii. the reliability of the information supplied in support of those reasons;
   iii. the date on which the reasons for absence became known to the defendant and what action the defendant thereafter took in response;
   iv. that trial in absence can and sometimes does result in acquittal;
   v. that if convicted the defendant can ask that the conviction be reopened in the interests of justice, for example if absence was involuntary;
   vi. if convicted the defendant has a right to a rehearing on appeal to the Crown Court.
e. where the defendant provides a medical note to excuse non-attendance the court must assess the provenance and reliability of the information contained therein and if necessary summons the author to attend court. The court must give reasons explaining why it has decided to proceed or not to proceed with the trial on the date it is listed. The reasons must be specific to the case.

5.4.13 **If the defendant is under 18:**
a. there is no presumption that the court should proceed in absence;
b. the potential for an acquittal may still be a relevant factor;
c. the potential for an application to re-open or appeal may also be a relevant matter;
d. the age, vulnerability, or experience of the defendant should be taken into account;
e. whether a parent or guardian is present, whether a parent or guardian ordinarily would be required to attend and whether such a person has attended a previous hearing;
f. the court should consider the interests of any co-defendant in the case proceeding;
g. the interests of any young and/or vulnerable witnesses who have attended.

Absence of witness (see A2.2.7)

5.4.14 Where the court is asked to adjourn because a witness has failed to attend, the court must:

a. rigorously investigate the steps taken to secure that witness' attendance, the fault for non-attendance is a relevant factor when deciding an application to adjourn;
b. critically examine the reasons given for absence and/or the likelihood of the witness attending should the case be adjourned;
c. consider the relevance of the witness to the case, and whether the witness's statement can be agreed or admitted, in whole or part, as hearsay;
d. consider whether proper notice has been given of the intention to call that witness;
e. consider whether an absent witness can be heard later in the trial;
f. where other witnesses have attended and the court has determined that the absent witness is required, consider hearing those witnesses who are present and adjourning the case part-heard, subject to that being possible within a reasonable timescale.

Need for additional evidence

5.4.15 It should rarely be the case that an application to adjourn based on a failure to serve evidence is made on the day of trial. The court is entitled to expect that evidence will have been served in good time and in accordance with the directions of the court. The court must consider whether the party who complains of the failure to serve evidence had informed the other party and the court in advance of the hearing. The court must conduct a rigorous inquiry into the nature of the evidence and must consider whether any of what is sought has been served, and if so when; the volume and the significance of what is sought; and the time likely to be needed for its consideration. In particular, the court must satisfy itself that any material still sought is relevant and that the party seeking it has a right to it.

5.4.16 In appropriate circumstances the court may refuse to admit evidence rather than adjourning the trial to allow it to be served. Applications to adjourn in order to obtain expert evidence should be rigorously scrutinised and it may not be appropriate to adjourn where the opinion sought is speculative.

Failure to comply with disclosure obligations (see A2.2.7)

5.4.17 Where a defendant complains of a prosecution failure to disclose material that ought to have been disclosed the court must first establish whether either party is applying for an adjournment as a result. If an adjournment is sought, the court should consider whether the matter can be resolved by providing disclosure at that stage. If it cannot, the court should consider whether the parties have complied with their obligations and should consider the relevance of fault.

5.4.18 If the prosecutor has complied or purported to comply with initial disclosure obligations, no further material is disclosable and consequently, in the absence of a defence statement served in accordance with s.6 Criminal Procedure and Investigations Act 1996, no application to adjourn should be granted. If the defendant has served a defence statement and asks for further disclosure, in consequence of the prosecutor's allegedly inadequate response or in consequence of a failure to respond at all, the court application must be made under s.8 Criminal Procedure and Investigations Act 1996 and **CrimPR 15.5**. The court should consider hearing such an application immediately, provided that there is sufficient time available for the application itself and then for the defence to consider any material disclosed in consequence of it.

A2.2 Additional case law

Whilst the directions supersede earlier judgments and are the primary point of reference, the following cases provide additional assistance.

A2.2.1 *Lack of explanation*

Because of the requirement for an explanation for the inability to proceed, an adjournment will not be granted when no explanation can be given (*R (Walden) and R (Stern) v Highbury Corner Magistrates' Court* [2003] EWHC 708 (Admin)). This applies as much to the Crown as to the defence.

A2.2.2 *Requirement for a fair trial*

On an application for an adjournment by the defence, the court in *R (Anderson) v Guildford Magistrates Court* [2015] EWHC 2454 (Admin) held that the issue was whether a fair trial could take place. Whilst speed was important an adjournment was granted where:

(1) The defence had voluntarily submitted a full and very detailed defence case statement even though initial disclosure had not yet been made.
(2) The defence had identified the need for two expert reports on the 'victim's' pathology (nature of the injury) and toxicology (drugs taken), and it was not for a court to prejudge whether these would be relevant or not.
(3) Other outstanding material identified a potential witness who might testify to the 'victim's' condition, and related to bad character.

This was notwithstanding that the not guilty plea had been entered on 16 April (by a duty solicitor), the trial was on 29 June, and the application to adjourn was made (by the defendant's own solicitor) on 1 June.

The power to adjourn was considered in *Bourne v Scarborough Magistrates' Court* [2017] EWHC 2828 (Admin) and it was held that the Crim PR allows a legal advisor to exercise this power. If the application was opposed, the adviser must be in possession of all the relevant facts and consider all the *CPS* v *Picton* criteria (including when the trial would be heard). If the defence seek an oral hearing that should normally be allowed, or at least written observations from the defence should be sought.

A2.2.3 *Requirement for accurate information*

Where the court is misled into granting an adjournment, it may reverse that decision even though in *DPP v Woods* [2017] EWHC 1070 (Admin) it meant that the Crown had to offer no evidence as its witnesses had been de-warned.

A2.2.4 *Diversion from prosecution*

Although courts are discouraged from allowing adjournments for this reason and there is no right to such an adjournment (*R (F) v CPS and the Chief Constable of Merseyside* (2004) 168 JP 93), such adjournments are regularly granted whenever the Crown Prosecution Service (CPS) on review agree that such an outcome is appropriate. This happens particularly where the charging decision has been made by the police or when defendants are receiving informed legal advice for the first time. It also applies when there are issues of mental disorder. Whilst a plea of not guilty can be entered, the Crown will often be willing to consider informed representations to comply with their duties under the Code for Crown Prosecutors.

Paragraph 3.6 of the Code for Crown Prosecutors states that:

Code for Crown Prosecutors, para 3.6

3.6 Prosecutors review every case they receive from the police or other investigators. Review is a continuing process and prosecutors must take account of any change in circumstances that occurs as the case develops. This includes what becomes known of the defence case, any further reasonable lines of inquiry that should be pursued, and receipt of any unused material that may undermine the prosecution case or assist the defence case, to the extent that charges should be altered or discontinued or the prosecution should not proceed. If a case is to be stopped, care should be taken when choosing the method of termination, as this can affect the victim's position under the Victims' Right to Review scheme. Wherever possible, prosecutors should consult the investigator when considering changing the charges or stopping the case. Prosecutors and investigators work closely together, but the final responsibility for the decision whether or not a case should go ahead rests with the CPS.

In addition, paragraph 9 of the Director's Guidance on Adult Conditional Cautions states that:

9. Prosecutor's post-charge review—cases that should have been considered for a Conditional Caution

9.1 Where an offender is charged with an offence, but it appears upon review by a prosecutor that a Conditional Caution is more appropriate, the reviewing prosecutor should direct an authorised person to offer a Conditional Caution. This includes any case where authorised persons ordinarily make that decision. The current prosecution should be adjourned whilst this action is taken. The authorised person shall then offer a caution with conditions as specified by the prosecutor. If it proves then not to be possible to administer the caution an alternative out of court disposal may not be offered and the prosecution must continue.

Note that there are particular provisions in relation to foreign offender conditional cautions.

A2.2.5 ***Legal aid***

A common issue that arises is in relation to adjournments for the purposes of legal aid being granted. Much will depend on the circumstances, and in particular, how much time the defendant has had, if any, to arrange appropriate representation. The court will also be mindful of payments that can be made to firms if legal aid is refused—thereby diluting the force of any argument that work would otherwise be unfunded. However, in *Stopya v District Court of Lublin Poland* [2012] EWHC 1787 (Admin) it was held that 'delays occasioned by means testing which are not occasioned by the fault of the requested person or his legal advisers cannot be held against the requested person'.

A2.2.6 *Absence of the defendant*

The issues were re-examined and confirmed in *Killick v West London Magistrates' Court* [2012] EWHC 3864 (Admin):

> Section 11(1)(b) and (2A) of the Magistrates' Courts Act 1980 allow the court to proceed in the absence of a defendant unless it appears contrary to the interests of justice, but it should not do so if it considers that there is an acceptable reason for his failure to attend. The jurisdiction must be exercised with the utmost care and caution. The case should not proceed without the court satisfying itself that the claim for an adjournment may properly be rejected and that no unfairness will thereby be done.
>
> Where a defendant wished to resist a criminal charge and is shown by medical evidence to be unfit to attend court either as a result of involuntary illness or incapacity, it would be very rarely, if ever, right for the court to exercise its discretion in favour of proceeding. If the court suspects the grounds to be spurious or inadequate, it should express its doubts to give the defence a chance to resolve them. The court must distinguish genuine grounds from those that are spurious and designed to frustrate the process. If the court concludes the latter is the case, it may proceed as if there is a truly compelling reason for doing so, notwithstanding the justified non-attendance. If a court proceeds, it should set aside the order under section 142 of the Magistrates' Court Act 1980 if compelling medical evidence is then produced.

Criminal Practice Direction 5.4.12 e contains specific provisions on the production of medical certificates.

A2.2.7 *Witnesses*

Where a party was unable, through no fault of his own, to call an important witness, an adjournment should be granted to give an opportunity for that witness to be traced and steps taken to secure attendance (*Khurshied v Peterborough Magistrates' Court* [2009] EWHC 1136 (Admin) and *Nadour v Chester Magistrates' Court* [2009] EWHC 1505 (Admin)). In *Essen v DPP* [2005] EWHC 1077 (Admin), the court was concerned with a failure of the CPS, due to administrative error, to warn its witnesses for trial. The court held that in the absence of some other counter-prevailing factor an adjournment ought not to be granted. The fact that a crime may go unpunished is not sufficient as:

> in that case no prosecutor, however dilatory, need attend to the requirement to be ready for trial on the set date. . . The prejudice to the defendant [of an adjournment in those circumstances] was manifest. The CPS had no ground for seeking clemency. It was the sole author of its own misfortune.

A prosecutor should always be given some time to make inquiries as to why a witness is not present (*R v Swansea Justices, ex p DPP*, *The Times*, 30 March 1990). See CPD 5.4.14.

A2.2.8 ***Disclosure***

The defence must identify the possible significance of missing disclosure. If the prosecution have failed to carry out their statutory duties in relation to disclosure under the CPIA 1996, an adjournment may be granted, on the Crown's application (*Swash v DPP* [2009] EWHC 803 (Admin)). A wholesale failure on the part of the prosecution to comply with its disclosure obligations may require the prosecution to offer no evidence but the defence must have followed the correct formal disclosure procedures (*DPP v Graham Petrie* [2015] EWHC 48 (Admin)). The courts may exclude all prosecution evidence under s 78 Police and Criminal Evidence Act 1984 as it may then be unfair in the proceedings to admit that evidence alone at trial (*R (Ibrahim) v Feltham Magistrates' Court* [2001] EWHC 130 (Admin)). In *R v Boardman* [2015] EWCA Crim 175, a case where material disclosed very late then required expert analysis, all the key prosecution evidence was excluded under this provision.

See also A16.

A2.2.9 ***Ambush defence***

If a defendant raises matters for the first time in the proceedings (so-called ambush defences), the court is fully justified in adjourning the matter in order to allow the prosecution to deal with them properly (eg *R (Lawson) v Stratford Magistrates' Court* [2007] EWHC 2490 (Admin), where compliance with signage regulations in relation to a prosecution for speeding was raised for the first time in cross-examination). The general principles are established by the series of decisions in *R v Gleeson* [2003] EWCA Crim 3357, *R v Chorley Justices* [2006] EWHC 1795 (Admin), and *Malcolm v DPP* [2007] EWHC 363 (Admin).

In *R (Taylor) v Southampton Magistrates' Court* [2008] EWHC 3006 (Admin), it was held that, during a trial for failing to comply with a notice under s 172 Road Traffic Act 1988, a District Judge was right to adjourn the case in order for the prosecution to be able to gather evidence (if such evidence existed) to prove service of the notice. There was no question of bias, even though the court acted of its own motion. In this case there was no issue of 'ambush', the prosecution having not only been put to proof of all issues but the specific issue having been raised. That was not enough for the court in this instance, in the absence of a positive defence case that the notice had not in fact been served. The case should be contrasted with *R (Decani) v City of London Magistrates' Court* [2017] EWHC 3422 (Admin) where notice of the issue had been given and the Divisional Court held that the Crown should have been refused an adjournment.

See *Blackstone's Criminal Practice 2026* D5.2

A3 Admissibility and Exclusion of Evidence

A3.1 Admissibility and exclusion

A written document (in this instance a drink/drug driving form) referred to in a read statement can be an exhibit even if it is not expressly referred to as an exhibit in the statement (*Clarke v CPS* [2024] EWHC 704 (Admin)).

Given that magistrates deal with questions of both fact and law, the *voir dire* procedure adopted in the Crown Court is not always appropriate in summary proceedings when issues of admissibility arise. The timing of any challenge is a matter for the court, and whilst there is no right to have issues of admissibility determined as a preliminary issue (*R v Epping and Ongar Justices, ex p Manby* [1986] Crim LR 555), s 8A Magistrates' Courts Act 1980 provides for pre-trial rulings on issues of admissibility. Previous rulings on admissibility can be reversed, but this should happen only exceptionally (see A9 for relevant provisions and cases).

When a party is seeking to exclude evidence under s 76 Police and Criminal Evidence Act 1984 (PACE), a *voir dire* will be required as there is no discretion under s 76 (as opposed to s 78) and the prosecution carry the burden of disproving unfairness (*Vel v Owen* [1987] Crim LR 496).

When a party is inviting a court to exercise its discretion to exclude evidence under s 78 PACE, the court has a choice as to whether to deal with the issue when it arises or once all evidence has been heard. The *voir dire* procedure is appropriate to such applications, as an accused may otherwise be denied the opportunity to remain silent in relation to the substantive matter. *Halawa v Federation Against Copyright Theft* [1995] 1 Cr App R 496 established the relevant principles.

Police and Criminal Evidence Act 1984, s 78

78 (1) In any proceedings the court may refuse to allow evidence on which the prosecution proposes to rely to be given if it appears to the court that, having regard to all the circumstances, including the circumstances in which the evidence was obtained, the admission of the evidence would have such an adverse effect on the fairness of the proceedings that the court ought not to admit it.

It should be noted that s 78 may only be used to exclude prosecution evidence, not that led by a co-defendant.

Blackstone's Magistrates' Court Handbook 2026. Bartholomew Dalton and Caroline Liggins, Oxford University Press. © Oxford University Press 2026.
DOI: 10.1093/oso/9780198963943.003.0003

A4 Allocation and Plea before Venue

(For sending and transfer procedures see A26.)

A4.1 Cases that must be sent to the Crown Court

The court must send the case to the Crown Court if:

- there is an indictable-only offence;
- a notice has been served under s 51B (serious fraud) or s 51C (children) of the Crime and Disorder Act 1998; or
- the offence is related to an indictable/notice offence for which the defendant or another defendant is sent for trial (unless the defendant appears on a subsequent occasion when there is a discretion);
- the defendant is charged with an either-way offence or relevant (imprisonable or disqualifiable) summary offence, and is or has been sent to the Crown Court for a related offence;
- the defendant is jointly charged with another defendant who is or has been sent to the Crown Court for a related offence;
- the defendant is jointly charged or is charged with a related offence with a child defendant who is or has been sent to the Crown Court for trial.

In each case where there is a co-defendant, the duty exists when the defendants appear on the same occasion, but becomes a discretion if this defendant appears on a subsequent occasion.

A4.2 Cases that may be sent to the Crown Court

A plea before venue is conducted for all other either-way offences. Under Crim PR 3.16(3) and 9.11(2) the defendant may request an indication as to whether a custodial or non-custodial sentence is more likely in a procedure similar to the procedure for a *Goodyear* (2005 EWCA Crim 888) indication in the Crown Court. The court is not bound to give such an indication. The defendant is asked to indicate a plea. The plea to an either-way matter must, *until the implementation of written procedures by the Judicial Review and Courts Act 2022*, be indicated by the defendant personally and not by a lawyer on their behalf (s 17A MCA 1980 and *Westminster City Council v Owadally* [2017] EWHC 1092 (Admin)), although under s 17B MCA 1980, an advocate can indicate a plea on an adult defendant's behalf to an either-way offence if that defendant's disorderly behaviour makes it impossible to conduct the proceedings in his presence, or (Sch 3 MCA 1980) the defendant is a company.

A4.3 Where there is a guilty plea

If the indication of plea is guilty, the court proceeds to sentence, and this may include a committal for sentence if Crown Court powers are required to deal with the defendant. It shall commit for sentence if the offence is a specified offence and the dangerous offender provisions apply on the facts of the particular case. Sections 14 (insufficient powers), 15 (dangerous offenders), 18 (further either way offences when

Blackstone's Magistrates' Court Handbook 2026. Bartholomew Dalton and Caroline Liggins, Oxford University Press. © Oxford University Press 2026.
DOI: 10.1093/oso/9780198963943.003.0004

defendant already before Crown Court) and 20 (other offences when committed for sentence on other matters) of the Sentencing Act 2020 governs the process whereby the magistrates' court can commit a defendant to the Crown Court to be sentenced. These sections also set out the circumstances where the Crown Court would have the same powers as if the defendant had been convicted on indictment, and where the Court would be limited to the sentencing powers of the magistrates' court.

It will be rare that a defendant saying that they have "done nothing wrong" at the same time as entering a guilty plea will be sufficient to render a plea equivocal (*R v Johnson* [2022] EWCA Crim 790). However, the court should always take care that unrepresented defendants understand the elements of the offences, particularly when there are mental health issues or learning disabilities involved.

Section 12 of MCA 1980 has been expanded, and once in force, it will allow charged defendants of a summary offence to plead guilty by written notice under Judicial Review and Courts Act 2022.

A4.4 **Not guilty or no indication of plea**

If the indication of plea is not guilty, *there is a new procedure which has been introduced by the Judicial Review and Courts Act 2022. Under s 17BA MCA 1980, once in force, an accused or their legal representative may choose to give an indication that the accused would not consent to summary trial. If such an indication is given, the case is forthwith sent to the Crown Court.* Until that time the court proceeds to allocation. If there is no indication of plea, it is treated as a plea of not guilty.

- The court receives representations from the Crown, which may include details of previous convictions of the defendant, and from the defence (see Figure 1). The court determines, in accordance with s 19 MCA 1980 and the Allocation Guidelines, whether the case is more suitable for summary trial or trial on indictment.

A4.4.1 ***Allocation procedure (s 19 MCA 1980)***

The court must hear representations from all parties before considering whether jurisdiction ought to be accepted or declined. The procedure where there is more than one charge or more than one defendant is set out in rule 9.2 of the Criminal Procedure Rules.

A4.4.2 ***Allocation guideline***

The Sentencing Council has issued a definitive guideline in relation to the allocation of cases between the magistrates' court and Crown Court.

> It is important to ensure that all cases are tried at the appropriate level.
>
> 1. In general, either-way offences should be tried summarily unless:
>   - the outcome would clearly be a sentence in excess of the court's powers for the offence(s) concerned after taking into account personal mitigation and any potential reduction for a guilty plea; or
>   - for reasons of unusual legal, procedural, or factual complexity, the case should be tried in the Crown Court. This exception may apply in cases where a very substantial fine is the likely sentence. Other circumstances where this exception will apply

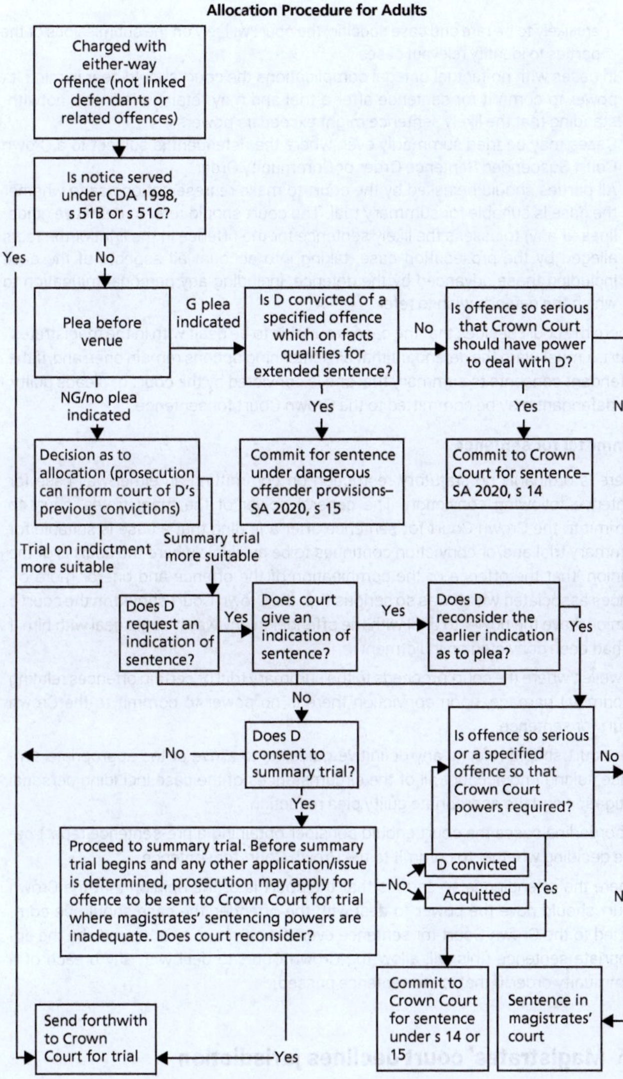

Figure 1 Allocation procedure for adults

are likely to be rare and case specific; the court will rely on the submissions of the parties to identify relevant cases.

2. In cases with no factual or legal complications the court should bear in mind its power to commit for sentence after a trial and may retain jurisdiction notwithstanding that the likely sentence might exceed its powers.
3. Cases may be tried summarily even where the defendant is subject to a Crown Court Suspended Sentence Order or Community Order.
4. All parties should be asked by the court to make representations as to whether the case is suitable for summary trial. The court should refer to definitive guidelines (if any) to assess the likely sentence for the offence in the light of the facts alleged by the prosecution case, taking into account all aspects of the case including those advanced by the defence, including any personal mitigation to which the defence wish to refer.

Where the court decides that the case is suitable to be dealt with in the magistrates' court, it must warn the defendant that all sentencing options remain open and, if the defendant consents to summary trial and is convicted by the court or pleads guilty, the defendant may be committed to the Crown Court for sentence.

Committal for sentence

There is ordinarily no statutory restriction on committing an either-way case for sentence following conviction. The general power of the magistrates' court to commit to the Crown Court for sentence after a finding that a case is suitable for summary trial and/or conviction continues to be available where the court is of the opinion 'that the offence or the combination of the offence and one or more offences associated with it was so serious that the Crown Court should, in the court's opinion, have the power to deal with the offender in any way it could deal with him if he had been convicted on indictment'.

However, where the court proceeds to the summary trial of certain offences relating to criminal damage, upon conviction there is no power to commit to the Crown Court for sentence.

The court should refer to any definitive guideline to arrive at the appropriate sentence, taking into account all of the circumstances of the case including personal mitigation and the appropriate guilty plea reduction.

In borderline cases the court should consider obtaining a pre-sentence report before deciding whether to commit to the Crown Court for sentence.

Where the offending is so serious that the court is of the opinion that the Crown Court should have the power to deal with the offender, the case should be committed to the Crown Court for sentence even if a community order may be the appropriate sentence (this will allow the Crown Court to deal with any breach of a community order, if that is the sentence passed).

A4.5 Magistrates' court declines jurisdiction

If the court declines jurisdiction, it must send the case to the Crown Court. For the procedure on sending see **A26**.

A4.6 Magistrates' court accepts jurisdiction

If the court accepts jurisdiction, the defendant may request an indication whether the court is considering a custodial sentence. If the court is willing to give an indication, the defendant must be invited to reconsider his plea. If the indication was non-custodial and a plea of guilty is indicated, the court may neither impose a custodial sentence nor commit for sentence.

- The defence must otherwise be asked if they consent to summary trial. This consent can, under s 23 MCA 1980, be given by the defendant's legal representative. If the defence elect trial on indictment, the case must be sent to the Crown Court. (See A26.)
- If the defence consent to summary trial, the Crown may make further representations that the trial should be on indictment if new factors become relevant. However, there can be no change of venue once the trial has begun or an application in relation to the trial has been made.

If the case remains summary there is a trial, and in the event of a conviction the court may sentence within its own powers, unless:

- there is a specified offence and the requirements for an extended sentence are met by the facts of the particular case; or
- new factors have arisen during the trial, making the initial decision to accept jurisdiction inappropriate.

This follows the case law on 'expectation' preventing a court from changing its mind (*R v Nottingham Magistrates' Court, ex p Davidson* [2000] 1 Cr App R (S) 167). Under these procedures the court will have been fully advised about the defendant's previous convictions, and as the Crown will have had opportunities to emphasise particular seriousness, it will therefore be difficult for the court to say that the decision to accept summary jurisdiction did not give rise to a legitimate expectation of disposal within magistrates' court powers (*Sheffield Magistrates' Court, ex p Ojo* (2000) 164 JP 659). However, the allocation guideline emphasises the powers to commit for sentence (see A4.4.2) and there may as a result now be no general expectation of a summary disposal. The power to commit for sentence certainly arises when there is an acceptance of jurisdiction that was so perverse as to be unlawful (*R (Nicholas) v Chester Magistrates' Court* [2009] EWHC 1504 (Admin)) or in total disregard of the relevant sentencing guideline (*Thornton v CPS* [2012] EWHC 346 (Admin)); or there have been new convictions since the allocation hearing; or the facts at trial were clearly more serious than originally described so that Crown Court sentencing powers are required.

A4.7 Either-way offences that must be tried summarily ss 22 and 22A MCA 1980

The court must determine venue for either-way offences but some either-way offences have venue dictated by value (criminal damage, save arson and damage to a memorial, aggravated vehicle-taking, and theft from a shop).

A4.7.1 *Criminal damage*

If the value of damage is less than £5,000, only summary trial will be offered. For multiple offences, the aggregate value must be considered (s 22(11) MCA 1980). A court has a discretion but not a duty to hear evidence in relation to value (*R v Canterbury Justices, ex p Klisiak* [1981] 2 All ER 129). Value does not include consequential loss flowing from destruction (*R v Colchester Magistrates' Court, ex p Abbott* [2001] Crim LR 564). Where it is not clear whether or not the value exceeds £5,000, the defendant will be permitted, if he so wishes, to elect Crown Court trial but the maximum ten-year sentence is then available (*R v Alden* [2002] EWCA Crim 412).

The definition of memorial appears at C6.5.

A4.7.2 ***Theft from a shop***

Theft from a shop that does not exceed an aggregate value of £200 is a hybrid offence in that it can only be tried summarily (without a power to commit for sentence) unless the defendant elects to be tried on indictment: s 22A MCA 1980. The aggregate value is calculated by adding the values of all the allegations placed before the court on a single occasion (*R v Harvey* [2020] EWCA Crim 354). If the defendant does elect for trial on indictment full sentencing powers are available.

Section 22A MCA 1980 provides:

Magistrates' Courts Act 1980, s 22A

22A Low-value shoplifting to be a summary offence

(1) Low-value shoplifting is triable only summarily.

(2) But where a person accused of low-value shoplifting is aged 18 or over, and appears or is brought before the court before the summary trial of the offence begins, the court must give the person the opportunity of electing to be tried by the Crown Court for the offence and, if the person elects to be so tried—

(a) subsection (1) does not apply, and

(b) the court must proceed in relation to the offence in accordance with section 51(1) of the Crime and Disorder Act 1998.

The definition of low-value shoplifting appears at C16.21.3.

An offence of low-value shoplifting only qualifies as such once the accused appears in court to answer the charge(s), it remains an either way offence until that point (*Candlish v DPP* [2022] EWHC 842 (Admin)).

Criminal Attempts Act 1981, s 1(5)

This section also applies to low-value shoplifting (which is defined in, and is triable only summarily by virtue of, s 22A MCA 1980).

A4.8 **Summary-only offences**

For the position in relation to summary-only offences that are related to a matter being sent see A26.1.

See *Blackstone's Criminal Practice 2026* D6

A5 **Amending Charge**

A5.1 **Amendment within the time limit**

Prosecutors do not have an unfettered right to seek to amend charges that are not subject to any limitation of time (i.e. indictable and indictable-only charges). Amendments should be granted only where the application is judged to be proper and appropriate (*R v Redbridge Justices, ex p Whitehouse* (1992) 94 Cr App R 332).

A5.2 **Amendment outside the time limit**

An amendment outside the time limit, in order to allow the prosecution to proceed with a summary-only offence which would otherwise be time barred, may be permitted, provided that the new offence is based on the 'same misdoing', that it is in the interests of justice to allow the amendment (*R v Scunthorpe Justices, ex p McPhee and Gallagher* (1998) 162 JP 635, DC), and the matter to be amended was preferred *within* the relevant time limit (*Dougall v CPS* [2018] EWHC 1367 (Admin)).

The following principles emerge from *Scunthorpe Justices*:

- the purpose of the six-month time limit imposed by s 127 MCA 1980 is to ensure that summary offences are charged and tried as soon as reasonably practicable after their alleged commission;
- where an information has been laid within the six-month period it can be amended after the expiry of that period;
- an information can be amended after the expiry of the six-month period, even to allege a different offence or different offences, provided that:
  - the different offence or offences allege the 'same misdoing' as the original offence; and
  - the amendment can be made in the interests of justice.

The phrase 'same misdoing' should not be construed too narrowly. It means that the new offence should arise out of the same (or substantially the same) facts as gave rise to the original offence.

In *Shaw v DPP* [2007] EWHC 207 (Admin), the court ruled that an amendment to charge an offence which was based on similar misdoing ought not to have been permitted, as the original offence carried only a financial penalty whereas the new offence carried imprisonment. The court ruled similarly in *DPP v Everest* [2005] EWHC 1124 (Admin), observing that the new offence carried a higher penalty, had a statutory defence that the defence had to establish, and that the defendant was not legally represented.

The amendment of a charge to substitute failing to provide a specimen of breath with failing to provide a specimen of urine was held to be proper in *Williams v DPP* [2009] EWHC 2354 (Admin), although the court did allow the appeal as the alteration had not been made in a timely fashion (applying *DPP v Hammerton* [2009] EWHC 921 (Admin)). By contrast in *Crann v CPS*

Blackstone's Magistrates' Court Handbook 2026. Bartholomew Dalton and Caroline Liggins, Oxford University Press. © Oxford University Press 2026.
DOI: 10.1093/oso/9780198963943.003.0005

[2013] EWHC 552 (Admin), a very late amendment was allowed as the offence was no more serious and had been anticipated.

When the prosecution seeks to change the name of a defendant out of time, a factual enquiry is necessary. The issue is whether there was a mistake as to identity, such as the wrong company in a group (when amendment is not permissible (see *Sainsbury's Supermarkets Ltd v HM Courts Service* [2006] EWHC 1749 (Admin)) or a misstatement of the name which could be amended, as in *Platinum Crown Investments Ltd v North East Essex Magistrates Court* [2017] EWHC 2761 (Admin).

See *Blackstone's Criminal Practice 2026* **D21.11**

A6 Appeals and Reopening

A6.1 Two routes of appeal under the Magistrates' Courts Act 1980; and judicial review availability

A6.1.1 *Appeals against conviction or sentence*

Under s 108 MCA 1980, an appeal against conviction and/or sentence lies as of right to the Crown Court. A notice of appeal must be served within 15 business days of sentence or committal for sentence. Section 113 MCA 1980 creates an obligation on the magistrates' court to consider an application for bail pending appeal in every case where a notice of appeal has been lodged in accordance with the Criminal Procedure Rules (Crim PR) 34.3 and a properly constituted application for bail is made (*Thomas v CPS* [2015] EWHC 4079 (Admin)).

If a custodial sentence is imposed it is not the normal practice to grant bail pending an appeal, and there is no statutory right to bail. Where the appeal is against conviction and the defendant was convicted after trial, many courts will look more favourably on bail pending appeal, particularly when the custodial sentence is short. In *R v Imdad Shah* (1980) 144 JP 460, the court rejected an argument that bail should be granted where the sentence was a short one and there was a risk that the sentence would be served prior to the appeal being heard. The court ruled that in such cases an early listing should be sought. By way of contrast, in *R (G) v Inner London Crown Court* [2003] EWHC 2715 (Admin) the applicant successfully judicially reviewed a decision by a Crown Court to refuse bail in a 'short sentence' case.

A6.1.2 *Appeals by way of case stated*

Provision is made for appeals by way of case stated by s 111 MCA 1980 and Crim PR 35. The application, complying with Crim PR 35(2), must be made within 15 business days of the decision sought to be appealed. This is a strict and non-extendable time limit (*Mishra v Colchester MC* [2017] EWHC 2869 (Admin)) and time runs from the giving of the decision and not from the giving of written reasons (*R v Ziegler* [2019] EWHC 19 (Admin)). The decision must be a final determination going to an issue of law or excess of jurisdiction (*R (Highbury Poultry Farm Produce Ltd) v Telford Magistrates Court* [2018] EWHC 3122 (Admin)). The making of an application rules out any appeal on the facts under **A6.1.1**. A magistrates' court representation order covers the costs of seeking a case.

A6.1.3 *Judicial review*

The distinction between an appeal by way of case stated and an application for judicial review, and the circumstances in which they should be used, was considered in *Downes v RSPCA* [2017] EWHC 3622 (Admin). In *R (Parashar) v Sunderland Magistrates Court* [2019] EWHC 514 (Admin) the court considered that judicial review may be an appropriate remedy where:

Blackstone's Magistrates' Court Handbook 2026. Bartholomew Dalton and Caroline Liggins, Oxford University Press. © Oxford University Press 2026.
DOI: 10.1093/oso/9780198963943.003.0006

(a) it is properly arguable that the ability of the defendant to present his defence is so seriously compromised by the decision under challenge that an unfair trial is inevitable; and
(b) where an important point of principle is raised, likely to affect other cases; and
(c) where the case had some other exceptional feature which justifies the intervention of the High Court.

The threshold for exceptionality is less high where the application is made pre-trial. In *R (Tesco Stores Ltd) v Birmingham Magistrates Court* [2019] EWHC 3755 (Admin) the court held that it must look at all of the relevant circumstances and determine whether, by exercising its power to consider a judicial review of an interlocutory decision of a criminal court, it can further the overriding objective of dealing with cases justly. 'Dealing with a case justly of course involves consideration of managing cases efficiently and cost efficiently.'

See *Blackstone's Criminal Practice 2026* D29

A6.2 Reopening cases

A6.2.1 *Jurisdiction*

Magistrates' Courts Act 1980, s 142

142 Power of magistrates' court to re-open cases to rectify mistakes, etc.

(1) A magistrates' court may vary or rescind a sentence or other order imposed or made by it when dealing with an offender if it appears to the court to be in the interests of justice to do so, and it is hereby declared that this power extends to replacing a sentence or order which for any reason appears to be invalid by another which the court has power to impose or make.

(1A) The power conferred on a magistrates' court by subsection (1) above shall not be exercisable in relation to any sentence or order imposed or made by it when dealing with an offender if—
(a) the Crown Court has determined an appeal against—
(i) that sentence or order;
(ii) the conviction in respect of which that sentence or order was imposed or made; or
(iii) any other sentence or order imposed or made by the magistrates' court when dealing with the offender in respect of that conviction (including a sentence or order replaced by that sentence or order); or
(b) the High Court has determined a case stated for the opinion of that court on any question arising in any proceeding leading to or resulting from the imposition or making of the sentence or order.

(2) Where a person is convicted by a magistrates' court and it subsequently appears to the court that it would be in the interests of justice that the case should be heard again by different justices, the court may so direct.

(2A) The power conferred on a magistrates' court by subsection (2) above shall not be exercisable in relation to a conviction if—
(a) the Crown Court has determined an appeal against—
(i) the conviction; or
(ii) any sentence or order imposed or made by the magistrates' court when dealing with the offender in respect of the conviction; or

(b) the High Court has determined a case stated for the opinion of that court on any question arising in any proceeding leading to or resulting from the conviction.

A6.2.2 *Principles*

Section 142 MCA 1980 relates to criminal proceedings and has no application to other areas of magistrates' court jurisdiction such as liability orders (*Liverpool City Council v Plemora Distribution Ltd* [2002] EWHC 2467 (Admin)), and detention and forfeiture in relation to proceeds of crime. A defendant who has been convicted in absence can properly attempt to reopen under this section. Culpability on the part of the offender is relevant to whether it is in the interests of justice to reopen, but it is not determinative. It will normally be in the interests of justice for a defendant to be able to defend himself, and unless the evidence indicates that his absence from trial is deliberate and voluntary, a rehearing would normally be the appropriate course (*R (Morsby) v Tower Bridge Magistrates' Court* [2007] EWHC 2766 (Admin)). See also *R (Manorgate Ltd) v Thames Magistrates' Court* [2013] EWHC 535 (Admin). Any inconvenience to the court in allowing a reopening can never outweigh the interests of justice (*R (Blick) v Doncaster Magistrates' Court* (2008) 172 JP 651). Section 142(2) MCA 1980 does not require a mistake in every case but merely that rectification be in the interests of justice. However, there must be new material before the court (*R (Nkromah) v Willesden Magistrates Court* [2014] EWHC 4455 (Admin)).

Persons made subject to a hospital order under s 37(3) Mental Health Act 1983 fall within the definition of 'offender', and a person can use s 142 MCA 1980 to reopen a hearing determining the issue under the Mental Health Act (*R (Bartram) v Southend Magistrates' Court* [2004] EWHC 2691 (Admin)). An order to commit an offender to prison for non-satisfaction of a confiscation order made under the Proceeds of Crime Act 2002 in the Crown Court is capable of being reopened.

The court has power to revisit the issue of a warrant following non-payment of fines. A court does not have the power to rescind a costs order made in favour of a defendant who was not convicted as the section related only to orders post-conviction (*Coles v East Penwith Justices, The Times*, 27 July 1998).

A prosecutor cannot apply to reopen proceedings that have previously been withdrawn (*R (Green and Green Scaffolding Ltd) v Staines Magistrates' Court* (2008) 172 JP 353).

The nature of the remedy afforded under MCA 1980 is akin to a 'slip rule', allowing a court to rectify a clear mistake or injustice. An applicant who entered an unequivocal plea of guilty cannot apply to reopen a plea under this section (*R v Croydon Youth Court, ex p DPP* [1997] 2 Cr App R 411), unless the plea was inappropriate and so now equivocal; however, this exception did not apply where the allegation was of professional impropriety by the defendant's legal representative as this did not fall within the word 'mistake' (*Williamson v City of Westminster Magistrates' Court* [2012] EWHC 1444 (Admin)).

Section 142 should not be used to advance new arguments, neither should it be used as an 'appeal' mechanism (*Zykin v CPS* [2009] EWHC 1469 (Admin); *R v Chajed* [2013] EWHC 188 (Admin)). Applications based on a change of law between conviction and application should not be entertained. The section may not be used to revisit an interlocutory ruling, but only after the conclusion of the case (*R (Poskitt) v Reading Magistrates' Court* [2018] EWHC 984 (Admin)). Section 142 can only be used in relation to determinations made by the Magistrates' Court, not those of the Crown Court (*H v DPP* [2021] EWHC 147 (Admin)).

A6.2.3 *Applications*

The procedure for an application under s 142 is provided by Crim PR 44.3.

There is no statutory time limit on reopening, but the former 28-day rule should act as a guideline. Applications made much beyond this date might properly be refused on interests of justice grounds, as '[d]elay in matters of this sort is always harmful, memories fade, records may be lost and the essence of doing justice is that it should be done expeditiously' (*R v Ealing Magistrates' Court, ex p Sahota* [1997] EWHC 993 (Admin)). It is not, however, a decisive factor. It is not enough for the magistrates simply to say that the length of time is such that it is no longer proper to open the case under s 142. More substantial reasoning than that has to be given, so that the applicant (and any court on appeal) can understand why it is no longer proper to deal with the matter.

It is possible for the section to apply when, in hindsight, the decision to proceed was made in error because all the facts that had a bearing on the exercise of judicial discretion were not known to the court. The power arises when the earlier decision would not have been reached had the full facts been known and the reason for that was not the defendant's fault (*R (Rathor) v Southampton Magistrates Court* [2018] EWHC 3278 (Admin)).

Applications may be made by both defence and prosecution, but the exercise of such discretion in favour of a prosecutor will be rare, and can never extend to the overturning of an acquittal. A prosecutor could properly make an application to reopen where the court had erroneously failed to impose penalty points or some other appropriate order. Similarly, if the court had been unaware of factors relevant to sentence, it could be invited to reopen sentence, even if that meant a risk that it would be increased. However, if it is appropriate for the powers under s 142 to be used to increase sentence then the power must be exercised very speedily (*R (Holme) v Liverpool Magistrates' Court* [2004] EWHC 3131 (Admin), where the court declined to allow the prosecution to exercise the power).

A6.2.4 *Interests of justice*

Justices are given wide discretion in determining what are relevant factors in relation to interests of justice, but decisions must be based on sound judicial reasoning. A defendant's late arrival at court was held not to be a proper ground, in itself, to refuse a rehearing (*R v Camberwell Green Magistrates' Court, ex p Ibrahim* (1984) 148 JP 400). Factors a court ought to consider include:

- why the convicted person did not appear at the original trial (if that was the case);
- timeliness of the application;
- reason for any delay;
- importance of the decision being questioned—note that the importance to all parties, including defendant, prosecution, and other interested parties (such as victim), should be assessed;
- inconvenience and prejudice caused to opposing parties;
- whether a more appropriate appeal remedy is available. It will not normally be appropriate to allow a reopening where a defendant is denied a right of appeal due to an unequivocal guilty plea (*R v Croydon Youth Court, ex p DPP* [1997] 2 Cr App R 411).

In addition, the court must always consider rule 1 of the Crim PR and the overriding objective.

A6.2.5 *Effect of reopening*

A conviction will be set aside, as will any sentence or ancillary orders flowing from it. The matter is treated as adjourned for trial. Justices who sat on the original hearing, or the hearing to reopen, cannot sit on the adjourned trial. The prosecution retain the right to offer no evidence and the court lacks power to insist that a prosecutor proceeds with the case (*R (Rhodes-Presley) v South Worcestershire Magistrates' Court* [2008] EWHC 2700 (Admin)).

If a sentence or order is reopened, the court may vary or rescind the original finding and substitute any other lawful sentence or order that would have been available to the court at the original hearing. The new orders take effect from the date of the old order unless the court directs otherwise. A court must be careful not to offend against any legitimate expectation given to the offender (*Jane v Broome, The Times*, 2 November 1988).

A6.3 Reopening of guilty plea

The procedure is set out in Crim PR 24.10. The relevant issues were considered in *Wilson v CPS* 2020 EWHC 820 (QB). The discretion to permit a change of plea should be 'exercised sparingly and only in clear cases . . . if the defendant could establish that he pleaded guilty without understanding elements of the offence, or without intending to admit that he was guilty of what was alleged, then it might be appropriate to allow him to withdraw his guilty plea'. Legal representation 'may be a relevant factor . . . If there has been improper pressure to plead guilty, a defendant might be permitted to vacate his plea. If incorrect legal advice has been given that a certain factual basis would not amount to a defence, the plea may be set aside'.

The court has the power to direct that a guilty plea be vacated even when the defendant does not request so or even opposes it, but it is unlikely to be appropriate to do so to 'recuse the prosecution from a muddle of their own making' (*R v Gould and others* [2021] EWCA Crim 447).

In *S (An Infant) v Recorder of Manchester* [1971] AC 481, the court held that:

- the power to reopen plea was a discretionary one;
- the power ought to be used sparingly;
- the power is available up until sentence has been passed;
- the question for the court is whether justice requires the change of plea to be permitted.

See *Blackstone's Criminal Practice 2026* **D23.23**

A7 Bad Character

A7.1 Introduction

The admissibility of bad character is regulated by ss 98–113 of the Criminal Justice Act (CJA) 2003, but s 27(3) Theft Act 1968 remains available to the Crown in cases of handling. The common law rules are now subsidiary to the statutory regime. The Act is concerned with the admission of bad character in relation to:

- the defendant;
- any co-defendant;
- a person other than a defendant in the case.

The Criminal Procedure Rules (Crim PR Part 21) provide the regime for the admission of evidence of bad character. The court has the power to exclude otherwise admissible evidence of bad character on the grounds of non-compliance, if the effect would be to prejudice a party, for example by way of ambush defence (*R v Musone* [2007] EWCA Crim 1237). Provided that there is no prejudice, a court is free to admit evidence of bad character if to do so would satisfy the overriding objective of Crim PR 1. Attempts to argue that evidence ought to be admitted following procedural non-compliance only in exceptional cases have been rejected (*R (Robinson) v Sutton Coldfield Magistrates' Court* [2006] EWHC 307 (Admin)). In *Robinson*, the court did say, however, that:

> a court would ordinarily wish to know when the relevant enquiries had been initiated, and in broad terms why they have not been completed within the time allowed. Any application for an extension will be closely scrutinised by the court. A party seeking an extension cannot expect the indulgence of the court unless it clearly sets out the reasons why it is seeking that indulgence.

A7.2 What is bad character?

The CJA 2003 defines 'bad character' as the commission of an offence or other 'reprehensible behaviour'. It is important to note the effect of s 98 (see A7.3), which has the effect of excluding much bad character evidence from the statutory scheme, allowing for its admissibility subject only to the normal rules of probity and relevance.

In considering whether or not a party has committed an offence, regard can be had to:

- previous convictions;
- previous police cautions or youth cautions;
- offences for which the person has not been tried;
- offences for which the person has been acquitted (*R v Z* [2000] 2 AC 483) or found unfit to be tried (*R v Renda* [2005] EWCA Crim 2826).

Other examples include telling lies, taking illegal drugs (*R v AJC* [2006] EWCA Crim 284), being sexually promiscuous (*R v Ball* [2005] EWCA Crim 2826), and collecting photographs of people being violently attacked (*R v Saleem* [2007] EWCA Crim 1923). In *R v M* [2014] EWCA Crim 1407, it was held

Blackstone's Magistrates' Court Handbook 2026. Bartholomew Dalton and Caroline Liggins, Oxford University Press. © Oxford University Press 2026.
DOI: 10.1093/oso/9780198963943.003.0007

that attempted suicide and probably self-harming do not amount to reprehensible behaviour but excessive drinking and illegal drug taking do fall within the meaning of the term. The Act also covers those with a disposition towards reprehensible conduct, for example an admission that a person is sexually attracted to children (*R v S* [2007] EWCA Crim 1387; but see also *R v Fox* [2009] EWCA Crim 653, where it was stated that such evidence ought not to be admitted).

It is important to note that a defendant is entitled to dispute that he is guilty of a matter that has resulted in conviction (or caution); the procedure for doing so is discussed in *R v C* [2010] EWCA Crim 2971.

There are some particular considerations at play when admitting police cautions as evidence of bad character. In *R v Olu and others* [2010] EWCA Crim 2975, the court held:

> We accept the submission that there is a very considerable difference not only between a caution and a conviction for the reasons given in the authorities to which we have referred, but there is also a very considerable difference between an admission contained in a caution without legal advice having been given and an admission made in a caution after legal advice or before a court by a plea. In such circumstances, the giving of legal advice or the formality of a court appearance will have made clear to the person the consequences of his admission. The processes that lead to a caution can differ widely between police area and police area; a court would be shutting its eyes to reality if it assumed that, where a person was not legally represented, the consequences of admitting an offence and accepting a caution were fully explained to a person in a manner that he understood the serious adverse consequences that would follow and what he was giving up by not exercising his right to legal advice—namely that what he was admitting would give him a criminal record, that the caution would be maintained on his PNC record for very many years and that it would be used against his interests in certain circumstances.

Penalty notices for disorder cannot, in themselves, be adduced as evidence of bad character and do not represent an admission (*R v Hamer* [2010] EWCA Crim 2053); *Hewson v Commissioner of the Police of the Metropolis* [2018] EWHC 471 (Admin)) neither can unsubstantiated allegations contained in crime reports (*R v Braithwaite* [2010] EWCA Crim 1082).

A7.3 **Bad character excluded from application**

Section 98 provides:

Criminal Justice Act 2003, s 98

98 'Bad character'

References in this Chapter to evidence of a person's 'bad character' are to evidence of, or of a disposition towards, misconduct on his part, other than evidence which—

(a) has to do with the alleged facts of the offence with which the defendant is charged, or

(b) is evidence of misconduct in connection with the investigation or prosecution of that offence.

This means that the allegation itself (obviously of misconduct) does not need to be subject to an application to admit bad character. The section also covers:

- evidence of a previous conviction that might be a component of the offence alleged (eg a conviction for assault against a child in relation to a cruelty charge concerning that same child: *R v R* [2006] EWCA Crim 3196);
- preparatory acts (eg purchase of a murder weapon);
- background evidence (eg an act that provided motive for the offence: *R v Saleem* [2007] EWCA Crim 1923 and *R v McNeill* [2007] EWCA Crim 2927);
- On gang membership and activity see *R v Heslop* 2022 EWCA Crim 897;
- a temporal connection is not essential for the evidence to be 'to do' with the offence if it goes to provide the motive, but it is otherwise if it is being used as evidence of propensity (*R v Sule* [2012] EWCA Crim 1130).

A7.4 Non-defendant's bad character

Section 100 provides:

Criminal Justice Act 2003, s 100

100 Non-defendant's bad character

(1) In criminal proceedings evidence of the bad character of a person other than the defendant is admissible if and only if—
 (a) it is important explanatory evidence,
 (b) it has substantial probative value in relation to a matter which—
  (i) is a matter in issue in the proceedings, and
  (ii) is of substantial importance in the context of the case as a whole, or
 (c) all parties to the proceedings agree to the evidence being admissible.

(2) For the purposes of subsection (1)(a) evidence is important explanatory evidence if—
 (a) without it, the court or jury would find it impossible or difficult properly to understand other evidence in the case, and
 (b) its value for understanding the case as a whole is substantial.

(3) In assessing the probative value of evidence for the purposes of subsection (1)(b) the court must have regard to the following factors (and to any others it considers relevant)—
 (a) the nature and number of the events, or other things, to which the evidence relates;
 (b) when those events or things are alleged to have happened or existed;
 (c) where—
  (i) the evidence is evidence of a person's misconduct, and
  (ii) it is suggested that the evidence has probative value by reason of similarity between that misconduct and other alleged misconduct, the nature and extent of the similarities and the dissimilarities between each of the alleged instances of misconduct;
 (d) where—
  (i) the evidence is evidence of a person's misconduct,
  (ii) it is suggested that that person is also responsible for the misconduct charged, and
  (iii) the identity of the person responsible for the misconduct charged is disputed, the extent to which the evidence shows or tends to show that the same person was responsible each time.

(4) Except where subsection (1)(c) applies, evidence of the bad character of a person other than the defendant must not be given without leave of the court.

A non-defendant includes a person who is not a witness in the case (*R v R Ahmed* [2017] EWCA Crim 1515). In deciding whether to allow cross-examination of a defence witness on their bad character there were two issues:

- whether creditworthiness is a matter in issue which is of substantial importance in the context of the case as a whole. If it is,
- the second question is whether the bad character relied on is of substantial probative value in relation to that issue.

When the prosecution seeks to invoke s 100, s 78 Police and Criminal Evidence Act (PACE) 1984 may be used to avoid too much focus on the nature of the previous offending (*R v Murphy (Anthony)* [2020] EWCA Crim 137).

A7.5 Defendant's bad character

Section 101 provides:

Criminal Justice Act 2003, s 101

101 Defendant's bad character

(1) In criminal proceedings evidence of the defendant's bad character is admissible if, but only if—
  (a) all parties to the proceedings agree to the evidence being admissible,
  (b) the evidence is adduced by the defendant himself or is given in answer to a question asked by him in cross-examination and intended to elicit it,
  (c) it is important explanatory evidence,
  (d) it is relevant to an important matter in issue between the defendant and the prosecution,
  (e) it has substantial probative value in relation to an important matter in issue between the defendant and a co-defendant,
  (f) it is evidence to correct a false impression given by the defendant, or
  (g) the defendant has made an attack on another person's character.
(2) Sections 102 to 106 contain provision supplementing subsection (1).
(3) The court must not admit evidence under subsection (1)(d) or (g) if, on an application by the defendant to exclude it, it appears to the court that the admission of the evidence would have such an adverse effect on the fairness of the proceedings that the court ought not to admit it.
(4) On an application to exclude evidence under subsection (3) the court must have regard, in particular, to the length of time between the matters to which that evidence relates and the matters which form the subject of the offence charged.

A7.6 Important explanatory evidence

Section 102 provides:

Criminal Justice Act 2003, s 102

102 'Important explanatory evidence'

For the purposes of section 101(1)(c) evidence is important explanatory evidence if—
(a) without it, the court or jury would find it impossible or difficult properly to understand other evidence in the case, and
(b) its value for understanding the case as a whole is substantial.

A case which is truly one of propensity cannot and must not be dressed up as a case of important explanatory evidence. To say the evidence fills out the picture is not the same as saying that the rest of the picture is either impossible or difficult to see without it (*R v Lee* [2012] EWCA Crim 316).

A7.7 Matter in issue between defendant and prosecution

Section 103 provides:

Criminal Justice Act 2003, s 103

103 Matter in issue between the defendant and the prosecution

(1) For the purposes of section 101(1)(d) the matters in issue between the defendant and the prosecution include—
   (a) the question whether the defendant has a propensity to commit offences of the kind with which he is charged, except where his having such a propensity makes it no more likely that he is guilty of the offence;
   (b) the question whether the defendant has a propensity to be untruthful, except where it is not suggested that the defendant's case is untruthful in any respect.

(2) Where subsection (1)(a) applies, a defendant's propensity to commit offences of the kind with which he is charged may (without prejudice to any other way of doing so) be established by evidence that he has been convicted of—
   (a) an offence of the same description as the one with which he is charged, or
   (b) an offence of the same category as the one with which he is charged.

(3) Subsection (2) does not apply in the case of a particular defendant if the court is satisfied, by reason of the length of time since the conviction or for any other reason, that it would be unjust for it to apply in his case.

(4) For the purposes of subsection (2)—
   (a) two offences are of the same description as each other if the statement of the offence in a written charge or indictment would, in each case, be in the same terms;
   (b) two offences are of the same category as each other if they belong to the same category of offences prescribed for the purposes of this section by an order made by the Secretary of State.

(5) A category prescribed by an order under subsection (4)(b) must consist of offences of the same type.

(6) Only prosecution evidence is admissible under section 101(1)(d).

Whilst the matter in issue includes propensity, the provision is more likely to be relevant to ruling out a defence such as innocent association (*R v Vo* [2013] EWCA Crim 2292); self-defence (*R v Cox* [2014] EWCA Crim 804); or identity (*R Richardson* [2014] EWCA Crim 1785). It may assist to establish the credibility of the complainant (*R v Blake* [2014] EWCA Crim 2341). It must not be used to bolster a weak case (see *R v H* [2014] EWCA Crim 420).

R v Mitchell [2016] UKSC 55 confirms that the issue for a court, asked to find bad character evidence from the propensity of a defendant to commit acts of the kind in question, was whether they were sure to the criminal standard that propensity existed. It was not necessary to prove the facts of each incident beyond reasonable doubt or that one incident should be considered separately from the others. However, propensity remains an incidental issue and could not alone establish guilt. In that case the evidence was used to challenge a defence of self-defence when the defendant had made extensive use of knives in the past.

A7.8 Matter in issue between the defendant and a co-defendant

Section 104 provides:

Criminal Justice Act 2003, s 104

104 'Matter in issue between the defendant and a co-defendant'

(1) Evidence which is relevant to the question whether the defendant has a propensity to be untruthful is admissible on that basis under section 101(1) only if the nature or conduct of his defence is such as to undermine the co-defendant's defence.

(2) Only evidence—
- (a) which is to be (or has been) adduced by the co-defendant, or
- (b) which a witness is to be invited to give (or has given) in cross-examination by the co-defendant, is admissible under section 101(1)(e).

A7.9 Evidence to correct a false impression

Section 105 provides:

Criminal Justice Act 2003, s 105

105 'Evidence to correct a false impression'

(1) For the purposes of section 101(1)(f)—
- (a) the defendant gives a false impression if he is responsible for the making of an express or implied assertion which is apt to give the court or jury a false or misleading impression about the defendant;
- (b) evidence to correct such an impression is evidence which has probative value in correcting it.

(2) A defendant is treated as being responsible for the making of an assertion if—
- (a) the assertion is made by the defendant in the proceedings (whether or not in evidence given by him),
- (b) the assertion was made by the defendant—
  - (i) on being questioned under caution, before charge, about the offence with which he is charged, or
  - (ii) on being charged with the offence or officially informed that he might be prosecuted for it, and evidence of the assertion is given in the proceedings,
- (c) the assertion is made by a witness called by the defendant,
- (d) the assertion is made by any witness in cross-examination in response to a question asked by the defendant that is intended to elicit it, or is likely to do so, or
- (e) the assertion was made by any person out of court, and the defendant adduces evidence of it in the proceedings.

(3) A defendant who would otherwise be treated as responsible for the making of an assertion shall not be so treated if, or to the extent that, he withdraws it or disassociates himself from it.

(4) Where it appears to the court that a defendant, by means of his conduct (other than the giving of evidence) in the proceedings, is seeking to give the court or jury an impression about himself that is false or misleading, the court may if it

appears just to do so treat the defendant as being responsible for the making of an assertion which is apt to give that impression.
(5) In subsection (4) 'conduct' includes appearance or dress.
(6) Evidence is admissible under section 101(1)(f) only if it goes no further than is necessary to correct the false impression.
(7) Only prosecution evidence is admissible under section 101(1)(f).

Material is only admissible (s 105(6)) if it goes no further than is necessary to correct the false impression (*R v Omotoso* [2018] EWCA Crim 1394).

A7.10 **Attack on another person's character**

Section 106 provides:

Criminal Justice Act 2003, s 106

106 'Attack on another person's character'

(1) For the purposes of section 101(1)(g) a defendant makes an attack on another person's character if—
  (a) he adduces evidence attacking the other person's character,
  (b) he (or any legal representative appointed under section 38(4) of the Youth Justice and Criminal Evidence Act 1999 (c. 23) to cross-examine a witness in his interests) asks questions in cross-examination that are intended to elicit such evidence, or are likely to do so, or
  (c) evidence is given of an imputation about the other person made by the defendant—
    (i) on being questioned under caution, before charge, about the offence with which he is charged, or
    (ii) on being charged with the offence or officially informed that he might be prosecuted for it.
(2) In subsection (1) 'evidence attacking the other person's character' means evidence to the effect that the other person—
  (a) has committed an offence (whether a different offence from the one with which the defendant is charged or the same one), or
  (b) has behaved, or is disposed to behave, in a reprehensible way; and 'imputation about the other person' means an assertion to that effect.
(3) Only prosecution evidence is admissible under section 101(1)(g).

Only issues raised in evidence, and not during a procedural application, may be taken into account (*R v Omotoso* [2018] EWCA Crim 1394).

See *Blackstone's Criminal Practice 2026* F15

A7.11 **Handling: special rules**

Theft Act 1968, s 27

(3) Where a person is being proceeded against for handling stolen goods (but not for any offence other than handling stolen goods), then at any stage of the proceedings, if evidence has been given of his having or arranging to have in his possession the goods the subject of the charge, or of his undertaking or assisting in, or arranging to undertake or assist in, their retention, removal, disposal or

> realisation, the following evidence shall be admissible for the purpose of proving that he knew or believed the goods to be stolen goods:—
> (a) evidence that he has had in his possession, or has undertaken or assisted in the retention, removal, disposal or realisation of, stolen goods from any theft taking place not earlier than twelve months before the offence charged; and
> (b) (provided that seven days' notice in writing has been given to him of the intention to prove the conviction) evidence that he has within the five years preceding the date of the offence charged been convicted of theft or of handling stolen goods.

A7.11.1 Key points

Handling must be the only offence in issue. The provision goes only to proof of guilty knowledge, not dishonesty or possession (*Duffas* (1994) 158 JP 245). Only the details admissible by reason of s 73(2) PACE 1984 should be admitted (*Hacker* [1994] 1 All ER 45). *Hacker* also confirms that s 78 PACE 1984 can be used to exclude the evidence if it is unfair in the proceedings to admit it.

A8 Bail

A8.1 Introduction

The starting point is that there is a presumption in favour of bail being granted in criminal proceedings (see A8.2 for the position in relation to defendants charged with murder appearing before a magistrates' court). The exceptions to that right under Sch 1 to the Bail Act 1976 are summarized in the following table:

Exception	Imprisonable—Pt I	Imprisonable—Pt IA triable only summarily	Non-imprisonable—Pt II
Fail to answer bail	Yes, but where there is a real likelihood of custody (para 2(1)(a))	Previously failed to answer bail in criminal proceedings and consequently court believes will fail to answer if bailed now, but only where real likelihood of custody (para 2)	Previously failed to answer bail in criminal proceedings and consequently court believes will fail to answer bail now (para 2)
Offend while on bail	Yes, but where real likelihood of custody (para 2(1)(b))	On bail at the date of the offence and consequently court believes would commit an offence on bail, but only if a real likelihood of custody (para 3)	NA
Interfere with witnesses or obstruct course of justice	Yes, but where real likelihood of custody (para 2(1)(c))	NA	NA
Substantial grounds for believing that if released on bail would commit an offence likely to cause physical or mental injury to an associated person, or cause an associated person to fear physical or mental injury	Yes (para 2ZA)	Yes (para 4)	NA

Blackstone's Magistrates' Court Handbook 2026. Bartholomew Dalton and Caroline Liggins, Oxford University Press. © Oxford University Press 2026.
DOI: 10.1093/oso/9780198963943.003.0008

Exception	Imprisonable—Pt I	Imprisonable—Pt IA triable only summarily	Non-imprisonable—Pt II
Arrested for breach of bail in same proceedings and substantial grounds to believe would fail to appear, commit offences, or interfere with witnesses or obstruct the course of justice	Yes, but must be a real likelihood of custody; if offence carries a life term the court may not grant bail unless satisfied there is no significant risk of failure to appear (para 6)	Yes, but must be real likelihood of custody (para 7)	Yes, including committing the offence by engaging in conduct likely to cause physical or mental injury to an associated person (paras 5 and 6)
Indictable or either-way offence and defendant on bail at the time of the offence	Yes, but note that if the offence carries a life term the court may not grant bail unless it is satisfied that there is no significant risk of an offence on bail. Must be a real likelihood of custody (para 2A)	NA	NA
Own protection or welfare	Yes (para 3)	Yes (para 5)	Yes (para 3)
Serving sentence	Yes (para 4)	Yes (para 6)	Yes (para 4)
Insufficient information	Yes (para 5)	Yes (para 8)	NA
Reports	Yes (para 7)	NA	NA
Drugs scheme	Yes (para 6A)	Yes (para 9)	NA
Homicide or rape	No bail unless exceptional circumstances justified if charged or convicted of a CJPOA 1994, s 25 offence and previous convictions for a s 25 offence	NA	NA
Murder	Not in the magistrates' court	NA	NA

A8.1.1 *General exceptions*

That presumption does not apply in the following cases:

- in extradition proceedings where the person is alleged to have been convicted of the offence;
- following committal to the Crown Court for sentence or for breach of a Crown Court order;

- after conviction, unless the proceedings are adjourned for inquiries to be made or a report to be prepared for sentence;
- on appeal against conviction or sentence.

Where a defendant aged 18 or over has tested positive for heroin, cocaine, or crack cocaine, and is unwilling to undergo an assessment of his drug misuse and/or any proposed follow-up treatment, different rules apply. The defendant cannot be granted bail unless the court is satisfied that there is no significant risk of an offence being committed while on bail.

Bail may be granted only in exceptional circumstances where a defendant is charged with or convicted of an offence of:

- murder, or
- attempted murder, or
- manslaughter, or
- rape, or
- attempted rape,

and the defendant has been previously convicted in the United Kingdom of any such offence or of culpable homicide. (If the previous conviction was manslaughter or culpable homicide, the provision applies only if the defendant received a sentence of imprisonment/long-term detention.) Convictions in EU member states can be taken into account.

Bail need not be granted to a person on bail at the time of committing an indictable offence (Sch 1, para 2A Bail Act 1976). Sections 14 and 15 of the Criminal Justice Act 2003 are partially in force and currently apply *only* to those charged with offences carrying life imprisonment.

Criminal Justice Act 2003, s 14

14 Offences committed on bail

(1) For paragraph 2A of Part 1 of Schedule 1 to the 1976 Act (defendant need not be granted bail where he was on bail on date of offence) there is substituted—

'2A(1) If the defendant falls within this paragraph he may not be granted bail unless the court is satisfied that there is no significant risk of his committing an offence while on bail (whether subject to conditions or not).

- The defendant falls within this paragraph if—

(a) he is aged 18 or over, and

(b) it appears to the court that he was on bail in criminal proceedings on the date of the offence.'

(2) After paragraph 9 of that Part there is inserted— '9AA(1) This paragraph applies if—

(a) the defendant is a child or young person, and

(b) it appears to the court that he was on bail in criminal proceedings on the date of the offence.

(2) In deciding for the purposes of paragraph 2(1) of this Part of this Schedule whether it is satisfied that there are substantial grounds for believing that the defendant, if released on bail (whether subject to conditions or not), would commit an offence while on bail, the court shall give particular weight to the fact that the defendant was on bail in criminal proceedings on the date of the offence.'

Criminal Justice Act 2003, s 15(1) and (2)

15 Absconding by persons released on bail

(1) For paragraph 6 of Part 1 of Schedule 1 to the 1976 Act (defendant need not be granted bail if having been released on bail he has been arrested in pursuance of section 7) there is substituted—

'6(1) If the defendant falls within this paragraph, he may not be granted bail unless the court is satisfied that there is no significant risk that, if released on bail (whether subject to conditions or not), he would fail to surrender to custody.

(2) Subject to sub-paragraph (3) below, the defendant falls within this paragraph if—

(a) he is aged 18 or over, and

(b) it appears to the court that, having been released on bail in or in connection with the proceedings for the offence, he failed to surrender to custody.

(3) Where it appears to the court that the defendant had reasonable cause for his failure to surrender to custody, he does not fall within this paragraph unless it also appears to the court that he failed to surrender to custody at the appointed place as soon as reasonably practicable after the appointed time . . .'

(2) After paragraph 9AA of that Part (inserted by section 14(2)) there is inserted—

'9AB (1) Subject to sub-paragraph (2) below, this paragraph applies if—

(a) the defendant is a child or young person, and

(b) it appears to the court that, having been released on bail in or in connection with the proceedings for the offence, he failed to surrender to custody

(2) Where it appears to the court that the defendant had reasonable cause for his failure to surrender to custody, this paragraph does not apply unless it also appears to the court that he failed to surrender to custody at the appointed place as soon as reasonably practicable after the appointed time.

(3) In deciding for the purposes of paragraph 2(1) of this Part of this Schedule whether it is satisfied that there are substantial grounds for believing that the defendant, if released on bail (whether subject to conditions or not), would fail to surrender to custody, the court shall give particular weight to—

(a) where the defendant did not have reasonable cause for his failure to surrender to custody, the fact that he failed to surrender to custody, or

(b) where he did have reasonable cause for his failure to surrender to custody, the fact that he failed to surrender to custody at the appointed place as soon as reasonably practicable after the appointed time. . .'

A8.2 Right to apply for bail

An application for bail may be made at the first hearing of the case before a magistrates' court, save in respect of a defendant facing a charge of murder (or murder and any other charge(s)), in which case the issue of bail must be resolved before a Crown Court judge within 48 hours (excluding public holidays) beginning the day after the defendant's appearance in the magistrates' court (s 115 Coroners and Justice Act 2009). If bail is refused, an application may be made at the subsequent hearing, and may be based on the same grounds as the first. A refusal of bail on the grounds of insufficient information should not be counted as a decision to refuse bail, thereby exhausting one of the two attempts (*R v Calder Justices, ex p Kennedy* (1992) 156 JP 716). Similarly, a remand in absence should be discounted (*R v Dover and East Kent Justices, ex p Dean* (1991) 156 JP 357).

Note, however, that if a fully argued application is not made by the defendant at the first hearing, the effect is that one opportunity to argue for bail is lost, meaning that if bail is refused at the subsequent hearing, the two opportunities for bail have been spent. Similarly, if an argument is made at the first hearing but not at the second hearing, there is no right to a second application for bail at the third hearing. Advocates should always obtain certificates of full argument in order to support any further Crown Court bail application (s 5(6A) Bail Act 1976). This should appear on the bail form issued by the court. Following two refusals to grant bail, further applications may be made if there are new arguments as to fact or law (Sch 1, Pt IIA Bail Act 1976). This includes but is not limited to a change in circumstances, for example:

- change in the case alleged against the defendant (*R v Reading Crown Court, ex p Malik* [1981] QB 451 and *R v Slough Justices, ex p Duncan* [1981] QB 451);
- increased surety (*R v Isleworth Crown Court, ex p Commissioners of Customs and Excise, The Times*, 27 July 1990);
- passage of time (*Neumeister v Austria (No 1)* (1979–80) 1 EHRR 91).

In *R (B) v Brent Youth Court* [2010] EWHC 1893 (Admin), the court held that a change of address presented for residence purposes amounted to a change of circumstances. It was not necessary that any new factor be exceptional in nature. The correct test is whether there are any new considerations which were not before the court when the accused was last remanded in custody. Similarly, an argument that the prosecution case against the defendant was significantly weaker than at first presented would qualify as a new argument. The court ended by saying that:

> even if the Bench had been entitled to form the view that each and every argument as to fact or law was an argument which it had heard previously, it manifestly failed to go on to consider whether, notwithstanding that, it should nonetheless consider substantively a bail application, given the provisions of Section 44 [Children and Young Persons Act 1933], having regard to the welfare of a child or young person.

A8.3 Grounds for refusing bail

The seriousness of the offence (and the likely penalty) cannot of itself justify a refusal of bail on the inference that the person is likely to abscond (*Lettelier v France* (1992) 14 EHRR 83), although a judge is perfectly entitled to regard that as a significant factor (*R (Thompson) v Central Criminal Court* [2005] EWHC 2345 (Admin)). Before bail can be refused on the grounds of interfering with witnesses or obstructing justice, the prosecution must point to an identifiable risk and provide supporting evidence (*Clooth v Belgium* (1991) 14 EHRR 717). The court should not take the prosecution case at its highest, but rather follow the statute and consider the strength overall of the prosecution evidence (*R (E) v Wood Green Crown Court* [2013] EWHC 1869 (Admin)). Bail should only be refused for a defendant's own protection, depending on the circumstances, in exceptional circumstances and for a short time such that there were no reasonably available means other than detention to afford protection (*Archer v CPM* [2020] EWHC 1567 (QB)).

R (Iqbal) v Canterbury Crown Court [2020] EWHC 452 (Admin) confirms the normal rules apply upon charge, by requisition, even when there has been a very lengthy period of release under investigation.

In deciding whether to refuse bail the relevant considerations include (Sch 1, para 9 Bail Act 1976):

- the nature and seriousness of the offence or default (and the probable method of dealing with the defendant for it);
- the character, antecedents, associations, and community ties of the defendant;
- the defendant's record as respects the fulfilment of his obligations under previous grants of bail in criminal proceedings:
  - except in the case of a defendant whose case is adjourned for inquiries or a report, the strength of the evidence of his having committed the offence or having defaulted;
- the court is satisfied that there are substantial grounds for believing that the defendant, if released on bail (whether subject to conditions or not), would commit an offence while on bail, it is a relevant consideration that there is a risk that the defendant may do so by engaging in conduct that would, or would be likely to, cause physical or mental injury to any person other than the defendant;
- any other considerations that appear to be relevant.

A8.3.1 *Classifying the offence*

There are three categories of offences to consider:

- indictable imprisonable offences (Sch 1, Pt 1);
- summary-only imprisonable offences (which includes offences triable summarily only due to the value of the offence, eg criminal damage) (Sch 1, Pt 1A), although it is unclear whether the hybrid offence of low-value theft from a shop falls into this group because of the defendant's right to elect; and
- summary-only non-imprisonable offences (Sch 1, Pt II).

A8.4 Indictable imprisonable offences

Bail cannot be refused if there is no real prospect that the defendant will be sentenced to a custodial sentence in the proceedings.

A court may refuse bail on the grounds:

- that the defendant is already a serving prisoner (para 4 remand); or
- that there is insufficient information on which to base a decision (para 5 remand).

Refusal of bail can be for the defendant's own protection or, for a defendant under 18 years of age, his own welfare (para 3 remand).

Bail may be refused if there are substantial grounds for believing that, if released on bail, the defendant would:

- fail to surrender;

- commit further offences;
- commit an offence on bail by engaging in conduct that would or would be likely to cause physical or mental injury to an associated person, or that an associated person would fear physical or mental injury—under s 62 Family Law Act 1996, 'associated person' includes:
  - those who are or have been married to each other or in a civil partnership,
  - present or former cohabitants,
  - those who live or have lived in the same household other than as employees, tenants, or lodgers,
  - relatives,
  - those who are or have been engaged to marry or enter into a civil partnership,
  - those who have or have had intimate personal relationships of significant duration,
  - the parents of children and those with parental responsibility,
  - parties to the same family proceedings; or
- interfere with witnesses or otherwise obstruct the course of justice.

Bail may also be refused if the offender was:

- on bail at the time of the offence;
- arrested for breach of bail in the same proceedings and there are substantial grounds to believe he would fail to appear, commit offences, or interfere with witnesses or obstruct the course of justice.

A8.5 Summary-only imprisonable offences

Bail cannot be refused if there is no real prospect that the defendant will be sentenced to a custodial sentence in the proceedings.

Bail can be refused on one or more of the following grounds only:

- failure to surrender (if the defendant has previously failed to surrender);
- commission of further offences (if the instant offence was committed on bail);
- fear of commission of offences likely to cause an associated person to suffer or fear physical or mental injury;
- the defendant's own protection (for his own welfare if aged under 18);
- the defendant is serving custody;
- fear of failure to surrender, commission of offences, interference with witnesses, or obstruction of justice (if the defendant has been arrested for breach of bail in respect of the instant offence); and
- lack of sufficient information.

A8.6 Summary-only non-imprisonable offences (Sch 1, Pt II)

Bail can be denied only if there has been a previous failure to surrender in the proceedings and the court believes that if granted bail the defendant would fail to surrender again, or:

- for the defendant's own protection (for his own welfare if aged under 18);

- where the defendant is already in custody;
- where, following a breach of bail, or the defendant absconding, there are substantial grounds for believing that if released on bail the defendant would:
  - fail to surrender,
  - commit further offences, or
  - interfere with witnesses or otherwise obstruct the course of justice.

A8.7 Conditional bail

Conditional bail may be imposed if the court believes that it is necessary because there is a risk that:

- the defendant will fail to surrender; a surety should only be used for this reason (*R (Shea) v Winchester Crown Court* [2013] EWHC 1050 (Admin));
- the defendant will commit an offence while on bail;
- the defendant would interfere with witnesses or obstruct justice;
- the defendant would not cooperate with the making of pre-sentence or other reports; or
- the defendant would not attend appointments with his legal adviser.

A person granted bail on a charge of murder must be required to undergo a psychiatric examination (s 3(6A) Bail Act 1976).

A8.8 Insufficient information

The accused need not be granted bail if the court is satisfied that, owing to lack of time since the commencement of the proceedings, it has not been practicable to obtain sufficient information for taking the bail decision. This may apply if the defence need to confirm an address, or immigration status, or the mental health of the defendant; or the police have enquiries outstanding which might make the allegation more serious. There is no restriction in the Bail Act which has the effect of limiting the number of times on which the provision can be used. While it should not allow the police to delay their enquiries, it has the benefit of not counting as a bail application.

A8.9 Pre-release conditions

Bail Act 1976, ss 3 and 8

3 General provisions

(1) A person granted bail in criminal proceedings shall be under a duty to surrender to custody, and that duty is enforceable in accordance with section 6 of this Act.

. . .

(4) He may be required, before release on bail, to provide a surety or sureties to secure his surrender to custody.

. . .

8 Bail with sureties

(1) This section applies where a person is granted bail in criminal proceedings on condition that he provides one or more surety or sureties for the purpose of securing that he surrenders to custody.

(2) In considering the suitability for that purpose of a proposed surety, regard may be had (amongst other things) to—
  (a) the surety's financial resources;
  (b) his character and any previous convictions of his; and
  (c) his proximity (whether in point of kinship, place of residence or otherwise) to the person for whom he is to be surety.

(3) Where a court grants a person bail in criminal proceedings on such a condition but is unable to release him because no surety or no suitable surety is available, the court shall fix the amount in which the surety is to be bound and subsections (4) and (5) below, or in a case where the proposed surety resides in Scotland subsection (6) below, shall apply for the purpose of enabling the recognizance of the surety to be entered into subsequently.

(4) Where this subsection applies the recognizance of the surety may be entered into before such of the following persons or descriptions of persons as the court may by order specify or, if it makes no such order, before any of the following persons, that is to say—
  (a) where the decision is taken by a magistrates' court, before a justice of the peace, a justices' clerk or a police officer who either is of the rank of inspector or above or is in charge of a police station or, if magistrates' courts rules so provide, by a person of such other description as is specified in the rules . . .

(5) Where a surety seeks to enter into his recognizance before any person in accordance with subsection (4) above but that person declines to take his recognizance because he is not satisfied of the surety's suitability, the surety may apply to—
  (a) the court which fixed the amount of the recognizance in which the surety was to be bound, or
  (b) a magistrates' court for that court to take his recognizance and that court shall, if satisfied of his suit-ability, take his recognizance . . .

(7) Where, in pursuance of subsection (4) or (6) above, a recognizance is entered into otherwise than before the court that fixed the amount of the recognizance, the same consequences shall follow as if it had been entered into before that court. A surety may be taken by a police officer under these provisions unless the court otherwise orders.

Courts will wish to see some evidence of a surety's means. A surety must understand the risks to them, including of imprisonment, if the defendant fails to appear and the recognizance cannot be found.

For the convenience of all parties sureties should normally be made continuous for each hearing at which the defendant is required to attend.

A surety may only be used to secure attendance and is not appropriate to prevent further offences (*R (Shea) v Winchester Crown Court* [2013] EWHC 1050 (Admin)).

A8.9.1 *Security*

This may be money or items of value. The Money Laundering Regulations require that those handling the money (including a court) are satisfied as to its source. There is no limitation on what may be provided as the security, though jointly owned property may not be accepted. The courts are ill equipped to hold substantial securities and solicitors will often give undertakings, backed by irrevocable authorities from the owner of the security, to account to the court should the defendant fail to appear.

A8.10 Electronic monitoring

Section 3AB Bail Act 1976 deals with electronic monitoring for adults; and s 3AC is applicable to all defendants. The court must be satisfied that without electronic monitoring bail would not be granted.

A8.11 Prosecution appeals against the grant of bail

The Bail (Amendment) Act 1993 allows a prosecutor to appeal the grant of bail in any case where the offence is imprisonable. The prosecution must have objected to bail, and following the grant of bail, must orally in court state their intention to appeal the decision. A written notice must be served on both the court and the defendant within two hours of the oral notice having been given. A delay of five minutes in giving an oral indication to the court (and after the defendant had been taken from the courtroom) was deemed to comply with the Act in *R v Isleworth Crown Court, ex p Clarke* [1998] 1 Cr App R 257. In *R (Cardin) v Birmingham Crown Court* [2017] EWHC 2101 (Admin) it was held that the two hours was to be liberally interpreted where there was no fault on the part of the Crown. This confirmed the decision in *R (Jeffrey) v Crown Court at Warwick* [2002] EWHC 2469, where it was held that s 1(7) of the Act should have read into it the following words:

> unless such failure was caused by circumstances outside the control of the prosecution and not due to any fault on its part.

Service of the written notice on a jailer who hands the notice to a defendant suffices, and solicitors who accept such notices do so on the implicit understanding that they will be immediately communicated to the defendant.

A8.12 Breach of bail conditions

Offences in relation to bail are dealt with at **C3**.

Bail Act 1976, s 7

(4) a person arrested in pursuance of subsection (3) above—
   (a) shall, except where he was arrested within 24 hours of the time appointed for him to surrender to custody, be brought as soon as practicable and in any event within 24 hours after his arrest before a justice of the peace; and
   (b) in the said excepted case shall be brought before the court at which he was to have surrendered to custody.

(5) A justice of the peace before whom a person is brought under subsection (4) above may, subject to subsection (6) below, if of the opinion that that person—
   (a) is not likely to surrender to custody, or
   (b) has broken or is likely to break any condition of his bail, remand him in custody or commit him to custody, as the case may require, or alternatively, grant him bail subject to the same or to different conditions, but if not of that opinion shall grant him bail subject to the same conditions (if any) as were originally imposed.

(5A) A justice of the peace may not remand a person in, or commit a person to, custody under subsection (5) if—
 (a) the person has attained the age of eighteen,
 (b) the person was released on bail in non-extradition proceedings,
 (c) the person has not been convicted of an offence in those proceedings, and
 (d) it appears to the justice of the peace that there is no real prospect that the person will be sentenced to a custodial sentence in the proceedings.

(6) Where a person brought before a justice under subsection (4) or (4B) is a child or young person and the justice does not grant him bail, subsection (5) above shall have effect subject to the provisions of section 91 of the Legal Aid, Sentencing and Punishment of Offenders Act 2012 (remands of children otherwise than on bail).

(7) In reckoning for the purposes of this section any period of 24 hours, no account shall be taken of Christmas Day, Good Friday or any Sunday.

Following an alleged breach of bail conditions, the defendant must be brought before a magistrates' court within 24 hours of arrest. This means that the hearing must commence at court within those 24 hours, and any delay must result in the defendant's automatic release from custody (*R v Governor of Glen Parva Young Offender Institution, ex p G (A Minor)* [1998] 2 Cr App R 349). A court can, however, bring a defendant into the dock and then adjourn the hearing until later in the court list but there is no power to adjourn to another day (*R (Hussein) v Derby Magistrates' Court* [2001] 1 WLR 254). According to *R (Culley) v Dorchester Crown Court* [2007] EWHC 109 (Admin) the breach of bail proceedings must be concluded within 24 hours. However, this decision was criticized in *obiter* in *McElkerney v Highbury Corner Magistrates' Court* [2009] EWHC 2621 (Admin). A magistrates' court has no power simply to commit an offender to the Crown Court in order for the breach to be decided (*R v Teeside Magistrates' Court, ex p Ellison* (2001) 165 JP 355).

Only one magistrate need deal with an alleged bail breach, and there is no requirement for formal evidence to be called by prosecution or defence. There is no defence of 'reasonable excuse' in relation to the breaking of bail conditions (*R (Vickers) v West London Magistrates' Court* [2004] Crim LR 63), although the reasons for breach would be relevant to the determination of whether or not to grant bail again.

In *R v Liverpool Justices, ex p DPP* (1992) 95 Cr App R 222, the court laid down the following guidance for a court to follow when considering bail breaches:

- strict rules of evidence did not apply and hearsay was admissible;
- the court must consider the type of evidence called and take account of the fact that there had been no cross-examination;
- the prosecution and defence can call witnesses if they so wish, and the other party has the right to cross-examine;
- the defendant has a right to give oral evidence.

In practice a statement will be made. No issue in relation to hearsay arises (*R (Thomas) v Greenwich Magistrates' Court* [2009] EWHC 1180 (Admin)).

If the breach is not proved, the defendant must be released on the same conditions as existed previously. If the breach is proved, that does not mean an automatic remand into custody; *R (DPP) v Havering Magistrates' Court* [2001] 1 WLR 805 confirms that it is simply a factor to be considered when the court decides whether or not it should re-bail the defendant and on what conditions. The statute does not require that they be more stringent.

Since August 2023 issues have arisen regarding the expiry of time to deal with proceedings on arrest for breach of bail under s 7 Bail Act 1976. There is nothing in the section which requires the application to be concluded in that time and nothing extrinsic to it which would justify such a reading, quite the opposite. Bringing before a judge/magistrates should be something more than merely showing the defendant to the bench and then taking him back to the cells for an application to be made later in the day; that is clearly not within the spirit of the Act. However, once the application has started, the hearing can be put back until later in the day, but no later than that.

A8.13 Criminal Procedure Rules applicable to the grant of bail

Part 14 of the Criminal Procedure Rules applies to bail.

A8.14 Provision of bail for youths

The rules relating to the provision of bail for youths are discussed in B2.

A8.15 Appeals in relation to bail

A8.15.1 *Appeal against conditional bail*

If a defendant is dissatisfied with the conditions of bail he may appeal to the Crown Court, provided that he has first applied to a magistrates' court to vary those conditions and has been unsuccessful. An appeal lies only in relation to the following conditions:

- residence (but not in relation to any bail hostel);
- surety or security;
- curfew;
- non-contact.

In other circumstances it may be necessary to apply for a judicial review.

A8.15.2 *Appeal against refusal of bail*

Following full argument in the magistrates' court (and a certificate of full argument having been issued; Crim PR 14.4(4) requires that the document confirming the refusal of bail contain such a certificate), an appeal lies as of right to the Crown Court.

There is no longer any appeal route to the High Court, save in an exceptional case by way of judicial review.

A8.15.3 *Bail pending appeal*

The procedure for making an application in the magistrates' court is at s 113 MCA 1980. *Thomas v CPS* [2015] EWHC 4079 (Admin) confirms that this provision creates an entitlement to apply for bail pending appeal in every case in which such a properly constituted application is made and places an obligation on the magistrates' court, whether by the sentencing tribunal or otherwise, to consider an application for bail pending appeal in every case where a properly constituted application for bail is made at the magistrates' court. It does not follow that in every case it would be necessary to hold an oral hearing on the application.

See *Blackstone's Criminal Practice 2026* D7

A9 **Binding Rulings**

Section 8A MCA 1980 deals with pre-trial rulings and s 8B allows a magistrates' court to make or vary binding rulings.

Sections 8A and 8B MCA 1980 provide:

Magistrates' Courts Act 1980, ss 8A and 8B

8A Power to make rulings at pre-trial hearing

(1) For the purposes of this section a hearing is a pre-trial hearing if—
  (a) it relates to an information—
    (i) which is to be tried summarily, and
    (ii) to which the accused has pleaded not guilty, and
  (b) it takes place before the start of the trial.

(2) . . .

(3) At a pre-trial hearing, a magistrates' court may make a ruling as to any matter mentioned in subsection (4) if—
  (a) the condition in subsection (5) is met,
  (b) the court has given the parties an opportunity to be heard, and
  (c) it appears to the court that it is in the interests of justice to make the ruling.

(4) The matters are—
  (a) any question as to the admissibility of evidence;
  (b) any other question of law relating to the case.

(5) . . .

(6) A ruling may be made under this section—
  (a) on an application by a party to the case, or
  (b) of the court's own motion.

(7) For the purposes of this section and section 8B, references to the prosecutor are to any person acting as prosecutor, whether an individual or body.

8B Effect of rulings at pre-trial hearing

(1) Subject to subsections (3) and (6), a ruling under section 8A has binding effect from the time it is made until the case against the accused or, if there is more than one, against each of them, is disposed of.

(2) The case against an accused is disposed of if—
  (a) he is acquitted or convicted,
  (b) the prosecutor decides not to proceed with the case against him, or
  (c) the information is dismissed.

(3) A magistrates' court may discharge or vary (or further vary) a ruling under section 8A if—
  (a) the condition in section 8A(5) is met,
  (b) the court has given the parties an opportunity to be heard, and
  (c) it appears to the court that it is in the interests of justice to do so.

(4) The court may act under subsection (3)—
  (a) on an application by a party to the case, or
  (b) of its own motion.

(5) No application may be made under subsection (4)(a) unless there has been a material change of circumstances since the ruling was made or, if a previous application has been made, since the application (or last application) was made.

(6) A ruling under section 8A is discharged in relation to an accused if—
  (a) the magistrates' court commits or sends him to the Crown Court for trial for the offence charged in the information, or
  (b) a count charging him with the offence is included in an indictment by virtue of section 40 of the Criminal Justice Act 1988.

Blackstone's Magistrates' Court Handbook 2026. Bartholomew Dalton and Caroline Liggins, Oxford University Press. © Oxford University Press 2026.
DOI: 10.1093/oso/9780198963943.003.0009

Because of the binding nature of these rulings, it is not open to a later bench simply to reverse the ruling because it would have reached a different conclusion.

In *Brett v DPP* [2009] EWHC 440 (Admin), the court took a far less restrictive approach than that taken in previous cases in holding a judge to have erred in feeling that he was bound by a previous ruling under s 8A MCA 1980. However, a later court cannot simply annul a previous decision on the sole ground that it simply disagrees with it (*CPS v Gloucester Justices and Loveridge* [2008] EWHC 1488 (Admin)). In *R (Jones) v South East Surrey Local Justice Area* [2010] EWHC 916 (Admin), the court, having previously disallowed a prosecution application to adjourn, later granted it due to the fact that the information presented on the renewed application was different and that it was in the interests of justice that the previous ruling be reversed.

Where the court acts of its own motion to vary a previous ruling, the grounds for discharge or variation are simply the interests of justice; and where an application is made by a party, there is an additional requirement for proof of material change of circumstances (*CPS v Gloucester Justices and Alan Loveridge* [2008] EWHC 1488 (Admin)).

The decision of a magistrates' court to reverse its earlier decision was upheld when the court found the original application by the Crown to adjourn a trial was materially misleading (*DPP v Woods* [2017] EWHC 1070 (Admin)).

See *Blackstone's Criminal Practice 2026* D21.33

A10 Case Management

A10.1 Identification of the defendant

Under Crim PR 5, there is no standalone rule on the 'Identification of the defendant'. The new rules state that all participants in a criminal case have a duty to actively manage the case, which includes identifying and narrowing the issues, including the identity of the defendant. Crim PR 24.15(2) provides that where the court imposes a custodial sentence the court shall require the defendant to provide their nationality. Failure to do so, without reasonable excuse, is an offence under s 86A Courts Act 2003.

A10.2 Overview

All parties are expected to manage cases proactively through the system. This applies as much in road traffic cases as in any criminal case (*R (Hassani) v West London Magistrates' Court* [2017] EWHC 1270 (Admin)). The most notable impact has been to limit the use of so-called ambush defences. However, a strong defendant, aware of the risks, is still able to put the Crown to proof.

For information on the completion of the preparation for effective trial form, see **Appendix 1**.

A10.3 Application of the rules to civil proceedings

The Crim PR have no application in relation to civil proceedings in the magistrates' court, and the Civil Procedure Rules do not apply either. However, Rule 3A of the Magistrates' Courts Rules 1981 provides the court with case management powers identical to those enjoyed in relation to criminal cases.

A10.4 Alternative and additional charges

When the Crown prefers an aggravated offence and in the alternative the underlying offence, the latter should be adjourned *sine die* if the court convicts on the more serious matter. If the defendant offers a plea to the lesser offence it should be noted but not taken (*Henderson v CPS* [2016] EWHC 464 (Admin)).

When the Crown prefers an additional charge it must comply with Crim PR 7.3(3).

A10.5 The overriding objective and case management

Crim PR 1 and 3 deal with the overriding objective and case management powers. Extracts from these rules are reproduced in **Appendix 2**.

A10.6 Prosecution witnesses

Once the Crown has served witness statements as initial details of the prosecution case, it must, if the defence so request, call or at least tender as witnesses all those whose statements have been served, unless the statement is

Blackstone's Magistrates' Court Handbook 2026. Bartholomew Dalton and Caroline Liggins, Oxford University Press. © Oxford University Press 2026.
DOI: 10.1093/oso/9780198963943.003.0010

to be read or the witness is not capable of belief (*R v Russell Jones* [1995] 3 All ER 239). If the prosecution choose not to call a particular witness, and the court is satisfied that the interests of justice require that the witness be called, and that it would be unfair to the defence not to do so, the court may in appropriate cases call the witness itself (*R v Haringey Justices ex p DPP* [1996] 1 All ER 828). These cases were not referred to in *Azzaz v DPP* [2015] EWHC 3016 when the case proceeded without the unwilling complainant, there being another witness to the events. Neither party made a hearsay application in relation to the statement of the missing witnesses nor sought to follow the procedure in *Haringey Justices*. The result of any cross-examination was speculative.

A10.7 Defence case statements

These are not obligatory in summary proceedings but if given should be served within 14 days of initial disclosure by the Crown. An application for further disclosure under s 8 CPIA 1996 cannot be made unless a defence case statement has been served (see **A16**).

A10.8 Defence witnesses—notification of intention to call

Section 6C CPIA 1996 imposes duties on a defendant intending to call defence witnesses at trial. Failure to comply is most likely to result in an adjournment and wasted costs, so solicitors should ensure that they have taken all reasonable steps to ensure that a defendant is made aware of his obligations to provide such information. Notice of the name, address, and date of birth, if available, should be given in summary proceedings within 14 days of initial disclosure. A form is prescribed at Criminal Procedure Rules forms 15.4. It is likely that the prosecution will supply such information to the police. There is a code of practice for arranging and conducting interviews of witnesses notified by the accused, and this governs police conduct.

A10.8.1 *Time limits*

The Criminal Procedure and Investigations Act 1996 (Defence Disclosure Time Limits) Regulations 2011, Reg 3 provides for time limits and extensions. The time for service begins with the day on which the prosecutor complies or purports to comply with s 3 Criminal Procedure and Investigations Act 1996 (initial duty of the prosecutor to disclose) and expires at the end of 14 days.

A10.9 Failure by the Crown to appear or proceed

Section 15 MCA 1980 provides that:

15 Non-appearance of prosecutor:

Where at the time and place appointed for the trial or adjourned trial of an information the accused appears or is brought before the court and the prosecutor does not appear, the court may dismiss the information or, if evidence has been received on a previous occasion, proceed in the absence of the prosecutor.

DPP v Bird [2015] EWHC 4077 (Admin) states that a magistrates' court may only dismiss a charge

- after hearing evidence;
- where the prosecution offers no evidence or is not able to proceed and the case is not adjourned or;
- where the prosecution does not appear at the time and place appointed for trial.

Section 9 MCA 1980 confirms that the summary trial of an information begins with the entry of a plea.

A10.10 **Procedure at trial**

Crim PR 24.3 requires that both prosecution and defence prepare their cases because, at the start of a trial,

(a) the prosecutor may summarize the prosecution case, concisely identifying the relevant law, outlining the facts, and indicating the matters likely to be in dispute;
(b) to help the members of the court to understand the case and resolve any issue in it, the court may invite the defendant concisely to identify what is in issue.

The rest of the procedure for a trial is set out in the remainder on Crim PR 24.3.

A10.11 **Vulnerable persons**

Criminal Practice Direction

6.1 Vulnerable people in the courts

6.1.1 However, many other people giving evidence in a criminal case, whether as a witness or defendant, may require assistance: the court is required to take 'every reasonable step' to encourage and facilitate the attendance of witnesses and to facilitate the participation of any person, including the defendant (Rule 3.8(4)(a) and (b)). This includes enabling a witness or defendant to give their best evidence, and enabling a defendant to comprehend the proceedings and engage fully with his or her defence. The pre-trial and trial process should, so far as necessary, be adapted to meet those ends. Regard should be had to the welfare of a young defendant as required by section 44 of the Children and Young Persons Act 1933, and generally to Parts 1 and 3 of the Criminal Procedure Rules (the overriding objective and the court's powers of case management).

Under Part 3 of the Rules, the court must identify the needs of witnesses at an early stage (Rule 3.2(2)(b)) and may require the parties to identify arrangements to facilitate the giving of evidence and participation in the trial (Crim PR 3.11). There are various statutory special measures that the court may utilise to assist a witness in giving evidence. Crim PR Part 18 gives the procedures to be followed. Courts should note the 'primary rule' which requires the court to give a direction for a special measure to assist a child witness or qualifying witness and that in such cases an application to the court is not required (Crim PR 18.9).

6.1.4–6.1.11 [Provides for ground rules hearings to plan the questioning of a vulnerable witness or defendant.]

6.2 Intermediaries

[Sets out detailed provisions for the use of intermediaries. The process of appointment should begin with assessment by an intermediary and a an expert report (psychiatric/psychological). The report will make recommendations to address the communication needs of the witness or defendant during trial. (See also **A27**.)]

6.4 Vulnerable defendants

[Sets out provisions for vulnerable defendants before the trial, sentencing, or appeal.]

Note: there is a Judicial Protocol: Expedition of Cases Involving Witnesses Under 10 Years.

A10.12 Case law

The courts deprecate any attempts to take a tactical advantage.

In *Writtle v DPP* [2009] EWHC 236 (Admin), the court held:

> the present regime of case management should in general ensure that the issues in the case are identified well before a hearing. There will, of course, be cases where something occurs in the course of a trial which may properly give rise to a new issue, but this was not such a case. The days when the defence can assume that they will be able successfully to ambush the prosecution are over.

The court adopted the earlier ruling in *Malcolm v DPP* [2007] EWHC 363 (Admin), in which Burnton J stated that it is the duty of the defence to make clear to the prosecution and the court at an early stage both the defence and the issues it raises.

In *DPP v Bury Magistrates' Court* [2007] EWHC 3256 (Admin), the court deprecated the practice of the defence of failing to notify the court of prosecution failures when certifying a case ready for trial, in order to take a tactical advantage. Further, that defence breach of the rules may have an impact on the amount of any costs to be recovered (in this case wasted costs).

In *R (Lawson) v Stratford Magistrates' Court* [2007] EWHC 2490 (Admin), it was held that a court was correct to allow a prosecution adjournment in order to address issues raised for the first time by the defence during a closing speech. The issues related to signage and device calibration.

A10.13 Effects on the admissibility of evidence

There is no power under the Rules to make hearsay statements admissible other than by a proper application of the hearsay provisions of the CJA 2003. *T v R* [2012] EWCA Crim 2358 confirms that a failure to comply with procedural rules could not affect the law on the admissibility of evidence. This is confirmed in relation to expert evidence (form SFR1) by *Hunt v CPS* [2018] EWHC 3341 (Admin).

The court should have regard to s 114(2) CJA 2003.

For the answers given on a preparation for effective trial (PET) form to be admissible, a properly formulated application must be made to admit the hearsay evidence contained in that answer (*Valiati v DPP; KM v DPP* [2018] EWHC 2908 (Admin) and see **Appendix** 1). An unfair advantage must normally have been obtained from the way the form was completed.

Evidence cannot be admitted merely because no issue on it has been identified on the PET form. Being unhelpful was not a concession as to the truth of a statement (*Randell v DPP* [2018] EWHC 1048 (Admin)).

A failure to serve defence notices does not render the evidence inadmissible. The sanctions are adverse comment, cross-examination, and inference (*R (Tinnion) v Reading Crown Court* [2010] EWHC 2930 (Admin); *R v Ullah* [2011] EWCA Crim 3275).

A10.14 Other consequences

A failure by a defendant to serve a defence statement did not amount to a contempt of court on either the part of the advocate or defendant (*R v Rochford* [2010] EWCA Crim 1928 and *Joseph Hill & Co* [2013] EWCA Crim 775). In *SVS Solicitors* [2012] EWCA Crim 319, a wasted costs order was upheld in a case where the solicitors were said to be complicit in their client's disobedience of the Rules, failing to file a counter-notice to an application to admit hearsay evidence. The court stated (albeit *obiter*) that a solicitor instructed by a client to ignore the requirements of the Crim PR should withdraw from the case. It is wise to seek directions from the court in that eventuality.

See *Blackstone's Criminal Practice 2026* D4.7

A11 Civil Orders

A full list of possible civil proceedings, and the relevant statutes, appears at **A19.1**. These proceedings are prescribed by reg 9 Criminal Legal Aid (General) Regulations 2013, so that criminal legal aid is available on forms CRM 14 and 15. Many orders may also be made on conviction, and these appear in **Part D**. This section deals with civil orders that may be made on short notice. All are handled as civil proceedings.

A11.1 Closure orders

It should be noted that applications for closure orders will only be prescribed proceedings for the purposes of reg 9 Criminal Legal Aid (General) Regulations 2013 where a person has engaged in, or is likely to engage in, behaviour that constitutes a criminal offence on the premises. This will include where the closure order relates to criminal behaviour and a combination of other grounds; but not closure orders that relate to nuisance or disorderly behaviour only, unless they amount to a common law public nuisance.

Anti-social Behaviour Crime and Policing Act 2014, ss 76, 80, and 81

76 Power to issue closure notices

(1) A police officer of at least the rank of inspector, or the local authority, may issue a closure notice if satisfied on reasonable grounds—
  (a) that the use of particular premises has resulted, or (if the notice is not issued) is likely soon to result, in nuisance to members of the public, or
  (b) that there has been, or (if the notice is not issued) is likely soon to be, disorder near those premises associated with the use of those premises, and that the notice is necessary to prevent the nuisance or disorder from continuing, recurring or occurring.

80 Power of court to make closure orders

(1) Whenever a closure notice is issued an application must be made to a magistrates' court for a closure order (unless the notice has been cancelled under section 78).
(2) An application for a closure order must be made—
  (a) by a constable, if the closure notice was issued by a police officer;
  (b) by the authority that issued the closure notice, if the notice was issued by a local authority.
(3) The application must be heard by the magistrates' court not later than 48 hours after service of the closure notice.
(4) In calculating when the period of 48 hours ends, Christmas Day is to be disregarded.
(5) The court may make a closure order if it is satisfied—
  (a) that a person has engaged, or (if the order is not made) is likely to engage, in disorderly, offensive or criminal behaviour on the premises, or
  (b) that the use of the premises has resulted, or (if the order is not made) is likely to result, in serious nuisance to members of the public, or
  (c) that there has been, or (if the order is not made) is likely to be, disorder near those premises associated with the use of those premises, and that the order

Blackstone's Magistrates' Court Handbook 2026. Bartholomew Dalton and Caroline Liggins, Oxford University Press. © Oxford University Press 2026.
DOI: 10.1093/oso/9780198963943.003.0011

is necessary to prevent the behaviour, nuisance or disorder from continuing, recurring or occurring.

(6) A closure order is an order prohibiting access to the premises for a period specified in the order.

The period may not exceed 3 months.

(7) A closure order may prohibit access—
  (a) by all persons, or by all persons except those specified, or by all persons except those of a specified description;
  (b) at all times, or at all times except those specified;
  (c) in all circumstances, or in all circumstances except those specified.

(8) A closure order—
  (a) may be made in respect of the whole or any part of the premises;
  (b) may include provision about access to a part of the building or structure of which the premises form part.

(9) The court must notify the relevant licensing authority if it makes a closure order in relation to premises in respect of which a premises licence is in force.

81 Temporary orders

(1) This section applies where an application has been made to a magistrates' court under section 80 for a closure order.

(2) If the court does not make a closure order it may nevertheless order that the closure notice continues in force for a specified further period of not more than 48 hours, if satisfied—
  (a) that the use of particular premises has resulted, or (if the notice is not continued) is likely soon to result, in nuisance to members of the public, or
  (b) that there has been, or (if the notice is not continued) is likely soon to be, disorder near those premises associated with the use of those premises, and that the continuation of the notice is necessary to prevent the nuisance or disorder from continuing, recurring or occurring.

(3) The court may adjourn the hearing of the application for a period of not more than 14 days to enable—
  (a) the occupier of the premises,
  (b) the person with control of or responsibility for the premises, or
  (c) any other person with an interest in the premises, to show why a closure order should not be made.

(4) If the court adjourns the hearing under subsection (3) it may order that the closure notice continues . . .

A11.1.1 ***Breach of a closure order is a criminal offence (see C2.17.2)***

See *Blackstone's Criminal Practice 2026* D25.49

A11.2 **Domestic abuse**

A11.2A ***Domestic violence protection orders***

Note: these will be available until the introduction of Domestic Abuse protection notices and orders by the Domestic Abuse Act 2021.

Crime and Security Act 2010, ss 27 and 28

27 Application for a domestic violence protection order

(1) If a DVPN (Domestic Violence protection notice) has been issued, a constable must apply for a domestic violence protection order ('a DVPO').
(2) The application must be made by complaint to a magistrates' court.
(3) The application must be heard by the magistrates' court not later than 48 hours after the DVPN was served pursuant to section 25(2).
(4) In calculating when the period of 48 hours mentioned in subsection (3) ends, Christmas Day, Good Friday, any Sunday and any day which is a bank holiday in England and Wales under the Banking and Financial Dealings Act 1971 are to be disregarded.
(5) A notice of the hearing of the application must be given to (the respondent) P.
(6) The notice is deemed given if it has been left at the address given by P (when asked at the time of service of the DVPN).
(7) But if the notice has not been given because no address was given by P under section 25(3), the court may hear the application for the DVPO if the court is satisfied that the constable applying for the DVPO has made reasonable efforts to give P the notice.
(8) The magistrates' court may adjourn the hearing of the application.
(9) If the court adjourns the hearing, the DVPN continues in effect until the application has been determined.
(10) On the hearing of an application for a DVPO, section 97 of the Magistrates' Courts Act 1980 (summons to witness and warrant for his arrest) does not apply in relation to a person for whose protection the DVPO would be made, except where the person has given oral or written evidence at the hearing.

28 Conditions for and contents of a domestic violence protection order

(1) The court may make a DVPO if two conditions are met.
(2) The first condition is that the court is satisfied on the balance of probabilities that P has been violent towards, or has threatened violence towards, an associated person.
(3) The second condition is that the court thinks that making the DVPO is necessary to protect that person from violence or a threat of violence by P.
(4) Before making a DVPO, the court must, in particular, consider—
   (a) the welfare of any person under the age of 18 whose interests the court considers relevant to the making of the DVPO (whether or not that person is an associated person), and
   (b) any opinion of which the court is made aware—
      (i) of the person for whose protection the DVPO would be made, and
      (ii) in the case of provision included by virtue of subsection (8), of any other associated person who lives in the premises to which the provision would relate.
(5) But the court may make a DVPO in circumstances where the person for whose protection it is made does not consent to the making of the DVPO.
(6) A DVPO must contain provision to prohibit P from molesting the person for whose protection it is made.
(7) Provision required to be included by virtue of subsection (6) may be expressed so as to refer to molestation in general, to particular acts of molestation, or to both.
(8) If P lives in premises which are also lived in by a person for whose protection the DVPO is made, the DVPO may also contain provision—
   (a) to prohibit P from evicting or excluding from the premises the person for whose protection the DVPO is made,
   (b) to prohibit P from entering the premises, (c) to require P to leave the premises, or

(d) to prohibit P from coming within such distance of the premises as may be specified in the DVPO.

(9) A DVPO must state that a constable may arrest P without warrant if the constable has reasonable grounds for believing that P is in breach of the DVPO.

(10) A DVPO may be in force for—

(a) no fewer than 14 days beginning with the day on which it is made, and

(b) no more than 28 days beginning with that day.

(11) A DVPO must state the period for which it is to be in force.

Chief Constable of Cleveland Police v Jemmett [2024] EWHC 1172 (Admin) provides guidance in relation to making a DVPO when the "protected person" doesn't support the making of the order. In this case the court had been wrong to not make the DVPO.

A11.2A.1 *Breach Proceedings*

Any breach of a domestic violence protection order is dealt with under s 63 MCA 1980 which provides for a penalty of up to £50 per day that the breach continues to a maximum of £5,000 or for committal to custody for a maximum of two months.

The section provides no defence of reasonable excuse so it is important that such protections are drafted into the original order. The court has a discretion whether to impose any penalty but cases should be proved to the criminal standard as they can result in imprisonment.

A11.2B *Domestic abuse protection notices and orders*

In force from the implementation of the Domestic Abuse Act 2021.

A11.2B.1 *Breach of domestic abuse notice*

Domestic Abuse Act 2021

S 26 Breach of notice

(1) *If a constable has reasonable grounds for believing that a person is in breach of a domestic abuse protection notice, the constable may arrest the person without warrant.*

(2) *A person arrested by virtue of subsection (1) must be held in custody and brought before the appropriate magistrates' court—*

(a) *before the end of the period of 24 hours beginning with the time of the arrest, or*

(b) *if earlier, at the hearing of the application for a domestic abuse protection order against the person. . . (see section 28(3)).*

(4) *In calculating when the period of 24 hours mentioned in subsection (2)(a) ends, the following days are to be disregarded—*

(a) *any Sunday,*

(b) *Christmas Day,*

(c) *Good Friday, and*

(d) *any day which is a bank holiday in England and Wales under the Banking and Financial Dealings Act 1971.*

(5) *If the person is brought before the court as mentioned in subsection (2)(a), the court may remand the person.*

(For power to remand a person brought before the court as mentioned in subsection (2)(b), see section 29(8).)

(7) *The court may, when remanding the person on bail, require the person to comply, before release on bail or later, with any requirements that appear to the court to be necessary to secure that the person does not interfere with witnesses or otherwise obstruct the course of justice.*

(8) *Sections 57A(2) and 57C of the Crime and Disorder Act 1998 (use of live link at preliminary hearings where accused is at police station) apply in relation to hearings arising by virtue of subsection (2)(a) as they apply in relation to preliminary hearings in a magistrates' court (within the meaning of section 57A(3) of that Act), but as if—*

(a) *any reference in section 57C of that Act to being in police detention in connection with an offence were a reference to being held in custody under subsection (2) above, and*

(b) *subsections (4), (10) and (11) of that section were omitted.*

S 29 Applications where domestic abuse protection notice has been given

(8) *If—*

(a) *P is brought before the court at the hearing of the application as a result of P's arrest by virtue of section 26(1) (arrest for breach of domestic abuse protection notice), and*

(b) *the court adjourns the hearing, the court may remand P.*

30 Remand under section 29(8) of person arrested for breach of notice

(1) *This section applies where—*

(a) *as a result of a person being given a domestic abuse protection notice under section 22, a chief officer of police has applied for a domestic abuse protection order against the person, and*

(b) *the magistrates' court remands the person under section 29(8) . . .*

(3) *If the court has reason to suspect that a medical report will be required, the power to remand the person may be exercised for the purpose of enabling a medical examination to take place and a report to be made.*

(4) *If the person is remanded in custody for that purpose, the adjournment may not be for more than 3 weeks at a time.*

(5) *If the person is remanded on bail for that purpose, the adjournment may not be for more than 4 weeks at a time.*

(6) *If the court has reason to suspect that the person is suffering from mental disorder within the meaning of the Mental Health Act 1983, the court has the same power to make an order under section 35 of that Act (remand to hospital for report on accused's mental condition) as it has under that section in the case of an accused person (within the meaning of that section).*

(7) *The court may, when remanding the person on bail, require the person to comply, before release on bail or later, with any requirements that appear to the court to be necessary to secure that the person does not interfere with witnesses or otherwise obstruct the course of justice.*

A11.2B.2 *Domestic abuse protection orders on application*

Domestic Abuse Act 2021

28 (1) A court may make a domestic abuse protection order under this section against a person ('P') on an application made to it in accordance with this section.

(2) *An application for an order under this section may be made by—*

(a) *the person for whose protection the order is sought;*

(b) *the appropriate chief officer of police (see subsection (4));*
(c) *a person specified in regulations made by the Secretary of State;*
(d) *any other person with the leave of the court to which the application is to be made.*

(3) *Where P is given a domestic abuse protection notice by a member of a relevant police force under section 22, the chief officer of police in relation to that force must apply for a domestic abuse protection order against P . . .*

(6) *An application made by a chief officer of police for an order under this section must be made by complaint to a magistrates' court . . . .*

(8) *Where an application is made to a magistrates' court in accordance with this section—*
(a) *the magistrates' court may adjourn the hearing of the application;*
(b) *on the hearing of the application, section 97 of the Magistrates' Courts Act 1980 (summons to witness and warrant for arrest) does not apply in relation to the person for whose protection the order is sought, except where the person has given oral or written evidence at the hearing.*

Applications where domestic abuse protection notice has been given

29 (1) This section applies where, as a result of a person ('P') being given a domestic abuse protection notice under section 22, a chief officer of police is required by section 28(3) to apply for a domestic abuse protection order against P.

(2) *The application must be heard by the magistrates' court not later than 48 hours after the notice was given to P.*
(3) *In calculating when the period of 48 hours mentioned in subsection (2) ends, the following days are to be disregarded—*
(a) *any Sunday,*
(b) *Christmas Day,*
(c) *Good Friday, and*
(d) *any day which is a bank holiday in England and Wales under the Banking and Financial Dealings Act 1971.*

(4) P must be given a notice of the hearing of the application.
(5) The notice under subsection (4) is to be treated as having been given if it has been left at the address given by P under section 25(4).
(6) But if the notice has not been given because P did not give an address under section 25(4), the court may hear the application if satisfied that the chief officer of police has made reasonable efforts to give P the notice.
(7) If the court adjourns the hearing of the application, the domestic abuse protection notice continues in effect until the application has been determined or withdrawn . . . .

Conditions for making an order

32 (1) The court may make a domestic abuse protection order under section 28 or 31 against a person ('P') if conditions A and B are met.

(2) *Condition A is that the court is satisfied on the balance of probabilities that P has been abusive towards a person aged 16 or over to whom P is personally connected.*
(3) *Condition B is that the order is necessary and proportionate to protect that person from domestic abuse, or the risk of domestic abuse, carried out by P.*
(4) *It does not matter—*
(a) *whether the abusive behaviour referred to in subsection (2) took place in England and Wales or elsewhere, or*
(b) *whether it took place before or after the coming into force of this section.*
(5) *A domestic abuse protection order may not be made against a person who is under the age of 18.*

Matters to be considered before making an order

33 (1) Before making a domestic abuse protection order against a person ('P'), the court must, among other things, consider the following—

(a) *the welfare of any person under the age of 18 whose interests the court considers relevant to the making of the order (whether or not that person and P are personally connected);*

(b) *any opinion of the person for whose protection the order would be made—*

(i) *which relates to the making of the order, and*

(ii) *of which the court is made aware;*

(c) *in a case where the order includes provision relating to premises lived in by the person for whose protection the order would be made, any opinion of a relevant occupant—*

(i) *which relates to the making of the order, and*

(ii) *of which the court is made aware.*

(2) *In subsection (1)(c) 'relevant occupant' means a person other than P or the person for whose protection the order would be made—*

(a) *who lives in the premises, and*

(b) *who is personally connected to—*

(i) *the person for whose protection the order would be made, or*

(ii) *if P also lives in the premises, P.*

(3) *It is not necessary for the person for whose protection a domestic abuse protection order is made to consent to the making of the order.*

Provision that may be made by orders

35 (1) A court may by a domestic abuse protection order impose any requirements that the court considers necessary to protect the person for whose protection the order is made from domestic abuse or the risk of domestic abuse.

'Requirement' includes any prohibition or restriction.

(2) *The court must, in particular, consider what requirements (if any) may be necessary to protect the person for whose protection the order is made from different kinds of abusive behaviour.*

(3) *Subsections (4) to (6) contain examples of the type of provision that may be made under subsection (1), but they do not limit the type of provision that may be so made.*

(4) *A domestic abuse protection order may provide that the person against whom the order is made ('P')—*

(a) *may not contact the person for whose protection it is made;*

(b) *may not come within a specified distance of any premises in England or Wales in which that person lives;*

(c) *may not come within a specified distance of any other specified premises, or any other premises of a specified description, in England or Wales.*

'Specified' means specified in the order.

(5) *If P lives in premises in England or Wales in which the person for whose protection the order is made also lives, the order may contain provision—*

(a) *prohibiting P from evicting or excluding that person from the premises;*

(b) *prohibiting P from entering the premises;*

(c) *requiring P to leave the premises.*

(6) *A domestic abuse protection order may require P to submit to electronic monitoring in England and Wales of P's compliance with other requirements imposed by the order.*

In this Part a requirement imposed by virtue of this subsection is referred to as an 'electronic monitoring requirement'.

(7) *Sections 36 and 37 contain further provision about the requirements that may be imposed by a domestic abuse protection order.*

36 Further provision about requirements that may be imposed by orders

(1) *Requirements imposed on a person by a domestic abuse protection order must, so far as practicable, be such as to avoid—*
  (a) *conflict with the person's religious beliefs;*
  (b) *interference with the person's work or with the person's attendance at an educational establishment;*
  (c) *conflict with the requirements of any other court order or injunction to which the person may be subject.*

(2) *A domestic abuse protection order that imposes a requirement to do something on a person ('P') must specify the person who is to be responsible for supervising compliance with that requirement.*

(3) *Before including such a requirement in a domestic abuse protection order, the court must receive evidence about its suitability and enforceability from the person to be specified under subsection (2) . . .*

37 Further provision about electronic monitoring requirements

(1) *Subsections (2) to (4) apply for the purpose of determining whether a court may impose an electronic monitoring requirement on a person ('P') in a domestic abuse protection order.*

(2) *The requirement may not be imposed in P's absence.*

(3) *If there is a person (other than P) without whose co-operation it would be impracticable to secure the monitoring in question, the requirement may not be imposed without that person's consent . . .*

Duration and geographical application of orders

38 (1) A domestic abuse protection order takes effect on the day on which it is made.

This is subject to subsection (2).

(2) *If, on the day on which a domestic abuse protection order ('the new order') is made against a person, the person is subject to another domestic abuse protection order ('the previous order'), the new order may be made so as to take effect on the previous order ceasing to have effect.*

(3) *A domestic abuse protection order has effect—*
  (a) *for a specified period,*
  (b) *until the occurrence of a specified event, or*
  (c) *until further order.*

'Specified' means specified in the order.

(4) *A domestic abuse protection order may also specify periods for which particular requirements imposed by the order have effect.*

(5) *But a domestic abuse protection order may not provide for an electronic monitoring requirement to have effect for more than 12 months.*

(6) *Subsection (5) is subject to any variation of the order under section 44.*

(7) *A requirement imposed by a domestic abuse protection order has effect in all parts of the United Kingdom unless expressly limited to a particular locality.*

A11.2B.3 Key points

- *Breach of domestic abuse protection order is a criminal offence* (see **C2.5**).
- *Special measures are available for proceedings in relation to a domestic abuse protection order in accordance with s 49 Domestic Abuse Act 2021.*
- *'Domestic abuse' is defined by s 1 Domestic Abuse Act 2021. 'Personally connected' is defined by s 2. Section 3 identifies children subject to domestic abuse.*

A11.3 **Stalking Protection Orders**

Stalking Protection Act 2019, s 1

1 Applications for orders

(1) A chief officer of police may apply to a magistrates' court for an order (a 'stalking protection order') in respect of a person (the 'defendant') if it appears to the chief officer that—
- (a) the defendant has carried out acts associated with stalking,
- (b) the defendant poses a risk associated with stalking to another person, and
- (c) there is reasonable cause to believe the proposed order is necessary to protect another person from such a risk (whether or not the other person was the victim of the acts mentioned in paragraph (a)).

(2) A stalking protection order is an order which, for the purpose of preventing the defendant from carrying out acts associated with stalking—
- (a) prohibits the defendant from doing anything described in the order, or
- (b) requires the defendant to do anything described in the order.

(3) A chief officer of police for a police area in England and Wales may apply for a stalking protection order only in respect of a person—
- (a) who resides in the chief officer's police area, or
- (b) who the chief officer believes is in that area or is intending to come to it.

(4) A risk associated with stalking—
- (a) may be in respect of physical or psychological harm to the other person;
- (b) may arise from acts which the defendant knows or ought to know are unwelcome to the other person even if, in other circumstances, the acts would appear harmless in themselves.

(5) It does not matter—
- (a) whether the acts mentioned in subsection (1)(a) were carried out in a part of the United Kingdom or elsewhere, or
- (b) whether they were carried out before or after the commencement of this section.

(6) See section 2A of the Protection from Harassment Act 1997 for examples of acts associated with stalking.

3 Duration of orders

(1) A stalking protection order has effect—
- (a) for a fixed period specified in the order, or
- (b) until a further order.

(2) Where a fixed period is specified it must be a period of at least 2 years beginning with the day on which the order is made.

(3) Different periods may be specified in relation to different prohibitions or requirements.

6 Content of orders

A stalking protection order and an interim stalking protection order must specify—
- (a) the date on which the order is made;
- (b) whether it has effect for a fixed period and, if it does, the length of that period;
- (c) each prohibition or requirement that applies to the defendant;
- (d) whether any prohibition or requirement is expressly limited to a particular locality and, if it is, what the locality is;
- (e) whether any prohibition or requirement is subject to a fixed period which differs from the period for which the order has effect and, if it is, what that period is.

A11.4 Procedure

The procedure for a contested hearing is governed by s 53 MCA 1980 and rule 14 Magistrates' Court Rules 1981. Under rule 14 the defendant may call evidence and address the court in a contested hearing. Section 54 MCA 1980 covers adjournments and ss 55 to 57 deal with non-appearance of parties.

By s 2(1) Civil Evidence Act 1995 and Crim PR Part 31.6, a party which proposes to adduce hearsay evidence must give notice of that intention to the other party or parties. A failure does not affect the admissibility of the evidence but may be taken into account in considering the exercise of its powers with respect to the course of proceedings and costs and as a matter adversely affecting the weight to be given to the evidence.

The Magistrates' Court (Hearsay Evidence in Civil Proceedings) Rules 1999 provide time limits:

- 21 days before the hearing date: notice of the intention to give hearsay evidence;
- within seven days: counter-notice with reasons why there should be cross-examination and a party must also give notice of any intention to attack the credibility of a hearsay witness.

Procedural safeguards were recommended in R (Cleary) v Highbury Corner Magistrates' Court [2006] EWHC 1869 (Admin) on the service of evidence, the use of hearsay evidence, and disclosure:

> As to the service of evidence fairness requires that the police must normally serve written versions of the evidence they propose to adduce in sufficient time before the hearing to enable the defendant fairly to deal with it.
>
> As to hearsay evidence, this is in principle admissible under section 1 of the Civil Evidence Act 1995. But, by section 2(1), a party proposing to adduce hearsay evidence in civil proceedings has to give the other party notice of that fact and, on request, such particulars of or relating to the evidence as is reasonable and practicable in the circumstances for the purpose of enabling him to deal with any matters arising from it being hearsay. Syntactically, the 'reasonable and practicable' requirement applies to the notice as well as the particulars.
>
> Section 3 provides that the rules may provide that another party to the proceedings may with the leave of the court call as a witness and cross-examine the maker of the hearsay statement. Thus to expect to adduce, as hearsay, evidence of a person who is not identified offends the spirit if not the letter of section 3, since a defendant cannot seek leave to call and cross-examine a witness whose identity is not revealed . . . an easy assumption that hearsay evidence is routine in these cases risks real injustice. The willingness of a civil court to admit hearsay evidence carries with it inherent dangers. It is much more difficult for a court to assess the truth of what they are being told if the original maker of the statement does not attend to be cross-examined. More attention should be paid by claimants to the need to state by convincing direct evidence why it is not reasonable and practicable to produce the original maker of the statement as a witness. Magistrates should have these matters well in mind. The use of the words 'if any' in section 4 of the 1995 Act shows that some hearsay evidence may be given no weight at all. Credible direct evidence of a defendant in an application for a closure order may well carry greater weight than

uncross-examined hearsay from an anonymous witness or several anonymous witnesses (as to hearsay generally in civil proceedings see **A11.5**).

The police should disclose documents which clearly and materially affect their case adversely or support the defendant's case.

The Magistrates' Court Rules 1981 gives the court the power to:

- Allow or require anyone to take part in proceedings by live link if it is satisfied that it is in the interests of justice to do so (Rule 3B);
- Allow a witness special measures if it is satisfied that it is in the interests of justice to do so (Rule 3C).

A11.5 **Evidence**

A11.5.1 ***Hearsay***

Civil behaviour orders such as closure orders and domestic violence protection orders are now commonplace in criminal courts, and very often involve issues of hearsay. Hearsay evidence in these cases is not regulated by the Criminal Justice Act 2003 but, in so far as it relates to ancillary orders in criminal proceedings, by Part 31 of the Criminal Procedure Rules; and by the Civil Evidence Act 1995.

A11.5.2 ***Challenging the weight to be attached to hearsay evidence***

Regard should be had to s 4 Civil Evidence Act 1995, which provides:

Civil Evidence Act 1995, s 4

4 Considerations relevant to weighing of hearsay evidence

(1) In estimating the weight (if any) to be given to hearsay evidence in civil proceedings the court shall have regard to any circumstances from which any inference can reasonably be drawn as to the reliability or otherwise of the evidence.

(2) Regard may be had, in particular, to the following—

(a) whether it would have been reasonable and practicable for the party by whom the evidence was adduced to have produced the maker of the original statement as a witness;

(b) whether the original statement was made contemporaneously with the occurrence or existence of the matters stated;

(c) whether the evidence involves multiple hearsay;

(d) whether any person involved had any motive to conceal or misrepresent matters;

(e) whether the original statement was an edited account, or was made in collaboration with another or for a particular purpose;

(f) whether the circumstances in which the evidence is adduced as hearsay are such as to suggest an attempt to prevent proper evaluation of its weight.

A11.5.3 ***Credibility and previous inconsistent statements***

Sections 5(2) and 6 Civil Evidence Act 1995 provide:

Civil Evidence Act 1995, ss 5(2) and 6

5 Competence and credibility

(2) Where in civil proceedings hearsay evidence is adduced and the maker of the original statement, or of any statement relied upon to prove another statement, is not called as a witness—
   (a) evidence which if he had been so called would be admissible for the purpose of attacking or supporting his credibility as a witness is admissible for that purpose in the proceedings; and
   (b) evidence tending to prove that, whether before or after he made the statement, he made any other statement inconsistent with it is admissible for the purpose of showing that he had contradicted himself. Provided that evidence may not be given of any matter of which, if he had been called as a witness and had denied that matter in cross-examination, evidence could not have been adduced by the cross-examining party.

6 Previous statements of witness

(1) Subject as follows, the provisions of this Act as to hearsay evidence in civil proceedings apply equally (but with any necessary modifications) in relation to a previous statement made by a person called as a witness in the proceedings.
(2) A party who has called or intends to call a person as a witness in civil proceedings may not in those proceedings adduce evidence of a previous statement made by that person, except—
   (a) with the leave of the court, or
   (b) for the purpose of rebutting a suggestion that his evidence has been fabricated. This shall not be construed as preventing a witness statement (that is, a written statement of oral evidence which a party to the proceedings intends to lead) from being adopted by a witness in giving evidence or treated as his evidence.
(3) Where in the case of civil proceedings section 3, 4 or 5 of the Criminal Procedure Act 1865 applies, which make provision as to—
   (a) how far a witness may be discredited by the party producing him,
   (b) the proof of contradictory statements made by a witness, and
   (c) cross-examination as to previous statements in writing, this Act does not authorise the adducing of evidence of a previous inconsistent or contradictory statement otherwise than in accordance with those sections.

This is without prejudice to any provision made by rules of court under section 3 above (power to call witness for cross-examination on hearsay statement).

(4) Nothing in this Act affects any of the rules of law as to the circumstances in which, where a person called as a witness in civil proceedings is cross-examined on a document used by him to refresh his memory, that document may be made evidence in the proceedings.
(5) Nothing in this section shall be construed as preventing a statement of any description referred to above from being admissible by virtue of section 1 as evidence of the matters stated.

A12 Commencing Proceedings: Time Limits

A12.1 Time limits

A12.1.1 *Overview*

Generally speaking, under s 127 Magistrates' Courts Act 1980, summary-only proceedings must be started within 6 months of the criminality complained of. If there is a dispute as to whether the proceedings have been commenced within the time limit, their validity must be proved by the Crown to the criminal standard (*Atkinson v DPP* [2014] EWHC 1457 (Admin)). If there is doubt as to whether an information has been laid in time, it must be resolved in favour of the defendant (*Lloyd v Young* [1963] Crim LR 703). However, *Young v DPP* [2020] EWHC 976 (Admin) confirms that a written charge under s 29 CJA 2003 is a public document and so admissible to prove its date of issue.

The following principles emerge from the case law:

- the date of the offence is excluded from the time calculation (*Radcliffe v Bartholomew* [1892] 1 QB 161);
- in relation to a continuing offence, it is the date of the last act identified and known to the prosecution that is relevant (*DPP v Baker* [2004] EWHC 2782 (Admin); *Luton Borough Council v Altavon Luton Ltd* [2019] EWHC 2415 (Admin));
- month means calendar month;
- limitation ends at midnight on the last day.

A requisition is 'issued' once fully prepared in the CPS office. It will not be out of time if not sent to the court within 6 months of the offence (*Brown v DPP* [2019] EWHC 798 (Admin)). The same principle applies when an additional written charge is laid, even though the Crown had not attached a requisition (*DPP v McFarlane* [2019] EWHC 1895).

The 6-month time limit does not apply to allegations of criminal damage of whatever value as they are either-way offences that, under £5,000 in value, may only be tried summarily (*DPP v Bird* 2015 EWHC 4077 (Admin)) or low-value theft from shops (*Candlish v DPP* [2022] EWHC 842 (Admin)) (C16.21.3). It was said in *Candlish* that an egregious delay in charging may amount to an abuse of process (A1.2.6).

See A5 for the rules relating to amendment of a charge to substitute an offence that would otherwise be time-barred.

Blackstone's Magistrates' Court Handbook 2026. Bartholomew Dalton and Caroline Liggins, Oxford University Press. © Oxford University Press 2026.
DOI: 10.1093/oso/9780198963943.003.0012

A12.1.2 *Common assault exception*

Criminal Justice Act, s 39A

39A Time limit for prosecution of common assault or battery in domestic abuse cases

(1) This section applies to proceedings for an offence of common assault or battery where—
  (a) the alleged behaviour of the accused amounts to domestic abuse, and
  (b) the condition in subsection (2) or (3) is met.

(2) The condition in this subsection is that—
  (a) the complainant has made a witness statement with a view to its possible admission as evidence in the proceedings, and
  (b) the complainant has provided the statement to—
    (i) a constable of a police force, or
    (ii) a person authorised by a constable of a police force to receive the statement.

(3) The condition in this subsection is that—
  (a) the complainant has been interviewed by—
    (i) a constable of a police force, or
    (ii) a person authorised by a constable of a police force to interview the complainant, and
  (c) a video recording of the interview has been made with a view to its possible admission as the complainant's evidence in chief in the proceedings.

(4) Proceedings to which this section applies may be commenced at any time which is both—
  (a) within two years from the date of the offence to which the proceedings relate, and
  (b) within six months from the first date on which either of the conditions in subsection (2) or (3) was met.

(5) This section has effect despite section 127(1) of the Magistrates' Court Act 1980 (limitation of time).

(6) In this section—
"domestic abuse" has the meaning given by section 1 of the Domestic Abuse Act 2021;
"police force" has the meaning given by section 3(3) of the Prosecution of Offences Act 1985;
"video recording" has the meaning given by section 63(1) of the Youth Justice and Criminal Evidence Act 1999;
"witness statement" means a written statement that satisfies the conditions in section 9(2)(a) and (b) of the Criminal Justice Act 1967.

This provision applies to all offences committed on or after 28 June 2022.

A12.1.3 *Other Exceptions*

A large number of offences that can be tried only summarily are, in certain circumstances, exempt from the six-month time bar.

In relation to some offences, time runs only from when an offence is 'discovered' by the prosecutor, which means when there was a reasonable belief that an offence had been committed (*Tesco Stores Ltd v London Borough of Harrow* (2003) 167 JP 657, DC). Where the relevant statute provides for a certificate to be signed by a prosecutor as to when he first had knowledge of the relevant facts, and there is a defence challenge to such a certificate, the matter should be dealt with by an application to stay the case for abuse (*Lamont-Perkins v RSPCA* [2012] EWHC 1002 (Admin)). *Letherbarrow v Warwickshire County Council* [2015] EWHC 4820 (Admin) held that, where the time ran from the date on which evidence that a prosecutor considers sufficient to justify proceeding comes to his knowledge, the date referred to is that on which a decision-maker considered the evidence and not the date on which any employee became aware of the case. A prosecutor must be distinguished from an investigator. That decision is not merely whether there is a *prima facie* case but effectively the application of both parts of a prosecutor's duty (both evidential and public interest tests) to review a case before authorising a prosecution.

Where multiple prosecutors review a case, unless further inquiries result in different evidence being placed before a later prosecutor, the time limit will run from the date that the first prosecutor made the initial review (see *DPP v Jinks* [2024] EWHC 3341 (Admin) in relation to s 127(5) Communications Act 2003).

The matter as further considered in *CPS v Woodward* [2017] EWHC 1008 (Admin) which held that it is for the prosecutor to show, to the relevant standard of proof, that there has been compliance. If there has been non-compliance, the prosecution is invalid. The prosecution may surmount the time bar hurdle by either of two means. The first is the issue of a certificate. The second is the adducing of evidence of fact showing who made the decision that a prosecution was justified and when. A certificate is not essential.

Where reliance is placed upon a certificate, then:

1. The certificate must strictly comply with the statutory requirements; and it must comply on its face, in the sense that deficiencies cannot be remedied by reference to extrinsic evidence.
2. A valid certificate is determinative of the matter unless the certificate is inaccurate on its face (i.e. plainly wrong on its face and patently misleading), or can be shown to be fraudulent. A certificate or further certificates may be issued or reissued at any time, at least until the close of the prosecution case.

In *Downes v RSPCA* [2017] EWHC 3622 (Admin) the court stated that the circumstances in which it will be proper to try to go behind the certificate are likely to be few and far between, and encouraged courts to deal robustly with suggestions that certificates are wrong so as to be susceptible to challenge.

However, 'the conclusive evidence provisions must not be manipulated to deprive a defendant of the benefit of a time-bar defence' and are 'not a charter for paper-shuffling [although] abuse of process is and should remain a separate question concerned with the fairness of the procedure and of the trial.' (*R (on the application of Chesterfield Poultry Ltd) v Sheffield Magistrates' Court* [2019] EWHC 2953 (Admin)).

See *Blackstone's Criminal Practice 2026* **D21.17**

A13 Costs

Detailed provisions in relation to costs are contained in the Practice Direction (Costs in Criminal Proceedings) 2015 EWCA Crim 1568 (as amended) and in Crim PR Part 45.

A13.1 Statutory basis for awarding defence costs (defence costs orders)

Section 16(1) of the Prosecution of Offences Act 1985 provides:

Prosecution of Offences Act 1985, s 16(1)

16 Defence costs

(1) Where—

(a) an information laid before a justice of the peace for any area, charging any person with an offence, is not proceeded with;

(b) a magistrates' court dealing summarily with an offence dismisses the information; that court or, in a case falling within paragraph (a) above, a magistrates' court for that area, may make an order in favour of the accused for a payment to be made out of central funds in respect of his costs (a 'defendant's costs order').

Section 16(1) does not apply to proceedings in respect to breach of community penalty as the information does not charge a person with an offence. Similarly, the provision has no application in relation to civil proceedings (eg in relation to domestic violence protection orders).

Costs should generally be awarded to a defendant who can satisfy s 16(1). This includes:

- where the case is withdrawn so that a caution can be administered (*R (Stoddard) v Oxford Magistrates' Court* (2005) 169 JP 683);
- where there is a stay for abuse of process (*R (RE Williams & Sons (Wholesale) Ltd) v Hereford Magistrates' Court* [2008] EWHC 2585 (Admin));
- where a case is resolved by way of bind over (*Emohare v Thames Magistrates' Court* [2009] EWHC 689 (Admin)).

In *R (Spiteri) v Basildon Crown Court* [2009] EWHC 665 (Admin), it was held that a costs order could not be refused on the sole ground that the applicant had brought the proceedings upon himself, as more was required, such as the defendant's having misled the prosecution as to the strength of the case against him. A similar point arose in *Dowler v Mersey Rail* [2009] EWHC 558 (Admin), where the court ruled that, when refusing costs, courts should give reasons for the refusal contemporaneously with the ruling. In *R (Rees) v Snaresbrook Crown Court* [2012] EWHC 3879 (Admin), the court left open the possibility of refusing a defence costs order where the defendant had committed perjury or succeeded by ambushing the Crown.

A court should not limit the amount of costs recoverable from central funds to those of the final hearing, at which a bind over was accepted, where the

Blackstone's Magistrates' Court Handbook 2026. Bartholomew Dalton and Caroline Liggins, Oxford University Press. © Oxford University Press 2026.
DOI: 10.1093/oso/9780198963943.003.0013

Crown would not have discontinued the proceedings (*Newcombe v CPS* [2013] EWHC 2160 (Admin)).

A13.1.1 *Orders against a party to pay costs thrown away*

Such orders may benefit defendants who suffer financial prejudice as a result of CPS actions or failures to act.

Section 19 Prosecution of Offences Act 1985 provides:

Prosecution of Offences Act 1985, s 19

19 Provision for orders as to costs in other circumstances

(1) The Lord Chancellor may by regulations make provision empowering magistrates' courts . . . in any case where the court is satisfied that one party to criminal proceedings has incurred costs as a result of an unnecessary or improper act or omission by, or on behalf of, another party to the proceedings, to make an order as to the payment of those costs.

The Regulations are the Costs in Criminal Cases (General) Regulations 1986.

Costs Practice Direction 4.1.1

Costs against a party to the proceedings

A magistrates' court . . . may order the payment of any costs incurred as a result of any unnecessary or improper act or omission by or on behalf of any party to the proceedings as distinct from his legal representative: section 19 of the Act and regulation 3 of the General Regulations. In ***R (Commissioners of Customs and Excise) v Leicester Crown Court*** [2001] EWHC 33 (Admin) the court suggested a four-stage approach: (a) Has there been an unnecessary or improper, act or omission? (b) As a result have any costs been incurred by another party? (c) If the answers to (a) and (b) are 'yes', should the court exercise its discretion to order the party responsible to meet the whole or any part of the relevant costs, and if so what specific sum is involved? (d) What amount of costs should be paid?

In *DPP v Denning* (1991) 2 QB 532 an act was defined as unnecessary or improper if events would not have occurred if the party had conducted itself properly, or which should otherwise have been properly avoided (*R (Haigh) v City of Westminster Magistrates Court* [2017] EWHC 232 (Admin)).

The word 'improper' does not necessarily connote some grave impropriety. In *R (Singh) v Ealing Magistrates' Court* [2014] EWHC 1443 (Admin) it was held that a mere mistake without repetition can be grounds for a costs order under s 19 if additional costs arise from someone on the prosecution side not conducting the case properly. It is not an answer to be unsure whether the CPS or police are responsible. The prosecution is indivisible. The section does, however, contain a discretion not a duty to make an order if there is a satisfactory explanation.

In considering an application under s 19 Prosecution of Offences Act 1985 the principles to be applied in respect of an application under that section and Regulation 3 were set out in *Evans v Serious Fraud Office* [2015] EWHC 263

(QB) and in *R v Cornish and Maidstone and Tunbridge Wells NHS Trust* [2016] EWHC 779 (QB) and apply in both public and private prosecutions (*Asif v Ditta* [2021] EWCA Crim 1091). It should be noted that these cases were concerned with an application for the total costs of a failed prosecution. More common will be applications in relation to unnecessary hearings or extra work caused by the failure of a party to comply in a timely fashion with an order of the court. It is suggested that failure to comply with a court order amounts to impropriety, as a party, however busy, can always apply for further time.

Prosecution of Offences Act 1985, s 19A

Costs against legal representatives etc

(1) In any criminal proceedings—

. . .

(c) a magistrates' court, may disallow, or (as the case may be) order the legal or other representative concerned to meet, the whole of any wasted costs or such part of them as may be determined in accordance with regulations.

. . .

(3) In this section—

'wasted costs' means any costs incurred by a party—

(a) as a result of any improper, unreasonable, or negligent act or omission on the part of any representative or any employee of a representative; or

(b) which, in the light of any such act or omission occurring after they were incurred, the court considers it is unreasonable to expect that party to pay.

The Practice Direction (Costs in Criminal Proceedings) 2015 EWCA Crim 1568 deals with wasted costs in paragraph 4.2:

Practice Direction (Costs in Criminal Proceedings) 2015 EWCA Crim 1568

Part 4.2.4

(iv) A three-stage test or approach is recommended when a wasted costs order is contemplated:

(a) Has there been an improper, unreasonable or negligent act or omission?

(b) As a result have any costs been incurred by a party?

(c) If the answers to (a) & (b) are 'yes', should the court exercise its discretion to disallow or order the representative to meet the whole or any part of the relevant costs, and if so what specific sum is involved?

. . .

(vi) The judge must specify the sum to be allowed or ordered. Alternatively the relevant available procedure should be substituted should it be impossible to fix the sum.

Part 4.2.5

(i) The primary object is not to punish but to compensate, albeit as the order is sought against a non party, it can from that perspective be regarded as penal.

. . .

(iv) Because of the penal element a mere mistake is not sufficient to justify an order, there must be a more serious error.

. . .

(vi) The normal civil standard of proof applies but if the allegation is one of serious misconduct or crime clear evidence will be required to meet that standard.

In *Ridehalgh v Horsefield* [1994] Ch 205 the court stated:

> Improper, unreasonable or negligent: . . . In our view the meaning of these expressions is not open to serious doubt.
>
> 'Improper' means, but is not confined to, conduct which would ordinarily be held to justify disbarment, striking off, suspension from practice or other serious professional penalty. It covers any significant breach of a substantial duty imposed by a relevant code of professional conduct. But it is not in our judgment limited to that. Conduct which would be regarded as improper according to the consensus of professional (including judicial) opinion can be fairly stigmatised as such whether or not it violates the letter of a professional code.
>
> 'Unreasonable': conduct cannot be described as unreasonable simply because it leads in the event to an unsuccessful result or because other more cautious legal representatives would have acted differently. The acid test is whether the conduct permits of a reasonable explanation. If so, the course adopted may be regarded as optimistic and as reflecting on a practitioner's judgment, but it is not unreasonable.
>
> 'negligent' should be understood in an untechnical way to denote failure to act with the competence reasonably to be expected of ordinary members of the profession. [A]n applicant for a wasted costs order under this head need[s to prove what]he would have to prove in an action for negligence: 'advice, acts or omissions in the course of their professional work which no member of the profession who was reasonably well-informed and competent would have given or done or omitted to do'; an error 'such as no reasonably well-informed and competent member of that profession could have made'. . . Conduct which is unreasonable may also be improper, and conduct which is negligent will very frequently be (if it is not by definition) unreasonable. We do not think any sharp differentiation between these expressions is useful or necessary or intended.

Under the provisions of s 19B Prosecution of Offences Act 1985, to make a wasted costs order against a third party the court must find serious misconduct as required by s 19B Prosecution of Offenders Act 1986. There must therefore be a history of failure to address an underlying issue (*R v Allied Language Solutions* (2013) (QB)).

A13.2 **Costs in relation to civil complaints**

Section 64 MCA 1980 provides:

> **Magistrates' Courts Act 1980, s 64**
>
> **64 Power to award costs and enforcement of costs**
>
> (1) On the hearing of a complaint, a magistrates' court shall have power in its discretion to make such order as to costs—
> (a) on making the order for which the complaint is made, to be paid by the defendant to the complainant;
> (b) on dismissing the complaint, to be paid by the complainant to the defendant,
> as it thinks just and reasonable; but if the complaint is for an order for the periodical payment of money, or for the revocation, revival or variation of such an order, or for the enforcement of such an order, the court may, whatever adjudication it makes, order either party to pay the whole or any part of the other's costs.
>
> (2) The amount of any sum ordered to be paid under subsection (1) above shall be specified in the order, or order of dismissal, as the case may be.

The discretion here is narrower than under s 16 Prosecution of Offences Act 1985 (see A13.1), and can be invoked if the court makes an order or dismisses the complaint, or the proceedings are withdrawn (s 52 Courts Act 1971). Applicants may also rely upon *Baxendale-Walker v Law Society* [2007] 3 All ER 330 (and other similar cases) to avoid costs on the basis that they are public bodies acting in the wider public interest and should not be exposed to the risk of adverse costs orders:

- in relation to civil proceedings commenced under the Proceeds of Crime Act 2002 (*Perinpanathan v City of Westminster Magistrates' Court* [2010] EWCA Civ 40) in relation to cash seizure cases that have been successfully defended;
- in relation to proceedings under s 1 Crime and Disorder Act 1998 (ASBO application) (*Manchester City Council v Manchester Magistrates' Court* [2009] EWHC 1866 (Admin));
- in withdrawal cases—see *Chief Constable of Warwickshire v MT* [2015] EWHC 2303 (Admin).

The relevant factors were considered in *City of Bradford v Booth* [2000] EWHC 44 (Admin):

> Where a complainant has successfully challenged . . . an administrative decision by a police or regulatory authority acting honestly, reasonably, properly and on grounds that reasonably appeared to be sound, in exercise of its public duty, the court should consider, in addition to any other relevant fact or circumstances, both (i) the financial prejudice to the particular complainant in the particular circumstances if an order for costs is not made in his favour; and (ii) the need to encourage public authorities to make and stand by honest, reasonable and apparently sound administrative decisions made in the public interest without fear of exposure to undue financial prejudice.

A13.3 Costs in relation to witnesses

Costs in relation to character witnesses' attendance at court can be recovered only when the court has certified that the interests of justice required the witnesses' attendance (Costs in Criminal Cases (General) Regulations 1986 (SI 1986/1335), reg 15). Advocates should ensure that an application is made to the court either prior to or immediately after the witnesses' attendance.

See *Blackstone's Criminal Practice 2026* D33

A14 Court-Appointed Legal Representatives

A14.1 Overview

In circumstances defined by s 34 Youth Justice and Criminal Evidence Act 1999 (complainants in proceedings for sexual offences); s 35 (child complainants and other child witnesses); and s 36 (more generally), a defendant is prohibited from cross-examining witnesses. In the event that the defendant has declined or is not eligible for legal funding, the court has power under s 38 to appoint a legal representative to carry out this function on behalf of the court.

A14.2 Key points

Fees for this work are authorized under s 19 Prosecution of Offences Act 1985 and are as agreed by the court or allowed following taxation at private client rates. Solicitors should not agree to fees that are less than those that would be allowed for in line with civil guideline costs rates. A duty solicitor can be required to conduct such cases but should ensure that they have sufficient time to undertake the work professionally.

In *Abbas v CPS* [2015] EWHC 579 (Admin), the court held that to allow for effective cross-examination there was a need for a pre-trial conference and also for presence at pre-trial applications such as over bad character or disclosure. Under the amended rule payment is possible until the conclusion of cross-examination. In *R v Andrews* [2016] 4 Costs LR 705, the costs judge held that cross-examination of a witness continues until such time as any such witness might be recalled, noting that trials involving defendants in person tend to be chaotic.

Criminal Procedure Rule 23 applies. It identifies the information to which the representative is entitled.

A14.3 Statutory provisions

Youth Justice and Criminal Evidence Act 1999, ss 34, 35, 36, and 38

34 Complainants in proceedings for sexual offences

No person charged with a sexual offence may in any criminal proceedings cross-examine in person a witness who is the complainant, either—

(a) in connection with that offence, or

(b) in connection with any other offence (of whatever nature) with which that person is charged in the proceedings.

35 Child complainants and other child witnesses

(1) No person charged with an offence to which this section applies may in any criminal proceedings cross-examine in person a protected witness, either—

  (a) in connection with that offence, or

  (b) in connection with any other offence (of whatever nature) with which that person is charged in the proceedings.

Blackstone's Magistrates' Court Handbook 2026. Bartholomew Dalton and Caroline Liggins, Oxford University Press. © Oxford University Press 2026.
DOI: 10.1093/oso/9780198963943.003.0014

(2) For the purposes of subsection (1) a 'protected witness' is a witness who—
 (a) either is the complainant or is alleged to have been a witness to the commission of the offence to which this section applies, and
 (b) either is a child or falls to be cross-examined after giving evidence in chief (whether wholly or in part)—
  (i) by means of a video recording made (for the purposes of section 27) at a time when the witness was a child, or
  (ii) in any other way at any such time.

(3) The offences to which this section applies are—
 (a) any offence under—
  (iv) any of sections 33 to 36 Sexual Offences Act 1956,
  (v) the Protection of Children Act 1978;
  (vi) part 1 of the Sexual Offences Act 2003 or any relevant superseded enactment; or
  (vii) sections 1 and 2 of the Modern Slavery Act 2015;
 (b) kidnapping, false imprisonment or an offence under section 1 or 2 of the Child Abduction Act 1984;
 (c) any offence under section 1 of the Children and Young Persons Act 1933;
 (d) any offence (not within any of the preceding paragraphs) which involves an assault on, or injury or a threat of injury to, any person.

(4) In this section 'child' means—
 (a) where the offence falls within subsection (3)(a), a person under the age of 17; or
 (b) where the offence falls within subsection (3)(b), (c) or (d), a person under the age of 14.

(5) For the purposes of this section 'witness' includes a witness who is charged with an offence in the proceedings.

36 Direction prohibiting accused from cross-examining particular witness

(1) This section applies where, in a case where neither of sections 34 and 35 operates to prevent an accused in any criminal proceedings from cross-examining a witness in person—
 (a) the prosecutor makes an application for the court to give a direction under this section in relation to the witness, or
 (b) the court of its own motion raises the issue whether such a direction should be given.

(2) If it appears to the court—
 (a) that the quality of evidence given by the witness on cross-examination—
  (i) is likely to be diminished if the cross-examination (or further cross-examination) is conducted by the accused in person, and
  (ii) would be likely to be improved if a direction were given under this section, and
 (b) that it would not be contrary to the interests of justice to give such a direction,
 the court may give a direction prohibiting the accused from cross-examining (or further cross-examining) the witness in person.

(3) In determining whether subsection (2)(a) applies in the case of a witness the court must have regard, in particular, to—
 (a) any views expressed by the witness as to whether or not the witness is content to be cross-examined by the accused in person;
 (b) the nature of the questions likely to be asked, having regard to the issues in the proceedings and the defence case advanced so far (if any);
 (c) any behaviour on the part of the accused at any stage of the proceedings, both generally and in relation to the witness;
 (d) any relationship (of whatever nature) between the witness and the accused;

(e) whether any person (other than the accused) is or has at any time been charged in the proceedings with a sexual offence or an offence to which section 35 applies, and (if so) whether section 34 or 35 operates or would have operated to prevent that person from cross-examining the witness in person;
(f) any direction under section 19 which the court has given, or proposes to give, in relation to the witness.

(4) For the purposes of this section—
(a) 'witness', in relation to an accused, does not include any other person who is charged with an offence in the proceedings; and
(b) any reference to the quality of a witness's evidence shall be construed in accordance with section 16(5). . . .

38 Defence representation for purposes of cross-examination

(1) This section applies where an accused is prevented from cross-examining a witness in person by virtue of section 34, 35 or 36.

(2) Where it appears to the court that this section applies, it must—
(a) invite the accused to arrange for a legal representative to act for him for the purpose of cross-examining the witness; and
(b) require the accused to notify the court, by the end of such period as it may specify, whether a legal representative is to act for him for that purpose.

(3) If by the end of the period mentioned in subsection (2)(b) either—
(a) the accused has notified the court that no legal representative is to act for him for the purpose of cross-examining the witness, or
(b) no notification has been received by the court and it appears to the court that no legal representative is to so act, the court must consider whether it is necessary in the interests of justice for the witness to be cross-examined by a legal representative appointed to represent the interests of the accused.

(4) If the court decides that it is necessary in the interests of justice for the witness to be so cross-examined, the court must appoint a qualified legal representative (chosen by the court) to cross-examine the witness in the interests of the accused.

(5) A person so appointed shall not be responsible to the accused.

See *Blackstone's Criminal Practice 2026* F7

A15 Custody Time Limits

A15.1 Overview

Category	Time limit
Cases sent to the Crown Court	An overall time limit of 182 days applies, which includes any time spent in custody at the magistrates' court.
Either-way offences	Maximum 56 days from first appearance to hearing evidence in a summary trial (unless case was originally destined for sending and court reverts to summary trial after 56 days have elapsed, in which case the limit is 70 days).
Summary-only offences	56 days to start of summary trial.
Youths	As above, save that indictable-only cases that are tried summarily in the youth court are subject to the same time limits as either-way cases (R v Stratford Youth Court, ex p S (A Minor) [1998] 1 WLR 1758).

A15.2 Statutory framework

Section 22 of the Prosecution of Offence Act 1985 provides

(3) The appropriate court may, at any time before the expiry of a time limit imposed by the regulations, extend, or further extend, that limit; but the court shall not do so unless it is satisfied—

(a) that the need for the extension is due to—

(i) the illness or absence of the accused, a necessary witness, a judge or a magistrate;

(ii) a postponement which is occasioned by the ordering by the court of separate trials in the case of two or more accused or two or more offences; or

(iii) some other good and sufficient cause; and

(b) that the prosecution has acted with all due diligence and expedition.

A15.3 Exceptions

Defendants who abscond from prison, or who have been released on bail following expiry of a custody time limit, but are then remanded following a breach of bail, do not enjoy the protections offered by custody time limits.

If a person is granted bail and is later remanded into custody, the earlier period on remand will count towards the custody time limit.

Custody time limits start at the end of the first day of remand and expire at midnight on the last day. A time limit expiring on one of the following days will be treated as having expired on the next preceding day which is not one of those days: a Saturday, a Sunday, Christmas Day, Good Friday, or a bank holiday.

Blackstone's Magistrates' Court Handbook 2026. Bartholomew Dalton and Caroline Liggins, Oxford University Press. © Oxford University Press 2026.
DOI: 10.1093/oso/9780198963943.003.0015

A15.4 Extending custody time limits

In general, the following considerations are relevant:

- the prosecution should give two days' notice of an intention to apply, but lack of notice is not fatal to the application and the court retains a discretion to extend the time limits (*R v Governor of Canterbury Prison, ex p Craig* [1991] 2 QB 195);
- there is no power to extend once a time limit has lapsed (*R v Sheffield Justices, ex p Turner* [1991] 2 WLR 987);
- the court must be satisfied, on a balance of probabilities, that the need for the extension is due to the illness or absence of the accused, a necessary witness, a judge or magistrate; or a postponement which is occasioned by the ordering of separate trials, or some other good and sufficient cause; and that the prosecution have acted with all due diligence and expedition;
- the following have been held not to amount to good and sufficient cause, certainly in cases that are routine (*R (McAuley) v Coventry Crown Court* [2012] EWHC 680 (Admin) and *R (Raeside) v Luton Crown Court* [2012] EWHC 1064 (Admin)): lack of court time, listing difficulties attributable to the nature of the case, lack of a suitably experienced judge (or lack of any judge at all). Absent exceptional circumstances, resource difficulties do not amount to a good and sufficient cause.
- The words 'good' and 'sufficient' must be separately considered. Even when good cause exists, whether there is sufficient cause will depend on factors which include:

  (a) The likely duration of the delay before trial;
  (b) Whether there has been any previous extension of the CTL;
  (c) The age and antecedents of the defendant;
  (d) The likely sentence in the event of conviction. A defendant should rarely be kept in custody if he had served, or come close to serving, the likely sentence were he convicted;
  (e) The underlying reasons why bail was refused;
  (f) Any particular vulnerabilities of the defendant which make remand in custody particularly difficult (*DPP v Crown Court at Woolwich* [2020] EWHC 3243 (Admin)).

A15.5 Effect of release

A release is in consequence of an expiry of the CTL when an application to extend a CTL is refused or no application is made. If the defendant is later arrested CTL do not apply (although an application for bail may be made). Where bail is granted other than by expiry of the CTL, the CTL clock is merely paused whilst the defendant is on bail (*R (Jabbar) v Sheffield CC* [2022] EWHC 516 (Admin)).

See *Blackstone's Criminal Practice 2026* D15.7

A16 Disclosure

A16.1 Overview

Disclosure comes in stages:

(1) Initial disclosure of the prosecution case.
(2) Common law disclosure.
(3) Disclosure in relation to unused material.
(4) Consideration also has to be given to third party disclosure.

A16.2 Initial details of the prosecution case

Part 8 of the Crim PR requires that initial disclosure should be available no later than the start of the day of the first hearing.

Part 8 provides for disclosure of such information in relation to all cases in a magistrates' court. Criminal Practice Direction 5.1.1 requires that there is sufficient information to assist the court to identify real issues and give directions for an effective magistrates' court or Crown Court trial.

Frequent problems arise in relation to the service of video and other recorded evidence. If the Crown is not relying on the undisclosed video evidence then no issue in relation to initial disclosure arises. In any event, the prosecution are under a duty to serve only a summary of their case, not the case in its entirety. The defendant's remedy is to enter a not guilty plea and put the Crown to proof.

A16.3 Extent of disclosure

Part 8 of the Crim PR provides:

Criminal Procedure Rules, Pt 8

8.1 When this Part applies

This Part applies in a magistrates' court.

8.2

(1) The prosecutor must serve initial details of the prosecution case on the court officer—
  (a) as soon as practicable; and
  (b) in any event, no later than the beginning of the day of the first hearing.
(2) Where a defendant requests those details, the prosecutor must serve them on the defendant—
  (a) as soon as practicable; and
  (b) in any event, no later than the beginning of the day of the first hearing.
(3) Where a defendant does not request those details, the prosecutor must make them available to the defendant at, or before, the beginning of the day of the first hearing.

Blackstone's Magistrates' Court Handbook 2026. Bartholomew Dalton and Caroline Liggins, Oxford University Press. © Oxford University Press 2026.
DOI: 10.1093/oso/9780198963943.003.0016

8.3 Content of initial details

Initial details of the prosecution case must include—
(a) where, immediately before the first hearing in the magistrates' court, the defendant was in police custody for the offence charged—
  (i) a summary of the circumstances of the offence, and
  (ii) the defendant's criminal record, if any;
(b) where paragraph (a) does not apply—
  (i) a summary of the circumstances of the offence,
  (ii) any account given by the defendant in interview, whether contained in that summary or in another document,
  (iii) any written witness statement or exhibit that the prosecutor then has available and considers material to plea, or to the allocation of the case for trial, or to sentence,
  (iv) the defendant's criminal record, if any, and
  (v) any available statement of the effect of the offence on a victim, a victim's family or others.

8.4

(1) This rule applies where—
  (a) the prosecutor wants to introduce information contained in a document listed in rule 8.3; and
  (b) the prosecutor has not—
    (i) served that document on the defendant, or
    (ii) made that information available to the defendant.
(2) The court must not allow the prosecutor to introduce that information unless the court first allows the defendant sufficient time to consider it.

See *Blackstone's Criminal Practice 2026* **D5.22**

A16.4 Common law disclosure

There is a common law duty, recognized by paragraph 78 of the Attorney-General's Guidelines on Disclosure 2022 (see **A16.8**), to disclose material which may assist the defence at bail hearings or in the early preparation of their case or in mitigation. Following the decision in *R v DPP, ex p Lee* [1999] 2 All ER 737, the prosecutor must always be alive to the need to make disclosure of material of which he is aware (either from his own consideration of the papers or because his attention has been drawn to it by the defence), and which he, as a responsible prosecutor, recognizes should be disclosed at an earlier stage. Examples include:

- previous convictions of a complainant or deceased if that information could reasonably be expected to assist the defence when applying for bail;
- material which will enable the defence to make preparations for trial which may be significantly less effective if disclosure is delayed (eg names of eye-witnesses who the prosecution do not intend to use);
- the withdrawal of support for the prosecution by a witness.

This material must be revealed to the prosecutor for service on the defence with the initial details of the prosecution case.

A16.5 Disclosure of unused material

Prosecution disclosure of unused material following a not guilty plea is regulated under s 3(1)(a) CPIA 1996. Guidance is given by the Judicial Protocol on disclosure of unused material and the Attorney-General's Guidelines on disclosure 2022. The Attorney-General's Guidelines, paragraphs 81 and 82 emphasize the need for early engagement between the defence and prosecution. There is a presumption in favour of disclosure of the list of items set out in paragraph 86 of the Attorney-General's Guidelines (see **A16.8**).

Criminal Procedure and Investigations Act 1996, s 3(1)(a)

3 Initial duty of prosecutor to disclose

(1) The prosecutor must—

(a) disclose to the accused any prosecution material which has not previously been disclosed to the accused and which might reasonably be considered capable of undermining the case for the prosecution against the accused or of assisting the case for the accused. . . .

In the magistrates' court there is no duty to serve a defence case statement but in the absence of one, a prosecutor may not be able to discover which information might be disclosable. Particular problems arise with CCTV. Courts are unlikely to adjourn for CCTV where its content is purely speculative. If an early request was made, forensic advantage could be taken of its absence (*DPP v Petrie* [2015] EWHC 48 (Admin)). However, it is otherwise when the CCTV has been referred to in interview by the police, or has been viewed by the police who decided not to retain it because it did not assist their case, without performing their duty to consider whether it might assist the defendant's case. The court considered that the trial in the latter situation would not be fair (*R v Birmingham* [1992] Crim LR 117)).

A failure to disclose in accordance with the statutory scheme may lead to an adjournment (see **A2.2**). In the alternative, courts may exclude all or any prosecution evidence under s 78 Police and Criminal Evidence Act 1984 where there has been a failure in accordance with statutory time limits to provide initial or further disclosure, and this makes the trial unfair (*R (Ibrahim) v Feltham MC* [2001] EWHC 130 (Admin) and *R v Boardman* [2015] EWCA Crim 175). The need for a defence case statement cannot arise until initial disclosure had been served by the Crown.

A16.6 Section 8 disclosure applications

A party aggrieved in relation to prosecution disclosure can apply to the court under s 8 1996 Act, but *must* serve a defence case statement in order to do so. See Directions 5.4.17 and 5.4.18.

Criminal Procedure and Investigations Act 1996, s 8

8 Application by accused for disclosure

(1) This section applies where the accused has given a defence statement under section 5, 6 or 6B and the prosecutor has complied with section 7A(5) or purported to comply with it or has failed to comply with it.

(2) If the accused has at any time reasonable cause to believe that there is prosecution material which is required by section 7A to be disclosed to him and has not been, he may apply to the court for an order requiring the prosecutor to disclose it to him.

(3) For the purposes of this section prosecution material is material—

- (a) which is in the prosecutor's possession and came into his possession in connection with the case for the prosecution against the accused,
- (b) which, in pursuance of a code operative under Part II, he has inspected in connection with the case for the prosecution against the accused, or
- (c) which falls within subsection (4).

(4) Material falls within this subsection if in pursuance of a code operative under Part II the prosecutor must, if he asks for the material, be given a copy of it or be allowed to inspect it in connection with the case for the prosecution against the accused.

(5) Material must not be disclosed under this section to the extent that the court, on an application by the prosecutor, concludes it is not in the public interest to disclose it and orders accordingly.

(6) Material must not be disclosed under this section to the extent that it is material the disclosure of which is prohibited by section 17 of the Regulation of Investigatory Powers Act 2000.

In road traffic cases, in the absence of some specific evidence which indicates that there is a problem with the Intoximeter EC/IR machine, extensive exploration of technicalities will normally be a waste of time (*R (Hassani) v West London MC* [2017] EWHC 1270 (Admin)). The issues were explored extensively in *R (DPP) v Manchester and Salford MC* [2017] EWHC 1708 (Admin) which held:

> It is not enough to say that the defence case is that the amount drunk would not put the defendant over the limit or anywhere near it, and therefore the machine must be unreliable. What the evidence needed to do, in order to provide a basis for such a disclosure order was to address two critical features:
>
> The first requirement is the basis for contending how the device might produce a printout which, on its face, demonstrated that it was operating in proper fashion, but which could generate a very significantly false positive reading, where, on the defence case, the true reading would have been well below the prosecution limit.
>
> The second requirement is to identify how the material which was sought could assist to demonstrate how that might have happened.

DPP v Walsall MC [2019] EWHC 3317 (Admin) emphasizes the need to comply with Crim PR 19.4 and to have regard to Criminal Practice Direction (see Part 6).

A16.7 Third party disclosure

A16.7.1 *CPIA Code of Practice*

CPIA Code of Practice

3.5 In conducting an investigation, the investigator should pursue all reasonable lines of inquiry, whether these point towards or away from the suspect. What is reasonable in each case will depend on the particular circumstances . . .

3.6 If the officer in charge of an investigation believes that other persons may be in possession of material that may be relevant to the investigation, and if this has not been obtained under paragraph 3.5 above, he should ask the disclosure officer to inform them of the existence of the investigation and to invite them to retain the material in case they receive a request for its disclosure. The disclosure officer should inform the prosecutor that they may have such material. However, the officer in charge of an investigation is not required to make speculative enquiries of other persons; there must be some reason to believe that they may have relevant material. That reason may come from information provided to the police by the accused or from other inquiries made or from some other source.

. . .

4.3 Negative information is often relevant to an investigation. If it may be relevant it must be recorded. An example might be a number of people present in a particular place at a particular time who state that they saw nothing unusual.

A16.7.2 *Attorney-General's Guidelines on Disclosure*

The principles of accessing third party material are set out in three steps at paragraphs 28 to 34.

Step 1: Establishing a Reasonable Line of Inquiry
Step 2: Establishing Relevance
Step 3: Balancing Rights

A16.7.3 *Case law*

In *R v Alibhai* [2004] EWCA Crim 681, the Court of Appeal held that under the CPIA 1996 the prosecutor is only under a duty to disclose a third party's material if that material had come into the prosecutor's possession and the prosecutor was of the opinion that such material satisfied the disclosure test. Before taking steps to obtain third party material, the Court emphasized that it must be shown that there was a suspicion that the third party not only had relevant material and that the material was not merely neutral or damaging to the accused, but it also satisfied the disclosure test.

Furthermore, *R v Alibhai* states that even if there is the necessary suspicion, the prosecutor has a 'margin of consideration' as to what steps to take in any particular case and was not thus under an absolute obligation to obtain material that was suspected to satisfy the disclosure test.

There may be cases where the investigator, disclosure officer, or prosecutor believes that a third party (eg a local authority, a social services department, a hospital, a doctor, a school, a provider of forensic services) has material or information which might be relevant to the prosecution case. In such cases, investigators, disclosure officers, and prosecutors should take reasonable steps to identify, secure, and consider material held by any third party where it appears to the investigator, disclosure officer, or prosecutor that (a) such material exists, and (b) it may be relevant to an issue in the case.

A16.7.4 *Statutory procedure to obtain third party material*

If material evidence is in the hands of a third party a summons may be issued under s 97 Magistrates Courts Act 1980 (see **A31**). The statutory requirements in s 97 are more stringent than the disclosure test. Items sought under the summons procedure must be 'likely to be material evidence' (which the House of Lords in *R v Derby Magistrates' Court ex p B* [1995] 4 All ER 526 has construed to mean 'immediately admissible per se').

A16.8 Guidance on disclosure of unused material

The Attorney-General's Guidelines on Disclosure

84. In deciding whether material satisfies the disclosure test, consideration should include:
    a. The use that might be made of it in cross-examination;
    b. Its capacity to support submissions that could lead to:
        i. The exclusion of evidence;
        ii. A stay of proceedings, where the material is required to allow a proper application to be made;
        iii. A court or tribunal finding that any public authority had acted incompatibly with the accused's rights under the European Convention of Human Rights;
    c. Its capacity to suggest an explanation or partial explanation of the accused's actions;
    d. Its capacity to undermine the reliability or credibility of a prosecution witness;
    e. The capacity of the material to have a bearing on scientific or medical evidence in the case.
85. Material relating to the accused's mental or physical health, intellectual capacity, or to any ill treatment which the accused may have suffered when in the investigator's custody is likely to meet the test for disclosure.

    Material should not be viewed in isolation as, whilst items taken alone may not be reasonably considered capable of undermining the prosecution case or assisting the case for the accused, several items together can have that effect.

Material which is likely to meet the test for disclosure

86. The following material is likely to include information which meets the test for disclosure:
    a) records which are derived from tapes or recordings of telephone messages (for example, 999 calls) containing descriptions of an alleged offence or offender;
    b) any incident logs relating to the allegation;

c) crime reports and crime report forms, or where not already contained within the crime report:
   - an investigation log;
   - any record or note made by an investigator (including police notebook entries and other handwritten notes) on which they later make a statement or which relates to contact with suspects, victims or witnesses;
   - an account of an incident or information relevant to an incident noted by an investigator in manuscript or electronically;
   - records of actions carried out by officers (such as house-to-house interviews, CCTV or forensic enquiries) noted by a police officer in manuscript or electronically;
   - CCTV footage, or other imagery, of the incident in action;

d) the defendant's custody record or voluntary attendance record;

e) any previous accounts made by a complainant or by any other witnesses;

f) interview records (written records, or audio or video tapes, of interviews with actual or potential witnesses or suspects);

g) any material casting doubt on the reliability of a witness, eg relevant previous convictions and relevant cautions of any prosecution witnesses and any co-accused.

87. When providing CCTV footage, or other imagery, of the incident in action as material which is likely to meet the test for disclosure, investigators should include all relevant body-worn footage that is not provided as evidence. It may be that the entirety of the footage contains both relevant and irrelevant material. Irrelevant footage should not be provided to prosecutors in the first instance. It may be the footage requires clipping or editing to achieve this. Where multiple body worn cameras capture the same content, it may be that only one set of footage needs be provided. The remainder should be listed clearly on the unused material schedule. This decision must be made on a case-by-case basis, as it may be that similar but distinct footage has been captured, in which case multiple sets of footage should be provided.

The judicial protocol on disclosure 2013

The section on magistrates' courts states:

Judicial Protocol on the Disclosure of Unused Material in Criminal Cases, paras 30–33, 35–36

30. The principles relating to disclosure apply equally in the magistrates' courts. It follows that whilst disclosure of unused material in compliance with the statutory test is undoubtedly essential in order to achieve justice, it is critical that summary trials are not delayed or made over-complicated by misconceived applications for, or inappropriate disclosure of, prosecution material.

31. Magistrates will rely on their legal advisers for guidance, and the latter should draw the attention of the parties and the court to the statutory provisions and the applicable case law. Cases raising disclosure issues of particular complexity should be referred to a District Judge (Magistrates' Courts), if available.

32. Although service of a defence statement is voluntary for summary trials (section 6 CPIA), the defendant cannot make an application for specific disclosure under section 8 CPIA, and the court cannot make any orders in this regard, unless a proper defence statement has been provided. It follows that although providing a defence statement is not mandatory, it remains a critical stage in the disclosure process. If disclosure issues are to be raised by the defence, a defence statement must be served well in advance of the trial date. Any section 8 application must be made in strict compliance with the Rules.

33. The case-management forms used in the magistrates' courts fulfil some of the functions of a defence statement, and the prosecution must take into account the information provided as to the defence case when conducting its ongoing review of unused material. As the Court of Appeal noted in ***R v Newell*** (supra), admissions can be made in the Trial Preparation Form and the defence is able to identify the matters that are not in issue. Admissions made in these circumstances may be admissible during the trial. However, other information on the form that does not come within the section relating to admissions should . . . not generally be introduced as part of the evidence at trial. However, the contents of the Trial Preparation Form do not replace the need to serve a defence statement if the defendant seeks to apply for disclosure under section 8 CPIA.

35. Although CCTV footage frequently causes difficulties, it is to be treated as any other category of unused material and it should only be disclosed if the material meets the appropriate test for disclosure under the CPIA. The defence should either be provided with copies of the sections of the CCTV or afforded an opportunity to view them. If the prosecution refuses to disclose CCTV material that the defence considers to be disclosable, the courts should not make standard or general directions requiring the prosecutor to disclose material of this kind in the absence of an application under section 8. When potentially relevant CCTV footage is not in the possession of the police, the guidance in relation to third party material will apply, although the police remain under a duty to pursue all reasonable lines of inquiry, including those leading away from a suspect, whether or not defence requests are made.

36. The previous convictions of witnesses and any disciplinary findings against officers in the case are frequently disclosable and care should be taken to disclose them as appropriate. Documents such as crime reports or records of emergency calls should not be provided on a routine basis, for instance as part of a bundle of disclosed documents, irrespective of whether the material satisfies the appropriate test for disclosure. Defence advocates should not request this material in standard or routine correspondence, and instead focused consideration should be given to the circumstances of the particular case. Unjustified requests for disclosure of material of this kind are routinely made, frequently leading to unnecessary delays and adjournments. The prosecution should always consider whether the request is properly made out.

See *Blackstone's Criminal Practice 2026* **D9**

A17 Hearsay

A17.1 Overview

Hearsay evidence in criminal proceedings is regulated by ss 114–126 CJA 2003. The main legislative provisions are set out in A17.3.

A17.2 Criminal Procedure Rules

Part 20 of the Criminal Procedure Rules regulates the admission of hearsay evidence:

Criminal Procedure Rules, Pt 20

20.2 (1) This rule applies where a party wants to introduce hearsay evidence for admission under any of the following sections of the Criminal Justice Act 2003—
- (a) section 114(1)(d) (evidence admissible in the interests of justice);
- (b) section 116 (evidence where a witness is unavailable);
- (c) section 117(1)(c) (evidence in a statement prepared for the purposes of criminal proceedings);
- (d) section 121 (multiple hearsay).

A17.3 Legislative scheme

Sections 114–120 CJA 2003 are the main statutory provisions.

Criminal Justice Act 2003, s 114

114 Admissibility of hearsay evidence

(1) In criminal proceedings a statement not made in oral evidence in the proceedings is admissible as evidence of any matter stated if, but only if—
- (a) any provision of this Chapter or any other statutory provision makes it admissible,
- (b) any rule of law preserved by section 118 makes it admissible,
- (c) all parties to the proceedings agree to it being admissible, or
- (d) the court is satisfied that it is in the interests of justice for it to be admissible.

(2) In deciding whether a statement not made in oral evidence should be admitted under subsection (1)(d), the court must have regard to the following factors (and to any others it considers relevant)—
- (a) how much probative value the statement has (assuming it to be true) in relation to a matter in issue in the proceedings, or how valuable it is for the understanding of other evidence in the case;
- (b) what other evidence has been, or can be, given on the matter or evidence mentioned in paragraph (a);
- (c) how important the matter or evidence mentioned in paragraph (a) is in the context of the case as a whole;
- (d) the circumstances in which the statement was made;
- (e) how reliable the maker of the statement appears to be;
- (f) how reliable the evidence of the making of the statement appears to be;
- (g) whether oral evidence of the matter stated can be given and, if not, why it cannot;
- (h) the amount of difficulty involved in challenging the statement;

Blackstone's Magistrates' Court Handbook 2026. Bartholomew Dalton and Caroline Liggins, Oxford University Press. © Oxford University Press 2026.
DOI: 10.1093/oso/9780198963943.003.0017

(i) the extent to which that difficulty would be likely to prejudice the party facing it.

(3) Nothing in this Chapter affects the exclusion of evidence of a statement on grounds other than the fact that it is a statement not made in oral evidence in the proceedings.

It will rarely be appropriate to use s 114 in order to circumvent s 116 (cases where a witness is unavailable) (*R v Ibrahim* [2010] EWCA Crim 1176). This principle takes on a particular importance in the magistrates' court in relation to 'missing' or reluctant witnesses (eg in domestic abuse cases). While there would be occasions when, in domestic abuse proceedings, it would be necessary to admit hearsay evidence from the complainant the correct procedures must be followed. Section 114(1)(d) CJA 2003 (the interest of justice) could not be considered until all due enquiries and applications had been made and evidence heard under s 116 (*R v Jones (Kane)* [2015] EWCA Crim 1317). Section 114 should not be used simply to bypass other procedures available to the prosecution, for example the witness summons. In *R v Freeman* [2010] EWCA Crim 1997, the court quashed a conviction where s 114 was used in relation to a witness who had retracted his previous statement. Section 114(d) can be used where a hostile witness refuses to answer questions (*R v Muldoon* [2021] EWCA Crim 381).

Regard must be had to all of the criteria in s 114(2), although not all factors need be decided in favour of admissibility.

Section 114(2)(e) requires the court to consider the reliability of the maker of the statement. The principles were considered further in *R v Riat and others* [2012] EWCA Crim 1509. The court must:

- be satisfied that there is proper statutory basis for admitting hearsay;
- identify if there is any material assisting in the test of credibility (s 124);
- consider as appropriate any interests of justice test;
- if there is no specific gateway, consider s 114(1)(d);
- consider any application to exclude under s 78 Police and Criminal Evidence Act 1984 or s 126 CJA 2003.

The criteria in s 114(2) are a useful aide-mémoire in identifying the relevant issues.

A focused decision must be made considering:

- the importance of the evidence in the case;
- the risks of unreliability;
- issues as to whether the reliability of the maker of the statement can be tested and assessed.

Of particular relevance are:

- the circumstances of the making of the hearsay statement,
- interest or disinterest of the maker,
- the existence of supporting evidence,
- information on the reliability of the maker,
- any means of testing reliability.

Section 114(2)(g) does not prohibit the court from admitting business documents under s 114(1)(d), as an alternative to adjourning the matter so that the documents' creator could be called to give evidence where the crucial facts were not in dispute, even though the evidence could not be admitted under s 117 (*Salem and another v London Borough of Camden* [2021] EWHC 2530 (Admin)).

Criminal Justice Act 2003, ss 115 and 116

115 Statements and matters stated

(1) In this Chapter references to a statement or to a matter stated are to be read as follows.
(2) A statement is any representation of fact or opinion made by a person by whatever means; and it includes a representation made in a sketch, photofit or other pictorial form.
(3) A matter stated is one to which this Chapter applies if (and only if) the purpose, or one of the purposes, of the person making the statement appears to the court to have been—
  (a) to cause another person to believe the matter, or
  (b) to cause another person to act or a machine to operate on the basis that the matter is as stated.

The essential questions as to what is hearsay were identified in *R v Twist* [2011] EWCA Crim 1143:

(1) Identify the relevant fact/matter it is sought to prove.
(2) Is there a statement of that matter?
(3) If yes, was one of the purposes of the maker of the communication that the recipient or any other person should believe that matter or act upon it as true?

In *R v Midmore* [2017] EWCA Crim 533 a text was sent to a third party saying 'this one is the face melter', with a photograph of a chemical. In relation to the three elements, it was held:

(1) It established the defendant's shared intention to use the acid for a criminal as opposed to an innocent propose;
(2) It was an implied representation of intention, not just a comment from which intention could be inferred; *but*
(3) The third test was not met on the facts.

Similarly in *R v Noble and Johnson* [2016] EWCSA Crim 2219, a text message from a girlfriend of the defendant setting out an implication that the defendant was in a certain place and had a firearm was not hearsay as it was not intended that the defendant should believe it—he already knew—or act upon it.

A17.3.1 *Witnesses unable to attend*

116 Cases where a witness is unavailable

(1) In criminal proceedings a statement not made in oral evidence in the proceedings is admissible as evidence of any matter stated if—

(a) oral evidence given in the proceedings by the person who made the statement would be admissible as evidence of that matter,
(b) the person who made the statement (the relevant person) is identified to the court's satisfaction, and
(c) any of the five conditions mentioned in subsection (2) is satisfied.

(2) The conditions are—
(a) that the relevant person is dead;
(b) that the relevant person is unfit to be a witness because of his bodily or mental condition;
(c) that the relevant person is outside the United Kingdom and it is not reasonably practicable to secure his attendance;
(d) that the relevant person cannot be found although such steps as it is reasonably practicable to take to find him have been taken;
(e) that through fear the relevant person does not give (or does not continue to give) oral evidence in the proceedings, either at all or in connection with the subject matter of the statement, and the court gives leave for the statement to be given in evidence.

(3) For the purposes of subsection (2)(e) 'fear' is to be widely construed and (for example) includes fear of the death or injury of another person or of financial loss.

(4) Leave may be given under subsection (2)(e) only if the court considers that the statement ought to be admitted in the interests of justice, having regard—
(a) to the statement's contents,
(b) to any risk that its admission or exclusion will result in unfairness to any party to the proceedings (and in particular to how difficult it will be to challenge the statement if the relevant person does not give oral evidence),
(c) in appropriate cases, to the fact that a direction under section 19 of the Youth Justice and Criminal Evidence Act 1999 (c. 23) (special measures for the giving of evidence by fearful witnesses etc) could be made in relation to the relevant person, and
(d) to any other relevant circumstances.

(5) A condition set out in any paragraph of subsection (2) which is in fact satisfied is to be treated as not satisfied if it is shown that the circumstances described in that paragraph are caused—
(a) by the person in support of whose case it is sought to give the state in evidence, or
(b) by a person acting on his behalf, in order to prevent the relevant person giving oral evidence in the proceedings (whether at all or in connection with the subject matter of the statement).

In considering whether it is reasonably practicable to secure the attendance of a witness, the court must consider what steps have, and have not, been taken. The reasonableness will be judged in relation to many factors, including the resources available to the party (*R v Maloney* [1994] Crim LR 525).

Even where the attendance of a witness is not practicable (or some other factor in s 116 is present), the court should then go on to consider s 126 of the Act and s 78 PACE 1984 in order to decide whether the evidence ought, in fairness, to be admitted. Section 126 CJA 2003, giving a discretion to exclude hearsay evidence, should also be used to exclude material that is barely relevant, which lacked significant probative value. The test was the same for the Crown and for the defence (unlike s 78 PACE) (*R v Drinkwater* [2016] EWCA Crim 16).

A17.3.2 *Business documents*

Criminal Justice Act 2003, ss 117 and 118

117 Business and other documents

(1) In criminal proceedings a statement contained in a document is admissible as evidence of any matter stated if—
 (a) oral evidence given in the proceedings would be admissible as evidence of that matter,
 (b) the requirements of subsection (2) are satisfied, and
 (c) the requirements of subsection (5) are satisfied, in a case where subsection (4) requires them to be.

(2) The requirements of this subsection are satisfied if—
 (a) the document or the part containing the statement was created or received by a person in the course of a trade, business, profession or other occupation, or as the holder of a paid or unpaid office,
 (b) the person who supplied the information contained in the statement (the relevant person) had or may reasonably be supposed to have had personal knowledge of the matters dealt with, and
 (c) each person (if any) through whom the information was supplied from the relevant person to the person mentioned in paragraph (a) received the information in the course of a trade, business, profession or other occupation, or as the holder of a paid or unpaid office.

(3) The persons mentioned in paragraphs (a) and (b) of subsection (2) may be the same person.

(4) The additional requirements of subsection (5) must be satisfied if the statement—
 (a) was prepared for the purposes of pending or contemplated criminal proceedings, or for a criminal investigation, but
 (b) was not obtained pursuant to—
  (i) a request under section 7 of the Crime (International Co-operation) Act 2003,
  (ii) an order under paragraph 6 of Schedule 13 to the Criminal Justice Act 1988, *(or)*
  (iii) an order under Part 2 of the Criminal Justice (European Investigation Order) Regulations 2017, ***or***
  (iv) ***an overseas production order under the Crime (Overseas Production Orders) Act 2019.***
 (all of which relate to overseas evidence)

(5) The requirements of this subsection are satisfied if—
 (a) any of the five conditions mentioned in section 116(2) is satisfied (absence of relevant person etc), or
 (b) the relevant person cannot reasonably be expected to have any recollection of the matters dealt with in the statement (having regard to the length of time since he supplied the information and all other circumstances).

(6) A statement is not admissible under this section if the court makes a direction to that effect under subsection (7).

(7) The court may make a direction under this subsection if satisfied that the statement's reliability as evidence for the purpose for which it is tendered is doubtful in view of—
 (a) its contents,
 (b) the source of the information contained in it,
 (c) the way in which or the circumstances in which the information was supplied or received, or
 (d) the way in which or the circumstances in which the document concerned was created or received.

If the Crown seeks to rely on a forensic match on central records, a statement confirming that match does not meet the requirements of s 117. There must also be evidence of the taking of that earlier forensic material from the defendant (*Chester-Nash v CPS* [2000] WL 571246).

A17.3.3 *Common law exceptions*

118 Preservation of certain common law categories of admissibility

(1) The following rules of law are preserved.

Public information etc

(1) Any rule of law under which in criminal proceedings—
- (a) published works dealing with matters of a public nature (such as histories, scientific works, dictionaries and maps) are admissible as evidence of facts of a public nature stated in them,
- (b) public documents (such as public registers, and returns made under public authority with respect to matters of public interest) are admissible as evidence of facts stated in them,
- (c) records (such as the records of certain courts, treaties, Crown grants, pardons and commissions) are admissible as evidence of facts stated in them, or
- (d) evidence relating to a person's age or date or place of birth may be given by a person without personal knowledge of the matter.

Reputation as to character

(2) Any rule of law under which in criminal proceedings evidence of a person's reputation is admissible for the purpose of proving his good or bad character.

[*Note*. The rule is preserved only so far as it allows the court to treat such evidence as proving the matter concerned. The good character of a non-defendant may be admitted if it is relevant to an issue in the case such as consent or self-defence (*R v Mader* [2018] EWCA Crim 2454).]

Reputation or family tradition

(3) Any rule of law under which in criminal proceedings evidence of reputation or family tradition is admissible for the purpose of proving or disproving—
- (a) pedigree or the existence of a marriage,
- (b) the existence of any public or general right, or
- (c) the identity of any person or thing.

[*Note*: The rule is preserved only so far as it allows the court to treat such evidence as proving or disproving the matter concerned.]

Res gestae

(4) Any rule of law under which in criminal proceedings a statement is admissible as evidence of any matter stated if—
- (a) the statement was made by a person so emotionally overpowered by an event that the possibility of concoction or distortion can be disregarded,
- (b) the statement accompanied an act which can be properly evaluated as evidence only if considered in conjunction with the statement, or
- (c) the statement relates to a physical sensation or a mental state (such as intention or emotion).

Confessions etc

(5) Any rule of law relating to the admissibility of confessions or mixed statements in criminal proceedings.

Admissions by agents etc

(6) Any rule of law under which in criminal proceedings—
   (a) an admission made by an agent of a defendant is admissible against the defendant as evidence of any matter stated, or
   (b) a statement made by a person to whom a defendant refers a person for information is admissible against the defendant as evidence of any matter stated.

Common enterprise

(7) Any rule of law under which in criminal proceedings a statement made by a party to a common enterprise is admissible against another party to the enterprise as evidence of any matter stated.

Expert evidence

(8) Any rule of law under which in criminal proceedings an expert witness may draw on the body of expertise relevant to his field.
(9) With the exception of the rules preserved by this section, the common law rules governing the admissibility of hearsay evidence in criminal proceedings are abolished.

No notice was required to admit *res gestae* evidence under s 118(1)(4) CJA 2003. The law was described in *R v Andrews* [1987] AC 281 and the court had considered whether the complainant was a person so emotionally overpowered that the court could rule out concoction or distortion. In *Barnaby v DPP* [2015] EWHC 232 (Admin) the magistrates had been correct to admit the content of three 999 calls and of the first statements by the victim to police when they arrived six minutes after the calls. This decision was confirmed in *Ibrahim v CPS* [2016] EWHC 1750 (Admin) when the district judge found that the phone call had been made in the immediate aftermath of the assault. The issue must be answered by considering the circumstances in which the particular statement is made; because the *res gestae* principle deals with events that are so unusual, startling, or dramatic as to dominate the thoughts of the victim so that the utterance was an instinctive reaction to them, giving no real opportunity for reasoned reflection. The time between the event and the statement is obviously a factor, but there may be special features quite apart from the time factor that relate to the possibility of concoction or distortion. In *Morgan v DPP* [2016] EWHC 3414 (Admin) hearsay evidence was admitted when an allegation was made an hour after the incident in issue after considering the relevant issues which included:

- the demeanour of the complainant,
- the content of the 999 call,
- the body-worn camera film,
- the way the complainant behaved during the call and with police,
- the fact that she had remained outside the address for an hour for fear that the defendant was still there.

However, *res gestae* may not be used until the court has examined the reason that the witness does not attend the trial (*Wills and another v CPZS* [2016] EWHC 3779 (Admin)).

If the Crown has not made enquiries as to whether the complainant is willing to give evidence and, if not, why, the court will not usually be in a position to make a proper judgment on whether to admit the evidence as *res gestae* or not (*Vilhete v CPS* [2024] EWHC 2171 (Admin)).

In *DPP v Barton* [2024] EWHC 1350 (Admin), it was held that it was not an abuse for the prosecution to rely on *res gestae* of a witness present in court but not called as a prosecution witness by the prosecution. Nor is prosecution obliged to call a witness when it is anticipated with good reason that their evidence will be untruthful.

A17.3.4 ***Prior statements***

Criminal Justice Act 2003, ss 119 and 120

119 Inconsistent statements

(1) If in criminal proceedings a person gives oral evidence and—
  (a) he admits making a previous inconsistent statement, or
  (b) a previous inconsistent statement made by him is proved by virtue of section 3, 4 or 5 of the Criminal Procedure Act 1865 (c. 18), the statement is admissible as evidence of any matter stated of which oral evidence by him would be admissible.

(2) If in criminal proceedings evidence of an inconsistent statement by any person is given under section 124(2)(c), the statement is admissible as evidence of any matter stated in it of which oral evidence by that person would be admissible.

In *Griffiths v CPS* [2018] EWHC 3062 (Admin), a complainant was treated as a hostile witness and her earlier statements were put to her. In a questionable analysis they were admitted under s 119 CJA 2003. Her retraction statement did not say the earlier statements were untrue. The bench was entitled to have regard to them as representing the truth even though there was no chance for the defence to cross-examine her on them. She had made in them admissions against herself which went to their credibility. It is difficult, however, to find a prior inconsistent statement.

Section 119 CJA 2003 cannot be used to introduce earlier statements made when a hostile witness refuses to answer questions (*R v Muldoon* (see **A17.3**)), but note that on the facts the witnesses' previous statements were admitted under s 114(1)(d) CJA 2003.

120 Other previous statements of witnesses

(1) This section applies where a person (the witness) is called to give evidence in criminal proceedings.

(2) If a previous statement by the witness is admitted as evidence to rebut a suggestion that his oral evidence has been fabricated, that statement is admissible as evidence of any matter stated of which oral evidence by the witness would be admissible.

(3) A statement made by the witness in a document—
  (a) which is used by him to refresh his memory while giving evidence,
  (b) on which he is cross-examined, and
  (c) which as a consequence is received in evidence in the proceedings, is admissible as evidence of any matter stated of which oral evidence by him would be admissible.

(4) A previous statement by the witness is admissible as evidence of any matter stated of which oral evidence by him would be admissible, if—
  (a) any of the following three conditions is satisfied, and
  (b) while giving evidence the witness indicates that to the best of his belief he made the statement, and that to the best of his belief it states the truth.

(5) The first condition is that the statement identifies or describes a person, object or place.

(6) The second condition is that the statement was made by the witness when the matters stated were fresh in his memory but he does not remember them, and cannot reasonably be expected to remember them, well enough to give oral evidence of them in the proceedings.

(7) The third condition is that—
 (a) the witness claims to be a person against whom an offence has been committed,
 (b) the offence is one to which the proceedings relate,
 (c) the statement consists of a complaint made by the witness (whether to a person in authority or not) about conduct which would, if proved, constitute the offence or part of the offence,
 (d) [repealed]
 (e) the complaint was not made as a result of a threat or a promise, and
 (f) before the statement is adduced the witness gives oral evidence in connection with its subject matter.

(8) For the purposes of subsection (7) the fact that the complaint was elicited (for example, by a leading question) is irrelevant unless a threat or a promise was involved.

139 Use of documents to refresh memory

(1) A person giving oral evidence in criminal proceedings about any matter may, at any stage in the course of doing so, refresh his memory of it from a document made or verified by him at an earlier time if—
 (a) he states in his oral evidence that the document records his recollection of the matter at that earlier time, and
 (b) his recollection of the matter is likely to have been significantly better at that time than it is at the time of his oral evidence.

(2) Where—
 (a) a person giving oral evidence in criminal proceedings about any matter has previously given an oral account, of which a sound recording was made, and he states in that evidence that the account represented his recollection of the matter at that time,
 (b) his recollection of the matter is likely to have been significantly better at the time of the previous account than it is at the time of his oral evidence, and
 (c) a transcript has been made of the sound recording.

Where a person giving evidence seeks to refresh his memory in accordance with s 139 'from a document made or verified by him at an earlier time', verification involves a question of fact as to whether the witness has at an earlier time when the matter was fresh in his mind satisfied himself that the document that he wishes to use as a memory-refresher accurately recorded his recollection of the events in question. Evidence of verification may typically include the witness's signature on the document, but that is simply one form of evidence (*Cummings (Davina) v CPS* [2016] EWHC 3624 (Admin)). Provided there is compliance with s 139, copy documents may be used to refresh memory if the secondary document is likely to be an accurate reflection of the content of the original, provided that the witness verified either the original or the secondary document at a time when his or her recall was better than at the time of giving oral evidence. Whether or not the document becomes evidence in the case, the court will always consider and give appropriate weight to any discrepancy or risk of discrepancy between its content and an original or source document of which it is a copy or from which it is derived (*DPP v Sugden* [2018] EWHC 544 (Admin)).

See *Blackstone's Criminal Practice 2026* F16

A18 Identification Evidence

A18.1 *Turnbull* direction: visual identification

In *R v Turnbull* (1976) 63 Cr App R 132, the court laid down the following guidance:

> First, whenever the case against an accused depends wholly or substantially on the correctness of one or more identifications of the accused which the defence alleges to be mistaken, the judge should warn the jury of the special need for caution before convicting the accused in reliance on the correctness of the identification or identifications. In addition he should instruct them as to the reason for the need for such a warning and should make some reference to the possibility that a mistaken witness can be a convincing one and that a number of such witnesses can all be mistaken. Provided this is done in clear terms the judge need not use any particular form of words.
>
> Secondly, the judge should direct the jury to examine closely the circumstances in which the identification by each witness came to be made. How long did the witness have the accused under observation? At what distance? In what light? Was the observation impeded in any way, as for example, by passing traffic or a press of people? Had the witness ever seen the accused before? How often? If only occasionally, had he any special reason for remembering the accused? How long elapsed between the original observation and the subsequent identification to the police? Was there any material discrepancy between the description of the accused given to the police by the witness when first seen by them and his actual appearance? If in any case, whether it is being dealt with summarily or on indictment, the prosecution has reason to believe that there is such a material discrepancy it should supply the accused or his legal advisers with particulars of the description the police were first given. In all cases if the accused asks to be given particulars of such descriptions, the prosecution should supply them. Finally, he should remind the jury of any specific weaknesses which had appeared in the identification evidence.
>
> Recognition may be more reliable than identification of a stranger; but even when the witness is purporting to recognise someone whom he knows, the jury should be reminded that mistakes in recognition of close relatives and friends are sometimes made. All these matters go to the quality of the identification evidence. If the quality is good and remains good at the close of the accused's case, the danger of a mistaken identification is lessened; but the poorer the quality, the greater the danger.
>
> In our judgment when the quality is good as for example when the identification is made after a long period of observation, or in satisfactory conditions by a relative, a neighbour, a close friend, a workmate and the like, the jury can safely be left to assess the value of the identifying evidence even though there is no other evidence to support it: provided always, however, that an adequate warning has been given about the special need for caution.
>
> Were the Courts to adjudge otherwise, affronts to justice would frequently occur. A few examples, taken over the whole spectrum of criminal activity, will illustrate what the effects upon the maintenance of law and order would be if any law were enacted that no person could be convicted on evidence of visual identification alone.

Blackstone's Magistrates' Court Handbook 2026. Bartholomew Dalton and Caroline Liggins, Oxford University Press. © Oxford University Press 2026.
DOI: 10.1093/oso/9780198963943.003.0018

A18.2 Audio identification

For the protections necessary when there is evidence of voice recognition, reference should be made to *Flynn and St John* [2008] EWCA Crim 970. But such evidence may be admitted, with appropriate warnings, when the quality of the recording is good and the length sufficient (*R v Kapikanya (Alick)* [2015] EWCA Crim 1507).

A18.3 Social media identification

In Facebook identification cases, reference should be made to *R v Alexander and McGill* [2012] EWCA Crim 2768.

See *Blackstone's Criminal Practice 2026* F19

A19 **Legal Aid**

A19.1 **Overview**

Legal aid is available for criminal proceedings. The Legal Aid Agency publishes a Criminal Legal Aid Manual which is regularly updated. Criminal proceedings are defined by the Legal Aid, Sentencing and Punishment of Offenders Act 2012 as including the following:

Legal Aid, Sentencing and Punishment of Offenders Act 2012, s 14

14 Criminal proceedings

In this Part 'criminal proceedings' means—

(a) proceedings before a court for dealing with an individual accused of an offence,
(b) proceedings before a court for dealing with an individual convicted of an offence, including proceedings in respect of a sentence or order,
(c) proceedings for dealing with an individual under the Extradition Act 2003,
(d) proceedings for binding an individual over to keep the peace or to be of good behaviour under section 115 of the Magistrates' Courts Act 1980 and for dealing with an individual who fails to comply with an order under that section,
(e) proceedings on an appeal brought by an individual under section 44A of the Criminal Appeal Act 1968 (appeal in case of death of appellant),
(f) proceedings on a reference under section 36 of the Criminal Justice Act 1972 on a point of law following the acquittal of an individual on indictment,
(g) proceedings for contempt committed, or alleged to have been committed, by an individual in the face of a court, and
(h) such other proceedings, before any court, tribunal or other person, as may be prescribed.

The proceedings referred to in s 14(h) are set out at reg 9 of the Criminal Legal Aid (General) Regulations 2013 (SI 2013/9):

Criminal Legal Aid (General) Regulations 2013, reg 9

Criminal proceedings

9. The following proceedings are criminal proceedings for the purposes of section 14(h) of the Act (criminal proceedings)—
   (a) civil proceedings in a magistrates' court arising from a failure to pay a sum due or to obey an order of that court where such failure carries the risk of imprisonment;
   (b) proceedings under sections 14B, 14D, 14G, 14H, 21B and 21D of the Football Spectators Act 1989 in relation to banning orders and references to a court;
   (c) proceedings under section 5A of the Protection from Harassment Act 1997 in relation to restraining orders on acquittal;
   (f) proceedings in relation to parenting orders made under section 8(1)(b) of the Crime and Disorder Act 1998 where an order under section 330 of the Sentencing Code or a sexual harm prevention order under section 103A of the Sexual Offences Act 2003 or Chapter 2 of Part 11 of the Sentencing Code is made;

Blackstone's Magistrates' Court Handbook 2026. Bartholomew Dalton and Caroline Liggins, Oxford University Press. © Oxford University Press 2026.
DOI: 10.1093/oso/9780198963943.003.0019

(fa) proceedings under sections 342H and 342I of the Sentencing Code in relation to serious violence reduction orders;
(g) proceedings under section 366 of the Sentencing Code in relation to parenting orders made on the conviction of a child;
(h) proceedings under section 9(5) of the Crime and Disorder Act 1998 or section 374 of the Sentencing Code to discharge or vary a parenting order made as set out in sub-paragraph (f) or (g);
(i) proceedings under section 366(10) of the Sentencing Code in relation to an appeal against a parenting order made as set out in sub-paragraph (f) or (g);
(j) proceedings under section 368 of the Sentencing Code in relation to parenting orders for failure to comply with orders under section 90 of that Code;
(ja) proceedings in a youth court (or on appeal from such a court) in relation to the breach or potential breach of a provision of an injunction under Part 1 of the Anti-social Behaviour, Crime and Policing Act 2014 where the person who is subject to the injunction is aged under 14;
(k) proceedings under sections 80, 82, 83 and 84 of the Anti-social Behaviour, Crime and Policing Act 2014 in relation to closure orders made under section 80(5)(a) of that Act where a person has engaged in, or is likely to engage in behaviour that constitutes a criminal offence on the premises;
(ka) proceedings under paragraph 3 of Schedule 2 to the Female Genital Mutilation Act 2003 in relation to female genital mutilation protection orders made other than on conviction and related appeals;
(kb) proceedings under paragraph 6 of Schedule 2 to the Female Genital Mutilation Act 2003 in relation to female genital mutilation protection orders made under paragraph 3 of that Schedule;
(l) proceedings under sections 20, 22, 26 and 28 of the Anti-social Behaviour Act 2003 in relation to parenting orders—
   (i) in cases of exclusion from school; or
   (ii) in respect of criminal conduct and anti-social behaviour;
(m) proceedings under sections 97, 100 and 101 of the Sexual Offences Act 2003 in relation to notification orders and interim notification orders;
(n) proceedings under sections 103A, 103E, 103F and 103H of the Sexual Offences Act 2003 or sections 345, 350, and 353 of the Sentencing Code in relation to sexual harm prevention orders;

. . .

(p) proceedings under sections 122A, 122D, 122E and 122G of the Sexual Offences Act 2003 in relation to sexual risk orders;

. . .

(r) proceedings under section 13 of the Tribunals, Courts and Enforcement Act 2007 on appeal against a decision of the Upper Tribunal in proceedings in respect of—
   (i) a decision of the Financial Conduct Authority
   (ia) a decision of the Prudential Regulation Authority;
   (ii) a decision of the Bank of England; or
   (iii) a decision of a person in relation to the assessment of any compensation or consideration under the Banking (Special Provisions) Act 2008 or the Banking Act 2009;
(s) proceedings before the Crown Court or the Court of Appeal in relation to serious crime prevention orders under sections 19, 20, 21 and 24 of the Serious Crime Act 2007;
(t) proceedings under sections 100, 101, 103, 104 and 106 of the Criminal Justice and Immigration Act 2008 in relation to violent offender orders and interim violent offender orders;
(u) proceedings under sections 26, 27 and 29 of the Crime and Security Act 2010 in relation to—

(i) domestic violence protection notices; or
(ii) domestic violence protection orders;

(ua) proceedings under sections 14(1)(b) and (c), 15 and 20 to 22 of the Modern Slavery Act 2015 in relation to slavery and trafficking prevention orders;
(ub) proceedings under sections 23 and 27 to 29 of the Modern Slavery Act 2015 in relation to slavery and trafficking risk orders;

. . .

(ud) proceedings under sections 1, 4, 5 and 7 of the Stalking Protection Act 2019 in relation to stalking protection orders and interim stalking protection orders, and
(v) any other proceedings that involve the determination of a criminal charge for the purposes of Article 6(1) of the European Convention on Human Rights.

This provision (v) includes proceedings for contempt other than in the face of the court in the High Court.

Legal aid is subject to a merits test, and means assessment in some cases. There is no means assessment:

- for those under 18 years;
- for those in receipt of income support;
- for those in receipt of income-based employment and support allowance (ESA);
- for those in receipt of income-based job-seeker's allowance (JSA);
- for those in receipt of guaranteed state pension credit; or
- for those in receipt of Universal Credit.

Legal aid extends automatically to the Crown Court if the case is committed for sentence (note that there is no additional contribution payable in respect of these Crown Court proceedings).

Legal aid automatically extends, without a merits test, to any case sent to the Crown Court, but proceedings in the Crown Court are subject to a means test. A contribution may then be required or legal aid be refused.

Appeals to the Crown Court require a fresh legal aid application to be lodged, and are subject to interests of justice and means criteria. A contribution may be payable in the Crown Court, dependent on means, or legal aid be refused.

A19.2 **The interests of justice test**

When assessing whether the grant of representation is in the interests of justice, regard should be had to the provisions of s 17(2) Legal Aid, Sentencing and Punishment of Offenders Act 2012 (the *Widgery* criteria). The defendant must be able to demonstrate one or more of the following:

- It is likely that I will lose my liberty.
- I have been given a sentence that is suspended or non-custodial. If I break this, the court may be able to deal with me for the original offence.
- It is likely that I will lose my livelihood.
- It is likely that I will suffer serious damage to my reputation.
- A substantial question of law may be involved.

- I may not be able to understand the court proceedings or present my own case.
- I may need witnesses to be traced or interviewed on my behalf.
- The proceedings may involve expert cross-examination of a prosecution witness.
- It is in the interests of another person that I am represented.
- Any other reasons.

Refusal on the basis of the interests of justice test can be appealed to justices or an officer of the Crown Court (Criminal Legal Aid (General) Regulations 2013 (SI 2013/9), regs 29 and 30), and regard should be had to the following:

- the likely penalty, not the theoretical maximum: *R v Highgate Justices, ex p Lewis* [1977] Crim LR 611. Where a defendant has received many prison sentences for identical offending it is irrational to refuse legal aid as it is likely that they will lose their livelihood (*R (David Sonn) v West London Magistrates' Court* [2000] CLW 40/13);
- in *R (Punatar) v Horseferry Road Magistrates' Court* [2002] EWHC 1196 (Admin), the solicitor attended court to defend an imprisonable matter and submitted an application for representation at the end of those proceedings. At that stage the imprisonable matter had been replaced by a non-imprisonable one and legal aid was refused. The court held that the refusal was wrong in law; the court should not apply hindsight but instead look at what had been in the mind of the solicitor when he made the decision to attend court;
- a 16-year-old would not have the skills to cross-examine a police officer effectively: *Scunthorpe Justices, ex p S, The Times*, 5 March 1998;
- in *R (GKR Law Solicitors) v Liverpool Magistrates' Court* [2008] EWHC 2974 (Admin), the court held that it was appropriate to grant representation to a defendant in relation to a special reasons hearing, where a witness in the case was the defendant's 12-year-old son. The child was a witness entitled to and requiring special measures, and consideration would need to be given to video-interviewing the young witness in order to ensure best evidence was given; such measures would be outside the competence and resources of the defendant;
- in *R v Chester Magistrates' Court, ex p Ball* (1999) 163 JP 757, it was said that any defendant of previous good character pleading not guilty to a charge equal to, or more significant than, s 5 Public Order Act 1986 in terms of nature and seriousness should be granted legal aid regardless of his social or professional standing. This is very unlikely to include non-imprisonable road traffic or regulatory offences;
- in *R v Gravesend Magistrates' Court ex p Baker* (1977) 161 JP 765 the defendant was charged with driving with excess alcohol and put forward special reasons based on spiked drinks. The court held that the applicant should be granted legal aid because a scientific expert would be required and the assistance of a solicitor would be necessary to identify witnesses, to take proper proofs, and to extract the defence in the witness box.

A19.3 **Transfer of representation**

The law is contained in reg 14 Criminal Legal Aid (Determinations by a Court and Choice of Representative) Regulations 2013 (SI 2013/614):

Criminal Legal Aid (Determinations by a Court and Choice of Representative) Regulations 2013, reg 14

Change of provider

14 (1) Subject to paragraph (2), where an individual has selected a provider in criminal proceedings, the right conferred by section 27(4) of the Act does not include a right to select a provider in place of the original provider.

(1) The relevant court may determine that the individual can select a provider in place of the original provider in the circumstances set out in paragraphs (3) or (4).

(2) The circumstances are that the relevant court determines that—
  - (a) there has been a breakdown in the relationship between the individual and the original provider such that effective representation can no longer be provided by the original provider; or
  - (b) there is some other compelling reason why effective representation can no longer be provided by the original provider.

(3) The circumstances are that the relevant court determines that—
  - (a) the original provider—
    - (i) considers there to be a duty to withdraw from the case in accordance with the provider's professional rules of conduct; or
    - (ii) is no longer able to represent the individual through circumstances outside the provider's control; and
  - (b) the original provider has supplied the relevant court with details as to—
    - (i) the nature of any such duty to withdraw from the case; or
    - (ii) the particular circumstances that render the provider unable to represent the individual.

Solicitors seeking a transfer must exercise a proper and independent judgment when considering whether the supplicant's grounds were justified: *R (Sanjari) v Birmingham CC* [2015] EWHC 2037 (Admin).

Part 46 of the Crim PR provides the relevant procedure.

See *Blackstone's Criminal Practice 2026* **D32**

A20 Mental Disorder

A20.1 CPS legal guidance

In October 2019 the CPS published detailed guidance: Mental Health: Suspects and Defendants with Mental Health Conditions or Disorders, applying the following principles to all aspects of the criminal justice process.

'This guidance identifies the principles relevant to the decision to prosecute, and any prosecution which follows, of individuals who have:

- A mental disorder as defined by the Mental Health Act 2007
- A learning disability
- A learning difficulty
- Autism Spectrum Disorder
- An acquired brain injury
- Dementia
- Other mental health, cognitive, or neurodiverse conditions.

This guidance therefore seeks to inform the decision to prosecute in respect of a span of conditions which comprise disorders, disabilities, impairments, injuries, and diseases, which relate both to the brain and the mind.

Outside the ambit of this guidance, prosecutors will more broadly have regard to the mental functioning of a suspect or defendant even where this is not reflected in a recognized condition: when assessing the individual suspects *mens rea*; when considering their maturity—in the case of young adults who continue to mature into their mid-twenties—and in recognizing neurodiversity, the variations in the human brain and the mental functions of suspects and defendants.

There is a very wide span of mental health conditions or disorders, and each will impact on individuals in different ways. The fact that someone has a mental health condition or disorder may be relevant to the offence, but it may not. For this reason, prosecutors should approach each case on its own facts and merits and assess the nature, extent, and effect of the condition on an individual, together with the circumstances of the particular offences. Mental health conditions or disorders are not always a constant: they may fluctuate, including being different at the time of an alleged offence to the different stages of any prosecution.

While some mental health conditions or disorders are distinct and easily defined, there are also crossovers and individuals may have a number of related conditions. For example, autism is often diagnosed alongside other conditions, such as learning disabilities and/or difficulties. Multiple complex issues may be involved, for instance personality disorder or post-traumatic stress disorder, combined with substance misuse. Where this is the case, it will be important to understand the combined impact on the behaviour and capabilities of the individual concerned'.

Blackstone's Magistrates' Court Handbook 2026. Bartholomew Dalton and Caroline Liggins, Oxford University Press.
DOI: 10.1093/oso/9780198963943.003.0020

A20.2 **Fitness to plead**

In a strict legal sense the issue of fitness to plead does not arise in the magistrates' court as the relevant legislation does not provide for any summary procedures. For the courts powers see **D19.1**.

If the offence is an either-way offence the court may decline jurisdiction, but the defendant will not be able to consent to summary trial. However, if the accused is being tried for an imprisonable offence, and it is shown that the accused did the act or made the omission charged, *Lincoln (Kesteven) Justices, ex p O'Connor* [1983] 1 WLR 335 confirms that he can be made subject to a hospital order under s 37(3) Mental Health Act 1983.

Subject to having obtained two satisfactory reports, and the court can remand under s 35 Mental Health Act 1983 for that purpose, the court can then go on to make a hospital order under s 37(3). The stages are:

- raise issue of mental disorder;
- prove that the accused did the act or made the omission charged;
- obtain requisite medical assessment;
- make hospital order.

The prosecution will be required to prove only the *actus reus* of the offence (*R v Antoine* [2000] 2 All ER 208, HL). If the prosecution cannot prove the act or omission, the defendant must be discharged.

In the alternative, if the Crown will not follow that route, the defendant can plead not guilty and put the Crown to proof of the mental element.

The procedure under s 37(3) Mental Health Act 1983 is not available for indictable-only offences.

A20.3 **Fitness to stand trial**

If the defendant does not require a hospital/guardianship order under s 37(3) and suffers from mental disorder or some other significant impairment of intelligence, he may be able to participate in criminal proceedings if necessary with adaptations to the trial process tailored to suit his particular needs; see Criminal Practice Direction 3D–3F (**A10.12** and **A27**), including the use of an intermediary. However, if the defendant's illness or disability is so severe that he will be unable to participate in any way in his trial, then the CPS should be invited to consider discontinuing the proceedings, or the court could stay the proceedings on the grounds of an abuse of process, or of its own volition adjourn the case *sine die*.

A20.4 **Insanity**

Loake v CPS [2017] EWHC 2855 (Admin) confirms that insanity is available as a defence to all offences in the magistrates' court, because the M'Naghten Rules are not limited to *mens rea* but recognize the principle that criminal punishment should be imposed only upon those who are responsible for their actions (he does not know what he is doing is wrong, ie conduct being contrary to law). However, the defendant does not have an absolute right to have the issue determined at trial if the court feels that a disposal under s 37(3) Mental Health Act 1983 might be more appropriate. There is no 'special verdict' of not guilty by reason of insanity; a finding of insanity prevents conviction (*R (Singh) v Stratford Magistrates' Court* [2007] EWHC 1582 (Admin)).

A20.5 **Medical reports**

In order to decide whether the person should be tried or made subject to the fitness to plead procedure, the court may need to consider the report of a medical practitioner, and a remand to hospital under s 11 Powers of Criminal Courts (Sentencing) Act 2000 may be ordered. The appropriate procedures and requirements are set out in Crim PR Rule 3.10. Procedures at the sentencing stage are set out at Crim PR 28.8. Solicitors may choose to commission their own expert to preserve client privilege.

Powers of Criminal Courts (Sentencing) Act 2000, s 11

11 Remand by magistrates' court for medical examination

(1) If, on the trial by a magistrates' court of an offence punishable on summary conviction with imprisonment, the court—
  (a) is satisfied that the accused did the act or made the omission charged, but
  (b) is of the opinion that an inquiry ought to be made into his physical or mental condition before the method of dealing with him is determined, the court shall adjourn the case to enable a medical examination and report to be made, and shall remand him.

(2) An adjournment under subsection (1) above shall not be for more than three weeks at a time where the court remands the accused in custody, nor for more than four weeks at a time where it remands him on bail.

(3) Where on an adjournment under subsection (1) above the accused is remanded on bail, the court shall impose conditions under paragraph (d) of section 3(6) of the Bail Act 1976 and the requirements imposed as conditions under that paragraph shall be or shall include requirements that the accused—
  (a) undergo medical examination by a registered medical practitioner or, where the inquiry is into his mental condition and the court so directs, two such practitioners; and
  (b) for that purpose attend such an institution or place, or on such practitioner, as the court directs and, where the inquiry is into his mental condition, comply with any other directions which may be given to him for that purpose by any person specified by the court or by a person of any class so specified.

A20.6 **Legal aid**

The Legal Aid Agency's (LAA's) criminal legal aid manual confirms:

Criminal Legal Aid Manual, paras 3.5.6 and 3.5.7

3.5.6 Signing the form

For audit purposes and ***with the exception of applicants with severe mental health problems,*** the applicant must sign the application form in all cases . . .

3.5.7 Applicants with mental health problems

There are some applicants who, because of mental health problems, are unable to give instructions to their solicitor, to understand the declaration, and/or are unable to sign the applicant declaration form. It is likely that these applicants will be detained under the Mental Health Act or will be being kept under medical supervision. Where the applicant lacks capacity, within the meaning of the Mental Capacity Act 2005, to instruct a solicitor as their representative and to sign the applicant declaration form, the LAA's contract does allow the solicitor to get someone else to sign the application on the applicant's behalf (see 4.25(b) of Specification of the 2017 Standard Crime Contract). The applicant declaration form may be signed by

- The applicant's attorney or deputy appointed under the Mental Capacity Act 2005
- The applicant's nearest relative or guardian
- A person acting as a litigation friend
- Any other person who is acting in the applicant's best interest and who has sufficient knowledge of the applicant's financial affairs to be able to sign the declaration on the applicant's behalf.

The solicitor or any other member, employee, or associate of the solicitor's firm cannot sign the form. In addition to the signature, the third party must also be in a position to provide details of the applicant's finances or the application form will be rejected. The person signing the form takes on the responsibility for providing evidence of the applicant's income and capital, so that the applicant's means may be determined. This will include evidence of any income and/or capital assets. As the CRM14 eForm does not currently allow for the applicant's signature to be bypassed in these circumstances solicitors should confirm that the applicant has signed but record in the further information field (that appears before you confirm that you wish to submit the eForm) the name of the person signing on the applicant's behalf and their relationship to the applicant, and explain why this was necessary. In cases where the applicant does not have sufficient capacity to instruct a solicitor, is unwilling or physically unable to sign the applicant declaration form themselves and there is no one available to sign on the applicant's behalf, then special circumstances may apply. We recognise the difficulties faced by the solicitor in obtaining information in these circumstances. A solicitor who wishes to act for the client in this situation should complete the CRM14 eForm to the best of their ability on the information provided. To avoid rejection of the eForm, for any mandatory questions where you are unsure of the answer you may select 'No' or enter '0.00' or 'not known' but you should then provide further explanation of your understanding of the applicant's circumstances in the further information field that appears before you confirm that you wish to submit the eForm. Similarly, solicitors should confirm that the applicant has signed but provide an explanation as to why the applicant has not actually signed the applicant declaration form. Should you experience any difficulty completing the form in this way you should contact the National Crime Team for assistance (see Section 1: Key Players for contact details). The NCT will work with you to build a picture of the applicant's circumstances and assess the level of risk the client presents. Whilst we do not expect the solicitor to commission a mental health report, if you are able to provide a copy of any existing reports, this can assist in achieving a resolution. If the applicant has been assessed by the court's own psychiatric team, then providing this report can also be useful. Such reports can be uploaded with the eForm as with other types of evidence. We understand that it may not be possible to provide reports in every case; however, we ask that reasonable attempts to do so have been made. In the absence of any reports we will require as much detail as the solicitor is reasonably able to provide. For instance, how the applicant has been supporting themselves financially, where and with whom they have been living, have they been diagnosed with a mental illness, are they known to mental health services, have they been sectioned previously, how does their illness manifest itself, and in particular how does it affect their ability to instruct the solicitor and understand the declaration. This will enable the NCT to work with the solicitor to achieve an acceptable solution. Please note: legal advisers and judges do not have the authority to accept unsigned forms for applicants in these circumstances, please see Criminal Legal Aid (Determinations by a Court and Choice of Representative) Regulations 2013 for further details.

A20.7 **Force in mental health units**

Under the Mental Health Units (Use of Force) Act 2018 a police officer who assists staff must wear and have operational body-worn video. A failure goes to the admissibility of evidence.

A20.8 **Discontinuance or diversion**

In considering these issues, the CPS legal guidance provides that in reaching decisions to prosecute in cases where mental health or disability is a live issue prosecutors should firstly consider any evidence concerning the nature and degree of the defendant's mental ill health or disability, and the relationship between this and their conduct, and reach a preliminary view on culpability. Prosecutors should also consider the impact of a prosecution where there is evidence of its likely interaction with a suspect's mental health, particularly in a case where there is evidence that it can be exacerbated, or it is degenerating.

Prosecutors should then turn to consider:

- The seriousness of the offence
- The likelihood of repetition
- The need to safeguard the public or those providing care

Seriousness is not made out simply where the outcome of proceedings is likely to result in more than a nominal/minor penalty. It requires an assessment of the overall seriousness of the offence which will depend on the facts and merits of each individual allegation. Violent, sexual, or offences involving weapons, save for the most minor, are likely to be serious; dishonesty or public order offences may require more careful assessment. The Code provides at 4.14(b) and (c) for considerations relevant to seriousness, namely an assessment of culpability and harm.

An assessment of the likelihood of repetition should be informed by evidence addressing the following if possible:

- Any history of similar and/or recent behaviour
- Any proposed treatment of the suspect, the aim of that treatment, and its potential impact on offending behaviour
- The suspect's history of engagement with, and response to, treatment
- The suspect's current response to treatment

An absence of susceptibility to treatment, and/or engagement with treatment, is an absence of a factor tending against prosecution, rather than a factor tending in favour.

The evidence should also address the risk of causing harm to others. A prosecution is more likely to be in the public interest where the risk of harm to others through reoffending is high.

Prosecutors should consider what weight to attach to seriousness, likelihood of reoffending, and the need to safeguard and reach a conclusion, considering these in the round.

Prosecutors should also take into account any evidence of an adverse impact on the suspect's health or disability of a prosecution. It does not serve public confidence in the administration of justice to pursue proceedings which are likely to have a significant detrimental impact on the health of the defendant, including the proceedings themselves as well as any likely sentence.

Prosecutors should take into account the views expressed by the victim about the impact that the offence has had. The circumstances of the victim are highly relevant, including whether the victim was a person serving the public at the material time and whether the victim was the subject of a hate crime.

The likelihood of a nominal penalty or other order (in particular, if that is the likely outcome of a not guilty by reason of insanity verdict, a finding that a defendant who is not fit to plead did the act alleged, or of the court ordering treatment which the defendant is already receiving) will not necessarily be determinative. Prosecutors should have regard to the following:

- Deterrence may legitimately and importantly be achieved by subjecting the suspect's conduct to scrutiny in proceedings conducted in open court and formally recording the outcome;
- This must be balanced against an assessment of the impact of doing so upon the defendant. That impact may be detrimental to the defendant which will tend against prosecution; there may be evidence that it will assist to ensure the defendant takes responsibility for their actions and does not appear to excuse them. Deterrence may also be secured by means other than court proceedings;
- Justice may be achieved for victims by the formal finding of a court, following the hearing of evidence in open court, that a defendant has done the acts alleged, even if not guilty by reason of insanity or being unfit to plead. The views of victims must where possible be taken into account. These should be informed by the purpose and likely outcome of any hearing;
- Public confidence in the administration of justice may be upheld in finding a defendant did the acts alleged against him through the mechanism provided by Parliament to provide a legal defence for, or accommodate, accused persons who have serious mental health conditions or disorders. It may have a wider importance to the community and public at large in hearing the allegations and having them tested; and
- There is a public interest in a judicial determination of allegations and in hearing the evidence of complainants in a case.

Prosecutors should test the suggestion that a nominal penalty is likely, in appropriate cases. For instance, a defendant's treatment may be ongoing whether a prosecution follows or not and so any further order may appear to be nominal. However, the finding of a court of the commission of a crime during the course of that treatment may inform the future treatment and management of an offender than if the case is not proceeded with. A finding or conviction can have a bearing on forensic risk assessments of a patient, as without such a finding or conviction it may be argued, for example at a tribunal hearing where discharge is sought, that there is no evidence of the commission of an alleged offence. Prosecutors may also have regard to other orders which may be available upon conviction, including restraining orders (also available upon acquittal—but not where the defendant is unfit to plead or following a special verdict) and criminal behaviour orders. Prosecutors should consider carefully the position where a defendant has been receiving treatment for a long period of time—the hospital order will continue but no further treatment is required—as to whether a prosecution remains proportionate.

Where a nominal penalty is likely but a prosecution is nonetheless to follow, this must be clearly set out when authorizing charge and explained to the court. Cases should be kept under continuing review, and if there is a change of circumstance particularly a decision is likely to be revisited, but equally it is important to proceed with cases and avoid unnecessary adjournments where, notwithstanding a likely nominal penalty, a prosecution is to proceed.

The Code for Crown Prosecutors indicates that, in applying the public interest test, prosecutors should also have regard when considering culpability as to whether the suspect is, or was at the time of the offence, suffering from any significant mental or physical ill-health as in some circumstances this may mean that it is less likely that a prosecution is required. However, prosecutors will also need to consider how serious the offence was, whether it is likely to be repeated, and the need to safeguard the public or those providing care to such persons.

See *Blackstone's Criminal Practice 2026* **D20.75** and **E22**

A21 **Misbehaviour at Court**

A21.1 **Misbehaviour during allocation and summary trial**

Section 18(3) MCA 1980 provides:

> **Magistrates' Courts Act 1980, s 18(3)**
>
> **18 Initial procedure on information against adult for offence triable either way**
>
> ...
>
> (3) The court may proceed in the absence of the accused in accordance with such of the provisions of sections 19 to 22 below as are applicable in the circumstances if the court considers that by reason of his disorderly conduct before the court it is not practicable for the proceedings to be conducted in his presence; and subsections (3) to (5) of section 23 below, so far as applicable, shall have effect in relation to proceedings conducted in the absence of the accused by virtue of this subsection (references in those subsections to the person representing the accused being for this purpose read as references to the person, if any, representing him).
>
> ...
>
> A similar power exists in relation to youths by reason of s 24B(1) MCA 1980.

A21.2 **Contempt of Court Act 1981**

Section 12 Contempt of Court Act 1981 provides:

> **Contempt of Court Act 1981, s 12**
>
> **12 Offences of contempt of magistrates' courts**
>
> (1) A magistrates' court has jurisdiction under this section to deal with any person who—
>
> (a) wilfully insults the justice or justices, any witness before or officer of the court or any solicitor or counsel having business in the court, during his or their sitting or attendance in court or in going to or returning from the court; or
>
> (b) wilfully interrupts the proceedings of the court or otherwise misbehaves in court.
>
> (2) In any such case the court may order any officer of the court, or any constable, to take the offender into custody and detain him until the rising of the court; and the court may, if it thinks fit, commit the offender to custody for a specified period not exceeding one month or impose on him a fine not exceeding £2,500, or both.
>
> (2A) A fine imposed under subsection (2) above shall be deemed, for the purposes of any enactment, to be a sum adjudged to be paid by a conviction.
>
> (4) A magistrates' court may at any time revoke an order of committal made under subsection (2) and, if the offender is in custody, order his discharge.
>
> (5) Section 123 of the Sentencing Code (limit on fines in respect of young persons) and the following provisions of the Magistrates' Courts Act 1980 apply in relation to an order under this section as they apply in relation to a sentence on conviction or finding of guilty of an offence; and those provisions of the Magistrates' Courts Act 1980 are section 36 (restriction on fines in respect of young persons);

Blackstone's Magistrates' Court Handbook 2026. Bartholomew Dalton and Caroline Liggins, Oxford University Press. © Oxford University Press 2026.
DOI: 10.1093/oso/9780198963943.003.0021

> sections 75 to 91 (enforcement); section 108 (appeal to Crown Court); section 136 (overnight detention in default of payment); and section 142(1) (power to rectify mistakes).

It should be noted that there is no power to adjourn, and the matter must be dealt with before the end of the court day. There will be few cases that cannot be handled adequately by a suitable apology. See also Part 48 of the Crim PR.

Essential procedures, before any court considers a committal application, were set out in *Re L (a child); Re Oddin* [2016] EWCA Civ 173, including:

- there is complete clarity at the outset as to precisely what the foundation of the alleged contempt is;
- consideration is given to the question of whether the judge hearing the committal application should do so, or whether it should be heard by another judge;
- the accused has been given the opportunity to secure legal representation;
- that the standard of proof applied is the criminal standard; and
- any committal order sets out what the findings are that establish the contempt.

For procedures where the contempt is not in the face of the court see *R v Yaxley-Lennon* [2018] EWCA Crim 1356.

See *Blackstone's Criminal Practice 2026* **B14.83**

A22 Presence of Defendant and Prosecutor in Court

A22.1 General principles

Under provisions of the Judicial Review and Courts Act 2022, once in force, many hearings may take place in the absence of the defendant and cases in relation to defendants on bail may be sent in their absence to the Crown Court.

If a defendant has been bailed to attend court, his presence is mandatory unless and until it is excused by the court. Where a defendant on bail fails to appear, a warrant may be issued for his arrest. However, various exceptions apply.

Statutory provisions are contained in s 129 MCA 1980:

> **Magistrates' Court Act 1980, s 129**
>
> **129 Further remand**
>
> (1) If a magistrates' court is satisfied that any person who has been remanded is unable by reason of illness or accident to appear or be brought before the court at the expiration of the period for which he was remanded, the court may, in his absence, remand him for a further time; and section 128(6) above shall not apply.
>
> (2) Notwithstanding anything in section 128(1) above, the power of a court under subsection (1) above to remand a person on bail for a further time—
>
> (a) where he was granted bail in criminal proceedings, includes power to enlarge the recognizance of any surety for him to a later time;
>
> (3) Where a person remanded on bail is bound to appear before a magistrates' court at any time and the court has no power to remand him under subsection (1) above, the court may in his absence—
>
> (a) where he was granted bail in criminal proceedings, appoint a later time as the time at which he is to appear and enlarge the recognizances of any sureties for him to that time;
>
> and the appointment of the time or the enlargement of his recognizance shall be deemed to be a further remand.
>
> (4) Where a magistrates' court sends a person to the Crown Court for trial on bail and the recognizance of any surety for him has been conditioned in accordance with paragraph (a) of subsection (4) of section 128 above, the court may, in the absence of the surety, enlarge his recognizance so that he is bound to secure that the person so sent for trial appears also before the Crown Court.

On summons and certain other matters, the defendant may be represented by a legal representative.

Section 122 MCA 1980 provides:

> **Magistrates' Courts Act 1980, s 122**
>
> **122 Appearance by counsel or solicitor**
>
> (1) A party to any proceedings before a magistrates' court may be represented by a legal representative.

Blackstone's Magistrates' Court Handbook 2026. Bartholomew Dalton and Caroline Liggins, Oxford University Press. © Oxford University Press 2026.
DOI: 10.1093/oso/9780198963943.003.0022

(2) Subject to subsection (3) below, an absent party so represented shall be deemed not to be absent.
(3) Appearance of a party by legal representative shall not satisfy any provision of any enactment or any condition of a recognizance expressly requiring his presence.

For allocation hearings see **A4.2.** *Until the implementation of the Judicial Review and Courts Act 2022 (which allows for proceedings in writing)* the defendant must personally enter the plea to an either-way offence.

A22.2 **Defendants in custody**

A further remand of a defendant in custody can be ordered if there is illness or accident in accordance with s 129 MCA 1980. There is no limit to the length of a remand under this provision.

However, further powers exist in s 128.

Magistrates Courts Act 1980, s 128

128(3A)

Subject to subsection (3B) below, where a person has been remanded in custody and the remand was not a remand under section 128A below for a period exceeding 8 clear days, the court may further remand him (otherwise than in the exercise of the power conferred by that section) on an adjournment under section 5, 10(1) 17C or 18(4) above without his being brought before it if it is satisfied—

(a) that he gave his consent, either in response to a question under subsection (1C) above or otherwise, to the hearing and determination in his absence of any application for his remand on an adjournment of the case under any of those provisions; and
(b) that he has not by virtue of this subsection been remanded without being brought before the court on more than two such applications immediately preceding the application which the court is hearing; and

. . .

(d) that he has not withdrawn his consent to their being so heard and determined.

(3B) The court may not exercise the power conferred by subsection (3A) above if it appears to the court, on an application for a further remand being made to it, that the person to whom the application relates has no legal representative acting for him in the case (whether present in court or not).

(3C) Where—
(a) a person has been remanded in custody on an adjournment of a case under section 5, 10(1) 17C or 18(4) above; and
(b) an application is subsequently made for his further remand on such an adjournment; and
(c) he is not brought before the court which hears and determines the application; and
(d) that court is not satisfied as mentioned in subsection (3A) above, the court shall adjourn the case and remand him in custody for the period for which it stands adjourned.

(3D) An adjournment under subsection (3C) above shall be for the shortest period that appears to the court to make it possible for the accused to be brought before it.

(3E) Where—

(a) on an adjournment of a case under section 5, 10(1) 17C or 18(4) above a person has been remanded in custody without being brought before the court; and
(b) it subsequently appears—
  (i) to the court which remanded him in custody; or
  (ii) to an alternate magistrates' court to which he is remanded under section 130 below, that he ought not to have been remanded in custody in his absence, the court shall require him to be brought before it at the earliest time that appears to the court to be possible.

A22.3 Defendant's presence at trial

Section 11 MCA 1980 details the court's powers when a defendant does not appear for trial:

Magistrates' Courts Act 1980, s 11

11 Non-appearance of accused: general provisions

(1) Subject to the provisions of this Act, where at the time and place appointed for the trial or adjourned trial of an information the prosecutor appears but the accused does not—
  (a) if the accused is under 18 years of age, the court may proceed in his absence; and
  (b) if the accused has attained the age of 18 years, the court shall proceed in his absence unless it appears to the court to be contrary to the interests of justice to do so.

This is subject to subsections (2), (2A), (3), and (4).

(2) Where a summons has been issued, the court shall not begin to try the information in the absence of the accused unless either it is proved to the satisfaction of the court, on oath or in such other manner as may be prescribed, that the summons was served on the accused within what appears to the court to be a reasonable time before the trial or adjourned trial or the accused has appeared on a previous occasion to answer to the information.
(2A) The court shall not proceed in the absence of the accused if it considers that there is an acceptable reason for his failure to appear.
(3) In proceedings to which this subsection applies, the court shall not in a person's absence sentence him to imprisonment or detention in a detention centre or make a detention and training order or an order under paragraph 8(2)(a) or (b) of Schedule 12 to the Criminal Justice Act 2003 that a suspended sentence passed on him shall take effect.
(3A) But where a sentence or order of a kind mentioned in subsection (3) is imposed or given in the absence of the offender, the offender must be brought before the court before being taken to a prison or other institution to begin serving his sentence (and the sentence or order is not to be regarded as taking effect until he is brought before the court).
(4) In proceedings to which this subsection applies, the court shall not in a person's absence impose any disqualification on him, except on resumption of the hearing after an adjournment under section 10(3) above; and where a trial is adjourned in pursuance of this subsection the notice required by section 10(2) above shall include notice of the reason for the adjournment . . .

In deciding whether or not to proceed in the defendant's absence, the court has to have regard to the following principles (*R v Jones and others* [2002]

UKHL 5; *Shirzadeh v Maidstone Magistrates' Court* [2003] EWHC 2216 (Admin)):

- the nature and circumstances of the defendant's behaviour in absenting himself from the trial or disrupting it, as the case may be, and in particular, whether his behaviour was deliberate, voluntary, and such as plainly waived his right to appear;
- (in the case of a defendant aged under 18 years) whether an adjournment might result in the defendant being caught or attending voluntarily and/or not disrupting the proceedings;
- (in the case of a defendant aged under 18 years) the likely length of such an adjournment;
- whether the defendant, though absent, is, or wishes to be, legally represented at the trial or has, by his conduct, waived his right to representation;
- whether an absent defendant's legal representatives are able to receive instructions from him during the trial and the extent to which they are able to present his defence (*Note*: it is a matter for the professional judgement of the advocate whether they should continue to represent the absent defendant (*R v Ulcay* [2007] EWCA Crim 2379));
- the extent of the disadvantage to the defendant in not being able to give his account of events, having regard to the nature of the evidence against him;
- the risk of the jury reaching an improper conclusion about the absence of the defendant;
- the seriousness of the offence, which affects defendant, victim, and public;
- the general public interest and the particular interest of victims and witnesses that a trial should take place within a reasonable time of the events to which it relates;
- the effect of delay on the memories of witnesses;
- where there is more than one defendant and not all have absconded, the undesirability of separate trials, and the prospects of a fair trial for the defendant(s) who are present.

The court in *Shirzadeh* identified four additional factors relevant to trial in the magistrates' court:

> [first] that there ought to be less risk from either a trained lay justice or a district judge in drawing an impermissible inference from a defendant's absence; secondly, in a magistrates' court the finder of fact may ask its own questions and test the evidence of prosecution witnesses; thirdly, a defendant in summary proceedings can apply to set aside any resulting conviction under section 142 of the Magistrates' Courts Act 1980; and fourthly, a defendant in summary proceedings has an automatic right of appeal to the Crown Court.

The decision to try a person in his absence must be exercised with great care and only in cases such as where the absence was a deliberate absconding (*R (Drinkwater) v Solihull Magistrates' Court* [2012] EWHC 765 (Admin)). (See also case law in A2.)

A22.4 **Statutory declarations**

Where a defendant is convicted in absence, having not known of the summons or proceedings, including within a single justice procedure, he may apply to the court for the conviction to be set aside. Section 14 MCA 1980 provides:

Magistrates' Courts Act 1980, s 14

14 Proceedings invalid where accused did not know of them

(1) Where a summons has been issued under section 1 above and a magistrates' court has begun to try the information to which the summons relates, then, if—

(a) the accused, at any time during or after the trial, makes a statutory declaration that he did not know of the summons or the proceedings until a date specified in the declaration, being a date after the court has begun to try the information; and

(b) within 21 days of that date the declaration is served on the designated officer for the court, without prejudice to the validity of the information, the summons and all subsequent proceedings shall be void.

. . .

(3) If on the application of the accused it appears to a magistrates' court (which for this purpose may be composed of a single justice) that it was not reasonable to expect the accused to serve such a statutory declaration as is mentioned in subsection (1) above within the period allowed by that subsection, the court may accept service of such a declaration by the accused after that period has expired; and a statutory declaration accepted under this subsection shall be deemed to have been served as required by that subsection.

(4) Where any proceedings have become void by virtue of subsection (1) above, the information shall not be tried again by any of the same justices.

The procedure is provided for by Criminal Procedure Rule 44.2.

A22.5 **Failure by the prosecutor to appear or proceed**

Section 15 MCA 1980 provides that:

15 Non-appearance of prosecutor

(1) Where at the time and place appointed for the trial or adjourned trial of an information the accused appears or is brought before the court and the prosecutor does not appear, the court may dismiss the information or, if evidence has been received on a previous occasion, proceed in the absence of the prosecutor.

DPP v Bird [2015] EWHC 4077 (Admin) states that a magistrates' court may only dismiss a charge

- after hearing evidence,
- where the prosecution offers no evidence or is not able to proceed and the case is not adjourned, or
- where the prosecution does not appear at the time and place appointed for trial.

Section 9 MCA 1980 confirms that the summary trial of an information begins with the entry of a plea.

See *Blackstone's Criminal Practice 2026* **D22.12**

A23 Pre-Charge Hearings

A23.1 Funding

Advocacy assistance, without a means test, is available for all the hearings in this section.

A23.2 Warrants of further detention and extended warrants of further detention

Police and Criminal Evidence Act 1984, ss 43 and 44

43

(1) Where, on an application on oath made by a constable and supported by an information, a magistrates' court is satisfied that there are reasonable grounds for believing that the further detention of the person to whom the application relates is justified, it may issue a warrant of further detention authorising the keeping of that person in police detention.

(2) A court may not hear an application for a warrant of further detention unless the person to whom the application relates—
- (a) has been furnished with a copy of the information; and
- (b) has been brought before the court for the hearing . . .

. . .

(4) A person's further detention is only justified for the purposes of this section or section 44 below if—
- (a) his detention without charge is necessary to secure or preserve evidence relating to an offence for which he is under arrest or to obtain such evidence by questioning him;
- (b) an offence for which he is under arrest is an indictable offence; and
- (c) the investigation is being conducted diligently and expeditiously.

(5) Subject to subsection (7) below, an application for a warrant of further detention may be made—
- (a) at any time before the expiry of 36 hours after the relevant time; or
- (b) in a case where—
  - (i) it is not practicable for the magistrates' court to which the application will be made to sit at the expiry of 36 hours after the relevant time; but
  - (ii) the court will sit during the 6 hours following the end of that period, at any time before the expiry of the said 6 hours . . .

(7) If—
- (a) an application for a warrant of further detention is made after the expiry of 36 hours after the relevant time; and
- (b) it appears to the magistrates' court that it would have been reasonable for the police to make it before the expiry of that period, the court shall dismiss the application.

(8) Where on an application such as is mentioned in subsection (1) above a magistrates' court is not satisfied that there are reasonable grounds for believing that the further detention of the person to whom the application relates is justified, it shall be its duty—
- (a) to refuse the application; or
- (b) to adjourn the hearing of it until a time not later than 36 hours after the relevant time.

Blackstone's Magistrates' Court Handbook 2026. Bartholomew Dalton and Caroline Liggins, Oxford University Press. © Oxford University Press 2026.
DOI: 10.1093/oso/9780198963943.003.0023

(9) The person to whom the application relates may be kept in police detention during the adjournment.

(10) A warrant of further detention shall—

(a) state the time at which it is issued;

(b) authorise the keeping in police detention of the person to whom it relates for the period stated in it.

(11) Subject to subsection (12) below, the period stated in a warrant of further detention shall be such period as the magistrates' court thinks fit, having regard to the evidence before it.

(12) The period shall not be longer than 36 hours.

(13) If it is proposed to transfer a person in police detention to a police area other than that in which he is detained when the application for a warrant of further detention is made, the court hearing the application shall have regard to the distance and the time the journey would take.

(14) Any information submitted in support of an application under this section shall state—

(a) the nature of the offence for which the person to whom the application relates has been arrested;

(b) the general nature of the evidence on which that person was arrested;

(c) what inquiries relating to the offence have been made by the police and what further inquiries are proposed by them;

(d) the reasons for believing the continued detention of that person to be necessary for the purposes of such further inquiries.

(15) Where an application under this section is refused, the person to whom the application relates shall forthwith be charged or, subject to subsection (16) below, released,

(a) without bail unless the pre-conditions for bail are satisfied, or

(b) on bail if those pre-conditions are satisfied.

(16) A person need not be released under subsection (15) above—

(a) before the expiry of 24 hours after the relevant time; or

(b) before the expiry of any longer period for which his continued detention is or has been authorised under section 42 above.

(17) Where an application under this section is refused, no further application shall be made under this section in respect of the person to whom the refusal relates, unless supported by evidence which has come to light since the refusal.

44 Extension of warrants of further detention

(1) On an application on oath made by a constable and supported by an information a magistrates' court may extend a warrant of further detention issued under section 43 above if it is satisfied that there are reasonable grounds for believing that the further detention of the person to whom the application relates is justified.

(2) Subject to subsection (3) below, the period for which a warrant of further detention may be extended shall be such period as the court thinks fit, having regard to the evidence before it.

(3) The period shall not—

(a) be longer than 36 hours; or

(b) end later than 96 hours after the relevant time.

(4) Where a warrant of further detention has been extended under subsection (1) above, or further extended under this subsection, for a period ending before 96 hours after the relevant time, on an application such as is mentioned in that subsection a magistrates' court may further extend the warrant if it is satisfied as there mentioned; and subsections (2) and (3) above apply to such further extensions as they apply to extensions under subsection (1) above.

(5) A warrant of further detention shall, if extended or further extended under this section, be endorsed with a note of the period of the extension.
(6) Subsections (2), (3) and (14) of section 43 above shall apply to an application made under this section as they apply to an application made under that section.
(7) Where an application under this section is refused, the person to whom the application relates shall forthwith be charged or, subject to subsection (8) below, released, (a) without bail unless the pre-conditions for bail are satisfied, or
 (b) on bail if those pre-conditions are satisfied.
(8) A person need not be released under subsection (7) above before the expiry of any period for which a warrant of further detention issued in relation to him has been extended or further extended on an earlier application made under this section.

See *Blackstone's Criminal Practice 2026* **D1.40**

A23.3 Warrants of further detention and extensions in terrorist cases

Terrorism Act 2000, s 41

41 Arrest without warrant

(1) A constable may arrest without a warrant a person whom he reasonably suspects to be a terrorist.
(2) Where a person is arrested under this section the provisions of Schedule 8 (detention: treatment, review and extension) shall apply.
(3) Subject to subsections (4) to (7), a person detained under this section shall (unless detained under any other power) be released not later than the end of the period of 48 hours beginning–.
 (a) with the time of his arrest under this section, or
 (b) if he was being detained under Schedule 7 when he was arrested under this section, with the time when his examination under that Schedule began.
(4) If on a review of a person's detention under Part II of Schedule 8 the review officer does not authorise continued detention, the person shall (unless detained in accordance with subsection (5) or (6) or under any other power) be released.
(5) Where a police officer intends to make an application for a warrant under paragraph 29 of Schedule 8 extending a person's detention, the person may be detained pending the making of the application.
(6) Where an application has been made under paragraph 29 or 36 of Schedule 8 in respect of a person's detention, he may be detained pending the conclusion of proceedings on the application.
(7) Where an application under paragraph 29 or 36 of Schedule 8 is granted in respect of a person's detention, he may be detained, subject to paragraph 37 of that Schedule, during the period specified in the warrant.
(8) The refusal of an application in respect of a person's detention under paragraph 29 or 36 of Schedule 8 shall not prevent his continued detention in accordance with this section.

Schedule 8 Terrorism Act 2000, paras 29–36

29 (1) Each of the following–
 (a) in England and Wales, a Crown Prosecutor, . . .

(d) in any part of the United Kingdom, a police officer of at least the rank of superintendent, may apply to a judicial authority for the issue of a warrant of further detention under this Part.

(2) A warrant of further detention—

(a) shall authorise the further detention under section 41 of a specified person for a specified period, and

(b) shall state the time at which it is issued.

(3) Subject to sub-paragraph (3A) and paragraph 36, the specified period in relation to a person shall be the period of seven days beginning—

(a) with the time of his arrest under section 41, or

(b) if he was being detained under Schedule 7 when he was arrested under section 41, with the time when his examination under that Schedule began.

(3A) A judicial authority may issue a warrant of further detention in relation to a person which specifies a shorter period as the period for which that person's further detention is authorised if—

(a) the application for the warrant is an application for a warrant specifying a shorter period; or

(b) the judicial authority is satisfied that there are circumstances that would make it inappropriate for the specified period to be as long as the period of seven days mentioned in sub-paragraph (3)

(4) In this Part 'judicial authority' means—

(a) in England and Wales . . . a District Judge (Magistrates' Courts) who is designated for the purpose of this Part by the Lord Chief Justice of England and Wales

Time limit

30 (1) An application for a warrant shall be made—

(a) during the period mentioned in section 41(3), or

(b) within six hours of the end of that period.

(2) The judicial authority hearing an application made by virtue of sub-paragraph (1)(b) shall dismiss the application if he considers that it would have been reasonably practicable to make it during the period mentioned in section 41(3).

(3) For the purposes of this Schedule, an application for a warrant is made when written or oral notice of an intention to make the application is given to a judicial authority.

Notice

31 An application for a warrant may not be heard unless the person to whom it relates has been given a notice stating—

(a) that the application has been made,

(b) the time at which the application was made,

(c) the time at which it is to be heard, and

(d) the grounds upon which further detention is sought.

Grounds for extension

32 (1) A judicial authority may issue a warrant of further detention only if satisfied that—

(a) there are reasonable grounds for believing that the further detention of the person to whom the application relates is necessary as mentioned in sub-paragraph (1A), and

(b) the investigation in connection with which the person is detained is being conducted diligently and expeditiously.

(1A) The further detention of a person is necessary as mentioned in this sub-paragraph if it is necessary—

(a) to obtain relevant evidence whether by questioning him or otherwise;

(b) to preserve relevant evidence; or

(c) pending the result of an examination or analysis of any relevant evidence or of anything the examination or analysis of which is to be or is being carried out with a view to obtaining relevant evidence.

(2) In this paragraph 'relevant evidence' means, in relation to the person to whom the application relates, evidence which—

(a) relates to his commission of an offence under any of the provisions mentioned in section 40(1)(a), or

(b) indicates that he is a person falling within section 40(1)(b) . . .

Representation

33 (3) A judicial authority may exclude any of the following persons from any part of the hearing—

(a) the person to whom the application relates;

(b) anyone representing him.

(4) A judicial authority may, after giving an opportunity for representations to be made by or on behalf of the applicant and the person to whom the application relates, direct—

(a) that the hearing of the application must be conducted, and

(b) that all representations by or on behalf of a person for the purposes of the hearing must be made, by such means (whether a live television link or other means) falling within sub-paragraph (5) as may be specified in the direction and not in the presence (apart from by those means) of the applicant, of the person to whom the application relates or of any legal representative of that person.

Information

34 (1) The person who has made an application for a warrant may apply to the judicial authority for an order that specified information upon which he intends to rely be withheld from—

(a) the person to whom the application relates, and

(b) anyone representing him.

(2) Subject to sub-paragraph (3), a judicial authority may make an order under sub-paragraph (1) in relation to specified information only if satisfied that there are reasonable grounds for believing that if the information were disclosed—

(a) evidence of an offence under any of the provisions mentioned in section 40(1)(a) would be interfered with or harmed,

(b) the recovery of property obtained as a result of an offence under any of those provisions would be hindered,

(c) the recovery of property in respect of which a forfeiture order could be made under section 23 or 23A would be hindered,

(d) the apprehension, prosecution or conviction of a person who is suspected of falling within section 40(1)(a) or (b) would be made more difficult as a result of his being alerted,

(e) the prevention of an act of terrorism would be made more difficult as a result of a person being alerted,

(f) the gathering of information about the commission, preparation or instigation of an act of terrorism would be interfered with, or

(g) a person would be interfered with or physically injured.

(3) A judicial authority may also make an order under sub-paragraph (1) in relation to specified information if satisfied that there are reasonable grounds for believing that—

(a) the detained person has benefited from his criminal conduct, and

(b) the recovery of the value of the property constituting the benefit would be hindered if the information were disclosed.

(3A) For the purposes of sub-paragraph (3) the question whether a person has benefited from his criminal conduct is to be decided in accordance with Part 2 or 3 of the Proceeds of Crime Act 2002.

(4) The judicial authority shall direct that the following be excluded from the hearing of the application under this paragraph—
(a) the person to whom the application for a warrant relates, and
(b) anyone representing him.

Adjournments

35 (1) A judicial authority may adjourn the hearing of an application for a warrant only if the hearing is adjourned to a date before the expiry of the period mentioned in section 41(3).
(2) This paragraph shall not apply to an adjournment under paragraph 33(2).

Extensions of warrants

36 (1) Each of the following—
(a) in England and Wales, a Crown Prosecutor, . . .
(d) in any part of the United Kingdom, a police officer of at least the rank of superintendent, may apply. . . for the extension or further extension of the period specified in a warrant of further detention.
(1A) The person to whom an application under sub-paragraph (1) may be made is—
(a) a judicial authority;
(2) Where the period specified is extended, the warrant shall be endorsed with a note stating the new specified period.
(3) Subject to sub-paragraph (3AA), the period by which the specified period is extended or further extended shall be the period which—
(a) begins with the time specified in sub-paragraph (3A); and
(b) ends with whichever is the earlier of—
(i) the end of the period of seven days beginning with that time; and
(ii) the end of the period of 14 days beginning with the relevant time. (3A) The time referred to in sub-paragraph (3)(a) is—
(a) in the case of a warrant specifying a period which has not previously been extended under this paragraph, the end of the period specified in the warrant, and
(b) in any other case, the end of the period for which the period specified in the warrant was last extended under this paragraph.
(3AA) A judicial authority . . . may extend or further extend the period specified in a warrant by a shorter period than is required by sub-paragraph (3) if—
(a) the application for the extension is an application for an extension by a period that is shorter than is so required; or
(b) the judicial authority. . . is satisfied that there are circumstances that would make it inappropriate for the period of the extension to be as long as the period so required.
(3B) In this paragraph 'the relevant time', in relation to a person, means—
(a) the time of his arrest under section 41, or
(b) if he was being detained under Schedule 7 when he was arrested under section 41, the time when his examination under that Schedule began.
(4) Paragraphs 30(3) and 31 to 34 shall apply to an application under this paragraph as they apply to an application for a warrant of further detention . . .
(5) A judicial authority. . . may adjourn the hearing of an application under sub-paragraph (1) only if the hearing is adjourned to a date before the expiry of the period specified in the warrant.
(6) Sub-paragraph (5) shall not apply to an adjournment under paragraph 33(2).

A23.4 **Appeals against pre-charge bail decisions**

A23.4.1 ***Pre-charge bail conditions***

An application to the court, by way of appeal, from the decision to impose conditions on the grant of police bail, is provided for by s 47 PACE 1984.

Police and Criminal Evidence Act 1984, s 47

(1C) Subsections (1D) to (1F) below apply where a person released on bail under section 37, 37C(2)(b) or 37CA(2)(b) above is on bail subject to conditions.

. . .

(1E) A magistrates' court may, on an application by or on behalf of the person, vary the conditions of bail; and in this subsection 'vary' has the same meaning as in the Bail Act 1976.

(1F) Where a magistrates' court varies the conditions of bail under subsection (1E) above, that bail shall not lapse but shall continue subject to the conditions as so varied.

The procedure is provided for by rule 14.6 of the Crim PR.

A23.4.2 ***Extension of pre-charge bail time limits***

The procedures are set out in ss 47ZC and 47ZF–J of PACE and Crim PR Parts 14.21 and 22.For any extension to be granted the court must be satisfied that conditions B–D in s 47ZC and the provisions of s 47ZF(7) are met. The Criminal Procedure (Amendment) Rules 2023 (CPAR 2023) came into force on 3 April 2023 and have now brought about significant changes to the way that pre-charge bail is managed. Sections 47ZA and 47ZB of the Police and Criminal Evidence Act 1984 limit the period for which a person may be subject to pre-charge bail. This period may be extended in specific circumstances by a senior police officer/court. This was overhauled in 2020 by the Police, Crime, Sentencing and Courts Act 2022 which lengthened the time period for which people can be subject to pre-charge bail. Additionally, pre-charge bail can also be extended by police officers of the rank of inspector and above for up to six months, and by officers of the rank of superintendent or above by up to nine months (ss 47ZC and 47ZD of the 1984 Act). The CPAR 2023 (s 47ZF of the 1984 Act) has now further extended the period for which a person can be kept on pre-charge bail by a magistrates' court. They replaced all references to '12 months' in the Crim PR to '24 months'.

Police and Criminal Evidence Act 1984

47ZC

. . .

(3) Condition B is that the decision-maker has reasonable grounds for believing—
   (a) in a case where the person in question is or is to be released on bail under section 37(7)*[*(c)*]**(b)* or 37CA(2)(b), that further time is needed for making a decision as to whether to charge the person with the relevant offence, or
   (b) otherwise, that further investigation is needed of any matter in connection with the relevant offence.

(4) Condition C is that the decision-maker has reasonable grounds for believing—

(a) in a case where the person in question is or is to be released on bail under section 37(7)*[(c)](b)* or 37CA(2)(b), that the decision as to whether to charge the person with the relevant offence is being made diligently and expeditiously, or

(b) otherwise, that the investigation is being conducted diligently and expeditiously.

(5) Condition D is that the decision-maker has reasonable grounds for believing that the release on bail of the person in question is necessary and proportionate in all the circumstances (having regard, in particular, to any conditions of bail which are, or are to be, imposed).

47ZF Applicable bail period: first extension of limit by court

(1) This section applies in relation to a person if—

[. . .]

(b) a senior officer has authorised an extension of the applicable bail period in relation to the person under section 47ZDA (standard cases)

(ba) an appropriate decision maker has authorised an extension of the applicable bail period in relation to a person under section 47ZDB or

(c) a qualifying police officer has authorised an extension of the applicable bail period in relation to the person under section 47ZE (cases designated as exceptionally complex).

(2) Before the applicable bail period in relation to the person ends a qualifying applicant may apply to a magistrates' court for it to authorise an extension of the applicable bail period in relation to the person under this section. . . .

(4) The (applicable bail period) is to end—

(a) in a case falling within subsection (1) (b), at the end of the period of 12 months beginning with the person's bail start date;

(b) in a case falling within subsection (1) (ba) *or* (c), at the end of the period of 18 months beginning with the person's bail start date.

(5) If the court is satisfied that . . . it may authorise the applicable bail period to be extended as specified in subsection (6).

(6) The applicable bail period is to end—

(a) in a case falling within subsection (1) (b), at the end of the period of 18 months beginning with the person's bail start date;

(b) in a case falling within subsection (1) (ba) *or* (c), at the end of the period of 24 months beginning with the person's bail start date.

(7) A case falls within this subsection if the nature of the decision or further investigations mentioned in condition B means that that decision is unlikely to be made or those investigations completed if the applicable bail period in relation to the person is not extended as specified in subsection (6).

47ZG Applicable bail period: subsequent extensions of limit by court

(1) Subsections (2) to (6) apply where a court has authorised an extension of the applicable bail period in relation to a person under section 47ZF.

(2) Before the applicable bail period in relation to the person ends a qualifying applicant may apply to a magistrates' court for it to authorise an extension of the applicable bail period in relation to the person under this section.

(3) . . . the court may authorise the applicable bail period to be extended as specified in subsection (4).

(4) The applicable bail period is to end at the end of the period of 3 months beginning with the end of the current applicable bail period in relation to the person. . . .

(6) The applicable bail period is to end at the end of the period of 6 months beginning with the end of the current applicable bail period in relation to the person.

(7) Where a court has authorised an extension of the applicable bail period . . . a qualifying applicant may make further applications . . .

47ZH Sections 47ZF and 47ZG: withholding sensitive information

(1) This section applies where a qualifying applicant makes an application to a magistrates' court under section 47ZF or 47ZG in relation to a person.
(2) The qualifying applicant may apply to the court for it to authorise the specified information to be withheld from the person and any legal representative of the person.
(3) The court may grant an application under subsection (2) only if satisfied that there are reasonable grounds for believing that the specified information is sensitive information.
(4) For the purposes of this section information is sensitive information if its disclosure would have one or more of the following results—
  (a) evidence connected with an indictable offence would be interfered with or harmed;
  (b) a person would be interfered with or physically injured;
  (c) a person suspected of having committed an indictable offence but not yet arrested for the offence would be alerted;
  (d) the recovery of property obtained as a result of an indictable offence would be hindered.
(5) In this section 'specified information' means the information specified in the application under subsection (2).

47ZI Sections 47ZF to 47ZH: proceedings in magistrates' court

(1) An application made to a magistrates' court under section 47ZF or 47ZG in relation to a person is to be determined by a single justice of the peace on written evidence unless subsection (2) or (3) applies.
(2) This subsection applies if—
  (a) the effect of the application would be to extend the applicable bail period in relation to the person so that it ends at or before the end of the period of 24 months beginning with the person's bail start date, and
  (b) a single justice of the peace considers that the interests of justice require an oral hearing.
(3) This subsection applies if—
  (a) the effect of the application would be to extend the applicable bail period in relation to the person so that it ends after the end of the period of 24 months beginning with the person's bail start date, and
  (b) the person, or the person who made the application, requests an oral hearing.
(4) If subsection (2) or (3) applies, the application is to be determined by two or more justices of the peace sitting otherwise than in open court.
(5) Where an application under section 47ZF or 47ZG in relation to a person is to be determined as mentioned in subsection (4), the justices may direct that the person and any legal representative of the person be excluded from any part of the hearing.
(6) The justices may give a direction under subsection (5) only if satisfied that there are reasonable grounds for believing that sensitive information would be disclosed at the part of the hearing in question.
(7) An application under section 47ZH is to be determined by a single justice of the peace on written evidence unless the justice determines that the interests of justice require an oral hearing.
(8) If the justice makes a determination under subsection (7)—
  (a) the application is to be determined by two or more justices of the peace sitting otherwise than in open court, and
  (b) the justices hearing the application must direct that the person to whom the application relates and any legal representative of the person be excluded from the hearing.
(9) In this section 'sensitive information' has the meaning given in section 47ZH(4).

47ZJ Sections 47ZF and 47ZG: late applications to magistrates' court

(1) This section applies where—
   (a) an application under section 47ZF or 47ZG is made to a magistrates' court before the end of the applicable bail period in relation to a person, but
   (b) it is not practicable for the court to determine the application before the end of that period.

(2) The court must determine the application as soon as is practicable.

(3) The applicable bail period in relation to the person is to be treated as extended until the application is determined.

(4) If it appears to the court that it would have been reasonable for the application to have been made in time for it to have been determined by the court before the end of the applicable bail period in relation to the person, it may refuse the application.

A24 Remand Periods

A24.1 Continuing investigations

The power under s 128(7) and (8) MCA 1980 to remand to police custody does not arise until the court has decided that bail cannot be granted and must relate to allegations that are not already before the court. The court should then consider whether the remand should be to custody or to a police station, depending on whether further evidence is likely to be obtained, and if to a police station how long is required, with 3 days being the maximum for an adult and 24 hours for a child (s 91(5) Legal Aid Sentencing and Punishment of Offenders Act 2012).

Under s 152 Criminal Justice Act 1988 the courts have power to commit a person facing certain drugs offences to police custody for up to 192 hours.

A24.2 Prior to conviction

A24.2.1 *In custody*

The courts may remand to custody for a maximum of 8 clear days on first remand.

A defendant may subsequently be remanded to custody for up to 28 clear days, provided the next stage in the proceedings will be dealt with. If it is known that the next stage cannot be dealt with in that period then 8-day remands will have to follow, until such time as completion of the next stage within 28 days is achievable.

However, the defendant can agree not to be produced for these hearings.

A further subsequent remand to custody for 28 clear days is allowed if the defendant is already in custody serving a sentence and will not be released before that date.

A24.2.2 *On bail*

The courts may remand on bail for 8 days, or longer if the defendant consents.

A24.3 Upon sending

After a case has been sent to the Crown Court, the magistrates have the power to adjourn for a period up to the date of trial. It is important to note that the expression 'remand' has a particular meaning within the MCA 1980, and the court is not remanding a person when it sends someone for trial—therefore, when a court sends a person for trial during his first appearance, it can do so in custody for a period in excess of 8 days.

For remands in absence see **A22**.

A24.4 During trial

No limit (s 10 MCA 1980).

Blackstone's Magistrates' Court Handbook 2026. Bartholomew Dalton and Caroline Liggins, Oxford University Press. © Oxford University Press 2026.
DOI: 10.1093/oso/9780198963943.003.0024

A24.5 Post-conviction

Maximum 3 weeks if in custody; 4 weeks if on bail.

See *Blackstone's Criminal Practice 2026* **D5.38–D5.44**

A25 **Reporting Restrictions**

A25.1 **Youths**

Section 39 Children and Young Persons Act 1933 has been disapplied from criminal proceedings. The law in relation to child defendants in the adult court is set out in s 45 Youth Justice and Criminal Evidence Act 1999 (see **B8**).

A25.1.1 ***Lifetime reporting restrictions in criminal proceedings for witnesses and victims under 18***

Section 45A Youth Justice and Criminal Evidence Act 1999 provides:

Youth Justice and Criminal Evidence Act 1999, s 45A

Power to restrict reporting of criminal proceedings for lifetime of witnesses and victims under 18

(1) This section applies in relation to—
  (a) any criminal proceedings in any court (other than a service court) in England and Wales, and
  (b) any proceedings (whether in the United Kingdom or elsewhere) in any service court.
(2) The court may make a direction ('a reporting direction') that no matter relating to a person mentioned in subsection (3) shall during that person's lifetime be included in any publication if it is likely to lead members of the public to identify that person as being concerned in the proceedings.
(3) A reporting direction may be made only in respect of a person who is under the age of 18 when the proceedings commence and who is—
  (a) a witness, other than an accused, in the proceedings;
  (b) a person against whom the offence, which is the subject of the proceedings, is alleged to have been committed.
(4) For the purposes of subsection (2), matters relating to a person in respect of whom the reporting direction is made include—
  (a) the person's name,
  (b) the person's address,
  (c) the identity of any school or other educational establishment attended by the person,
  (d) the identity of any place of work of the person, and
  (e) any still or moving picture of the person.
(5) The court may make a reporting direction in respect of a person only if it is satisfied that—
  (a) the quality of any evidence given by the person, or
  (b) the level of co-operation given by the person to any party to the proceedings in connection with that party's preparation of its case, is likely to be diminished by reason of fear or distress on the part of the person in connection with being identified by members of the public as a person concerned in the proceedings.
(6) In determining whether subsection (5) is satisfied, the court must in particular take into account—
  (a) the nature and alleged circumstances of the offence to which the proceedings relate;
  (b) the age of the person;
  (c) such of the following as appear to the court to be relevant—
    (i) the social and cultural background and ethnic origins of the person,

Blackstone's Magistrates' Court Handbook 2026. Bartholomew Dalton and Caroline Liggins, Oxford University Press.
DOI: 10.1093/oso/9780198963943.003.0025

(ii) the domestic, educational and employment circumstances of the person, and
(iii) any religious beliefs or political opinions of the person;
(d) any behaviour towards the person on the part of—
(i) an accused,
(ii) members of the family or associates of an accused, or
(iii) any other person who is likely to be an accused or a witness in the proceedings.

(7) In determining that question the court must in addition consider any views expressed—
(a) by the person in respect of whom the reporting restriction may be made, and
(b) where that person is under the age of 16, by an appropriate person other than an accused.

(8) In determining whether to make a reporting direction in respect of a person, the court must have regard to—
(a) the welfare of that person,
(b) whether it would be in the interests of justice to make the direction, and
(c) the public interest in avoiding the imposition of a substantial and unreasonable restriction on the reporting of the proceedings.

(9) A reporting direction may be revoked by the court or an appellate court.

(10) The court or an appellate court may by direction ('an excepting direction') dispense, to any extent specified in the excepting direction, with the restrictions imposed by a reporting direction.

(11) The court or an appellate court may only make an excepting direction if—
(a) it is satisfied that it is necessary in the interests of justice to do so, or
(b) it is satisfied that—
(i) the effect of the reporting direction is to impose a substantial and unreasonable restriction on the reporting of the proceedings, and
(ii) it is in the public interest to remove or relax that restriction.

(12) No excepting direction shall be given under subsection (11)(b) by reason only of the fact that the proceedings have been determined in any way or have been abandoned.

(13) In determining whether to make an excepting direction in respect of a person, the court or the appellate court must have regard to the welfare of that person.

(14) An excepting direction—
(a) may be given at the time the reporting direction is given or subsequently, and
(b) may be varied or revoked by the court or an appellate court.

A25.2 **Adults**

A25.2.1 ***Withholding names or other details***

Under s 11 Contempt of Court Act 1981, where a court exercises its powers to allow a name or any other matter to be withheld from the public in criminal proceedings, the court may make such directions as are necessary prohibiting the publication of that name or matter in connection with the proceedings.

In *Re Times Newspapers Ltd* [2008] EWCA Crim 2559 the court held that it is an important aspect of open justice that a defendant's name should be made public. However, the court may in appropriate circumstances order the identity of a defendant, or their address, to be protected from publicity. The power to do so is a common law power.

The Judicial College has published the following guidance:

> 4.4 . . . Section 11 can only be invoked where the court allows a name or matter to be withheld from being mentioned in open court. It follows that there is no power to prohibit publication of any name or other matter which has been given in open court in the proceedings. For this reason, applications for an order under s. 11 may be heard in private provided there is good reason for doing so.
>
> Section 11 does not itself give the court power to withhold a name or other matter from the public. The power to do this must exist either at common law or from some other statutory provision.

Consistent with the requirement to protect the open justice principle and freedom of expression, courts should only make an order under s 11 where the nature or circumstances of the proceedings are such that hearing all evidence in open court would frustrate or render impractical the administration of justice. It follows that a defendant in a criminal trial must be named save in rare circumstances. It is not appropriate therefore to invoke the s 11 power to withhold matters for the benefit of a defendant's feelings or comfort or to prevent financial damage, or damage to reputation resulting from proceedings concerning a person's business. Nor can the power be invoked to prevent identification and embarrassment of the defendant's children, because of the defendant's public profile.

Where the ground for seeking a s 11 order is that the identification of a witness or a defendant will expose that person to a real and immediate risk to his life, engaging the state's duty to protect life under Article 2 of the European Convention on Human Rights (ECHR), the court will consider whether the fear is objectively well founded. In practical terms, the applicant will have to provide clear and cogent evidence to show that publication of his name will create or materially increase a risk of death or serious injury.

In appropriate cases consideration should be given to s 46 Youth Justice and Criminal Evidence Act 1999 if the evidence of a witness may be affected by fear that the identity of her children may become known. *Re ITN News* [2013] EWCA Crim 773 (Admin) confirms that this does not follow automatically from a special measures direction but requires a separate fact-finding exercise.

The court must balance the Article 10 rights of free expression and the Article 8 rights of the child. Particular weight is attached to the interests of the child if their interests were likely on the facts to be harmed, but there was a presumption that there should be open justice. In *R (A) v Lowestoft Magistrates' Court* [2013] EWHC 659 an elected councillor with a caution already was drunk in charge of a child. The child was under three years of age and would know nothing of the publicity. By contrast, in *Z v News Group Newspapers* [2013] EWHC 1150 (Fam), when a mother of eight children was involved in a benefit fraud, claiming by reference to disabilities and incapacities of those children, all of whom were innocent of any involvement, the balance was in favour of preventing the children (and so the mother) being named. The heavy burden to prevent publicity had been met, not least because the medical conditions of the children would be extensively examined and some of them were vulnerable. However, once the mother had been convicted the balance was in favour of naming her.

In rare circumstances, the right to private and family life under Article 8 ECHR may mean that normal media reporting has to be curtailed, but injunctions to cover these cases are dealt with by the High Court rather than the criminal courts. In *A v BBC* [2014] UKSC 325 the Supreme Court held that s 11 Contempt of Court Act 1981 could be used to protect a person's ECHR rights and not only to protect the public interest. It was not necessary for a restriction to have been in place for those who attended court. In this case the identification of the defendant would, on her deportation, have endangered her Article 3 rights and given her new grounds to seek asylum.

The court may in appropriate circumstances limit information to protect a person's safety or commercial interests, or to prevent disclosure of intimate personal details of a complainant. Each case turned on its own facts and involved a balancing exercise.

A25.2.2 ***Postponement of reports***

Section 4(2) Contempt of Court Act 1981 provides:

> **Contempt of Court Act 1981, s 4(2)**
>
> **4 Contemporary reports of proceedings**
>
> (2) In any such proceedings the court may, where it appears to be necessary for avoiding a substantial risk of prejudice to the administration of justice in those proceedings, or in any other proceedings pending or imminent, order that the publication of any report of the proceedings, or any part of the proceedings, be postponed for such period as the court thinks necessary for that purpose.
>
> . . .

The provision was considered in *R. v Sarker; Re BBC* [2018] EWCA Crim 1341. The word 'substantial' does not mean 'weighty'. It means 'not insubstantial' or 'not minimal'. It is important to focus on what prejudice it is said would be occasioned by the reports sought to be postponed. Applications must be made in accordance with rules 6.4 and 6.5 of the Crim PR.

The explanation for why the order is necessary needs to address, clearly (and ordinarily in writing):

(i) how contemporaneous, fair, and accurate reports of the trial will cause a substantial risk of prejudice, and
(ii) why a postponement order would avoid the identified risk of prejudice.

When dealing with applications for reporting restrictions, the default position is the general principle that all proceedings in courts and tribunals are conducted in public.

Even if an order would achieve the objective, the judge still has to consider whether the risk could satisfactorily be overcome by some less restrictive means. If so, it cannot be said to be 'necessary' to take the more drastic approach: if the judge is satisfied that there is no other way of eliminating the perceived risk of prejudice, it still does not necessarily follow that an order has to be made. The judge may still have to ask whether the degree of risk contemplated should be regarded as being 'the lesser of two evils'. It is at this stage that value judgements may have to be made as to the priority between the competing public interests, fair trial, and freedom of expression/open justice.

See *Blackstone's Criminal Practice 2026* D3.123

A26 Sending and Transfer for Trial

A26.1 Overview

In the following instances the court may decline or be deprived of jurisdiction to try a matter:

- indictable-only (and related) matters—sent to the Crown Court;
- either-way (if related) matters where jurisdiction is declined or the defendant has elected Crown Court trial—sent to the Crown Court;
- summary-only (if related) matters in defined circumstances—sent to the Crown Court;
- transfer cases—transferred to the Crown Court;
- voluntary bill of indictment (not covered in this book).

Either-way matters are related if they could be tried on the same indictment. By contrast, summary matters are related if they 'arise out of circumstances which are the same or connected with those giving rise to the indictable offence'.

Method	Notes
Sending. Section 51 of the Crime and Disorder Act 1998	The court will send any indictable-only matter, along with any related either-way and defined summary only matters. This may involve sending one or more co-defendants, who shall be sent if appearing at the same time and may be sent if appearing on another occasion. Note: A sending is not a remand within the meaning of MCA 1980, ss 128, 128A, and therefore the initial 8-day limitation on a remand in custody does not apply. An either-way offence is related to an indictable offence if the charge for the either-way offence could be joined in the same indictment as the charge for the indictable offence. A summary offence is related to an indictable offence if it arises out of circumstances which are the same as or connected with those giving rise to the indictable offence. The court can send related summary offences only if they are imprisonable or carry discretionary or obligatory disqualification from driving. In the case of a youth charged with an adult (not necessarily on the same occasion), the youth will be sent if it is in the interests of justice to try him with the adult. When sending cases a clear distinction must be made between either-way offences and summary-only cases (of which low-value shoplifting is one) (R v Maxwell [2017] EWCA Crim 1233).
Transfer cases. Note: See ss 51B and 51C of the Crime and Disorder Act 1998	Applicable to fraud cases and child cases.

Blackstone's Magistrates' Court Handbook 2026. Bartholomew Dalton and Caroline Liggins, Oxford University Press. © Oxford University Press 2026.
DOI: 10.1093/oso/9780198963943.003.0026

A26.2 Case management

When sending a case to the Crown Court, the magistrates have certain management responsibilities, including to ask whether the defendant intends to plead guilty in the Crown Court (Crim PR 9.7). Because a discount for guilty plea can be reduced if a plea is not entered or indicated at the first hearing in the magistrates' court, even in indictable-only matters, very careful consideration should be given to the completion of the case management form identifying, when possible, the issues in the case and which are in dispute.

A reminder is to review the revised and updated Better Case Management Handbook which is intended to remind everyone of those principles and to identify good practice. Those who sit in the magistrates' courts or Crown Court, as well as those who practice in criminal law, MUST apply these principles.

A26.3 Relevant case law

- Represented defendants need not be physically present in court for sending proceedings, but whether the accused is to be present or absent is a matter for the court to decide (*R v Umerji* [2021] EWCA Crim 598) *Under provisions introduced by the Judicial Review and Courts Act 2022, once in force, a defendant on bail may be sent in absence provided that the requirements of s 51(2B) Crime and Disorder Act 1998 are met.*
- Where a person is arrested for an either-way offence and commits a summary-only assault while at the police station, there is no basis for dealing with the summary-only matter at the Crown Court; it did not arise out of the same facts, neither was it part of a series of offences, so s 40(1) Criminal Justice Act 1988 did not apply (*R v Walton* [2011] EWCA Crim 2832).
- An offence under s 6 Bail Act 1976 does not relate to the substantive offence for which bail was granted and so cannot be sent for trial to the Crown Court (*R v Osman* [2017] EWCA Crim 2178). See also *R v Merritt* [2019] EWCA Crim 1514 which confirms that low-value shoplifting may not be sent because of either-way offences committed at the police station.

A26.4 Relevant legislation

The relevant legislation is set out in Crime and Disorder Act 1998, ss 50A–51D.

See *Blackstone's Criminal Practice 2026* **D10**

A27 Special Measures and Vulnerable Witnesses

A27.1 Special measures

Sections 16 and 17 Youth Justice and Criminal Evidence Act 1999 provide for special measures. Those aged under 18 may always benefit, as well as those meeting the requirements for incapacity (s 16). Witnesses who seek assistance may always benefit if the allegation is of the serious offences listed in the Youth Justice and Criminal Evidence Act 1999, Sch 1A, which will usually be tried in the Crown Court, as well as those who otherwise meet the criteria (s 17). Under Part 3 of the Criminal Procedure Rules, the courts are required to facilitate the participation of anyone taking part, both witnesses and defendant(s).

Youth Justice and Criminal Evidence Act 1999, ss 16 and 17

16 Witnesses eligible for assistance on grounds of age or incapacity

(1) For the purposes of this Chapter a witness in criminal proceedings (other than the accused) is eligible for assistance by virtue of this section—
   (a) if under the age of 18 at the time of the hearing; or
   (b) if the court considers that the quality of evidence given by the witness is likely to be diminished by reason of any circumstances falling within subsection (2).

(2) The circumstances falling within this subsection are—
   (a) that the witness—
      (i) suffers from mental disorder within the meaning of the Mental Health Act 1983, or
      (ii) otherwise has a significant impairment of intelligence and social functioning;
   (b) that the witness has a physical disability or is suffering from a physical disorder.

(3) In subsection (1)(a) 'the time of the hearing', in relation to a witness, means the time when it falls to the court to make a determination for the purposes of section 19(2) in relation to the witness.

(4) In determining whether a witness falls within subsection (1)(b) the court must consider any views expressed by the witness.

(5) In this Chapter references to the quality of a witness's evidence are to its quality in terms of completeness, coherence and accuracy; and for this purpose 'coherence' refers to a witness's ability in giving evidence to give answers which address the questions put to the witness and can be understood both individually and collectively.

17 Witnesses eligible for assistance on grounds of fear or distress about testifying

(1) For the purposes of this Chapter a witness in criminal proceedings (other than the accused) is eligible for assistance by virtue of this subsection if the court is satisfied that the quality of evidence given by the witness is likely to be diminished by reason of fear or distress on the part of the witness in connection with testifying in the proceedings.

(2) In determining whether a witness falls within subsection (1) the court must take into account, in particular—

Blackstone's Magistrates' Court Handbook 2026. Bartholomew Dalton and Caroline Liggins, Oxford University Press. © Oxford University Press 2026.
DOI: 10.1093/oso/9780198963943.003.0027

(a) the nature and alleged circumstances of the offence to which the proceedings relate;
(b) the age of the witness;
(c) such of the following matters as appear to the court to be relevant, namely—
(i) the social and cultural background and ethnic origins of the witness,
(ii) the domestic and employment circumstances of the witness, and
(iii) any religious beliefs or political opinions of the witness;
(d) any behaviour towards the witness on the part of—
(i) the accused,
(ii) members of the family or associates of the accused, or
(iii) any other person who is likely to be an accused or a witness in the proceedings.

(3) In determining that question the court must in addition consider any views expressed by the witness.

(4) Where the complainant in respect of an offence listed in subsection (4A) is a witness in proceedings relating to that offence (or to that offence and any other offences), the witness is eligible for assistance in relation to those proceedings by virtue of this subsection unless the witness has informed the court of the witness's wish not to be so eligible by virtue of this subsection.

(4A) The offences are—
(a) a sexual offence;
(b) an offence under section 1 or 2 of the Modern Slavery Act 2015;
(c) any other offence where it is alleged that the behaviour of the accused amounted to domestic abuse within the meaning of the Domestic Abuse Act 2021 (see section 1 of that Act).

(5) A witness in proceedings relating to a relevant offence (or to a relevant offence and any other offences) is eligible for assistance in relation to those proceedings by virtue of this subsection unless the witness has informed the court of the witness's wish not to be so eligible by virtue of this subsection.

(6) For the purposes of subsection (5) an offence is a relevant offence if it is an offence described in Schedule 1A.

The following special measures are available in the magistrates' court:

	Section 16 witnesses (children and vulnerable adults)	**Section 17 witnesses (intimidated/fear or distress)**
Section 23—screening witness from accused	Full availability	Full availability
Section 24—evidence via live link	Full availability	Full availability
Section 25—evidence given in private	Full availability	Full availability
Section 26—removal of wigs/gowns	Not applicable	Not applicable
Section 27—video-recorded evidence-in-chief	Full availability	Full availability
Section 28—video-recorded cross-examination and re-examination	Available in some Crown and limited Youth Courts	Available for limited offences in some Crown Courts

	Section 16 witnesses (children and vulnerable adults)	Section 17 witnesses (intimidated/fear or distress)
Section 29—examination through an intermediary	Full availability	Not applicable
Section 30—aids to communication	Full availability	Not applicable

A27.2 **Witness anonymity**

Sections 86–95 Coroners and Justice Act 2009 provide for the making and discharge of witness anonymity orders. These are to be regarded as a special measure of last practicable resort (*R v Mayers* [2008] EWCA Crim 2989).

See *Blackstone's Criminal Practice 2026* D14

A28 Submission of No Case

A28.1 Test for no case to answer

In *R v Galbraith* (1981) 73 Cr App R 124, the court laid down the following test:

(1) If there is no evidence that the crime alleged has been committed by the defendant, there is no difficulty. The judge will of course stop the case.

(2) The difficulty arises where there is some evidence but it is of a tenuous character, for example because of inherent weakness, or vagueness, or because it is inconsistent with other evidence.

  (a) Where the judge comes to the conclusion that the prosecution evidence, taken at its highest, is such that a jury properly directed could not properly convict upon it, it is his duty, upon a submission being made, to stop the case.

  (b) Where, however, the prosecution evidence is such that its strength or weakness depends on the view to be taken of a witness's reliability, or other matters which are generally speaking within the province of the jury and where on one possible view of the facts there is evidence upon which a jury could properly come to the conclusion that the defendant is guilty, then the judge should allow the matter to be tried by the jury.

It follows that we think the second of the two schools of thought is to be preferred.

A28.2 Dismissal of case

A magistrates' court might only dismiss a charge in the following circumstances (*DPP v Bird* [2015] EWHC 4077 (Admin)):

1 after hearing evidence;
2 where the prosecution had offered no evidence; or is not able to proceed and the case had not been adjourned; or
3 where the prosecution had not appeared at the time and place appointed for trial.

See *Blackstone's Criminal Practice 2026* **D16.53**

Blackstone's Magistrates' Court Handbook 2026. Bartholomew Dalton and Caroline Liggins, Oxford University Press. © Oxford University Press 2026.
DOI: 10.1093/oso/9780198963943.003.0028

A29 **Transfer/Remittal of Criminal Cases**

A29.1 **Transfer between courts**

Section 27A MCA 1980 provides for transfer between magistrates' courts:

> **Magistrates' Courts Act 1980, s 27A**
>
> **27A Power to transfer criminal proceedings**
>
> (1) Where a person appears or is brought before a magistrates' court—
> (a) to be tried by the court for an offence, or
> (b) for the court to inquire into the offence as examining justices, the court may transfer the matter to another magistrates' court.
>
> (2) The court may transfer the matter before or after beginning the trial or inquiry.
>
> (3) But if the court transfers the matter after it has begun to hear the evidence and the parties, the court to which the matter is transferred must begin hearing the evidence and the parties again . . .

A29.2 **Transfer of custodial remand hearings**

> **Magistrates Courts Act 1980, s 130**
>
> **130 Transfer of remand hearings**
>
> (1) A magistrates' court adjourning a case under section 5, 10(1), or 18(4) above, and remanding the accused in custody, may, if he has attained the age of 17, order that he be brought up for any subsequent remands before an alternate magistrates' court nearer to the prison where he is to be confined while on remand.
>
> (2) The order shall require the accused to be brought before the alternate court at the end of the period of remand or at such earlier time as the alternate court may require.
>
> (3) While the order is in force, the alternate court shall, to the exclusion of the court which made the order, have all the powers in relation to further remand (whether in custody or on bail) and which that court would have had but for the order.
>
> (4) The alternate court may, on remanding the accused in custody, require him to be brought before the court which made the order at the end of the period of remand or at such earlier time as that court may require; and, if the alternate court does so, or the accused is released on bail, the order under subsection (1) above shall cease to be in force. . . .

A29.3 **Remittal of convicted defendants**

Provision is made for the remittal of convicted defendants by s 10 Sentencing Act 2020:

> **Sentencing Act 2020, s 28**
>
> **28 Power of magistrates' court to remit case to another magistrates' court for sentence**
>
> (1) Subsection (2) applies where—

Blackstone's Magistrates' Court Handbook 2026. Bartholomew Dalton and Caroline Liggins, Oxford University Press.
DOI: 10.1093/oso/9780198963943.003.0029

(a) a person aged 18 or over has been convicted by a magistrates' court ('the convicting court') of a relevant offence ('the present offence'),
(b) it appears to the convicting court that some other magistrates' court ('the other court') has convicted the offender of another relevant offence in respect of which the other court has not—
 (i) passed sentence on the offender,
 (ii) committed the offender to the Crown Court for sentence, nor
 (iii) dealt with the offender in any other way, and
(c) the other court consents to the offender's being remitted to it under this section.

(2) The convicting court may remit the offender to the other court to be dealt with in respect of the present offence by the other court instead of by the convicting court.

(3) In subsection (1), 'relevant offence', in relation to the convicting court or the other court, means an offence which is punishable by that court with—
(a) imprisonment, or
(b) driving disqualification.

For this purpose, an offence is punishable by a court with driving disqualification if the court has a power or duty to order the offender to be disqualified under section 34, 35 or 36 of the Road Traffic Offenders Act 1988 (disqualification for certain motoring offences) in respect of it.

(4) Where the convicting court remits the offender to the other court under this section the other court may deal with the offender in any way in which it could deal with the offender if it had convicted the offender of the present offence.

This is subject to subsection (7).

(5) The power conferred on the other court by subsection (4) includes, where applicable, the power to remit the offender under this section to another magistrates' court in respect of the present offence.

(6) Where the convicting court has remitted the offender under this section, the other court may remit the offender back to the convicting court; and where it does so subsections (4) and (5) (so far as applicable) apply with the necessary modifications.

(7) Nothing in this section prevents the convicting court from making a restitution order (see section 147) by virtue of the offender's conviction of the present offence.

(8) In this section 28 of the Sentencing Act 'conviction' includes a finding under section 11(1) of the Powers of Criminal Courts (Sentencing) Act 2000 (remand for medical examination) that the person in question did the act or made the omission charged, and 'convicted' is to be read accordingly

See *Blackstone's Criminal Practice 2026* **D21.5**

A30 Video/Live Links

A30.1 Criminal Justice Act 2003 s 51

51 Directions for live links in criminal proceedings

(1) The court may, by a direction, require or permit a person to take part in eligible criminal proceedings through—
  (a) a live audio link, or
  (b) a live video link . . .
(3) In this Part "eligible criminal proceedings" means—
  (a) a preliminary hearing,
  (b) a summary trial, . . .
  (k) a hearing before a magistrates' court or the Crown Court which is held after the defendant has entered a plea of guilty,
  (l) a hearing under section 142(1) or (2) of the Magistrates' Courts Act 1980, . . .
  (n) any hearing following conviction held for the purpose of making a decision about bail in respect of the person convicted,
  (o) a sentencing hearing (see section 56(1)), or
  (p) an enforcement hearing (see section 56(1)).
(4) The court may not give a direction under this section unless—
  (a) the court is satisfied that it is in the interests of justice for the person to whom the direction relates to take part in the proceedings in accordance with the direction through the live audio link or live video link,
  (b) the parties to the proceedings have been given the opportunity to make representations, and
  (c) if so required by section 52(9), the relevant youth offending team has been given the opportunity to make representations.
(5) In deciding whether to give a direction under this section, the court must consider—
  (a) any guidance given by the Lord Chief Justice, and
  (b) all the circumstances of the case.
(6) Those circumstances include in particular—
  (a) the availability of the person to whom the direction would relate,
  (b) any need for that person to attend in person,
  (c) the views of that person,
  (d) the suitability of the facilities at the place where that person would take part in the proceedings in accordance with the direction,
  (e) whether that person would be able to take part in the proceedings effectively if the person took part in accordance with the direction,
  (f) in the case of a direction relating to a witness—
    (i) the importance of the witness's evidence to the proceedings, and
    (ii) whether the direction might tend to inhibit any party to the proceedings from effectively testing the witness's evidence, and
  (g) the arrangements that would or could be put in place for members of the public to see or hear the proceedings as conducted in accordance with the direction.

Blackstone's Magistrates' Court Handbook 2026. Bartholomew Dalton and Caroline Liggins, Oxford University Press. © Oxford University Press 2026.
DOI: 10.1093/oso/9780198963943.003.0030

A30.2 The Lord Chief Justice's guidance

Statutory criteria

3. A live link direction may only be made in respect of those who are taking part in the proceedings (including counsel, solicitors, witnesses and defendants). It may not be made for those who are not taking part in the proceedings (eg public observers or journalists). Those who are not taking part in the proceedings are entitled to apply to observe the proceedings remotely under section 85A of the Courts Act 2003. Separate guidance is in place in respect of such requests.
4. The court may only make a live link direction if:
   (a) the parties to the proceedings (and where the defendant is under 18, the relevant youth offending team) have been given the opportunity to make representations, and
   (b) the court is satisfied that it would be in the interests of justice.

Application of statutory criteria

5. In deciding whether the statutory criteria are met, the court must consider this guidance and all the circumstances of the case (section 51(5)). In particular, the court must consider (as appropriate to the circumstances of the individual case) (section 51(6)):
   (a) The availability of the person to whom the direction would relate,
   (b) Any need for that person to attend in person,
   (c) The views of that person,
   (d) The suitability of the facilities at the place where that person would take part in the proceedings in accordance with the direction,
   (e) Whether that person would be able to take part in the proceedings effectively if the person took part in accordance with the direction,
   (f) In the case of a direction relating to a witness—
      (i) the importance of the witness's evidence to the proceedings, and
      (ii) whether the direction might tend to inhibit any party to the proceedings from effectively testing the witness's evidence, and
   (g) the arrangements that would or could be put in place for members of the public to see or hear the proceedings as conducted in accordance with the direction.
6. The process for seeking representations need not be elaborate. In some cases, the written request might make it clear that it is agreed, or might include the representations that all parties wish to make. In other cases, the parties (and, where appropriate, the youth offending team/youth justice service) can be asked by email from the court staff to submit any written representations. Where the request is made orally in the course of the hearing then oral representations from all parties can be obtained there and then.
7. It will not be in the interests of justice to make a live link direction unless live link facilities are available and are in working order, and will allow all participants to hear and (in the case of a video live link) see each other clearly, with no distractions, and the person attending by live link has the necessary technology available and is able to operate it. Nor is it likely to be in the interests of justice to make a live link direction unless a member of staff is available (without unreasonably impacting on other work) to set up the live link, test that it is working, and monitor its operation. In some instances, a participant in criminal proceedings may have a disorder or disability that prevents effective participation via live link. In those instances, too, it will not be in the interests of justice to make a live link direction.
8. Defendants: It may be in the interests of justice to allow or require a defendant to attend hearings (particularly preliminary hearings) by live link so as to avoid

delays and disruption. As well as the parties' representations, the court will wish to take account of any mental health or other medical assessment before deciding if a live link is in the interests of justice. Pre and post court conferences between advocate and defendant may not be able to take place effectively by live link: where such conferences are desirable a live link is less likely to be in the interests of justice.

9. Factors to consider in deciding whether the defendant should attend a sentencing hearing via live link include: the potential penalty; ensuring the explanations of sentence can be given satisfactorily for all participants and for the public; and the preferences of the maker of any Victim Personal Statement which is to be read.
10. In the case of children, arrangements must be made in advance of any live link hearing to enable the youth offending worker to be at the secure establishment where the child is in custody. In the event that such arrangements are not practicable, the child offending worker must have sufficient access to the child via the live link booth before and after the hearing.
11. It is rarely appropriate for a child to be sentenced over a live link. Potentially, this may be acceptable where the child is
    (i) already serving a custodial sentence and either the sentence to be imposed is bound to be a further custodial sentence, or a non-custodial sentence is likely to be imposed which will have no material impact on the sentence being served;
    (ii) detained in a secure establishment a long way from court, and being produced would materially affect them,
    (iii) so disturbed their production would be a significant detriment to their welfare.
12. Advocates: The interests of justice are wider than the circumstances of the individual case. They include the efficient despatch of business and the availability of judicial, staff, technical and other resources. So, provided that it would not cause any detriment to the individual case, it may well be in the interests of justice to allow an advocate to attend by live link if that will enable the advocate to undertake other work at another court centre on the same day. However, if the defendant is required to attend a hearing in person, then the interests of justice will usually require the defence advocate also to attend in person.
13. Mentions, bail applications, ground rules hearings, CTL extensions, uncontested POCAs and hearings involving legal argument only will generally be suitable for remote attendance by all advocates. . . Sentencing hearings will require case-by-case consideration.
14. Advocates must adopt the court dress and standards of conduct that would be applied if they were in the courtroom. The court must be able to communicate with all advocates throughout the time the list is being heard. Advocates must be ready and available as soon as the case is called on.
15. Witnesses: A live link may be used as a special measure under section 24 of the Youth Justice and Criminal Evidence Act 1999. Even when not used as a special measure, the court may allow a witness to give evidence by live link where that is in the interests of justice (for example to save a witness from a long journey to court where all parties agree the evidence can be given remotely, or to allow a medical expert witness (or any other witness) to give evidence without having to take the entire day off work). Where a live link direction is given for a witness, the witness must give evidence by the live link unless the live link direction is revoked (section 52(2), (4)).

A30.3 Key points

Rules 3.35 to 3.39 of the Criminal Procedure Rules set out the procedure in relation to live links.

R v Kadir [2022] EWCA Crim 1244 confirms that WhatsApp may be allowed as a live link in accordance with s 51.

See *Blackstone's Criminal Practice 2026* D15.40

A31 Witnesses, Issue of Summons, or Warrant

A31.1 Power to require attendance

Magistrates' Courts Act 1980, s 97

97 Summons to witness and warrant for his arrest

(1) Where a justice of the peace is satisfied that—

(a) any person in England or Wales is likely to be able to give material evidence, or produce any document or thing likely to be material evidence, at the summary trial of an information or hearing of a complaint or of an application under the Adoption and Children Act 2002 (c. 38) by a magistrates' court, and

(b) it is in the interests of justice to issue a summons under this subsection to secure the attendance of that person to give evidence or produce the document or thing, the justice shall issue a summons directed to that person requiring him to attend before the court at the time and place appointed in the summons to give evidence or to produce the document or thing.

(2) If a justice of the peace is satisfied by evidence on oath of the matters mentioned in subsection (1) above, and also that it is probable that a summons under that subsection would not procure the attendance of the person in question, the justice may instead of issuing a summons issue a warrant to arrest that person and bring him before such a court as aforesaid at a time and place specified in the warrant; but a warrant shall not be issued under this subsection where the attendance is required for the hearing of a complaint or of an application under the Adoption and Children Act 2002 (c. 38).

(2A) A summons may also be issued under subsection (1) above if the justice is satisfied that the person in question is outside the British Islands but no warrant shall be issued under subsection (2) above unless the justice is satisfied by evidence on oath that the person in question is in England or Wales.

(2B) A justice may refuse to issue a summons under subsection (1) above in relation to the summary trial of an information if he is not satisfied that an application for the summons was made by a party to the case as soon as reasonably practicable after the accused pleaded not guilty.

(2C) In relation to the summary trial of an information, subsection (2) above shall have effect as if the reference to the matters mentioned in subsection (1) above included a reference to the matter mentioned in subsection (2B) above.

(3) On the failure of any person to attend before a magistrates' court in answer to a summons under this section, if—

(a) the court is satisfied by evidence on oath that he is likely to be able to give material evidence or produce any document or thing likely to be material evidence in the proceedings; and

(b) it is proved on oath, or in such other manner as may be prescribed, that he has been duly served with the summons, and that a reasonable sum has been paid or tendered to him for costs and expenses; and

(c) it appears to the court that there is no just excuse for the failure, the court may issue a warrant to arrest him and bring him before the court at a time and place specified in the warrant.

If any person attending or brought before a magistrates' court refuses without just excuse to be sworn or give evidence, or to produce any document or thing, the court may commit him to custody until the expiration of such

Blackstone's Magistrates' Court Handbook 2026. Bartholomew Dalton and Caroline Liggins, Oxford University Press. © Oxford University Press 2026.
DOI: 10.1093/oso/9780198963943.003.0031

period not exceeding one month as may be specified in the warrant or until he sooner gives evidence or produces the document or thing or impose on him a fine not exceeding £2,500 or both.

Conduct money should be served with any summons sufficient to enable the person to attend court.

The power to compel production of documents relates only to material evidence, and should not be used to compel the production of documents solely for the purpose of cross-examination (*R v Skegness Magistrates' Court, ex p Cardy* [1985] RTR 49). See also Part 17 of the Crim PR.

The alternative approach is to require the Crown to accept its responsibilities under paragraph 3.5 of the Code of Practice issued under the Criminal Procedure and Investigations Act 1996 to pursue all reasonable lines of enquiry, a duty recognized by paragraphs 46 to 48 of the Judicial Protocol on Disclosure of Unused Material (see A16).

In *R v Dania* [2019] EWCA Crim 796 the court considered what amounted to material evidence and whether it was in the interests of justice for a summons to issue. The issues included whether the evidence was peripheral and whether there was clear evidence to show the witness was incapable of being believed.

See *Blackstone's Criminal Practice 2026* D21.26

Part B

Youths in the Adult Court

B1 Age of Offender and the Position of Those Attaining 18

B1.1 Ascertainment of age

The age of the offender is important in relation to the court's power to impose different types of sentence. It is the duty of a court to determine their age when a young person is brought before the court. In most cases there is no dispute and a simple confirmation of the child's date of birth will suffice. The court is, however, able to hear evidence on the issue. Section 405 SA 2020 provides that a person is to be deemed to be whatever age the person appears to the court to be. In general, the decision maker must seek to elicit the general background to the young person, including his family circumstances and history, his educational background, and his activities during the previous few years. Ethnic and cultural information may also be important. If there is reason to doubt the applicant's statement as to his age, the decision maker will have to test and assess his credibility. Compliance with s 99 Children and Young Persons Act 1933 requires much more than superficial observation of the defendant in court and the court must be provided with all the relevant evidence (*R v Mohammed (Adnan Abdushahur)* [2021] EWCA Crim 1375). If there is a real doubt about the defendant's age, directions should be given for an age assessment to be carried out, usually through the Youth Offending Team (YOT) (*R (M) v Hammersmith MC* [2017] EWHC 1359 (Admin)). If the age is later found to be incorrect, this has no bearing on any orders made by the court (s 99 Children and Young Persons Act 1933).

B1.2 Child becoming an adult during course of proceedings

B1.2.1 *Attaining 18 before first court appearance*

Notwithstanding the defendant's age at the date of allegation or charge, where a defendant is 18 years of age at the date of the first court appearance the hearing is in the adult magistrates' court. Section 24(1) Magistrates' Courts Act 1980 ('summary trial of information against child or young person for indictable offence') applies only to those who are under 18 years at the date of the first appearance in court. The youth court has no jurisdiction (*R v Amersham Juvenile Court, ex p Wilson* [1981] 2 All ER 315). This applies where the defendant does not appear and a warrant is issued prior to the defendant's 18th birthday. The charge must be laid again in the adult court (*R v Uxbridge Youth Court, ex p H* [1998] EWHC (Admin) 341).

B1.2.2 *Attaining 18 during court proceedings*

The relevant date is the date on which the plea is taken and/or the venue is determined. If the defendant attains 18 after the first appearance at court and the offence is indictable, and no plea has been taken/venue has not been

Blackstone's Magistrates' Court Handbook 2026. Bartholomew Dalton and Caroline Liggins, Oxford University Press. © Oxford University Press 2026.
DOI: 10.1093/oso/9780198963943.003.0032

determined, the adult sending and venue procedures apply. This includes the right to elect trial by jury (*Re Daley* [1983] 1 AC 327; *R v West London Justices, ex p Siley-Winditt* [2000] Crim LR 926).

Where the prosecution, during the course of the proceedings, seek to lay a new charge based on the same facts, the new charge must be laid in the adult court (*R v Chelsea Justices, ex p DPP* [1963] 3 All ER 657).

B1.3 Sentence

Sentencing Children and Young People: Definitive Guideline

SCG Guideline: Overarching Principles—Available

Sentences, para 6

6. Crossing a significant age threshold between commission of offence and sentence

6.1 There will be occasions when an increase in the age of a child or young person will result in the maximum sentence on the date of the finding of guilt being greater than that available on the date on which the offence was committed (primarily turning 12, 15, or 18 years old).

6.2 In such situations the court should take as its starting point the sentence likely to have been imposed on the date at which the offence was committed. This includes young people who attain the age of 18 between the commission and the finding of guilt of the offence but when this occurs the purpose of sentencing adult offenders has to be taken into account, which is: the punishment of offenders; the reduction of crime (including its reduction by deterrence); the reform and rehabilitation of offenders; the protection of the public; and the making of reparation by offenders to persons affected by their offences.

6.3 When any significant age threshold is passed it will rarely be appropriate that a more severe sentence than the maximum that the court could have imposed at the time the offence was committed should be imposed. However, a sentence at or close to that maximum may be appropriate.

B1.3.1 *Sentencing principles*

For the purposes of sentence, the relevant age is the age of the defendant at the date of conviction or guilty plea (*R v Danga* [1992] QB 476), not the date of offence. As a matter of public policy, however, the courts have been willing to sentence having regard to the offence date, as opposed to conviction date. In *R v Ghafoor* [2002] EWCA Crim 1857, the court said:

> The starting point is the sentence that the defendant would have been likely to receive if he had been sentenced at the date of the commission of the offence. It has been described as a 'powerful factor'. That is for the obvious reason that . . . the philosophy of restricting sentencing powers in relation to young persons reflects both (a) society's acceptance that young offenders are less responsible for their actions and therefore less culpable than adults, and (b) the recognition that, in consequence, sentencing them should place greater emphasis on rehabilitation and less on retribution and deterrence than in the case of adults. It should be noted that the 'starting point' is not the maximum sentence that could lawfully have been imposed, but the sentence that the offender would have been likely to receive.

In *R v Bowker* [2007] EWCA Crim 1608, the court said that *Ghafoor* was a powerful starting point but other factors (such as the need for deterrent sentencing, as to which see: Sentencing Children and Young People: Definitive Guideline) may justify departing from it.

In *R v ZA* [2023] EWCA Crim 596 there was collective failure of counsel and court. Sentencing young people is a difficult and time-consuming endeavour, if it is to be done properly in accordance with Sentencing Council guidance. Sentencing notes were not full, accurate, nor did they reference the relevant (and correct) guidelines, case law, and processes. What came out of this case was that it is wrong to treat young people as 'mini-adults'.

In *R v Ahmed* [2023] EWCA Crim 281 it was held that whatever the person's age at time of conviction and sentence, the children and young person guidelines must be followed unless not in the interests of justice. The court must have regard to the maximum sentence at time of offending. The starting point should be the sentence likely to be imposed shortly after the offence. If detention is not available at the time, the court cannot pass a custodial sentence. The court is not bound by the maximum sentence at the time, which is only to be exceeded with good reasons.

B1.3.2 ***Breach of conditional discharge***

Where a court activates a conditional discharge, the relevant age for the purpose of resentencing is that of the offence (Sentencing Act 2020, s 402).

See *Blackstone's Criminal Practice 2026* E15.2

B2 Bail

With the following exceptions, the bases on which the Crown may oppose bail, and on which an application for bail, whether unconditional or conditional, may be made for a child appearing in the adult court, are the same as for an adult (see A8).

Under transitional arrangements, if the offence carries a sentence of life imprisonment and at the time of the offence the defendant was on bail, Sch 1, paras 9AA and 9AB to the Bail Act 1976 (as amended) provide:

Bail Act 1976, Sch 1, paras 9AA and 9AB

9AA (1) This paragraph applies if—
(a) the defendant is a child or young person, and
(b) it appears to the court that he was on bail in criminal proceedings on the date of the offence.

(2) In deciding for the purposes of paragraph 2(1) of this Part of this Schedule whether it is satisfied that there are substantial grounds for believing that the defendant, if released on bail (whether subject to conditions or not), would commit an offence while on bail, the court shall give particular weight to the fact that the defendant was on bail in criminal proceedings on the date of the offence.

9AB (1) Subject to sub-paragraph (2) below, this paragraph applies if—
(a) the defendant is a child or young person, and
(b) it appears to the court that, having been released on bail in or in connection with the proceedings for the offence, he failed to surrender to custody.

(2) Where it appears to the court that the defendant had reasonable cause for his failure to surrender to custody, this paragraph does not apply unless it also appears to the court that he failed to surrender to custody at the appointed place as soon as reasonably practicable after the appointed time.

(3) In deciding for the purposes of paragraph 2(1) of this Part of this Schedule whether it is satisfied that there are substantial grounds for believing that the defendant, if released on bail (whether subject to conditions or not), would fail to surrender to custody, the court shall give particular weight to—
(a) where the defendant did not have reasonable cause for his failure to surrender to custody, the fact that he failed to surrender to custody, or
(b) where he did have reasonable cause for his failure to surrender to custody, the fact that he failed to surrender to custody at the appointed place as soon as reasonably practicable after the appointed time.

(4) . . .

If electronic monitoring is to be a condition of bail, the court must comply with s 3AA Bail Act 1976.

Bail Act 1976, ss 3AA(1)–(5)

3AA Conditions for the imposition of electronic monitoring requirements: children and young persons

(1) A court may not impose electronic monitoring requirements on a child or young person unless each of the following conditions is met.

(2) The first condition is that the child or young person has attained the age of twelve years.

Blackstone's Magistrates' Court Handbook 2026. Bartholomew Dalton and Caroline Liggins, Oxford University Press. © Oxford University Press 2026.
DOI: 10.1093/oso/9780198963943.003.0033

(3) The second condition is that—
 (a) the child or young person is charged with or has been convicted of a violent or sexual offence, or an offence punishable in the case of an adult with imprisonment for a term of fourteen years or more; or
 (b) he is charged with or has been convicted of one or more imprisonable offences which, together with any other imprisonable offences of which he has been convicted in any proceedings—
  (i) amount, or
  (ii) would, if he were convicted of the offences with which he is charged, amount, to a recent history of repeatedly committing imprisonable offences while remanded on bail or to local authority accommodation.

(4) The third condition is that the court is satisfied that the necessary provision for dealing with the person concerned can be made under arrangements for the electronic monitoring of persons released on bail that are currently available in each local justice area which is a relevant area.

(5) The fourth condition is that a youth offending team has informed the court that in its opinion the imposition of electronic monitoring requirements will be suitable in the case of the child or young person.

B2.1 Refusal of bail

If a child is refused bail, the Legal Aid, Sentencing and Punishment of Offenders Act 2012, Part 3, Chapter 3 provides for the regime (see **B2.1.8** for ss 91–102).

It should be noted that remands both to local authority accommodation and to youth detention accommodation are custodial remands, and that time limits for such remands and custody time limits apply. In the case of a child charged with murder, where the court has no power to grant bail, the court will still determine where the child is to be remanded (*R (A) v Lewisham Youth Court* [2011] EWHC 1193 (Admin)) and there is no limit under the Bail Act 1976 to the number of occasions on which consideration can be given to this issue.

B2.1.1 *Youth remands*

Where a child is not released on bail, s 91 Legal Aid, Sentencing and Punishment of Offenders Act 2012 requires the court to remand the child to local authority accommodation in accordance with s 92, unless one of the sets of conditions set out in ss 98 to 101 is fulfilled (see **B2.1.8**), in which case the court may instead remand the child to youth detention accommodation (see Figure 2). Under s 92(2), a court that remands a child to local authority accommodation must designate the local authority that is to receive the child.

B2.1.2 *Remand to local authority accommodation*

The remand may be without conditions, but if appropriate, under s 93 Legal Aid, Sentencing and Punishment of Offenders Act 2012, after consultation with the designated local authority, the court may require:

- the child to comply with any conditions that could be imposed under section 3(6) of the Bail Act 1976;
- the child to comply with any conditions required for the purpose of securing compliance with electronic monitoring;
- the designated local authority to comply with any requirements to secure the child's compliance with a condition; and
- the designated local authority not to place the child with a named person.

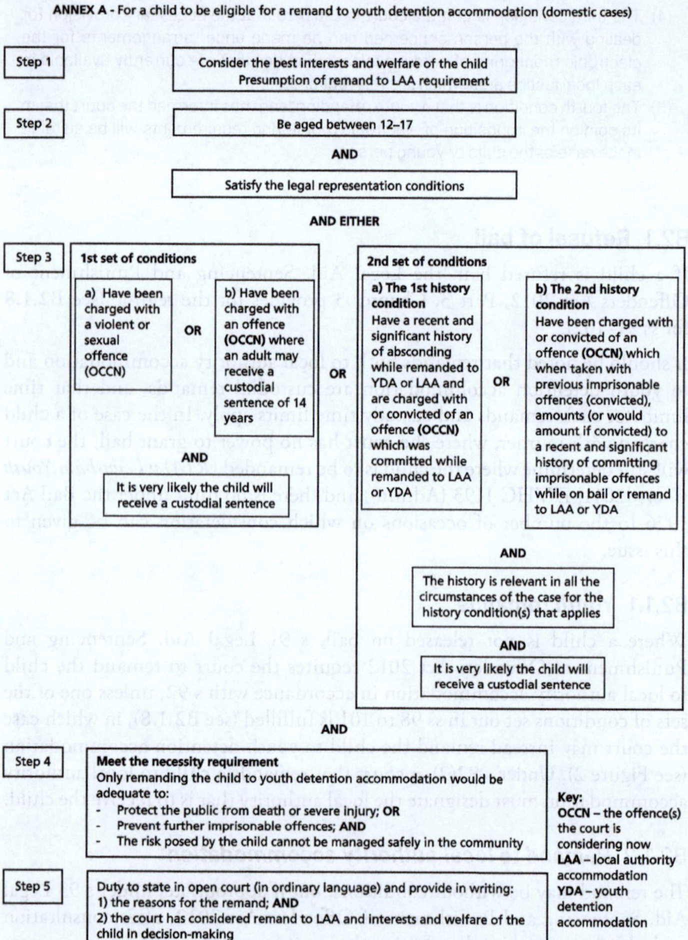

Figure 2 Remand to youth detention accommodation

An application may be made to the court in respect of a child who has been remanded to local authority accommodation to impose, vary, or revoke conditions.

B2.1.3 *Electronic monitoring as a condition of bail whilst remanded to local authority accommodation*

The court may not impose electronic monitoring of a child's compliance with a condition imposed under s 93 unless the conditions set out in s 94 (see B2.1.8) are satisfied.

B2.1.4 *Failure to surrender*

Where a child who is remanded on bail fails to surrender to court without reasonable cause, s 6 Bail Act 1976 will apply (see C3).

B2.1.5 *Breach of conditions of remand to local authority accommodation*

Under s 97 Legal Aid, Sentencing and Punishment of Offenders Act 2012, a constable may arrest a child without a warrant if the child has been remanded to local authority accommodation with conditions and the constable has reasonable grounds to suspect that the child has broken any of those conditions. The child must be brought before the court as soon as practicable and within 24 hours of the child's arrest. Where that 24-hour period includes the time appointed for the child's original court appearance then the child should appear before that same court.

If the court is of the opinion that a child has broken any of the conditions of a remand to local authority accommodation, the court may once again consider the conditions of bail and may attach new conditions to the remand to local authority accommodation or, if the conditions in ss 98–101 are met, remand the child to youth detention accommodation.

If the court is not of the opinion that the child has broken any of the conditions of his remand to local authority accommodation, it must remand the child subject to the original conditions imposed.

B2.1.6 *10- to 11-year-olds*

A child aged 10 to 11 years may only be remanded on bail or to local authority accommodation. If a child reaches the age of 12 during the course of a remand, it is possible that he may then be remanded to youth detention accommodation at the next court appearance should the relevant conditions (ss 98–101 Legal Aid, Sentencing and Punishment of Offenders Act 2012) be met.

B2.1.7 *Secure accommodation*

A child aged between 10 and 17 years who is remanded to local authority accommodation may be placed in secure local authority accommodation if the designated local authority obtains a court order permitting this under s 25 Children Act 1989 (as modified by the Children (Secure Accommodation) Regulations 1991 (SI 1991/1505)).

Section 25 Children Act 1989 provides:

Children Act 1989, s 25

25 Use of accommodation for restricting liberty

(1) Subject to the following provisions of this section, a child who is being looked after by a local authority or local authority in Wales may not be placed, and, if placed, may not be kept, in accommodation in England provided for the purpose of restricting liberty ('secure accommodation') unless it appears—
 (a) that—
  (i) he has a history of absconding and is likely to abscond from any other description of accommodation; and
  (ii) if he absconds, he is likely to suffer significant harm; or
 (b) that if he is kept in any other description of accommodation he is likely to injure himself or other persons.

(2) The Secretary of State may by regulations—
 (a) specify a maximum period—
  (i) beyond which a child may not be kept in secure accommodation in England without the authority of the court; and
  (ii) for which the court may authorise a child to be kept in secure accommodation in England;
 (b) empower the court from time to time to authorise a child to be kept in secure accommodation in England for such further period as the regulations may specify; and
 (c) provide that applications to the court under this section shall be made only by local authorities or local authorities in Wales.

(3) It shall be the duty of a court hearing an application under this section to determine whether any relevant criteria for keeping a child in secure accommodation are satisfied in his case.

(4) If a court determines that any such criteria are satisfied, it shall make an order authorising the child to be kept in secure accommodation and specifying the maximum period for which he may be so kept.

(5) On any adjournment of the hearing of an application under this section, a court may make an interim order permitting the child to be kept during the period of the adjournment in secure accommodation.

(6) No court shall exercise the powers conferred by this section in respect of a child who is not legally represented in that court unless, having been informed of his right to apply for the provision of representation under Part 1of LASPO 2012 and having had the opportunity to do so, he refused or failed to apply . . .

B2.1.8 *The statutory remand scheme*

Section 157 of the Police, Crime, Sentencing and Courts Act 2022 (PCSCA) amends the relevant provisions of the Legal Aid, Sentencing and Punishment of Offenders Act 2012 (LASPO), ss 91–102, by introducing statutory duties to consider the best interests and welfare of the child in the remand decision and to record the reasons for a custodial remand. The new provisions also increase the thresholds of the sentencing condition, the previous offending condition (second set of conditions), and the necessity condition. The new provisions bring the sentencing condition to both LASPO tests. PCSCA tightens the tests to be applied by the courts in order to remand children and young people into custodial remand. Under the current provisions, courts dealing with children and young people are required to first consider bail in the usual way. Pursuant to s 91 LASPO, if bail is refused, the child must be remanded into local authority accommodation unless either of the sets of conditions set out in s 98 and s 99 of LASPO apply (ss 100 and 101 for extradition).

PCSCA amends LASPO in the following ways:

1. Duty to consider the interests and welfare of the child before imposing a custodial remand (s 91(4A)).
2. The sentencing condition to the first set of conditions for a remand to youth detention accommodation (s 98).
3. The sentencing condition that now applies to both sets of conditions contains a higher threshold.
4. The threshold for the second history condition (second set of conditions) is increased.
5. The necessity condition threshold is increased.
6. PCSCA introduces a statutory requirement on the court to record its reasons for imposing a custodial remand.

91 Remands of children otherwise than on bail

(1) This section applies where—
  (a) a court deals with a child charged with or convicted of one or more offences by remanding the child, and
  (b) the child is not released on bail.

(2) This section also applies where—
  (a) a court remands a child in connection with extradition proceedings, and
  (b) the child is not released on bail.

(3) Subject to subsection (4), the court must remand the child to local authority accommodation in accordance with section 92.

(4) The court may instead remand the child to youth detention accommodation in accordance with section 102 where—
  (a) in the case of a child remanded under subsection (1), the first or second set of conditions for such a remand (see sections 98 and 99) is met in relation to the child, or
  (b) in the case of a child remanded under subsection (2), the first or second set of conditions for such a remand in an extradition case (see sections 100 and 101) is met in relation to the child.

(4A) Before deciding whether to remand a child to youth detention accommodation in accordance with section 102 the court must consider the interests and welfare of the child.

(5) This section is subject to section 128(7) of the Magistrates' Courts Act 1980 (remands to police detention for periods of not more than 3 days); but that provision has effect in relation to a child as if for the reference to 3 clear days there were substituted a reference to 24 hours.

(6) In this Chapter, 'child' means a person under the age of 18.

(7) References in this Chapter (other than in relation to extradition proceedings) to the remand of a child include a reference to—
  (a) the sending of a child for trial, and
  (b) the committal of a child for sentence, and related expressions are to be construed accordingly

...

93 Conditions etc on remands to local authority accommodation

(1) A court remanding a child to local authority accommodation may require the child to comply with any conditions that could be imposed under section 3(6) of the Bail Act 1976 if the child were then being granted bail.

(2) The court may also require the child to comply with any conditions imposed for the purpose of securing the electronic monitoring of the child's compliance with the conditions imposed under subsection (1) if—

(a) in the case of a child remanded under section 91(1) (proceedings other than extradition proceedings), the requirements in section 94 are met, or

(b) in the case of a child remanded under section 91(2) (extradition proceedings), the requirements in section 95 are met . . .

94 Requirements for electronic monitoring

(1) The requirements referred to in section 93(2)(a) (requirements for imposing electronic monitoring condition: non-extradition cases) are those set out in subsections (2) to (6).

(2) The first requirement is that the child has reached the age of twelve.

(3) The second requirement is that the offence mentioned in section 91(1), or one or more of those offences, is an imprisonable offence.

(4) The third requirement is that—

(a) the offence mentioned in section 91(1), or one or more of those offences, is a violent or sexual offence or an offence punishable in the case of an adult with imprisonment for a term of 14 years or more, or

(b) the offence or offences mentioned in section 91(1), together with any other imprisonable offences of which the child has been convicted in any proceedings, amount or would, if the child were convicted of that offence or those offences, amount to a recent history of committing imprisonable offences while on bail or subject to a custodial remand.

(5) The fourth requirement is that the court is satisfied that the necessary provision for electronic monitoring can be made under arrangements currently available in each local justice area which is a relevant area.

(6) The fifth requirement is that a youth offending team has informed the court that, in its opinion, the imposition of an electronic monitoring condition will be suitable in the child's case . . .

98 First set of conditions for a remand to youth detention accommodation

(1) For the purposes of section 91(4)(a), the first set of conditions for a remand to youth detention accommodation is met in relation to a child if each of the following is met in relation to the child—

(a) the age condition (see subsection (2)),

(aa) the sentencing condition (see subsection (2A),

(b) the offence condition (see subsection (3)),

(c) the necessity condition (see subsection (4)), and

(d) the first or second legal representation condition (see subsections (5) and (6)).

(2) The age condition is that the child has reached the age of twelve.

(2A) The sentencing condition is that it appears to the court that it is very likely that the child will be sentenced to a custodial sentence for the offence mentioned in section 91(1) or one or more of those offences.

(3) The offence condition is that the offence mentioned in section 91(1), or one or more of those offences—

(a) is a violent sexual or terrorism offence, or

(b) is an offence punishable in the case of an adult with imprisonment for a term of 14 years or more.

(4) The necessity condition is that the court is of the opinion, after considering all the options for the remand of the child, that only remanding the child to youth detention accommodation would be adequate—
  (a) to protect the public from death or serious personal injury (whether physical or psychological) occasioned by further offences committed by the child, or
  (b) to prevent the commission by the child of imprisonable offences and that the risks posed by the child cannot be managed safely in the community.
(5) The first legal representation condition is that the child is legally represented before the court.
(6) The second legal representation condition is that the child is not legally represented before the court and—
  (a) representation was provided to the child under Part 1 of this Act for the purposes of the proceedings, but was withdrawn—
    (i) because of the child's conduct, or
    (ii) because it appeared that the child's financial resources were such that the child was not eligible for such representation,
  (b) the child applied for such representation and the application was refused because it appeared that the child's financial resources were such that the child was not eligible for such representation, or
  (c) having been informed of the right to apply for such representation and having had the opportunity to do so, the child refused or failed to apply.

99 Second set of conditions for a remand to youth detention accommodation

(1) For the purposes of section 91(4)(a), the second set of conditions for a remand to youth detention accommodation is met in relation to a child if each of the following is met in relation to the child—
  (a) the age condition (see subsection (2)),
  (b) the sentencing condition (see subsection (3)),
  (c) the offence condition (see subsection (4)),
  (d) the first or second history condition or both (see subsections (5) and (6)),
  (e) the necessity condition (see subsection (7)), and
  (f) the first or second legal representation condition (see subsections (8) and (9)).
(2) The age condition is that the child has reached the age of twelve.
(3) The sentencing condition is that it appears to the court that it is very likely that the child will be sentenced to a custodial sentence for the offence mentioned in section 91(1) or one or more of those offences.
(4) The offence condition is that the offence mentioned in section 91(1), or one or more of those offences, is an imprisonable offence.
(5) The first history condition is that—
  (a) the child has a recent and significant history of absconding while subject to a custodial remand and it appears to the court that the history is relevant in all the circumstances of the case, and
  (b) the offence mentioned in section 91(1), or one or more of those offences, is alleged to be or has been found to have been committed while the child was remanded to local authority accommodation or youth detention accommodation.
(6) The second history condition is that the offence or offences mentioned in section 91(1), together with any other imprisonable offences of which the child has been convicted in any proceedings, amount or would, if the child were convicted of that offence or those offences, amount to a recent and significant history of committing imprisonable offences while on bail or subject to a custodial remand, and this appears to the court relevant in all the circumstances of the case.

(7) The necessity condition is that the court is of the opinion, after considering all the options for the remand of the child, that only remanding the child to youth detention accommodation would be adequate—
  (a) to protect the public from death or serious personal injury (whether physical or psychological) occasioned by further offences committed by the child, or
  (b) to prevent the commission by the child of imprisonable offences and that the risks posed by the child cannot be managed safely in the community.

(8) The first legal representation condition is that the child is legally represented before the court.

(9) The second legal representation condition is that the child is not legally represented before the court and—
  (a) representation was provided to the child under Part 1 of this Act for the purposes of the proceedings, but was withdrawn—
    (i) because of the child's conduct, or
    (ii) because it appeared that the child's financial resources were such that the child was not eligible for such representation,
  (b) the child applied for such representation and the application was refused because it appeared that the child's financial resources were such that the child was not eligible for such representation, or
  (c) having been informed of the right to apply for such representation and having had the opportunity to do so, the child refused or failed to apply.

(10) In this Chapter 'custodial sentence' means a sentence or order mentioned in section 222(1) of the Sentencing Code.

(11) The reference in subsection (5)(b) to a child being remanded to local authority accommodation or youth detention accommodation includes—
  (a) a child being remanded to local authority accommodation under section 23 of the Children and Young Persons Act 1969, and
  (b) a child being remanded to prison under that section as modified by section 98 of the Crime and Disorder Act 1998 or under section 27 of the Criminal Justice Act 1948.

B3 Breach of Orders, and New Offences Committed during an Order

See Appendix 1 of Sentencing Children and Young People: Definitive Guideline.

B3.1 General limitation on re-sentencing (Sentencing Act 2020, s 402)

402 Powers to re-sentence

(1) Where under this Code a court has power to re-sentence an offender for an offence, the court may deal with the offender in any way in which it could deal with the offender—
    (a) if the offender had just been convicted by or before it of the offence, and
    (b) in a case where the offender was aged under 18 when in fact convicted of the offence, as if the offender were the same age as when in fact convicted.

B3.2 Referral orders

B3.2.1 *Which court will handle the case?*

Sentencing Act 2020, s 108

S 108 . . . 'the appropriate court', in relation to any referral of an offender back to court, means—
    (a) if the offender is aged under 18 when first appearing before the court in pursuance of the referral back, a youth court acting in the local justice area in which it appears to the youth offender panel that the offender resides or will reside;
    (b) otherwise, a magistrates' court (other than a youth court) acting in that area.

B3.2.2 *Referral order—breach proceedings*

Sentencing Act 2020, Sch 4 Pt 1

In dealing with the child for such an offence, the appropriate court 'may deal with them in any way in which he could have been dealt with for that offence by the court which made the order' (Sch 4, Pt 1, para 7(4)). This provision disapplies the obligation to impose a referral order.

The court must be satisfied that the youth justice's services panel was entitled to make the finding of breach of the referral order, or that any discretion was exercised reasonably. Where a court is revoking and re-sentencing an offender, the court has the powers of the youth court, whatever the age of the defendant. As an alternative to revocation the court can impose a fine of up to £2,500 or the contract period may be increased up to a maximum of 12 months (Sentencing Act (SA) 2020, Sch 4, para 9) and the court must have regard to the circumstances of the referral back and the extent of any compliance with it. The court may take no action.

Blackstone's Magistrates' Court Handbook 2026. Bartholomew Dalton and Caroline Liggins, Oxford University Press. © Oxford University Press 2026.
DOI: 10.1093/oso/9780198963943.003.0034

B3.2.3 *Conviction while subject to a referral order*

See SA 2020, Sch 4, Pt 2, paras 14–17.

The court sentencing for the new offence may extend the compliance period of the referral order. The total period may not exceed 12 months. If sentencing for the new offence in any other way (other than by an absolute or conditional discharge), the referral order may be revoked, but it may also be allowed to continue. The court may, if it is in the interests of justice, deal with the child in any manner in which the offender could have been dealt with by the original court. The extent of any compliance must be taken into account.

See *Blackstone's Criminal Practice 2026* E4.7

B3.3 Youth rehabilitation order

B3.3.1 *Which court will handle the case?*

Sentencing Act 2020, Sch 7, para 5(4) (Criminal Justice and Immigration Act 2008, Sch 2, para 5(3))

(4) . . . 'appropriate court' means—
- (a) if the offender is aged under 18, a youth court acting in the relevant local justice area, and
- (b) if the offender is aged 18 or over, a magistrates' court (other than a youth court) acting in that local justice area.

In a youth rehabilitation order (YRO) case, a warning is required if the supervising officer finds there is a failure to comply without reasonable excuse. If, following a further, second warning within the 12-month 'warned period', there is then a third failure to comply without reasonable excuse, the officer must refer the case to court for breach proceedings, although Youth Justice Service will have additional discretion in exceptional circumstances following a third failure to comply. The officer also has the discretion to refer the case to court at an earlier warning stage.

B3.3.2 *Youth rehabilitation order—breach proceedings Powers of the court (SA 2020, Sch 7)*

When dealing with the breach of a YRO, the court has the following options:

- no action;
- a fine of up to £2,500;
- amend the YRO, but not with Intensive Supervision and Surveillance Requirement (ISSR) or Intensive Fostering, unless that already applies;
- revoke the YRO and re-sentence, within the powers of the original (sentencing) court.

Custody is an option for breach of a YRO only if the original offence is imprisonable or, in the case of a non-imprisonable offence, if, following 'wilful and persistent' non-compliance (SA 2020, Sch 7; Criminal Justice and Immigration Act 2008, Sch 2), a YRO with an ISSR or Intensive Fostering provision is made and that further YRO is then also subject to non-compliance. The court, if passing a custodial sentence, must state that a YRO with an ISSR or Intensive Fostering provision is not appropriate and the reasons why. This is in addition to meeting the existing criteria, that is, the court forming the opinion that the offence(s) is so serious that a community sentence cannot be justified.

Paragraph 6 provides:

Sentencing Act 2020 (Criminal Justice and Immigration Act 2008), Sch 7, para 6 Powers of magistrates' court

6(1) This paragraph applies where—
- (a) an offender appears or is brought before a youth court or other magistrates' court under paragraph 5, and
- (b) it is proved to the satisfaction of the court that the offender has breached a requirement of the youth rehabilitation order without reasonable excuse, and must be read with paragraphs 8 to 11.

(2) The court may deal with the case under sub-paragraph (5). . . . (5) Where the court deals with the case under this sub-paragraph, it may deal with the offender in respect of the breach in any one of the following ways—
- (a) by ordering the offender to pay a fine of an amount not exceeding £2,500;
- (b) by amending the terms of the youth rehabilitation order to add or substitute any requirement which it could include in a youth rehabilitation order if, applying the relevant assumptions, it were now making such an order in respect of the relevant offence;
- (c) by re-sentencing the offender for the relevant offence.

(6) In this paragraph—
'relevant offence' means the offence in respect of which the youth rehabilitation order was made, and the 'relevant assumptions' are that—
- (a) the court has just convicted the offender of the relevant offence, and
- (b) the offender is the same age as when in fact convicted of that offence.

(7) Sub-paragraph (5)(b) is subject to paragraph 10.

(8) In dealing with the offender under sub-paragraph (5), the court must take into account the extent to which the offender has complied with the requirements of the youth rehabilitation order.

(9) Where the court—
- (a) deals with the offender under sub-paragraph (5)(b), and
- (b) does not act in the offender's home local justice area, it may exercise the power in paragraph 15 (amendment by reason of change of residence) as if it were the appropriate court for the purposes of that paragraph.

(10) Where the court deals with the offender under sub-paragraph (5)(c), it must revoke the offender may appeal to the Crown Court against a sentence imposed under sub-paragraph (5)(c).

Restriction of powers in paragraphs 6 and 7 where treatment required

8 (1) Sub-paragraph (2) applies where the offender—
- (a) is required by a treatment requirement of the youth rehabilitation order to submit to treatment, and
- (b) has refused to undergo any surgical, electrical or other treatment.

(2) The offender is not to be treated for the purposes of paragraph 6 or 7 as having breached the requirement on the ground only of that refusal if, in the opinion of the court, the refusal was reasonable having regard to all the circumstances.

(3) In this paragraph, 'treatment requirement' means—
  (a) a mental health treatment requirement,
  (b) a drug treatment requirement, or
  (c) an intoxicating substance treatment requirement.

Fines imposed under paragraphs 6 and 7

9 (1) A fine imposed under paragraph 6(5)(a) or 7(2)(a) is to be treated, for the purposes of any enactment, as being a sum adjudged to be paid by a conviction.

(2) Where—
  (a) a court is dealing with an offender for breach of a requirement of a youth rehabilitation order,
  (b) the offender is aged under 18, and (c) but for this sub-paragraph, the court would impose a fine under paragraph 6(5)(a) or 7(2)(a), section 380 (order for payment by parent or guardian) applies to the fine.

Powers in paragraphs 6 and 7 to impose other requirements: further provisions

10 (1) This paragraph applies where— (a) the magistrates' court deals with the offender under paragraph 6(5)(b), . . .

(2) Paragraphs 6(5)(b) and 7(2)(b) have effect subject to any provision that applies to the court in making a youth rehabilitation order as if the court were imposing the requirements on making the order.

That is subject to the following provisions of this paragraph and to paragraph 11.

(3) Subject to sub-paragraph (4), any requirement imposed under paragraph 6(5)(b) or 7(2)(b) must be capable of being complied with before the end date.

(4) In dealing with an offender under paragraph 6(5)(b) or 7(2)(b) the court may substitute a later date for the end date.

(5) A date substituted under sub-paragraph (4)—
  (a) must not be more than 6 months after the existing end date;
  (b) subject to that, may be more than 3 years after the date on which the order took effect.

(6) Once the power in sub-paragraph (4) has been exercised in relation to the order, it may not be exercised again in relation to it by any court.

(7) Where—
  (a) in dealing with the offender under paragraph 6(5)(b) or 7(2)(b), the court imposes an unpaid work requirement, and
  (b) the youth rehabilitation order does not already contain an unpaid work requirement, the number of hours for which the offender may be required to work under the requirement (see paragraph 10(3) of Schedule 6) must not, in aggregate, be less than 20.

(8) The court may not under paragraph 6(5)(b) or 7(2)(b) impose—
  (a) an extended activity requirement, or
  (b) a fostering requirement, if the order does not already impose such a requirement.

(9) Sub-paragraph (10) applies where—
  (a) the order includes a fostering requirement (the 'original Requirement'), and
  (b) under paragraph 6(5)(b) or 7(2)(b) the court proposes to substitute a new fostering requirement ('the substitute requirement') for the original requirement.

(10) The fostering period (see paragraph 26(3) of Schedule 6) for the substitute requirement must end—
  (a) within 18 months beginning with the day on which the original requirement first took effect, and 268
  (b) before the offender reaches the age of 18.

Powers in paragraphs 6 and 7 to re-sentence: further provisions relating to intensive supervision and surveillance

11 (1) This paragraph applies where—

(a) the court is dealing with the offender under paragraph 6(5)(c) or 7(2)(c) for an offence, and

(b) the offender has wilfully and persistently failed to comply with the youth rehabilitation order.

(2) The court may impose a youth rehabilitation order with intensive supervision and surveillance even if—

(a) the offence is not an imprisonable offence, or

(b) the court is not of the opinion mentioned in section 180(2)(a) (custodial sentence otherwise appropriate).

(3) If—

(a) the order is a youth rehabilitation order with intensive supervision and surveillance, and

(b) the offence is an imprisonable offence, the court may impose a custodial sentence even if it is not of the opinion mentioned in section 230(2) (threshold for imposing discretionary custodial sentence).

(4) If—

(a) the order is a youth rehabilitation order with intensive supervision and surveillance which was imposed by virtue of sub-paragraph (2), and

(b) the offence is not an offence punishable with imprisonment, the court's powers under paragraph 6(5)(c) or 7(2)(c) to deal with the offender for the offence include power to make a detention and training order for a term not exceeding 4 months.

B3.4 Youth rehabilitation orders made in the Crown Court

B3.4.1 *Breach proceedings—powers of the court*

Sentencing Act 2020, s 189 (Criminal Justice and Immigration Act 2008, Sch 1, para 36) and Sentencing Act 2020, Sch 7

189 Power for Crown Court to direct magistrates' court supervision

(1) This section applies where the Crown Court makes a youth rehabilitation order otherwise than on appeal from a magistrates' court.

(2) The Crown Court may include a direction that the order is to be subject to magistrates' court supervision.

Sentencing Act 2020, Sch 7, para 2(b)

(b) a youth rehabilitation order is 'subject to magistrates' court supervision' if it—

(i) was made by a magistrates' court, or

(ii) was made by the Crown Court and includes a direction under that section.

If the order is subject to magistrates' court supervision, it may deal with the matter under SA 2020 Sch 6 as set out above but in addition.

Sentencing Act 2020, Sch 7, para 6(3) (Criminal Justice and Immigration Act 2008, Sch 2, para 7)

(3) If the youth rehabilitation order was made by the Crown Court, the court may instead—

(a) commit the offender to custody, or
(b) release the offender on bail, until the offender can be brought or appear before the Crown Court

B3.4.2 *Conviction while subject to a youth rehabilitation order*

If the defendant is convicted of a new offence while subject to a YRO, the court has power to revoke the sentence and re-sentence. If the sentence was imposed in the Crown Court, it must commit to the Crown Court for sentence, unless the Crown Court made an order allowing the magistrates' court to deal with any breach under SA 2020, s 189.

Sentencing Act 2020, Sch 7, paras 21 and 22 (Criminal Justice and Immigration Act 2008, Sch 2, para 18)

21 (1) This paragraph applies if—
(a) the existing youth rehabilitation order is subject to magistrates' court supervision, and
(b) the convicting court is dealing with the offender for the further offence.
(2) If it appears to the convicting court to be in the interests of justice to do so, having regard to circumstances which have arisen since the youth rehabilitation order was made, the convicting court may—
(a) revoke the youth rehabilitation order, or
(b) both—
(i) revoke the youth rehabilitation order, and
(ii) re-sentence the offender for the offence in respect of which the order was made . . .
(5) If the convicting court deals with the offender under sub-paragraph (2)(b), it must take into account the extent to which the offender has complied with the requirements of the order.
(6) A person sentenced under sub-paragraph (2)(b) for an offence may appeal to the Crown Court against the sentence.
22 (1) Sub-paragraph (2) applies if—
(a) the existing youth rehabilitation order was made by the Crown Court but is subject to magistrates' court supervision, and
(b) the convicting court would, but for this paragraph, deal with the offender for the further offence.
(2) The convicting court may, instead of proceeding under paragraph 21—
(a) commit the offender to custody, or
(b) release the offender on bail, until the offender can be brought before the Crown Court.
(3) Sub-paragraph (4) applies if the youth rehabilitation order is a Crown Court youth rehabilitation order.
(4) The convicting court may—
(a) commit the offender to custody, or
(b) release the offender on bail, until the offender can be brought or appear before the Crown Court.

See *Blackstone's Criminal Practice 2026* E11.27

B3.5 Detention and training order: breach of the supervision requirements

B3.5.1 *Which court handles the case?*

SA 2020, Sch 12, para 2 provides that such matters must be dealt with by the youth court, even if the defendant has reached the age of 18 years.

B3.5.2 *Detention and training order—new offences*

Sentencing Act 2020, Sch 12, para 7(1)–(7) (PCC SA 2000, s 105(1)–(4))

Offence after release for supervision or during further supervision period

7 (1) This paragraph applies where an offender commits an imprisonable offence ('the new offence')—
(a) after having been released for supervision under a detention and training order but before the date on which the term of the order ends, or
(b) during a period of supervision under a further supervision order.
(2) The court which deals with the offender for the new offence may order the offender to be detained for all or part of the period mentioned in sub-paragraph (3).
(3) That period is the period which—
(a) begins with the date of the order under sub-paragraph (2), and
(b) is equal in length to the period between—
(i) the date on which the new offence was committed, and
(ii) the date on which the term of the detention and training order, or the period of supervision, mentioned in subsection (1) ends.
(4) A court may make an order under sub-paragraph (2) whether or not it passes any other sentence on the offender.
(5) Detention under sub-paragraph (2) is to be in such youth detention accommodation as the Secretary of State may determine.
(6) The period for which an offender is ordered under sub-paragraph (2) to be detained—
(a) must, as the court may direct—
(i) be served before and be followed by, or
(ii) be served concurrently with, any sentence imposed for the new offence, and
(b) in either case, is to be disregarded in determining the appropriate length of that sentence.
(7) Where the new offence is found to have been committed—
(a) over a period of 2 or more days, or
(b) at some time during a period of 2 or more days, it is be taken for the purposes of this paragraph to have been committed on the last of those days. . . .

See *Blackstone's Criminal Practice 2026* **E15.20**

B4 Jurisdiction of the Adult Magistrates' Court over Children

B4.1 Children in the adult court alone

A child or young person, who is not jointly charged with an adult and who is refused bail at the police station, may appear in an adult court when no youth court is sitting. The adult court may deal with the young person only for the purposes of making a decision with regard to a remand. It must then remit the young person to the next available youth court (s 46(2) Children and Young Persons Act 1933) (see further B6).

B4.2 Jointly charged with an adult

A child or young person *must* appear before the adult court if jointly charged with an adult.

A child or young person *may* appear before the adult court if:

- charged with aiding or abetting an adult;
- an adult is charged with aiding or abetting the child or young person;
- charged with an offence arising out of the same circumstances as those giving rise to proceedings against an adult

(s 46 Children and Young Persons Act 1933 and s 18 Children and Young Persons Act 1963).

B4.2.1 *What is a joint charge?*

It is not necessary for the charge to specify that the offence was committed 'jointly' or 'together with' the adult concerned (*R v Rowlands* [1972] 1 All ER 306).

Where there is a charge of taking a motor vehicle without consent or aggravated vehicle-taking, the driver and any passengers charged with allowing themselves to be carried are jointly charged (*R v Peterborough Justices, ex p Allgood* (1995) 159 JP 627, QBD).

B4.3 Severance of a child from an adult

B4.3.1 *Sendings*

When the court sends the adult but is not obliged to send the child, it shall, after following the plea before venue procedures (see B5), send the child too if it considers it necessary in the interests of justice to do so (s 51(7) Crime and Disorder Act 1998).

Relevant issues have been identified by the Sentencing Council in two Guidelines which mirror each other: The Allocation Guideline and the Definitive Guideline on Sentencing Children and Young People, paragraphs 2.11–2.14.

Blackstone's Magistrates' Court Handbook 2026. Bartholomew Dalton and Caroline Liggins, Oxford University Press. © Oxford University Press 2026.
DOI: 10.1093/oso/9780198963943.003.0035

Sentencing Children and Young People: Definitive Guideline, paras 2.11–2.14

2.11 The proper venue for the trial of any child or young person is normally the youth court. Subject to statutory restrictions, that remains the case where a child or young person is jointly charged with an adult. If the adult is sent for trial to the Crown Court, the court should conclude that the child or young person must be tried separately in the youth court unless it is in the interests of justice for the child or young person and the adult to be tried jointly.

2.12 Examples of factors that should be considered when deciding whether to send the child or young person to the Crown Court (rather than having a trial in the youth court) include:

- whether separate trials will cause injustice to witnesses or to the case as a whole (consideration should be given to the provisions of ss 27 and 28 of the Youth Justice and Criminal Evidence Act 1999);
- the age of the child or young person; the younger the child or young person, the greater the desirability that the child or young person be tried in the youth court;
- the age gap between the child or young person and the adult; a substantial gap in age militates in favour of the child or young person being tried in the youth court;
- the lack of maturity of the child or young person;
- the relative culpability of the child or young person compared with the adult and
- whether the alleged role played by the child or young person was minor; and/or the lack of previous findings of guilt on the part of the child or young person.

2.13 The court should bear in mind that the youth court now has a general power to commit for sentence (as discussed at paragraph 2.9); in appropriate cases this will permit a sentence to be imposed by the same court on adults and children and young people who have been tried separately.

2.14 The court should follow the plea before venue procedure (see flowcharts on page 217) prior to considering whether it is in the interests of justice for the child or young person and the adult to be tried jointly.

B4.4 **Summary trials**

If an adult and the child plead not guilty to a joint charge, the trial must take place in the adult court (s 46(1)(a) Children and Young Persons Act 1933). It may do so if the allegation is of aiding and abetting, or arises out of the same circumstances (s 46(1)(b) Children and Young Persons Act 1933; s 18(a) and (b) Children and Young Persons Act 1963). (See **B4.2**.)

If the child pleads guilty or is found guilty, the adult court may sentence under its limited powers or remit to the youth court (s 8(6) Powers of Criminal Courts (Sentencing) Act 2000).

If the adult pleads guilty and the child not guilty, it is to be expected that the court will remit to the youth court for trial (s 29(2) Magistrates' Courts Act 1980) (see **B6**).

B4.5 Remittal

All cases not sent to the Crown Court, sentenced within the limited powers of the adult court (see **B9**), or listed for trial with an adult will be remitted to the youth court (see **B6**).

B5 **Managing the Case**

In order to handle the case appropriately, the steps shown in Figure 3 must be followed where the child is jointly charged with an adult. If the adult faces an indictable-only offence he must be sent to the Crown Court before dealing with this procedure. If the adult faces an either-way offence, this procedure should be followed but any plea should be taken first from the adult.

B5.1 **Sending to the Crown Court**

The court *must* forthwith send the case to the Crown Court if the child is charged with:

- homicide;
- an offence attracting a minimum sentence under the Sentencing Act (SA) 2020, s 311 (s 51A Firearms Act 1968) or s 29(3) Violent Crime Reduction Act 2006, provided the child was aged at least 16 at the date of the offence;
- a specified offence and on the facts of the case an extended sentence may be required (so that for youths, a minimum sentence of four years would be required) (the dangerous offender provisions); *or*
- if notice has been given by the Crown under s 51B (serious fraud) or s 51C (children) of the Crime and Disorder Act 1998 (see **B5.5**).

When a child or young person is sent for trial, the court may also send for trial any either-way or summary offence for which he is charged if:

- it appears to the court to be related to the indictable-only offence; *and*
- in the case of a summary offence, it is punishable with imprisonment or involves obligatory or discretionary disqualification from driving (s 51(6) and (11) Crime and Disorder Act 1998—see **B5.5**).

B5.1.1 **Key points**

- An offence of murder, attempted murder, manslaughter, causing or allowing the death of a child or vulnerable adult, or infanticide must be sent to the Crown Court for trial (s 24(1) MCA 1980), along with any other offences with which the defendant is charged at the same time, if the charges for both offences could be joined in the same indictment (s 24(1A) MCA 1980).
- The relevant offences under the Firearms Act 1968 are set out in SA 2020, Sch 20 (s 51A of that Act).:

Sentencing Act 2020, Sch 20

PART 1

1 An offence under section 5(1)(a), (ab), (aba), (ac), (ad), (ae), (af) or (c) of the Firearms Act 1968 (offence of having in possession, purchasing or acquiring, weapon or ammunition) committed on or after 22 January 2004.

Blackstone's Magistrates' Court Handbook 2026. Bartholomew Dalton and Caroline Liggins, Oxford University Press.
DOI: 10.1093/oso/9780198963943.003.0036

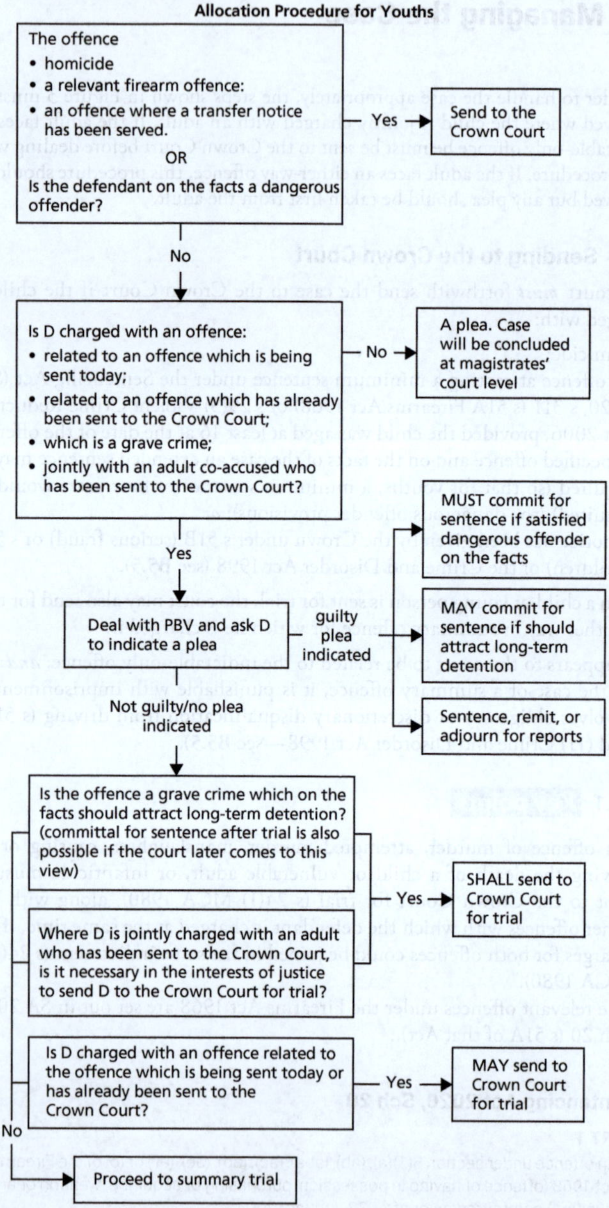

Figure 3 Allocation procedure for youths

2 An offence under section 5(1A)(a) of the Firearms Act 1968 (offence of having in possession, purchasing or acquiring firearm disguised as another object) committed on or after 22 January 2004.

3 An offence under section 5(2A) of the Firearms Act 1968 (manufacture, sale or transfer of firearm or ammunition, or possession etc for sale or transfer) committed in respect of a relevant firearm or relevant ammunition.

4(1) An offence under any of the provisions of the Firearms Act 1968 listed in sub-paragraph (2) committed on or after 6 April 2007 in respect of a relevant firearm or relevant ammunition.

(2) Those provisions are—section 16 (possession of firearm or ammunition with intent to injure);
section 16A (possession of firearm with intent to cause fear or violence);
section 17 (use of firearm to resist arrest);
section 18 (carrying firearm with criminal intent);
section 19 (carrying a firearm in a public place);
section 20(1) (trespassing in a building with firearm).

5 An offence under section 28 of the Violent Crime Reduction Act 2006 (using someone to mind a weapon), where the dangerous weapon in respect of which the offence was committed was a relevant firearm.

PART 2

INTERPRETATION OF SCHEDULE

6 In this Schedule—
'relevant firearm' means a firearm specified in any of the following provisions of section 5 of the Firearms Act 1968 (weapons subject to general prohibition)—
(a) subsection (1)(a), (ab), (aba), (ac), (ad), (ae) or (af);
(b) subsection (1A)(a);
'relevant ammunition' means ammunition specified in subsection (1)(c) of that section.

For this purpose, 'firearm' and 'ammunition' have the same meanings as in the Firearms Act 1968.

B5.2 Other indictable and all summary matters

The court must proceed to plea before venue if the case could be sent; or take a plea if it is a summary-only offence. This applies even when appearing jointly with an adult, though if both plead not guilty the court will have to consider whether it is appropriate to join the cases.

Tottenham Youth Court, ex p Fawzy [1999] 1 WLR 1350 confirms that the adult court must make the decision on venue. There is no power to remit the child to the youth court for that court to make the mode of trial decision.

B5.3 Guilty plea indications

If a guilty plea is indicated, the court should proceed to sentence if the court's powers are sufficient (see **B9**) or remit to the youth court (see **B6**) *unless*:

- the offence is a specified offence under the dangerous offender provisions and on the developing facts an extended sentence may be required (so that for a child a minimum sentence of at least four years may be required), in which case it *must* commit to the Crown Court for sentence;

- the offence is related to an offence which is being sent that day, or related to a matter which has already been sent, in which case it *may* commit to the Crown Court for sentence;
- the offence is capable of being a grave crime, in which case it *may* commit for sentence if on the facts the offence might attract a sentence of long-term detention.

If the child pleads guilty and the adult is committed for sentence under SA 2020, s 18 (s 4 Powers of Criminal Courts (Sentencing) Act (PCCSA) 2000), he must be remitted for sentence to the youth court, unless either he is committed to the Crown Court for seriousness or dangerousness, or the court imposes a discharge, referral order, financial penalty, or bind over (SA 2020, s 25 (s 8 PCCSA 2000).

B5.3.1 Key points

- Offences are *grave crimes* (SA 2020, s 249) if they comprise:
  - an offence punishable in the case of a person aged 21 or over with imprisonment for 14 years or more, not being an offence the sentence for which is fixed by law; or
  - an offence under s 3 Sexual Offences Act 2003 ('the 2003 Act') (sexual assault); or
  - an offence under s 13 2003 Act (child sex offences committed by children or young persons); or
  - an offence under s 25 2003 Act (sexual activity with a child family member); or
  - an offence under s 26 2003 Act (inciting a child family member to engage in sexual activity); or
  - an offence under subsection (1)(a), (ab), (aba), (ac), (ad), (ae), (af), or (c) of s 5 Firearms Act 1968 (prohibited weapons), or under subsection (1A)(a) of that section; or
  - an offence under s 51A(1A)(b), (e), or (f) Firearms Act 1968, which was committed in respect of a firearm or ammunition specified in s 5(1), (ab), (aba), (ac), (ad), (ae), (af), or (c), or s 5(1A)(a) of that Act; or
  - an offence under s 28 Violent Crime Reduction Act 2006 (using someone to mind a weapon).
- An offence requiring a sentence of 'long-term detention' because it should substantially exceed two years:
  - in determining whether a sentence of more than two years would be imposed, the court should ask itself what sentence was realistically possible, bearing in mind the sentencing range (*CPS v Newcastle Upon Tyne Youth Court* [2010] EWHC 2773 (Admin));
  - the fact that a particular child aged 12 to 14 years could not receive a detention and training order is not a ground for refusing jurisdiction when a sentence of more than two years' detention is not required; children of this age should not be detained save in wholly exceptional circumstances

(*R (B) v Norfolk Youth Court* and CPS [2013] EWHC 1459 (Admin));

- in *BH v Llandudno Youth Court* [2014] EWHC 1833 (Admin) the court considered all the relevant authorities and applied the guideline, emphasizing that the correct question is, bearing in mind the age and the previous good character of the child concerned (there an 11-year-old facing an allegation of inducing a boy under 13 to engage in a sexual act against s 8 Sexual Offences Act 2003), and any other mitigation that is known and uncontentious, and bearing in mind aggravating factors, is there a real prospect that the Crown Court would exercise its powers under s 91 PCC(S) Act 2000 (now see s 22 SA 2020) to impose custody? It concluded that there was not;
- *R v H* [2014] EWCA Crim 2292 confirmed that while detention may have been appropriate for a 15-year-old in the same circumstances, a defendant who was 14 years old at the time of the offence had a youth rehabilitation order substituted. This was notwithstanding the seriousness of the burglary by 15 to 20 youths who entered a dwelling house and threatened violence, and his brandishing a carving knife to make his escape. He did not have 'a particularly bad record'—assaults on his mother; theft convictions; and various reprimands and warnings so as to be 'just' a persistent offender. The mitigation was a plea at the first opportunity; his being the only one arrested and being in the presence of much older boys who had serious criminal records and of whom he was in fear about attempting to separate himself;
- reference should be made to the definitive guideline at **B5.4**.

See *Blackstone's Criminal Practice 2026* **D24.19**

B5.4 Not guilty and no plea indications

If a child is jointly charged with an adult who has been sent to the Crown Court, the court must first consider if the offence is a grave crime which on the facts should attract a sentence of long-term detention; and if it is, the court *must* send for trial. This is now subject to the provisions of the Definitive Guideline.

Definitive Guideline on Sentencing Children and Young People, para 12.10

2.10 Before deciding whether to send the case to the Crown Court or retain jurisdiction in the youth court, the court should hear submissions from the prosecution and defence. As there is now a power to commit grave crimes for sentence the court should no longer take the prosecution case at its highest when deciding whether to retain jurisdiction. In most cases it is likely to be impossible to decide whether there is a real prospect that a sentence in excess of two years' detention will be imposed without knowing more about the facts of the case and the circumstances of the child or young person. In those circumstances the youth court should retain jurisdiction and commit for sentence if it is of the view, having heard more about the facts and the circumstances of the child or young person, that its powers of sentence are insufficient.

> Where the court decides that the case is suitable to be dealt with in the youth court it must warn the child or young person that all available sentencing options remain open and, if found guilty, the child or young person may be committed to the Crown Court for sentence.
>
> Children and young people should only be sent for trial or committed for sentence to the Crown Court when charged with or found guilty of an offence of such gravity that a custodial sentence substantially exceeding two years is a realistic possibility. For children aged 10 or 11, and children/young people aged 12–14 who are not persistent offenders, the court should take into account the normal prohibition on imposing custodial sentences.

If the child has not been sent for that reason but is jointly charged with an adult and it is necessary in the interests of justice (see **B4.3.1**) to send the child to the Crown Court for trial, the court must then send the child for that reason.

If the child is charged with an offence related to an offence which is sent that day, or has already been sent, the court *may* send to the Crown Court for trial.

In all other cases the court should proceed to summary trial or, if there is to be no effective trial of the adult, remit to the youth court (see **B6**).

B5.5 **Statutory provisions**

Refer to MCA 1980, ss 24A–24C and Crime and Disorder Act 1998, ss 51–51C. *Under amendments to s 51A Crime and Disorder Act 1998, once in force, a case involving a defendant on bail may be sent to the Crown Court in the absence of the defendant provided the conditions in s 51A(3B) are met.*

B6 Remittal to the Youth Court for Trial/Sentence

Under s 46 Children and Young Persons Act 1933 the magistrates' court shall remit to:

- a youth court acting for the same place as the remitting court; or
- a youth court acting for the place where the young offender habitually resides, except when:
  - (a) a charge made jointly against a child or young person and a person who has attained the age of eighteen years shall be heard by a magistrates' court other than a youth court; and
  - (b) where a child or young person is charged with an offence, the charge may be heard by a magistrates' court which is not a youth court if a person who has attained the age of eighteen years is charged at the same time with aiding, abetting, causing, procuring, allowing or permitting that offence; and
  - (c) where, in the course of any proceedings before any magistrates' court other than a youth court, it appears that the person to whom the proceedings relate is a child or young person, nothing in this subsection shall be construed as preventing the court, if it thinks fit so to do, from proceeding with the hearing and determination of those proceedings.

It is generally good practice to remit for sentence to the young person's local court.

A power to remit to the youth court for trial is granted under s 29 Magistrates' Courts Act 1980 where there will be no effective trial of an adult in relation to a joint charge either because the adult(s) plead guilty or are sent to the Crown Court.

A duty to remit exists under the Sentencing Act 2020, s 25, for sentencing where the adult court's limited powers are not regarded as sufficient (see **B6**).

Sentencing Act 2020, s 25

Power and duty to remit offenders aged under 18 to youth courts for sentence

(1) This section applies where a person aged under 18 is convicted by or before a court ('the convicting court') of an offence other than homicide . . .

(4) If the convicting court is a magistrates' court other than a youth court—
- (a) it may remit the offender to a youth court, and
- (b) must do so unless subsection (5) applies.

(5) This subsection applies where the convicting court—
- (a) would be required by section 85(1)(a) to make a referral order if it did not remit the offender to a youth court, or
- (b) is of the opinion that the case is one which can properly be dealt with by means of—
  - (i) an order for absolute discharge or an order for conditional discharge,
  - (ii) a fine, or

Blackstone's Magistrates' Court Handbook 2026. Bartholomew Dalton and Caroline Liggins, Oxford University Press. © Oxford University Press 2026.
DOI: 10.1093/oso/9780198963943.003.0037

(iii) an order (under section 376) requiring the offender's parent or guardian to enter into a recognizance to take proper care of, and exercise proper control over, the offender, with or without any other order that the court has power to make when making an order for absolute discharge or an order for conditional discharge.

B7 Parents and Guardians

B7.1 Definition of parent/guardian

B7.1.1 *Parent*

There is no definition of who is a 'parent', but it is likely to include a person with parental responsibility under the Children Act 1989.

B7.1.2 *Guardian*

Children and Young Persons Act 1933, s 107(1)

107 Interpretation

'Guardian', in relation to a child or young person, includes any person who, in the opinion of the court having cognisance of any case in relation to the child or young person or in which the child or young person is concerned, has for the time being the care of the child or young person . . .

B7.2 Requiring attendance at court

Children and Young Persons Act 1933, s 34A

34A Attendance at court of parent or guardian

(1) Where a child or young person is charged with an offence or is for any other reason brought before a court, the court—
   (a) may in any case; and
   (b) shall in the case of a child or a young person who is under the age of sixteen years, require a person who is a parent or guardian of his to attend at the court during all the stages of the proceedings, unless and to the extent that the court is satisfied that it would be unreasonable to require such attendance, having regard to the circumstances of the case.

(2) In relation to a child or young person for whom a local authority have parental responsibility and who—
   (a) is in their care; or
   (b) is provided with accommodation by them in the exercise of any functions (in particular those under the Children Act 1989) which are social service functions within the meaning of the Local Authority Social Services Act 1970, the reference in subsection (1) above to a person who is a parent or guardian of his shall be construed as a reference to that authority or, where he is allowed to live with such a person, as including such a reference.

In this subsection 'local authority' and 'parental responsibility' have the same meanings as in the Children Act 1989.

In the Definitive Guideline on Sentencing Children and Young People, it is stated:

Blackstone's Magistrates' Court Handbook 2026. Bartholomew Dalton and Caroline Liggins, Oxford University Press. © Oxford University Press 2026.
DOI: 10.1093/oso/9780198963943.003.0038

Definitive Guideline on Sentencing Children and Young People, paras 3.1 and 3.2

3.1 For any child or young person aged under 16 appearing before court there is a statutory requirement that parents/guardians attend during all stages of proceedings, unless the court is satisfied that this would be unreasonable having regard to the circumstances of the case. The court may also enforce this requirement for a young person aged 16 and above if it deems it desirable to do so.

3.2 Although this requirement can cause a delay in the case before the court it is important it is adhered to. If a court does find exception to proceed in the absence of a responsible adult then extra care must be taken to ensure the outcomes are clearly communicated to and understood by the child or young person.

B7.3 Responsibility for financial orders (s 380 SA 2020)

Where the defendant is aged under 16 years, the court *must* order the parent or guardian to pay the fine, costs, surcharge, and compensation if ordered unless:

- he cannot be found; or
- it would be unreasonable to make an order for payment having regard to the circumstances of the case.

Where the defendant is aged 16 or 17 years, the court *may* order the parent or guardian to pay the fine, costs, surcharge, and compensation if ordered unless:

- he cannot be found; or
- it would be unreasonable to make an order for payment having regard to the circumstances of the case.

The court may make such an order in the absence of the parent or guardian where the court has required attendance but they have not attended.

Section 128 SA 2020 states that before making a financial order against a parent or guardian, the court may require details of their circumstances through a financial circumstances order. If there is no cooperation with this inquiry, the court may make such determination as it thinks fit.

Courts need not order parents to pay the victim surcharge if they are the victims of the crime. The liability may be delayed, possibly until the child reaches 18 (see Ministry of Justice Circular 18/13).

B7.3.1 *When is it 'unreasonable' to make a financial order?*

In *R v Sheffield Crown Court, ex p Clarkson* [1986] Cr App R (S) 454, a compensation order payable by a mother who 'had done what she could to keep her son from criminal ways' was quashed. She was also of limited means, and the order meant that it would have taken her more than two years to pay.

In *TA v DPP* [1997] 1 Cr App R (S) 1, [1996] Crim LR 606, QBD, the parent of a child accommodated by the local authority under section 20 of the Children Act 1989 was not reasonably to be ordered to pay a financial penalty.

In *R (M) v Inner London Crown Court* [2003] EWHC 301 (Admin), the policy underlying the legislation meant that it was in the public interest that the financial order be recovered from the parent unless there were special circumstances which made that inappropriate.

In *R v JB* [2004] EWCA Crim 14, there seems to be an assumption that in the absence of parental fault it would be unreasonable to order the parent to pay.

B7.4 Local authorities

A local authority is responsible for payment of financial orders where the authority has parental responsibility for the defendant and the defendant is in the authority's care or is accommodated by it.

An order remanding a young person to the care of the local authority does not confer parental responsibility on the local authority. Parental responsibility is acquired only with a full care order (*North Yorkshire County Council v Selby Youth Court* [1994] 1 All ER 991, QBD).

B7.4.1 *When is it 'unreasonable' to make a financial order?*

In *D and R v DPP* [1995] 16 Cr App R (S) 1040, [1995] Crim LR 748, a local authority that had done everything it reasonably and properly could to protect the public from the criminal behaviour of a young person in its care could not be expected to assume responsibility for financial orders.

In *Bedfordshire County Council v DPP* [1996] 1 Cr App R (S) 322, [1995] Crim LR 962, the court stated that a causal link between the authority's lack of care and the offending needs to be established before the court should order payment of the financial penalty by the authority.

In *Marlowe Child and Family Services Ltd v DPP* [1998] Crim LR 594, a company contracted by the local authority to look after the young person could not be ordered to pay a financial order.

B8 Reporting Restrictions

In the adult court, unlike the youth court, discretionary provisions apply. The court must specifically apply the restrictions which relate to the identification of victims, other witnesses, and defendants by stating in open court that it is doing so. The conflicting demands of Articles 8 and 10 of the European Convention on Human Rights (ECHR) must be balanced (see A25.2.1). Section 39 Children and Young Persons Act 1933 has been disapplied from criminal proceedings, and the relevant provisions are now ss 45 and 45A Youth Justice and Criminal Evidence Act 1999. The latter is considered at A25.1.1.

Youth Justice and Criminal Evidence Act 1999, s 45

45 Power to restrict reporting of criminal proceedings involving persons under 18

(1) This section applies (subject to subsection (2)) in relation to—
- (a) any criminal proceedings in any court (other than a service court) in England and Wales

(2) This section does not apply in relation to any proceedings to which section 49 of the Children and Young Persons Act 1933 applies.

(3) The court may direct that no matter relating to any person concerned in the proceedings shall while he is under the age of 18 be included in any publication if it is likely to lead members of the public to identify him as a person concerned in the proceedings.

(4) The court or an appellate court may by direction ('an excepting direction') dispense, to any extent specified in the excepting direction, with the restrictions imposed by a direction under subsection (3) if it is satisfied that it is necessary in the interests of justice to do so.

(5) The court or an appellate court may also by direction ('an excepting direction') dispense, to any extent specified in the excepting direction, with the restrictions imposed by a direction under subsection (3) if it is satisfied—
- (a) that their effect is to impose a substantial and unreasonable restriction on the reporting of the proceedings, and
- (b) that it is in the public interest to remove or relax that restriction; but no excepting direction shall be given under this subsection by reason only of the fact that the proceedings have been determined in any way or have been abandoned.

(6) When deciding whether to make—
- (a) a direction under subsection (3) in relation to a person, or
- (b) an excepting direction under subsection (4) or (5) by virtue of which the restrictions imposed by a direction under subsection (3) would be dispensed with (to any extent) in relation to a person, the court or (as the case may be) the appellate court shall have regard to the welfare of that person.

(7) For the purposes of subsection (3) any reference to a person concerned in the proceedings is to a person—
- (a) against or in respect of whom the proceedings are taken, or
- (b) who is a witness in the proceedings.

(8) The matters relating to a person in relation to which the restrictions imposed by a direction under subsection (3) apply (if their inclusion in any publication is likely to have the result mentioned in that subsection) include in particular—
- (a) his name,
- (b) his address,

Blackstone's Magistrates' Court Handbook 2026. Bartholomew Dalton and Caroline Liggins, Oxford University Press.
DOI: 10.1093/oso/9780198963943.003.0039

(c) the identity of any school or other educational establishment attended by him,
(d) the identity of any place of work, and
(e) any still or moving picture of him.

(9) A direction under subsection (3) may be revoked by the court or an appellate court.

(10) An excepting direction—
(a) may be given at the time the direction under subsection (3) is given or subsequently; and
(b) may be varied or revoked by the court or an appellate court.

Considering earlier statutory provisions, the following principles were set out in *R (Y) v Aylesbury Crown Court* [2012] EWHC 1140 (Admin):

- The defendant had to satisfy the court that there was a good reason for restriction.
- The good reason for a young person would in most cases be his welfare. Publicity would have significant effects on the young person's prospects and opportunities.
- The court must have regard to Article 10 ECHR. A restriction order must be necessary and proportionate, and for a pressing social need. There was a public interest in knowing the outcome of proceedings.
- There is a balance to be struck. Prior to conviction it was unlikely that there should be publicity. After conviction, the age of the defendant and seriousness of the crime would be particularly relevant.
- Partial publicity was possible.
- If there was an even balance there should be no publicity.

B9 Sentencing

B9.1 Overview

Only the following sentencing options are available in relation to children appearing in the adult court. Any case requiring a greater sentence must be remitted to the youth court (see **B6**).

Age (last birthday)	10–13	14	15	16–17
Absolute discharge	Yes	Yes	Yes	Yes
Conditional discharge (note that a conditional discharge cannot be imposed if the offender has received a final warning/ youth caution in the previous 24 months unless exceptional circumstances are found). A conditional discharge in respect to a youth can be for a maximum period of 3 years.	Yes	Yes	Yes	Yes
Fine	Yes: maximum £250. Order must be made against parent/ guardian unless unreasonable in the circumstances	Yes: maximum £1,000. Order must be made against parent/ guardian unless unreasonable in the circumstances	Yes: maximum £1,000. Order must be made against parent/ guardian unless unreasonable in the circumstances	Yes: maximum £1,000
Referral order	Yes	Yes	Yes	Yes

Blackstone's Magistrates' Court Handbook 2026. Bartholomew Dalton and Caroline Liggins, Oxford University Press.
DOI: 10.1093/oso/9780198963943.003.0040

B9.2 Victim surcharge

The court must add the relevant victim surcharge which for youths is as follows:

Offenders under 18 years at the time the offence was committed	Victim surcharge for offences:	
	Before 16 June 2022	on or after 16 June 2022
A conditional discharge	£17	£20
A fine	£22	£26
Referral order	£22	£26

B9.3 Referral orders

The adult court (unless it remits to the youth court) shall make a referral order in circumstances where, in the youth court, such an order must be made. This obligation arises under s 84 SA 2020 (s 17(1) PCCSA 2000) where:

- the offence is punishable with imprisonment;
- the offender has pleaded guilty to the offence(s);
- the court is not imposing an absolute or conditional discharge, a hospital order, or a custodial sentence;
- the offender has never previously been convicted (in the United Kingdom) of an offence or bound over.

B9.4 Ancillary powers

In addition to exercising these powers, the court may make ancillary orders such as:

- an order (under s 376 SA 2020 (s 150 PCCSA 2000)) binding over a parent or guardian to take proper care of the youth and exercise proper care over him, or a parenting order;
- ancillary orders such as disqualification from driving, endorsement of a driving licence, and to pay compensation and costs.

See *Blackstone's Criminal Practice 2026* D24.96

B10 Summary Trials Involving Children

Before the trial of a child in the adult court can begin, it is necessary to check the ability of the child to understand the procedure.

B10.1 Capacity of the child to take part

It is necessary to consider the child's intellectual capacity to understand the proceedings.

There have been a number of cases where the defence have sought to raise a capacity issue, namely, that the defendant, whether due to immaturity or mental capacity, is unable to understand the proceedings, such that it would be an abuse of process to continue on the ground that he could not have a fair trial.

The elements of a fair trial (in this regard) are:

- the defendant had to understand what he is said to have done wrong;
- the court had to be satisfied that the defendant, when he had done wrong by act or omission, had the means of knowing that was wrong;
- he had to understand what, if any, defences were available to him;
- he had to have a reasonable opportunity to make relevant representations if he wished;
- he had to have the opportunity to consider what representation he wished to make once he understood the issues involved;
- he had, therefore, to be able to give proper instructions and to participate by way of providing answers to questions and suggesting questions to his lawyers in the circumstances of the trial as they arose.

The following guidance on how to approach the issue was issued by the court in *CPS v P* [2007] EWHC 946 (Admin):

- the fitness to plead procedure (in so far as it applies in the magistrates' court—see **A20**) does not provide a complete answer to the defendant who lacks capacity, as there are fair trial issues to consider under Article 6 ECHR;
- in an exceptional case there may be grounds to stay a case as an abuse of process if the child lacks capacity;
- medical evidence on the issue is not decisive;
- before considering a stay, the court should consider conducting a fact-finding exercise with a view to a medical disposal under the Mental Health Act 1983 in appropriate cases.

It can be seen, therefore, that only in cases where the capacity issue is not linked to mental health, or a mental health disposal is not appropriate, will a court consider a stay of proceedings.

Blackstone's Magistrates' Court Handbook 2026. Bartholomew Dalton and Caroline Liggins, Oxford University Press. © Oxford University Press 2026.
DOI: 10.1093/oso/9780198963943.003.0041

B10.2 Assistance to the defendant

B10.2.1 *Live link direction for vulnerable young defendants*

The court has power to allow a vulnerable young defendant to give evidence via live link (Youth Justice and Criminal Evidence Act 1999, s 33A). An application is made under section 33A on the basis that the defendant's ability to participate effectively is compromised by his level of intellectual ability or social functioning. The fact that the defendant has a temper and does not like being challenged by authority is not a characteristic of social functioning. An expert report on communication with young people is not essential but can be of assistance (*R v Rahman* [2015] EWCA Crim 15).

In the case of *Kadir* [2022] EWCA Crim 1244 the Court of Appeal Criminal Division gave important guidance on the use of live link evidence from abroad and, more specifically, the use of WhatsApp.

This decision translates not only as an acknowledgement by the courts of the ever-growing presence of social media in people's everyday lives, but also as an effort to utilize the technological tools made available by the internet, to improve access to justice. It is likely to be particularly effective for younger witnesses, as it would allow them to testify in an alternative environment more suited to their needs. See the Direction 5.5, where it is lawful and in the interests of justice to do so, courts should exercise their statutory and other powers to conduct hearings by live link, The Live Link in Criminal Courts Guidance issued by the Lord Chief Justice must be complied with.

Youth Justice and Criminal Evidence Act 1999, s 33A

33A Live link directions

(1) This section applies to any proceedings (whether in a magistrates' court or before the Crown Court) against a person for an offence.

(2) The court may, on the application of the accused, give a live link direction if it is satisfied—
- (a) that the conditions in subsection (4) or, as the case may be, subsection (5) are met in relation to the accused, and
- (b) that it is in the interests of justice for the accused to give evidence through a live link.

(3) A live link direction is a direction that any oral evidence to be given before the court by the accused is to be given through a live link.

(4) Where the accused is aged under 18 when the application is made, the conditions are that—
- (a) his ability to participate effectively in the proceedings as a witness giving oral evidence in court is compromised by his level of intellectual ability or social functioning, and
- (b) use of a live link would enable him to participate more effectively in the proceedings as a witness (whether by improving the quality of his evidence or otherwise).

(5) Where the accused has attained the age of 18 at that time, the conditions are that—
- (a) he suffers from a mental disorder (within the meaning of the Mental Health Act 1983) or otherwise has a significant impairment of intelligence and social function,

(b) he is for that reason unable to participate effectively in the proceedings as a witness giving oral evidence in court, and

(c) use of a live link would enable him to participate more effectively in the proceedings as a witness (whether by improving the quality of his evidence or otherwise).

(6) While a live link direction has effect the accused may not give oral evidence before the court in the proceedings otherwise than through a live link.

(7) The court may discharge a live link direction at any time before or during any hearing to which it applies if it appears to the court to be in the interests of justice to do so (but this does not affect the power to give a further live link direction in relation to the accused).

The court may exercise this power of its own motion or on an application by a party.

(8) The court must state in open court its reasons for—

(a) giving or discharging a live link direction, or

(b) refusing an application for or for the discharge of a live link direction, and, if it is a magistrates' court, it must cause those reasons to be entered in the register of its proceedings.

B10.2.2 *Examination of accused through intermediary*

In *R (C) v Sevenoaks Youth Court* [2009] EWHC 3088 (Admin), the court held that an intermediary could be appointed under the court's common law power to ensure a fair trial process, until such time as statutory provisions are brought into force. In *R (AS) v Great Yarmouth Youth Court* [2011] EWHC 2059 (Admin), the court held that it was irrational to ignore the need for an intermediary of a child suffering from attention deficit and hyperactive disorder (ADHD).

B10.3 **Further assistance**

The Criminal Practice Directions give further assistance. The relevant provisions are in section 6.2. See also Crim PR 18.19 to 18.24. Further information is in Intermediaries: Step by Step (Toolkit 16; The Advocate's Gateway, 2015) and chapter 2 of the Equal Treatment Bench Book (Judicial College, May 2025 update). See Crim PR 18 *R v Cox, R (OP) v Ministry of Justice* [2014] EWHC 1944 (Admin), and *R v Rashid* [2017] EWCA Crim 2 for other measures designed to accommodate the needs of a vulnerable defendants.

Part C
Offences

C1 Animal Offences

C1.1 Animal cruelty

Sections 4, 5, 6, 7, 8, and 9 Animal Welfare Act 2006 provide for offences in relation to unnecessary suffering, mutilation, docking of dogs' tails, administration of poisons, and fighting.

Animal Welfare Act 2006, ss 4(1)–(2), 5(1)–(2), (6), 6(1)–(12), 7, 8, and 9

4 Unnecessary suffering

(1) A person commits an offence if—
- (a) an act of his, or a failure of his to act, causes an animal to suffer,
- (b) he knew, or ought reasonably to have known, that the act, or failure to act, would have that effect or be likely to do so,
- (c) the animal is a protected animal, and
- (d) the suffering is unnecessary.

(2) A person commits an offence if—
- (a) he is responsible for an animal,
- (b) an act, or failure to act, of another person causes the animal to suffer,
- (c) he permitted that to happen or failed to take such steps (whether by way of supervising the other person or otherwise) as were reasonable in all the circumstances to prevent that happening, and
- (d) the suffering is unnecessary . . .

5 Mutilation

(1) A person commits an offence if—
- (a) he carries out a prohibited procedure on a protected animal;
- (b) he causes such a procedure to be carried out on such an animal.

(2) A person commits an offence if—
- (a) he is responsible for an animal,
- (b) another person carries out a prohibited procedure on the animal, and
- (c) he permitted that to happen or failed to take such steps (whether by way of supervising the other person or otherwise) as were reasonable in all the circumstances to prevent that happening.

. . .

(6) Nothing in this section applies to the removal of the whole or any part of a dog's tail.

6 Docking of dogs' tails

(1) A person commits an offence if—
- (a) he removes the whole or any part of a dog's tail, otherwise than for the purpose of its medical treatment;
- (b) he causes the whole or any part of a dog's tail to be removed by another person, otherwise than for the purpose of its medical treatment.

(2) A person commits an offence if—
- (a) he is responsible for a dog,
- (b) another person removes the whole or any part of the dog's tail, otherwise than for the purpose of its medical treatment, and
- (c) he permitted that to happen or failed to take such steps (whether by way of supervising the other person or otherwise) as were reasonable in all the circumstances to prevent that happening.

Blackstone's Magistrates' Court Handbook 2026. Bartholomew Dalton and Caroline Liggins, Oxford University Press. © Oxford University Press 2026.
DOI: 10.1093/oso/9780198963943.003.0042

(3) Subsections (1) and (2) do not apply if the dog is a certified working dog that is not more than 5 days old.
(4) For the purposes of subsection (3), a dog is a certified working dog if a veterinary surgeon has certified, in accordance with regulations made by the appropriate national authority, that the first and second conditions mentioned below are met.
(5) The first condition referred to in subsection (4) is that there has been produced to the veterinary surgeon such evidence as the appropriate national authority may by regulations require for the purpose of showing that the dog is likely to be used for work in connection with—
    (a) law enforcement,
    (b) activities of Her Majesty's armed forces,
    (c) emergency rescue,
    (d) lawful pest control, or
    (e) the lawful shooting of animals.
(6) The second condition referred to in subsection (4) is that the dog is of a type specified for the purposes of this subsection by regulations made by the appropriate national authority.
(7) It is a defence for a person accused of an offence under subsection (1) or to show that he reasonably believed that the dog was one in relation to which subsection (3) applies.
(8) A person commits an offence if—
    (a) he owns a subsection (3) dog, and
    (b) fails to take reasonable steps to secure that, before the dog is 3 months old, it is identified as a subsection (3) dog in accordance with regulations made by the appropriate national authority.
(9) A person commits an offence if—
    (a) he shows a dog at an event to which members of the public are admitted on payment of a fee,
    (b) the dog's tail has been wholly or partly removed (in England and Wales or elsewhere), and
    (c) removal took place on or after the commencement day.
(10) Where a dog is shown only for the purpose of demonstrating its working ability, subsection (9) does not apply if the dog is a subsection (3) dog.
(11) It is a defence for a person accused of an offence under subsection (9) to show that he reasonably believed—
    (a) that the event was not one to which members of the public were admitted on payment of an entrance fee,
    (b) that the removal took place before the commencement day, or
    (c) that the dog was one in relation to which subsection (10) applies.
(12) A person commits an offence if he knowingly gives false information to a veterinary surgeon in connection with the giving of a certificate for the purposes of this section.

7 Administration of poisons etc

(1) A person commits an offence if, without lawful authority or reasonable excuse, he—
    (a) administers any poisonous or injurious drug or substance to a protected animal, knowing it to be poisonous or injurious, or
    (b) causes any poisonous or injurious drug or substance to be taken by a protected animal, knowing it to be poisonous or injurious.
(2) A person commits an offence if—
    (a) he is responsible for an animal,
    (b) without lawful authority or reasonable excuse, another person administers a poisonous or injurious drug or substance to the animal or causes the animal to take such a drug or substance, and

(c) he permitted that to happen or, knowing the drug or substance to be poisonous or injurious, he failed to take such steps (whether by way of supervising the other person or otherwise) as were reasonable in all the circumstances to prevent that happening.

(3) In this section, references to a poisonous or injurious drug or substance include a drug or substance which, by virtue of the quantity or manner in which it is administered or taken, has the effect of a poisonous or injurious drug or substance.

8 Fighting etc

(1) A person commits an offence if he—
- (a) causes an animal fight to take place, or attempts to do so;
- (b) knowingly receives money for admission to an animal fight;
- (c) knowingly publicises a proposed animal fight;
- (d) provides information about an animal fight to another with the intention of enabling or encouraging attendance at the fight;
- (e) makes or accepts a bet on the outcome of an animal fight or on the likelihood of anything occurring or not occurring in the course of an animal fight;
- (f) takes part in an animal fight;
- (g) has in his possession anything designed or adapted for use in connection with an animal fight with the intention of its being so used;
- (h) keeps or trains an animal for use for in connection with an animal fight;
- (i) keeps any premises for use for an animal fight.

(2) A person commits an offence if, without lawful authority or reasonable excuse, he is present at an animal fight.

(3) A person commits an offence if, without lawful authority or reasonable excuse, he—
- (a) knowingly supplies a video recording of an animal fight,
- (b) knowingly publishes a video recording of an animal fight,
- (c) knowingly shows a video recording of an animal fight to another, or
- (d) possesses a video recording of an animal fight, knowing it to be such a recording, with the intention of supplying it.

(4) Subsection (3) does not apply if the video recording is of an animal fight that took place—
- (a) outside Great Britain, or
- (b) before the commencement date.

(5) Subsection (3) does not apply—
- (a) in the case of paragraph (a), to the supply of a video recording for inclusion in a programme service;
- (b) in the case of paragraph (b) or (c), to the publication or showing of a video recording by means of its inclusion in a programme service;
- (c) in the case of paragraph (d), by virtue of intention to supply for inclusion in a programme service.

. . .

(7) In this section—

'animal fight' means an occasion on which a protected animal is placed with an animal, or with a human, for the purpose of fighting, wrestling or baiting; . . .

'programme service' has the same meaning as in the Communications Act 2003 (c. 21);

'video recording' means a recording, in any form, from which a moving image may by any means be reproduced and includes data stored on a computer disc or by other electronic means which is capable of conversion into a moving image.

(8) In this section—
- (a) references to supplying or publishing a video recording are to supplying or publishing a video recording in any manner, including, in relation to a video recording in the form of data stored electronically, by means of transmitting such data;

(b) references to showing a video recording are to showing a moving image reproduced from a video recording by any means.

9 Duty of person responsible for animal to ensure welfare

(1) A person commits an offence if he does not take such steps as are reasonable in all the circumstances to ensure that the needs of an animal for which he is responsible are met to the extent required by good practice.

(2) For the purposes of this Act, an animal's needs shall be taken to include—
 (a) its need for a suitable environment,
 (b) its need for a suitable diet,
 (c) its need to be able to exhibit normal behaviour patterns,
 (d) any need it has to be housed with, or apart from, other animals, and
 (e) its need to be protected from pain, suffering, injury and disease.

(3) The circumstances to which it is relevant to have regard when applying subsection
 (1) include, in particular—
 (a) any lawful purpose for which the animal is kept, and
 (b) any lawful activity undertaken in relation to the animal.

(4) Nothing in this section applies to the destruction of an animal in an appropriate and humane manner.

EW s 4, 5, 6(1), 6(2), 7, and 8

SO s 9, but note that a magistrates' court may try an information relating to an offence under this Act if the information is laid:

(a) before the end of the period of 3 years beginning with the date of the commission of the offence; and
(b) before the end of the period of 6 months beginning with the date on which evidence which the prosecutor thinks is sufficient to justify the proceedings comes to his knowledge.

ss 4, 5, 6(1), 6(2), 7, and 8: Fine and/or 12 months'/5 years' imprisonment

s 9: Fine and/or 6 months' imprisonment

C1.1.1 *Sentencing*

SCG Animal cruelty

C1.1.2 Key points

General

- The 6-month limitation period for summary offences under this Act can be disapplied in certain circumstances (see s 31 of the 2006 Act, *RSPCA v Johnson* [2009] EWHC 2702 (Admin) and the cases at A12.1.3).
- References to a person responsible for an animal are to a person responsible for an animal, whether on a permanent or a temporary basis.
- References to being responsible for an animal include being in charge of it.
- A person who owns an animal shall always be regarded as being a person who is responsible for it.

- A person shall be treated as responsible for any animal for which a person under the age of 16 years of whom he has actual care and control is responsible.
- Protected animal refers to an animal commonly domesticated in the British Isles, under the control of man, or not living in a wild state.

Section 4

Section 4 is to be interpreted so as to require the Crown to prove that the defendant knew or ought to have known that the suffering was unnecessary. *Riley v CPS* [2016] EWHC 2531 (Admin) confirms that an offence under s 4(1) has an element of *mens rea* (permitting unnecessary suffering) and so partners in a business could not be liable for events in their absence when there was no allegation of a systemic failure or a proper joint charge.

Section 8

Section 8(1)(h) is to be interpreted to include those who have actual physical possession as well as those who retain control of the animal while it is elsewhere. The keeper of an animal may have it in their own home or retain it in the home or place of another. Equally a person may themselves train the animal to fight or arrange for another to carry out the training for them. There is no sensible basis to restrict the interpretation of s 8(1)(h) to the person who has actual physical possession or actually does the training themselves; to do so would unnecessarily restrict the offence and the policy of the legislation to criminalize those who are involved in training animals to fight (*Wright v Reading Crown Court* [2017] EWHC 2643 (Admin)).

In *RSPCA v McCormick* [2016] EWHC 928 (Admin) 'animal fight' in s 8(7) was held to mean an occasion on which a protected animal (an animal under control) is placed with an animal, or a human, for the purpose of fighting, wrestling, or baiting. The effect is that the other animal must also be under some degree of control and not wild. The case confirmed that, while s 8(7) is aimed at animal fights that are organized or controlled, the payment of money does not have to be involved.

Section 9

The considerations to which it is relevant to have regard when determining for the purposes of this section whether suffering is unnecessary include:

- whether the suffering could reasonably have been avoided or reduced;
- whether the conduct which caused the suffering was in compliance with any relevant enactment or any relevant provisions of a licence or code of practice issued under an enactment;
- whether the conduct which caused the suffering was for a legitimate purpose, such as:
  - benefiting the animal, or
  - protecting a person, property, or another animal;
- whether the suffering was proportionate to the purpose of the conduct concerned;
- whether the conduct concerned was in all the circumstances that of a reasonably competent and humane person.

Nothing in this section applies to the destruction of an animal in an appropriate and humane manner.

A conviction should not be recorded under s 9, where the standard is objective, when there is a conviction under s 4 and the offending behaviour is no wider (*R (Gray and Gray) v Aylesbury Crown Court* [2013] EWHC 500 (Admin)).

The welfare offence in this section extends to non-farmed animals; similar provisions are found in the Welfare of Farmed Animals (England) Regulations 2000 (SI 2000/1870) (made under Part 1 of the Agriculture (Miscellaneous Provisions) Act 1968), which ensure the welfare of livestock situated on agricultural land. A duty to ensure welfare will therefore apply to all animals for which someone is responsible, as defined in s 3. Where someone is responsible for an animal, he has a duty to take steps that are reasonable in all the circumstances to ensure its needs are met to the extent required by good practice (s 9(1)).

Section 9(3) specifies certain matters to which the courts should have regard when considering whether a person has committed an offence under this section. The provision recognizes that some otherwise lawful practices may prevent or hinder a person from ensuring that all of the welfare needs specified in s 9(2) can be met, and requires the courts to take this into account when considering what is reasonable in the circumstances of the case.

Expenses:

Where there is a conviction under s 8, there is power to order the reimbursement of the expenses in keeping the animal (s 39 Animal Welfare Act 2006). Section 18 contains powers for the court to make orders for expenses where an animal is in distress. There are powers to make orders towards the expense of carrying out the court's orders in ss 33, 36, 37, 38, and 41. However, the cost of otherwise keeping an animal cannot be classified as prosecution costs (*R (Donovan) v Burnley Crown Court* [2014] EWHC 742 (Admin)).

C1.1.3 *Ancillary orders*

The High Court, commenting that the Sentencing Guideline did not assist on ancillary orders, gave the following guidance in relation to orders made under ss 33 and 34 Animal Welfare Act 2006 for s 9 cases in *Barker and another v RSPCA* [2018] EWHC 880:

(1) There can be an 'all animals' order, that is to say a prohibition against owning, keeping, etc. of any animals. An example in an extreme case would be a case where there was no insight whatever into the need to protect the welfare of the animals in question and a culture of uncaring indifference towards them. An 'all animals' prohibition is not wrong in principle in a section 9 case. A person's treatment of a dog may shed light on his likely treatment of a cat or a parrot.
(2) There can be an order covering some kinds of animals but not others.

(3) There can an exclusory order, that is to say an order prohibiting the ownership, etc of all animals except those of certain kinds by reference to their genus of species although under section 34(5) it is not permissible to prohibit the ownership etc of individual animals.

The purpose of the disqualification was protection, not punishment. It was for the sentencing courts to select what they considered the appropriate period of disqualification, up to and including disqualification for life.

C1.1.3.1 Deprivation order

Section 33 Animal Welfare Act 2006 provides for a convicted person to be deprived of his animals:

Animal Welfare Act 2006, s 33

33 Deprivation

(1) If the person convicted of an offence under any of sections 4, 5, 6(1) and (2), 7, 8 and 9 is the owner of an animal in relation to which the offence was committed, the court by or before which he is convicted may, instead of or in addition to dealing with him in any other way, make an order depriving him of ownership of the animal and for its disposal.

(2) Where the owner of an animal is convicted of an offence under section 34(9) because ownership of the animal is in breach of a disqualification under section 34(2), the court by or before which he is convicted may, instead of or in addition to dealing with him in any other way, make an order depriving him of ownership of the animal and for its disposal.

(3) Where the animal in respect of which an order under subsection (1) or (2) is made has any dependent offspring, the order may include provision depriving the person to whom it relates of ownership of the offspring and for its disposal.

(4) Where a court makes an order under subsection (1) or (2), it may—
  (a) appoint a person to carry out, or arrange for the carrying out of, the order;
  (b) require any person who has possession of an animal to which the order applies to deliver it up to enable the order to be carried out;
  (c) give directions with respect to the carrying out of the order;
  (d) confer additional powers (including power to enter premises where an animal to which the order applies is being kept) for the purpose of, or in connection with, the carrying out of the order;
  (e) order the offender to reimburse the expenses of carrying out the order.

(5) Directions under subsection (4)(c) may—
  (a) specify the manner in which an animal is to be disposed of, or
  (b) delegate the decision about the manner in which an animal is to be disposed of to a person appointed under subsection (4)(a) . . . .

(8) In subsection (1), the reference to an animal in relation to which an offence was committed includes, in the case of an offence under section 8, an animal which took part in an animal fight in relation to which the offence was committed.

(9) In this section, references to disposing of an animal include destroying it.

C1.1.3.2 Disqualification order

Section 34 Animal Welfare Act 2006 provides for disqualification orders to be made against convicted persons, thereby making it an offence for them to be involved with owning, keeping, or otherwise in the control of animals:

Animal Welfare Act 2006, s 34

34 Disqualification

(1) If a person is convicted of an offence to which this section applies, the court by or before which he is convicted may, instead of or in addition to dealing with him in any other way, make an order disqualifying him under any one or more of subsections (2) to (4) for such period as it thinks fit.

(2) Disqualification under this subsection disqualifies a person—

(a) from owning animals,

(b) from keeping animals,

(c) from participating in the keeping of animals, and

(d) from being party to an arrangement under which he is entitled to control or influence the way in which animals are kept.

(3) Disqualification under this subsection disqualifies a person from dealing in animals.

(4) Disqualification under this subsection disqualifies a person—

(a) from transporting animals, and

(b) from arranging for the transport of animals.

(5) Disqualification under subsection (2), (3) or (4) may be imposed in relation to animals generally, or in relation to animals of one or more kinds.

(6) The court by which an order under subsection (1) is made may specify a period during which the offender may not make an application under section 43(1) for termination of the order.

(7) The court by which an order under subsection (1) is made may—

(a) suspend the operation of the order pending an appeal, or

(b) where it appears to the court that the offender owns or keeps an animal to which the order applies, suspend the operation of the order, and of any order made under section 35 in connection with the disqualification, for such period as it thinks necessary for enabling alternative arrangements to be made in respect of the animal.

. . .

(9) A person who breaches a disqualification imposed by an order under subsection (1) commits an offence [carrying a . . . fine and/or 6 months' imprisonment (s 32(2))].

(10) This section applies to an offence under any of sections 4, 5, 6(1) and (2), 7, 8, 9 and 13(6) and subsection (9).

SO

Fine and/or 6 months' imprisonment (see s 32(2))

C1.1.3.2.1 *Sentencing*

SCG **Breach of disqualification from keeping an animal**

C1.1.3.2.2 Key points: Sentencing

When considering making a disqualification order under s 4 of the Act, regard can be had to any previous convictions (*Ward v RSPCA* [2010] EWHC 347). To be in breach of a disqualification order (s 34(2) of the Animal Welfare Act 2006) by participating in the keeping of animals or being party to an arrangement under which the defendant is entitled to control or influence the way in which animals are kept, there must be something more than contact with, or mere influence on the keeping of, the animals. There must be evidence of an entitlement to control the animals (*Patterson v RSPCA* [2013] EWHC 4531 (Admin)).

The High Court, in *Barker and another v RSPCA* [2018] EWHC 880 (see C1.1.2), identified that the purpose of the disqualification was protection, not punishment. It was for the sentencing courts to select what they considered the appropriate period of disqualification, up to and including disqualification for life.

C1.1.3.3 Destruction orders

Sections 37 and 38 Animal Welfare Act 2006 allow for destruction orders to be made in appropriate cases:

Animal Welfare Act 2006, ss 37 and 38

37 Destruction in the interests of the animal

(1) The court by or before which a person is convicted of an offence under any of sections 4, 5, 6(1) and (2), 7, 8(1) and (2) and 9 may order the destruction of an animal in relation to which the offence was committed if it is satisfied, on the basis of evidence given by a veterinary surgeon, that it is appropriate to do so in the interests of the animal.

(2) A court may not make an order under subsection (1) unless—
  - (a) it has given the owner of the animal an opportunity to be heard, or
  - (b) it is satisfied that it is not reasonably practicable to communicate with the owner.

(3) Where a court makes an order under subsection (1), it may—
  - (a) appoint a person to carry out, or arrange for the carrying out of, the order;
  - (b) require a person who has possession of the animal to deliver it up to enable the order to be carried out;
  - (c) give directions with respect to the carrying out of the order (including directions about how the animal is to be dealt with until it is destroyed);
  - (d) confer additional powers (including power to enter premises where the animal is being kept) for the purpose of, or in connection with, the carrying out of the order;
  - (e) order the offender or another person to reimburse the expenses of carrying out the order.

(4) Where a court makes an order under subsection (1), each of the offender and, if different, the owner of the animal may—
  - (a) in the case of an order made by a magistrates' court, appeal against the order to the Crown Court;
  - (b) in the case of an order made by the Crown Court, appeal against the order to the Court of Appeal.

(5) Subsection (4) does not apply if the court by which the order is made directs that it is appropriate in the interests of the animal that the carrying out of the order should not be delayed.

(6) In subsection (1), the reference to an animal in relation to which an offence was committed includes, in the case of an offence under section 8(1) or (2), an animal which took part in an animal fight in relation to which the offence was committed.

38 Destruction of animals involved in fighting offences

(1) The court by or before which a person is convicted of an offence under section 8(1) or (2) may order the destruction of an animal in relation to which the offence was committed on grounds other than the interests of the animal.

(2) A court may not make an order under subsection (1) unless—
  (a) it has given the owner of the animal an opportunity to be heard, or
  (b) it is satisfied that it is not reasonably practicable to communicate with the owner.
(3) Where a court makes an order under subsection (1), it may—
  (a) appoint a person to carry out, or arrange for the carrying out of, the order;
  (b) require a person who has possession of the animal to deliver it up to enable the order to be carried out;
  (c) give directions with respect to the carrying out of the order (including directions about how the animal is to be dealt with until it is destroyed);
  (d) confer additional powers (including power to enter premises where the animal is being kept) for the purpose of, or in connection with, the carrying out of the order;
  (e) order the offender or another person to reimburse the expenses of carrying out the order.
(4) Where a court makes an order under subsection (1) in relation to an animal which is owned by a person other than the offender, that person may—
  (a) in the case of an order made by a magistrates' court, appeal against the order to the Crown Court;
  (b) in the case of an order made by the Crown Court, appeal against the order to the Court of Appeal.
(5) In subsection (1), the reference to an animal in relation to which the offence was committed includes an animal which took part in an animal fight in relation to which the offence was committed.

See *Blackstone's Criminal Practice 2026* **B20.17**

C1.2 Dangerous dogs

C1.2.1 *Dogs bred for fighting*

Dangerous Dogs Act 1991, s 1

(1) This section applies to—
  (a) any dog of the type known as the pit bull terrier;
  (b) any dog of the type known as the Japanese tosa; and
  (c) any dog of any type designated for the purposes of this section by an order of the Secretary of State, being a type appearing to him to be bred for fighting or to have the characteristics of a type bred for that purpose.
(2) No person shall—
  (a) breed, or breed from, a dog to which this section applies;
  (b) sell or exchange such a dog or offer, advertise or expose such a dog for sale or exchange;
  (c) make or offer to make a gift of such a dog or advertise or expose such a dog as a gift;
  (d) allow such a dog of which he is the owner or of which he is for the time being in charge to be in a public place without being muzzled and kept on a lead; or
  (e) abandon such a dog of which he is the owner or, being the owner or for the time being in charge of such a dog, allow it to stray.
(3) After [30 November 1991] no person shall have any dog to which this section applies in his possession or custody except—
  (a) in pursuance of the power of seizure conferred by the subsequent provisions of this Act; or

(b) in accordance with an order for its destruction made under those provisions;

(c) but the Secretary of State shall by order make a scheme for the payment to the owners of such dogs who arrange for them to be destroyed before that day of sums specified in or determined under the scheme in respect of those dogs and the cost of their destruction.

(4) Subsection (2)(b) and (c) above shall not make unlawful anything done with a view to the dog in question being removed from the United Kingdom before the day appointed under subsection (3) above.

(5) The Secretary of State may by order provide that the prohibition in subsection (3) above shall not apply in such cases and subject to compliance with such conditions as are specified in the order and any such provision may take the form of a scheme of exemption containing such arrangements (including provision for the payment of charges or fees) as he thinks appropriate.

(6) A scheme under subsection (3) or (5) above may provide for specified functions under the scheme to be discharged by such persons or bodies as the Secretary of State thinks.

(6A) A scheme under subsection (3) or (5) may in particular include provision requiring a court to consider whether a person is a fit and proper person to be in charge of a dog appropriate.

(7) Any person who contravenes this section is guilty of an offence and liable on summary conviction to imprisonment for a term not exceeding six months or a fine or both except that a person who publishes an advertisement in contravention of subsection (2)(b) or (c)—

(a) shall not on being convicted be liable to imprisonment if he shows that he published the advertisement to the order of someone else and did not himself devise it; and

(b) shall not be convicted if, in addition, he shows that he did not know and had no reasonable cause to suspect that it related to a dog to which this section applies.

SO

Fine and/or 6 months' imprisonment

Key points: Sentencing In relation to an offence under s 1(2)(b) or (c), see s 1(7) which limits liability and sentence in certain circumstances.

Key points

- For 'type' see *Crown Court at Knightsbridge, ex p Dune* [1993] 4 All ER 491

- There are no defences in relation to s 1 (see *DPP v Kellett* (1994) 158 JP 1138 (intoxication) and *Cichon v DPP* [1994] Crim LR (welfare of the animal—unmuzzling to allow the dog to be sick)).

C1.2.1.1 *Sentencing*

SCG **Possession of a prohibited dog/Breeding, selling, exchanging or advertising a prohibited dog**

C1.2.1.2 *Ancillary orders (see C1.2.3)*

The guideline advises that ancillary orders available include:

Disqualification from having a dog

The court **may** disqualify the offender from having custody of a dog for such period as it thinks fit. The test the court should consider is whether the offender is a fit and proper person to have custody of a dog.

Destruction order/contingent destruction order

In any case where the offender is not the owner of the dog, the owner must be given an opportunity to be present and make representations to the court. The court **shall** make a destruction order unless the court is satisfied that the dog would not constitute a danger to public safety. In reaching a decision, the court should consider the relevant circumstances, which must include:

- the temperament of the dog and its past behaviour;
- whether the owner of the dog, or the person for the time being in charge of it, is a fit and proper person to be in charge of the dog;

and **may** include:

- other relevant circumstances.

If the court is satisfied that the dog would not constitute a danger to public safety, it **shall** make a contingent destruction order requiring that the dog be exempted from the prohibition on possession or custody within the requisite period.

Where the court makes a destruction order, it **may** appoint a person to undertake destruction and order the offender to pay what it determines to be the reasonable expenses of destroying the dog and keeping it pending its destruction.

Fit and proper person

In determining whether a person is a fit and proper person to be in charge of a dog the following non-exhaustive factors may be relevant:

- any relevant previous convictions, cautions, or penalty notices;
- the nature and suitability of the premises that the dog is to be kept at by the person;
- where the police have released the dog pending the court's decision, whether the person has breached conditions imposed by the police; and
- any relevant previous breaches of court orders.

Note: the court must be satisfied that the person who is assessed by the court as a fit and proper person can demonstrate that they are the owner or the person ordinarily in charge of that dog at the time the court is considering whether the dog is a danger to public safety. Someone who has previously not been in charge of the dog should not be considered for this assessment, because it is an offence under the Dangerous Dogs Act 1991 to make a gift of a prohibited dog.

C1.2.2 *Dangerous Dogs Act 1991*

Keeping dogs under proper control, s 3

(1) If a dog is dangerously out of control in any place in England or Wales (whether or not a public place)—
   (a) the owner; and
   (b) if different, the person for the time being in charge of the dog, is guilty of an offence, or, if the dog while so out of control injures any person or assistance dog, an aggravated offence, under this subsection.

(1A) A person ('D') is not guilty of an offence under subsection (1) in a case which is a householder case.

(1B) For the purposes of subsection (1A) 'a householder case' is a case where—
   (a) the dog is dangerously out of control while in or partly in a building, or part of a building, that is a dwelling or is forces accommodation (or is both), and
   (b) at that time—
      (i) the person in relation to whom the dog is dangerously out of control ('V') is in, or is entering, the building or part as a trespasser, or
      (ii) D (if present at that time) believed V to be in, or entering, the building or part as a trespasser.

Section 76(8B) to (8F) of the Criminal Justice and Immigration Act 2008 (use of force at place of residence) apply for the purposes of this subsection as they apply for the purposes of subsection (8A) of that section (and for those purposes the reference in section 76(8D) to subsection (8A)(d) is to be read as if it were a reference to paragraph (b)(ii) of this subsection).

(2) In proceedings for an offence under subsection (1) above against a person who is the owner of a dog but was not at the material time in charge of it, it shall be a defence for the accused to prove that the dog was at the material time in the charge of a person whom he reasonably believed to be a fit and proper person to be in charge of it.

. . .

(4) A person guilty of an offence under subsection (1) above other than an aggravated offence is liable on summary conviction to imprisonment for a term not exceeding six months or a fine. . . or both; and a person guilty of an aggravated offence under that subsection is liable—
   (a) on summary conviction, to imprisonment for a term not exceeding six months or a fine or both;
   (b) on conviction on indictment, to imprisonment for a term not exceeding the relevant maximum specified in subsection (4A)

   or a fine or both.

(4A) For the purposes of subsection (4)(b), the relevant maximum is—
   (a) 14 years if a person dies as a result of being injured;
   (b) 5 years in any other case where a person is injured;
   (c) 3 years in any case where an assistance dog is injured (whether or not it dies).

(5) It is hereby declared for the avoidance of doubt that an order under section 2 of the Dogs Act 1871 (order on complaint that dog is dangerous and not kept under proper control)—
   (a) may be made whether or not the dog is shown to have injured any person; and
   (b) may specify the measures to be taken for keeping the dog under proper control, whether by muzzling, keeping on a lead, excluding it from specified places or otherwise.

(6) If it appears to a court on a complaint under section 2 of the said Act of 1871 that the dog to which the complaint relates is a male and would be less dangerous if neutered the court may under that section make an order requiring it to be neutered.

(7) The reference in section 1(3) of the Dangerous Dogs Act 1989 (penalties) to failing to comply with an order under section 2 of the said Act of 1871 to keep a dog under proper control shall include a reference to failing to comply with any other order made under that section; but no order shall be made under that section by virtue of subsection (6) above where the matters complained of arose before the coming into force of that subsection.

SO Non-aggravated offence

EW Aggravated offence

Non-aggravated offence: Fine and/or 6 months' imprisonment
Aggravated offence: Fine and/or 12 months' imprisonment/imprisonment as specified in s 4A

Key points: Sentencing

An offence is aggravated if the dog injures a person or assistance dog.

Dangerous Dogs Act 1991, s 3(4) and (4A)

(4) A person guilty of an offence under subsection (1) above other than an aggravated offence is liable on summary conviction to imprisonment for a term not exceeding six months or a fine . . . or both; and a person guilty of an aggravated offence under that subsection is liable—
   (a) on summary conviction, to imprisonment for a term not exceeding six months or a fine or both;
   (b) on conviction on indictment, to imprisonment for a term not exceeding the relevant maximum specified in subsection (4A)

   or a fine or both.

(4A) For the purposes of subsection (4)(b), the relevant maximum is—
   (a) 14 years if a person dies as a result of being injured;
   (b) 5 years in any other case where a person is injured;
   (c) 3 years in any case where an assistance dog is injured (whether or not it dies).

C1.2.2.1 Key points

- 'Dangerously out of control' is defined under s 10(3) of the Act:

Dangerous Dogs Act 1991, s 10(3)

(3) For the purposes of this Act a dog shall be regarded as dangerously out of control on any occasion on which there are grounds for reasonable apprehension that it will injure any person or assistance dog, whether or not it actually does so, but references to a dog injuring a person or assistance dog or there being grounds for reasonable apprehension that it will do so do not include references to any case in which the dog is being used for a lawful purpose by a constable or a person in the service of the Crown.

- As this is a strict liability offence the conduct of any person injured is irrelevant (Royal Mail Group v Watson [2021] EWHC 2098 (Admin) which also considers who is trespasser).
- Although s 3 creates an offence of strict liability, there must still be some causal connection between having charge of the dog and the occurrence of the serious injury (*R v Robinson-Pierre* [2013] EWCA Crim 2396).
- The owner of the dog has a defence under s 3(2) if another fit and proper person was in charge of the dog at the material time. Whether a person is a fit and proper person will depend on all of the circumstances. The dog must have been left with an identifiable person; it was not sufficient merely to say that different members of a family looked after the dog at different times (*R v Huddart* [1999] Crim LR 568).
- It is irrelevant that the owner did not anticipate the behaviour of the dog (*R v Bezzina* (1994) 158 JP 671).
- A person who relinquishes physical control of a dog by passing the lead to another may remain in joint control of the dog (*L v Crown Prosecution Service*, unreported, 10 February 2010). Plain evidence is required to demonstrate that control has been passed to another (*R v Huddart* [1999] Crim LR 568).
- Regard must be had to the behaviour of the dog and the degree of control exercised by its handler. The fact that the dog has not displayed any previous bad traits was of relevance but not conclusive (*R v Gedminintaite* [2008] EWCA Crim 814).

C1.2.2.2 *Sentencing guidelines*

SCG There are four separate sentencing guidelines for offences under s 3(1) Dangerous Dogs Act 1991:

- **Owner or person in charge of a dog dangerously out of control in any place where death is caused**
- **Owner or person in charge of a dog dangerously out of control in any place where a person is injured**
- **Owner or person in charge of a dog dangerously out of control in any place (whether or not a public place) where an assistance dog is injured or killed**
- **Owner or person in charge of a dog dangerously out of control in any place (whether or not a public place)**

Disqualification from having a dog

The court may disqualify the offender from having custody of a dog. The test the court should consider is whether the offender is a fit and proper person to have custody of a dog.

Destruction order/contingent destruction order

In any case where the offender is not the owner of the dog, the owner must be given an opportunity to be present and make representations to the court.

If the dog is a **prohibited dog** refer to the guideline for possession of a prohibited dog in relation to destruction/contingent destruction orders.

The court **shall** make a destruction order unless the court is satisfied that the dog would not constitute a danger to public safety.

In reaching a decision, the court should consider the relevant circumstances which **must** include:

- the temperament of the dog and its past behaviour;
- whether the owner of the dog, or the person for the time being in charge of it is a fit and proper person to be in charge of the dog;

and **may** include:

- other relevant circumstances.

If the court is satisfied that the dog would not constitute a danger to public safety and the dog is not prohibited, it **may** make a contingent destruction order requiring the dog be kept under proper control. A contingent destruction order may specify the measures to be taken by the owner for keeping the dog under proper control, which include:

- muzzling;
- keeping on a lead;
- neutering in appropriate cases; and
- excluding it from a specified place.

Where the court makes a destruction order, it **may** appoint a person to undertake destruction and order the offender to pay what it determines to be the reasonable expenses of destroying the dog and keeping it pending its destruction.

Fit and proper person

In determining whether a person is a fit and proper person to be in charge of a dog the following non-exhaustive factors may be relevant:

- any relevant previous convictions, cautions or penalty notices;
- the nature and suitability of the premises that the dog is to be kept at by the person;
- where the police have released the dog pending the court's decision whether the person has breached conditions imposed by the police; and
- any relevant previous breaches of court orders.

Other ancillary orders available (see **C1.2.3**) include:

C1.2.3 *Destruction and disqualification orders*

Dangerous Dogs Act 1991, s 4

(1) Where a person is convicted of an offence under section 1 or 3(1) above or of an offence under an order made under section 2 above the court—
  (a) may order the destruction of any dog in respect of which the offence was committed and, subject to subsection (1A) below, shall do so in the case of an offence under section 1 or an aggravated offence under section 3(1) above; and
  (b) may order the offender to be disqualified, for such period as the court thinks fit, for having custody of a dog.

(1A) Nothing in subsection (1)(a) above shall require the court to order the destruction of a dog if the court is satisfied—
  (a) that the dog would not constitute a danger to public safety; and
  (b) where the dog was born before 30 November 1991 and is subject to the prohibition in section 1(3) above, that there is a good reason why the dog has not been exempted from that prohibition.

(1B) For the purposes of subsection (1A)(a), when deciding whether a dog would constitute a danger to public safety, the court—
  (a) must consider—
    (i) the temperament of the dog and its past behaviour, and
    (ii) whether the owner of the dog, or the person for the time being in charge of it, is a fit and proper person to be in charge of the dog, and
  (b) may consider any other relevant circumstances.

(2) Where a court makes an order under subsection (1)(a) above for the destruction of a dog owned by a person other than the offender, the owner may appeal to the Crown Court against the order.

(3) A dog shall not be destroyed pursuant to an order under subsection (1)(a) above—
  (a) until the end of the period for giving notice of appeal against the conviction or, against the order; and
  (b) if notice of appeal is given within that period, until the appeal is determined or withdrawn, unless the offender and, in a case to which subsection (2) above applies, the owner of the dog give notice to the court that made the order that there is to be no appeal

. . .

4A Contingent destruction orders

Dangerous Dogs Act 1991, s 4A

(1) Where—
  (a) a person is convicted of an offence under section 1 above or an aggravated offence under section 3(1) above;
  (b) the court does not order the destruction of the dog under section 4(1)(a) above; and
  (c) in the case of an offence under section 1 above, the dog is subject to the prohibition in section 1(3) above,
  (d) the court shall order that, unless the dog is exempted from that prohibition within the requisite period, the dog shall be destroyed.

(2) Where an order is made under subsection (1) above in respect of a dog, and the dog is not exempted from the prohibition in section 1(3) above within the requisite period, the court may extend that period.

(3) Subject to subsection (2) above, the requisite period for the purposes of such an order is the period of two months beginning with the date of the order.

(4) Where a person is convicted of an offence under section 3(1) above, the court may order that, unless the owner of the dog keeps it under proper control, the dog shall be destroyed.

(5) An order under subsection (4) above—

   (a) may specify the measures to be taken for keeping the dog under proper control, whether by muzzling, keeping on a lead, excluding it from specified places or otherwise; and

   (b) if it appears to the court that the dog is a male and would be less dangerous if neutered, may require it to be neutered.

(6) Subsections (2) to (4) of section 4 above shall apply in relation to an order under subsection (1) or (4) above as they apply in relation to an order under subsection (1)(a) of that section.

C1.2.3.1 Key points

In relation to destruction orders, see the guidance issued by the Court of Appeal in *R v Flack* [2008] EWCA Crim 204 and *R v Davies* [2010] EWCA Crim 1923, reviewed in *Kelleher v DPP* [2012] EWHC 2978 (Admin) and *R (Killeen) v Birmingham Crown Court and others* [2018] EWHC 174 (Admin).

- Essentially the court must consider whether the dog constitutes a danger to the public. If it does not then no order is made. If it does, the court must consider whether a contingent destruction order would remove that danger. In the case of an aggravated offence, the burden of proof to show that the dog does not represent a danger is on the defence. The normal burden of proof applies in non-aggravated cases.
- It is sufficient that the danger is only to other dogs (*Briscoe v Shattock* (1998) 163 JP 201), but hunting and killing rabbits and other small animals is part of a dog's nature and does not make it dangerous (*Sansom v Chief Constable of Kent* [1981] Crim LR 617).

The breach of a contingent destruction order made previously does not automatically mean a destruction order should be made (*R v Fitzgerald* [2024] EWHC 869 (Admin)). Furthermore, a court is bound to consider uncontested expert evidence concluding that the dog in question would not pose a danger to public safety if various measures were taken, unless there is a reason why the conclusions can be fairly ignored or discounted.

See *Blackstone's Criminal Practice 2026* **B20**

C2 **Breach Offences**

C2.1 **Criminal behaviour order**

Sentencing Act 2020, s 339

339 Breach of order

(1) It is an offence for a person without reasonable excuse—
  (a) to do anything he or she is prohibited from doing by a criminal behaviour order, or
  (b) to fail to do anything he or she is required to do by a criminal behaviour order . . .

(3) If a person is convicted of an offence under this section, an order for conditional discharge under section 80 is not available to the court by or before which the person is convicted.

EW

Fine and/or 12 months'/5 years' imprisonment

C2.1.1 ***Sentencing***

SCG **Breach of a criminal behaviour order**

A conditional discharge may not be imposed.

C2.1.2 Key points

- The prosecution must be in a position to prove that the person before the court is the person in respect of whom the order was made (*Barber v CPS* [2004] EWHC 2605 (Admin)).
- In *R v Nicholson* [2006] EWCA Crim 1518, it was held that forgetfulness, misunderstanding, or ignorance could amount in law to a reasonable excuse.
- The fact that a person is appealing against the imposition of an order does not give rise to a reasonable excuse (*West Midlands Probation Board v Daly* [2008] EWHC 15 (Admin)).
- A belief that the order has come to an end is capable of amounting to a reasonable excuse (*Barber v CPS* [2004] EWHC 2605 (Admin)).
- Where conduct forming the breach would also be a criminal offence in its own right, a court was not bound by the maximum sentence available for that offence, but should have regard to proportionality. It would be wrong for a prosecutor to proceed with a breach of an order simply because it was thought that the penalty for the substantive offence was too lenient (*R v Stevens* [2006] EWCA Crim 255).
- The burden of negativing reasonable excuse, once raised by evidence by the defence, falls on the prosecution (*R v Charles* [2009] EWCA Crim 1570).

Blackstone's Magistrates' Court Handbook 2026. Bartholomew Dalton and Caroline Liggins, Oxford University Press. © Oxford University Press 2026.
DOI: 10.1093/oso/9780198963943.003.0043

- A defendant's state of mind is relevant to the issue of reasonable excuse (*JB v CPS* [2012] EWHC 72 (Admin)).

See *Blackstone's Criminal Practice 2026* D25.30

C2.2 Breach of protective orders

- **Restraining order**

> **Sentencing Act 2020, s 363**
>
> **363 Offence of breaching restraining order**
>
> (1) It is an offence for a person who is subject to a restraining order without reasonable excuse to do anything prohibited by the restraining order . . .
>
> (6) A court dealing with a person for an offence under this section may vary or discharge the restraining order by further order

EW

Fine and/or 12 months'/5 years' imprisonment

See *Blackstone's Criminal Practice 2026* E21.35

- **Non-molestation orders**

> **Family Law Act 1996, s 42A**
>
> (1) A person who without reasonable excuse does anything that he is prohibited from doing by a non-molestation order is guilty of an offence.
>
> (2) In the case of a non-molestation order made by virtue of section 45(1) [ex parte orders], a person can be guilty of an offence under this section only in respect of conduct engaged in at a time when he was aware of the existence of the order.

EW

Fine and/or 12 months'/5 years' imprisonment

C2.2.1 *Sentencing*

SCG Breach of protective order

C2.2.2 Key points

- A delusional schizophrenic's belief that his neighbour was committing crime could not be regarded as a reasonable excuse for such a breach, and the test of whether his conduct breached an order was objective. The belief was relevant to sentence, however (*R v Grazanfer* [2015] EWCA Crim 642).

- When considering a breach of a restraining order the word 'harass' in an order is to be read, as it would be under the Protection from Harassment Act 1997, so that a defendant would not be in breach of the order if he could make good the defence under s 1(3)(c) of that Act that, in the particular circumstances, the pursuit of the course of conduct had been reasonable (*R v O'Neill* [2016] EWCA Crim 92).
- The words of an order are to be strictly interpreted. Shouting abuse is not a breach of a restriction not to *send* intimidating letters (*R v Anekore* [2019] EWCA Crim 1657).
- A reasonable excuse may exist when a defendant makes an honest mistake or did not know of circumstances that gave rise to a breach, unless they ought to have known of them (*R v Damji* [2020] EWCA Crim 1774).

See *Blackstone's Criminal Practice 2026* B14.138

C2.3 Breach of sexual harm prevention order (SHPO)

Sentencing Act 2020, s 354

354 Offence: breach of sexual harm prevention order

(1) A person commits an offence if, without reasonable excuse, the person—
   (a) does anything that the person is prohibited from doing by a sexual harm prevention order, or
   (b) fails to do something that the person is required to do by a sexual harm prevention order. . . .

(5) An order for conditional discharge is not available in respect of an offence under this section.

EW

Fine and/or 12 months'/5 years' imprisonment

A conditional discharge may not be imposed.

An order must be observed until set aside even if made without jurisdiction, as per *R v Wilkes* [2022] EWCA Crim 525.

C2.3.1 *Sentencing*

SCG **Breach of a sexual harm prevention order**

See *Blackstone's Criminal Practice 2026* E21.30

C2.4 Breach of sexual risk order

Sexual Offences Act 2003, s 122H

122H Offence: breach of sexual risk order or interim sexual risk order etc

(A1) A person who, without reasonable excuse—
- (a) does anything that the person is prohibited from doing by a sexual risk order or an interim sexual risk order, or
- (b) fails to do something that the person is required to do by a sexual risk order or an interim sexual risk order,

commits an offence.

(1) A person who, without reasonable excuse, does anything that the person is prohibited from doing by—
- (c) a risk of sexual harm order,
- (d) an interim risk of sexual harm order,

commits an offence.

(1A) A person who, without reasonable excuse, does anything that the person is required to do by a risk of sexual harm order that has been renewed or varied as mentioned in section 136ZJ(7) commits an offence.

EW

Fine and/or 12 months'/5 years' imprisonment

C2.4.1

In the absence of sentencing guidelines, courts should have regard to the guideline for breach of SHPO and then make a fact-sensitive adjustment if needed.

C2.5 Breach of Sexual Offences Act 2003 notification requirements

See C15.25.

C2.6 Breach of domestic abuse protection orders and notification requirements

Note in relation to breach of domestic violence protection orders (see A11.2B.2)

Domestic Abuse Act 2021 s 39

39 Breach of Order

(1) *A person who is subject to a domestic abuse protection order commits an offence if without reasonable excuse the person fails to comply with any requirement imposed by the order.*

(2) *In a case where the order was made against the person without that person being given notice of the proceedings, the person commits an offence under this section only in respect of behaviour engaged in at a time when the person was aware of the existence of the order.*

(See also section 45(8) and (9), which makes similar provision where an order has been varied.)

(3) *Where a person is convicted of an offence under this section in respect of any behaviour, that behaviour is not punishable as a contempt of court.*

(4) *A person may not be convicted of an offence under this section in respect of any behaviour which has been punished as a contempt of court . . .*

(8) *In proceedings for an offence under this section, a copy of the original domestic abuse protection order, certified by the proper officer of the court that made it, is admissible as evidence of its having been made and of its contents to the same extent that oral evidence of those matters is admissible in those proceedings.*

43 Offences relating to notification

(1) *A person ('P') commits an offence if P—*
  (a) *fails, without reasonable excuse, to comply with a requirement imposed by or under section 41, or*
  (b) *notifies the police, in purported compliance with such a requirement, of any information which P knows to be false.*

EW

12 months' imprisonment and/or a fine/5 years' imprisonment

A conditional discharge may not be imposed for an offence under s 39.

C2.6.1 *Sentencing*

SCG **Breach of protective order**

C2.7 Breach of a Modern Slavery Act protection order

Modern Slavery Act 2015, s 30

(1) A person who, without reasonable excuse, does anything that the person is prohibited from doing . . . commits an offence.

EW

12 months' imprisonment and/or a fine/5 years' imprisonment

A conditional discharge may not be imposed.

C2.8 Breach of a female genital mutilation protection order

Female Genital Mutilation Act 2003, s 5A and Sch 2, para 4(1)

4(1) A person who without reasonable excuse does anything that the person is prohibited from doing by an FGM protection order is guilty of an offence.

EW

12 months' imprisonment and/or a fine/5 years' imprisonment

C2.9 Breach of a forced marriage protection order

Family Law Act 1996, s 63CA

(1) A person who without reasonable excuse does anything that the person is prohibited from doing by a forced marriage protection order is guilty of an offence.
(2) In the case of a forced marriage protection order made [ex parte] a person can be guilty of an offence under this section only in respect of conduct engaged in at a time when the person was aware of the existence of the order.

EW

12 months' imprisonment and/or a fine/5 years' imprisonment

C2.10 Serious crime prevention order

Serious Crime Act 2007, s 25

(1) A person who, without reasonable excuse, fails to comply with a serious crime prevention order commits an offence.

EW

12 months' imprisonment and/or a fine/5 years' imprisonment

C2.11 Breach of a football banning order

Football Spectators Act 1989, s 14J

(1) A person subject to a banning order who fails to comply with—
 (a) any requirement imposed by the order, or
 (b) any requirement imposed under section 19(2B) or (2C) below, is guilty of an offence.

SO In its definitive guideline on breach offences, the Sentencing Council has suggested that reference should be made to the penalties for breach of a criminal behaviour order and the penalty adjusted to take account of the maximum available sentences.

6 months and/or a fine

See *Blackstone's Criminal Practice 2026* E21.7

C2.12 Breach of bail

See C3.1.

C2.13 **Breach of dispersal order**

Anti-social Behaviour Crime and Policing Act 2014

34 Authorisations to use powers under section 35

(1) A police officer of at least the rank of inspector may authorise the use in a specified locality, during a specified period of not more than 48 hours, of the powers given by section 35.
'Specified' means specified in the authorisation.

(2) An officer may give such an authorisation only if satisfied on reasonable grounds that the use of those powers in the locality during that period may be necessary for the purpose of removing or reducing the likelihood of—
  (a) members of the public in the locality being harassed, alarmed or distressed, or
  (b) the occurrence in the locality of crime or disorder.

(3) In deciding whether to give such an authorisation an officer must have particular regard to the rights of freedom of expression and freedom of assembly set out in Articles 10 and 11 of the Convention.
'Convention' has the meaning given by section 21(1) of the Human Rights Act 1998.

(4) An authorisation under this section—
  (a) must be in writing,
  (b) must be signed by the officer giving it, and
  (c) must specify the grounds on which it is given.

35 Directions excluding a person from an area

(1) If the conditions in subsections (2) and (3) are met and an authorisation is in force under section 34, a constable in uniform may direct a person who is in a public place in the locality specified in the authorisation—
  (a) to leave the locality (or part of the locality), and
  (b) not to return to the locality (or part of the locality) for the period specified in the direction ('the exclusion period').

(2) The first condition is that the constable has reasonable grounds to suspect that the behaviour of the person in the locality has contributed or is likely to contribute to—
  (a) members of the public in the locality being harassed, alarmed or distressed, or
  (b) the occurrence in the locality of crime or disorder.

(3) The second condition is that the constable considers that giving a direction to the person is necessary for the purpose of removing or reducing the likelihood of the events mentioned in subsection (2)(a) or (b).

(4) The exclusion period may not exceed 48 hours.

The period may expire after (as long as it begins during) the period specified in the authorisation under section 34.

(5) A direction under this section—
  (a) must be given in writing, unless that is not reasonably practicable;
  (b) must specify the area to which it relates;
  (c) may impose requirements as to the time by which the person must leave the area and the manner in which the person must do so (including the route).

(6) The constable must (unless it is not reasonably practicable) tell the person to whom the direction is given that failing without reasonable excuse to comply with the direction is an offence.

(7) If the constable reasonably believes that the person to whom the direction is given is under the age of 16, the constable may remove the person to a place where the person lives or a place of safety.

(8) Any constable may withdraw or vary a direction under this section; but a variation must not extend the duration of a direction beyond 48 hours from when it was first given.
(9) Notice of a withdrawal or variation of a direction—
  (a) must be given to the person to whom the direction was given, unless that is not reasonably practicable, and
  (b) if given, must be given in writing unless that is not reasonably practicable.
(10) In this section 'public place' means a place to which at the material time the public or a section of the public has access, on payment or otherwise, as of right or by virtue of express or implied permission.
(11) In this Part "exclusion period" has the meaning given by subsection (1)(b).

36 Restrictions

(1) A constable may not give a direction under section 35 to a person who appears to the constable to be under the age of 10.
(2) A constable may not give a direction under section 35 that prevents the person to whom it is given having access to a place where the person lives.
(3) A constable may not give a direction under section 35 that prevents the person to whom it is given attending at a place which the person is—
  (a) required to attend for the purposes of the person's employment, or a contract of services to which the person is a party,
  (b) required to attend by an obligation imposed by or under an enactment or by the order of a court or tribunal, or
  (c) expected to attend for the purposes of education or training or for the purposes of receiving medical treatment, at a time when the person is required or expected (as the case may be) to attend there.
(4) A constable may not give a direction to a person under section 35 if the person is one of a group of persons who are—
  (a) engaged in conduct that is lawful under section 220 of the Trade Union and Labour Relations (Consolidation) Act 1992 (peaceful picketing), or
  (b) taking part in a public procession of the kind mentioned in subsection (1) of section 11 of the Public Order Act 1986 in respect of which—
    (i) written notice has been given in accordance with that section, or
    (ii) written notice is not required to be given as provided by subsections (1) and (2) of that section.
(5) In deciding whether to give a direction under section 35 a constable must have particular regard to the rights of freedom of expression and freedom of assembly set out in Articles 10 and 11 of the Convention.
'Convention' has the meaning given by section 21(1) of the Human Rights Act 1998.

. . .

. . .

39 Offences

(1) A person given a direction under section 35 who fails without reasonable excuse to comply with it commits an offence.
(3) A person given a direction under section 37 who fails without reasonable excuse to comply with it commits an offence.

SO

s 39(1) level 4 fine/3 months' imprisonment

s 39(3) level 2 fine

C2.13.1 *Sentencing*

The Guideline for breach offences states in relation to this offence

> A court is . . . entitled to use, and may be assisted by, a guideline for an analogous offence subject to differences in the elements of the offences and the statutory maxima.
>
> In sentencing this breach offence the court should refer to the sentencing approach in step one of the guideline for breach of a criminal behaviour order to determine culpability and harm, and determine an appropriate sentence bearing in mind the maximum penalty for the offence.

C2.13.2 Key points

- The power to issue dispersal notices has also been given to police community support officers (s 40).
- To prove an offence under s 39 it must be established that the officer issuing the dispersal notice was acting lawfully. This means that the prosecution must prove the validity of the authorization (*Carter v DPP* [2009] EWHC 2197 (Admin)) and the reasonableness of the grounds for issuing the notice to the particular defendant (*Buckley v DPP* [2006] EWHC 1888 (Admin)).
- Unless there were exceptional circumstances, reasonable [grounds] under s 34 had normally to depend, in part at least, on some behaviour of the group which indicates in some way or other that harassment, alarm, or intimidation had or was likely to occur (*Buckley v DPP*).

Blackstone's Criminal Practice 2024 **B11.146**

C2.14 Breach of a serious disruption prevention order

Public Order Act 2023, s27

27 Offences relating to a serious disruption prevention order

(1) Where a serious disruption prevention order has effect in respect of a person ("P"), P commits an offence if P—
  (a) fails without reasonable excuse to do anything P is required to do by the order,
  (b) without reasonable excuse does anything P is prohibited from doing by the order, or
  (c) notifies to the police, in purported compliance with the order, any information which P knows to be false.

SO

6 months' imprisonment and/or fine

C2.15 Breach of a stalking protection order and notification requirements

Stalking Protection Act 2019, s 8

(1) A person who, without reasonable excuse, breaches a stalking protection order or an interim stalking protection order commits an offence.

EW

12 months' imprisonment and/or a fine/5 years' imprisonment

Stalking Protection Act 2019, s 11

11 Offences relating to notification

(1) A person commits an offence if the person—
  (a) fails, without reasonable excuse, to comply with [notification requirements] or with [requirement to give fingerprints or photographs], or
  (b) notifies to the police, in purported compliance with [notification requirements] any information which the person knows to be false.

EW

12 months' imprisonment and/or a fine/5 years

A conditional discharge may not be imposed.

C2.15.1 *Sentencing*

SCG Breach of protective order

C2.16 Breach of serious violence reduction orders

SA 2020, s 342G

342G Offences relating to a serious violence reduction order

(1) Where a serious violence reduction order is in effect, the offender commits an offence if the offender—
  (a) fails without reasonable excuse to do anything the offender is required to do by the order,
  (b) without reasonable excuse does anything the offender is prohibited from doing by the order,
  (c) notifies to the police, in purported compliance with the order, any information which the offender knows to be false,
  (d) tells a constable that they are not subject to a serious violence reduction order, or
  (e) intentionally obstructs a constable in the exercise of any power conferred by section 342E.

EW

12 months and/or a fine/2 years' imprisonment

A conditional discharge may not be imposed.

C2.17 Other breach offences

SCG Breach offences

C2.17.1 *Breach of disqualification from acting as a director*

Company Directors Disqualification Act 1986, s 13

EW

12 months and/or a fine/2 years' imprisonment

C2.17.1.1 *Sentencing*

SCG **Breach of disqualification from acting as a director**

C2.17.2 *Other offences*

The Sentencing Council guideline on breach has the following additional comments:

> Where an offence is not covered by a sentencing guideline a court is also entitled to use, and may be assisted by, a guideline for an analogous offence subject to differences in the elements of the offences and the statutory maxima.

In sentencing the following breach offences, the court should refer to the sentencing approach in step one of the guideline for breach of a criminal behaviour order to determine culpability and harm, and determine an appropriate sentence bearing in mind the maximum penalty for the offence.

Community protection notice Part 4, Chapter 1 Anti-social Behaviour, Crime and Policing Act 2014 (stops a person, business or organisation committing ASB which spoils the community's quality of life.)	Triable summarily only	A person guilty of an offence under this section is liable on summary conviction—to a fine not exceeding level 4 on the standard scale, in the case of an individual; to a fine of up to £20,000, in the case of a body. (If dealt with by way of fixed penalty, a fixed penalty notice of up to £100.)
Breach of public spaces protection order Part 4, Chapter 2 Anti-social Behaviour, Crime and Policing Act 2014 (stops people committing ASB in a particular public place.)	Triable summarily only	A person guilty of an offence under this section is liable on summary conviction to a fine not exceeding level 3 on the standard scale. (If dealt with by way of fixed penalty, a fixed penalty notice of up to £100.)
Closure power Part 4, Chapter 3 Anti-social Behaviour, Crime and Policing Act 2014 (allows the police or local council to close premises where ASB is being committed, or is likely to be committed.)	Triable summarily only	A person guilty of obstructing a person acting under s 79 or 85(1) is liable on summary conviction—(a) to imprisonment for a period not exceeding 3 months, or (b) to a fine. A person who is guilty of remaining on or entering premises in contravention of a closure order is liable on summary conviction—(a) to imprisonment for a period not exceeding 6 months [51 weeks], or (b) to a fine, or to both.

C3 Administration of Justice

C3.1 Bail: failure to surrender

Bail Act 1976, s 6(1) and (2)

6 Offence of absconding by person released on bail

(1) If a person who has been released on bail in criminal proceedings fails without reasonable cause to surrender to custody he shall be guilty of an offence.

(2) If a person who—
  (a) has been released on bail in criminal proceedings, and
  (b) having reasonable cause therefor, has failed to surrender to custody, fails to surrender to custody at the appointed place as soon after the appointed time as is reasonably practicable he shall be guilty of an offence.

SO But with power to commit to the Crown Court. However, a Bail Act offence is not 'related to' the substantive matter in which bail was granted and must be tried in the court that granted bail (*R v Osman* [2017] EWCA Crim 2178).

Fine and/or 3 months'/12 months' imprisonment

C3.1.1 *Sentencing*

SCG **Failure to surrender to bail**

C3.1.2 Key points

- The appropriate procedures are set out in CPD III 14C.
- Courts should arrange for the surrender to bail to occur on appearance in the court room and not before on signing in with a court official. The effect is that those who arrive late, but whose cases are not called, will not be committing an offence. This reconciles *DPP v Richards* [1988] 3 All ER 406 (magistrates' courts) *with R v Scott Evans* [2011] 1 WLR 1192 (Crown Courts) as appears below.
- In *R v Scott* [2007] EWCA Crim 2757, the court rejected an argument that surrendering to bail 30 minutes late was *de minimis* so as to make proceeding with a Bail Act charge *Wednesbury* unreasonable. The court held:

> We are prepared for the sake of argument to accept the possibility that there could be circumstances where a defendant's late arrival at court was so truly marginal that it would be Wednesbury unreasonable to pursue it but it would be a rare case. Even if a delay is small it can still cause inconvenience and waste of time. If a culture of lateness is tolerated the results can be cumulative and bad for the administration of justice.

- In *R v Gateshead Justices, ex p Usher* [1981] Crim LR 491, DC, a period of seven minutes was held to be *de minimis*; however, in *Scott* the court said

Blackstone's Magistrates' Court Handbook 2026. Bartholomew Dalton and Caroline Liggins, Oxford University Press. © Oxford University Press 2026.
DOI: 10.1093/oso/9780198963943.003.0044

that no gloss should be placed on the clear wording in the Bail Act and *Usher* established no clear principle of law.

- Proof of *bail* terms: s 6 Bail Act 1976 provides:

Bail Act 1976, s 6(8) and (9)

6 Offence of absconding by person released on bail

(8) In any proceedings for an offence under subsection (1) or (2) above a document purporting to be a copy of the part of the prescribed record which relates to the time and place appointed for the person specified in the record to surrender to custody and to be duly certified to be a true copy of that part of the record shall be evidence of the time and place appointed for that person to surrender to custody.

(9) For the purposes of subsection (8) above—
 (a) 'the prescribed record' means the record of the decision of the court, officer or constable made in pursuance of section 5(1) of this Act;
 (b) the copy of the prescribed record is duly certified if it is certified by the appropriate officer of the court or, as the case may be, by the constable who took the decision or a constable designated for the purpose by the officer in charge of the police station from which the person to whom the record relates was released.

- In *R v Liverpool Justices, ex p Santos*, *The Times*, 23 January 1997, the court held that reliance on mistaken information provided by a solicitor may be found a reasonable excuse for failing to surrender. All relevant factors would need to be considered, and a mistake on the part of a solicitor in calculating the bail date did not automatically excuse the defendant's non-attendance.
- A failure to give the defendant a written bail notice does not amount to a reasonable excuse. Defendants have a personal obligation to stay in touch with their solicitors and the court and to surrender (*R v Balaam* [2022] EWCA Crim 692).
- A genuine, albeit mistaken, belief that bail was to another date would not amount to a reasonable excuse (*Laidlaw v Atkinson*, *The Times*, 2 August 1986).
- A reasonable excuse need be proved only to the civil standard (*R v Carr-Bryant* (1944) 29 Cr App R 76).
- A person who had overtly subjected himself to the court's direction (see *R v Central Criminal Court, ex p Guney* [1995] 2 All ER 577), or reported to court officials as directed, had surrendered to custody (see *DPP v Richards* [1988] QB 701 in relation to the magistrates' court). If the defendant later left court, no offence would be committed (although the court could issue a warrant for arrest). It is not essential that there be a formal surrender to an official (*R v Rumble* [2003] EWCA Crim 770), but simply arriving at the court at the proper time may not be enough (*R v Render* (1987) 84 Cr App R 294). In *Evans* [2011] EWCA Crim 2842, the court made clear that in the Crown Court a defendant who advises the usher and his own lawyer of his presence but then leaves, does not surrender to bail. He must be identified before the judge, or surrender to the dock officer.
- If a person is acquitted of the offence for which he was on bail, that does not mitigate the penalty for failing to surrender (*R v Maguire* [1993] RTR 306).

- Under s 68 Policing and Crime Act 2017 it is an either-way offence carrying 12 months' imprisonment, if a person is on bail in respect of an offence mentioned in s 41(1) or (2) Counter-Terrorism Act 2008, and their release on bail is subject to a travel restriction condition and they fail to comply with that condition.

See *Blackstone's Criminal Practice 2026* D7.97

C3.2 Contempt of court

C3.2.1 *Magistrates' Court Act 1980, s 97*

(4) If any person attending or brought before a magistrates' court refuses without just excuse to be sworn or give evidence, or to produce any document or thing, the court may commit him to custody until the expiration of such period not exceeding one month as may be specified in the warrant or until he sooner gives evidence or produces the document or thing or impose on him a fine not exceeding £2,500 or both.

See *Blackstone's Criminal Practice 2026* D21.31

C3.2.2 *Contempt of Court Act 1981, s 12*

(1) A magistrates' court has jurisdiction under this section to deal with any person who—
  (a) wilfully insults the justice or justices, any witness before or officer of the court or any solicitor or counsel having business in the court, during his or their sitting or attendance in court or in going to or returning from the court; or
  (b) wilfully interrupts the proceedings of the court or otherwise misbehaves in court.
(2) In any such case the court may order any officer of the court, or any constable, to take the offender into custody and detain him until the rising of the court; and the court may, if it thinks fit, commit the offender to custody for a specified period not exceeding one month or impose on him a fine not exceeding £2,500, or both.

See *Blackstone's Criminal Practice 2026* B14.89

C3.3 Escape from lawful custody

At common law it is an offence to escape from legal custody.

IO

Life

GC

C3.3.1 Key points

- The prosecution must prove that the defendant was in custody, that he knew (or was reckless as to whether he was or not); that the custody was lawful; and that he intentionally escaped from it (*R v Dhillon* [2005] EWCA Crim 2996).

- The escape may be from police custody following arrest (*R v Timmis* [1976] Crim LR 129).
- A prisoner is deemed to be in legal custody while he is confined in, or is being taken to or from, any prison or young offender institution (s 13 Prison Act 1952).
- Whether a person can be said to be in custody at any particular time is a question of fact to be decided by reference to the circumstances of each individual case. For a person to be in custody, his liberty must be subject to such restraint or restriction that he can be said to be confined by another in the sense that that person's immediate freedom of movement is under the direct control of another (*E v DPP* [2002] EWHC 433 (Admin)).
- A youth refused bail and remanded to local authority accommodation with a security requirement (now a remand to youth detention accommodation under s 91(5) Legal Aid, Punishment and Sentencing of Offenders Act 2012) but not placed in such accommodation as no placement was available was in lawful custody when he absented himself from court (*E v DPP*).
- A youth refused bail and remanded to local authority accommodation who had been collected from the cells by a Youth Offending Team worker and told to wait while she arranged a placement was held to be in lawful custody (*H v DPP* [2003] EWHC 878 (Admin)).

See *Blackstone's Criminal Practice 2026* B14.74

C3.4 Perverting the course of justice

It is an offence at common law to do an act tending and intended to pervert the course of public justice.

IO

Life

GC

C3.4.1 *Sentencing*

SCG Perverting the course of justice

C3.4.2 Key points

- Making false allegations against another person, intending that he be prosecuted or knowing that he might be, would constitute an offence (*R v Rowell* [1978] 1 WLR 132).
- Where it is alleged that a false allegation has been made, the prosecution must show that the defendant intended that the police take it seriously. It is not necessary to prove that the defendant intended anyone to be arrested (*R v Cotter* [2002] EWCA Crim 1033).

- False complaints which do not risk the arrest of an innocent person might in certain circumstances be more appropriately charged as wasting police time (see C3.4 *R v Cotter*).
- There must be a positive action taken by the defendant, acquiescence is not sufficient (*R v Headley* [1996] RTR 173).
- Where there is found to be an intention to impede police investigations before an investigation has begun, there is an intention to pervert the course of public justice (*R v Rafique* (1993) 97 Cr App R 395).
- The course of justice includes the police investigation of a possible crime. An act that makes that investigation more difficult, or which may mislead the police in their investigation, may tend to pervert the course of justice (*R v T* [2011] EWCA Crim 729).
- When dealing with a suspected false sexual allegation reference should be made to the detailed CPS Legal Guidance *Perverting the Course of Justice: Charging in Cases Involving Rape and/or Domestic Violence Allegations.*

See *Blackstone's Criminal Practice 2026* B14.29

C3.5 **Wasting police time**

Criminal Law Act 1967, s 5

(2) Where a person causes any wasteful employment of the police by knowingly making to any person a false report tending to show that an offence has been committed, or to give rise to apprehension for the safety of any persons or property, or tending to show that he has information material to any police inquiry, he shall be liable . . .

SO

6 months' imprisonment/level 4 fine

C3.5.1

- No proceedings shall be instituted for an offence under this section except by or with the consent of the DPP (s 5(3)).

See *Blackstone's Criminal Practice 2026* B14.82

C3.6 **Witness intimidation**

Criminal Justice and Public Order Act 1994, s 51(1)–(5) 51 Intimidation, etc of witnesses, jurors and others

(1) A person commits an offence if—
  (a) he does an act which intimidates, and is intended to intimidate, another person ('the victim'),

(b) he does the act knowing or believing that the victim is assisting in the investigation of an offence or is a witness or potential witness or a juror or potential juror in proceedings for an offence, and
(c) he does it intending thereby to cause the investigation or the course of justice to be obstructed, perverted or interfered with.

(2) A person commits an offence if—
(a) he does an act which harms, and is intended to harm, another person or, intending to cause another person to fear harm, he threatens to do an act which would harm that other person,
(b) he does or threatens to do the act knowing or believing that the person harmed or threatened to be harmed ('the victim'), or some other person, has assisted in an investigation into an offence or has given evidence or particular evidence in proceedings for an offence, or has acted as a juror or concurred in a particular verdict in proceedings for an offence, and
(c) he does or threatens to do it because of that knowledge or belief.

(3) For the purposes of subsections (1) and (2) it is immaterial that the act is or would be done, or that the threat is made—
(a) otherwise than in the presence of the victim, or
(b) to a person other than the victim.

(4) The harm that may be done or threatened may be financial as well as physical (whether to the person or a person's property) and similarly as respects an intimidatory act which consists of threats.

(5) The intention required by subsection (1)(c) and the motive required by subsection (2)(c) above need not be the only or the predominating intention or motive with which the act is done or, in the case of subsection (2), threatened.

EW

Fine and/or 12 months'/5 years' imprisonment

C3.6.1 *Sentencing*

SCG **Witness intimidation**

C3.6.2 Key points

For there to be an offence under s 51(1) Criminal Justice and Public Order Act 1994 the witness, etc must be proved to have been intimidated. Intent alone is not enough. It might, however, be possible to establish an attempt (*R v ZN* [2013] EWCA Crim 989).

The suspect cannot commit the offence where he wrongly believes there to be an investigation in progress, as it requires the belief to be correct (*R v Singh (B)* [1999] Crim LR 681 CA).

Physical harm under ss 51(1) and (4) must involve some physical injury (*R v Normanton* [1998] Crim LR 220 CA).

See *Blackstone's Criminal Practice 2026* B14.50

C4 Communication Network Offences

C4.1 Improper use of public electronic communications network

Communications Act 2003, s 127(1) and (2)

127 Improper use of public electronic communications network

(1) A person is guilty of an offence if he—
  - (a) sends by means of a public electronic communications network a message or other matter that is grossly offensive or of an indecent, obscene or menacing character; or
  - (b) causes any such message or matter to be so sent.

(2) A person is guilty of an offence if, for the purpose of causing annoyance, inconvenience or needless anxiety to another, he—
  - (c) persistently makes use of a public electronic communications network.

SO

Fine and/or 6 months' imprisonment

C4.1.1 *Sentencing*

SCG Communication network offences

C4.1.2 *Time limits (see also A12.1.2)*

Communications Act 2003, s 127

(5) An information or complaint relating to an offence under this section may be tried by a magistrates' court in England and Wales or Northern Ireland if it is laid or made—
  - (a) before the end of the period of 3 years beginning with the day on which the offence was committed, and
  - (b) before the end of the period of 6 months beginning with the day on which evidence comes to the knowledge of the prosecutor which the prosecutor considers sufficient to justify proceedings . . .

(7) A certificate of a prosecutor as to the date on which evidence described in subsection (5)(b) or (6)(b) came to his or her knowledge is conclusive evidence of that fact.

See *DPP v Jinks* [2024] EWHC 3341 (Admin) (at **A12.1.2**) in relation to s 127(5) Communications Act 2003 and multiple prosecutors conducting reviews.

C4.1.3 Key points

- In *DPP v Collins* [2006] UKHL 40, the court held that to be guilty of an offence under s 127:
  - the defendant must have intended his words to be offensive to those to whom they related; or
  - must be aware that they might be taken to be so.

Blackstone's Magistrates' Court Handbook 2026. Bartholomew Dalton and Caroline Liggins, Oxford University Press. © Oxford University Press 2026.
DOI: 10.1093/oso/9780198963943.003.0045

It does not matter if the material sent was not received. The question of whether something is in fact offensive is to be determined by reference to whether or not reasonable persons would find the message grossly offensive, judged by the standards of an open and just multiracial society.

- In *DPP v Smith (Kingsley Anthony)* [2017] EWHC 359 (Admin) the court emphasized that in deciding whether a particular message is grossly offensive, a court needs to be careful not to criminalize speech that, however contemptible, is no more than offensive.

  It has to be asked whether taking account of the context and all the relevant circumstances, and applying the standards of a reasonable person in an open and just multiracial and multifaith society, it is proved that a particular message was grossly offensive to those to whom it related or was of a menacing character, and whether it would have created a sense of apprehension or fear in a person of reasonable fortitude who received or read it:

  - Parliament cannot have intended to criminalize the conduct of a person using language which is, for reasons unknown to him, grossly offensive to those to whom it relates, or which may even be thought, however wrongly, to represent a polite or acceptable usage. On the other hand, a culpable state of mind will ordinarily be found where a message is couched in terms showing an intention to insult those to whom the message relates, or giving rise to the inference that a risk of doing so must have been recognized by the sender. The same will be true where facts known to the sender of a message about an intended recipient render the message peculiarly offensive to that recipient, or likely to be so, whether or not the message in fact reaches the recipient.
  - While it is an offence to send by public electronic communication network a message of a menacing character (Communications Act 2003, s 127(1)(a)), the mental element requires the sender either to have intended that the message be of a menacing character, or to have been aware or to have recognized the risk that it might create fear or apprehension in any reasonable member of the public who reads or sees it.
  - If the message was intended as a joke, however poor, the offence will rarely be made out (*Chambers v DPP* [2012] EWHC 2157 (QB)).
  - For a call to be menacing within s 127(1)(a) Communications Act 2003 it must be more than offensive or nasty and anti-Semitic (*Karsten v Wood Green Crown Court* [2014] EWHC 2900 (Admin)).
- Private messages consensually exchanged on a medium such as WhatsApp between purely private persons (not public officials, such as police officers, discussing policing matters, as was the situation in this case) are very likely to have a reasonable expectation of privacy and difficult questions may arise as to whether the interference with Article 8 ECHR rights can be justified (*obiter* in *Cobban v DPP* [2024] EWHC 1908 (Admin)).
- See *R v Casserly* [2024] EWCA Crim 25 (C4.5 below) in relation to grossly offensive in a political context
- The question was whether a message had been sent that was intended to be, or which he was aware might be, grossly offensive to members of the public who saw it. The offence does not particularly require any element of racism, although racism is potentially relevant to the extent to which

the sender of the message intended or was aware that the message was not simply offensive but grossly offensive. The offence might be made out by a video without any soundtrack (*DPP v Bussetti* [2021] EWHC 2140 (Admin)).

- The purpose of s 127(2)(c) is to prohibit the abuse of facilities for no other purpose than to annoy, cause inconvenience, or cause needless anxiety. The focus was not on the content of any communication, but rather its purpose and the way in which that purpose was put into effect. Examples of the kinds of behaviour that would fall within the scope of s 127(2)(c) were repeated instances of prank calls, silent calls, heavy breathing, and other common forms of nuisance phone call containing no meaningful content. Content would not always be irrelevant but there was no offence under s 127(2)(c) of posting annoying tweets.
- A series of communications had to have an element of frequency. There also had to be a connecting theme or factor if the messages were to count as 'persistent' (*Scottow v CPS* [2020] EWHC 3421 (Admin)).
- 'Sending' includes uploading a video. Creating a hyperlink fell within the section if it amounted to endorsing its content with intent that the content be seen (*R (Chablos) v CPS* [2019] EWHC 3094 (Admin)).

See *Blackstone's Criminal Practice 2026* **B18.28**

C4.2 False communications offence

Online Safety Act 2023, s 179

179 False communications offence

(1) A person commits an offence if—
  (a) the person sends a message (see section 182),
  (b) the message conveys information that the person knows to be false,
  (c) at the time of sending it, the person intended the message, or the information in it, to cause non-trivial psychological or physical harm to a likely audience, and
  (d) the person has no reasonable excuse for sending the message.

(2) For the purposes of this offence an individual is a "likely audience" of a message if, at the time the message is sent, it is reasonably foreseeable that the individual—
  (a) would encounter the message, or
  (b) in the online context, would encounter a subsequent message forwarding or sharing the content of the message.

(3) In a case where several or many individuals are a likely audience, it is not necessary for the purposes of subsection (1)(c) that the person intended to cause harm to any one of them in particular (or to all of them).

(4) See section 180 for exemptions from the offence under this section [relating to news publishers, broadcast licence holders, cinema etc.].

SO

Fine and/or 6 months' imprisonment

C4.2.1 *Time limits (see also A12.1.2)*

Online Safety Act 2023, s 179

(7) Proceedings for an offence under this section may be brought within the period of 6 months beginning with the date on which evidence sufficient in the opinion of the prosecutor to justify the proceedings comes to the prosecutor's knowledge.

(8) But such proceedings may not be brought by virtue of subsection (7) more than 3 years after the commission of the offence.

(9) A certificate signed by the prosecutor as to the date on which the evidence in question came to the prosecutor's knowledge is conclusive evidence of the date on which it did so; and a certificate to that effect and purporting to be so signed is to be treated as being so signed unless the contrary is proved.

C4.2.2 Key points

Online Safety Act, s 182

182 Interpretation of sections 179 to 181

(2) A person "sends a message" if the person—
- (a) sends, transmits or publishes a communication (including an oral communication) by electronic means, or
- (b) sends, or gives to an individual, a letter or a thing of any other description,

and references to a message are to be read accordingly.

(3) A person also "sends a message" if the person—
- (a) causes a communication (including an oral communication) to be sent, transmitted or published by electronic means, or
- (b) causes a letter or a thing of any other description to be—
  - (i) sent, or
  - (ii) given to an individual.

(4) But a provider of an internet service by means of which a communication is sent, transmitted or published is not to be regarded as a person who sends a message.

(5) "Encounter", in relation to a message, means read, view, hear or otherwise experience the message.

(6) It does not matter whether the content of a message is created by the person who sends it (so for example, in the online context, an offence may be committed by a person who forwards another person's direct message or shares another person's post).

(7) In the application of sections 179 to 181 to the sending by electronic means of a message consisting of or including a hyperlink to other content—
- (a) references to the message are to be read as including references to content accessed directly via the hyperlink, and
- (b) an individual who is a likely audience in relation to the hyperlink for the purposes of section 179 is to be assumed to be a likely audience in relation to the linked content.

(8) In the application of sections 179 to 181 to the sending of an item on which data is stored electronically, references to the message are to be read as including content accessed by means of the item to which the recipient is specifically directed by the sender (and in this subsection "sending" includes "giving", and "sender" is to be read accordingly).

(9) In the online context, the date on which a person commits an offence in relation to a message is the date on which the message is first sent by the person.

C4.3 Threatening communications offence

Online Safety Act 2023, s 181

181 Threatening communications offence

(1) A person commits an offence if—
- (a) the person sends a message (see section 182),
- (b) the message conveys a threat of death or serious harm, and
- (c) at the time of sending it, the person—
  - (i) intended an individual encountering the message to fear that the threat would be carried out (whether or not by the person sending the message), or
  - (ii) was reckless as to whether an individual encountering the message would fear that the threat would be carried out (whether or not by the person sending the message).

(2) "Serious harm" means—
- (a) serious injury amounting to grievous bodily harm within the meaning of the Offences against the Person Act 1861,
- (b) rape,
- (c) assault by penetration within the meaning of section 2 of the Sexual Offences Act 2003, or
- (d) serious financial loss.

EW

Fine and/or 12 months'/5 years' imprisonment

C4.3.1 Key points

Defence where a threat of serious financial loss conveyed:

Online Safety Act 2023, s 181(3) and (4)

(3) In proceedings for an offence under this section relating to a threat of serious financial loss, it is a defence for the person to show that—
- (a) the threat was used to reinforce a reasonable demand, and
- (b) the person reasonably believed that the use of the threat was a proper means of reinforcing the demand.

(4) If evidence is adduced which is sufficient to raise an issue with respect to the defence under subsection (3), the court must assume that the defence is satisfied unless the prosecution proves beyond reasonable doubt that it is not.

See C4.2.2 above in relation to interpretation.

C4.4 Sending indecent material through the post

Postal Services Act 2000, s 85

85 Prohibition on sending certain articles by post

(1) A person commits an offence if he sends by post a postal packet which encloses any creature, article or thing of any kind which is likely to injure other postal packets in course of their transmission by post or any person engaged in the business of a postal operator.

(2) Subsection (1) does not apply to postal packets which enclose anything permitted (whether generally or specifically) by the postal operator concerned.

(3) A person commits an offence if he sends by post a postal packet which encloses—
- (a) any indecent or obscene print, painting, photograph, lithograph, engraving, cinematograph film or other record of a picture or pictures, book, card or written communication, or
- (b) any other indecent or obscene article (whether or not of a similar kind to those mentioned in paragraph (a)).

(4) A person commits an offence if he sends by post a postal packet which has on the packet, or on the cover of the packet, any words, marks or designs which are of an indecent or obscene character.

(5) A person who commits an offence under this section shall be liable—
- (a) on summary conviction, to a fine not exceeding the statutory maximum,
- (b) on conviction on indictment, to a fine or to imprisonment for a term not exceeding twelve months or to both.

EW

Summary trial: Fine

On indictment: Fine and/or 12 months' imprisonment

C4.4.1 Key points

Whether something is obscene is to be judged objectively.

The section is compatible with Article 10 ECHR (*R v Kirk* [2006] EWCA Crim 725).

See *Blackstone's Criminal Practice 2026* B18.26

C4.5 Indecent or offensive or threatening letters, etc

Malicious Communications Act 1988, s 1

1 Offence of sending letters etc with intent to cause distress or anxiety

(1) Any person who sends to another person—
- (a) a letter, electronic communication or article of any description which conveys—
  - (i) a message which is indecent or grossly offensive;
- (b) any article or electronic communication which is, in whole or part, of an indecent or grossly offensive nature, is guilty of an offence if his purpose, or

one of his purposes, in sending it is that it should, so far as falling within paragraph (a) or (b) above, cause distress or anxiety to the recipient or to any other person to whom he intends that it or its contents or nature should be communicated.

(2A) In this section 'electronic communication' includes—

(a) any oral or other communication by means of an electronic communications network; and

(b) any communication (however sent) that is in electronic form.

(3) In this section references to sending include references to delivering or transmitting and to causing to be sent, delivered or transmitted and 'sender' shall be construed accordingly.

EW

Fine and/or 12 months'/2 years' imprisonment

C4.5.1 Key points

- A message on a website can amount to an offence contrary to s 1 and the offence can cover statements of fact or expressions of opinion (*R v BLC* [2024] EWCA Crim 1186).
- See *Connolly v DPP* [2008] 1 WLR 276 for Articles 9 (religion) and 10 (free speech) considerations. Articles 9(2) and 10(2) allow for restrictions on the relevant rights.
- According to *R v Casserly* [2024] EWCA Crim 25 whether a communication is so grossly offensive that it amounts to a criminal offence and loses the protection of freedom of speech, would depend on its content, the context in which it was sent and the purpose(s) of the sender, particularly relevant in this case were:
  - (i) Political communications and holding politicians to account are an important part of a democratic society.
  - (ii) Those receiving communications in a political context should have a thicker skin than ordinary citizens.
  - (iii) The use of strong language, even that which is offensive, shocking or extremely rude, may not be enough to amount to the offence charged.
  - (iv) Accordingly, the prosecution has to meet a very high threshold. It would only be possible for the communication to be grossly offensive if it went well beyond robust scrutiny of an elected politician in the performance of their elected role.
  - (v) It was not enough for the prosecution to prove the communication was likely to have caused distress or anxiety and the defendant either knew it was likely to have that effect or did not give thought to whether it would, in order to be guilty at least part of the defendant's objective(s) in sending the email must be to cause distress or anxiety.

See *Blackstone's Criminal Practice 2026* **B18.34**

C4.6 Offence of encouraging or assisting serious self-harm

Online Safety Act 2023, s 184

184 Offence of encouraging or assisting serious self-harm

(1) A person (D) commits an offence if—
- (a) D does a relevant act capable of encouraging or assisting the serious self-harm of another person, and
- (b) D's act was intended to encourage or assist the serious self-harm of another person.

(2) D "does a relevant act" if D—
- (a) communicates in person,
- (b) sends, transmits or publishes a communication by electronic means,
- (c) shows a person such a communication,
- (d) publishes material by any means other than electronic means,
- (e) sends, gives, shows or makes available to a person—
  - (i) material published as mentioned in paragraph (d), or
  - (ii) any form of correspondence, or
- (f) sends, gives or makes available to a person an item on which data is stored electronically.

(3) "Serious self-harm" means self-harm amounting to—
- (a) in England and Wales ... grievous bodily harm within the meaning of the Offences Against the Person Act 1861 . . .

(4) The person referred to in subsection (1)(a) and (b) need not be a specific person (or class of persons) known to, or identified by, D.

(5) D may commit an offence under this section whether or not serious self-harm occurs.

(6) If a person (D1) arranges for a person (D2) to do an act that is capable of encouraging or assisting the serious self-harm of another person and D2 does that act, D1 is to be treated as also having done it.

(7) In the application of subsection (1) to an act by D involving an electronic communication or a publication in physical form, it does not matter whether the content of the communication or publication is created by D (so for example, in the online context, the offence under this section may be committed by forwarding another person's direct message or sharing another person's post).

(8) In the application of subsection (1) to the sending, transmission or publication by electronic means of a communication consisting of or including a hyperlink to other content, the reference in subsection (2)(b) to the communication is to be read as including a reference to content accessed directly via the hyperlink.

(9) In the application of subsection (1) to an act by D involving an item on which data is stored electronically, the reference in subsection (2)(f) to the item is to be read as including a reference to content accessed by means of the item to which the person in receipt of the item is specifically directed by D.

(10) A provider of an internet service by means of which a communication is sent, transmitted or published is not to be regarded as a person who sends, transmits or publishes it.

(11) Any reference in this section to doing an act that is capable of encouraging the serious self-harm of another person includes a reference to doing so by threatening another person or otherwise putting pressure on another person to seriously self-harm. "Seriously self-harm" is to be interpreted consistently with subsection (3).

(12) Any reference to an act in this section, except in subsection (3), includes a reference to a course of conduct, and references to doing an act are to be read accordingly.

(13) In subsection (3) "act" includes omission.

EW

Fine and/or 12 months'/5 years' imprisonment

C5 **Computer Misuse**

C5.1 Unauthorized access to computer material

Computer Misuse Act 1990, s 1

(1) A person is guilty of an offence if—
- (a) he causes a computer to perform any function with intent to secure access to any program or data held in any computer or to enable any such access to be secured;
- (b) the access he intends to secure or to enable to be secured is unauthorised; and
- (c) he knows at the time when he causes the computer to perform the function that that is the case.

(2) The intent a person has to have to commit an offence under this section need not be directed at—
- (a) any particular program or data;
- (b) a program or data of any particular kind; or
- (c) a program or data held in any particular computer.

EW

Fine and/or 12 months'/2 years' imprisonment

C5.1.1 Key points

- For the offence to be made out there must be an interaction with the computer's programs but the interaction need not be successful.
- A public interest defence cannot be read into the statute (*R v Coltman* [2018] EWCA Crim 2059).
- s 1 was designed to combat all forms of unauthorized access to the actual data involved (*Bow Street Stipendiary Magistrate ex p United States* [2000] 2 AC 216).
- Definitions are provided in s 17 Computer Misuse Act 1990.

C5.2 Unauthorized access with intent to commit or facilitate commission of further offences

Computer Misuse Act 1990, s 2

(1) A person is guilty of an offence under this section if he commits an offence under section 1 above ('the unauthorised access offence') with intent—
- (a) to commit an offence to which this section applies; or
- (b) to facilitate the commission of such an offence (whether by himself or by any other person);

and the offence he intends to commit or facilitate is referred to below in this section as the further offence.

(2) This section applies to offences—
- (a) for which the sentence is fixed by law; or

Blackstone's Magistrates' Court Handbook 2026. Bartholomew Dalton and Caroline Liggins, Oxford University Press.
DOI: 10.1093/oso/9780198963943.003.0046

(b) for which a person who has attained the age of twenty-one years and has no previous convictions may be sentenced to imprisonment for a term of five years but for the restrictions imposed by section 33 of the Magistrates' Courts Act 1980).

(3) It is immaterial for the purposes of this section whether the further offence is to be committed on the same occasion as the unauthorised access offence or on any future occasion.

(4) A person may be guilty of an offence under this section even though the facts are such that the commission of the further offence is impossible.

EW

Fine and/or 12 months'/5 years' imprisonment

C5.3 Unauthorised acts impairing the operation of a computer

Computer Misuse Act 1990, s 3

3 (1) A person is guilty of an offence if—
- (a) he does any unauthorised act in relation to a computer;
- (b) at the time when he does the act he knows that it is unauthorised; and
- (c) either subsection (2) or subsection (3) below applies.

(2) This subsection applies if the person intends by doing the act—
- (a) to impair the operation of any computer;
- (b) to prevent or hinder access to any program or data held in any computer;
- (c) to impair the operation of any such program or the reliability of any such data; or
- (d) to enable any of the things mentioned in paragraphs (a) to (c) above to be done.

(3) This subsection applies if the person is reckless as to whether the act will do any of the things mentioned in paragraphs (a) to (d)of subsection (2) above.

(4) The intention referred to in subsection (2) above, or the recklessness referred to in subsection (3) above, need not relate to—
- (a) any particular computer;
- (b) any particular program or data; or
- (c) a program or data of any particular kind.

(5) In this section—
- (a) a reference to doing an act includes a reference to causing an act to be done;
- (b) 'act' includes a series of acts;
- (c) a reference to impairing, preventing or hindering something includes a reference to doing so temporarily.

EW

Fine and/or 12 months'/10 years' imprisonment

C5.3.1 Key points

The offence is made out if a bogus email is placed on another person's computer (*Zezev and Yarimaka v Governor of HMP Brixton* [2002] EWHC 589 (Admin)).

C5.4 Making, supplying, or obtaining articles for use in offence under section 1, 3, or 3ZA Computer Misuse Act 1990

Computer Misuse Act 1990, s 3A

(1) A person is guilty of an offence if he makes, adapts, supplies or offers to supply any article intending it to be used to commit, or to assist in the commission of, an offence under section 1, 3 or 3ZA.

(2) A person is guilty of an offence if he supplies or offers to supply any article believing that it is likely to be used to commit, or to assist in the commission of, an offence under section 1, 3 or 3ZA.

(3) A person is guilty of an offence if he obtains any article—

(a) intending to use it to commit, or to assist in the commission of, an offence under section 1, 3 or 3ZA, or

(b) with a view to its being supplied for use to commit, or to assist in the commission of, an offence under section 1, 3 or 3ZA.

(4) In this section 'article' includes any program or data held in electronic form.

EW

Fine and/or 12 months'/2 years' imprisonment

See *Blackstone's Criminal Practice 2026* **B17.14**

C6 **Criminal Damage**

C6.1 Destroying or damaging property

See *Blackstone's Criminal Practice 2026* **B8**

C6.1A *Destroying or damaging property: basic offence*

Criminal Damage Act 1971, s 1 (1) Destroying or damaging property

(1) A person who without lawful excuse destroys or damages any property belonging to another intending to destroy or damage any such property or being reckless as to whether any such property would be destroyed or damaged shall be guilty of an offence.

(2) A person who without lawful excuse destroys or damages any property, whether belonging to himself or another—

(a) intending to destroy or damage any property or being reckless as to whether any property would be destroyed or damaged; and

(b) intending by the destruction or damage to endanger the life of another or being reckless as to whether the life of another would be thereby endangered;

shall be guilty of an offence.

(3) An offence committed under this section by destroying or damaging property by fire shall be charged as arson.

IO s 1(2)

EW Racially aggravated (see C6.1.B) or offence is under s 1(1) and value is over £5,000, involves arson, or destroying or damaging a memorial.

SO If value does not exceed £5,000 and offence is under s 1(1) and does not involve arson or destroying or damaging a memorial; the offence remains an indictable offence for all other purposes (*Fennell* [2000] EWCA Crim 3544) such as for time limits (*DPP v Bird* [2015] EWHC 4077 (Admin)), committing an attempt and costs.

s 1(2): Life

Racially aggravated offence: Fine and/or 12 months'/14 years' imprisonment

If either way non-aggravated offence: Fine and/or 12 months'/ 10 years' imprisonment

If summary only: Level 4 fine and/or 3 months' imprisonment

Blackstone's Magistrates' Court Handbook 2026. Bartholomew Dalton and Caroline Liggins, Oxford University Press. © Oxford University Press 2026.
DOI: 10.1093/oso/9780198963943.003.0047

C6.1B *Damaging or destroying property: aggravated offence*

Crime and Disorder Act 1998, s 30

(1) A person is guilty of an offence under this section if he commits an offence under section 1(1) of the Criminal Damage Act 1971 (destroying or damaging property belonging to another) which is racially or religiously aggravated for the purposes of this section.

EW

12 months' imprisonment and/or fine/14 years' imprisonment

C6.1.2 *Sentencing*

The guidelines for endangering life and threats to cause criminal damage appear at C6.2 and C6.3.

C6.1.2.1 Arson (criminal damage by fire)

Note: Courts should consider requesting a report from: liaison and diversion services, a medical practitioner, or where it is necessary, ordering a psychiatric report, to ascertain both whether the offence is linked to a mental disorder or learning disability (to assist in the assessment of culpability) and whether any mental health disposal should be considered

SCG Arson (criminal damage by fire)

C6.1.2.2 Criminal damage (other than by fire) value not exceeding £5,000: basic and aggravated offences

Note: Where an offence of criminal damage is added to the indictment at the Crown Court the statutory maximum sentence is 10 years' custody regardless of the value of the damage.

SCG Criminal damage (other than by fire) value not exceeding £5,000/ Racially or religiously aggravated criminal damage

C6.1.2.3 Criminal damage (other than by fire) value exceeding £5,000

SCG Criminal damage (other than by fire) value exceeding £5,000/ Racially or religiously aggravated criminal damage

C6.2 Criminal damage (by endangering life) Criminal Damage Act 1971, s 1(2)

IO See C6.1.

Life

C6.2.1 *Sentencing*

SCG **Arson/criminal damage with intent to endanger life or reckless as to whether life endangered**

Courts should consider requesting a report from: liaison and diversion services, a medical practitioner, or where it is necessary, ordering a psychiatric report, to ascertain both whether the offence is linked to a mental disorder or learning disability (to assist in the assessment of culpability) and whether any mental health disposal should be considered.

C6.3 Threats to destroy or damage property

Criminal Damage Act 1971, s 2

2 Threats to destroy or damage property

A person who without lawful excuse makes to another a threat, intending that that other would fear it would be carried out—

(a) to destroy or damage any property belonging to that other or a third person; or

(b) to destroy or damage his own property in a way which he knows is likely to endanger the life of that other or third person;

shall be guilty of an offence.

EW

Fine and/or 12 months'/10 years' imprisonment

See *Blackstone's Criminal Practice 2026* **B8.31**

C6.3.1 *Sentencing*

SCG **Threats to destroy or damage property**

In cases of threats to cause damage by fire, courts should consider requesting a report from: liaison and diversion services, a medical practitioner, or where it is necessary, ordering a psychiatric report, to ascertain both whether the offence is linked to a mental disorder or learning disability (to assist in the assessment of culpability) and whether any mental health disposal should be considered.

C6.4 Possessing anything with intent to destroy or damage property

Criminal Damage Act 1971, s 3

3 Possessing anything with intent to destroy or damage property

A person who has anything in his custody or under his control intending without lawful excuse to use it or cause or permit another to use it—

(a) to destroy or damage any property belonging to some other person; or
(b) to destroy or damage his own or the user's property in a way which he knows is likely to endanger the life of some other person;

shall be guilty of an offence.

EW

Fine and/or 12 months'/10 years' imprisonment

See *Blackstone's Criminal Practice 2026* **B8.36**

C6.5 Key points

- There is no bar on charging attempted criminal damage where, due to value, the matter can be tried summarily only (*R v Bristol Justices, ex p E* [1999] 1 WLR 390).
- Lawful excuse is defined in s 5:

Criminal Damage Act 1971, s 5(1)–(5)

5 'Without lawful excuse'

(1) This section applies to any offence under section 1(1) above and any offence under section 2 or 3 above other than one involving a threat by the person charged to destroy or damage property in a way which he knows is likely to endanger the life of another or involving an intent by the person charged to use or cause or permit the use of something in his custody or under his control so to destroy or damage property.

(2) A person charged with an offence to which this section applies, shall, whether or not he would be treated for the purposes of this Act as having a lawful excuse apart from this subsection, be treated for those purposes as having a lawful excuse—

(a) if at the time of the act or acts alleged to constitute the offence he believed that the person or persons whom he believed to be entitled to consent to the destruction of or damage to the property in question had so consented, or would have so consented to it if he or they had known of the destruction or damage and its circumstances; or

(b) if he destroyed or damaged or threatened to destroy or damage the property in question or, in the case of a charge of an offence under section 3 above, intended to use or cause or permit the use of something to destroy or damage it, in order to protect property belonging to himself or another or a right or interest in property which was or which he believed to be vested in himself or another, and at the time of the act or acts alleged to constitute the offence he believed—

(i) that the property, right or interest was in immediate need of protection; and

(ii) that the means of protection adopted or proposed to be adopted were or would be reasonable having regard to all the circumstances.

(3) For the purposes of this section it is immaterial whether a belief is justified or not if it is honestly held.

(4) For the purposes of subsection (2) above a right or interest in property includes any right or privilege in or over land, whether created by grant, licence or otherwise.

(5) This section shall not be construed as casting doubt on any defence recognised by law as a defence to criminal charges.

- A person can avail himself of the defence of lawful excuse, notwithstanding the fact that he was intoxicated (*Jaggard v Dickinson* (1981) 72 Cr App R 33). The test is subjective, that is, whether the belief is held honestly, not whether it is justified or reasonable. Conduct due to mental illness resulting from alcohol psychosis or hallucinosis may not be reckless if the defendant was thereby not aware of the risk (*R v Coley* [2013] EWCA Crim 223).
- Whether a person is acting to protect property has an objective element (*R v Hunt* (1977) 66 Cr App R 105).
- It is clear that s 5(5) is intended to cover the situation whereby damage is caused to protect life or prevent injury (*R v Baker*, The Times, 26 November 1996).
- Damage does not need to be destruction and encompasses harm that is not permanent, such as graffiti. If expense or inconvenience is involved in putting right the matter then damage will have been caused (eg stamping on a policeman's helmet so that it had to be pushed back into shape). Damaging something that can be restored (eg deleting a computer program) constitutes damage (*Cox v Riley* (1986) 83 Cr App R 54). Spitting on a police officer's uniform is unlikely to cause damage (*A v R* [1978] Crim LR 689). The soaking of a blanket and the flooding of the floor of a police cell were held to amount to damage in *R v Fiak* [2005] EWCA Crim 2381, and the daubing of water-soluble paint on a pavement was equally found to amount to damage in *Hardman v Chief Constable of Avon and Somerset* [1986] Crim LR 330.
- Determining whether something has been damaged is a matter of fact and degree to be determined by the magistrates or the jury (*Roe v Kingerlee* [1986] Crim LR 735).
- For the purposes of s 5(2), the defendant must be sure that the owner would consent, and the belief that the owner 'might (or should) have consented' is insufficient (*AG's Reference (No. 1 of 2023)* [2024] EWCA Crim 243). Also, the term 'circumstances' includes an objective element and does not include the merits, urgency or importance of any matter about which the defendant may be protesting. The political or philosophical beliefs of the defendant are irrelevant.

- Causing significant damage to property during a protest falls outside ECHR protection. Minor or temporary damage caused during a protest requires a case-specific assessment of proportionality, but such assessment will very rarely be needed (AG's Reference (No 1 of 2022) [2022] EWCA Crim 1259).
- It is an offence to damage jointly owned property. Section 10 provides:

Criminal Damage Act 1971, s 10

10 Interpretation

(1) In this Act 'property' means of a tangible nature, whether real or personal, including money and—
  (a) including wild creatures which have been tamed or are ordinarily kept in captivity, and any other wild creatures or their carcasses if, but only if, they have been reduced into possession which has not been lost or abandoned or are in the course of being reduced into possession; but
  (b) not including mushrooms growing wild on any land or flowers, fruit or foliage of a plant growing wild on any land.

  For the purposes of this subsection 'mushroom' includes any fungus and 'plant' includes any shrub or tree.

(2) Property shall be treated for the purposes of this Act as belonging to any person—
  (a) having the custody or control of it;
  (b) having in it any proprietary right or interest (not being an equitable interest arising only from an agreement to transfer or grant an interest); or
  (c) having a charge on it.

(3) Where property is subject to a trust, the persons to whom it belongs shall be so treated as including any person having a right to enforce the trust.

(4) Property of a corporation sole shall be so treated as belonging to the corporation notwithstanding a vacancy in the corporation.

(5) For the purposes of this Act a modification of the contents of a computer shall not be regarded as damaging any computer or computer storage medium unless its effect on that computer or computer storage medium impairs its physical condition.

- Whether a threat has been made under s 2(a) is to be assessed objectively with reference to the words and actions of the defendant (*R v Cakmak* [2002] EWCA Crim 500).
- In relation to possession of anything with intent to destroy or damage a conditional intent will suffice (*R v Buckingham* (1976) 63 Cr App R 159).
- The prosecution will have proved that the defendant was reckless if, having regard to all the available evidence, the court is sure:
  - that he was aware of a risk that property would be destroyed/damaged; and
  - that in the circumstances which were known to him it was unreasonable for him to take that risk.

  This test allows for some of the personal characteristics of a defendant to be taken into account (see *R v G* [2003] UKHL 50).
- In relation to criminal damage to a memorial:

Magistrates Courts Act 1980, s 22

(11A) s 22 In paragraph 1 of Schedule 2 'memorial' means—

(a) a building or other structure, or any other thing, erected or installed on land (or in or on any building or other structure on land), or

(b) a garden or any other thing planted or grown on land, which has a commemorative purpose

(11B) For the purposes of that paragraph, any moveable thing (such as a bunch of flowers) which—

(a) is left in, on or at a memorial within the meaning of subsection (11A), and (b) has (or can reasonably be assumed to have) a commemorative purpose, is also to be regarded as a memorial.

(11C) For the purposes of subsections (11A) and (11B)—

(a) references to a building or a structure include a reference to part of a building or part of a structure (as the case may be), and

(b) something has a commemorative purpose if at least one of its purposes is to commemorate—

(i) one or more individuals or animals (or a particular description of individuals or animals), or

(ii) an event or a series of events (such as an armed conflict).

(11D) It is immaterial for the purposes of subsection (11C)(b)(i) whether or not any individuals or animals concerned are or were (at any material time)— (a) living or deceased, or (b) capable of being identified.

C7 **Drugs**

See *Blackstone's Criminal Practice 2026* **B19**

C7.1 Key points: General defence

- A statutory defence is provided by s 28 Misuse of Drugs Act 1971:

> **Misuse of Drugs Act 1971, s 28**
>
> **28 Proof of lack of knowledge etc to be a defence in proceedings for certain offences**
>
> (1) This section applies to offences under any of the following provisions of this Act, that is to say section 4(2) and (3), section 5(2) and (3), section 6(2) and section 9.
>
> (2) Subject to subsection (3) below, in any proceedings for an offence to which this section applies it shall be a defence for the accused to prove that he neither knew of nor suspected nor had reason to suspect the existence of some fact alleged by the prosecution which it is necessary for the prosecution to prove if he is to be convicted of the offence charged.
>
> (3) Where in any proceedings for an offence to which this section applies it is necessary, if the accused is to be convicted of the offence charged, for the prosecution to prove that some substance or product involved in the alleged offence was the controlled drug which the prosecution alleges it to have been, and it is proved that the substance or product in question was that controlled drug, the accused—
>
> (a) shall not be acquitted of the offence charged by reason only of proving that he neither knew nor suspected nor had reason to suspect that the substance or product in question was the particular controlled drug alleged; but
>
> (b) shall be acquitted thereof—
>
> (i) if he proves that he neither believed nor suspected nor had reason to suspect that the substance or product in question was a controlled drug; or
>
> (ii) if he proves that he believed the substance or product in question to be a controlled drug, or a controlled drug of a description, such that, if it had in fact been that controlled drug or a controlled drug of that description, he would not at the material time have been committing any offence to which this section applies.
>
> (4) Nothing in this section shall prejudice any defence which it is open to a person charged with an offence to which this section applies to raise apart from this section.

- In considering a defence under s 28(3)(b), self-induced intoxication should not be considered (*R v Young* [1984] 2 All ER 164).

C7.2 Key points: Sentencing

- A minimum sentence of seven years must, unless exceptional circumstances apply, be imposed where an adult is convicted of a Class A drug trafficking offence (which excludes possession alone) if the offender has been convicted

Blackstone's Magistrates' Court Handbook 2026. Bartholomew Dalton and Caroline Liggins, Oxford University Press.
DOI: 10.1093/oso/9780198963943.003.0048

of two other drug trafficking offences in the circumstances set out in **D20**. Such offences may be tried on indictment only

- Sentences are prescribed by Sch 4 to the Misuse of Drugs Act 1971 in the table below.

C7.3 Drugs—class A: fail to attend/remain for initial or follow-up assessment

Drugs Act 2005, s 12(1)–(3)

12 Attendance at initial assessment

This section applies if a person is required to attend an initial assessment and remain for its duration by virtue of section 9(2).

(3) A person is guilty of an offence if without good cause—
  (a) he fails to attend an initial assessment at the specified time and place, or
  (b) he attends the assessment at the specified time and place but fails to remain for its duration.

SO

Level 4 fine and/or 3 months' imprisonment

Drugs Act 2005, s 14(1) and (3)

14 Attendance at follow-up assessment

(b) This section applies if a person is required to attend a follow-up assessment and remain for its duration by virtue of section 10(2).

...

(3) A person is guilty of an offence if without good cause—
  (a) he fails to attend a follow-up assessment at the specified time and place, or
  (b) he attends the assessment at the specified time and place but fails to remain for its duration.

...

SO

Level 4 fine and/or 3 months' imprisonment

MISUSE OF DRUGS ACT 1971, Sch 4 Schedule 4 Prosecution and Punishment of Offences						
Section Creation Offence	**General Nature of Offence**	**Mode of Prosecution**	**Punishment**			
			Class A drug involved	Class B drug involved	Class C drug involved	General
Section 4(2)	Production, or being concerned in the production, of a controlled drug.	(a) Summary	12 months or fine, or both	12 months or fine, or both	3 months or £2,500, or both	
		(b) On indictment	Life	14 years	14 years	
Section 4(3)	Supplying or offering to supply a controlled drug or being concerned in the doing of either activity by another.	(a) Summary	12 months or fine, or both	12 months or fine, or both	3 months or £2,500, or both	
		(b) On indictment	Life	14 years	14 years	
Section 5(2)	Having possession of a controlled drug.	(a) Summary	12 months or fine, or both	12 months or fine, or both	3 months or £1,000 fine, or both	
		(b) On indictment	7 years	5 years	2 years	
Section 5(3)	Having possession of a controlled drug with intent to supply it to another.	(a) Summary	12 months or fine, or both	12 months or fine, or both	3 months or £2,500, or both	
		(b) On indictment	Life	14 years	14 years	
Section 6(2)	Cultivation of cannabis plant.	(a) Summary				12 months or fine, or both
		(b) On indictment				14 years
Section 8	Being the occupier, or concerned in the management, of premises and permitting or suffering certain activities to take place there.	(a) Summary	12 months or fine, or both	12 months or fine, or both	3 months or £2,500, or both	
		(b) On indictment	14 years	14 years	14 years	

C7.3.1 *Sentencing*

SCG Drugs—class A—fail to attend/remain for assessment

Note that this guideline refers to s 12 offences only.

C7.4 Drugs—class A: fail/refuse to provide a sample

There are a considerable number of condition precedents that need to be satisfied before a lawful request for a sample can be made.

Police and Criminal Evidence Act 1984, s 63B

63B Testing for presence of Class A drugs

(1) A sample of urine or a non-intimate sample may be taken from a person in police detention for the purpose of ascertaining whether he has any specified Class A drug in his body if—
   (a) either the arrest condition or the charge condition is met;
   (b) both the age condition and the request condition are met; and
   (c) the notification condition is met in relation to the arrest condition, the charge condition or the age condition (as the case may be).

(1A) The arrest condition is that the person concerned has been arrested for an offence but has not been charged with that offence and either—
   (a) the offence is a trigger offence; or
   (b) a police officer of at least the rank of inspector has reasonable grounds for suspecting that the misuse by that person of a specified Class A drug caused or contributed to the offence and has authorised the sample to be taken.

(2) The charge condition is either—
   (a) that the person concerned has been charged with a trigger offence; or
   (b) that the person concerned has been charged with an offence and a police officer of at least the rank of inspector, who has reasonable grounds for suspecting that the misuse by that person of any specified Class A drug caused or contributed to the offence and has authorised the sample to be taken.

(3) The age condition is—
   (a) if the arrest condition is met, that the person concerned has attained the age of 18;
   (b) if the charge condition is met, that he has attained the age of 14.

(4) The request condition is that a police officer has requested the person concerned to give the sample.

(4A) ...

(4B) ...

(5) Before requesting the person concerned to give a sample, an officer must—
   (a) warn him that if, when so requested, he fails without good cause to do so he may be liable to prosecution, and
   (b) in a case within subsection (1A)(b) or (2)(b) above, inform him of the giving of the authorisation and of the grounds in question.

(5A) ...

(5B) ...

(5C) Despite subsection (1)(a) above, a sample may be taken from a person under this section if—
   (c) he was arrested for an offence (the first offence),
   (d) the arrest condition is met but the charge condition is not met,
   (e) before a sample is taken by virtue of subsection (1) above he would (but for his arrest as mentioned in paragraph (d) below) be required to be released from police detention,

(f) he continues to be in police detention by virtue of his having been arrested for an offence not falling within subsection (1A) above, and

(g) the sample is taken before the end of the period of 24 hours starting with the time when his detention by virtue of his arrest for the first offence began.

(5D) A sample must not be taken from a person under this section if he is detained in a police station unless he has been brought before the custody officer.

(6) A sample may be taken under this section only by a person prescribed by regulations made by the Secretary of State by statutory instrument.

(6A) . . .

(6B) . . .

(7) . . .

(8) A person who fails without good cause to give any sample which may be taken from him under this section shall be guilty of an offence.

SO

Level 4 fine and/or 3 months' imprisonment

C7.4.1 *Sentencing*

SCG **Drugs—class A—fail/refuse to provide a sample**

C7.5 Drugs—fraudulent evasion of a prohibition by bringing into or taking out of the United Kingdom a controlled drug

Misuse of Drugs Act 1971, s 3

3 Restriction of importation and exportation of controlled drugs

(1) Subject to subsection (2) below—

a. the importation of a controlled drug; and

b. the exportation of a controlled drug, are hereby prohibited.

(2) Subsection (1) above does not apply—

a. to the importation or exportation of a controlled drug which is for the time being excepted from paragraph (a) or, as the case may be, paragraph (b) of subsection (1) above by regulations under section 7 of this Act or by provision made in a temporary class drug order by virtue of section 7A; or

b. to the importation or exportation of a controlled drug under and in accordance with the terms of a licence issued by the Secretary of State and in compliance with any conditions attached thereto.

Customs and Excise Management Act 1979, s 170(2)

170 Penalty for fraudulent evasion of duty, etc

(2) Without prejudice to any other provision of the Customs and Excise Acts 1979, if any person is, in relation to any goods, in any way knowingly concerned in any fraudulent evasion or attempt at evasion—

(a) of any duty chargeable on the goods;

(b) of any prohibition or restriction for the time being in force with respect to the goods under or by virtue of any enactment; or
(c) of any provision of the Customs and Excise Acts 1979 applicable to the goods,
he shall be guilty of an offence under this section and may be detained.

EW

Class A: 12 months' imprisonment and/or £20,000 or three times the value of the drugs if greater/life

Class B: 12 months' imprisonment and/or £20,000 or three times the value of the drugs if greater/14 years' imprisonment

Class C: 3 months' imprisonment and/or three times the value of the drugs or £500 if greater/14 years

GC If Class A or B

C7.5.1 *Sentencing*

SCG **Fraudulent evasion of a prohibition by bringing into or taking out of the UK a controlled drug**

C7.5.2 Key points

- The suspect may be mistaken as to the nature of the substance being trafficked, and a belief, albeit mistaken, that that item was not at the time prohibited may provide a defence (*R v Taaffe* (1984) 78 Cr App R 301 and *R v Forbes* [2001] UKHL 40, by analogy).
- It is not necessary to prove that the suspect knew the precise category of what was being smuggled, simply that it was prohibited (*R v Hussain* (1969) 53 Cr App R 448). The offence is analysed in *R v Datson* [2022] EWCA Crim 1248.
- Where a charge is instead brought under the 1971 Act rather than the 1979 Act, a defence under s 28 of the 1971 Act may apply.

C7.6 Drugs—supplying, offering to supply and possession with intent to supply

Misuse of Drugs Act 1971, ss 4(3) and 5(3)

4 Restriction of production and supply of controlled drugs

(3) Subject to section 28 of this Act, it is an offence for a person—
(a) to supply or offer to supply a controlled drug to another in contravention of subsection (1) above; or
(b) to be concerned in the supplying of such a drug to another in contravention of that subsection; or
(c) to be concerned in the making to another in contravention of that subsection of an offer to supply such a drug.

. . .

5 Restriction of possession of controlled drugs (with intent to supply)

(4) Subject to section 28 of this Act, it is an offence for a person to have a controlled drug in his possession, whether lawfully or not, with intent to supply it to another in contravention of section 4(1) of this Act.

EW

See table in C7.3

C7.6.1 *Sentencing*

Note:

Sentencing Act 2020, s 71

71 Supply of controlled drug near school premises or involving child

(1) This section applies where—
   (a) a court is considering the seriousness of an offence under section 4(3) of the Misuse of Drugs Act 1971 (supplying controlled drug etc), and
   (b) the offender was aged 18 or over when the offence was committed.
(2) If condition A or B is met, the court—
   (a) must treat the fact that the condition is met as an aggravating factor, and
   (b) must state in open court that the offence is so aggravated.
(3) Condition A is that the offence was committed on or in the vicinity of school premises at a relevant time.
(4) For the purposes of subsection (3)—
   'relevant time', in relation to school premises, is—
   (a) any time when the school premises are in use by persons under the age of 18;
   (b) one hour before the start and one hour after the end of any such time;
   'school' has the same meaning as it has in section 4A of the Misuse of Drugs Act 1971;
   'school premises' means land used for the purposes of a school excluding any land occupied solely as a dwelling by a person employed at the school.
(5) Condition B is that in connection with the commission of the offence the offender used a courier who, when the offence was committed, was aged under 18.
(6) For the purposes of subsection (5), a person uses a courier in connection with an offence under section 4(3) of the Misuse of Drugs Act 1971 if the person causes or permits another person ('the courier')—
   (a) to deliver a controlled drug to a third person, or
   (b) to deliver a drug-related consideration to the person or a third person.
(7) For the purposes of subsection (6), a drug-related consideration is a consideration of any description which—
   (a) is obtained in connection with the supply of a controlled drug, or
   (b) is intended to be used in connection with obtaining a controlled drug.
(8) In this section, 'controlled drug' and 'supply' have the same meanings as in the Misuse of Drugs Act 1971.

SCG **Supply a controlled drug**

C7.6.2 Key points

- Purchasing drugs on behalf of a third party, and passing those drugs to that party, even for no profit, amounts to supply.
- So-called social supply should be charged as simple possession. In *R v Denslow* [1998] Crim LR 566 the court observed:

> We wonder why it was thought necessary to charge supply in the circumstances of this case. How could it possibly serve the interests of the public that there should be either a trial or if not a trial as conventionally understood a hearing to determine this matter of law? It was inevitable that the appellant would be dealt with at worst as though he were in possession of the drugs and, as turned out in this case, as though he were without any criminal responsibility for that particular part of the transaction. We are told that a plea had been offered to a charge of possession. It ought to have been accepted. We hope that those words will be borne in mind by prosecuting authorities in the future.

- A person who places drugs in the hands of a third party merely for safe keeping does not supply drugs (*R v Maginnis* [1987] AC 303).
- An offer to supply can be made by words or conduct, and once made cannot be withdrawn.
- To be concerned in the supply of drugs under s 4(3)(b) Misuse of Drugs Act 1971 does not require proof of an actual supply but rather involvement in the process of supply. It is not limited to actual or past supply (*R v Martin (Dwain Ashley)* [2014] EWCA Crim 1940 and *R v Abi-Khalil* [2017] EWCA Crim 17).

C7.7 Drugs—production of a controlled drug and cultivation of cannabis

Misuse of Drugs Act 1971, ss 4(2)(a), (b), and 6

4 Restriction of production and supply of controlled drugs

(2) Subject to section 28 of this Act, it is an offence for a person—
  (a) to produce a controlled drug in contravention of subsection (1) above; or
  (b) to be concerned in the production of such a drug in contravention of that subsection by another.

6 Restriction of cultivation of cannabis plant

(1) Subject to any regulations under section 7 of this Act for the time being in force, it shall not be lawful for a person to cultivate any plant of the genus Cannabis.
(2) Subject to section 28 of this Act, it is an offence to cultivate any such plant in contravention of subsection (1) above.

EW

GC

See table at C7.3

C7.7.1 *Sentencing*

SCG **Production of a controlled drug/Cultivation of cannabis plant**

C7.7.2 Key points

- In sentencing cases involving the cultivation of cannabis it is the capacity to produce that is central rather than the quantity (*R v Wiseman* [2013] EWCA Crim 2499).
- It is the plant that must be cultivated, not the cannabis produced from the plant.
- The accused does not need to know that the plant was in fact cannabis (*R v Champ* (1981) 73 Cr App R 267). A simple act such as placing a plant in a protected environment (e.g. a bedroom where it is shielded from the elements) or watering the soil is a positive act encouraging growth (*Taylor v Chief Constable of Kent* (1981) 72 Cr App R 318).
- The defence of necessity (commonly pleaded by sufferers of certain illnesses) is not a defence available in law for this charge (*R v Quayle and others* [2006] 1 All ER 988).

C7.8 Drugs—permitting premises to be used

Misuse of Drugs Act 1971, s 8

8 Occupiers etc of premises to be punishable for permitting certain activities to take place there

A person commits an offence if, being the occupier or concerned in the management of any premises, he knowingly permits or suffers any of the following activities to take place on those premises, that is to say—

(a) producing or attempting to produce a controlled drug in contravention of section 4(1) of this Act;

(b) supplying or attempting to supply a controlled drug to another in contravention of section 4(1) of this Act, or offering to supply a controlled drug to another in contravention of section 4(1);

(c) preparing opium for smoking;

(d) smoking cannabis, cannabis resin or prepared opium.

EW

GC

See table at C7.3

C7.8.1 *Sentencing*

SCG **Permitting premises to be used**

C7.8.2 Key points

Where the allegation is permitting premises to be used for the supply of drugs, in order to establish the offence the Crown must prove not only that the defendant knowingly permitted the supply of the drugs, but also that a supply of the drugs had actually taken place on the premises (*R v McGee* [2012] EWCA Crim 613 (Class A); *R v Auguiste* [2003] EWCA Crim 3329 (Class B). The prohibited activity may include offering to supply drugs, which on the facts might be inferred, and supply included the whole process of supply (*R v McNaught* [2018] EWCA Crim 1588).

C7.9 Drugs—possession of a controlled drug

Misuse of Drugs Act 1971, s 5(2) and (4)

5 Restriction of possession of controlled drugs

(2) Subject to section 28 of this Act [see C6.1] and to subsection (4) below, it is an offence for a person to have a controlled drug in his possession in contravention of subsection (1) above.

. . .

(4) In any proceedings for an offence under subsection (2) above in which it is proved that the accused had a controlled drug in his possession, it shall be a defence for him to prove—
  (a) that, knowing or suspecting it to be a controlled drug, he took possession of it for the purpose of preventing another from committing or continuing to commit an offence in connection with that drug and that as soon as possible after taking possession of it he took all such steps as were reasonably open to him to destroy the drug or to deliver it into the custody of a person lawfully entitled to take custody of it; or
  (b) that, knowing or suspecting it to be a controlled drug, he took possession of it for the purpose of delivering it into the custody of a person lawfully entitled to take custody of it and that as soon as possible after taking possession of it he took all such steps as were reasonably open to him to deliver it into the custody of such a person.

EW

See table at C7.3

C7.9.1 *Sentencing*

SCG Possession of a controlled drug

C7.9.2 Key points

A person must know that he is in possession of the drug; therefore a person holding drugs believing that they were something else would not be guilty (assuming the court believed the defendant). Note, however, that suspicion would be sufficient (see s 28 Misuse of Drugs Act 1971); and see later on containers.

- A person who 'forgot' that he had drugs would still be in possession of those drugs, but a person who had no knowledge at all would not (*R v Martindale* [1986] 3 All ER 25).
- A person need not be in physical possession of a drug, provided he is in control (sole or joint): see s 37(3) Misuse of Drugs Act 1971. It is not sufficient that the defendant might have knowledge of a confederate's possession of drugs; the test is whether the drugs were part of a common pool from which all could draw (*R v Searle* [1971] Crim LR 592).
- The fact that the quantity of drug was so minuscule as to be incapable of being used does not amount to a defence (*R v Boyesen* [1982] AC 768); it is merely an indication that the defendant may not have had knowledge of its presence.
- If a person is in possession of a container and he knows there is something inside, he will be in possession of the contents, even if he does not know their characteristics (*R v Lambert* [2002] 2 AC 545). If, however, the defendant had no right to open the container, he may not be in possession of its contents (*Warner v Metropolitan Police Commissioner* [1969] 2 AC 256), nor if he believed the contents to be different from what in fact they were (*R v McNamara* (1988) 87 Cr App R 246) and see s 28 Misuse of Drugs Act 1971 at C7.1.
- Possession of drugs for religious purposes is not afforded any special protection under the European Convention (*R v Taylor* [2002] 1 Cr App R 519). Using restricted drugs (eg cannabis) for medicinal purposes does not make possession lawful (*AG's Reference (No 2 of 2004)* [2005] EWCA Crim 1415) but there may be public interest arguments why prosecution should not take place.

See *Blackstone's Criminal Practice 2026* B19.23

C7.10 Prosecution and Punishment of Misuse of Drugs Act Offences

C7.10.1 *Obstruction under the Misuse of Drugs Act 1971*

Section 23(4) Misuse of Drugs Act 1971 provides:

Misuse of Drugs Act 1971, s 23(4)

23 Powers to search and obtain evidence

(4) A person commits an offence if he—
  (a) intentionally obstructs a person in the exercise of his powers under this section; or
  (b) conceals from a person acting in the exercise of his powers under subsection (1) above any such books, documents, stocks or drugs as are mentioned in that subsection; or
  (c) without reasonable excuse (proof of which shall lie on him) fails to produce any such books or documents as are so mentioned where their production is demanded by a person in the exercise of his power under that subsection.

EW

12 months' imprisonment and/or fine/2 years' imprisonment

C7.10.2 Key points

For there to be obstruction, the officer must be acting in the execution of his office. The officer must comply strictly with the requirements of the Police and Criminal Evidence Act 1984 in relation to a stop and search (*R v Bristol* [2007] EWHC 3214 (Admin); *B v DPP* [2008] EWHC 1655 (Admin); *R (Michaels) v Highbury Corner Magistrates' Court* [2009] EWHC 2928 (Admin)).

C7.11 Drugs—psychoactive substances

Psychoactive Substances Act 2016, ss 1, 4–9

1 Overview

(1) This Act contains provision about psychoactive substances.
(2) Section 2 defines what is meant by a 'psychoactive substance'.
(3) Sections 4 to 10 contain provision about offences relating to psychoactive substances. S 6 has been replaced by SA 2020 s 72.
(4) Section 11 provides for exceptions to those offences.
(5) Sections 12 to 35 contain powers for dealing with prohibited activities in respect of psychoactive substances, in particular powers to give prohibition notices and make prohibition orders.
(6) Sections 36 to 54 contain enforcement powers.

. . .

Offences

4 Producing a psychoactive substance

(1) A person commits an offence if—
  (a) the person intentionally produces a psychoactive substance,
  (b) the person knows or suspects that the substance is a psychoactive substance, and
  (c) the person—
    (i) intends to consume the psychoactive substance for its psychoactive effects, or
    (ii) knows, or is reckless as to whether, the psychoactive substance is likely to be consumed by some other person for its psychoactive effects.
(2) This section is subject to section 11 (exceptions to offences).

5 Supplying, or offering to supply, a psychoactive substance

(1) A person commits an offence if—
  (a) the person intentionally supplies a substance to another person,
  (b) the substance is a psychoactive substance,
  (c) the person knows or suspects, or ought to know or suspect, that the substance is a psychoactive substance, and
  (d) the person knows, or is reckless as to whether, the psychoactive substance is likely to be consumed by the person to whom it is supplied, or by some other person, for its psychoactive effects.
(2) A person ('P') commits an offence if—
  (a) P offers to supply a psychoactive substance to another person ('R'), and

(b) P knows or is reckless as to whether R, or some other person, would, if P supplied a substance to R in accordance with the offer, be likely to consume the substance for its psychoactive effects.

(3) For the purposes of subsection (2)(b), the reference to a substance's psychoactive effects includes a reference to the psychoactive effects which the substance would have if it were the substance which P had offered to supply to R.

(4) This section is subject to section 11 (exceptions to offences).

7 Possession of psychoactive substance with intent to supply

(1) A person commits an offence if—
   (a) the person is in possession of a psychoactive substance,
   (b) the person knows or suspects that the substance is a psychoactive substance, and
   (c) the person intends to supply the psychoactive substance to another person for its consumption, whether by any person to whom it is supplied or by some other person, for its psychoactive effects.

(2) This section is subject to section 11 (exceptions to offences).

8 Importing or exporting a psychoactive substance

(1) A person commits an offence if—
   (a) the person intentionally imports a substance, (b) the substance is a psychoactive substance,
   (c) the person knows or suspects, or ought to know or suspect, that the substance is a psychoactive substance, and
   (d) the person—
      (i) intends to consume the psychoactive substance for its psychoactive effects, or
      (ii) knows, or is reckless as to whether, the psychoactive substance is likely to be consumed by some other person for its psychoactive effects.

(2) A person commits an offence if—
   (a) the person intentionally exports a substance,
   (b) the substance is a psychoactive substance,
   (c) the person knows or suspects, or ought to know or suspect, that the substance is a psychoactive substance, and
   (d) the person—
      (i) intends to consume the psychoactive substance for its psychoactive effects, or
      (ii) knows, or is reckless as to whether, the psychoactive substance is likely to be consumed by some other person for its psychoactive effects.

(3) In a case where a person imports or exports a controlled drug suspecting it to be a psychoactive substance, the person is to be treated for the purposes of this section as if the person had imported or exported a psychoactive substance suspecting it to be such a substance.

In this subsection 'controlled drug' has the same meaning as in the Misuse of Drugs Act 1971.

(4) Section 5 of the Customs and Excise Management Act 1979 (time of importation, exportation, etc) applies for the purposes of this section as it applies for the purposes of that Act.

(5) This section is subject to section 11 (exceptions to offences).

9 Possession of a psychoactive substance in a custodial institution

(1) A person commits an offence if—

(a) the person is in possession of a psychoactive substance in a custodial institution,
(b) the person knows or suspects that the substance is a psychoactive substance, and
(c) the person intends to consume the psychoactive substance for its psychoactive effects.

(2) In this section 'custodial institution' has the same meaning as in section 6.
(3) This section is subject to section 11 (exceptions to offences). . . .

EW ss 4–9

ss 4–8: 12 months' imprisonment and/or fine/7 years' imprisonment
s 9: 12 months' imprisonment and/or fine/2 years' imprisonment

C7.11.1 *Sentencing*

Note: aggravating factor under s 5.

Sentencing Act 2020, s 72

72 Supply of psychoactive substance in certain circumstances

(1) This section applies where—
(a) a court is considering the seriousness of an offence under section 5 of the Psychoactive Substances Act 2016 (supplying psychoactive substance, etc.), and
(b) the offender was aged 18 or over when the offence was committed.

(2) If condition A, B or C is met the court—
(a) must treat the fact that the condition is met as an aggravating factor, and
(b) must state in open court that the offence is so aggravated.

(3) Condition A is that the offence was committed on or in the vicinity of school premises at a relevant time.

(4) For the purposes of subsection (3)—
'relevant time', in relation to school premises, means—
(a) any time when the school premises are in use by persons under the age of 18;
(b) one hour before the start and one hour after the end of any such time;
'school' has the same meaning as in section 6 of the Psychoactive Substances Act 2016;
'school premises' means land used for the purposes of a school excluding any land occupied solely as a dwelling by a person employed at the school.

(5) Condition B is that, in connection with the offence, the offender used a courier who, when the offence was committed, was aged under 18.

(6) For the purposes of subsection (5), a person uses a courier in connection with an offence under section 5 of the Psychoactive Substances Act 2016 if the person causes or permits another person ('the courier')—
(a) to deliver a substance to a third person, or
(b) to deliver a drug-related consideration to the person or a third person.

(7) For the purposes of subsection (6), a drug-related consideration is a consideration of any description which—
(a) is obtained in connection with the supply of a psychoactive substance, or
(b) is intended to be used in connection with obtaining a psychoactive substance.

(8) Condition C is that the offence was committed in a custodial institution.
(9) For the purposes of subsection (8), 'custodial institution' means any of the following—
  (a) a prison;
  (b) a young offender institution, secure training centre or secure college;
  (c) a removal centre, short-term holding facility or pre-departure accommodation (each, as defined in section 147 of the Immigration and Asylum Act 1999);
  (d) service custody premises (as defined in section 300(7) of the Armed Forces Act 2006).
(10) In this section 'psychoactive substance' has the same meaning as in the Psychoactive Substances Act 2016 (see section 2 of that Act)

SCG **Producing a psychoactive substance/Importing or exporting a psychoactive substance**

C7.11.2 Key points

Psychoactive Substances Act 2016, ss 2, 3, and 11

2 Meaning of 'psychoactive substance' etc

(1) In this Act 'psychoactive substance' means any substance which—
  (a) is capable of producing a psychoactive effect in a person who consumes it, and
  (b) is not an exempted substance (see section 3).
(2) For the purposes of this Act a substance produces a psychoactive effect in a person if, by stimulating or depressing the person's central nervous system, it affects the person's mental functioning or emotional state; and references to a substance's psychoactive effects are to be read accordingly.
(3) For the purposes of this Act a person consumes a substance if the person causes or allows the substance, or fumes given off by the substance, to enter the person's body in any way.

A psychoactive substance may produce its effect by directly or indirectly stimulating or depressing the central nervous system (*R v Rochester* [2018] EWCA Crim 1936).

3 Exempted substances

s(1) In this Act 'exempted substance' means a substance listed in Schedule 1.

. . .

[SCHEDULE 1 Section 3—summary

EXEMPTED SUBSTANCES

Controlled drugs

Medicinal products

Alcohol

Nicotine and tobacco products

Caffeine

Food, including drink;]

. . .

Nitrous oxide is not necessarily a medicinal product under the Human Medicines Regulations 2012 and so is not automatically excluded from the effect of the Psychoactive Substances Act 2016. The substance must, to be an offence, be intended to be consumed its psychoactive effects and not for one of its lawful uses. The Crown must prove the unlawful intention (*R v Chapman and others* [2017] EWCA Crim 1743).

11 Exceptions to offences

(1) It is not an offence under this Act for a person to carry on any activity listed in subsection (3) if, in the circumstances in which it is carried on by that person, the activity is an exempted activity.

(2) In this section 'exempted activity' means an activity listed in Schedule 2.

(3) The activities referred to in subsection (1) are—

- (a) producing a psychoactive substance;
- (b) supplying such a substance;
- (c) offering to supply such a substance;
- (d) possessing such a substance with intent to supply it;
- (e) importing or exporting such a substance;
- (f) possessing such a substance in a custodial institution (within the meaning of section 9) . . .

[Schedule 2 EXEMPTED ACTIVITIES—summary

Healthcare-related activities

Research]

C8 Education Act

C8.1 School non-attendance

Education Act 1996, s 444(1), (1A), (1B), (2), (2A), and (3)

444 Offence: failure to secure regular attendance at school of registered pupil

(1) If a child of compulsory school age who is a registered pupil at a school fails to attend regularly at the school, his parent is guilty of an offence.

(1A) If in the circumstances mentioned in subsection (1) the parent knows that his child is failing to attend regularly at the school and fails to cause him to do so, he is guilty of an offence.

(1B) It is a defence for a person charged with an offence under subsection (1A) to prove that he had a reasonable justification for his failure to cause the child to attend regularly at the school.

(2) Subsections (2A) to (6) below apply in proceedings for an offence under this section in respect of a child who is not a boarder at the school at which he is a registered pupil.

(2A) The child shall not be taken to have failed to attend regularly at the school by reason of his absence from the school at any time if the parent proves that at that time the child was prevented from attending by reason of sickness or any unavoidable cause.

(3) The child shall not be taken to have failed to attend regularly at the school by reason of his absence from the school—
  (a) with leave, or
  (b) [repealed]
  (c) on any day exclusively set apart for religious observance by the religious body to which his parent belongs.

SO

s 444(1): Level 3 fine

s 444(1A): Level 4 fine and/or 3 months' imprisonment

C8.1.1 *Sentencing*

SCG School non-attendance

C8.1.2 Key points

- The offence under section 444(1) is strict liability, but the prosecution have the burden of proof. In *Isle of Wight Council v Platt* [2017] UKSC 28, the Supreme Court held that children fail to attend regularly at school under section 444 Education Act 1996 when they fail to attend on every day when required to do so in accordance with the rules prescribed by the school, unless they have permission to be absent or some other reasonable excuse.

Blackstone's Magistrates' Court Handbook 2026. Bartholomew Dalton and Caroline Liggins, Oxford University Press.
DOI: 10.1093/oso/9780198963943.003.0049

- Difficulties in getting a child to school due to the child's behavioural and psychological difficulties did not equate to an unavoidable cause (s 444(1)), neither did it provide a defence under section 444(2A) (*Islington London Borough Council v TD* [2011] EWHC 990 (Admin)). Unavoidable cause had to relate to the child, not the parent, and had to be something in the nature of an emergency. A child's chaotic lifestyle could not provide the defence of unavoidable cause for absence from school. The defence of reasonable justification to the aggravated version of the offence should only be considered if the general defence to both levels of the offence failed (*West Sussex County Council v C* [2013] EWHC 1757(Admin)).
- In relation to section 444(1A), the parent will have only an evidential burden to satisfy, the prosecution having then to prove to the criminal standard that the defence is not made out (*R (P) v Liverpool City Magistrates' Court* [2006] EWHC 2732 (Admin)).

C8.2 Education Act: failure to comply with school attendance order

Education Act 1996, s 443(1) and (2)

443 Offence: failure to comply with school attendance order

(1) If a parent on whom a school attendance order is served fails to comply with the requirements of the order, he is guilty of an offence, unless he proves that he is causing the child to receive suitable education otherwise than at school.

(2) If, in proceedings for an offence under this section, the parent is acquitted, the court may direct that the school attendance order shall cease to be in force.

SO

Level 3 fine

C9 **Harassment Offences**

C9.1 **Harassment (without violence)**

Protection from Harassment Act 1997, ss 1 and 2(1)

1 Prohibition of harassment

(1) A person must not pursue a course of conduct—
 (a) which amounts to harassment of another, and
 (b) which he knows or ought to know amounts to harassment of the other.

(1A) A person must not pursue a course of conduct —
 (a) which involves harassment of two or more persons, and
 (b) which he knows or ought to know involves harassment of those persons, and
 (c) by which he intends to persuade any person (whether or not one of those mentioned above)—
  (i) not to do something that he is entitled or required to do, or
  (ii) to do something that he is not under any obligation to do.

(2) For the purposes of this section or section 2A(2)(c), the person whose course of conduct is in question ought to know that it amounts to or involves harassment of another if a reasonable person in possession of the same information would think the course of conduct amounted to harassment of the other.

(3) Subsection (1) or (1A) does not apply to a course of conduct if the person who pursued it shows—
 (a) that it was pursued for the purpose of preventing or detecting crime,
 (b) that it was pursued under any enactment or rule of law or to comply with any condition or requirement imposed by any person under any enactment, or
 (c) that in the particular circumstances the pursuit of the course of conduct was reasonable.

2 Offence of harassment

(1) A person who pursues a course of conduct in breach of section 1 or 1A is guilty of an offence.

EW Racially or religiously aggravated offence

SO Non-aggravated offence

Racially or religiously aggravated offence: Fine and/or 6 months'/2 years' imprisonment

Non-aggravated offence: Fine and/or 6 months' imprisonment

C9.1.1 ***Sentencing***

SCG Harassment/stalking

Where offence committed in a domestic context, also refer to the Overarching principles: Domestic abuse guideline.

Blackstone's Magistrates' Court Handbook 2026. Bartholomew Dalton and Caroline Liggins, Oxford University Press. © Oxford University Press 2026.
DOI: 10.1093/oso/9780198963943.003.0050

C9.1.2 Key points

- The question of what constitutes a course of conduct has been considered in a number of cases, and the answer will always be fact-sensitive. In *R v Curtis* [2010] EWCA Crim 123, the court allowed a defence appeal where the defendant, in the context of there being a volatile relationship, had been responsible for six incidents over a period of nine months. The court held that the conduct must be unacceptable to a degree which would sustain criminal liability and also must be oppressive, and went on to say:

> Courts are well able to separate the wheat from the chaff at an early stage of the proceedings. They should be astute to do so. In most cases courts should have little difficulty in applying the 'close connection' test. Where the claim meets that requirement, and the quality of the conduct said to constitute harassment is being examined, courts will have in mind that irritations, annoyances, even a measure of upset, arise at times in everybody's day-to-day dealings with other people. Courts are well able to recognise the boundary between conduct which is unattractive, even unreasonable, and conduct which is oppressive and unacceptable. To cross the boundary from the regrettable to the unacceptable the gravity of the misconduct must be of an order which would sustained *[sic]* criminal liability under section 2.

- References to harassing a person include alarming the person or causing the person distress (s 7). The person whose course of conduct is in question ought to know that it will cause another to fear that violence will be used against him on any occasion, if a reasonable person in possession of the same information would think the course of conduct would cause the other so to fear on that occasion.
- *R v O'Neill* [2016] EWCA Crim 92 confirmed that the definition in s 7 is inclusive and not exhaustive. 'Harassment' is generally understood to involve improper, oppressive, and unreasonable conduct that is targeted at an individual and calculated to produce the consequences described in s 7. Harassment cannot simply be equated with 'causing alarm or distress'. The danger of doing this is that not all conduct, even if unattractive, unreasonable, and causing alarm or distress, will be of an order justifying the sanction of the criminal law. By s 1(3) Act '. . . reasonable and/or lawful courses of conduct may be excluded'. But the Crown does not need to prove that a defendant's conduct is unreasonable.
- *DPP v Heaton* [2024] EWHC 1808 (Admin) concerned an arrangement that the defendant should know that his relationship with the complainant was over for good if she blocked his business phone number. The court held this arrangement was not immutable. Even though the complainant had appreicated the defendant's persistence in trying to get them back together on previous occasions, the defendant's behaviour—calling her over 20 times over two days and banging on her door repeatedly on another day, after she had asked for him to leave her alone—was extreme and the defendant should have known his conduct went beyond what was acceptable.
- In *Sledziewski v Persons Unknown (Going by Chapona)* [2024] EWHC 1955 (KB) the court gave detailed guidance on 'citizen journalism'. In this case, videos posted online in relation to a driving incident are unlikely to

amount to harassment, unless the posts are so oppressive as to amount to a conscious or negligent abuse of press freedom.

- Complaining to a victim's employer and/or professional regulator can amount to harassment and stalking as long as the complaints cause distress. However, appropriate complaints will almost always fall under the defence of reasonableness (*R v Musharraf* [2022] EWCA Crim 1482).
- The defence of M'Naghten Rules insanity was considered in *Loake v CPS* [2017] EWHC 2855 (Admin). The defence is available to a defendant charged with an offence of harassment under s 2 but the 'course' of conduct may make it very difficult to meet the requirements for insanity in relation to each separate event (see also A20).
- The naming of two complainants in one charge is not duplicitous, but unlike the charge under s 4, there need only be conduct against at least two people on at least one occasion each (*DPP v Dunn* (2008) 165 JP 130).

See *Blackstone's Criminal Practice 2026* B2.201

C9.2 Harassment—putting people in fear of violence

Protection from Harassment Act 1997, s 4

4 Putting people in fear of violence

(1) A person whose course of conduct causes another to fear, on at least two occasions, that violence will be used against him is guilty of an offence if he knows or ought to know that his course of conduct will cause the other so to fear on each of those occasions . . .

(2) For the purposes of this section, the person whose course of conduct is in question ought to know that it will cause another to fear that violence will be used against him on any occasion if a reasonable person in possession of the same information would think the course of conduct would cause the other so to fear on that occasion.

(3) It is a defence for a person charged with an offence under this section to show that—

(a) his course of conduct was pursued for the purpose of preventing or detecting crime,

(b) his course of conduct was pursued under any enactment or rule of law or to comply with any condition or requirement imposed by any person under any enactment, or

(c) the pursuit of his course of conduct was reasonable for the protection of himself or another or for the protection of his or another's property.

EW

Racially or religiously aggravated offence: Fine and/or 12 months'/14 years' imprisonment

Non-aggravated offence: Fine and/or 12 months'/10 years' imprisonment

DO

GC Racially or religiously aggravated offence

C9.2.1 *Sentencing*

Where offence committed in a domestic context, also refer to the Overarching principles: Domestic abuse guideline,

SCG **Harassment (fear of violence)/ Stalking (fear of violence)**

C9.2.2 Key points

- See the key points in **C8.1.2.**
- In *R v Widdows* [2011] EWCA Crim 1500, the court held that the concept of harassment is at the core of the 1997 Act—though the word is not used in s 4—and considered the explanation of 'harassment' in *Majrowski v Guy's and St Thomas' NHS Trust* [2007] 1 AC 224 ('stalkers, racial abusers, disruptive neighbours, bullying at work and so forth') and in *Thomas v News Group Newspapers Ltd* [2001] EWCA Civ 1233 (where the practice of stalking was said to be a prime example). The section is not normally appropriate for use as a means of criminalizing conduct, not charged as violence, during incidents in a long and predominantly affectionate relationship in which both parties persisted and wanted to continue.
- In *R v Haque* [2011] EWCA Crim 1871, the following requirements were identified for there to be proof of harassment in s 4:
  - the conduct must be targeted at an individual;
  - conduct must be calculated to produce the consequences in s 7 (alarm or distress);
  - conduct must have been oppressive and unreasonable;
  - provocation may possibly be relevant to causation and reasonableness;
  - there must also be proof that the defendant knew or ought to have known that conduct would cause the complainant to fear violence.
- It is a defence for a person charged with an offence under s 4 to show that:
  - his course of conduct was pursued for the purpose of preventing or detecting crime. There is a test of rationality to this defence which applies a minimum objective standard to the relevant person's mental processes. It imposes a requirement for good faith and an absence of arbitrariness. Detection or prevention need not be the sole purpose but it must be a dominant purpose of the defendant (*Hayes v Willoughby* [2012] UKSC 17);
  - his course of conduct was pursued under any enactment or rule of law, or to comply with any condition or requirement imposed by any person under any enactment; or
  - the pursuit of his course of conduct was reasonable for the protection of himself or another, or for the protection of his or another's property.
- The naming of two complainants in one charge under s 4 is not duplicitous, but at least one of the complainants must have feared violence on at least two occasions (*Caurti v DPP* [2002] EWHC 867 (Admin)).

See *Blackstone's Criminal Practice 2026* **B2.217**

C9.3 Stalking

The offences of stalking mirror the approach of the basic and aggravated forms of the harassment offences set out at **C8.1** and **C8.2**.

The defences in s 1(3) Protection from Harassment Act 1997 are available (see **C8.1**).

C9.3.1 *The basic offence*

Protection from Harassment Act 1997, s 2A

2A Offence of stalking

(1) A person is guilty of an offence if—
  (a) the person pursues a course of conduct in breach of section 1(1), and
  (b) the course of conduct amounts to stalking.

(2) For the purposes of subsection (1)(b) (and section 4A(1)(a)) a person's course of conduct amounts to stalking of another person if—
  (a) it amounts to harassment of that person,
  (b) the acts or omissions involved are ones associated with stalking, and
  (c) the person whose course of conduct it is knows or ought to know that the course of conduct amounts to harassment of the other person.

(3) The following are examples of acts or omissions which, in particular circumstances, are ones associated with stalking—
  (a) following a person,
  (b) contacting, or attempting to contact, a person by any means,
  (c) publishing any statement or other material—
    (i) relating or purporting to relate to a person, or
    (ii) purporting to originate from a person,
  (d) monitoring the use by a person of the internet, email or any other form of electronic communication,
  (e) loitering in any place (whether public or private),
  (f) interfering with any property in the possession of a person,
  (g) watching or spying on a person.

…

(6) This section is without prejudice to the generality of section 2.

EW Racially or religiously aggravated offence

SO Non-aggravated offence

Racially or religiously aggravated offence: Fine and/or 12 months'/2 years' imprisonment

Non-aggravated offence: Fine and/or 6 months' imprisonment

C9.3.2 *Sentencing*

SCG **Harassment/Stalking**

C9.3.3 *Aggravated stalking*

Protection from Harassment Act 1997, s 4A

4A Stalking involving fear of violence or serious alarm or distress

(1) A person ('A') whose course of conduct—
  (a) amounts to stalking, and
  (b) either—
    (i) causes another ('B') to fear, on at least two occasions, that violence will be used against B, or
    (ii) causes B serious alarm or distress which has a substantial adverse effect on B's usual day-to-day activities, is guilty of an offence if A knows or ought to know that A's course of conduct will cause B so to fear on each of those occasions or (as the case may be) will cause such alarm or distress.

(2) For the purposes of this section A ought to know that A's course of conduct will cause B to fear that violence will be used against B on any occasion if a reasonable person in possession of the same information would think the course of conduct would cause B so to fear on that occasion.

(3) For the purposes of this section A ought to know that A's course of conduct will cause B serious alarm or distress which has a substantial adverse effect on B's usual day-to-day activities if a reasonable person in possession of the same information would think the course of conduct would cause B such alarm or distress.

(4) It is a defence for A to show that—
  (a) A's course of conduct was pursued for the purpose of preventing or detecting crime,
  (b) A's course of conduct was pursued under any enactment or rule of law or to comply with any condition or requirement imposed by any person under any enactment, or
  (c) the pursuit of A's course of conduct was reasonable for the protection of A or another or for the protection of A's or another's property.

...

(8) This section is without prejudice to the generality of section 4.

EW

Racially or religiously aggravated offence: Fine and/or 12 months'/14 years' imprisonment

Non-aggravated offence: Fine and/or 12 months'/10 years' imprisonment

DO

GC If racially or religiously aggravated

C9.3.4 *Sentencing*

SCG **Harassment (fear of violence)/Stalking (fear of violence)**

C9.3.5 Key points

In *R v Qosja* [2016] EWCA Crim 1543 it was held that the aggravated offence is made out if a person, whose course of conduct amounts to stalking, causes another to fear on at least two occasions that violence will be used. This is wide enough to cover a person who is caused to fear on a particular occasion that violence will be used on an uncertain future date. This does not need to be a specific threat of violence but the requirement is that they fear that violence will (rather than may be) used.

Section 4A requires no objective conduct on the part of a defendant beyond stalking. The remainder of the statutory test is concerned with the effect on the mind of the complainant, and the knowledge, or constructive knowledge, of the defendant. The question that arises is the actual effect on the mind of the victim. As regards the requirement in s 4A(1)(a)(i) that the person fears, on at least two occasions, that violence will be used against him or her, evidence of a threat to use sexually explicit material was not evidence of a fear of violence. That a complainant feared that she would be 'hunted down' by the appellant was not, unless more was said, evidence of a fear of violence, although it might have been evidence of a fear of stalking or harassment. It is not enough to establish that conditions existed that might reasonably have engendered a fear of violence: that will be so in many stalking cases. The court must be sure that such a fear was actually engendered. The offence requires proof of a specific state of mind on the part of the complainant, not merely proof of circumstances that might reasonably engender that state of mind (*Pendlebury v DPP* [2018] EWHC 3567 (Admin)).

C10 Immigration and Document Offences

C10.1 Illegal entry and deception

Immigration Act 1971, ss 24, 24A, and 24B

24 Illegal entry and similar offences

(A1) A person who knowingly enters the United Kingdom in breach of a deportation order commits an offence.

(B1) A person who—

(a) requires leave to enter the United Kingdom under this Act, and

(b) knowingly enters the United Kingdom without such leave, commits an offence.

(C1) A person who—

(a) has only a limited leave to enter or remain in the United Kingdom, and

(b) knowingly remains beyond the time limited by the leave, commits an offence.

(D1) A person who—

(a) requires entry clearance under the immigration rules, and

(b) knowingly arrives in the United Kingdom without a valid entry clearance, commits an offence.

(E1) *A person who—*

(a) *is required under immigration rules not to travel to the United Kingdom without an ETA [electronic travel authorisation] that is valid for the person's journey to the United Kingdom, and*

(b) *knowingly arrives in the United Kingdom without such an ETA, commits an offence.*

(1) A person who is not a British citizen shall be guilty of an offence

(b) if, having only a limited leave to enter or remain in the United Kingdom, he knowingly

fails to observe a condition of the leave;

(c) if, having lawfully entered the United Kingdom without leave by virtue of section 8(1) above, he remains without leave beyond the time allowed by section 8(1);

(d) if, without reasonable excuse, he fails to comply with any requirement imposed on him under Schedule 2 to this Act to report to a medical officer of health, or to attend, or submit to a test or examination, as required by such an officer;

(f) if he disembarks in the United Kingdom from a ship or aircraft after being placed on board under Schedule 2 or 3 to this Act with a view to his removal from the United Kingdom;

(g) if he embarks in contravention of a restriction imposed by or under an Order in Council under section 3(7) of this Act;

(h) if the person is on immigration bail within the meaning of Schedule 10 to the Immigration Act 2016 and without reasonable excuse, the person breaches a bail condition within the meaning of that Schedule.

(1A) A person commits an offence under subsection[(C1) above on the day when he first knows that the time limited by his leave has expired and continues to commit it throughout any period during which he is in the United Kingdom thereafter; but a person shall not be prosecuted under that provision more than once in respect of the same limited leave.

Blackstone's Magistrates' Court Handbook 2026. Bartholomew Dalton and Caroline Liggins, Oxford University Press. © Oxford University Press 2026.
DOI: 10.1093/oso/9780198963943.003.0051

24A Deception

(1) A person who is not a British citizen is guilty of an offence if, by means which include deception by him—
  (a) he obtains or seeks to obtain leave to enter or remain in the United Kingdom; or
  (b) he secures or seeks to secure the avoidance, postponement or revocation of enforcement action against him.

(2) his removal from the United Kingdom in consequence of directions or a deportation order.

24B Illegal working

(1) A person ('P') who is subject to immigration control commits an offence if—
  (a) P works at a time when P is disqualified from working by reason of P's immigration status, and
  (b) at that time P knows or has reasonable cause to believe that P is disqualified from working by reason of P's immigration status.

(2) For the purposes of subsection (1) a person is disqualified from working by reason of the person's immigration status if—
  (a) the person has not been granted leave to enter or remain in the United Kingdom, or
  (b) the person's leave to enter or remain in the United Kingdom—
    (i) is invalid,
    (ii) has ceased to have effect (whether by reason of curtailment, revocation, cancellation, passage of time or otherwise), or
    (iii) is subject to a condition preventing the person from doing work of that kind . . .

(8) The reference in subsection (1) to a person who is subject to immigration control is to a person who under this Act requires leave to enter or remain in the United Kingdom.

(9) Where a person is on immigration bail within the meaning of Part 1 of Schedule 10 to the Immigration Act 2016—
  (a) the person is to be treated for the purposes of subsection (2) as if the person had been granted leave to enter the United Kingdom, but
  (b) any condition as to the person's work in the United Kingdom to which the person's immigration bail is subject is to be treated for those purposes as a condition of leave . . .

(10) The reference in subsection (1) to a person working is to that person working—
  (a) under a contract of employment,
  (b) under a contract of apprenticeship,
  (c) under a contract personally to do work,
  (d) under or for the purposes of a contract for services,
  (e) for a purpose related to a contract to sell goods,
  (f) as a constable,
  (g) in the course of Crown employment,
  (h) as a relevant member of the House of Commons staff, or
  (i) as a relevant member of the House of Lords staff . . .

(13) In this section 'contract' means a contract whether express or implied and, if express, whether oral or in writing.

SO ss 24(1) and 25B

EW s 24(A1)–24(E1); 24A

ss 24(1) and 25B: Fine and/or 6 months' imprisonment

s 24(A1): Fine and/or 12 months'/5 years' imprisonment

s 24(B1)–(E1): Fine and/or 12 months'/4 years' imprisonment

s 24A: Fine and/or 12 months'/2 years' imprisonment

C10.1.1 Key points: Sentencing

In the absence of sentencing guidelines, *R v Ginar* [2023] EWCA Crim 1121 sets out detailed guidance about the correct approach for sentencing in relation to s 24(D1). The custody threshold will generally be passed and the starting point, prior to the consideration of case-specific aggravating and mitigating features or credit for guilty plea, will be 12 months' imprisonment.

C10.1.2 Key points

The burden of proving that entry was legal falls upon the defendant in relation to prosecutions commenced within six months of that entry (s 24(4)(b)). Enforcement action is defined in s 24A(2). Additional time limits are provided by s 28.

Section 24(D1) applies to those seeking asylum in the UK (*R v Mohamed* [2023] EWCA Crim 211).

The defence under s 31 Immigration and Asylum Act 1999 is available for offences under s 24A (see **C10.5.1**).

See *Blackstone's Criminal Practice 2026* **B22.35**

C10.2 Assisting unlawful entry

Immigration Act 1971, ss 25 and 25A

25 Assisting unlawful immigration to member state or United Kingdom

(1) A person commits an offence if he—
- (a) does an act which facilitates the commission of a breach or attempted breach of immigration law by an individual who is not a national of the United Kingdom,
- (b) knows or has reasonable cause for believing that the act facilitates the commission of a breach or attempted breach of immigration law by the individual, and
- (c) knows or has reasonable cause for believing that the individual is not a national of the United Kingdom.

(2) In subsection (1) 'immigration law' means a law which has effect in a member State or the United Kingdom and which controls, in respect of some or all persons who are not nationals of the State or, as the case may be, of the United Kingdom, entitlement to—
- (a) enter or arrive in the State or the United Kingdom
- (b) transit across the State or the United Kingdom or
- (c) be in the State or the United Kingdom.

. . .

(4) Subsection (1) applies to things done whether inside or outside the United Kingdom.

25A Helping asylum-seeker to enter United Kingdom

(1) A person commits an offence if—
  (a) he knowingly and for gain facilitates the arrival or attempted arrival in, or the entry or attempted entry into, the United Kingdom of an individual, and
  (b) he knows or has reasonable cause to believe that the individual is an asylum-seeker.

EW

Fine and/or 6 months'/life imprisonment

C10.2.1 Key points

Facilitation of a breach of immigration law under s 25 Immigration Act 1971 includes facilitating a breach by an asylum-seeker (*R v Bina* [2014] EWCA Crim 1444).

R v Ali [2013] EWCA Crim 43 confirms that, to prove an offence under s 25 Immigration Act 1971, it is not essential that breach actually occurs,

R v Boateng [2016] EWCA Crim 57 confirms that, for there to be an offence of facilitating the illegal entry of a person to the UK, it was not necessary that the person who enters be dishonest or aware of the position.

Section 25(1) includes the complete *mens rea* that the prosecution need to provide in order to secure a conviction. 'Immigration law' for the purposes of s 25(2) is not limited to breaches of ss 1 and 3 Immigration Act 1971 and includes the offence under s 24D1 (*R v Mohamed* [2023] EWCA Crim 211).

Section 25A(3) contains a defence for asylum organizations. Sections 25BA and s 25BB contain defences for rescuers and in relation to stowaways.

See *Blackstone's Criminal Practice 2026* **B22.45** and **B22.53**

C10.3 Possessing false passports, work permits, registration cards, etc

Immigration Act 1971, ss 26 and 26A

26 General offences in connection with administration of Act

(1) A person shall be guilty of an offence punishable on summary conviction with a fine or with imprisonment for not more than six months, or with both, in any of the following cases—
  (a) if, without reasonable excuse, he refuses or fails to submit to examination under Schedule 2 to this Act;
  (b) if, without reasonable excuse, he refuses to fails to furnish or produce any information in his possession, or any documents in his possession or control,

which he is on an examination under that Schedule required to furnish or produce;

(c) if on any such examination or otherwise he makes or causes to be made to an immigration officer or other person lawfully acting in the execution of a relevant enactment a return, statement or representation which he knows to be false or does not believe to be true;

(d) if, without lawful authority, he alters any certificate of entitlement, entry clearance, work permit or other document issued or made under or for the purposes of this Act, or uses for the purposes of this Act, or has in his possession for such use, any passport, certificate of entitlement, entry clearance, work permit or other document which he knows or has reasonable cause to believe to be false;

(e) if, without reasonable excuse, he fails to complete and produce a landing or embarkation card in accordance with any order under Schedule 2 to this Act;

(f) if, without reasonable excuse, he fails to comply with any requirement of regulations under section 4(3) or of an order under section 4(4) above;

(g) if, without reasonable excuse, he obstructs an immigration officer or other person lawfully acting in the execution of this Act.

(2) The extended time limit for prosecutions which is provided for by section 28 below shall apply to offences under subsection (1)(c) and

(a) above.

26A Registration card

...

(3) A person commits an offence if he—

(a) makes a false registration card,

(b) alters a registration card with intent to deceive or to enable another to deceive,

(c) has a false or altered registration card in his possession without reasonable excuse,

(d) uses or attempts to use a false registration card for a purpose for which a registration card is issued,

(e) uses or attempts to use an altered registration card with intent to deceive,

(f) makes an article designed to be used in making a false registration card,

(g) makes an article designed to be used in altering a registration card with intent to deceive or to enable another to deceive, or

(h) has an article within paragraph (f) or (g) in his possession without reasonable excuse.

(4) In subsection (3) 'false registration card' means a document which is designed to appear to be a registration card.

SO s 26

EW s 26A

卌 s 26 Fine and/or 6 months' imprisonment

s 26A(sub-ss (3)(a), (b), (d), (e), (f), or (g)): Fine and/or 12 months'/10 years' imprisonment

s 26A(sub-ss (3)(c) or (h)): Fine and/or 12 months'/2 years' imprisonment

C10.3.1 Key points

The 6-month time limit does not apply to offences under s 26(1)(c) and (d), or s 28(1)(a) and (c).

The defence under s 31 Immigration and Asylum Act 1999 is available for offences under s 26(1)(d) (see **C10.5.1**).

C10.4 Entering the UK without documentation

Asylum and Immigration (Treatment of Claimants, etc.) Act 2004, s 2

2 Entering United Kingdom without passport, &c [sic].

(1) A person commits an offence if at a leave or asylum interview he does not have with him an immigration document which—
 (a) is in force, and
 (b) satisfactorily establishes his identity and nationality or citizenship.

(2) A person commits an offence if at a leave or asylum interview he does not have with him, in respect of any dependent child with whom he claims to be travelling or living, an immigration document which—
 (a) is in force, and
 (b) satisfactorily establishes the child's identity and nationality or citizenship.

(3) But a person does not commit an offence under subsection (1) or (2) if—
 (a) the interview referred to in that subsection takes place after the person has entered the United Kingdom, and
 (b) within the period of three days beginning with the date of the interview the person provides to an immigration officer or to the Secretary of State a document of the kind referred to in that subsection.

(4) It is a defence for a person charged with an offence under subsection (1)—
 (a) to prove that he is —
  (i) an Irish citizen,
  (ii) has leave to enter or remain in the United Kingdom which was granted by virtue of residence scheme immigration rules, or
  (iii) is a frontier worker within the meaning of regulation 3 of the Citizens' Rights (Frontier Workers) (EU Exit) Regulations 2020,
 (c) to prove that he has a reasonable excuse for not being in possession of a document of the kind specified in subsection (1),
 (d) to produce a false immigration document and to prove that he used that document as an immigration document for all purposes in connection with his journey to the United Kingdom, or
 (e) to prove that he travelled to the United Kingdom without, at any stage since he set out on the journey, having possession of an immigration document.

(5) It is a defence for a person charged with an offence under subsection (2) in respect of a child—
 (a) to prove that the child is—
  (i) an Irish citizen,
  (ii) has leave to enter or remain in the United Kingdom which was granted by virtue of residence scheme immigration rules, or
  (iii) is a frontier worker within the meaning of regulation 3 of the Citizens' Rights (Frontier Workers) (EU Exit) Regulations 2020
 (c) to prove that the person has a reasonable excuse for not being in possession of a document of the kind specified in subsection (2),

(d) to produce a false immigration document and to prove that it was used as an immigration document for all purposes in connection with the child's journey to the United Kingdom, or

(e) to prove that he travelled to the United Kingdom with the child without, at any stage since he set out on the journey, having possession of an immigration document in respect of the child.

(6) Where the charge for an offence under subsection (1) or (2) relates to an interview which takes place after the defendant has entered the United Kingdom—

(a) subsections (4)(c) and (5)(c) shall not apply, but

(b) it is a defence for the defendant to prove that he has a reasonable excuse for not providing a document in accordance with subsection (3).

(7) For the purposes of subsections (4) to (6)—

(a) the fact that a document was deliberately destroyed or disposed of is not a reasonable excuse for not being in possession of it or for not providing it in accordance with subsection (3), unless it is shown that the destruction or disposal was—

(i) for a reasonable cause, or

(ii) beyond the control of the person charged with the offence, and

(b) in paragraph (a)(i) "reasonable cause" does not include the purpose of—

(i) delaying the handling or resolution of a claim or application or the taking of a decision,

(ii) increasing the chances of success of a claim or application, or

(iii) complying with instructions or advice given by a person who offers advice about, or facilitates, immigration into the United Kingdom, unless in the circumstances of the case it is unreasonable to expect non-compliance with the instructions or advice.

(8) A person shall be presumed for the purposes of this section not to have a document with him if he fails to produce it to an immigration officer or official of the Secretary of State on request.

...

(12) In this section—

- 'immigration document' means—
  (a) a passport, and
  (b) a document which relates to a national of a State other than the United Kingdom and which is designed to serve the same purpose as a passport, and
- 'leave or asylum interview' means an interview with an immigration officer or an official of the Secretary of State at which a person—
  (a) seeks leave to enter or remain in the United Kingdom, or
  (b) claims that to remove him from or require him to leave the United Kingdom would breach the United Kingdom's obligations under the Refugee Convention or would be unlawful under section 6 of the Human Rights Act 1998 (c. 42) as being incompatible with his Convention rights.
- 'residence scheme immigration rules' has the meaning given by section 17 of the European Union (Withdrawal Agreement) Act 2020

(13) For the purposes of this section—

(a) a document which purports to be, or is designed to look like, an immigration document, is a false immigration document, and

(b) an immigration document is a false immigration document if and in so far as it is used—

(i) outside the period for which it is expressed to be valid,

(ii) contrary to provision for its use made by the person issuing it, or

(iii) by or in respect of a person other than the person to or for whom it was issued.

EW

Fine and/or 12 months'/2 years' imprisonment

C10.4.1 Key points

There is a defence under the Asylum and Immigration (Treatment of Claimants) Act 2004 where the defendant could not obtain a valid immigration document in their own country (*Thet v DPP* [2006] EWHC 2701).

See *Blackstone's Criminal Practice 2026* **B22.58**

C10.5 Possession of false identity documents without reasonable excuse

Identity Documents Act 2010, ss 6 and 7

6 Possession of false identity documents, etc without reasonable excuse

(1) It is an offence for a person ('P'), without reasonable excuse, to have in P's possession or under P's control—
- (a) an identity document that is false,
- (b) an identity document that was improperly obtained, (c) an identity document that relates to someone else,
- (d) any apparatus which, to P's knowledge, is or has been specially designed or adapted for the making of false identity documents, or
- (e) any article or material which, to P's knowledge, is or has been specially designed or adapted to be used in the making of such documents.

. . .

7 Meaning of 'identity document'

(1) For the purposes of sections 4 to 6 'identity document' means any document that is or purports to be—
- (a) an immigration document,
- (b) a United Kingdom passport (within the meaning of the Immigration Act 1971),
- (c) a passport issued by or on behalf of the authorities of a country or territory outside the United Kingdom or by or on behalf of an international organisation,
- (d) a document that can be used (in some or all circumstances) instead of a passport,
- (e) a licence to drive a motor vehicle granted under Part 3 of the Road Traffic Act 1988 or under Part 2 of the Road Traffic (Northern Ireland) Order 1981, or
- (f) a driving licence issued by or on behalf of the authorities of a country or territory outside the United Kingdom.

(2) In subsection (1)(a) 'immigration document' means—
- (a) a document used for confirming the right of a person under the EU Treaties in respect of entry or residence in the United Kingdom,
- (b) a document that is given in exercise of immigration functions and records information about leave granted to a person to enter or to remain in the United Kingdom, or
- (c) a registration card (within the meaning of section 26A of the Immigration Act 1971).

(3) In subsection (2)(b) 'immigration functions' means functions under the Immigration Acts (within the meaning of the Asylum and Immigration (Treatment of Claimants, etc.) Act 2004).
(4) References in subsection (1) to the issue of a document include its renewal, replacement or re-issue (with or without modifications).
(5) In this section 'document' includes a stamp or label.
(6) The Secretary of State may by order amend the definition of 'identity document'.

EW

Fine and/or 12 months'/2 years' imprisonment

See *Blackstone's Criminal Practice 2026* **B22.67**

C10.5.1 *Defences*

C10.5.1.1 *Refugee Convention*

Immigration and Asylum Act 1999, s 31

31 Defences based on Article 31(1) of the Refugee Convention

(1) It is a defence for a refugee charged with an offence to which this section applies to show that, having come to the United Kingdom directly from a country where his life or freedom was threatened (within the meaning of the Refugee Convention), he—
  (a) presented himself to the authorities in the United Kingdom without delay;
  (b) showed good cause for his illegal entry or presence; and
  (c) made a claim for asylum as soon as was reasonably practicable after his arrival in the United Kingdom.
(2) If, in coming from the country where his life or freedom was threatened, the refugee stopped in another country outside the United Kingdom, subsection (1) applies only if he shows that he could not reasonably have expected to have sought protection under the Refugee Convention in that other country.
(3) In England and Wales and Northern Ireland the offences to which this section applies are any offence, and any attempt to commit an offence, under—
  (a) Part I of the Forgery and Counterfeiting Act 1981 (forgery and connected offences);
  (aa) section 4 or 6 of the Identity Documents Act 2010;
  (b) section 24A of the 1971 Act (deception); or
  (c) section 26(1)(d) of the 1971 Act (falsification of documents) . . . .
(4A) But this section does not apply to an offence by a refugee in the course of an attempt to leave the United Kingdom.
(5) A refugee who has made a claim for asylum is not entitled to the defence provided by subsection (1) in relation to any offence committed by him after making that claim.
(6) 'Refugee' has the same meaning as it has for the purposes of the Refugee Convention.
(7) If the Secretary of State has refused to grant a claim for asylum made by a person who claims that he has a defence under subsection (1), that person is to be taken not to be a refugee unless he shows that he is.

Key points

- Refugees are protected under Article 31 of the UN Convention relating to the status of refugees as recognized by these provisions. Section 37 Nationality and Borders Act 2022 defines a number of the terms in that Article and the earlier case law must be reconsidered in light of those provisions. However, s 37 does not provide a defence to s 24(D1) Immigration Act 1971 (*R v Mohamed* [2023] EWCA Crim 211).
- The defence was considered in *R v Matete* [2013] EWCA Crim 1372.
- The requirement that the claim for asylum must be made as soon as was reasonably practicable does not necessarily mean at the earliest possible moment (*Asfaw* [2008] UKHL 31).

  It follows that the fact a refugee stopped in a third country in transit is not necessarily fatal and may be explicable: for instance because they were under the control of people smugglers. The main touchstones by which exclusion from protection should be judged are the length of the stay in the intermediate country, the reasons for delaying there, and whether or not the refugee sought or found protection de jure or de facto from the persecution from which he or she was seeking to escape (*Asfaw*). The Court of Appeal has found that stays as long as three months in countries where a refugee could not reasonably be expected to seek asylum do not necessarily exclude reliance on the defence. Even where the third country is a signatory to the Refugee Convention, this is not necessarily fatal to the statutory defence. Short stopovers in 'safe' countries have been accepted by the Court of Appeal as falling within the description of 'in transit' for the purposes of the 'come directly' provision in s 31.

  The courts will consider the individual circumstances of the case, such as the length of the stay and the reason for delay in coming to the UK.
- The requirement that the refugee demonstrates 'good cause' for his illegal entry or presence in the UK will be satisfied by showing that he was reasonably travelling on false papers (*R v Uxbridge MC ex p Adimi* [2001] QB 667).
- In *R v Elmi* [2022] EWCA Crim 1428 it was confirmed that the defence only applies to refugees and not those with other forms of humanitarian protection. However, it may be available to those who were 'presumptive refugees' (i.e. those claiming asylum in good faith) at the time of the offence. It is for a jury to determine whether the defendant was a refugee at the relevant time and whether the defence is made out.

C10.5.1.2 *Documentary falsity*

- If the document itself is false then it is no defence in a case where the document was being used for establishing a registrable fact, that it bore the correct details of the defendant (*R v Jamalov*, 2010 EWCA Crim 309), but the defendant's ignorance of a document's falsity could amount to a reasonable cause for possessing it (*R v Unah* [2011] EWCA Crim 1837).

C10.5.1.3 *Trafficking*

- Applications to stay for abuse of process remain available to all victims of trafficking if there has been a failure to have due regard to CPS guidance or if there was no rational basis for departure by the prosecution from a conclusive grounds' decision, . It will then be assessed by the court by way of review on grounds corresponding to public law grounds (*R v AAD* [2022] EWCA Crim 106) (see **A1.1**).

See *Blackstone's Criminal Practice 2026* **B22.82**

C11 Prison Offences

C11.1 Conveyance of articles into prison

The Prison Act 1952 lists the following prohibited articles (s 40A):

List A articles	List B articles
(a) a controlled drug (as defined for the purposes of the Misuse of Drugs Act 1971); (b) an explosive; (c) any firearm or ammunition (as defined in s 57 of the Firearms Act 1968); (d) any other offensive weapon (as defined in s 1(9) of the Police and Criminal Evidence Act 1984).	(a) alcohol (as defined for the purposes of the Licensing Act 2003); (b) a mobile telephone; (c) a camera; (d) a sound-recording device. 'Camera' includes any device by means of which a photograph (as defined in s 40E) can be produced; 'sound-recording device' includes any device by means of which a sound-recording (as defined in s 40E) can be made. The reference in paragraph (b), (c), or (d) of List B to a device of any description includes a reference to— (a) a component part of a device of that description; or (b) an article designed or adapted for use with a device of that description (including any disk, film, or other separate article on which images, sounds, or information may be recorded).

- A List C article is any article or substance proscribed for the purposes of s 40A by prison rules. This includes electronic cigarettes, lighters, and matches

IO List A articles

EW List B articles

SO List C articles

List A articles: 10 years' imprisonment

List B articles: Fine and/or 12 months'/2 years' imprisonment

List C articles: Level 3 fine

Prison Act 1952, s 40B; s 40C

40B Conveyance etc. of List A articles into or out of prison

(1) A person who, without authorisation—
- (a) brings, throws or otherwise conveys a List A article into or out of a prison,
- (b) causes another person to bring, throw or otherwise convey a List A article into or out of a prison,
- (c) leaves a List A article in any place (whether inside or outside a prison) intending it to come into the possession of a prisoner, or
- (d) knowing a person to be a prisoner, gives a List A article to him, is guilty of an offence.

Blackstone's Magistrates' Court Handbook 2026. Bartholomew Dalton and Caroline Liggins, Oxford University Press. © Oxford University Press 2026.
DOI: 10.1093/oso/9780198963943.003.0052

40C Conveyance etc of List B or C articles into or out of prison

(1) A person who, without authorisation—
  (a) brings, throws or otherwise conveys a List B article into or out of a prison,
  (b) causes another person to bring, throw or otherwise convey a List B article into or out of a prison,
  (c) leaves a List B article in any place (whether inside or outside a prison) intending it to come into the possession of a prisoner, or
  (d) knowing a person to be a prisoner, gives a List B article to him, is guilty of an offence.

(2) A person who, without authorisation—
  (a) brings, throws or otherwise conveys a List C article into a prison intending it to come into the possession of a prisoner,
  (b) causes another person to bring, throw or otherwise convey a List C article into a prison intending it to come into the possession of a prisoner,
  (c) brings, throws or otherwise conveys a List C article out of a prison on behalf of a prisoner,
  (d) causes another person to bring, throw or otherwise convey a List C article out of a prison on behalf of a prisoner,
  (e) leaves a List C article in any place (whether inside or outside a prison) intending it to come into the possession of a prisoner, or
  (f) while inside a prison, gives a List C article to a prisoner, is guilty of an offence.

(3) A person who attempts to commit an offence under subsection (2) is guilty of that offence.

(4) In proceedings for an offence under this section it is a defence for the accused to show that—
  (a) he reasonably believed that he had authorisation to do the act in respect of which the proceedings are brought, or
  (b) in all the circumstances there was an overriding public interest which justified the doing of that act.

C11.1.2 Key points

R v Johnson [2017] EWCA Crim 189 confirms that whilst there is no stated mental element for the offence under s 40C, the offence will be made out if the Crown proves that person knew that they had a prohibited item. It was not necessary to prove that they knew the actual nature of the contents of a package.

Where an article might meet the classification of both List B and List C, the court should inquire first whether the item comes within the ambit of the more serious category, thereafter considering the lesser category if it is not within the definition of the former (*R v Salih and Hamasalih* [2020] EWCA Crim 658).

C11.2 Unauthorized possession of knives, etc in prison

Prison Act 1952, s 40CA

Unauthorised possession in prison of knife or offensive weapon

(1) A person who, without authorisation, is in possession of an article specified in subsection (2) inside a prison is guilty of an offence.

(2) The articles referred to in subsection (1) are—
   (a) any article that has a blade or is sharply pointed;
   (b) any other offensive weapon (as defined in section 1(9) of the Police and Criminal Evidence Act 1984).
(3) In proceedings for an offence under this section it is a defence for the accused to show that—
   (a) he reasonably believed that he had authorisation to be in possession of the article in question, or
   (b) in all the circumstances there was an overriding public interest which justified his being in possession of the article.
(4) In this section 'authorisation' means authorisation given for the purposes of this section; and subsections (1) to (3) of section 40E apply in relation to authorisations so given as they apply to authorisations given for the purposes of section 40D.

EW

Fine and/or 12 months'/4 years' imprisonment

See *Blackstone's Criminal Practice 2026* **B12.202**

C11.3 Throwing articles into prison

Prison Act 1952, s 40CB

40CB Throwing articles into prison

(1) A person who, without authorisation, throws any article or substance into a prison is guilty of an offence.
(2) For the purposes of subsection (1)—
   (a) the reference to an article or substance does not include a reference to a List A article, a List B article or a List C article (as defined by section 40A);
   (b) the reference to 'throwing' an article or substance into a prison includes a reference to doing anything from outside the prison that results in the article or substance being projected or conveyed over or through a boundary of the prison so as to land inside the prison.
(3) In proceedings for an offence under this section it is a defence for the accused to show that—
   (a) he reasonably believed that he had authorisation to do the act in respect of which the proceedings are brought, or
   (b) in all the circumstances there was an overriding public interest which justified the doing of that act.
(4) In this section 'authorisation' means authorisation given for the purposes of this section; and subsections (1) to (3) of section 40E apply in relation to authorisations so given as they apply to authorisations given for the purposes of section 40D.

EW

Fine and/or 12 months'/2 years' imprisonment

C11.4 Other offences relating to prison security

Prison Act 1952, s 40D

40D Other offences relating to prison security

(1) A person who, without authorisation—
   (a) takes a photograph, or makes a sound-recording, inside a prison, or
   (b) transmits, or causes to be transmitted, any image, sound or information from inside a prison by electronic communications for simultaneous reception outside the prison, is guilty of an offence.

(2) It is immaterial for the purposes of subsection (1)(a) where the recording medium is located.

(3) A person who, without authorisation—
   (a) brings or otherwise conveys a restricted document out of a prison or causes such a document to be brought or conveyed out of a prison . . . is guilty of an offence.

(3A) A person who, without authorisation, is in possession of any of the items specified in subsection (3B) inside a prison is guilty of an offence.

(3B) The items referred to in subsection (3A) are—
   (a) a device capable of transmitting or receiving images, sounds or information by electronic communications (including a mobile telephone);
   (b) a component part of such a device;
   (c) an article designed or adapted for use with such a device (including any disk, film or other separate article on which images, sounds or information may be recorded).

(4) In proceedings for an offence under this section it is a defence for the accused to show that—
   (a) he reasonably believed that he had authorisation to do the act in respect of which the proceedings are brought, or
   (b) in all the circumstances there was an overriding public interest which justified the doing of that act.

EW

Fine and/or 12 months'/2 years' imprisonment

C12 **Public Order**

C12.1 **Affray**

Public Order Act 1986, ss 3(1)–(4), 6(2) and (5)

3 Affray

(1) A person is guilty of affray if he uses or threatens unlawful violence towards another and his conduct is such as would cause a person of reasonable firmness present at the scene to fear for his personal safety.
(2) Where 2 or more persons use or threaten the unlawful violence, it is the conduct of them taken together that must be considered for the purposes of subsection (1).
(3) For the purposes of this section a threat cannot be made by the use of words alone.
(4) No person of reasonable firmness need actually be, or be likely to be, present at the scene

. . .

6 Mental element: miscellaneous

(2) A person is guilty of violent disorder or affray only if he intends to use or threaten violence or is aware that his conduct may be violent or threaten violence.
(5) For the purposes of this section a person whose awareness is impaired by intoxication shall be taken to be aware of that of which he would be aware if not intoxicated, unless he shows either that his intoxication was not self-induced or that it was caused solely by the taking or administration of a substance in the course of medical treatment.

EW

Fine and/or 12 months'/3 years' imprisonment

DO

C12.1.1 ***Sentencing***

SCG **Affray**

C12.1.2 Key points

- Section 6 provides that a threat cannot be made by the use of words alone.
- Affray may be committed in private as well as in public places. However, the fact that a third party could not be present may enable the court to hold that a hypothetical bystander would have viewed the threat as being restricted to the parties involved due to the turbulence of their relationship (*Leeson v DPP* [2010] EWHC 994 (Admin) where a conviction was quashed where L, who was drunk, had threatened a person with a knife in the bathroom of a private dwelling).

Blackstone's Magistrates' Court Handbook 2026. Bartholomew Dalton and Caroline Liggins, Oxford University Press. © Oxford University Press 2026.
DOI: 10.1093/oso/9780198963943.003.0053

- In *R v Sanchez* (1996) 160 JP 321, the court approved the following academic commentary:

> The offence of affray envisages at least three persons:(i) the person using or threatening unlawful violence; (ii) a person towards whom the violence or threat is directed; and (iii) a person of reasonable firmness who need not actually be, or be likely to be, present at the scene.

- The definition of 'affray' is very wide, and in *Sanchez* the court agreed that care has to be taken to avoid extending it so widely that it would cover every common assault:

> A common assault may be very trivial, so that it would not cause anyone to fear for his 'personal safety'. But where the assault threatens serious harm to the victim, there may be evidence of affray depending on the circumstances. The person of reasonable firmness present in a small room as in the present case might fear for his personal safety whereas the same person, observing the same conduct in an open space, would not. Thus the question in the present case was not whether a person of reasonable firmness in J's shoes would have feared for his personal safety but whether this hypothetical person, present in the room and seeing D's conduct towards J, would have so feared. The common law offence which it was intended to replace was, said the Law Commission, 'typically charged in cases of pitched street battles between rival gangs, spontaneous fights in public houses, clubs and at seaside resorts, and revenge attacks on individuals'. Reference should also be made to *R v Davison* [1992] Crim LR 31 and *R v Plavecz* [2002] Crim LR 837.

- If a group committed an affray, all taking part in unlawful violence, it was not necessary to attribute particular acts to any individual (*Dragjoshi v Croydon Magistrates Court* [2017] EWHC 2840 (QB)).
- The fact that a third party who is present does not feel afraid for their own safety is of evidential significance (*R v Blinkhorn* [2006] EWCA Crim 1416).
- The use, or threat, of unlawful violence must be directed at a person present at the scene for the offence of affray to be made out (*I v DPP* [2001] UKHL 10).

See *Blackstone's Criminal Practice 2026* **B11.23**

C12.2 Alcohol on coaches and trains

Sporting Events (Control of Alcohol etc) Act 1985, s 1(1)–(5)

1 Offences in connection with alcohol on coaches and trains

(1) This section applies to a vehicle which—
  (a) is a public service vehicle or railway passenger vehicle, and
  (b) is being used for the principal purpose of carrying passengers for the whole or part of a journey to or from a designated sporting event.

(2) A person who knowingly causes or permits alcohol to be carried on a vehicle to which this section applies is guilty of an offence—
  (a) if the vehicle is a public service vehicle and he is the operator of the vehicle or the servant or agent of the operator, or
  (b) if the vehicle is a hired vehicle and he is the person to whom it is hired or the servant or agent of that person.

(3) A person who has alcohol in his possession while on a vehicle to which this section applies is guilty of an offence.
(4) A person who is drunk on a vehicle to which this section applies is guilty of an offence.
(5) In this section 'public service vehicle' and 'operator' have the same meaning as in the Public Passenger Vehicles Act 1981.

SO

s 1(2) (causes or permits alcohol to be carried): Level 4 fine

s 1(3) (possession of alcohol): Level 3 fine and/or 3 months' imprisonment

s 1(4) (drunk): Level 2 fine

C12.3 **Begging**

Section 3 Vagrancy Act 1824, as amended by s 70 Criminal Justice Act 1982, provides:

Vagrancy Act 1824, s 3

Every person wandering abroad, or placing himself or herself in any public place, street, highway, court, or passage, to beg or gather alms, or causing or procuring or encouraging any child or children so to do; shall be deemed an idle and disorderly person within the true intent and meaning of this Act; and . . . it shall be lawful (to impose a fine).

SO

Level 3 fine

Note this offence is abolished by the PCSCA 2022 for offences committed on or after the implementation date for the relevant provision.

C12.4 **Causing a public nuisance**

PCSCA 2022, s 78

78 Intentionally or recklessly causing public nuisance

(1) A person commits an offence if—
  (a) the person— (i) does an act, or (ii) omits to do an act that they are required to do by any enactment or rule of law,
  (b) the person's act or omission—
    (i) creates a risk of, or causes, serious harm to the public or a section of the public, or
    (ii) obstructs the public or a section of the public in the exercise or enjoyment of a right that may be exercised or enjoyed by the public at large, and
  (c) the person intends that their act or omission will have a consequence mentioned in paragraph (b) or is reckless as to whether it will have such a consequence.
(2) In subsection (1)(b)(i) 'serious harm' means— (a) death, personal injury or disease, (b) loss of, or damage to, property, or (c) serious distress, serious annoyance, serious inconvenience or serious loss of amenity

(3) It is a defence for a person charged with an offence under subsection (1) to prove that they had a reasonable excuse for the act or omission mentioned in paragraph (a) of that subsection . . .
(6) The common law offence of public nuisance is abolished . . .

EW

Fine and/or 12 months'/10 years' imprisonment

C12.4.1 Key points: Sentencing

- In *R v Trowland and another* [2023] EWCA Crim 919 the court confirmed that particular caution is to be exercised in imposing a custodial sentence in non-violent protest cases. It is no part of the judicial function to evaluate (or comment on) the validity or merit of the cause(s) in support of which a protest is made. However, a conscientious motive on the part of protesters may be a relevant consideration, in particular where the offender is a law-abiding citizen apart from their protest activities. In such cases, a lesser sanction may be appropriate: a sense of proportion on the part of the offender in avoiding excessive damage or inconvenience may be matched by a relatively benign approach to sentencing. However, the more disproportionate or extreme the action taken by the protester, the less obvious is the justification for reduced culpability and more lenient sentencing. In this instance, sentences of 3 years' and 2 years 7 months' imprisonment for closing a bridge on the M25 for 40 hours were severe, but not manifestly excessive.

C12.4.2 Key points

- In *R v Smith* [2024] EWCA Crim 1040, it was confirmed that the focus should be on the risk of harm which was created, not on whether any harm was in fact caused. The risk must be real, not fanciful. A 'section of the public' is simply a group of persons within a larger group or body of persons and is distinct from a series of individuals. Whether a small group can fairly be described as 'a section of the public' will be a question of fact on a case-by-case basis.

See *Blackstone's Criminal Practice 2026* **B11.129**

C12.5 Disorderly behaviour (harassment, alarm, or distress)

Public Order Act 1986, s 5(1)

5 Harassment, alarm or distress

(1) A person is guilty of an offence if he—
  (a) uses threatening or abusive words or behaviour, or disorderly behaviour, or
  (b) displays any writing, sign or other visible representation which is threatening or abusive, within the hearing or sight of a person likely to be caused harassment, alarm or distress thereby.

SO

Racially or religiously aggravated offence: Level 4 fine

Non-aggravated offence: Level 3 fine

C12.5.1 *Sentencing*

SCG Disorderly behaviour

C12.5.2 Key points

Public Order Act 1986, s 5(3)

5 Harassment, alarm or distress

(3) It is a defence for the accused to prove—
- (a) that he had no reason to believe that there was any person within hearing or sight who was likely to be caused harassment, alarm or distress, or
- (b) that he was inside a dwelling and had no reason to believe that the words or behaviour used, or the writing, sign or other visible representation displayed, would be heard or seen by a person outside that or any other dwelling, or
- (c) that his conduct was reasonable.

Mental element

Section 6 provides:

Public Order Act 1986, s 6(4) and (5)

6 Mental element: miscellaneous

(4) A person is guilty of an offence under section 5 only if he intends his words or behaviour, or the writing, sign or other visible representation, to be threatening, or abusive, or is aware that it may be threatening, or abusive or (as the case may be) he intends his behaviour to be or is aware that it may be disorderly.

(5) For the purposes of this section a person whose awareness is impaired by intoxication shall be taken to be aware of that of which he would be aware if not intoxicated, unless he shows either that his intoxication was not self-induced or that it was caused solely by the taking or administration of a substance in the course of medical treatment.

- An offence under s 5 may be committed in a public or a private place, except that no offence is committed where the words or behaviour are used, or the writing, sign, or other visible representation is displayed, by a person inside a dwelling and the other person is also inside that or another dwelling. Subject to particular facts, a dwelling for the purposes of ss 8 and 5(2) does not include a garden to front or rear of a property (*DPP v Distill* [2017] EWHC 2244 (Admin)).
- The tone in which words are said will rarely be sufficient to convert an unpleasant altercation into a criminal offence if the words used are not themselves threatening or abusive. However, on the facts, holding a phone in the witness's face and causing them to feel intimidated and threatened by the prospect that the appellant might be streaming their images and that they might be subject to online abuse was sufficient for a conviction (*Hicks v DPP* [2023] EWHC 1089 (Admin)).

- The offence may be committed against a police officer but they are expected to show a degree of resilience (*Williams v CPS* [2018] EWHC 2869 (Admin), confirming *DPP v Orum* 1981 1 WLR 88).
- A person can be harassed without emotional upset (*Southard v Director of Public Prosecutions* [2006] EWHC 3449 (Admin)). In *Southard*, the defendant intervened in his brother's arrest, shouting 'fuck off' and 'fuck you' at the officer. The conviction was upheld. The harassment must not, however, be trivial (eg *R (R) v Director of Public Prosecutions* [2006] EWHC 1375 (Admin)—another case involving a police officer where the conviction was quashed).
- *Harvey v DPP* [2011] EWHC 3992 (Admin) confirms that it is not an offence under s 5 Public Order Act to use swear words in the presence of a police officer. The Crown must produce evidence of the likelihood of harassment, alarm, or distress. This cannot be implied for police officers or young people for whom they are a regular feature of life.
- Concealing a video camera in a changing room can amount to disorderly behaviour (*Vigon v Director of Public Prosecutions* (1997) 162 JP 115).
- For considerations under the European Convention on Human Rights (ECHR) (and in particular Art 10 ECHR), see *Abdul and others v Crown Prosecution Service* [2011] EWHC 247 (Admin). The following principles emerge from Article 10 ECHR jurisprudence (para 49 of the judgment):
  (i) The starting point is the importance of the right to freedom of expression.
  (ii) In this regard, it must be recognized that legitimate protest can be offensive at least to some—and on occasions must be, if it is to have impact. Moreover, the right to freedom of expression would be unacceptably devalued if it did no more than protect those holding popular, mainstream views; it must plainly extend beyond that so that minority views can be freely expressed, even if distasteful. [The context of the remarks is a key factor.]
  (iii) The justification for interference with the right to freedom of expression must be convincingly established. Accordingly, while Article 10 does not confer an unqualified right to freedom of expression, the restrictions contained in Article 10.2 are to be narrowly construed.
  (iv) There is not and cannot be any universal test for resolving when speech goes beyond legitimate protest, so attracting the sanction of the criminal law. The justification for invoking the criminal law is the threat to public order. Inevitably, the context of the particular occasion will be of the first importance.
  (v) The relevance of the threat to public order should not be taken as meaning that the risk of violence by those reacting to the protest is, without more, determinative; sometimes it may be that protesters are to be protected. That said, in striking the right balance when determining whether speech is 'threatening, abusive or insulting', the focus on minority rights should not result in overlooking the rights of the majority.
  (vi) Even if there is otherwise a prima facie case for contending that an offence has been committed under s 5, it is still for the Crown to establish that prosecution is a proportionate response, necessary for the preservation of public order.

If the line between legitimate freedom of expression and a threat to public order has indeed been crossed, freedom of speech will not have been impaired by 'ruling . . . out' threatening, abusive, or insulting speech. Thus a decision to discontinue a s 5 prosecution was not irrational where there was no risk of public disorder and the language was intemperate and offensive. That did not make it abusive under s 5 when read with Art 10 ECHR (*Campaign against Antisemitism v DPP* [2019] EWHC 9 (Admin)).

See *Blackstone's Criminal Practice 2026* **B11.52**

C12.6 Disorderly behaviour with intent to cause harassment, alarm, or distress

Public Order Act 1986, s 4A(1)

4A Intentional harassment, alarm or distress

(1) A person is guilty of an offence if, with intent to cause a person harassment, alarm or distress, he—
- (a) uses threatening, abusive or insulting words or behaviour, or disorderly behaviour, or
- (b) displays any writing, sign or other visible representation which is threatening, abusive or insulting, thereby causing that or another person harassment, alarm or distress.

EW Racially or religiously aggravated offence

SO Non-aggravated offence

Racially or religiously aggravated offence: Fine and/or 12 months'/2 years' imprisonment

Non-aggravated offence: Fine and/or 6 months' imprisonment

DO Racially or religiously aggravated offence

C12.6.1 *Sentencing*

SCG **Disorderly behaviour with intent to cause harassment, alarm or distress**

C12.6.2 Key points

Section 4A(3) provides:

Public Order Act 1986, s 4A(3)

4A Intentional harassment, alarm or distress

(3) It is a defence for the accused to prove—
- (a) that he was inside a dwelling and had no reason to believe that the words or behaviour used, or the writing, sign or other visible representation displayed, would be heard or seen by a person outside that or any other dwelling, or
- (b) that his conduct was reasonable.

- An offence under this section may be committed in a public or a private place, except that no offence is committed where the words or behaviour are used, or the writing, sign, or other visible representation is displayed, by a person inside a dwelling and the person who is harassed, alarmed, or distressed is also inside that or another dwelling.
- For considerations under the ECHR (and in particular Art 10 ECHR), see *Abdul and others v CPS* [2011] EWHC 247 (Admin) (**C12.5.2** above).
- In *R (DPP) v Manchester City Magistrates' Court* [2023] EWHC 2938 (Admin) it was confirmed that s 4A(3)(b) imposes a legal burden on the defence, but once it is established that there has been an interference with the defendant's ECHR rights the burden is the prosecution to prove the interference was proportionate and the court should carry out a fact-sensitive proportionality assessment.

See *Blackstone's Criminal Practice 2026* **B11.44**

C12.7 Intentional harassment, alarm or distress on account of sex

Public Order Act 1986, s 4B

4B Intentional harassment, alarm or distress on account of sex

(1) A person (A) is guilty of an offence under this section if—
(a) A commits an offence under section 4A (intentional harassment, alarm or distress), and
(b) A carried out the conduct referred to in section 4A(1) because of the relevant person's sex (or presumed sex).
(2) In subsection (1)—
"presumed" means presumed by A;
"the relevant person" means the person to whom A intended to cause harassment, alarm or distress.
(3) For the purposes of subsection (1)(b) it does not matter whether or not—
(a) A also carried out the conduct referred to in section 4A(1) because of any other factor not mentioned in subsection (1)(b), or
(b) A carried out the conduct referred to in section 4A(1) for the purposes of sexual gratification.

Not in force until implemented under the Protection from Sex-based Harassment in Public Act 2023.

EW

Fine and/or 12 months'/2 years' imprisonment

C12.8 Drunk and disorderly in a public place

Criminal Justice Act 1967, s 91(1), (2), and (4)

91 Drunkenness in a public place

(1) Any person who in any public place is guilty, while drunk, of disorderly behaviour. . . shall be liable on summary conviction to a fine not exceeding [level 3 on the standard scale].

(3) . . .

(4) In this section 'public place' includes any highway and any other premises or place to which at the material time the public have or are permitted to have access, whether on payment or otherwise.

SO

Level 3 fine

C12.8.1 ***Sentencing***

SCG **Drunk and disorderly in a public place**

C12.8.2 Key points

- In *Carroll v DPP* [2009] EWHC 554 (Admin), the court stated that:

4. The offence requires proof of three elements, namely that (1) the defendant was drunk; (2) he was in a public place; and (3) he was guilty of disorderly behaviour. Only the first and third elements call for further comment:

. . .

9. As to the first element in *Neale v E (A Minor)* (1983) 80 Crim App R 20, this court (Robert Goff LJ and Mann J, as they each then were) decided that the word 'drunk' should be given its ordinary and natural meaning. In the end, therefore, whether a defendant was drunk is a simple question of fact in each case. On familiar principles it is the voluntary consumption of alcohol which is the requisite *mens rea*, such as it is, of this most basic offence. If that voluntary consumption results in the defendant becoming drunk then the first element of the offence is proved.

10. As to the third element, there is no requirement for *mens rea* at all. What is required is proof that objectively viewed the defendant was guilty of disorderly behaviour. Specific drunken intent and recklessness are nothing to the point. The words 'disorderly behaviour' are again to be given their ordinary and natural meaning. In the end, therefore, it is a simple question of fact in each case: whether the defendant is guilty of disorderly behaviour.

See *Blackstone's Criminal Practice 2026* **B11.65**

C12.9 **Football-related offences**

Section 2 Sporting Events (Control of Alcohol etc) Act 1985 concerns possession of alcohol while entering or trying to enter a designated sports ground (s 2(1)), and being drunk in, or while trying to enter, a sports ground (s 2(2)); the Football Offences Act 1991 covers throwing of missiles (s 2), indecent or racialist chanting (s 3), and going onto prohibited areas (s 4); and the Criminal

Justice and Public Order Act 1994 deals with the unauthorized sale or attempted sale of tickets (s 166).

Sporting Events (Control of Alcohol etc) Act 1985, s 2(1), (1A), (2), and (3), 2A(1)

2 Offences in connection with alcohol, containers etc at sports grounds

(1) A person who has alcohol or an article to which this section applies in his possession—
   (a) at any time during the period of a designated sporting event when he is in any area of a designated sports ground from which the event may be directly viewed, or
   (b) while entering or trying to enter a designated sports ground at any time during the period of a designated sporting event at that ground, is guilty of an offence.

(1A) Subsection (1)(a) above has effect subject to section 5A(1) of this Act.

(2) A person who is drunk in a designated sports ground at any time during the period of a designated sporting event at that ground or is drunk while entering or trying to enter such a ground at any time during the period of a designated sporting event at that ground is guilty of an offence.

(3) This section applies to any article capable of causing injury to a person struck by it, being—
   (a) a bottle, can or other portable container (including such an article when crushed or broken) which—
      (i) is for holding any drink, and
      (ii) is of a kind which, when empty, is normally discarded or returned to, or left to be recovered by, the supplier, or
   (b) part of an article falling within paragraph (a) above; but does not apply to anything that is for holding any medicinal product (within the meaning of the Medicines Act 1968) or any veterinary medicinal product (within the meaning of the Veterinary Medicines Regulations 2006).

2A Fireworks etc

(1) A person is guilty of an offence if he has an article or substance to which this section applies in his possession—
   (a) at any time during the period of a designated sporting event when he is in any area of a designated sports ground from which the event may be directly viewed, or
   (b) while entering or trying to enter a designated sports ground at any time during the period of a designated sporting event at the ground.

(2) It is a defence for the accused to prove that he had possession with lawful authority.

(3) This section applies to any article or substance whose main purpose is the emission of a flare for purposes of illuminating or signalling (as opposed to igniting or heating) or the emission of smoke or a visible gas; and in particular it applies to distress flares, fog signals, and pellets and capsules intended to be used as fumigators or for testing pipes, but not to matches, cigarette lighters or heaters.

(4) This section also applies to any article which is a firework.

Football Offences Act 1991, ss 2, 3, and 4

2 Throwing of missiles

It is an offence for a person at a designated football match to throw anything at or towards—

(a) the playing area, or any area adjacent to the playing area to which spectators are not generally admitted, or

(b) any area in which spectators or other persons are or may be present, without lawful authority or lawful excuse (which shall be for him to prove).

3 Indecent or racialist chanting

(1) It is an offence to engage or take part in chanting of an indecent or racialist nature at a designated football match.

(2) For this purpose—

(a) 'chanting' means the repeated uttering of any words or sounds (whether alone or in concert with one or more others); and

(b) 'of a racialist nature' means consisting of or including matter which is threatening, abusive or insulting to a person by reason of his colour, race, nationality (including citizenship) or ethnic or national origins.

4 Going onto the playing area

It is an offence for a person at a designated football match to go onto the playing area, or any area adjacent to the playing area to which spectators are not generally admitted, without lawful authority or lawful excuse (which shall be for him to prove).

Criminal Justice and Public Order Act 1994, s 166

166 Sale of tickets by unauthorised persons

(1) It is an offence for an unauthorised person to—

(a) sell a ticket for a designated football match, or

(b) otherwise to dispose of such a ticket to another person.

(2) For this purpose—

(a) a person is 'unauthorised' unless he is authorised in writing to sell or otherwise dispose of tickets for the match by the organisers of the match;

(aa) a reference to selling a ticket includes a reference to—

(i) offering to sell a ticket;

(ii) exposing a ticket for sale;

(iii) making a ticket available for sale by another;

(iv) advertising that a ticket is available for purchase; and

(v) giving a ticket to a person who pays or agrees to pay for some other goods or services or offering to do so.

(b) a 'ticket' means anything which purports to be a ticket;

. . .

SO

s 2(1) and 2A(1) Sporting Events (Control of Alcohol etc) Act 1985: Level 3 fine and/or 3 months' imprisonment/level

s 2(2) Sporting Events (Control of Alcohol etc): Level 2 fine

Football Offences Act 1991 (throwing missile; indecent or racialist chanting; going onto prohibited areas): Level 3 fine

s 166 Criminal Justice and Public Order Act 1994 (unauthorised sale of tickets): Level 5 fine

C12.9.1 *Sentencing*

SCG **Football related offences**

See *Blackstone's Criminal Practice 2026* **B11.166**

C12.10 Interference with use or operation of key national infrastructure

Public Order Act 2023, s 7

7 Interference with use or operation of key national infrastructure

(1) A person commits an offence if—
 (a) they do an act which interferes with the use or operation of any key national infrastructure in England and Wales, and
 (b) they intend that act to interfere with the use or operation of such infrastructure or are reckless as to whether it will do so.

(2) It is a defence for a person charged with an offence under subsection (1) to prove that—
 (a) they had a reasonable excuse for the act mentioned in paragraph (a) of that subsection, or
 (b) the act mentioned in paragraph (a) of that subsection was done wholly or mainly in contemplation or furtherance of a trade dispute.

...

(4) For the purposes of subsection (1) a person's act interferes with the use or operation of key national infrastructure if it prevents the infrastructure from being used or operated to any extent for any of its intended purposes.

(5) The cases in which infrastructure is prevented from being used or operated for any of its intended purposes include where its use or operation for any of those purposes is significantly delayed.

(6) In this section "key national infrastructure" means—
 (a) road transport infrastructure,
 (b) rail infrastructure,
 (c) air transport infrastructure,
 (d) harbour infrastructure,
 (e) downstream oil infrastructure,
 (f) downstream gas infrastructure,
 (g) onshore oil and gas exploration and production infrastructure,
 (h) onshore electricity generation infrastructure, or
 (i) newspaper printing infrastructure.

Section 8 makes further provision about these kinds of infrastructure.

EW

Fine and/or 12 months' imprisonment

C12.10.1 Key points

Once the ingredients of the offence are made out, the court does not need to consider whether the conviction would be a proportionate interference with the defendant's convention rights under Articles 10 or 11 ECHR (*R v Sarti* [2025] EWCA Crim 61).

See *Blackstone's Criminal Practice 2026* **B13.89**

C12.11 Locking on/being equipped for locking on

Public Order Act 2023, ss 1 and 2

1 Offence of locking on

(1) A person commits an offence if—
  (a) they—
    (i) attach themselves to another person, to an object or to land,
    (ii) attach a person to another person, to an object or to land, or
    (iii) attach an object to another object or to land,
  (b) that act causes, or is capable of causing, serious disruption to—
    (i) two or more individuals, or
    (ii) an organisation,
  in a place other than a dwelling, and
  (c) they intend that act to have a consequence mentioned in paragraph (b) or are reckless as to whether it will have such a consequence.

(2) It is a defence for a person charged with an offence under subsection (1) to prove that they had a reasonable excuse for the act mentioned in paragraph (a) of that subsection.

...

(5) In this section "dwelling" means—
  (a) a building or structure which is used as a dwelling, or
  (b) a part of a building or structure, if the part is used as a dwelling,
  and includes any yard, garden, grounds, garage or outhouse belonging to and used with a dwelling.

2 Offence of being equipped for locking on

(1) A person commits an offence if they have an object with them in a place other than a dwelling with the intention that it may be used in the course of or in connection with the commission by any person of an offence under section 1(1) (offence of locking on).

...

(3) In this section "dwelling" has the same meaning as in section 1.

SO

s 1 (locking on): Fine and/or 6 months' imprisonment

s 2 (being equipped): Fine

See *Blackstone's Criminal Practice 2026* **B11.123**

C12.12 Obstruction of major transport works

Public Order Act 2023, ss 6 and 7

6 Obstruction etc of major transport works

(1) A person commits an offence if the person—
  (a) obstructs the undertaker or a person acting under the authority of the undertaker—
    (i) in setting out the lines of any major transport works,
    (ii) in constructing or maintaining any major transport works, or

(iii) in taking any steps that are reasonably necessary for the purposes of facilitating, or in connection with, the construction or maintenance of any major transport works, or

(b) interferes with, moves or removes any apparatus which—

(i) relates to the construction or maintenance of any major transport works, and

(ii) belongs to a person within subsection (5).

(2) It is a defence for a person charged with an offence under subsection (1) to prove that—

(a) they had a reasonable excuse for the act mentioned in paragraph (a) or (b) of that subsection, or

(b) the act mentioned in paragraph (a) or (b) of that subsection was done wholly or mainly in contemplation or furtherance of a trade dispute.

...

(5) to (10) [relevant definitions]

SO

Fine and/or 6 months' imprisonment

C12.13 Public assemblies

Public Order Act 1986, s 14

14 Imposing conditions on public assemblies

(1) Subsection (1A) applies if the senior police officer, having regard to the time or place at which and the circumstances in which any public assembly is being held or is intended to be held, reasonably believes that—

(a) it may result in serious public disorder, serious damage to property or serious disruption to the life of the community,

(aa) in the case of an assembly in England and Wales, the noise generated by persons taking part in the assembly may result in serious disruption to the activities of an organisation which are carried on in the vicinity of the assembly,

(ab) in the case of an assembly in England and Wales—

(i) the noise generated by persons taking part in the assembly may have a relevant impact on persons in the vicinity of the assembly, and

(ii) that impact may be significant, or

(b) the purpose of the persons organising it is the intimidation of others with a view to compelling them not to do an act they have a right to do, or to do an act they have a right not to do.

(1A) The senior police officer may give directions imposing on the persons organising or taking part in the assembly—

(a) in the case of an assembly in England and Wales, such conditions as appear to the officer necessary to prevent the disorder, damage, disruption, impact or intimidation mentioned in subsection (1);

...

(4) Subject to subsection (5A), a person who organises a public assembly and fails to comply with a condition imposed under this section is guilty of an offence, but it is a defence for him to prove that the failure arose from circumstances beyond his control.

(5) Subject to subsection (5A), a person who takes part in a public assembly and fails to comply with a condition imposed under this section is guilty of an offence, but it is a defence for him to prove that the failure arose from circumstances beyond his control.

(5A) A person is guilty of an offence under subsection (4) or (5) only if—

(a) in the case of a public assembly in England and Wales, at the time the person fails to comply with the condition the person knows or ought to know that the condition has been imposed;

. . .

(6) A person who incites another to commit an offence under subsection (5) is guilty of an offence.

SO

s 14(4) (organising): Level 4 fine and/or 6 months' imprisonment

s 14(5) (taking part): Level 4 fine

s 14(6) (inciting): Level 4 fine and/or 6 months' imprisonment

C12.13.1 Key points

There is no requirement on the prosecution to prove that a conviction under this section would be a proportionate interference with Articles 10 and 11 ECHR (*DPP v Eastburn* [2023] EWHC 1063 (Admin)).

C12.14 Obstructing stop and search (conducted without suspicion)

Public Order Act 2023, s 14

14 Offence relating to section 11

(1) A person commits an offence if the person intentionally obstructs a constable in the exercise of the constable's powers under section 11 [Public Order Act 2023 (powers to stop and search without suspicion)].

SO

Fine and/or 1 month's imprisonment

C12.15 Taxi touting/soliciting for hire

Criminal Justice and Public Order Act 1994, s 167

167 Touting for hire car services.

(1) Subject to the following provisions, it is an offence, in a public place, to solicit persons to hire vehicles to carry them as passengers.

(2) Subsection (1) above does not imply that the soliciting must refer to any particular vehicle nor is the mere display of a sign on a vehicle that the vehicle is for hire soliciting within that subsection . . . .

(6) In this section—
'public place' includes any highway and any other premises or place to which at the material time the public have or are permitted to have access (whether on payment or otherwise);

SO

Level 4 fine

C12.15.1 *Sentencing*

SCG Taxi touting/soliciting for hire

C12.15.2 Key points

Touting requires some form of invitation to a prospective hirer (*R (Oddy) v Bugbugs Ltd* [2003] EWHC 2865 (Admin)).

C12.16 Threatening behaviour, fear, or provocation of violence

Public Order Act 1986, ss 4(1), 6(3) and (5)

4 Fear or provocation of violence

(1) A person is guilty of an offence if he—
(a) uses towards another person threatening, abusive or insulting words or behaviour, or
(b) distributes or displays to another person any writing, sign or other visible representation which is threatening, abusive or insulting, with intent to cause that person to believe that immediate unlawful violence will be used against him or another by any person, or to provoke the immediate use of unlawful violence by that person or another, or whereby that person is likely to believe that such violence will be used or it is likely that such violence will be provoked.

. . .

6 Mental element: miscellaneous

(3) A person is guilty of an offence under section 4 only if he intends his words or behaviour, or the writing, sign or other visible representation, to be threatening, abusive or insulting, or is aware that it may be threatening, abusive or insulting.

. . .

(5) For the purposes of this section a person whose awareness is impaired by intoxication shall be taken to be aware of that of which he would be aware if not intoxicated, unless he shows either that his intoxication was not self-induced or that it was caused solely by the taking or administration of a substance in the course of medical treatment.

EW Racially or religiously aggravated offence

SO Non-aggravated offence

Racially or religiously aggravated offence: Fine and/or 12 months'/2 years' imprisonment

Non-aggravated offence: Fine and/or 6 months' imprisonment

DO Racially or religiously aggravated offence

C12.16.1 *Sentencing*

SCG **Threatening behaviour—fear or provocation of violence**

C12.16.2 Key points

- An offence under s 4 may be committed in a public or a private place, except that no offence is committed where the words or behaviour are used, or the writing, sign, or other visible representation is distributed or displayed, by a person inside a dwelling and the other person is also inside that or another dwelling.
- Subject to the Crown proving the use of threatening, etc words/behaviour and the *mens rea*, *Winn v DPP* (1992) 156 JP 881 confirmed that there are four ways in which the offence can be committed:
  - by intending to cause the person against whom the conduct is directed to believe that immediate unlawful violence will be used against him or another;
  - by intending to provoke the immediate use of unlawful violence by that person or another;
  - the person against whom the conduct is directed being likely to believe that immediate unlawful violence will be used; or
  - its being likely that immediate unlawful violence will be provoked.
- Actions taken in self-defence do not amount to unlawful violence.
- For the conduct to be used towards another, that other must be physically present (*Atkin v DPP* (1989) 89 Cr App R 199).
- The need for immediate unlawful violence means that it cannot be at some uncertain future time (*Horseferry Road Stipendiary Magistrate, ex p Siadatan* [1991] 1 QB 260), but it does not mean that it has to be instantaneous.
- For considerations under the European Convention on Human Rights (and in particular Art 10 ECHR), see *Abdul and others v CPS* [2011] EWHC 247 (Admin).

See *Blackstone's Criminal Practice 2026* B11.32

C12.17 Tunnelling etc

Public Order Act 2023, ss 3, 4, and 5

3 Offence of causing serious disruption by tunnelling

(1) A person commits an offence if—

(a) they create, or participate in the creation of, a tunnel,

(b) the creation or existence of the tunnel causes, or is capable of causing, serious disruption to—

(i) two or more individuals, or
(ii) an organisation,

in a place other than a dwelling, and

(c) they intend the creation or existence of the tunnel to have a consequence mentioned in paragraph (b) or are reckless as to whether its creation or existence will have such a consequence.

(2) It is a defence for a person charged with an offence under subsection (1) to prove that they had a reasonable excuse for creating, or participating in the creation of, the tunnel.

(3) Without prejudice to the generality of subsection (2), a person is to be treated as having a reasonable excuse for the purposes of that subsection if the creation of the tunnel was authorised by a person with an interest in land which entitled them to authorise its creation.

. . .

(5) For the purposes of this section—
(a) "tunnel" means an excavation that extends beneath land, whether or not—
(i) it is big enough to permit the entry or passage of an individual, or
(ii) it leads to a particular destination;
(b) an excavation which is created with the intention that it will become or connect with a tunnel is to be treated as a tunnel, whether or not—
(i) any tunnel with which it is intended to connect has already been created, or
(ii) it is big enough to permit the entry or passage of an individual.

(6) References in this section to the creation of an excavation include—
(a) the extension or enlargement of an excavation, and
(b) the alteration of a natural or artificial underground feature.

(7) This section does not apply in relation to a tunnel if or to the extent that it is in or under a dwelling.

(8) In this section "dwelling" has the same meaning as in section 1 (offence of locking on).

4 Offence of causing serious disruption by being present in a tunnel

(1) A person commits an offence if—
(a) they are present in a relevant tunnel having entered it after the coming into force of this section,
(b) their presence in the tunnel causes, or is capable of causing, serious disruption to—
(i) two or more individuals, or
(ii) an organisation,

in a place other than a dwelling, and

(c) they intend their presence in the tunnel to have a consequence mentioned in paragraph (b) or are reckless as to whether their presence there will have such a consequence.

(2) It is a defence for a person charged with an offence under subsection (1) to prove that they had a reasonable excuse for their presence in the tunnel.

(3) Without prejudice to the generality of subsection (2), a person ("P") is to be treated as having a reasonable excuse for the purposes of that subsection if P's presence in the tunnel was authorised by a person with an interest in land which entitled them to authorise P's presence there.

. . .

(5) For the purposes of this section—
(a) "tunnel" means an excavation that extends beneath land, whether or not it leads to a particular destination;
(b) an excavation which is created with the intention that it will become or connect with a tunnel is to be treated as a tunnel, whether or not any tunnel with which it is intended to connect has already been created.

(6) In this section "relevant tunnel" means a tunnel that was created for the purposes of, or in connection with, a protest (and it does not matter whether an offence has been committed under section 3 in relation to the creation of the tunnel).
(7) References in this section to the creation of an excavation include—
  (a) the extension or enlargement of an excavation, and
  (b) the alteration of a natural or artificial underground feature.
(8) This section does not apply in relation to a tunnel if or to the extent that it is in or under a dwelling.
(9) In this section "dwelling" has the same meaning as in section 1 (offence of locking on).

5 Offence of being equipped for tunnelling etc

(1) A person commits an offence if they have an object with them in a place other than a dwelling with the intention that it may be used in the course of or in connection with the commission by any person of an offence under section 3(1) or 4(1) (offences relating to tunnelling).

. . .

(4) In this section "dwelling" has the same meaning as in section 1 (offence of locking on).

EW ss 3 (causing serious disruption by tunnelling) and 4 (causing serious disruption by being present in a tunnel)

SO s 5 (being equipped for tunnelling)

s 3: Fine and/or 12 months'/3 years' imprisonment

s 4 Fine and/or 12 months'/3 years' imprisonment

s 5 Fine and/or 6 months' imprisonment

C12.18 Violent disorder

Public Order Act 1986, ss 2 and 6

2 Violent disorder

(1) Where three or more persons who are present together use or threaten unlawful violence and the conduct of them (taken together) is such as would cause a person of reasonable firmness present at the scene to fear for his personal safety, each of the persons using or threatening unlawful violence is guilty of violent disorder.
(2) It is immaterial whether or not the three or more use or threaten unlawful violence simultaneously.
(3) No person of reasonable firmness need actually be, be likely to be, present at the scene.
(4) Violent disorder may be committed in private as well as in public places.

6 Mental element: miscellaneous

(2) A person is guilty of violent disorder . . . only if he intends to use or threatens violence or is aware that his conduct may be violent or threatens violence.

. . .

(5) A person whose awareness is impaired by intoxication shall be taken to be aware of that of which he would be aware if not intoxicated, unless he shows either that his intoxication was not self-induced or that it was caused solely by the taking or administration of a substance in the course of medical treatment.

EW

Fine and/or 12 months'/5 years' imprisonment

C12.18.1 *Sentencing*

SCG Violent disorder

C12.18.2 Key points

- The offence of violent disorder does not require a common purpose and the expression 'present together' means no more than being in the same place at the same time; there is no requirement that there is a degree of cooperation between those who are using or offering violence (*R v NW* [2010] EWCA Crim 404).
- In *Allan v Ireland* (1984) 79 Cr App R 206 the Divisional Court held that a defendant's voluntary presence as part of a crowd engaged in threatening behaviour is capable of raising a prima facie case of participation, but mere voluntary presence is not sufficient to convict a defendant unless the court is satisfied that he at least also gave some overt encouragement to the others who were directly involved in the threatening behaviour. The prosecution must prove that (a) the relevant defendant intended to encourage and did encourage the offence by his presence, and (b) he was aware that his conduct (as opposed to the conduct of the group) might be violent or threatening behaviour (*R v Blackwood* [2002] EWCA Crim 3102).

See *Blackstone's Criminal Practice 2026* **B11.14**

C12.19 Wilful obstruction of the highway

Highways Act 1980 s 137

137 Penalty for wilful obstruction.

(1) If a person, without lawful authority or excuse, in any way wilfully obstructs the free passage along a highway he is guilty of an offence

. . . .

(1B) For the purposes of this section it does not matter whether free passage along the highway in question has already been temporarily restricted or temporarily prohibited (whether by a constable, a traffic authority or otherwise) . . . .

SO

Fine and/or 6 months' imprisonment

C12.19.1 Key points

- *DPP v Ziegler* [2019] UKSC 106 confirms that the Act must be read compatibly with the ECHR The defence of lawful excuse will be available when the interference with the rights under articles 10 and 11 is not proportionate. The extent of the disruption and whether it is intentional are relevant to the assessment of proportionality.

C13 **Road Traffic Offences—Definitions**

C13.1 **Accident**

'Accident' is to be given its ordinary meaning (*Chief Constable of West Midlands v Billingham* [1979] 1 WLR 747). A deliberate act can amount to an accident (*Chief Constable of Staffordshire v Lees* [1981] RTR 506). A physical impact is not necessary (*R v Currie* [2007] EWCA Crim 927), but the *de minimis* principle applies (*R v Morris* [1972] 1 WLR 228).

C13.2 **Causing**

Causing requires a positive act (*Ross Hillman Ltd v Bond* [1974] QB 435) committed with prior knowledge. *R v A* [2020] EWCA Crim 407 confirms that for there to be sufficient causation it is not necessary to foresee the precise circumstances of an incident but that an incident of that sort might occur.

C13.3 **Driver**

Section 192(1) Road Traffic Act 1988 provides:

> **Road Traffic Act 1988, s 192(1)**
>
> **192 General interpretation of Act**
>
> (1) . . .
>
> 'driver', where a separate person acts as a steersman of a motor vehicle, includes (except for the purposes of section 1 of this Act) that person as well as any other person engaged in the driving of the vehicle, and 'drive' is to be interpreted accordingly,
>
> . . .

A person supervising a driver will not be a driver unless he exercises some control over the vehicle (eg dual controls) (*Evans v Walkden* [1956] 1 WLR 1019).

C13.4 **Driving**

R v MacDonagh [1974] QB 448 defined 'driving' as use of the driver's controls for the purpose of directing the movement of the vehicle. The court gave the following guidance:

> There are an infinite number of ways in which a person may control the movement of a motor vehicle, apart from the orthodox one of sitting in the driving seat and using the engine for propulsion. He may be coasting down a hill with the gears in neutral and the engine switched off; he may be steering a vehicle which is being towed by another. As has already been pointed out, he may be sitting in the driving seat whilst others push, or half sitting in the driving seat but keeping one foot on the road in order to induce the car to move. Finally, as in the present case, he may be standing in the road and himself pushing the car with or without using the steering wheel to direct it. Although the word 'drive' must be given a wide meaning, the Courts must be alert to see that the net is not thrown so widely that it includes

Blackstone's Magistrates' Court Handbook 2026. Bartholomew Dalton and Caroline Liggins, Oxford University Press. © Oxford University Press 2026.
DOI: 10.1093/oso/9780198963943.003.0054

activities which cannot be said to be driving a motor vehicle in any ordinary use of that word in the English language.

As a person may be driving a stationary vehicle, it is a matter of fact to be decided in each case, and factors such as the reason for the vehicle stopping and the duration of the stop will be relevant (*Planton v DPP* [2002] RTR 107). Steering a vehicle being towed would amount to driving where there was an operational braking system (*McQuaid v Anderton* [1981] 1 WLR 154), as would freewheeling a vehicle down a hill while steering (*Saycell v Bool* [1948] 2 All ER 83). A person steering from the passenger seat is driving (*Tyler v Whatmore* [1976] RTR 83).

C13.5 **In charge**

In cases where the matter is not clear, the case of *DPP v Watkins* (1989) 89 Cr App R 112 should be considered in detail. The court laid down the following broad guidance:

Broadly there are two distinct classes of case. (1) If the defendant is the owner or lawful possessor of the vehicle or has recently driven it, he will have been in charge of it, and the question for the Court will be whether he is still in charge or whether he has relinquished his charge. Usually such a defendant will be prima facie in charge unless he has put the vehicle in someone else's charge. However, he would not be so if in all the circumstances he has ceased to be in actual control and there is no realistic possibility of his resuming actual control while unfit: eg if he is at home in bed for the night, if he is a great distance from the car, or if it is taken by another.

(2) If the defendant is not the owner, the lawful possessor, or recent driver but is sitting in the vehicle or is otherwise involved with it, the question for the Court is, as here, whether he has assumed being in charge of it. In this class of case the defendant will be in charge if, whilst unfit, he is voluntarily in de facto control of the vehicle or if, in the circumstances, including his position, his intentions and his actions, he may be expected imminently to assume control. Usually this will involve his having gained entry to the car and evinced an intention to take control of it. But gaining entry may not be necessary if he has manifested that intention some other way, eg by stealing the keys of a car in circumstances which show he means presently to drive it.

The circumstances to be taken into account will vary infinitely, but the following will be usually relevant:

(i) Whether and where he is in the vehicle or how far he is from it.
(ii) What he is doing at the relevant time.
(iii) Whether he is in possession of a key that fits the ignition.
(iv) Whether there is evidence of an intention to take or assert control of the car by driving or otherwise
(v) Whether any other person is in, at or near the vehicle and if so, the like particulars in respect of that person.

It will be for the Court to consider all the above factors with any others which may be relevant and reach its decision as a question of fact and degree.

C13.6 **Motor vehicle**

There is no statutory definition of 'vehicle' and therefore its ordinary meaning of a carriage or conveyance should apply. Where the statute uses the phrase 'motor vehicle', the definition to be found in s 185 Road Traffic Act (RTA) 1988 states that it is a 'mechanically propelled vehicle intended or adapted for use on roads'. The maximum speed of the vehicle is not a relevant factor (*DPP v King* [2008] EWHC 447 (Admin)). Section 20(1)(b) Chronically Sick and Disabled Persons Act 1970 means that a mechanically propelled invalid carriage, provided that it complies with the prescribed requirements and is being used in accordance with the prescribed conditions, is not a 'motor vehicle' for all the purposes of the RTA 1988 save for the sole and specific exception of s 22A, and is thus excluded from the ambit of the nine sections of the 1988 Act that apply to mechanically propelled vehicles, including offences of driving with excess alcohol (*Croitoru v CPS* [2016] EWHC 1645 (Admin)).

C13.7 **Owner**

This includes a person in possession of a vehicle under a hire or hire-purchase agreement.

C13.8 **Permitting**

A person permits use when he allows or authorizes use, or fails to take reasonable steps to prevent use. For permitting use with no insurance, the prosecution do not need to show that the person knew the driver to be uninsured. If, however, use is conditional (eg on the person having insurance), the outcome would be different (*Newbury v Davis* [1974] RTR 367).

C13.9 **Public place**

This is a place to which the public have access. However, the law draws a distinction between general public access and access for a defined group of persons. The law in this area is complex and voluminous, and advocates should always seek an adjournment where the answer is not clear. In *Richardson* [2018] EWHC 428 (Admin) the court held that the absence of barriers was not itself enough to make a car park a public place. The majority of the signage suggested otherwise.

C13.10 **Road**

This is defined as any highway or road to which the public have access. *Bowen v Isle of Wight Council* [2021] EWHC 3254 confirms that a road will be within the definition of 'road' in section 142 of the Road Traffic Regulation Act 1984, provided that the general public do as a matter of fact exercise access to it and provided that those members of the public 'have not obtained access either by overcoming a physical obstruction or in defiance of prohibition express or implied'. If the conditions are satisfied, it is irrelevant whether the presence of the public on the road was merely by the tolerance of the owners or whether the tolerance is to be taken to have given implicit permission. The following have been held to be a road:

- pedestrian pavement (*Randall v Motor Insurers' Bureau* [1968] 1 WLR 1900);

- grass verge at the side of a road (*Worth v Brooks* [1959] Crim LR 855);
- bridges over which a road passes.

It will be a matter of fact and degree as to whether something is a road, and whether or not the public have access. A car park will not generally be a road, even if there are roads running through it. In *Barrett v DPP*, 2009 EWHC 423 (Admin), the court held that a roadway running through a private caravan park, and facilitating entry to a beach, constituted a road.

A vehicle will be 'on' a road when part of the vehicle protrudes over a road (*Avery v CPS* [2011] EWHC 2388 (Admin)).

C13.11 Highway

This is defined as land over which there is a right of way on foot, by riding, or with vehicles and cattle. A highway includes: bridleways, footpaths, footways, walkways, carriageways, and driftways.

See generally *Blackstone's Criminal Practice 2026* C1

C14 **Road Traffic Offences**

C14.1 **Careless driving (drive without due care and attention)**

Road Traffic Act 1988, s 3

3 Careless, and inconsiderate, driving

If a person drives a mechanically propelled vehicle on a road or other public place without due care and attention, or without reasonable consideration for other persons using the road or place, he is guilty of an offence.

SO

Fine

Must endorse and may disqualify. If no disqualification, impose 3–9 points

C14.1.1 ***Sentencing***

SCG Careless driving

C14.1.2 Key points

- Careless driving is defined in the Act.

Section 3ZA(2)–(4) RTA1988 provides:

Road Traffic Act 1988, s 3ZA(2)–(4)

3ZA Meaning of careless, or inconsiderate, driving

. . .

(2) A person is to be regarded as driving without due care and attention if (and only if) the way he drives falls below what would be expected of a competent and careful driver.

(3) In determining for the purposes of subsection (2) above what would be expected of a careful and competent driver in a particular case, regard shall be had not only to the circumstances of which he could be expected to be aware but also to any circumstances shown to have been within the knowledge of the accused.

(4) A person is to be regarded as driving without reasonable consideration for other persons only if those persons are inconvenienced by his driving.

- Special provision is made for those driving for police purposes by s 3ZA (2A) through (2F).
- If death has resulted from the driving, any trial should await the conclusion of any inquest (*Smith v DPP* [2000] RTR 36).

Blackstone's Magistrates' Court Handbook 2026. Bartholomew Dalton and Caroline Liggins, Oxford University Press.
DOI: 10.1093/oso/9780198963943.003.0055

- Failure to drive in accordance with the Highway Code will generally amount to careless driving.
- An offence of careless driving can be tried alongside an offence of dangerous driving as an alternative. However, it is not clear as to why this is done in the magistrates' court, as the offence is a statutory alternative in any event.
- If the facts are such that in the absence of an explanation put forward by the defendant, or where that explanation is objectively inadequate, the only possible conclusion is that he was careless, he should be convicted (*DPP v Cox* (1993) 157 JP 1044).
- A court does not need to consider an alternative inference from facts, such as mechanical defect, without hearing evidence of the same (*DPP v Tipton* (1992) 156 JP 172).
- Whilst the condition of the driver is relevant and admissible, it is not sufficient of itself to prove that the way in which the defendant drove was careless (*Jones v CPS* [2019] EWHC 2826 (Admin)).

See *Blackstone's Criminal Practice 2026* C6.1

C14.2 Causing death by careless driving when under the influence of drink or drugs

RTA 1988 (s 3A)

IO

Life

Obligatory disqualification. Mandatory retest by way of extended test

DO

GC

C14.2.1 *Sentencing*

SCG **Causing death by careless driving when under the influence of drink or drugs**

C14.2.2 Key points

- The offence can be committed in eight separate ways.
- See **C14.3**, **C14.8**, and **C14.10** for details of constituent offences.
- On causation see **C13.2**.

See *Blackstone's Criminal Practice 2026* C3.20

C14.3 Causing death by dangerous driving

Road Traffic Act (RTA) 1988, s 1

IO

Life

Obligatory disqualification. Mandatory retest by way of extended test

DO

GC

C14.3.1 *Sentencing*

SCG Causing death by dangerous driving

C14.3.2 Key points

- One of the tests for dangerous driving as set out in s 2A RTAc1988 must be satisfied, producing a causal link to the death. See C14.6.2
- On causation see C13.2.

See *Blackstone's Criminal Practice 2026* C3.7

C14.4 Causing death by disqualified, careless, unlicensed/uninsured driving

Road Traffic Act 1988, ss 2B, 3ZB, and 3ZC

Causing death by:

- disqualified driving (s 3ZC);
- careless or inconsiderate driving (s 2B);
- unlicensed, or uninsured drivers (s 3ZB).

IO Causing death by disqualified driving

EW Causing death by careless, inconsiderate, unlicensed, or uninsured driving

Causing death by disqualified driving: Fine and/or 10 years' imprisonment

Causing death by careless or inconsiderate driving: Fine and/or 12 months'/5 years' imprisonment

Causing death by unlicensed or uninsured driving: Fine and/or 12 months'/2 years' imprisonment

Minimum disqualification of 12 months, discretionary retest, 3–11 penalty points.

C14.4.1 *Sentencing*

SCG **Causing death by driving: disqualified driving**

Causing death by careless or inconsiderate driving

Causing death by driving: unlicensed or uninsured drivers

C14.4.2 Key points

- Death must result from the act of driving but need not occur at the same time as the incident (*R v Jenkins* [2012] EWCA Crim 2909; dangerous parking).
- The driving must be more than a minimal cause of the death.
- Where the driver is faultless and the total responsibility for the death lies with the deceased, no offence is committed under s 3ZB (*R v Hughes* [2013] UKSC 56). *R v MH* [2011] EWCA Crim 1508 suggests it is open to the defence to argue that the defendant's contribution to the death was no more than minimal where, for example, in a stationary car or where the victim would have died anyway, say, because of a new act intervening.
- On causation see **C13.2**.

See *Blackstone's Criminal Practice 2026* **C3.52**

C14.5 Causing serious injury by careless, or inconsiderate, driving

Road Traffic Act 1988, s 2C

(1) A person who causes serious injury to another person by driving a mechanically propelled vehicle on a road or other public place without due care and attention, or without reasonable consideration for other persons using the road or place, is guilty of an offence.

(2) In this section 'serious injury' means—

(a) in England and Wales, physical harm which amounts to grievous bodily harm for the purposes of the Offences against the Person Act 1861 . . .

EW

Fine and/or 12 months'/2 years' imprisonment

There is obligatory disqualification but if avoided 3–11 points

C14.5.1 *Sentencing*

SCG **Causing serious injury by careless or inconsiderate driving**

C14.6 Causing serious injury by dangerous/disqualified driving

Road Traffic Act 1988, s 1A

1A Causing serious injury by dangerous driving

(1) A person who causes serious injury to another person by driving a mechanically propelled vehicle dangerously on a road or other public place is guilty of an offence.
(2) In this section 'serious injury' means—
  (a) in England and Wales, physical harm which amounts to grievous bodily harm for the purposes of the Offences against the Person Act 1861,
  (b) . . .

C14.6.1 *Causing serious injury by disqualified driving*

Road Traffic Act 1988, s 3ZD

(1) A person is guilty of an offence under this section if he or she—
  (a) causes serious injury to another person by driving a motor vehicle on a road, and
  (b) at that time, is committing an offence under section 103(1)(b) of this Act (driving while disqualified).
(2) In this section 'serious injury' means—
  (a) in England and Wales, physical harm which amounts to grievous bodily harm for the purposes of the Offences against the Person Act 1861.

EW

Serious injury by dangerous driving: Fine and/or 12 months'/5 years' imprisonment

Serious injury by disqualified driving: Fine and/or 12 months'/4 years' imprisonment

Obligatory disqualification for 24 months (with obligatory retest if dangerous driving). If no disqualification then 3–11 penalty points

C14.6.2 *Sentencing*

SCG **Causing serious injury by dangerous driving**

Causing serious injury by driving: disqualified drivers

C14.6.3 Key points

- Dangerous driving is defined by s 2A Road Traffic Act 1988. See **C14.7.2**
- On causation see **C13.2.**

See *Blackstone's Criminal Practice 2026* **C3.33**

C14.7 **Dangerous driving**

Road Traffic Act 1988, s 2

2 Dangerous driving

A person who drives a mechanically propelled vehicle dangerously on a road or other public place is guilty of an offence.

EW

Fine and/or 12 months'/2 years' imprisonment

Must endorse and disqualify for a minimum period of 12 months; must order extended retest; must disqualify for at least 2 years if offender has had two or more disqualifications for periods of 56 days or more in preceding 3 years

C14.7.1 *Sentencing*

SCG Dangerous driving

C14.7.2 Key points

Road Traffic Act 1988, s 2A

2A Meaning of dangerous driving

(1) For the purposes of sections 1, 1A and 2 above a person is to be regarded as driving dangerously if (and, subject to subsection (2) below, only if)—
  (a) the way he drives falls far below what would be expected of a competent and careful driver, and
  (b) it would be obvious to a competent and careful driver that driving in that way would be dangerous.

...

(2) A person is also to be regarded as driving dangerously for the purposes of sections 1, 1A and 2 above if it would be obvious to a competent and careful driver that driving the vehicle in its current state would be dangerous.
(3) In subsections (1) and (2) above 'dangerous' refers to danger either of injury to any person or of serious damage to property; and in determining for the purposes of those subsections what would be expected of, or obvious to, a competent and careful driver in a particular case, regard shall be had not only to the circumstances of which he could be expected to be aware but also to any circumstances shown to have been within the knowledge of the accused.
(4) In determining for the purposes of subsection (2) above the state of a vehicle, regard may be had to anything attached to or carried on or in it and to the manner in which it is attached or carried.

- The special skill (or indeed lack of skill) of a driver is an irrelevant circumstance when considering whether the driving is dangerous (*R v Bannister*

[2009] EWCA Crim 1571). However, special provision is made for those driving for police purposes by s 2A (1A) through (1F).

- The fact that the defendant had consumed alcohol is an admissible factor (*R v Webster* [2006] 2 Cr App R 103). Where drink is a major plank of the prosecution case, advocates should have regard to *R v McBride* [1962] 2 QB 167.
- Although it would not have been sufficient on its own, a passenger's lack of helmet whilst riding a motor scooter was properly considered when deciding that the driving was dangerous (*R v Holder* [2023] EWCA Crim 5).
- Where a vehicle's dangerous state is due to its official design and not use, it will not usually be appropriate to prosecute (*R v Marchant* [2004] 1 All ER 1187).
- A vehicle is being driven in a dangerous state if the driver is aware that his ability to control the vehicle might be impaired such that the standard of his driving might fall below the requisite standard (*R v Marison* [1997] RTR 457).
- CPS policy on prosecuting bad driving can be found on https://www.cps.gov.uk/prosecution-guidance/road-traffic-fatal-offences-and-bad-driving#a06.

See *Blackstone's Criminal Practice 2026* C3.43

C14.8 **Driving while disqualified**

Road Traffic Act 1988, s 103(1)

103 Obtaining licence, or driving, while disqualified

(1) A person is guilty of an offence if, while disqualified for holding or obtaining a licence, he—
  (a) obtains a licence, or
  (b) drives a motor vehicle on a road.

. . .

SO

s 103(1)(a): Level 3 fine

s 103(1)(b): Fine and/or 6 months' imprisonment.

Must endorse and may disqualify. If no disqualification, impose 6 points

C14.8.1 ***Sentencing***

SCG Drive whilst disqualified

C14.8.2 Key points

- When the guideline refers to Additional periods of disqualification the following guidance is given:

  To determine the overall period of disqualification

  1 determine the appropriate period of disqualification for the offence from the table above

  2 add any unexpired period of disqualification as at the date of sentence for this offence

  Where immediate custody is being imposed (for this or any other offence sentenced at the same time) to ensure the offender serves all the period of disqualification imposed for this offence once released from custody

  3 Add a period of disqualification equivalent to half of the custodial sentence imposed

  There is no statutory maximum period of disqualification.

- The prosecution do not need to prove that the defendant was aware of the prosecution that led to his being disqualified (*Taylor v Kenyon* [1952] 2 All ER 726); even where a driving licence has been returned to the defendant by mistake (*R v Bowsher* [1972] RTR 202). If the defendant was genuinely unaware and had no reason to anticipate one, prosecution is unlikely and an absolute discharge likely if one proceeds.
- Strict proof that the person disqualified by the court is the person now charged is required. This will normally arise from (a) admission, (b) fingerprints, (c) evidence of identity from someone in court when the disqualification was made (*R v Derwentside Justices, ex p Heaviside* [1996] RTR 384). Other evidence such as an unusual name will at least raise a prima facie case (*Olakunori v DPP* [1998] COD 443).
- A defendant's silence in interview (where he did not later rely on any fact) and his general attitude to the management of the case could not provide sufficient proof (*Mills v DPP* [2008] EWHC 3304 (Admin)).
- Consistency of personal details will normally be sufficient to raise a prima facie case. If the defendant calls no evidence to contradict that prima facie case, it will be open to the court to be satisfied that identity is proved (*Pattison v Director of Public Prosecutions* [2006] RTR 13).
- A solicitor could be called as a witness to confirm identity, although the practice is discouraged (*R (Howe) v South Durham Magistrates' Court* [2005] RTR 4).
- A mistaken belief by the defendant that he was not driving on a road will not amount to a defence (*R v Miller* [1975] 1 WLR 1222).
- The fact that a disqualification was later quashed on appeal does not provide a defence (*R v Thames Magistrates' Court, ex p Levy*, The Times, 17 July 1997).
- A bad character application in relation to the disqualification is not necessary as it has to do with the alleged facts of the offence (s 98 Criminal Justice Act 2003) (*DPP v Agyemang* [2009] EWHC 1542 (Admin)).

See *Blackstone's Criminal Practice 2026* **C6.40**

C14.9 Driving otherwise than in accordance with a licence

RTA 1988, s 87

87 Drivers of motor vehicles to have driving licences.

(1) It is an offence for a person to drive on a road a motor vehicle of any class otherwise than in accordance with a licence authorising him to drive a motor vehicle of that class.

(2) It is an offence for a person to cause or permit another person to drive on a road a motor vehicle of any class otherwise than in accordance with a licence authorising that other person to drive a motor vehicle of that class.

SO

Level 3 fine

Disqualification discretionary and endorsement obligatory (3–6 points) in a case where the offender's driving would not have been in accordance with any licence that could have been granted to him.

C14.9.1 *Sentencing*

SCG **Motoring offences appropriate for imposition of fine or discharge**

See *Blackstone's Criminal Practice 2026* C6.37

C14.9.2 *Restrictions applicable to children and young persons*

A person can apply for a driving licence up to three months before they can start driving.

C14.9.2.1 *Aged 16 years*

A person aged 16 years can apply for a provisional moped licence and take compulsory basic training (CBT) to start riding category AM and category Q mopeds. They must take a moped test within two years.

- Category AM mopeds have a maximum speed over 25km/h and no more than 45km/h.
- Category Q mopeds are two-or three-wheeled mopeds with a maximum speed of 25km/h.

C14.9.2.2 *Aged 17 years*

A person aged 17 years can apply for a provisional licence for a small motorbike (category A1). They then need to complete compulsory basic training (CBT) and take the A1 theory and practical tests within two years to get a full A1 licence.

- Category A1 covers motorbikes not exceeding: 125cc engine size/11kW power output/0.1kW/kg power to weight ratio.

A person aged 17 years can apply for a provisional licence to drive a car subject to the restrictions on that licence.

C14.9.2.3 *Restrictions on the use of a provisional licence*

A provisional licence has certain restrictions on its use.

A person with a provisional licence to drive a moped:

- must not drive a moped that has a maximum speed exceeding 25mph;
- must not drive a motorbike on a public road unless they have taken or are in the process of taking a compulsory basic training course;
- must not carry a passenger on the motorbike;
- must display 'L' plates ('D' plates in Wales) on the front and back of the vehicle;
- must not drive on a motorway.

A person with a provisional licence to drive a motorbike:

- must not drive a motorbike that is above 125cc;
- must not drive a motorbike on a public road unless they have taken or are in the process of taking a compulsory basic training course;
- must not carry a passenger on the motorbike;
- must display 'L' plates ('D' plates in Wales) on the front and back of the vehicle;
- must not drive on a motorway.

A person who has a provisional licence to drive a car or other vehicle (except a motorbike):

- must display 'L' plates on the front and back of the vehicle (or 'D' plates in Wales);
- must not drive on a motorway;
- if the vehicle has more than one seat, must have someone with them whenever they are driving. The person supervising must sit in the front passenger seat and be fit to drive the vehicle, for example, they must not be drunk. They must also be aged 21 or over and have had a full driving licence (for the type of vehicle being driven) for at least three years.

A person who has passed a driving test and is still waiting to receive a full licence is not subject to these restrictions.

C14.9.2.4 *Full driving licence*

In order to obtain a full licence to drive a moped a person must:

- pass the theory test for motorcycles; and
- pass the moped practical test.

In order to obtain a full licence to drive a motorcycle a person must:

- pass the theory test for motorcycles; and
- pass the motorcycle practical test.

In order to obtain a full driving licence to drive a car a person must:

- pass the theory test for cars; and
- pass the practical driving test.

C14.9.2.5 *New driver provisions (see D17.10)*

A person who builds up six or more penalty points within two years of passing their first driving test will automatically lose their licence. They will have to apply and pay for a new provisional licence and pass both theory and practical parts of the driving test again to obtain a full licence.

However, a period of disqualification does not trigger the new driver provisions.

C14.10 Excess alcohol/excess drugs

Road Traffic Act 1988, ss 5(1) and 5A

5 Driving or being in charge of a motor vehicle with alcohol concentration above prescribed limit

(1) If a person—
  (a) drives or attempts to drive a motor vehicle on a road or other public place, or
  (b) is in charge of a motor vehicle on a road or other public place, after consuming so much alcohol that the proportion of it in his breath, blood, or urine exceeds the prescribed limit he is guilty of an offence.

. . .

5A Driving or being in charge of a motor vehicle with concentration of specified controlled drug above specified limit

(1) This section applies where a person ('D')—
  (a) drives or attempts to drive a motor vehicle on a road or other public place, or
  (b) is in charge of a motor vehicle on a road or other public place, and there is in D's body a specified controlled drug.

(2) D is guilty of an offence if the proportion of the drug in D's blood or urine exceeds the specified limit for that drug.

The legal limit of alcohol in the body is: 35 micrograms (μg) per 100 millilitres of breath. 80 milligrams (mg) per 100 millilitres of blood. 107 milligrams per 100 millilitres of urine

The specified drugs and limits are:

Illicit drugs	
Benzoylecgonine	50 μg per litre of blood
Cocaine	10 μg per litre of blood
Delta–9–tetrahydrocannabinol (cannabis and cannabinol)	2 μg per litre of blood
Ketamine	20 μg per litre of blood
Lysergic acid diethylamide (LSD)	1 μg per litre of blood
Methylamphetamine	10 μg per litre of blood
Methylenedioxymethaphetamine (MDMA–ecstasy)	10 μg per litre of blood
Monoacetylmorphine (6–MAM–heroin and diamorphine)	5 μg per litre of blood

Illicit drugs	
Amphetamine	250 µg per litre of blood
General prescription drugs	
Clonazepam	50 µg per litre of blood
Diazepam	550 µg per litre of blood
Flunitrazepam	300 µg per litre of blood
Lorazepam	100 µg per litre of blood
Methadone	500 µg per litre of blood
Morphine	80 µg per litre of blood
Oxazepam	300 µg per litre of blood
Temazepam	1000 µg per litre of blood

SO

s 5 (drive/attempt to drive with excess alcohol):

Fine and/or 6 months' imprisonment

Obligatory disqualification (see below)

s 5 (being in charge with excess alcohol):

Level 4 fine and/or 3 months' imprisonment

Discretionary disqualification, 10 points

s 5A (drive/attempt to drive with excess drugs):

Fine and/or 6 months' imprisonment.

Obligatory disqualification (see below)

s 5A (in charge with excess drugs):

Level 4 fine and/or 3 months' imprisonment.

Discretionary disqualification; 10 points

See C14.18 for offence of being unfit through drink or drugs.

C14.10.1 *Sentencing: driving with excess alcohol*

SCG **Driving or Attempting to Drive with a specified drug above the specified limit**

Being in charge of a motor vehicle with a specified drug above the specified limit

C14.10.2 Key points

- Where there has been no consumption of alcohol between driving and testing, the alcohol reading is conclusive (s 15(2) Road Traffic Offenders Act 1988, and *Griffiths v DPP* [2002] EWHC 792 (Admin)). The presumption in s 15(2) applies only to trials and does not extend to a *Newton* hearing (*Goldsmith v DPP* [2009] EWHC 3010 (Admin)).
- Where there is post-driving consumption of alcohol, the defendant is able to 'back calculate' (s 15(3) Road Traffic Offenders Act 1988). There is a reversed burden and the defendant must prove, to the civil standard, that the excess alcohol was attributable to their post-driving consumption (see *DPP v Ridings* [2024] EWHC 498 (Admin)).
- Whilst normally the statutory procedures for the taking of samples should be strictly followed (*DPP v Murray* [1993] RTR 209) blood samples may be introduced when taken as part of medical procedures and the driver had denied that he or she had taken any drugs so that the formal procedure was not engaged (*R v Twigg* [2019] EWCA Crim 1553). The common law presumption of regularity requires a court to proceed on the basis that an evidential breath machine is in good working order and that its reading is reliable. That presumption is rebuttable if the defendant adduces "relevant" evidence that the reading was not reliable. Once a defendant does that, it is necessary for the prosecution then to prove, to the criminal standard, that the reading was reliable (*Ali v DPP* [2020] EWHC 2864 (Admin)).

C14.10.3 *Defences*

- Section 5(2)–(3) and s 5A(3)–(7) provides:

Road Traffic Act 1988, s 5(2)–(3)

5 Driving or being in charge of a motor vehicle with alcohol concentration above prescribed limit

(1) It is a defence for a person charged with an offence under subsection (1)(b) above to prove that at the time he is alleged to have committed the offence the circumstances were such that there was no likelihood of his driving the vehicle whilst the proportion of alcohol in his breath, blood or urine remained likely to exceed the prescribed limit.

(2) The court may, in determining whether there was such a likelihood as is mentioned in subsection (2) above, disregard any injury to him and any damage to the vehicle.

- Section 5A (3)–(7) provides:

Road Traffic Act 1988, s 5A(3)–(7)

(3) It is a defence for a person ('D') charged with an offence under this section to show that—
   (a) the specified controlled drug had been prescribed or supplied to D for medical or dental purposes,

(b) D took the drug in accordance with any directions given by the person by whom the drug was prescribed or supplied, and with any accompanying instructions (so far as consistent with any such directions) given by the manufacturer or distributor of the drug, and

(c) D's possession of the drug immediately before taking it was not unlawful under section 5(1) of the Misuse of Drugs Act 1971 (restriction of possession of controlled drugs) because of an exemption in regulations made under section 7 of that Act (authorisation of activities otherwise unlawful under foregoing provisions).

(4) The defence in subsection (3) is not available if D's actions were—

(a) contrary to any advice, given by the person by whom the drug was prescribed or supplied, about the amount of time that should elapse between taking the drug and driving a motor vehicle, or

(b) contrary to any accompanying instructions about that matter (so far as consistent with any such advice) given by the manufacturer or distributor of the drug.

(5) If evidence is adduced that is sufficient to raise an issue with respect to the defence in subsection (3), the court must assume that the defence is satisfied unless the prosecution proves beyond reasonable doubt that it is not.

(6) It is a defence for a person ("D") charged with an offence by virtue of subsection (1)(b) to prove that at the time D is alleged to have committed the offence the circumstances were such that there was no likelihood of D driving the vehicle whilst the proportion of the specified controlled drug in D's blood or urine remained likely to exceed the specified limit for that drug.

(7) The court may, in determining whether there was such a likelihood, disregard any injury to D and any damage to the vehicle.

- The burden of proof falls on the defendant (*Sheldrake v DPP* [2005] RTR 2).
- Duress is available as a defence. The defence will be available only for as long as the threat is active and a sober and reasonable person would have driven (*CPS v Brown* [2007] EWHC 3274 (Admin)).
- Automatism is available as a defence.

See *Blackstone's Criminal Practice 2026* C5.33 and C5.54

C14.11 Fail to give information of driver's identity as required

Road Traffic Act 1988, s 172

Duty to give information as to identity of driver etc in certain circumstances

(1) This section applies—

(a) to any offence under the preceding provisions of this Act except—

(i) an offence under Part V, or

(ii) an offence under section 13, 16, 51(2), 61(4), 67(9), 68(4), 96 or 120, and to an offence under section 178 of this Act,

(b) to any offence under sections 25, 26 or 27 of the Road Traffic Offenders Act 1988,

(c) to any offence against any other enactment relating to the use of vehicles on roads, and

(d) to manslaughter.

(2) Where the driver of a vehicle is alleged to be guilty of an offence to which this section applies—
   (a) the person keeping the vehicle shall give such information as to the identity of the driver as he may be required to give by or on behalf of a chief officer of police, and
   (b) any other person shall if required as stated above give any information which it is in his power to give and may lead to identification of the driver.

(3) Subject to the following provisions, a person who fails to comply with a requirement under subsection (2) above shall be guilty of an offence.

(4) [see **C14.11.1**]

(5) Where a body corporate is guilty of an offence under this section and the offence is proved to have been committed with the consent or connivance of, or to be attributable to neglect on the part of, a director, manager, secretary or other similar officer of the body corporate, or a person who was purporting to act in any such capacity, he, as well as the body corporate, is guilty of that offence and liable to be proceeded against and punished accordingly.

(6) Where the alleged offender is a body corporate, or the proceedings are brought against him by virtue of subsection (5) above or subsection (11) below, subsection (4) above shall not apply unless, in addition to the matters there mentioned, the alleged offender shows that no record was kept of the persons who drove the vehicle and that the failure to keep a record was reasonable.

(7) A requirement under subsection (2) may be made by written notice served by post; and where it is so made—
   (a) it shall have effect as a requirement to give the information within the period of 28 days beginning with the day on which the notice is served, and
   (b) the person on whom the notice is served shall not be guilty of an offence under this section if he shows either that he gave the information as soon as reasonably practicable after the end of that period or that it has not been reasonably practicable for him to give it.

(8) Where the person on whom a notice under subsection (7) above is to be served is a body corporate, the notice is duly served if it is served on the secretary or clerk of that body.

(9) For the purposes of section 7 of the Interpretation Act 1978 as it applies for the purposes of this section the proper address of any person in relation to the service on him of a notice under subsection (7) above is—
   (a) in the case of the secretary or clerk of a body corporate, that of the registered or principal office of that body or (if the body corporate is the registered keeper of the vehicle concerned) the registered address, and
   (b) in any other case, his last known address at the time of service.

(10) In this section—
'registered address', in relation to the registered keeper of a vehicle, means the address recorded in the record kept under the Vehicles Excise and Registration Act 1994 with respect to that vehicle as being that person's address, and
'registered keeper', in relation to a vehicle, means the person in whose name the vehicle is registered under that Act; and references to the driver of a vehicle include references to the rider of a cycle.

SO

Level 3 fine

6 points (no endorsement for limited companies)

SCG **Motoring offences appropriate for imposition of fine or discharge**

C14.11.1 Key points

- Section 172(4) provides:

Road Traffic Act 1988, s 172(4)

172 Duty to give information as to identity of driver etc in certain circumstances

(4) A person shall not be guilty of an offence by virtue of paragraph (a) of subsection (2) above if he shows that he did not know and could not with reasonable diligence have ascertained who the driver of the vehicle was.

- In *Krishevsky v DPP* [2014] EWHC 1755 (Admin) the court emphasized that the obligations under this provision arose on service and not on receipt.
- In *Duff v DPP* [2009] EWHC 675 (Admin), D's wife was served with a notice under s 172 Road Traffic Act 1988 requiring her to identify the name of the driver. D in fact replied to the notice, naming himself as the driver. As a result, a further s 172 notice was then served on D. Following legal advice, D did not respond to that notice and was subsequently convicted of failing to provide information. It was held that the conviction was sound, as the request to which he had in fact responded was a request of D's wife, not D himself.
- *Phiri v DPP* [2017] EWHC 2546 (Admin) confirms that a driver whose response is not received because he relied upon a third party to despatch it, is guilty of the offence.
- A driver is to be judged in relation to 172(4) by the actions he did or did not take only from the time of the police request to ascertain the identity of the driver, not before (*Atkinson v DPP* [2011] EWHC 3363 (Admin)). In *Lord Howard of Lympne v DPP* [2018] EWHC 100 (Admin) it was held that, although the form had no suitable box when the keeper was not sure who was the driver, a failure or inability to identify the driver constituted a breach of s 172(2)(a), and the keeper had committed an offence under s 172(3) but subject to establishing the defence under s 172(4). In establishing that defence, in a case where either husband or wife was driving (as they indicated in their s 172 replies), the court will be sharp to seek real evidence of diligent attempts to identify which was the driver at the relevant time: *Marshall v CPS* [2015] EWHC 2333 (Admin).
- For the defences available under s 172(7)(b), see *Purnell v Snaresbrook Crown Court* [2011] EWHC 934 (Admin) and *Whiteside v DPP* [2011] EWHC 3471 (Admin). *Whiteside* held that a lack of personal knowledge of the request was not itself a defence. But the defendant may be able to show that it was not reasonably practicable for him to have been aware of the notice and to provide the information sought.

See *Blackstone's Criminal Practice 2026* C2.12

C14.12 Fail to provide specimen for analysis

Road Traffic Act 1988, s 7(6) and (7)

7 Provision of specimens for analysis

(6) A person who, without reasonable excuse, fails to provide a specimen when required to do so in pursuance of this section is guilty of an offence.

(7) A constable must, on requiring any person to provide a specimen in pursuance of this section, warn him that a failure to provide it may render him liable to prosecution.

SO

Drive/attempt to drive:

Fine and/or 6 months' imprisonment.

Must endorse and disqualify for at least 12 months. Must disqualify for at least 2 years if offender has had two or more disqualifications for periods of 56 days or more in preceding 3 years. Must disqualify for at least 3 years if offender has been convicted of a relevant offence in preceding 10 years.

In-charge:

Level 4 fine and/or 3 months' imprisonment.

Must endorse and may disqualify. If no disqualification, impose 10 points.

C14.12.1 *Sentencing*

SCG **Fail to provide specimen for analysis (drive/attempt to drive)/Fail to provide specimen for analysis (in charge)**

C14.12.2 Key points

- A reasonable excuse for failing to provide must relate to inability due to physical or mental issues (*R v Lennard* [1973] RTR 252).
- The suspect need not in fact be the driver if relevant investigation is being conducted by the police.
- Failure to mention a medical reason at the time of refusal does not preclude a court from finding that a reasonable excuse existed, although it was a factor to be taken into account (*Piggott v DPP* [2008] RTR 16).
- Once a reasonable excuse is raised, it is for the prosecution to disprove it (*McKeon v DPP* [2008] RTR 14) but to require the Crown to disprove a defence of reasonable excuse (here in relation to needle phobia), the defence must lay an evidential basis, ie raise the issue by evidence. An assertion in the police station alone (during the statutory procedure) cannot meet that requirement (*R (Cuns) v Hammersmith Magistrates Court* [2016] EWHC 748 (Admin)).
- A failure to understand the statutory warning relating to prosecution may amount to a reasonable excuse if the accused's understanding of English is poor (*Chief Constable of Avon and Somerset v Singh* [1988] RTR 107); but if an accredited interpreter is present there is an (rebuttable) inference that the warning was understood (*Bielecki v DPP* [2011] EWHC 2245 (Admin)). Failure to understand due to intoxication will not suffice.
- The taking of a specimen does not have to be delayed (over and above a couple of minutes) for the purpose of taking legal advice (*R v Gearing* [2008] EWHC 1695 (Admin)).

See *Blackstone's Criminal Practice 2026* C5.25

C14.13 Fail to stop/report road accident

Road Traffic Act 1988, s 170

170 Duty of driver to stop, report accident and give information or documents

(1) This section applies in a case where, owing to the presence of a mechanically propelled vehicle on a road or other public place, an accident occurs by which—
  (a) personal injury is caused to a person other than the driver of that mechanically propelled vehicle, or
  (b) damage is caused—
    (i) to a vehicle other than that mechanically propelled vehicle or a trailer drawn by that mechanically propelled vehicle, or
    (ii) to an animal other than an animal in or on that mechanically propelled vehicle or a trailer drawn by that mechanically propelled vehicle, or
    (iii) to any other property constructed on, fixed to, growing in or otherwise forming part of the land on which the road or place in question is situated or land adjacent to such land.

(2) The driver of the mechanically propelled vehicle must stop and, if required to do so by any person having reasonable grounds for so requiring, give his name and address and also the name and address of the owner and the identification marks of the vehicle.

(3) If for any reason the driver of the mechanically propelled vehicle does not give his name and address under subsection (2) above, he must report the accident.

(4) A person who fails to comply with subsection (2) or (3) above is guilty of an offence.

(5) If, in a case where this section applies by virtue of subsection (1)(a) above, the driver of a motor vehicle does not at the time of the accident produce such a certificate of insurance or security, or other evidence, as is mentioned in section 165(2)(a) of this Act—
  (a) to a constable, or
  (b) to some person who, having reasonable grounds for so doing, has required him to produce it, the driver must report the accident and produce such a certificate or other evidence. This subsection does not apply to the driver of an invalid carriage.

(6) To comply with a duty under this section to report an accident or to produce such a certificate of insurance or security, or other evidence, as is mentioned in section 165(2)(a) of this Act, the driver—
  (a) must do so at a police station or to a constable, and
  (b) must do so as soon as is reasonably practicable and, in any case, within twenty-four hours of the occurrence of the accident.

(7) A person who fails to comply with a duty under subsection (5) above is guilty of an offence, but he shall not be convicted by reason only of a failure to produce a certificate or other evidence if, within seven days after the occurrence of the accident, the certificate or other evidence is produced at a police station that was specified by him at the time when the accident was reported.

(8) In this section 'animal' means horse, cattle, ass, mule, sheep, pig, goat or dog.

SO

Fine and/or 6 months' imprisonment

Must endorse and may disqualify. If no disqualification, impose 5–10 points.

C14.13.1 *Sentencing*

SCG Fail to stop/report road accident

C14.13.2 Key points

A driver who is unaware of the accident cannot commit an offence under these provisions (*Harding v Price* [1948] 1 KB 695); but if he later becomes aware of the accident, he must report it personally if he becomes aware within 24 hours (*DPP v Drury* [1989] RTR 165).

If a driver was genuinely unaware that an accident had occurred, or remained of the view that none had occurred (even in circumstances where someone informed that person that there had been an accident), there is no duty to report.

However, if the appellant was unaware of the accident because of her drunken state, she could not rely upon that as a defence where she is voluntarily intoxicated. This is a crime of basic intent (*Magee v CPS* [2014] EWHC 4089 (Admin)).

See *Blackstone's Criminal Practice 2026* C6.51

C14.13.3 *Power of police to stop vehicles*

Road Traffic Act 1988, s 163

(1) A person driving a mechanically propelled vehicle on a road must stop the vehicle on being required to do so by a constable in uniform or a traffic officer . . .

(3) If a person fails to comply with this section he is guilty of an offence.

SO

Level 5 fine

No endorsement

C14.14 No insurance, using, causing, or permitting

RTA 1988, s 143

143 Users of motor vehicles to be insured . . . .

(1) Subject to the provisions of this Part of this Act—
- (a) a person must not use a motor vehicle on a road or other public place unless there is in force in relation to the use of the vehicle by that person such a policy of insurance as complies with the requirements of this Part of this Act, and
- (b) a person must not cause or permit any other person to use a motor vehicle on a road or other public place unless there is in force in relation to the use of the vehicle by that other person such a policy of insurance as complies with the requirements of this Part of this Act.

Fine

Discretionary disqualification, 6–8 penalty points

C14.14.1 *Sentencing*

SCG **No insurance**

C14.14.2 Key points

- See **C13** for definitions.
- Proceedings may be brought within six months of a prosecutor forming the opinion that there is sufficient evidence of an offence having been committed (subject to an overall three-year time bar). See **A12.1.3**
- It is for a defendant to show that he was insured, once it is established that a motor vehicle was used on a road or other public place. However, in *DPP v Whittaker* [2015] EWHC 1850 (Admin) it was held that once the defence have proved the existence of a valid insurance policy, it is for the Crown to prove to the normal criminal standard that it does not cover the driving at issue.
- It is not necessary that the vehicle be capable of being driven (*Pumbien v Vines* [1996] RTR 37).
- Employed drivers have the following defence available to them:

Road Traffic Act 1988, s 143(3)

143 Users of motor vehicles to be insured or secured against third-party risks

(3) A person charged with using a motor vehicle in contravention of this section shall not be convicted if he proves—
   (a) that the vehicle did not belong to him and was not in his possession under a contract of hiring or of loan,
   (b) that he was using the vehicle in the course of his employment, and
   (c) that he neither knew nor had reason to believe that there was not in force in relation to the vehicle such a policy of insurance as is mentioned in subsection (1) above.

- Where a private hire licence was for a limited area but the defendant held an insurance policy for hire and reward, he was insured wherever he worked as s 148 Road Traffic Act 1988 invalidated any restriction in the policy to a particular area (*Oldham BC v Sajjad* [2016] EWHC 3597 (Admin)).

See *Blackstone's Criminal Practice 2026* **C6.46**

C14.15 Offences concerning the driver

Offence	Maximum	Points	Starting point	Special considerations
Fail to cooperate with preliminary (roadside) breath test	L3	4	B	
Fail to give information of driver's identity as required	L3	6	C	For limited companies, endorsement is not available; a fine is the only available penalty
Fail to produce insurance certificate	L4	–	A	Fine per offence, not per document
Fail to produce test certificate	L3	–	A	
Drive otherwise than in accordance with licence (where could be covered)	L3	–	A	
Drive otherwise than in accordance with licence (**C14.9**)	L3	3–6	A	Aggravating factor if no licence ever held

See *Blackstone's Criminal Practice 2026* C6

C14.16 Offences concerning the vehicle

The guidelines for some of the following offences differentiate between three types of offender when the offence is committed in the course of business: driver, owner-driver, and owner-company. For owner-drivers, the starting point is the same as for drivers; however, the court should consider an uplift of at least 25 per cent.

Offence	Maximum	Points	Starting point	Special considerations
No excise licence	L3 or 5 times annual duty, whichever is greater	–	A (1–3 months unpaid) B (4–6 months unpaid) C (7–12 months unpaid)	Add duty lost

Offence	Maximum	Points	Starting point	Special considerations
Fail to notify change of ownership to DVLA	L3	–	A	If offence committed in course of business: A (driver) A* (owner-driver) B (owner-company)
No test certificate	L3	–	A	If offence committed in course of business: A (driver) A* (owner-driver) B (owner-company)
Brakes defective Key points: it is sufficient only to prove that any part of the braking system is defective (Kennett v British Airports Authority [1975] Crim LR 106). The fact that everything possible (eg servicing) has been done in order to ensure that the vehicle is in good condition does not amount to a defence (Hawkins v Holmes [1974] RTR 436), as maintenance of the braking system is an absolute obligation on the driver (Green v Burnett [1954] 3 All ER 273).	L4	3	B	If offence committed in course of business: B (driver) B* (owner-driver) C (owner-company) L5 if goods vehicle
Steering defective	L4	3	B	If offence committed in course of business: B (driver) B* (owner-driver) C (owner-company) L5 if goods vehicle

Offence	Maximum	Points	Starting point	Special considerations
Tyres defective. It is a defence if the vehicle is not being used and there was no intention to use when the tyres were defective, regardless of the fact that the vehicle was on a road (Eden v Mitchell [1975] RTR 425). There is no requirement for the prosecution to have had the tyre examined by an authorized examiner as the issue was a simple question of fact (Phillips v Thomas [1974] RTR 28).	L4	3	B	If offence committed in course of business: B (driver) B* (owner-driver) C (owner-company) L5 if goods vehicle Penalty per tyre
Condition of vehicle/ accessories/ equipment involving danger of injury (Road Traffic Act 1988, s 40A)	L4	3	B	Must disqualify for at least 6 months if offender has one or more previous convictions for same offence within 3 years If offence committed in course of business: B (driver) B* (owner-driver) C (owner-company) L5 if goods vehicle
Exhaust defective	L3	–	A	If offence committed in course of business: A (driver) A* (owner-driver) B (owner-company)
Lights defective	L3	–	A	If offence committed in course of business: A (driver) A* (owner-driver) B (owner-company)

See *Blackstone's Criminal Practice 2026* C6

C14.17 Speeding

Road Traffic Regulation Act 1984, s 89(1)

SO

Level 3 fine (level 4 if motorway)

Discretionary disqualification, 3–6 points

C14.17.1 *Sentencing*

SCG Speeding

C14.17.2 Key points

- Necessity is available as a defence (*Moss v Howdle* [1997] SLT 782).
- Check that a notice of intended prosecution has been served in time.
- In relation to restricted roads (where a 30 mph speed limit applies) there must be a system of street lighting not more than 200 yards apart. If this matter is put in issue (but not otherwise), the prosecution must establish this beyond reasonable doubt.
- The 200-yard rule relates to a 'system of street lighting', so some lights may be more than 200 yards apart, it being a question of fact whether the 'system of lighting' as a whole complies. In *Briere v Hailstone* (1968) 112 SJ 767, a conviction was upheld even though 50 per cent of the lamps were incorrectly distanced. Similarly, the fact that one lamp was in disrepair did not affect a conviction (*Spittle v Kent County Constabulary* [1985] Crim LR 744).
- Save where the road is a restricted road, there needs to be signage in accordance with the regulations. A failure to provide adequate signage is fatal to any conviction. In *Jones v DPP* [2011] EWHC 50 (Admin), the court held that the relevant question to be answered by the court was:

  > Whether by the point on the road where the alleged offence took place (the point of enforcement) the driver by reference to the route taken thereto has been given (or drivers generally have been given) adequate guidance of the speed limit to be observed at that point on the road by the signs on the relevant part or parts of the road *in so far as (and thus to the extent that) those traffic signs comply with the Regulations?*

See *Blackstone's Criminal Practice 2026* C6.58

C14.18 Unfit through drink or drugs

Road Traffic Act 1988, s 4(1), (2), and (5)

4 Driving, or being in charge, when under influence of drink or drugs

(1) A person who, when driving or attempting to drive a mechanically propelled vehicle on a road or other public place, is unfit to drive through drink or drugs is guilty of an offence.

> (2) Without prejudice to subsection (1) above, a person who, when in charge of a mechanically propelled vehicle which is on a road or other public place, is unfit to drive through drink or drugs is guilty of an offence.
>
> . . .
>
> (5) For the purposes of this section, a person shall be taken to be unfit to drive if his ability to drive properly is for the time being impaired.

SO

Drive/attempt to drive:

Fine and/or 6 months' imprisonment.

Must endorse and disqualify for at least 12 months. Must disqualify for at least 2 years if offender has had two or more disqualifications for periods of 56 days or more in preceding years. Must disqualify for at least 3 years if offender has been convicted of a relevant offence in preceding 10 years.

In-charge:

Level 4 fine and/or 3 months' imprisonment.

Must endorse and may disqualify. If no disqualification, impose 10 points

C14.18.1 *Sentencing: driving or attempting to drive*

SCG **Unfit through drink or drugs (in charge)/Unfit through drink or drugs (in charge)**

C14.18.2 Key points

- No likelihood of driving while unfit provides a defence in law to the in-charge offence. Section 4(3) and (4) of the Road Traffic Act 1988 provides:

> **Road Traffic Act 1988, s 4(3) and (4)**
>
> **4 Driving, or being in charge, when under influence of drink or drugs**
>
> (3) For the purposes of subsection (2) above, a person shall be deemed not to have been in charge of a mechanically propelled vehicle if he proves that at the material time the circumstances were such that there was no likelihood of his driving it so long as he remained unfit to drive through drink or drugs.
>
> (4) The court may, in determining whether there was such a likelihood as is mentioned in subsection (3) above, disregard any injury to him and any damage to the vehicle.

- Drugs include normal medicines.
- Evidence of impairment to drive may be provided by both expert and lay witnesses. Note, however, that a lay witness can give evidence as to a person's demeanour (and how much he drank, for example) but not on the ultimate question of whether the person was 'fit' to drive.
- The results of any evidential specimens are admissible (Road Traffic Offenders Act 1988, ss 15 and 16).

See *Blackstone's Criminal Practice 2026* C5.58

C15 **Sexual Offences**

See *Blackstone's Criminal Practice 2026* **B3**

C15.1 Definitions

C15.1.1 *Consent*

The Sexual Offences Act (SOA) 2003 provides:

Sexual Offences Act 2003, ss 74, 75, 76

74 'Consent'

For the purposes of this Part, a person consents if he agrees by choice, and has the freedom and capacity to make that choice.

75 Evidential presumptions about consent

(1) If in proceedings for an offence to which this section applies it is proved—
  (a) that the defendant did the relevant act,
  (b) that any of the circumstances specified in subsection (2) existed, and
  (c) that the defendant knew that those circumstances existed,
the complainant is to be taken not to have consented to the relevant act unless sufficient evidence is adduced to raise an issue as to whether he consented, and the defendant is to be taken not to have reasonably believed that the complainant consented unless sufficient evidence is adduced to raise an issue as to whether he reasonably believed it.
(2) The circumstances are that—
  (a) any person was, at the time of the relevant act or immediately before it began, using violence against the complainant or causing the complainant to fear that immediate violence would be used against him;
  (b) any person was, at the time of the relevant act or immediately before it began, causing the complainant to fear that violence was being used, or that immediate violence would be used, against another person;
  (c) the complainant was, and the defendant was not, unlawfully detained at the time of the relevant act;
  (d) the complainant was asleep or otherwise unconscious at the time of the relevant act;
  (e) because of the complainant's physical disability, the complainant would not have been able at the time of the relevant act to communicate to the defendant whether the complainant consented;
  (f) any person had administered to or caused to be taken by the complainant, without the complainant's consent, a substance which, having regard to when it was administered or taken, was capable of causing or enabling the complainant to be stupefied or overpowered at the time of the relevant act.
(3) In subsection (2)(a) and (b), the reference to the time immediately before the relevant act began is, in the case of an act which is one of a continuous series of sexual activities, a reference to the time immediately before the first sexual activity began.

Blackstone's Magistrates' Court Handbook 2026. Bartholomew Dalton and Caroline Liggins, Oxford University Press. © Oxford University Press 2026.
DOI: 10.1093/oso/9780198963943.003.0056

76 Conclusive presumptions about consent

(1) If in proceedings for an offence to which this section applies it is proved that the defendant did the relevant act and that any of the circumstances specified in subsection (2) existed, it is to be conclusively presumed—
   (a) that the complainant did not consent to the relevant act, and
   (b) that the defendant did not believe that the complainant consented to the relevant act.

(2) The circumstances are that—
   (a) the defendant intentionally deceived the complainant as to the nature or purpose of the relevant act;
   (b) the defendant intentionally induced the complainant to consent to the relevant act by impersonating a person known personally to the complainant.

Only pressure and coercion, or two frauds, are capable of vitiating consent. These are frauds as to the identity of the perpetrator through impersonation; and fraud as to the nature of the sexual act. Such a deception relates to the physical performance of the sexual act and not to the risks or consequences associated with it. Thus there will be no consent if the deception is as to the use of a condom, or intent to withdraw, or gender at birth but it is otherwise if the deception is as to having a vasectomy or as to HIV status (*R (on the application of Monica) v DPP* [2018] EWHC 3469 (QB) and *R v Lawrance* [2020] EWCA Crim 971).

C15.1.2 *Sexual in nature*

Sexual Offences Act 2003, s 78

For the purposes of this Part (except sections 15A and 71), penetration, touching, or any other activity is sexual if a reasonable person would consider that—

(a) whatever its circumstances or any person's purpose in relation to it, it is because of its nature sexual, or
(b) because of its nature it may be sexual and because of its circumstances or the purpose of any person in relation to it (or both) it is sexual.

Acts which are automatically sexual within the meaning of s 78(a) would include penile penetration or oral sex. Where the act is not automatically sexual it was held in *R v H* [2005] EWCA Crim 732, [2005] 2 Cr App R 9 that two requirements must be satisfied: first, that the touching could reasonably be considered to be sexual; and, secondly, that the touching, because of its circumstances or the purpose of any person in relation to it (or both) was sexual.

C15.2 **Sentencing sexual offences against children**

Key points: Sentencing The correct approach to sentencing certain offences against children under the Sexual Offences Act 2003, when no sexual activity takes place, for instance, because the child is a fiction, was confirmed in *Reed and others* [2021] EWCA Crim 572.

Where a defendant sets out to sexually abuse a child, but in circumstances where the child happens to be an adult posing as a child, then the starting point for sentencing should be set by reference to the harm that the defendant intended to cause the fictional child. The fact that there was no real child for the defendant to abuse will then be reflected in a downward movement from that starting point. The extent of that reduction will be a matter for the court in individual cases to decide.

C15.3 Assault by penetration

Sexual Offences Act 2003, s 2

(1) A person (A) commits an offence if—
- (a) he intentionally penetrates the vagina or anus of another person (B) with a part of his body or anything else,
- (b) the penetration is sexual,
- (c) B does not consent to the penetration, and
- (d) A does not reasonably believe that B consents.

(2) Whether a belief is reasonable is to be determined having regard to all the circumstances, including any steps A has taken to ascertain whether B consents.

(3) Sections 75 and 76 apply to an offence under this section.

IO

Life

SON

DO

GC

C15.3.1 Key points

- Penetration is a continuing act from entry to withdrawal (s 79(2) SOA 2003).
- For the definition of 'sexual' and 'consent' see C15.1.1.

See *Blackstone's Criminal Practice 2026* B3.54

C15.4 Causing or inciting a child under 13 to engage in sexual activity

Sexual Offences Act 2003, s 8

8 Causing or inciting a child under 13 to engage in sexual activity

(1) A person commits an offence if—
- (a) he intentionally causes or incites another person (B) to engage in an activity,
- (b) the activity is sexual, and

> (c) B is under 13.
> (2) A person guilty of an offence under this section, if the activity caused or incited involved—
> (a) penetration of B's anus or vagina,
> (b) penetration of B's mouth with a person's penis,
> (c) penetration of a person's anus or vagina with a part of B's body or by B with anything else, or
> (d) penetration of a person's mouth with B's penis, is liable, on conviction on indictment, to imprisonment for life.

EW Save where penetration is involved when the offences become triable only on indictment

12 months' imprisonment and/or fine/14 years' imprisonment unless penetration involved then life

SON

DO

C15.4.1 *Sentencing*

SCG **Causing or inciting a child under 13 to engage in sexual activity**

C15.4.2 Key points

When incitement is alleged the essence of the offence is the intentional 'incitement', that is the intentional seeking to bring about something by encouragement or persuasion, by the defendant (*R v Walker (Simon John)* [2006] EWCA Crim 1907). The causing or inciting must be intentional . . . [and] [i]f the offence charged is that of intentional incitement the prosecution does not have to prove that defendant intended that the actual sexual activity should take place, because the essence of the offence is the intentional incitement of the person under 13 to engage in sexual activity. (*R v Grout* [2011] EWCA Crim 299)

Section 8 creates four different offences, each of which must be carried out intentionally. The first is causing penetrative sexual activity; the second is inciting such activity; the third is causing non-penetrative sexual activity; and the fourth is inciting such activity (*R v Grout* [2011] EWCA Crim 299).

See *Blackstone's Criminal Practice 2026* **B3.98**

C15.5 Child sex offences committed by children or young persons

Sexual Offences Act 2003, s 13

Child sex offences committed by children or young person

s 13(1) A person under 18 commits an offence if he does anything which would be an offence under any of ss 9 to 12 if he were aged 18.

EW

6 months' imprisonment and/or fine/5 years' imprisonment

SON If the offender is or has been sentenced, in respect of the offence, to imprisonment for a term of at least 12 months

DO

C15.6 Child sexual offences

See *Blackstone's Criminal Practice 2026* **B3.103**

C15.6.1 *Sexual activity with a child*

Sexual Offences Act 2003, s 9

9 Sexual activity with a child

(2) A person aged 18 or over (A) commits an offence if—
   (a) he intentionally touches another person (B),
   (b) the touching is sexual, and
   (c) either—
      (i) B is under 16 and A does not reasonably believe that B is 16 or over, or
      (ii) B is under 13.
(3) A person guilty of an offence under this section, if the touching involved—
   (a) penetration of B's anus or vagina with a part of A's body or anything else,
   (b) penetration of B's mouth with A's penis,
   (c) penetration of A's anus or vagina with a part of B's body, or
   (d) penetration of A's mouth with B's penis

EW But indictable only if the activity involves penetration

12 months' imprisonment and/or fine/14 years' imprisonment

SON

DO

See **C15.4** where offence committed by person under 18

C15.6.1.1 *Sentencing*

SCG **Sexual activity with a child/Causing or inciting a child to engage in sexual activity**

C15.6.2 *Causing or inciting child sexual activity*

> **Sexual Offences Act 2003, s 10**
>
> **Causing or inciting a child to engage in sexual activity**
>
> (1) A person aged 18 or over (A) commits an offence if—
> (a) he intentionally causes or incites another person (B) to engage in an activity,
> (b) the activity is sexual, and
> (c) either—
> (i) B is under 16 and A does not reasonably believe that B is 16 or over, or
> (ii) B is under 13.

EW But indictable only if the activity involves penetration

12 months' imprisonment and/or fine/14 years' imprisonment

SON

DO

GC

See **C15.4** where offence committed by person under 18.

C15.6.2.1 *Sentencing*

SCG **Sexual activity with a child/Causing or inciting a child to engage in sexual activity**

C15.6.3 *Engaging in sexual activity in presence of a child*

> **Sexual Offences Act 2003, s 11**
>
> **Engaging in sexual activity in the presence of a child**
>
> (1) A person aged 18 or over (A) commits an offence if—
> (a) he intentionally engages in an activity,
> (b) the activity is sexual,
> (c) for the purpose of obtaining sexual gratification, he engages in it—
> (i) when another person (B) is present or is in a place from which A can be observed, and
> (ii) knowing or believing that B is aware, or intending that B should be aware, that he is engaging in it, and
> (d) either—
> (i) B is under 16 and A does not reasonably believe that B is 16 or over, or
> (ii) B is under 13.

EW

12 months' imprisonment and/or fine/10 years' imprisonment

SON

DO

GC

See **C15.4** where offence committed by person under 18.

Key points

R v B and L [2018] EWCA Crim 1439 confirms that the offence under s 11(1) requires there to be a link between the 'purpose of obtaining sexual gratification' and the presence of the child.

C15.6.3.1 *Sentencing*

SCG **Engaging in sexual activity in the presence of a child/Causing a child to watch a sexual act**

C15.6.4 *Causing a child to watch*

Sexual Offences Act 2003, s 12

Causing a child to watch a sexual act

(1) A person aged 18 or over (A) commits an offence if—
   (a) for the purpose of obtaining sexual gratification, he intentionally causes another person (B) to watch a third person engaging in an activity, or to look at an image of any person engaging in an activity,
   (b) the activity is sexual, and
   (c) either—
      (i) B is under 16 and A does not reasonably believe that B is 16 or over, or
      (ii) B is under 13.

EW

12 months' imprisonment and/or fine/10 years' imprisonment

SON

DO

See **C15.4** where offence by person under 18.

C15.6.4.1 *Sentencing*

SCG **Engaging in sexual activity in the presence of a child/Causing a child to watch a sexual act**

C15.6.5 *Arranging or facilitating commission of a child offence*

Sexual Offences Act 2003, s 14 Arranging or facilitating commission of a child sex offence

(1) A person commits an offence if—
- (a) he intentionally arranges or facilitates something that he intends to do, intends another person to do, or believes that another person will do, in any part of the world, and
- (b) doing it will involve the commission of an offence under any of sections 5 to 13.

(2) A person does not commit an offence under this section if—
- (a) he arranges or facilitates something that he believes another person will do, but that he does not intend to do or intend another person to do, and
- (b) any offence within subsection (1)(b) would be an offence against a child for whose protection he acts.

(3) For the purposes of subsection (2), a person acts for the protection of a child if he acts for the purpose of—
- (a) protecting the child from sexually transmitted infection,
- (b) protecting the physical safety of the child,
- (c) preventing the child from becoming pregnant, or
- (d) promoting the child's emotional well-being by the giving of advice,

and not for the purpose of obtaining sexual gratification or for the purpose of causing or encouraging the activity constituting the offence within subsection (1)(b) or the child's participation in it.

EW

The penalty to which the person would be liable on conviction of the offence within subsection (1)(b)

SON

If the offender—
- (a) was 18 or over, or
- (b) is or has been sentenced, in respect of the offence, to imprisonment for a term of at least 12 months.

DO

C15.6.5.1 *Sentencing*

Sentencers should refer to the guideline for the applicable, substantive offence of arranging or facilitating under sections 5 to 13:

- Rape of a child under 13, Sexual Offences Act 2003, s 5 (see **C15.14.1**)
- Assault by penetration of a child under 13, Sexual Offences Act 2003, s 6 (see **C15.14.2**)
- Sexual assault of a child under 13, Sexual Offences Act 2003, s 7 (see **C15.23**)
- Causing or inciting a child under 13 to engage in sexual activity, Sexual Offences Act 2003, s 8 (see **C15.4**)

- Sexual activity with a child, Sexual Offences Act 2003, s 9 (see **C15.6.1**)
- Causing or inciting a child to engage in sexual activity, Sexual Offences Act 2003, s 10 (see **C15.6.2**)
- Engaging in sexual activity in the presence of a child, Sexual Offences Act 2003, s 11 (see **C15.6.3**)
- Causing a child to watch a sexual act, Sexual Offences Act 2003, s 12 (see **C15.6.4**)
- Child sex offences committed by children or young persons, Sexual Offences Act 2003, s 13 (see **C15.5**)

The level of harm should be determined by reference to the type of activity arranged or facilitated. Sentences commensurate with the applicable starting point and range will ordinarily be appropriate. For offences involving significant commercial exploitation and/or an international element, it may, in the interests of justice, be appropriate to increase a sentence to a point above the category range. In exceptional cases, such as where a vulnerable offender performed a limited role, having been coerced or exploited by others, sentences below the starting point and range may be appropriate. This guidance was clarified in *R v Privett* [2020] EWCA Crim 557 'the judge should, first, identify the category of harm on the basis of the sexual activity the defendant intended ("the level of harm should be determined by reference to the type of activity arranged or facilitated"), and, second, adjust the sentence in order to ensure it is "commensurate" with, or proportionate to, the applicable starting point and range if no sexual activity had occurred (including because the victim was fictional) ("sentences commensurate with the applicable starting point and range will ordinarily be appropriate").'

C15.7 **Exploitation of prostitution**

Sexual Offences Act 2003, ss 52 and 53

52 Causing or inciting prostitution for gain

(1) A person commits an offence if—
   (a) he intentionally causes or incites another person to become a prostitute in any part of the world, and
   (b) he does so for or in the expectation of gain for himself or a third person.

53 Controlling prostitution for gain

(1) A person commits an offence if—
   (a) he intentionally controls any of the activities of another person relating to that person's prostitution in any part of the world, and
   (b) he does so for or in the expectation of gain for himself or a third person.

EW

12 months' imprisonment and/or fine/7 years' imprisonment

DO

C15.7.1 *Sentencing*

SCG **Causing or inciting prostitution for gain/Controlling prostitution for gain**

See *Blackstone's Criminal Practice 2026* **B3.253**

C15.8 Causing a person to engage in sexual activity without consent

Sexual Offences Act 2003, s 4

4 Causing a person to engage in sexual activity without consent

(1) A person (A) commits an offence if—
   (a) he intentionally causes another person (B) to engage in an activity,
   (b) the activity is sexual,
   (c) B does not consent to engaging in the activity, and
   (d) A does not reasonably believe that B consents.

(2) Whether a belief is reasonable is to be determined having regard to all the circumstances, including any steps A has taken to ascertain whether B consents.

(3) Sections 75 and 76 apply to an offence under this section.

(4) A person guilty of an offence under this section, if the activity caused involved—
   (a) penetration of B's anus or vagina,
   (b) penetration of B's mouth with a person's penis,
   (c) penetration of a person's anus or vagina with a part of B's body or by B with anything else, or
   (d) penetration of a person's mouth with B's penis,

   is liable, on conviction on indictment, to imprisonment for life.

EW But indictable only if the activity involves penetration

12 months' imprisonment and/or fine/10 years' imprisonment (or life when penetration involved)

SON

DO

C15.8.1 *Sentencing*

SCG **Causing a person to engage in sexual activity without consent**

See *Blackstone's Criminal Practice 2026* **B3.71**

C15.9 Exposure

Sexual Offences Act 2003, s 66(1)

66 Exposure

(1) A person commits an offence if—
  (a) he intentionally exposes his genitals, and
  (b) he intends that someone will see them and be caused alarm or distress.

EW

12 months' imprisonment and/or fine/2 years' imprisonment

SON If—

(a) where the offender was under 18, he is or has been sentenced in respect of the offence to imprisonment for a term of at least 12 months;
(b) in any other case—
  (i) the victim was under 18, or
  (ii) the offender, is—
    (a) sentenced to a term of imprisonment,
    (b) detained in a hospital, or
    (c) made the subject of a community sentence of at least 12 months.

DO

C15.9.1 *Sentencing*

SCG Exposure

C15.9.2 Key points

- This offence is committed where an offender intentionally exposes his or her genitals and intends that someone will see them and be caused alarm or distress. It is gender-neutral, covering exposure of male or female genitalia to a male or female witness.

See *Blackstone's Criminal Practice 2026* B3.296

C15.10 Extreme pornography

Criminal Justice and Immigration Act 2008, ss 63, 65–66

63 Possession of extreme pornographic images

(1) It is an offence for a person to be in possession of an extreme pornographic image.
(2) An 'extreme pornographic image' is an image which is both—
  (a) pornographic, and

(b) an extreme image.

(3) An image is 'pornographic' if it is of such a nature that it must reasonably be assumed to have been produced solely or principally for the purpose of sexual arousal.

(4) Where (as found in the person's possession) an image forms part of a series of images, the question whether the image is of such a nature as is mentioned in subsection (3) is to be determined by reference to—

(a) the image itself, and

(b) (if the series of images is such as to be capable of providing a context for the image) the context in which it occurs in the series of images.

(5) So, for example, where—

(a) an image forms an integral part of a narrative constituted by a series of images, and

(b) having regard to those images as a whole, they are not of such a nature that they must reasonably be assumed to have been produced solely or principally for the purpose of sexual arousal,

the image may, by virtue of being part of that narrative, be found not to be pornographic, even though it might have been found to be pornographic if taken by itself.

(5A) In relation to possession of an image in . . . an 'extreme image' is an image which—

(a) falls within subsection (7) or (7A), and

(b) is grossly offensive, disgusting or otherwise of an obscene character.

(7) An image falls within this subsection if it portrays, in an explicit and realistic way, any of the following—

(a) an act which threatens a person's life,

(b) an act which results, or is likely to result, in serious injury to a person's anus, breasts or genitals,

(c) an act which involves sexual interference with a human corpse, or

(d) a person performing an act of intercourse or oral sex with an animal (whether dead or alive), and a reasonable person looking at the image would think that any such person or animal was real.

(7A) An image falls within this subsection if it portrays, in an explicit and realistic way, either of the following—

(a) an act which involves the non-consensual penetration of a person's vagina, anus or mouth by another with the other person's penis, or

(b) an act which involves the non-consensual sexual penetration of a person's vagina or anus by another with a part of the other person's body or anything else, and a reasonable person looking at the image would think that the persons were real.

(7B) For the purposes of subsection (7A)—

(a) penetration is a continuing act from entry to withdrawal;

(b) 'vagina' includes vulva.

(8) In this section 'image' means—

(a) a moving or still image (produced by any means); or

(b) data (stored by any means) which is capable of conversion into an image within paragraph (a).

(9) In this section references to a part of the body include references to a part surgically constructed (in particular through gender reassignment surgery).

(10) Proceedings for an offence under this section may not be instituted—

(a) in England and Wales, except by or with the consent of the Director of Public Prosecutions;

. . .

65 Defences: general

(1) Where a person is charged with an offence under section 63, it is a defence for the person to prove any of the matters mentioned in subsection (2).

(2) The matters are—
   (a) that the person had a legitimate reason for being in possession of the image concerned;
   (b) that the person had not seen the image concerned and did not know, nor had any cause to suspect, it to be an extreme pornographic image;
   (c) that the person—
      (i) was sent the image concerned without any prior request having been made by or on behalf of the person, and
      (ii) did not keep it for an unreasonable time.
(3) In this section 'extreme pornographic image' and 'image' have the same meanings as in section 63.

66 Defence: participation in consensual acts

(A1) Subsection (A2) applies where in England and Wales—
   (a) a person ('D') is charged with an offence under section 63, and
   (b) the offence relates to an image that portrays an act or acts within subsection (7)(a) to (c) or (7A) of that section (but does not portray an act within subsection (7)(d) of that section).
(A2) It is a defence for D to prove—
   (a) that D directly participated in the act or any of the acts portrayed, and
   (b) that the act or acts did not involve the infliction of any non-consensual harm on any person, and
   (c) if the image portrays an act within section 63(7)(c), that what is portrayed as a human corpse was not in fact a corpse, and
   (d) if the image portrays an act within section 63(7A), that what is portrayed as non-consensual penetration was in fact consensual, and
(3) For the purposes of this section harm inflicted on a person is 'non-consensual' harm if—
   (a) the harm is of such a nature that the person cannot, in law, consent to it being inflicted on himself or herself; or
   (b) where the person can, in law, consent to it being so inflicted, the person does not in fact consent to it being so inflicted.

EW

Fine and/or 12 months'/3 years' imprisonment (2 years if the offence relates to an image that does not portray any act within s 63(7)(a) or (b))

SON If the offender—

(a) was 18 or over, and
(b) is sentenced to imprisonment for a term of at least 2 years

C15.10.1 Key points

Section 63(3) means was the image produced for the purpose of sexually arousing anyone who comes to have it, be that the producer himself, a distributor, or an ultimate recipient. The section is designed to prevent the possession of such images by any person. The purpose of the subsection is to identify the types of image that are pornographic. The word 'pornographic' here deals with the assumed purpose of the image. The identity or purpose of the producer is immaterial; the circumstances in which the images are received are immaterial (*R v DB* [2016] EWCA Crim 474). There are two elements to be made out in order for an individual to have possession:

(1) the images must have been within the defendant's custody or control, ie so that he was capable of accessing them; and
(2) he must have known that he possessed an image or a group of images. Knowledge of the content of those images is not required to make out the basic ingredients of the offence; instead that issue is dealt with by the statutory defence under s 65(2) (*R v Okoro* [2019] EWCA Crim 1929).

See *Blackstone's Criminal Practice 2026* **B3.345**

C15.11 Indecent photographs of children

Protection of Children Act 1978, s 1(1)–(4)

1 Indecent photographs of children

(1) Subject to sections 1A and 1B, it is an offence for a person—
 (a) to take, or permit to be taken or to make, any indecent photograph or pseudo-photograph of a child; or
 (b) to distribute or show such indecent photographs or pseudophotographs; or
 (c) to have in his possession such indecent photographs or pseudophotographs, with a view to their being distributed or shown by himself or others; or
 (d) to publish or cause to be published any advertisement likely to be understood as conveying that the advertiser distributes or shows such indecent photographs or pseudo-photographs, or intends to do so.
(2) For purposes of this Act, a person is to be regarded as distributing an indecent photograph or pseudo-photograph if he parts with possession of it to, or exposes or offers it for acquisition by, another person.
(3) Proceedings for an offence under this Act shall not be instituted except by or with the consent of the Director of Public Prosecutions.
(4) Where a person is charged with an offence under subsection (1)(b) or (c), it shall be a defence for him to prove—
 (a) that he had a legitimate reason for distributing or showing the photographs or pseudo-photographs or (as the case may be) having them in his possession; or
 (b) that he had not himself seen the photographs or pseudo-photographs and did not know, nor had any cause to suspect, them to be indecent.

...

Criminal Justice Act 1988, s 160

160 Possession of indecent photograph of child

(1) Subject to section 160A, it is an offence for a person to have any indecent photograph or pseudo-photograph of a child in his possession.
(2) Where a person is charged with an offence under subsection (1) above, it shall be a defence for him to prove—
 (a) that he had a legitimate reason for having the photograph or pseudo-photograph in his possession; or
 (b) that he had not himself seen the photograph or pseudo-photograph and did not know, nor had any cause to suspect, it to be indecent; or

(c) that the photograph or pseudo-photograph was sent to him without any prior request made by him or on his behalf and that he did not keep it for an unreasonable time.

EW

Fine and/or 12 months'/10 years' imprisonment (5 years if s 160)

SON If—

(a) the indecent photographs or pseudo-photographs showed persons under 16, and
(b) the offender—
  (i) was 18 or over, or
  (ii) is sentenced in respect of the offence to imprisonment for a term of at least 12 months.

DO

C15.11.1 *Sentencing*

SCG **Possession of indecent photograph of child / Indecent photographs of children**

C15.11.2 Key points

- The meaning of possession and production in this guideline were considered in *R v Bateman* [2020] EWCA Crim 1333 concluding that:
  (1) mere downloading without more amounts to possession; (2) the taking of an image at source (for example the original image) is producing or creating that image; (3) because of the word 'include' in the explanatory note in the Guidelines the description in (2) is not a definitive statement of the circumstances when an image is produced or created; (4) the divide between possession and production/creation is not fixed in stone and the concepts are not mutually exclusive; common sense indicates that an image might start as a merely downloaded copy (and be possessed) but then be produced into something altogether different and more offensive. An image might be a hybrid of a possessed image and a created or produced image. When determining the correct categorization, a judge will thus need to form a view about the nature of the image and the extent to which it is merely downloaded, and/or the extent to which some creativity or production has been applied to it. That analysis will then enable the judge to apply the Guidelines in a calibrated manner.
- There were two types of *mens rea* required to prove an offence under s 1(1)(a) Protection of Children Act 1978. One was when making by downloading to a computer or telephone. The other was by photographing or filming the image. The former alone required proof of an awareness as to what was being downloaded (*R v PW* [2016] EWCA Crim 745).

- Under s 160 Criminal Justice Act 1988 there are two elements to be made out in order for an individual to have possession:
  (1) the images must have been within the defendant's custody or control, ie so that he was capable of accessing them; and
  (2) he must have known that he possessed an image or a group of images. Knowledge of the content of those images is not required to make out the basic ingredients of the offence; instead that issue is dealt with by the statutory defence under s 160(2) (*R v Okoro* [2019] EWCA Crim 1929).
- Photograph includes tracing or other image derived in whole or part from a photograph or pseudo-photograph.
- Whether a photograph is indecent depends on normally recognized standards of propriety.
- The age of the child may be relevant to the issue of indecency (*R v Owen* (1988) 88 Cr App R 291).
- The opening of an email or viewing of an image on the screen would amount to the making of an image if the defendant has the requisite knowledge of what he is doing.
- A person is not in possession of images if they have been deleted, if he is not able to recover those images (*R v Porter* [2006] EWCA Crim 560).
- A child is a person under 18 years of age (Sexual Offences Act 2003, s 45).
- In relying on the defence of legitimate reason the test of legitimacy is objective and the genuineness of the defendant's belief is not relevant to that issue *R v Toure* [2019] EWCA Crim 1961.
- Defences:
  S 1A Protection of Children Act 1978 and s 160A Criminal Justice Act 1988 provide for defences where the child is married or in a civil partnership with the defendant or they are living together as partners in an enduring family relationship. S 1B Protection of Children Act 1978 provides a defence for those involved in criminal investigations.

See *Blackstone's Criminal Practice 2026* B3.321

C15.12 Keeping a brothel used for prostitution

Sexual Offences Act 1956, s 33

33 Keeping a brothel

It is an offence for a person to keep a brothel, or to manage, or act or assist in the management of, a brothel.

SO

Level 3 fine and/or 3 months' imprisonment.

If previous conviction: Level 4 fine and/or 6 months' imprisonment

Sexual Offences Act 1956, s 33A

33A Keeping a brothel used for prostitution

(1) It is an offence for a person to keep, or to manage, or act or assist in the management of, a brothel to which people resort for practices involving prostitution (whether or not also for other practices).

EW

12 months' imprisonment and/or fine/7 years' imprisonment

C15.12.1 *Sentencing*

SCG Keeping a brothel used for prostitution

See *Blackstone's Criminal Practice 2026* **B3.357**

C15.13 Kerb crawling, paying for sexual services, loitering, and soliciting

Sexual Offences Act 2003, ss 51A and 53A

51A Soliciting

51A(1) It is an offence for a person in a street or public place to solicit another (B) for the purpose of obtaining B's sexual services as a prostitute.

(2) The reference to a person in a street or public place includes a person in a vehicle in a street or public place.

. . .

(4) In this section 'street' has the meaning given by section 1(4) of the Street Offences Act 1959.

53A Paying for sexual services of a prostitute subjected to force etc

53A(1) A person (A) commits an offence if—

(a) A makes or promises payment for the sexual services of a prostitute (B),

(b) a third person (C) has engaged in exploitative conduct of a kind likely to induce or encourage B to provide the sexual services for which A has made or promised payment, and

(c) C engaged in that conduct for or in the expectation of gain for C or another person (apart from A or B).

(2) The following are irrelevant—

(a) where in the world the sexual services are to be provided and whether those services are provided,

(b) whether A is, or ought to be, aware that C has engaged in exploitative conduct.

(3) C engages in exploitative conduct if—

(a) C uses force, threats (whether or not relating to violence) or any other form of coercion, or

(b) C practises any form of deception.

> **Street Offences Act 1959, s 1(1)**
>
> **1 Loitering or soliciting for purposes of prostitution**
>
> (1) It shall be an offence for a person aged 18 or over (whether male or female) persistently to loiter or solicit in a street or public place for the purpose of prostitution.

SO

Level 3 fine (for a first offence under Street Offences Act 1959, s 1, the fine is level 2)

See *Blackstone's Criminal Practice 2026* **B3.253**

C15.14 **Offences against child under 13**

There are three offences under ss 5–7 SOA 2003. It is not necessary to prove that the defendant knew that the complainant was under the age of 13 (*R v G* [2008] UKHL 37.). For s 7 see **C15.23**.

C15.14.1 ***Rape of child under 13***

> **Sexual Offences Act 2003, s 5**
>
> (1) A person commits an offence if—
> (a) he intentionally penetrates the vagina, anus, or mouth of another person with his penis, and
> (b) the other person is under 13.

IO

Life

For youths see the *Handbook of Youths in the Criminal Courts*

DO

GC

C15.14.2 ***Assault by penetration of a child under 13***

> **Sexual Offences Act 2003, s 6**
>
> (1) A person commits an offence if—
> (a) he intentionally penetrates the vagina or anus of another person with a part of his body or anything else,
> (b) the penetration is sexual, and
> (c) the other person is under 13.

IO

Life

For youths see the *Handbook of Youths in the Criminal Courts*

SON

DO

GC

C15.15 Outraging public decency

It is an offence at common law to commit in public an act that is lewd, obscene, or disgusting and of such a nature as to outrage minimum standards of public decency.

EW

12 months' imprisonment and/or a fine/life imprisonment

C15.15.1 *Sentencing*

- The guideline for exposure at SCG exposure may be relevant by way of analogy to conduct charged as the common law offence of outraging public decency.

C15.15.2 Key points

- It is not necessary for any particular member of the public to be outraged. To be public the act must be seen by at least one person and have been capable of being seen by more than one person. even if they do not in fact do so (*R v Hamilton* [2007] EWCA Crim 2062. Disgust need not be proved; it is sufficient that the act is merely capable of causing disgust (*R v Mayling* (1963) 47 Cr App R 102).
- The act need not happen in a public place.

See *Blackstone's Criminal Practice 2026* B3.351

C15.16 Possession of paedophile manual

Serious Crime Act 2015, s 69

69 Possession of paedophile manual

(1) It is an offence to be in possession of any item that contains advice or guidance about abusing children sexually.

(2) It is a defence for a person (D) charged with an offence under this section—

> (a) to prove that D had a legitimate reason for being in possession of the item;
> (b) to prove that—
>   (i) D had not read, viewed or (as appropriate) listened to the item, and
>   (ii) D did not know, and had no reason to suspect, that it contained advice or guidance about abusing children sexually; or
> (c) to prove that—
>   (i) the item was sent to D without any request made by D or on D's behalf, and
>   (ii) D did not keep it for an unreasonable time.
>
> . . .
>
> (4) Proceedings for an offence under this section may be brought—
>   (a) in England and Wales, only by or with the consent of the Director of Public Prosecutions;

C15.16.1 Key points

> **Serious Crime Act 2015, s 69**
>
> (8) In this section—,
> 'abusing children sexually' means doing anything that constitutes—
>   (a) an offence under Part 1 of the Sexual Offences Act 2003, or under Part 2, 3, against a person under 16, or
>   (b) an offence under section 1 of the Protection of Children Act 1978 involving indecent photographs (but not pseudo-photographs), or doing anything outside England and Wales that would constitute such an offence if done in England and Wales;
>
> 'item' includes anything in which information of any description is recorded; 'prohibited item' means an item within subsection (1).

EW

Fine and or 12 months'/3 years' imprisonment

SON

If the offender—
(a) was 18 or over, or
(b) is sentenced in respect of the offence to imprisonment for a term of at least 12 months

See *Blackstone's Criminal Practice 2026* B3.339

C15.17 Preparatory offences

See *Blackstone's Criminal Practice 2026* B3.272

C15.17.1 *Administering a substance with intent*

Sexual Offences Act 2003, s 61

(1) A person commits an offence if he intentionally administers a substance to, or causes a substance to be taken by, another person (B)—
   (a) knowing that B does not consent, and
   (b) with the intention of stupefying or overpowering B, so as to enable any person to engage in a sexual activity that involves B

EW

IIII 12 months' imprisonment and/or a fine/10 years' imprisonment

SON

C15.17.1.1 *Sentencing*

SCG Administering a substance with intent

C15.17.1.2 Key points

There is no need for sexual activity to take place for the offence to be made out. The absence of consent relates to the administration or taking of the substance, not to any sexual activity that may take place.

C15.17.2 *Committing an offence with intent to commit a sexual offence*

Sexual Offences Act 2003, s 62

(1) A person commits an offence under this section if he commits any offence with the intention of committing a relevant sexual offence.
(2) In this section, 'relevant sexual offence' means any offence under this Part (including an offence of aiding, abetting, counselling or procuring such an offence).

IO Where the offence is committed by kidnapping or false imprisonment

EW In other circumstances

IIII Where the offence is committed by kidnapping or false imprisonment: Life imprisonment

In other circumstances: 12 months' imprisonment and/or a fine/10 years' imprisonment

SON If—

(a) where the offender was under 18, he is or has been sentenced in respect of the offence to imprisonment for a term of at least 12 months;

(b) in any other case—
   (i) the intended offence was an offence against a person under 18, or
   (ii) the offender, in respect of the offence or finding, is or has been—
      (a) sentenced to a term of imprisonment,
      (b) detained in a hospital, or
      (c) made the subject of a community sentence of at least 12 months.

DO

C15.17.2.1 *Sentencing guideline*

SCG **Committing an offence with intent to commit a sexual offence**

The starting point and range should be commensurate with that for the preliminary offence actually committed but with an enhancement to reflect the intention to commit a sexual offence. The enhancement will vary depending on the nature and seriousness of the intended sexual offence but 2 years' custody is suggested as a suitable enhancement where the intent was to commit rape or assault by penetration.

C15.17.2.2 Key points

The Crown need not prove which sexual offence was intended (*Pacurar* [2016] EWCA Crim 569).

C15.17.3 *Trespass with intent to commit a sexual offence*

Sexual Offences Act 2003, s 63

(1) A person commits an offence if—
   (a) he is a trespasser on any premises,
   (b) he intends to commit a relevant sexual offence on the premises, and
   (c) he knows that, or is reckless as to whether, he is a trespasser.
(2) In this section—
   - 'premises' includes a structure or part of a structure;
   - 'relevant sexual offence' has the same meaning as in section 62;
   - 'structure' includes a tent, vehicle or vessel or other temporary or movable structure.

EW

12 months' imprisonment and/or fine/10 years' imprisonment

SON If—

(a) where the offender was under 18, he is or has been sentenced in respect of the offence to imprisonment for a term of at least 12 months;

(b) in any other case—
  (i) the intended offence was an offence against a person under 18, or
  (ii) the offender, in respect of the offence or finding, is or has been—
    (a) sentenced to a term of imprisonment,
    (b) detained in a hospital, or
    (c) made the subject of a community sentence of at least 12 months.

C15.17.3.1 ***Sentencing***

SCG Trespass with intent to commit a sexual offence

C15.17.3.2 **Key points**

The trespass must be at least reckless.

The Crown need not prove which sexual offence was intended (*R v Pacurar* [2016] EWCA Crim 569).

C15.18 **Prohibited images of children**

Coroners and Justice Act 2009, s 62

62 Possession of prohibited images of children

(1) It is an offence for a person to be in possession of a prohibited image of a child.
(2) A prohibited image is an image which—
  (a) is pornographic,
  (b) falls within subsection (6), and
  (c) is grossly offensive, disgusting or otherwise of an obscene character.
(3) An image is 'pornographic' if it is of such a nature that it must reasonably be assumed to have been produced solely or principally for the purpose of sexual arousal.
(4) Where (as found in the person's possession) an image forms part of a series of images, the question whether the image is of such a nature as is mentioned in subsection (3) is to be determined by reference to—
  (a) the image itself, and
  (b) (if the series of images is such as to be capable of providing a context for the image) the context in which it occurs in the series of images.
(5) So, for example, where—
  (a) an image forms an integral part of a narrative constituted by a series of images, and
  (b) having regard to those images as a whole, they are not of such a nature that they must reasonably be assumed to have been produced solely or principally for the purpose of sexual arousal,

  the image may, by virtue of being part of that narrative, be found not to be pornographic, even though it might have been found to be pornographic if taken by itself.
(6) An image falls within this subsection if it—
  (a) is an image which focuses solely or principally on a child's genitals or anal region, or
  (b) portrays any of the acts mentioned in subsection (7).

(7) Those acts are—
  (a) the performance by a person of an act of intercourse or oral sex with or in the presence of a child;
  (b) an act of masturbation by, of, involving or in the presence of a child;
  (c) an act which involves penetration of the vagina or anus of a child with a part of a person's body or with anything else;
  (d) an act of penetration, in the presence of a child, of the vagina or anus of a person with a part of a person's body or with anything else;
  (e) the performance by a child of an act of intercourse or oral sex with an animal (whether dead or alive or imaginary);
  (f) the performance by a person of an act of intercourse or oral sex with an animal (whether dead or alive or imaginary) in the presence of a child.

(8) For the purposes of subsection (7), penetration is a continuing act from entry to withdrawal.

(9) Proceedings for an offence under subsection (1) may not be instituted—
  (a) in England and Wales, except by or with the consent of the Director of Public Prosecutions;

...

EW

12 months' imprisonment and/or fine/3 years' imprisonment

SON

If the offender—
  (a) was 18 or over, and
  (b) is sentenced to imprisonment for a term of at least 2 years

C15.18.1 Key points

- Section 64 of the Coroners and Justice Act 2009 provides for the following defence:

Coroners and Justice Act 2009, s 64(1)

64 Defences

(1) Where a person is charged with an offence under section 62(1), it is a defence for the person to prove any of the following matters—
  (a) that the person had a legitimate reason for being in possession of the image concerned;
  (b) that the person had not seen the image concerned and did not know, nor had any cause to suspect, it to be a prohibited image of child;
  (c) that the person—
    (i) was sent the image concerned without any prior request having been made by or on behalf of the person, and
    (ii) did not keep it for an unreasonable time.

- Section 63 of the Act defines the meaning of 'image' and 'child'.

See *Blackstone's Criminal Practice 2026* **B3.333**

C15.19 **Rape**

Sexual Offences Act 2003, s 1

(1) A person (A) commits an offence if—
   (a) he intentionally penetrates the vagina, anus, or mouth of another person (B) with his penis,
   (b) B does not consent to the penet©ion, and
   (c) A does not reasonably believe that B consents.
(2) Whether a belief is reasonable is to be determined having regard to all the circumstances, including any steps A has taken to ascertain whether B consents.
(3) Sections 75 and 76 apply to an offence under this section.

IO

Life

SON

DO

GC

C15.19.1 ***Sentencing***

SCG Rape

For youths see the *Handbook of Youths in the Criminal Courts*

C15.19.2 Key points

- Penetration is a continuing act from entry to withdrawal (s 79(2) SOA 2003).
- For consent see **C15.1.1**.

See *Blackstone's Criminal Practice 2026* **B3.17**

C15.20 **Sending etc photograph or film of genitals**

Sexual Offences Act 2003, s 66A

66A Sending etc photograph or film of genitals

(1) A person (A) who intentionally sends or gives a photograph or film of any person's genitals to another person (B) commits an offence if—
   (a) A intends that B will see the genitals and be caused alarm, distress or humiliation, or
   (b) A sends or gives such a photograph or film for the purpose of obtaining sexual gratification and is reckless as to whether B will be caused alarm, distress or humiliation.

(2) References to sending or giving such a photograph or film to another person include, in particular—
  (a) sending it to another person by any means, electronically or otherwise,
  (b) showing it to another person, and
  (c) placing it for a particular person to find.
(3) "Photograph" includes the negative as well as the positive version.
(4) "Film" means a moving image.
(5) References to a photograph or film also include—
  (a) an image, whether made or altered by computer graphics or in any other way, which appears to be a photograph or film,
  (b) a copy of a photograph, film or image within paragraph (a), and
  (c) data stored by any means which is capable of conversion into a photograph, film or image within paragraph (a).

EW

12 months' imprisonment and/or a fine/2 years' imprisonment

SON

(a) where the offender was under 18, he is or has been sentenced, in respect of the offence, to imprisonment for a term of at least 12 months;
(b) in any other case—
  (i) if the victim was under 18, or
  (ii) the offender is—
    (a) sentenced to a term of imprisonment,
    (b) detained in a hospital, or
    (c) made the subject of a community sentence of at least 12 months.

DO

C15.21 **Sexual activity in a public lavatory**

Sexual Offences Act 2003, s 71(1) and (2)

71 Sexual activity in a public lavatory

(1) A person commits an offence if—
  (a) he is in a lavatory to which the public or a section of the public has or is permitted to have access, whether on payment or otherwise,
  (b) he intentionally engages in an activity, and,
  (c) the activity is sexual.
(2) For the purposes of this section, an activity is sexual if a reasonable person would, in all the circumstances but regardless of any person's purpose, consider it to be sexual.

SO

Fine and/or 6 months' imprisonment

C15.21.1 *Sentencing*

SCG Sexual activity in a public lavatory

C15.21.2 Key points

- This offence is committed where an offender intentionally engages in sexual activity in a public lavatory. It was introduced to give adults and children the freedom to use public lavatories for the purpose for which they are designed, without the fear of being an unwilling witness to overtly sexual behaviour of a kind that most people would not expect to be conducted in public. It is primarily a public order offence rather than a sexual offence.

See *Blackstone's Criminal Practice 2026* **B3.313**

C15.22 Sexual assault

Sexual Offences Act 2003, s 3(1)–(3)

3 Sexual assault

(1) A person (A) commits an offence if—
- (a) he intentionally touches another person (B),
- (b) the touching is sexual,
- (c) B does not consent to the touching, and
- (d) A does not reasonably believe that B consents.

(2) Whether a belief is reasonable is to be determined having regard to all the circumstances, including any steps A has taken to ascertain whether B consents.

(3) Sections 75 and 76 apply to an offence under this section.

EW

12 months' imprisonment and/or fine/10 years' imprisonment

SON

(a) where the offender was under 18, he is or has been sentenced, in respect of the offence, to imprisonment for a term of at least 12 months;

(b) in any other case—
- (i) if the victim was under 18, or
- (ii) the offender is—
  - (a) sentenced to a term of imprisonment,
  - (b) detained in a hospital, or
  - (c) made the subject of a community sentence of at least 12 months.

DO

GC

C15.22.1 *Sentencing*

SCG Sexual assault

C15.22.2 Key points

- A belief in consent arising from delusional psychotic illness must be objectively judged but the personality or disability of the defendant may be relevant to whether the belief was reasonably held where for instance it involved the reading of subtle social signals. An irrational belief can never meet the reasonableness test (*R v B* [2013] EWCA Crim 3).
- It is not necessary for the prosecution to prove, as an element of the offence of sexual assault, that the offender not only intentionally touched another person without their consent and without reasonable belief in their consent, and that the touching was sexual, but also that the offender additionally intended his touching of that person to be sexual. Instead, under section 78 (b), the accused's purpose in relation to the activity may be relevant if a reasonable person would consider that, given the nature of the activity, it may be sexual and, because of the accused's purpose, it was sexual (AG Ref No 1 of [2020] EWCA Crim 1665).

See *Blackstone's Criminal Practice 2026* **B3.63**

C15.23 Sexual assault of a child under 13

Sexual Offences Act 2003, s 7

Sexual assault of a child under 13

(1) A person commits an offence if—
- (a) he intentionally touches another person,
- (b) the touching is sexual, and
- (c) the other person is under 13.

EW

12 months' imprisonment and/or fine/14 years' imprisonment

SON If the offender—

(a) was 18 or over, or
(b) is or has been sentenced in respect of the offence to imprisonment for a term of at least 12 months

DO

GC

C15.23.1 *Sentencing*

SCG Sexual assault of a child under 13

See *Blackstone's Criminal Practice 2026* **B3.93**

C15.24 Sexual grooming

C15.24.1 *Meeting a child following sexual grooming etc*

Sexual Offences Act 2003, s 15

(1) A person aged 18 or over (A) commits an offence if—
- (a) A has met or communicated with another person (B) on one or more occasions and subsequently—
  - (i) A intentionally meets B,
  - (ii) A travels with the intention of meeting B in any part of the world or arranges to meet B in any part of the world, or
  - (iii) B travels with the intention of meeting A in any part of the world,
- (b) A intends to do anything to or in respect of B, during or after the meeting mentioned in paragraph (a)(i) to (iii) and in any part of the world, which if done will involve the commission by A of a relevant offence,
- (c) B is under 16, and
- (d) A does not reasonably believe that B is 16 or over.

(2) In subsection (1)—
- (a) the reference to A having met or communicated with B is a reference to A having met B in any part of the world or having communicated with B by any means from, to or in any part of the world;
- (b) 'relevant offence' means—
  - (i) an offence under this Part, . . .
  - (iii) anything done outside England and Wales which is not an offence within sub-paragraph (i) but would be an offence within sub-paragraph (i) if done in England and Wales . . .

EW

12 months' imprisonment and/or a fine/10 years' imprisonment

SON

DO

C15.24.1.1 *Sentencing*

SCG Meeting a child following sexual grooming

C15.24.2 *Sexual communications with a child*

Sexual Offences Act 2003, s 15A

15A Sexual communication with a child

(1) A person aged 18 or over (A) commits an offence if—
- (a) for the purpose of obtaining sexual gratification, A intentionally communicates with another person (B),
- (b) the communication is sexual or is intended to encourage B to make (whether to A or to another) a communication that is sexual, and
- (c) B is under 16 and A does not reasonably believe that B is 16 or over.

(2) For the purposes of this section, a communication is sexual if—
- (a) any part of it relates to sexual activity, or
- (b) a reasonable person would, in all the circumstances but regardless of any person's purpose, consider any part of the communication to be sexual; and in paragraph (a), 'sexual activity' means an activity that a reasonable person would, in all the circumstances but regardless of any person's purpose, consider to be sexual.

EW

12 months' imprisonment and/or a fine/2 years' imprisonment

SON

See *Blackstone's Criminal Practice 2026* **B3.134**

C15.24.2.1 *Sentencing*

SCG Sexual communication with a child

C15.25 Sex offenders register—fail to comply with notification requirements

Sexual Offences Act 2003, s 91(1)

91 Offences relating to notification

(1) A person commits an offence if he—
- (a) fails, without reasonable excuse, to comply with section 83(1), 84(1), 4(4)(b), 85(1) . . . 87(4) or 89(2)(b) or any requirement imposed by regulations made under section 86(1); or
- (b) notifies to the police, in purported compliance with section 83(1), 4(1) or 85(1), or any requirement imposed by regulations made under section 86(1), any information which he knows to be false.

EW

12 months' imprisonment and/or fine/5 years' imprisonment

C15.25.1 *Sentencing*

SCG Fail to comply with notification requirements

A conditional discharge cannot be imposed on breach.

C15.25.2 Key points

- A person who is subject to the notification requirements commits a criminal offence if he fails, without reasonable excuse, to:
  - make an initial notification, in accordance with s 83(1), of those matters set out in the Sexual Offences Act 2003 (Notification Requirements) (England and Wales) Regulations 2012;
  - notify a change of details in accordance with s 84(1);
  - make a renotification in accordance with s 85(1);
  - comply with any requirement imposed by regulations concerned with the notification of foreign travel (s 86(1));
  - notify the fact that a change did not happen as predicted when it had been notified in advance in accordance with s 84(4)(b);
  - allow a police officer to take his photograph or fingerprints (s 87(4));
  - ensure that a young offender on whose behalf he is required by a parental direction to comply with the notification requirements attends a police station when a notification is made (s 89(2)(b));
  - in the first four cases set out above, if he knowingly provides false information.
- The prescribed information includes names, addresses, date of birth, National Insurance number, bank accounts, debit and credit card details, and details of passports or other identity documents. Names include user names, pseudonyms, and handles on social media (*R v Smith* [2021] EWCA Crim 716).
- The offence occurs on the first day of breach and continues—only one breach can be prosecuted in such circumstances.

See *Blackstone's Criminal Practice 2026* E23.5

C15.26 Sharing or threatening to share intimate photograph or film

Sexual Offences Act 2023, s 66B

66B Sharing or threatening to share intimate photograph or film

(1) A person (A) commits an offence if—
  (a) A intentionally shares a photograph or film which shows, or appears to show, another person (B) in an intimate state,
  (b) B does not consent to the sharing of the photograph or film, and
  (c) A does not reasonably believe that B consents.

(2) A person (A) commits an offence if—
  (a) A intentionally shares a photograph or film which shows, or appears to show, another person (B) in an intimate state,
  (b) A does so with the intention of causing B alarm, distress or humiliation, and
  (c) B does not consent to the sharing of the photograph or film.

(3) A person (A) commits an offence if—
  (a) A intentionally shares a photograph or film which shows, or appears to show, another person (B) in an intimate state,
  (b) A does so for the purpose of A or another person obtaining sexual gratification,
  (c) B does not consent to the sharing of the photograph or film, and
  (d) A does not reasonably believe that B consents.

(4) A person (A) commits an offence if—
  (a) A threatens to share a photograph or film which shows, or appears to show, another person (B) in an intimate state, and
  (b) A does so—
    (i) with the intention that B or another person who knows B will fear that the threat will be carried out, or
    (ii) being reckless as to whether B or another person who knows B will fear that the threat will be carried out.

(5) Subsections (1) to (4) are subject to section 66C (exemptions).

(6) For the purposes of subsections (1) to (3) and section 66C(3)(b)—
  (a) "consent" to the sharing of a photograph or film includes general consent covering the particular act of sharing as well as specific consent to the particular act of sharing, and
  (b) whether a belief is reasonable is to be determined having regard to all the circumstances including any steps A has taken to ascertain whether B consents.

(7) Where a person is charged with an offence under subsection (4), it is not necessary for the prosecution to prove—
  (a) that the photograph or film mentioned in the threat exists, or
  (b) if it does exist, that it is in fact a photograph or film which shows or appears to show a person in an intimate state.

(8) It is a defence for a person charged with an offence under subsection (1) to prove that the person had a reasonable excuse for sharing the photograph or film.

(12) If on the trial of a person charged with an offence under subsection (2) or (3) a magistrates' court . . . finds the person not guilty of the offence charged, the magistrates' court . . . may find the person guilty of an offence under subsection (1).

SO s 66B(1)

EW s 66B(2), (3) and (4)

s 66B(1): Fine and/or 6 months' imprisonment

s 66B(2), (3) and (4): Fine and/or 12 months'/2 years' imprisonment

SON s 66B(3):

(a) where the offender was under 18, he is or has been sentenced, in respect of the offence, to imprisonment for a term of at least 12 months;
(b) in any other case—
  (i) if the victim was under 18, or
  (ii) the offender is—

(a) sentenced to a term of imprisonment,
(b) detained in a hospital, or
(c) made the subject of a community sentence of at least 12 months.

DO s 66B(2) and (3)

Key points

The following are exemptions to offences under s 66A(1)–(4):

Sexual Offences Act, s 66C

66C Sharing or threatening to share intimate photograph or film: exemptions

(1) A person (A) who shares a photograph or film which shows, or appears to show, another person (B) in an intimate state does not commit an offence under section 66B(1), (2) or (3) if—
  (a) the photograph or film was taken in a place to which the public or a section of the public had or were permitted to have access (whether on payment or otherwise),
  (b) B had no reasonable expectation of privacy from the photograph or film being taken, and
  (c) B was, or A reasonably believes that B was, in the intimate state voluntarily.

(2) For the purposes of subsection (1)(b), whether a person had a reasonable expectation of privacy from a photograph or film being taken is to be determined by reference to the circumstances that the person sharing the photograph or film reasonably believes to have existed at the time the photograph or film was taken.

(3) A person (A) who shares a photograph or film which shows, or appears to show, another person (B) in an intimate state does not commit an offence under section 66B(1), (2) or (3) if—
  (a) the photograph or film had, or A reasonably believes that the photograph or film had, been previously publicly shared, and
  (b) B had, or A reasonably believes that B had, consented to the previous sharing.

(4) A person (A) who shares a photograph or film which shows, or appears to show, another person (B) in an intimate state does not commit an offence under section 66B(1) if—
  (a) B is a person under 16,
  (b) B lacks, or A reasonably believes that B lacks, capacity to consent to the sharing of the photograph or film, and
  (c) the photograph or film is shared—
    (i) with a healthcare professional acting in that capacity, or
    (ii) otherwise in connection with the care or treatment of B by a healthcare professional.

(5) A person who shares a photograph or film which shows, or appears to show, a child in an intimate state does not commit an offence under section 66B(1) if the photograph or film is of a kind ordinarily shared between family and friends.

(6) A person who threatens to share a photograph or film which shows, or appears to show, another person in an intimate state does not commit an offence under section 66B(4) if, by reason of this section, the person would not commit an offence under section 66B(1), (2) or (3) by sharing the photograph or film in the circumstances conveyed by the threat.

C15.27 Voyeurism

Sexual Offences Act 2003, ss 67 and 67A

67 Voyeurism

(1) A person commits an offence if—
   (a) for the purpose of obtaining sexual gratification, he observes another person doing a private act, and
   (b) he knows that the other person does not consent to being observed for his sexual gratification.
(2) A person commits an offence if—
   (a) he operates equipment with the intention of enabling another person to observe, for the purpose of obtaining sexual gratification, a third person (B) doing a private act, and
   (b) he knows that B does not consent to his operating equipment with that intention.
(3) A person commits an offence if—
   (a) he records another person (B) doing a private act,
   (b) he does so with the intention that he or a third person will, for the purpose of obtaining sexual gratification, look at an image of B doing the act, and
   (c) he knows that B does not consent to his recording the act with that intention.
(4) A person commits an offence if he installs equipment, or constructs or adapts a structure or part of a structure, with the intention of enabling himself or another person to commit an offence under subsection (1).

67A Voyeurism: additional offences

(1) A person (A) commits an offence if—
   (a) A operates equipment beneath the clothing of another person (B),
   (b) A does so with the intention of enabling A or another person (C), for a purpose mentioned in subsection (3), to observe—
      (i) B's genitals or buttocks (whether exposed or covered with underwear), or
      (ii) the underwear covering B's genitals or buttocks,
   in circumstances where the genitals, buttocks or underwear would not otherwise be visible,
   and
   (c) A does so—
      (i) without B's consent, and
      (ii) without reasonably believing that B consents.
(2) A person (A) commits an offence if—
   (a) A records an image beneath the clothing of another person (B),
   (b) the image is of—
      (i) B's genitals or buttocks (whether exposed or covered with underwear), or
      (ii) the underwear covering B's genitals or buttocks,
   in circumstances where the genitals, buttocks or underwear would not otherwise be visible,
   (c) A does so with the intention that A or another person (C) will look at the image for a purpose mentioned in subsection (3), and
   (d) A does so—
      (i) without B's consent, and
      (ii) without reasonably believing that B consents.
(2A) A person (A) commits an offence if
   (a) A operates equipment,
   (b) A does so with the intention of enabling A or another person (C), for a purpose mentioned in subsection (3), to observe another (B) while B is breast-feeding a child, and

(c) A does so—
(i) without B's consent, and
(ii) without reasonably believing that B consents.

(2B) A person (A) commits an offence if—
(a) A records an image of another (B) while B is breast-feeding a child,
(b) A does so with the intention that A or another person (C) will look at the image for a purpose mentioned in subsection (3), and
(c) A does so—
(i) without B's consent, and
(ii) without reasonably believing that B consents.

(3) The purposes referred to in subsections (1) to (2B) [and (2)] are—
(a) obtaining sexual gratification (whether for A or C);
(b) humiliating, alarming or distressing B.

(3A) In this section a reference to B breast-feeding a child includes B rearranging B's clothing—
(a) in the course of preparing to breast-feed the child, or
(b) having just finished breast-feeding the child.

(3B) It is irrelevant for the purposes of subsections (2A) and (2B)—
(a) whether or not B is in a public place while B is breast-feeding the child,
(b) whether or not B's breasts are exposed while B is breast-feeding the child, and
(c) what part of B's body—
(i) is, or is intended by A to be, visible in the recorded image, or
(ii) is intended by A to be observed.

EW

s 67: 12 months' imprisonment and/or fine/2 years' imprisonment

s 67A: 12 months' imprisonment and/or fine/2 years' imprisonment

SON If—

(a) where the offender was under 18, he is or has been sentenced in respect of the offence to imprisonment for a term of at least 12 months;
(b) in any other case—
(i) the victim was under 18, or
(ii) the offender is or has been—
(a) sentenced to a term of imprisonment,
(b) detained in a hospital, or
(c) made the subject of a community sentence of at least 12 months. And in relation to s 67A the offence was committed for the purpose mentioned in s 67A(3)(a) (sexual gratification).

DO

C15.27.1 *Sentencing*

SCG Voyeurism

C15.27.2 Key points

Section 68 provides for the interpretation of key phrases:

Sexual Offences Act 2003, s 68

68 Voyeurism: interpretation

(1) For the purposes of section 67, a person is doing a private act if the person is in a place which, in the circumstances, would reasonably be expected to provide privacy, and—
  (a) the person's genitals, buttocks or breasts are exposed or covered only with underwear,
  (b) the person is using a lavatory, or
  (c) the person is doing a sexual act that is not of a kind ordinarily done in public.
  (1A) For the purposes of sections 67 and 67A, operating equipment includes enabling or securing its activation by another person without that person's knowledge.

(2) In section 67, 'structure' includes a tent, vehicle or vessel or other temporary or movable structure.

- Consent is defined under s 74 of the Act:

Sexual Offences Act 2003, s 74

74 'Consent' see C15.1.1

There can be a reasonable expectation of privacy even from a participant in the private act. In *R v Richards* [2020] EWCA Crim 95 it was alleged that consensual intercourse had been filmed without consent.

See *Blackstone's Criminal Practice 2026* **B3.300**

C16 **Dishonesty and Offences against Property**

C16.1 **Aggravated burglary**

Theft Act 1968, s 10

(1) A person is guilty of aggravated burglary if he commits any burglary and at the time has with him any firearm or imitation firearm, any weapon of offence, or any explosive; and for this purpose—
  - (a) 'firearm' includes an airgun or air pistol, and 'imitation firearm' means anything which has the appearance of being a firearm, whether capable of being discharged or not; and
  - (b) 'weapon of offence' means any article made or adapted for use for causing injury to or incapacitating a person, or intended by the person having it with him for such use; and
  - (c) 'explosive' means any article manufactured for the purpose of producing a practical effect by explosion or intended by the person having it with him for that purpose.

IO

Life

DO

GC

C16.1.1 ***Sentencing***

SCG Aggravated burglary

C16.1.2 Key points

The relevant time for consideration of an intent in relation to a 'weapon of offence' (not made or adapted to cause injury to the person) is the time of the theft and not of the entry (*R v Eletu and White* [2018] EWCA Crim 599).

See *Blackstone's Criminal Practice 2026* **B4.96**

C16.2 **Aggravated vehicle-taking**

Theft Act 1968, s 12A(1)–(3)

12A Aggravated vehicle-taking

(1) Subject to subsection (3) below, a person is guilty of aggravated taking of a vehicle if—
  - (a) he commits an offence under section 12(1) above (in this section referred to as a 'basic offence') in relation to a mechanically propelled vehicle; and

Blackstone's Magistrates' Court Handbook 2026. Bartholomew Dalton and Caroline Liggins, Oxford University Press.
DOI: 10.1093/oso/9780198963943.003.0057

(b) it is proved that, at any time after the vehicle was unlawfully taken (whether by him or another) and before it was recovered, the vehicle was driven, or injury or damage was caused, in one or more of the circumstances set out in paragraphs (a) to (d) of subsection (2) below.

(2) The circumstances referred to in subsection (1)(b) above are—
(a) that the vehicle was driven dangerously on a road or other public place;
(b) that, owing to the driving of the vehicle, an accident occurred by which injury was caused to any person;
(c) that, owing to the driving of the vehicle, an accident occurred by which damage was caused to any property, other than the vehicle;
(d) that damage was caused to the vehicle.

(3) A person is not guilty of an offence under this section if he proves that, as regards any such proven driving, injury or damage as is referred to in subsection (1)(b) above, either—
(a) the driving, accident or damage referred to in subsection (2) above occurred before he committed the basic offence; or
(b) he was neither in nor on nor in the immediate vicinity of the vehicle when that driving, accident or damage occurred.

EW Summary only if damage only and under £5,000

s 12A(2)(a), (c) and (d): 12 months' imprisonment and/or fine/2 years' imprisonment

s 12A(2)(b): 12 months' imprisonment and/or fine/2 years' imprisonment (14 years if accident caused death)

Must endorse and disqualify for at least 12 months. Must disqualify for at least 2 years if offender has had two or more disqualifications for periods of 56 days or more in preceding 3 years.

C16.2.1 *Sentencing*

SCG

Aggravated vehicle taking – death caused
Aggravated vehicle taking – injury caused
Aggravated vehicle taking – dangerous driving
Aggravated vehicle taking – vehicle/property damage caused

C16.2.2 Key points

- A magistrates' court can convict a defendant of the alternative offence of vehicle taking if it does not find the aggravating feature(s) (*H v Liverpool Youth Court* [2001] Crim LR 897).
- The allegation under s 12A Theft Act 1968 that there has been a taking and 'owing to the driving of the vehicle, an accident occurred by which injury was caused to any person' requires an element of fault in the driving. There must have been at least some act or omission in the control of the car which

involved some element of fault and which contributed in some more than minimal way (*R v Taylor* [2016] UKSC 5). This will apply equally to an accident in which damage is caused.

See *Blackstone's Criminal Practice 2026* B4.127

C16.3 Alcohol/ tobacco etc., fraudulently evade duty

Customs and Excise Management Act 1979, section 170

EW

12 months' imprisonment and/or £20,000 fine or three times the value of the goods, whichever is higher/14 years' imprisonment

C16.3.1 *Sentencing*

SCG Revenue fraud

SON If for adult offender prohibited goods include indecent photographs of children under 16.

C16.3.2 Key points

- It is not sufficient for the prosecution to show that the defendant was merely reckless (*R v Panayi* [1989] 1 WLR 187).
- It is irrelevant that the defendant does not know the precise nature of the goods being imported (*R v Shivpuri* [1987] AC 1).
- The burden of proving that duty has been paid falls on the defendant (s 154).
- The prosecution have the right to appeal sentence (*Customs and Excise Commissioners v Brunt* (1998) 163 JP 161).

See *Blackstone's Criminal Practice 2026* B16.39

C16.4 Blackmail

Theft Act 1968, s 21

(1) A person is guilty of blackmail if, with a view to gain for himself or another or with intent to cause loss to another, he makes any unwarranted demand with menaces; and for this purpose a demand with menaces is unwarranted unless the person making it does so in the belief—
    (a) that he has reasonable grounds for making the demand; and
    (b) that the use of the menaces is a proper means of reinforcing the demand.

(2) The nature of the act or omission demanded is immaterial, and it is also immaterial whether the menaces relate to action to be taken by the person making the demand.

IO

14 years' imprisonment

GC

See *Blackstone's Criminal Practice 2026* B5.47

C16.5 **Burglary**

Theft Act 1968, s 9(1) and (2)

9 Burglary

(1) A person is guilty of burglary if—
- (a) he enters any building or part of a building as a trespasser and with intent to commit any such offence as is mentioned in subsection (2) below; or
- (b) having entered any building or part of a building as a trespasser he steals or attempts to steal anything in the building or that part of it or inflicts or attempts to inflict on any person therein any grievous bodily harm.

(2) The offences referred to in subsection (1)(a) above are offences of stealing anything in the building or part of a building in question, of inflicting on any person therein any grievous bodily harm therein, and of doing unlawful damage to the building or anything therein.

IO If either the offence compromises the commission of, or an intention to commit, grievous bodily harm or in a dwelling if any person in the dwelling was subjected to violence or the threat of violence (Sch 1 para 28 Magistrates' Courts Act 1980).

Or if the offender:
- was 18 or over when he committed the offence,
- had previously been convicted of two other domestic burglary offences in England and Wales; one of those offences has been committed after conviction for the other and both of the previous domestic burglaries had been committed on or after 1 December 1999;

EW In other cases

12 months' imprisonment and/or fine/10 years' imprisonment (14 years if dwelling)

DO Where the burglary is committed with intent to inflict grievous bodily harm or do unlawful damage

C16.5.1 ***Sentencing***

SCG Non-domestic burglary/Domestic burglary

C16.5.2 *Sentencing: dwelling*

Because of its significance in present or future sentencing it is important that every case is correctly classified. Whether premises are a dwelling for these purposes is essentially a matter of fact and degree. The term does not require that the building to be occupied on the date of the entry if it is still furnished and ready for use as a home even if owned on a buy-to-let basis (*Hudson v CPS* [2017] EWHC 841 (Admin)). It may be possible for a dwelling to become derelict or a building site and a newly built house may also not be a dwelling (*obiter*, *Chipunza v R* [2021] EWCA Crim 597). An entry to a communal lobby area in flats is not a domestic burglary (*R v Ogungbile* [2017] EWCA Crim 1826). A dwelling is best classified as a building or part of a building in which a person is living and had made their home. This may be contrasted with transient occupation. Whether a hotel room is a dwelling will depend on the circumstances and degree of permanence of the residence there (*R v Chipunza*).

C16.5.3 Key points

- Entry can be partial (*R v Brown* [1985] Crim LR 212) and may be effected without any part of the body entering the building (eg cane and hook burglaries).
- For sentencing vandalism includes damage caused to gain entry (*R v Islam and Clayton* 2020 EWCA Crim 706).
- Trespass can be committed knowingly or recklessly (*R v Collins* [1973] QB 100).

See *Blackstone's Criminal Practice 2026* B4.75

C16.6 Electricity—abstract/use without authority

Theft Act 1968, s 13

13 Abstracting of electricity

A person who dishonestly uses without due authority, or dishonestly causes to be wasted or diverted, any electricity shall be guilty of an offence.

EW

12 months' imprisonment and/or fine/5 years' imprisonment

C16.6.1 *Sentencing*

SCG Abstracting electricity

See *Blackstone's Criminal Practice 2026* B4.140

C16.7 False accounting

Theft Act 1968, s 17(1)

17 False accounting

(1) Where a person dishonestly, with a view to gain for himself or another or with intent to cause loss to another,—
  (a) destroys, defaces, conceals or falsifies any account or any record or document made or required for any accounting purpose; or
  (b) in furnishing information for any purpose produces or makes use of any account, or any such record or document as aforesaid, which to his knowledge is or may be misleading, false or deceptive in a material particular,

…

EW

12 months' imprisonment and/or fine/7 years' imprisonment

C16.7.1 *Sentencing*

SCG Fraud

See *Blackstone's Criminal Practice 2026* **B6.3**

C16.8 False statement/representation to obtain social security benefit

Social Security Administration Act 1992, ss 111A and 112

111A Dishonest representations for obtaining benefit etc

(1) If a person dishonestly—
  (a) makes a false statement or representation; or
  (b) produces or furnishes, or causes or allows to be produced or furnished, any document or information which is false in a material particular;

with a view to obtaining any benefit or other payment or advantage under the relevant social security legislation (whether for himself or for some other person), he shall be guilty of an offence.

(1A) A person shall be guilty of an offence if—
  (a) there has been a change of circumstances affecting any entitlement of his to any benefit or other payment or advantage under any provision of the relevant social security legislation;
  (b) the change is not a change that is excluded by regulations from the changes that are required to be notified;
  (c) he knows that the change affects an entitlement of his to such a benefit or other payment or advantage; and
  (d) he dishonestly fails to give a prompt notification of that change in the prescribed manner to the prescribed person.

(1B) A person shall be guilty of an offence if—
  (a) there has been a change of circumstances affecting any entitlement of another person to any benefit or other payment or advantage under any provision of the relevant social security legislation;

(b) the change is not a change that is excluded by regulations from the changes that are required to be notified;
(c) he knows that the change affects an entitlement of that other person to such a benefit or other payment or advantage; and
(d) he dishonestly causes or allows that other person to fail to give a prompt notification of that change in the prescribed manner to the prescribed person.

(1C) This subsection applies where—
(a) there has been a change of circumstances affecting any entitlement of a person ('the claimant') to any benefit or other payment or advantage under any provision of the relevant social security legislation;
(b) the benefit, payment, or advantage is one in respect of which there is another person ('the recipient') who for the time being has a right to receive payments to which the claimant has, or (but for the arrangements under which they are payable to the recipient) would have, an entitlement; and
(c) the change is not a change that is excluded by regulations from the changes that are required to be notified.

(1D) In a case where subsection (1C) above applies, the recipient is guilty of an offence if—
(a) he knows that the change affects an entitlement of the claimant to a benefit or other payment or advantage under a provision of the relevant social security legislation;
(b) the entitlement is one in respect of which he has a right to receive payments to which the claimant has, or (but for the arrangements under which they are payable to the recipient) would have, an entitlement; and
(c) he dishonestly fails to give a prompt notification of that change in the prescribed manner to the prescribed person.

(1E) In a case where that subsection applies, a person other than the recipient is guilty of an offence if—
(a) he knows that the change affects an entitlement of the claimant to a benefit or other payment or advantage under a provision of the relevant social security legislation;
(b) the entitlement is one in respect of which the recipient has a right to receive payments to which the claimant has, or (but for the arrangements under which they are payable to the recipient) would have, an entitlement; and
(c) he dishonestly causes or allows the recipient to fail to give a prompt notification of that change in the prescribed manner to the prescribed person.

(1F) In any case where subsection (1C) above applies but the right of the recipient is confined to a right, by reason of his being a person to whom the claimant is required to make payments in respect of a dwelling, to receive payments of housing benefit—
(a) a person shall not be guilty of an offence under subsection (1D) or (1E) above unless the change is one relating to one or both of the following—
(i) the claimant's occupation of that dwelling;
(ii) the claimant's liability to make payments in respect of that dwelling; but
(b) subsections (1D)(a) and (1E)(a) above shall each have effect as if after 'knows' there were inserted 'or could reasonably be expected to know'.

(1G) For the purposes of subsections (1A) to (1E) above a notification of a change is prompt if, and only if, it is given as soon as reasonably practicable after the change occurs.

112 False representations for obtaining benefit etc

(1) If a person for the purpose of obtaining any benefit or other payment under the relevant social security legislation whether for himself or some other person, or for any other purpose connected with that legislation—
(a) makes a statement or representation which he knows to be false; or

(b) produces or furnishes, or knowingly causes or knowingly allows to be produced or furnished, any document or information which he knows to be false in a material particular, he shall be guilty of an offence.

(1A) A person shall be guilty of an offence if—

(a) there has been a change of circumstances affecting any entitlement of his to any benefit or other payment or advantage under any provision of the relevant social security legislation;

(b) the change is not a change that is excluded by regulations from the changes that are required to be notified;

(c) he knows that the change affects an entitlement of his to such a benefit or other payment or advantage; and

(d) he fails to give a prompt notification of that change in the prescribed manner to the prescribed person.

(1B) A person is guilty of an offence under this section if—

(a) there has been a change of circumstances affecting any entitlement of another person to any benefit or other payment or advantage under any provision of the relevant social security legislation;

(b) the change is not a change that is excluded by regulations from the changes that are required to be notified;

(c) he knows that the change affects an entitlement of that other person to such a benefit or other payment or advantage; and

(d) he causes or allows that other person to fail to give a prompt notification of that change in the prescribed manner to the prescribed person.

(1C) In a case where subsection (1C) of section 111A above applies, the recipient is guilty of an offence if—

(a) he knows that the change affects an entitlement of the claimant to a benefit or other payment or advantage under a provision of the relevant social security legislation;

(b) the entitlement is one in respect of which he has a right to receive payments to which the claimant has, or (but for the arrangements under which they are payable to the recipient) would have, an entitlement; and

(c) he fails to give a prompt notification of that change in the prescribed manner to the prescribed person.

(1D) In a case where that subsection applies, a person other than the recipient is guilty of an offence if—

(a) he knows that the change affects an entitlement of the claimant to a benefit or other payment or advantage under a provision of the relevant social security legislation;

(b) the entitlement is one in respect of which the recipient has a right to receive payments to which the claimant has, or (but for the arrangements under which they are payable to the recipient) would have, an entitlement; and

(c) he causes or allows the recipient to fail to give a prompt notification of that change in the prescribed manner to the prescribed person.

(1E) Subsection (1F) of section 111A above applies in relation to subsections (1C) and (1D) above as it applies in relation to subsections (1D) and (1E) of that section.

(1F) For the purposes of subsections (1A) to (1D) above a notification of a change is prompt if, and only if, it is given as soon as reasonably practicable after the change occurs.

Section 111A:

EW

Fine and/or 12 months'/7 years' imprisonment

Section 112:

SO

Fine and/or 3 months' imprisonment

C16.8.1 *Sentencing*

SCG s 111A: Benefit Fraud

s 112: False representation

Key points: Sentencing

R v Noel [2012] EWCA Crim 956 confirmed that a custodial sentence was not appropriate for an offence under s 112(1A)(2) (failing to notify change of circumstances) of the Social Security Amendment Act 1982 by a woman of good character, involving £12,500 over nearly 5 years. The committal to the Crown Court had been only for the purposes of confiscation. *R v Condomiti (Vitorio)* [2015] EWCA Crim 806 held that a legitimate entitlement to benefits not claimed is also a mitigating factor and is a form of set-off based against what the applicant would have received, had a claim been made.

C16.8.2 Key points

Allocation

Administrative penalties may be suitable (subject to an absence of aggravating factors) for offences to a value of £5,000, By the Social Security (Penalty as Alternative to Prosecution) (Maximum Amount) Order 2015 the maximum amount of the penalty that may be offered as an alternative to prosecution is set at £5,000 for matters occurring wholly on or after 1 April 2015.

- In *R v Laku* [2008] EWCA Crim 1748, L made false representations in order to claim benefits and was prosecuted under ss 111A and 111A(1A) of the Social Security Administration Act 1992. On subsequent claims he did not correct the falsehoods. Held: convictions under s 111A(1A) quashed; he had not failed to notify a change in circumstances as the same false circumstances that founded the convictions under s 111A continued.
- An offence under s 111A(1B) requires a positive act on the part of the defendant. Sitting back and doing nothing does not amount to (allowing) an offence (*R v Tilley* [2009] EWCA Crim 1426).
- The offence under s 112(1A) Social Security Administration Act 1992 was interpreted in *Coventry City Council v Vassell* [2011] EWHC 1542 (Admin), and is committed if:
- there is a change of circumstances affecting entitlement to benefit;
- that change is not excluded from reporting by regulations; and
- the defendant knows that change affects his entitlement to benefit; the court held this meant 'would' affect (not 'could' affect) that entitlement;

- in relation to the requirement that the defendant fails to give prompt notification in the prescribed manner to the prescribed person the court held that whether there was prompt notice is a matter of fact. In considering who is the prescribed person, the court confirmed that the DWP will not suffice if the regulations specify the local authority. However, the defendant must *know* who is the correct person for the offence to be committed. In considering that aspect, relevant issues include the information provided by the local authority and the unexpected continuation of benefit.

C16.8.3 *Time limits for prosecution*

The normal six-month time limit for summary-only offences is extended in relation to s 112 by s 116(2): On time limits see **A12.1.2**.

Social Security Administration Act 1992, s 116(2)–(3)

116 Legal proceedings

(2) Notwithstanding anything in any Act—
 (a) proceedings for an offence under this Act (other than proceedings to which paragraph (b) applies), or for an offence under the Jobseekers Act 1995, may be begun at any time within the period of 3 months from the date on which evidence, sufficient in the opinion of the Secretary of State to justify a prosecution for the offence, comes to his knowledge or within a period of 12 months from the commission of the offence, whichever period last expires; and
 (b) proceedings brought by the appropriate authority for an offence under this Act relating to housing benefit or council tax benefit may be begun at any time within the period of 3 months from the date on which evidence, sufficient in the opinion of the appropriate authority to justify a prosecution for the offence, comes to the authority's knowledge or within a period of 12 months from the commission of the offence, whichever period last expires.

(2A) Subsection (2) above shall not be taken to impose any restriction on the time when proceedings may be begun for an offence under section 111A above.

(3) For the purposes of subsection (2) above—
 (a) a certificate purporting to be signed by or on behalf of the Secretary of State as to the date on which such evidence as is mentioned in paragraph (a) of that subsection came to his knowledge shall be conclusive evidence of that date; and.
 (b) a certificate of the appropriate authority as to the date on which such evidence as is mentioned in paragraph (b) of that subsection came to the authority's knowledge shall be conclusive evidence of that date.

See *Blackstone's Criminal Practice 2026* **B16.58**

C16.9 Found on enclosed premises

Note these provisions will be repealed by the PCSCA 2022 for offences on or after the date of implementation of the relevant provision.

Vagrancy Act 1824, s 4

4 Persons committing certain offences to be deemed rogues and vagabonds

[The following is an abbreviated version of the original] . . . [E]very person wandering abroad and lodging in any barn or outhouse, or in any deserted or unoccupied building, or in the open air, or under a tent, or in any cart or waggon, and not giving a good account of himself or herself; every person being found in or upon any dwelling house, warehouse, coach-house, stable, or outhouse, or in any inclosed yard, garden, or area, for any unlawful purpose; . . . is guilty of an offence.

SO

Level 3 fine/3 months' imprisonment

C16.9.1 Key points

An unlawful purpose is to commit an offence. Hiding from the police is therefore not enough (*L v CPS* [2007] EWHC 1843 (Admin)).

See *Blackstone's Criminal Practice 2026* B4.95

C16.10 Fraud

Fraud Act 2006, ss 1(1) and (2), 2, 3, 4, and 5

1 Fraud

(1) A person is guilty of fraud if he is in breach of any of the sections listed in subsection (2) (which provide for different ways of committing the offence).
(2) The sections are—
  (a) section 2 (fraud by false representation),
  (b) section 3 (fraud by failing to disclose information), and
  (c) section 4 (fraud by abuse of position)

2 Fraud by false representation

(1) A person is in breach of this section if he—
  (a) dishonestly makes a false representation, and
  (b) intends, by making the representation—
    (i) to make a gain for himself or another, or
    (ii) to cause loss to another or to expose another to a risk of loss.
(2) A representation is false if—
  (a) it is untrue or misleading, and
  (b) the person making it knows that it is, or might be, untrue or misleading.
(3) 'Representation' means any representation as to fact or law, including a representation as to the state of mind of—
  (a) the person making the representation, or
  (b) any other person.
(4) A representation may be express or implied.

(5) For the purposes of this section a representation may be regarded as made if it (or anything implying it) is submitted in any form to any system or device designed to receive, convey or respond to communications (with or without human intervention).

3 Fraud by failing to disclose information

A person is in breach of this section if he—
(a) dishonestly fails to disclose to another person information which he is under a legal duty to disclose, and
(b) intends, by failing to disclose the information—
  (i) to make a gain for himself or another, or
  (ii) to cause loss to another or to expose another to a risk of loss.

4 Fraud by abuse of position

(1) A person is in breach of this section if he—
  (a) occupies a position in which he is expected to safeguard, or not to act against, the financial interests of another person,
  (b) dishonestly abuses that position, and
  (c) intends, by means of the abuse of that position—
    (i) to make a gain for himself or another, or
    (ii) to cause loss to another or to expose another to a risk of loss.
(2) A person may be regarded as having abused his position even though his conduct consisted of an omission rather than an act.

5 'Gain' and 'loss'

(1) The references to gain and loss in sections 2 to 4 are to be read in accordance with this section.
(2) 'Gain' and 'loss'—
  (a) extend only to gain or loss in money or other property;
  (b) include any such gain or loss whether temporary or permanent; and 'property' means any property whether real or personal (including things in action and other intangible property).
(3) 'Gain' includes a gain by keeping what one has, as well as a gain by getting what one does not have.
(4) 'Loss' includes a loss by not getting what one might get, as well as a loss by parting with what one has.

EW

Fine and/or 12 months'/10 years' imprisonment

C16.10.1 *Sentencing*

SCG Fraud

C16.10.2 Key points

The offence under s 2 requires that the defendant know that the representation was or might have been misleading. This is a subjective test. It is not a test of reasonableness or of what the defendant ought to have known. However, a defendant cannot close their eyes to obvious doubts about the genuineness of the representations (*R v Augunas* [2013] EWCA Crim 2046).

The facts must be considered in each case under s 3 to identify the relevant legal duty. *R v D* [2019] EWCA Crim 209 confirmed that here is no 'legal duty to disclose' within the meaning of s 3 Fraud Act 2006 to notify a change of circumstance in relation to council tax under the Local Government Finance Act 1992.

While an offence under s 4 does not require a fiduciary relationship, there must be something akin to one. The test is objective and does not depend on the views of the defendant. In *R v Valujevs* [2014] EWCA Crim 2888 it was held that gang-masters might meet the test where there is an interference by them with the payment of wages due.

See *Blackstone's Criminal Practice 2026* **B5.4**

C16.11 Going equipped for theft

Theft Act 1968, s 25(1)–(3), (5)

25 Going equipped for stealing etc

(1) A person shall be guilty of an offence if, when not at his place of abode, he has with him any article for use in the course of or in connection with any burglary or theft . . .

(3) Where a person is charged with an offence under this section, proof that he had with him any article made or adapted for use in committing a burglary or theft shall be evidence that he had it with him for such use.

(4) . . .

(5) For purposes of this section an offence under section 12(1) of this Act of taking a conveyance shall be treated as theft.

EW

12 months' imprisonment and/or fine/3 years' imprisonment

C16.11.1 *Sentencing*

SCG **Going equipped for theft or burglary**

C16.11.2 Key points

The article need not be intended for immediate use but it must be intended for future use (see *R v Ellames* [1974] 1 WLR 1391). Proof of intent is required and not mere contemplation of an offence (see *R v Hargreaves* [1985] Crim LR 243).

See *Blackstone's Criminal Practice 2026* **B4.150**

C16.12 Handling stolen goods

Theft Act 1968, s 22(1)

22 Handling stolen goods

(1) A person handles stolen goods if (otherwise than in the course of the stealing) knowing or believing them to be stolen goods he dishonestly receives the goods, or dishonestly undertakes or assists in their retention, removal, disposal or realisation by or for the benefit of another person, or if he arranges to do so.

EW

12 months' imprisonment and/or fine/14 years' imprisonment

C16.12.1 *Sentencing*

SCG Handling stolen goods

C16.12.2 Key points

- Mere suspicion that goods are stolen will not suffice.
- In *R v Hall* (1985) 81 Cr App R 260, belief was said to be present when someone thought: 'I cannot say for certain that those goods are stolen, but there can be no other reasonable conclusion in the light of all the circumstances of all I have heard and seen.' Similarly if the person admits that 'my brain is telling me [they are stolen] despite what I have heard'.
- If the defendant argues that he has paid an adequate consideration for the goods, it falls upon the prosecution to disprove (*Hogan v DPP* [2007] EWHC 978 (Admin)).

See *Blackstone's Criminal Practice 2026* B4.159

C16.13 Making, adapting, supplying, or offering to supply articles for fraud

Fraud Act 2006, s 7

7 Making or supplying articles for use in frauds

(1) A person is guilty of an offence if he makes, adapts, supplies or offers to supply any article—
  (a) knowing that it is designed or adapted for use in the course of or in connection with fraud, or
  (b) intending it to be used to commit, or assist in the commission of, fraud.

EW

Fine and/or 12 months'/10 years' imprisonment

C16.13.1 *Sentencing*

SCG Possession of articles for use in frauds/Making or supplying articles for use in frauds

C16.13.2 Key points

For definition of an 'article', see **C16.18.2**.

See *Blackstone's Criminal Practice 2026* **B5.25**

C16.14 Making off without payment

Theft Act 1978, s 3

3 Making off without payment

(1) Subject to subsection (3) below, a person who, knowing that payment on the spot for any goods supplied or service done is required or expected from him, dishonestly makes off without having paid as required or expected and with intent to avoid payment of the amount due shall be guilty of an offence.
(2) For purposes of this section 'payment on the spot' includes payment at the time of collecting goods on which work has been done or in respect of which service has been provided.
(3) Subsection (1) above shall not apply where the supply of the goods or the doing of the service is contrary to law, or where the service done is such that payment is not legally enforceable.

EW

12 months' imprisonment and/or fine/2 years' imprisonment

C16.14.1 *Sentencing*

SCG Making Off Without Payment

C16.14.2 Key points

The intention to avoid making payment means a permanent intention not to pay, so a person who genuinely disputes a bill and challenges someone to bring legal action cannot be said to have committed an offence.

See *Blackstone's Criminal Practice 2026* **B5.39**

C16.15 Money laundering

Proceeds of Crime Act 2002, ss 327–329

327 Concealing etc

(1) A person commits an offence if he—
- (a) conceals criminal property;
- (b) disguises criminal property;
- (c) converts criminal property;
- (d) transfers criminal property;
- (e) removes criminal property from England and Wales or from Scotland or from Northern Ireland.

(2) But a person does not commit such an offence if—
- (a) he makes an authorised disclosure under section 338 and (if the disclosure is made before he does the act mentioned in subsection (1)) he has the appropriate consent;
- (b) he intended to make such a disclosure but had a reasonable excuse for not doing so;
- (c) the act he does is done in carrying out a function he has relating to the enforcement of any provision of this Act or of any other enactment relating to criminal conduct or benefit from criminal conduct . . .

(2C) A deposit-taking body that does an act mentioned in paragraph (c) or (d) of subsection (1) does not commit an offence under that subsection if—
- (a) it does the act in operating an account maintained with it, and
- (b) the value of the criminal property concerned is less than the threshold amount determined under section 339A for the act.

(3) Concealing or disguising criminal property includes concealing or disguising its nature, source, location, disposition, movement or ownership or any rights with respect to it.

328 Arrangements

(1) A person commits an offence if he enters into or becomes concerned in an arrangement which he knows or suspects facilitates (by whatever means) the acquisition, retention, use or control of criminal property by or on behalf of another person.

(2) But a person does not commit such an offence if—
- (a) he makes an authorised disclosure under section 338 and (if the disclosure is made before he does the act mentioned in subsection (1)) he has the appropriate consent;
- (b) he intended to make such a disclosure but had a reasonable excuse for not doing so;
- (c) the act he does is done in carrying out a function he has relating to the enforcement of any provision of this Act or of any other enactment relating to criminal conduct or benefit from criminal conduct.

329 Acquisition, use and possession

(1) A person commits an offence if he—
- (a) acquires criminal property;
- (b) uses criminal property;
- (c) has possession of criminal property.

(2) But a person does not commit such an offence if—
- (a) he makes an authorised disclosure under section 338 and (if the disclosure is made before he does the act mentioned in subsection (1)) he has the appropriate consent;

> (b) he intended to make such a disclosure but had a reasonable excuse for not doing so;
> (c) he acquired or used or had possession of the property for adequate consideration;
> (d) the act he does is done in carrying out a function he has relating to the enforcement of any provision of this Act or of any other enactment relating to criminal conduct or benefit from criminal conduct.
>
> (3) For the purposes of this section—
> (a) a person acquires property for inadequate consideration if the value of the consideration is significantly less than the value of the property;
> (b) a person uses or has possession of property for inadequate consideration if the value of the consideration is significantly less than the value of the use or possession;
> (c) the provision by a person of goods or services which he knows or suspects may help another to carry out criminal conduct.

The critical definitions for these offences are contained in s 340 Proceeds of Crime Act 2002:

> **Proceeds of Crime Act 2002, s 340(2)–(4)(b)**
>
> **340 Interpretation**
>
> (2) Criminal conduct is conduct which—
> (a) constitutes an offence in any part of the United Kingdom, or
> (b) would constitute an offence in any part of the United Kingdom if it occurred there.
>
> (3) Property is criminal property if—
> (a) it constitutes a person's benefit from criminal conduct or it represents such a benefit (in whole or part and whether directly or indirectly), and
> (b) the alleged offender knows or suspects that it constitutes or represents such a benefit.
>
> (4) It is immaterial—
> (a) who carried out the conduct;
> (b) who benefited from it;
> ...

EW

Fine and/or 12 months'/14 years' imprisonment

C16.15.1 *Sentencing*

SCG Money laundering

Key points: Sentencing

Following *R v Cooper; R v Park; R v Fletcher* [2023] EWCA Crim 945, when sentencing a defendant for a money laundering offence contrary to ss 327 to 329 of the Proceeds of Crime Act 2002 in respect of the criminal benefit from offences for which the defendant also falls to be sentenced, the principle of totality should operate as follows:

(a) Where the 2002 Act offence adds nothing to the culpability and harm involved in the primary offence then there should be no additional penalty. In such a case it is appropriate to impose concurrent sentences, with no upward adjustment.

(b) Where the 2002 Act offence involves additional criminality (whether increasing the culpability or harm, or both) beyond that involved in the other offences for which sentences are imposed, an additional penalty should be imposed. The seriousness of the additional criminality is to be assessed by reference to the culpability of the offender and the harm caused by the 2002 Act offending. In such a case the sentencing judge may either impose concurrent sentences with an appropriate upward adjustment, or consecutive sentences, often with a downward adjustment.

C16.15.2 Key points

- As set out in *R (World Uyghur Congress) v National Crime Agency* [2024] EWCA Civ 715):

  The concept of 'criminal property' is not only very broadly expressed, but it is a fluid one which depends on the state of mind of the alleged offender. The property in question must not only be or represent a benefit from someone's criminal conduct, but the alleged offender must know or suspect that to be the case at the time of carrying out one of the activities prohibited by sections 327 to 329. This means that the same property can be criminal property in the hands of A but not criminal property in the hands of B, depending on their respective states of mind.

  ...

  The provision of 'adequate consideration' by someone who can rely on section 329(2)(c) does not preclude the property from being 'criminal property' in the hands of someone else with the requisite knowledge or suspicion.

- Knowledge of a potential breach of trust was not of itself the same as knowledge or suspicion of crime. That the defendant ought to have known is not enough (*Holt v Attorney General* [2014] UKPC 4).
- In *Wilkinson v DPP* [2006] EWHC 3012 (Admin), the court discouraged the use of this offence (with its requirement only for suspicion rather than belief) when a handling charge would adequately have reflected the seriousness of the offence.
- For there to be an offence there must be actual criminal conduct and the proceeds must already be the product of that crime (*R v Gabriel* [2006] EWCA Crim 229). However, a court might decide that 'clean' money had changed its nature and become 'criminal property' because it was obtained by fraud (*R v GH* [2015] UKSC 24). This case also confirmed that the money need not be 'criminal property' at the moment the parties come to a prohibited arrangement, but it must amount to 'criminal property' at the time the arrangement begins to operate upon it.
- *R v Ogden* [2016] EWCA Crim 6 confirms that an offence of conspiracy to convert criminal property (s 327 Proceeds of Crime Act 2000) is committed when A, who is in possession of controlled drugs, agrees to supply B with what B is aware is a controlled drug. The drugs are criminal property.

- There are two ways in which the Crown can prove that the property derives from crime. Either:
  - by showing that it derives from criminal conduct of a specific kind; or
  - by proving that the circumstances in which it was handled create an irresistible inference that it can only have derived from crime (*Kuchhadia v R* [2015] EWCA Crim 1252).
- *R v Rogers (Bradley)* [2014] EWCA Crim 1680 confirms that payments into a Spanish bank account by reason of frauds committed in England are amenable to the jurisdiction of the English courts, as ss 327–329 Proceeds of Crime Act 2002 have extraterritorial effect.
- Sections 327 and 328 provide defences, in defined circumstances, when the relevant criminal conduct occurred in a particular country or territory outside the United Kingdom.

See *Blackstone's Criminal Practice 2026* B21

C16.16 **Obtaining services dishonestly**

Fraud Act 2006, s 11(1) and (2)

11 Obtaining services dishonestly

(1) A person is guilty of an offence under this section if he obtains services for himself or another—
  (a) by a dishonest act, and
  (b) in breach of subsection (2).
(2) A person obtains services in breach of this subsection if—
  (a) they are made available on the basis that payment has been, is being or will be made for or in respect of them,
  (b) he obtains them without any payment having been made for or in respect of them or without payment having been made in full, and
  (c) when he obtains them, he knows—
    (i) that they are being made available on the basis described in paragraph (a), or
    (ii) that they might be, but intends that payment will not be made, or will not be made in full.

EW

Fine and/or 12 months'/5 years' imprisonment

C16.16.1 ***Sentencing***

The offence of *obtaining services dishonestly* may be committed in circumstances that otherwise could be charged as an offence contrary to s 1 Fraud Act 2006, or may be more akin to *making off without payment*, contrary to s 3 Theft Act 1978. For this reason, it has not been included specifically within any of the guidelines for fraud, and one of the following approaches should be used:

- where it involves conduct which can be characterized as a fraud offence (such as obtaining credit through fraud or payment card fraud), the court should apply the guideline for the relevant type of fraud (see SCG Fraud); or

- where the conduct could be characterized as *making off without payment* (ie where an offender, knowing that payment on the spot for any goods supplied or service done is required or expected, dishonestly makes off without having paid and with intent to avoid payment), the guideline for that offence should be used (SCG Making off without payment).

See *Blackstone's Criminal Practice 2026* **B5.32**

C16.17 **Pet Abduction**

Pet Abduction Act 2024, ss 1 and 2

1 Dog abduction

(1) A person (A) commits the offence of dog abduction if they—
 (a) take a dog so as to remove it from the lawful control of any person, or
 (b) detain a dog so as to keep it from the lawful control of any person who is entitled to have lawful control of it,
 and A and the dog are both in England or Northern Ireland at the time the dog is taken or detained.

(2) The offence of dog abduction is not committed if—
 (a) at any time before the taking or detention of the dog—
  (i) the person (A) who took or detained the dog,
  (ii) the person (B) from whose lawful control it was taken or detained, and
  (iii) the dog,
 all lived together in the same household,
 (a) A and B had been living together before the dog began to live with them,
 (b) A and B subsequently ceased to live together, and
 (c) A took or detained the dog at or after the time when A and B ceased to live together.

. . .

(8) In this section—
 (a) references to a person taking a dog include the person—
  (i) causing or inducing the dog to accompany the person or anyone else, or
  (ii) causing the dog to be taken, and
 (b) references to a person detaining a dog include the person—
  (i) causing or inducing the dog to remain with the person or anyone else, or
  (ii) causing the dog to be detained.

2 Cat abduction

(1) A person (A) commits the offence of cat abduction if—
 (a) they take a cat so as to remove it from the lawful control of any person, and
 (b) A and the cat are both in England or Northern Ireland at the time the cat is taken.

(2) The offence of cat abduction is not committed if—
 (a) at any time before the taking of the cat—
  (i) the person (A) who took the cat,
  (ii) the person (B) from whose lawful control it was taken, and
  (iii) the cat,
 all lived together in the same household,
 (b) A and B had been living together before the cat began to live with them,
 (c) A and B subsequently ceased to live together, and
 (d) A took the cat at or after the time when A and B ceased to live together.

. . .

(6) In this section, references to a person taking a cat include the person—
 (a) causing or inducing the cat to accompany the person or anyone else, or
 (b) causing the cat to be taken.

EW

Fine and/or 12 months'/5 years' imprisonment

C16.17.1 Key points

Defences:

Pet Abduction Act 2024, ss 1(3) and (4) and 2(3) and (4)

1 Dog abduction

(3) It is a defence for a person charged with the offence of dog abduction to show that the person had lawful authority or a reasonable excuse for taking or detaining the dog.
(4) In relation to England, it is a defence for a person charged with the offence of dog abduction by virtue of subsection (1)(b) to show that the person—
 (a) believed that the dog was a stray dog,
 (b) took all reasonable steps to comply with section 150(1) of the Environmental Protection Act 1990 (delivery of stray dogs to owner or officer of local authority), and
 (c) did not detain the dog for more than 96 hours (disregarding any period during which it is kept by virtue of section 150(2)(a) of that Act).

2 Cat abduction

(1) It is a defence for a person charged with the offence of cat abduction to show that the person had lawful authority or a reasonable excuse for taking the cat.
(2) A person is taken to have shown a fact mentioned in subsection (3) if—
 (a) sufficient evidence of the fact is adduced to raise an issue with respect to it, and
 (b) the contrary is not proved beyond reasonable doubt.

C16.18 Possession of articles for fraud

Fraud Act 2006, s 6

6 Possession etc of articles for use in frauds

(1) A person is guilty of an offence if he has in his possession or under his control any article for use in the course of or in connection with any fraud.

EW

Fine and/or 12 months'/5 years' imprisonment

C16.18.1 *Sentencing*

SCG **Possession of articles for use in frauds/Making or supplying articles for use in frauds**

C16.18.2 Key points

Section 8 provides:

> **Fraud Act 2006, s 8**
>
> **8 'Article'**
>
> (1) For the purposes of—
> (a) sections 6 and 7, and
> (b) the provisions listed in subsection (2), so far as they relate to articles for use in the course of or in connection with fraud, 'article' includes any program or data held in electronic form.

R v Sakalauskas [2013] EWCA Crim 2278 confirms that an 'article' in s 6 Fraud Act 2006 (as is the case under s 25 Theft Act 1968) meant any article that the defendant had with him for the purposes of fraud but not articles which he had possessed for that purpose in the past. However whilst the intention must be to use the article in connection with fraud at the time or in the future, they could include articles that were used to mislead a victim or created later to disguise a fraud (*R v Smith* [2020] EWCA Crim 38).

See *Blackstone's Criminal Practice 2026* **B5.22**

C16.19 Railway fare evasion

Regulation of Railways Act 1889, s 5(1) (failing to produce ticket) and (3) (travelling on railway without paying fare, with intent to avoid payment);

SO

Level 3 fine or 3 months' imprisonment (s 5(3) level 2 fine (s 5(1))

C16.19.1 *Sentencing*

SCG Railway fare evasion

C16.20 Robbery and assault with intent to rob

> **Theft Act 1968, s 8**
>
> (1) A person is guilty of robbery if he steals, and immediately before or at the time of doing so, and in order to do so, he uses force on any person or puts or seeks to put any person in fear of being then and there subjected to force.
> (2) A person guilty of robbery, or of an assault with intent to rob, shall on conviction on indictment be liable to imprisonment for life.

IO

Life

DO

GC

C16.20.1 *Sentencing*

SCG **Robbery—street and less sophisticated commercial/Robbery—professionally planned commercial/Robbery—dwelling**

A separate guideline applies for children and young people and appears in the *Handbook for Youths in the Criminal Courts.*

C16.20.2 Key points

- Force may be used indirectly, for example wrenching a bag from a victim's hand: *R v Clouden* [1987] Crim LR 56. Snatching a cigarette from the victim's hand was not robbery in *P v DPP* [2012] EWHC 1657 (Admin).
- Force must be used or threatened immediately before or at the time of stealing: *R v Vinall* [2011] EWCA Crim 6252.
- The force must be connected to the stealing: *R v Shendley* [1970] Crim LR 49.
- The elements of theft must be present: dishonesty, an intention to deprive permanently, and appropriation. See **C16.22**
- There must be intention or at least recklessness as to the use of force.

See *Blackstone's Criminal Practice 2026* **B4.66**

C16.21 Tax credit fraud

Tax Credits Act 2002, s 35

35 Offence of fraud

EW

Fine and/or 12 months'/7 years' imprisonment

C16.21.1 *Sentencing*

Consider **SCG Revenue fraud**

C16.21.2 Key points

- Disposing of the proceeds of fraud amounts to a fraudulent activity (*R v Kolapo* [2009] EWCA Crim 545).

- *R v Nolan and Howard* [2012] EWCA Crim 671 confirmed that the passive receipt of moneys and failure to report did not amount to 'fraudulent activity', which requires a positive act of misrepresentation with a view to gain. The statute requires behaviour calculated to achieve, rather than to capitalize on what had already been achieved.
- This is an offence of specific intention, requiring proof by the prosecution of 'knowledge'. Knowing connotes something more than mere recklessness (*R v Godir* [2018] EWCA Crim 2294).

C16.22 **Theft**

Theft Act 1968, s 1(1) and (2)

1 Basic definition of theft

(1) A person is guilty of theft if he dishonestly appropriates property belonging to another with the intention of permanently depriving the other of it; and 'thief' and 'steal' shall be construed accordingly.
(2) It is immaterial whether the appropriation is made with a view to gain, or is made for the thief's own benefit.

EW

卌 Low-value theft from a shop tried summarily: 6 months' imprisonment and/or a fine

Other offences: 12 months' imprisonment and/or fine/7 years' imprisonment

C16.22.1 ***Sentencing***

SCG Theft

Including:

Theft from the person

Theft in a dwelling

Theft in breach of trust

Theft from motor vehicle

Theft of a motor vehicle

Theft of a pedal bicycle

and all other s 1 Theft Act 1968 offences, but excluding theft from a shop or stall.

SCG **Theft from a shop or stall**

Key points: Sentencing

Targeting the same store three times in three weeks is not of itself evidence of 'significant planning' (*R v Gheorghe* [2021] EWCA Crim 1168). For there to be significant planning, one would normally expect to see some degree of sophistication.

C16.22.1.1 ***Prevalence***

There may be exceptional local circumstances that arise which may lead a court to decide that prevalence should influence sentencing levels. The pivotal issue in such cases will be the harm caused to the community. It is essential that the court, before taking account of prevalence:

- has supporting evidence from an external source, for example, community impact statements, to justify claims that a particular crime is prevalent in their area, and is causing particular harm in that community, and
- is satisfied that there is a compelling need to treat the offence more seriously than elsewhere

See *R v Bondzie* [2016] EWCA Crim 552.

C16.22.2 **Key points**

Dishonesty is interpreted in accordance with *Ivey v Genting Casinos (UK) Ltd* (t/ a Crockfords) [2017] UKSC 67 and *R v Barton and Booth* [2020] EWCA Crim 576.

The court must first ascertain (subjectively) the actual state of the individual's knowledge or belief as to the facts. Once the actual state of mind as to knowledge or belief as to facts is established, the question whether his conduct was honest or dishonest is to be determined by the fact-finder by applying the (objective) standards of ordinary decent people. There is no requirement that the defendant must appreciate that what he has done is, by those standards, dishonest. The court in *Barton* summarizes the law:

> 108. . . . All matters that lead an accused to act as he or she did will form part of the subjective mental state, thereby forming a part of the fact-finding exercise before applying the objective standard. That will include consideration, where relevant, of the experience and intelligence of an accused . . . the visitor to London who fails to pay for a bus journey believing it to be free (as it is, for example, in Luxembourg) would be no more dishonest than the diner or shopper who genuinely forgets to pay before leaving a restaurant or shop. The Magistrates or jury in such cases would first establish the facts and then apply an objective standard of dishonesty to those facts.

'Dishonestly' is considered in s 2 Theft Act 1968:

Theft Act 1968, s 2

2 'Dishonestly'

(1) A person's appropriation of property belonging to another is not to be regarded as dishonest—

(a) if he appropriates the property in the belief that he has in law the right to deprive the other of it, on behalf of himself or of a third person; or

(b) if he appropriates the property in the belief that he would have the other's consent if the other knew of the appropriation and the circumstances of it; or
(c) (except where the property came to him as trustee or personal representative) if he appropriates the property in the belief that the person to whom the property belongs cannot be discovered by taking reasonable steps.

(2) A person's appropriation of property belonging to another may be dishonest notwithstanding that he is willing to pay for the property. 'Appropriation' means the assumption of any of the rights of an owner (*R v Gomez* [1993] AC 442).

According to *R v Mahmud* [2024] EWCA Crim 130, in order for s 2 to apply, it is not necessary for a person to have said that they thought they were entitled to the property in law, using that express term. Most members of the public cannot be expected to be aware of the nuances of the civil law governing the passing of property. It will be a matter of inference in most cases as to whether a person holds a belief about legal entitlement or merely by reference to some non-legal concept of fairness.

The intention permanently to deprive is also considered in s 6 Theft Act 1968:

Theft Act 1968, s 6

6 'With the intention of permanently depriving the other of it'

(1) A person appropriating property belonging to another without meaning the other permanently to lose the thing itself is nevertheless to be regarded as having the intention of permanently depriving the other of it if his intention is to treat the thing as his own to dispose of regardless of the other's rights; and a borrowing or lending of it may amount to so treating it if, but only if, the borrowing or lending is for a period and in circumstances making it equivalent to an outright taking or disposal.

(2) Without prejudice to the generality of subsection (1) above, where a person, having possession or control (lawfully or not) of property belonging to another, parts with the property under a condition as to its return which he may not be able to perform, this (if done for purposes of his own and without the other's authority) amounts to treating the property as his own to dispose of regardless of the other's rights.

C16.22.3 ***Low-value shoplifting***

Low-value shoplifting is triable only summarily unless an adult defendant elects for trial on indictment.

Magistrates' Courts Act 1980, s 22A

(3) 'Low-value shoplifting' means an offence under section 1 of the Theft Act 1968 in circumstances where—
(a) the value of the stolen goods does not exceed £200,
(b) the goods were being offered for sale in a shop or any other premises, stall, vehicle or place from which there is carried on a trade or business, and
(c) at the time of the offence, the person accused of low-value shoplifting was, or was purporting to be, a customer or potential customer of the person offering the goods for sale.

(4) For the purposes of subsection (3)(a)—
(a) the value of the stolen goods is the price at which they were being offered for sale at the time of the offence, and

(b) where the accused is charged on the same occasion with two or more offences of low-value shoplifting, the reference to the value involved has effect as if it were a reference to the aggregate of the values involved . . .

The value of the stolen goods is calculated by adding the values of all the allegations placed before the court on a single occasion (*R v Harvey* [2020] EWCA Crim 354). It is possible in law to attempt this offence (Criminal Attempts Act 1981, s 1(5)). Low-value shoplifting offences are not subject to the six-month time limit for starting a prosecution for summary-only offences under the MCA 1980, s 127. (*Candlish v DPP* [2022] EWHC 842 (Admin).)

SO unless an adult defendant elects for trial on indictment

6 months' imprisonment and/or fine

In the Crown Court if the defendant elects (or the aggregate value exceeds £200) 7 years but should not normally exceed 12 months (*R v Chamberlin* [2017] EWCA Crim 39). Only the defendant can elect for Crown Court trial.

See *Blackstone's Criminal Practice 2026* B4.1

C16.23 **Trespass against property**

C16.23.1 ***Squatting***

Legal Aid, Sentencing and Punishment of Offenders Act 2012, s 144

144 Offence of squatting in a residential building

(1) A person commits an offence if—
  (a) the person is in a residential building as a trespasser having entered it as a trespasser,
  (b) the person knows or ought to know that he or she is a trespasser, and
  (c) the person is living in the building or intends to live there for any period.

(2) The offence is not committed by a person holding over after the end of a lease or licence (even if the person leaves and re-enters the building).

(3) For the purposes of this section—
  (a) 'building' includes any structure or part of a structure (including a temporary or moveable structure), and
  (b) a building is 'residential' if it is designed or adapted, before the time of entry, for use as a place to live.

(4) For the purposes of this section the fact that a person derives title from a trespasser, or has the permission of a trespasser, does not prevent the person from being a trespasser.

SO

Fine and/or 6 months' imprisonment

C16.23.2 Key points

It will be necessary to check that there was not even an informal licence; and whether a person intends to 'live' rather than stay temporarily will be a matter of fact in each case.

See *Blackstone's Criminal Practice 2026* B13.31

C16.23.3 *Aggravated trespass*

Criminal Justice and Public Order Act 1994, s 68(1) and (2)

68 Offence of aggravated trespass

(1) A person commits the offence of aggravated trespass if he trespasses on land and, in relation to any lawful activity which persons are engaging in or are about to engage in on that or adjoining land, does there anything which is intended by him to have the effect—
  (a) of intimidating those persons or any of them so as to deter them or any of them from engaging in that activity,
  (b) of obstructing that activity, or
  (c) of disrupting that activity.

(2) Activity on any occasion on the part of a person or persons on land is 'lawful' for the purposes of this section if he or they may engage in the activity on the land on that occasion without committing an offence or trespassing on the land.

SO

Level 4 fine and/or 3 months' imprisonment

C16.23.4 Key points

- There are four elements to the offence (*Richardson v DPP* [2014] UKSC 8; *Barnard v DPP* [2000] Crim LR 371):
  - The defendant must trespass on land,
  - Where a lawful activity is engaged,
  - With the intention to have any one of the three effects specified (*Tilly v DPP* [2001] EWHC 821 (Admin)),
  - Commit an act towards that end. This must be distinct from the act of trespass (*Peppersharp v DPP* [2012] EWHC 474 (Admin)). However, a mass entry and demonstration would, on particular facts, meet this need if there was an intimidatory effect to prevent people from engaging in a lawful activity (*Bauer and others* [2013] EWHC 634 (Admin)).
- It is not necessary for the prosecution to prove that the defendant either knew they were or was reckless as to whether they were trespassing (*DPP v Bailey and others* [2022] EWHC 3302 (Admin)).
- Actual disruption is not required if the necessary intention is proved (*Winder v DPP* (1996) 160 JP 713).

- In *Tilly v DPP* [2001] EWHC 821 (Admin) it was held that activity takes place only if there is someone physically on the land who is not allowed to go on with what he is entitled to do. However, in *DPP v Highbury Corner Magistrates' Court (Stephenson-Clarke and others, interested parties)* [2022] EWHC 3207 (Admin) it was said in *obiter* that it is open to argument that the offence may be committed where the person undertaking the lawful activity is not physically present on the land, particularly where, for example, the offence is based on an anticipated lawful activity.
- The offence is compatible with the ECHR. There is no requirement for the Crown to prove proportionality with convention rights (*DPP v Cuciurean* [2022] EWHC 736 (Admin)).
- If the defence are relying on the lack of lawful activity as a defence they must, by evidence, raise the issue of a specific criminal offence in English law, by the landowner. If that is done the burden passes to the Crown to disprove that proposition to the criminal standard. Not every incidental or collateral criminal offence can properly be said to affect the lawfulness of an activity, nor to render it criminal. It will do so only when the criminal offence is integral to the core activity carried on. It will not do so when there is some incidental or collateral offence, which is remote from the activity (*Richardson v DPP* [2014] UKSC 8).
- The defence must provide evidence of actual use or enjoyment of the way as of right for 20 years before there is any burden on the Crown to establish that it is not a highway (*DPP v Instone* 2022 EWHC 1840 (Admin))

See *Blackstone's Criminal Practice 2026* **B13.45**

C16.24 TWOC (vehicle-taking without consent)

Theft Act 1968, s 12(1), (5), (6), and (7)

12 Taking motor vehicle or other conveyance without authority

(1) Subject to subsections (5) and (6) below, a person shall be guilty of an offence if, without having the consent of the owner or other lawful authority, he takes any conveyance for his own or another's use or knowing that any conveyance has been taken without such authority, drives it or allows himself to be carried in or on it.

...

(5) Subsection (1) above shall not apply in relation to pedal cycles; but, subject to subsection (6) below, a person who, without having the consent of the owner or other lawful authority, takes a pedal cycle for his own or another's use, or rides a pedal cycle knowing it to have been taken without such authority, shall on summary conviction be liable to a fine not exceeding level 3 on the standard scale.

(6) A person does not commit an offence under this section by anything done in the belief that he has lawful authority to do it or that he would have the owner's consent if the owner knew of his doing it and the circumstances of it.

(7) For purposes of this section—

(a) 'conveyance' means any conveyance constructed or adapted for the carriage of a person or persons whether by land, water or air, except that it does not include a conveyance constructed or adapted for use only under the control of a person not carried in or on it, and 'drive' shall be construed accordingly; and

(b) 'owner', in relation to a conveyance which is the subject of a hiring agreement or hire-purchase agreement, means the person in possession of the conveyance under that agreement.

SO

Fine and/or 6 months' imprisonment

C16.24.1 *Sentencing*

SCG **Vehicle taking without consent**

C16.24.2 Key points

This offence is summary only, but subject to the following exception in relation to limitation period. On time limits see **A12.1.2**. Section 12(4A)–(4C) of the Act provides:

Theft Act 1968, s 12(4A)–(4C)

(4A) Proceedings for an offence under subsection (1) above (but not proceedings of a kind falling within subsection (4) above) in relation to a mechanically propelled vehicle—

(a) shall not be commenced after the end of the period of three years beginning with the day on which the offence was committed; but

(b) subject to that, may be commenced at any time within the period of six months beginning with the relevant day.

(4B) In subsection (4A)(b) above 'the relevant day' means—

(a) in the case of a prosecution for an offence under subsection (1) above by a public prosecutor, the day on which sufficient evidence to justify the proceedings came to the knowledge of any person responsible for deciding whether to commence any such prosecution;

(b) in the case of a prosecution for an offence under subsection (1) above which is commenced by a person other than a public prosecutor after the discontinuance of a prosecution falling within paragraph (a) above which relates to the same facts, the day on which sufficient evidence to justify the proceedings came to the knowledge of the person who has decided to commence the prosecution or (if later) the discontinuance of the other prosecution;

(c) in the case of any other prosecution for an offence under subsection (1) above, the day on which sufficient evidence to justify the proceedings came to the knowledge of the person who has decided to commence the prosecution.

(4C) For the purposes of subsection (4A)(b) above a certificate of a person responsible for deciding whether to commence a prosecution of a kind mentioned in subsection (4B)(a) above as to the date on which such evidence as is mentioned in the certificate came to the knowledge of any person responsible for deciding whether to commence any such prosecution shall be conclusive evidence of that fact.

- There must be movement for a vehicle to be taken (*R v Bogacki* [1973] QB 832). The vehicle must be taken as a conveyance (*R v Stokes* [1983] RTR 59). The burden of proving that the defendant did not have a belief that he had the authority of the owner lies on the Crown once the defendant has raised the issue by evidence (*R v Gannon* (1987) 87 Cr App R 254). The belief must exist at the time of the taking (*R v Ambler* [1979] RTR 217).
- Formal evidence of ownership may not be necessary where it is possible to infer from the facts that the cycle had not been abandoned: *Sturrock v DPP* [1996] RTR 216.

See *Blackstone's Criminal Practice 2026* **B4.116**

C16.25 Unauthorized use of trade mark, etc

Trade Marks Act 1994, s 92(1)–(4)

92 Unauthorised use of trade mark, etc in relation to goods

(1) A person commits an offence who with a view to gain for himself or another, or with intent to cause loss to another, and without the consent of the proprietor—
  (a) applies to goods or their packaging a sign identical to, or likely to be mistaken for, a registered trade mark, or
  (b) sells or lets for hire, offers or exposes for sale or hire or distributes goods which bear, or the packaging of which bears, such a sign, or
  (c) has in his possession, custody or control in the course of a business any such goods with a view to the doing of anything, by himself or another, which would be an offence under paragraph (b).

(2) A person commits an offence who with a view to gain for himself or another, or with intent to cause loss to another, and without the consent of the proprietor—
  (a) applies a sign identical to, or likely to be mistaken for, a registered trade mark to material intended to be used—
    (i) for labelling or packaging goods,
    (ii) as a business paper in relation to goods, or
    (iii) for advertising goods, or
  (b) uses in the course of a business material bearing such a sign for labelling or packaging goods, as a business paper in relation to goods, or for advertising goods, or
  (c) has in his possession, custody or control in the course of a business any such material with a view to the doing of anything, by himself or another, which would be an offence under paragraph (b).

(3) A person commits an offence who with a view to gain for himself or another, or with intent to cause loss to another, and without the consent of the proprietor—
  (a) makes an article specifically designed or adapted for making copies of a sign identical to, or likely to be mistaken for, a registered trade mark, or
  (b) has such an article in his possession, custody or control in the course of a business,

knowing or having reason to believe that it has been, or is to be, used to produce goods, or material for labelling or packaging goods, as a business paper in relation to goods, or for advertising goods.

(4) A person does not commit an offence under this section unless—
  (a) the goods are goods in respect of which the trade mark is registered, or

(b) the trade mark has a reputation in the United Kingdom and the use of the sign takes or would take unfair advantage of, or is or would be detrimental to, the distinctive character or the repute of the trade mark.

(5) It is a defence for a person charged with an offence under this section to show that he believed on reasonable grounds that the use of the sign in the manner in which it was used, or was to be used, was not an infringement of the registered trade mark.

EW

Fine and/or 12 months'/10 years' imprisonment

C16.25.1 *Sentencing*

SCG Trade marks unauthorised use of etc.

C16.25.2 Key points

It is a defence for a person charged with an offence under s 92 to show that he believed on reasonable grounds that the use of the sign in the manner in which it was used, or was to be used, was not an infringement of the registered trade mark. In order to be able to satisfy the statutory defence under s 95(2) Trade Marks Act 1994, the defendant must show not only that he had an honest belief that the trade marks did not infringe registered trade marks, but also that he had reasonable grounds for so believing. Section 97 makes provision for the forfeiture of counterfeit goods and packaging.

R v C and others [2017] UKSC 58 holds that a criminal offence can be committed where the proprietor of the registered trade mark has given his consent to the application of the sign that is its registered trade mark, or has itself applied its own registered trade mark, to the goods, but has not given his consent to the sale, distribution, or possession of them.

See *Blackstone's Criminal Practice 2026* B6.100

C16.26 Use of threat or violence for the purpose of securing entry to premises

Criminal Law Act 1977, s 6

6 Violence for securing entry

(1) Subject to the following provisions of this section, any person who, without lawful authority, uses or threatens violence for the purpose of securing entry into any premises for himself or for any other person is guilty of an offence, provided that—

(a) there is someone present on those premises at the time who is opposed to the entry which the violence is intended to secure; and

(b) the person using or threatening the violence knows that that is the case.

(1A) Subsection (1) above does not apply to a person who is a displaced residential occupier or a protected intending occupier of the premises in question or who is acting on behalf of such an occupier; and if the accused adduces sufficient evidence that he was, or was acting on behalf of, such an occupier he shall be presumed to be, or to be acting on behalf of, such an occupier unless the contrary is proved by the prosecution.

(2) Subject to subsection (1A) above, the fact that a person has any interest in or right to possession or occupation of any premises shall not for the purposes of subsection (1) above constitute lawful authority for the use or threat of violence by him or anyone else for the purpose of securing his entry into those premises.

(3) (repealed).

(4) It is immaterial for the purposes of this section—
- (a) whether the violence in question is directed against the person or against property; and
- (b) whether the entry which the violence is intended to secure is for the purpose of acquiring possession of the premises in question or for any other purpose.

SO

Fine and/or 6 months' imprisonment

C16.26.1

The terms premises, displaced residential occupier, and protected intending occupier are defined by ss 12 and 12A Criminal Law Act 1977.

See *Blackstone's Criminal Practice 2026* B13.23

C16.27 **Vehicle interference**

Criminal Attempts Act 1981, s 9(1) and (2)

9 Interference with vehicles

(1) A person is guilty of the offence of vehicle interference if he interferes with a motor vehicle or trailer or with anything carried in or on a motor vehicle or trailer with the intention that an offence specified in subsection (2) below shall be committed by himself or some other person.

(2) The offences mentioned in subsection (1) above are—
- (a) theft of the motor vehicle or trailer or part of it;
- (b) theft of anything carried in or on the motor vehicle or trailer; and
- (c) an offence under section 12(1) of the Theft Act 1968 (taking and driving away without consent);

and, if it is shown that a person accused of an offence under this section intended that one of those offences should be committed, it is immaterial that it cannot be shown which it was.

SO

Level 4 fine and/or 3 months' imprisonment

C16.27.1 *Sentencing*

SCG Vehicle interference

See *Blackstone's Criminal Practice 2026* B4.136

C16.28 Vehicle licence/registration fraud

Vehicle Excise and Registration Act 1994, s 44(1) and (2)

44 Forgery and fraud

(1) A person is guilty of an offence if he forges, fraudulently alters, fraudulently uses, fraudulently lends or fraudulently allows to be used by another person anything to which subsection (2) applies

(2) This subsection applies to—

. . .

(d) a registration mark,

(e) a registration document, and

(f) a trade plate (including a replacement trade plate).

EW

Fine only/2 years' imprisonment

Note: There are offences carrying the same penalties under s 173 (forgery of documents, etc.). Under s 174 (making certain false statements, etc, and withholding certain material information) Road Traffic Act 1988, the penalties are 12 months' imprisonment/fine/2 years.

C16.28.1 *Sentencing*

SCG Vehicle licence/registration fraud

See *Blackstone's Criminal Practice 2026* C4.9

C17 Offences against the Person

C17.1 General matters

C17.1.1 *Defences*

Key points: General defence The following defences should be considered:

- **Consent**, although *R v Brown* [1994] 1 AC 212 limits the application of this defence in sado-masochistic situations. It remains available, for instance, in sport or medical treatment, or where a wife agrees to be 'branded' (*R v Wilson* [1996] 2 Cr App R 241), but in addition s 71 Domestic Abuse Act 2021 provides:

Domestic Abuse Act 2021

S 71 Consent to serious harm for sexual gratification not a defence

. . .

(2) It is not a defence that V consented to the infliction of the serious harm for the purposes of obtaining sexual gratification (but see subsection (4)) . . .
(4) Subsection (2) does not apply in the case of an offence under section 20 or 47 of the 1861 Act where—
  (a) the serious harm consists of, or is a result of, the infection of V with a sexually transmitted infection in the course of sexual activity, and
  (b) V consented to the sexual activity in the knowledge or belief that D had the sexually transmitted infection.
(5) For the purposes of this section it does not matter whether the harm was inflicted for the purposes of obtaining sexual gratification for D, V or some other person.
(6) Nothing in this section affects any enactment or rule of law relating to other circumstances in which a person's consent to the infliction of serious harm may, or may not, be a defence to a relevant offence.

- **Lawful correction or chastisement in England,** but subject to s 58 Children Act 2004.

Children Act 2004, s 58(1)– (2)

58 Reasonable punishment in England

1. In relation to any offence specified in subsection (2), battery of a child taking place in England cannot be justified on the ground that it constituted reasonable punishment.
2. The offences referred to in subsection (1) are—
  (a) an offence under section 18 or 20 of the Offences against the Person Act 1861 (c. 100) (wounding and causing grievous bodily harm);
  (b) an offence under section 47 of that Act (assault occasioning actual bodily harm);
  (c) an offence under section 1 of the Children and Young Persons Act 1933 (c. 12) (cruelty to persons under 16).

Blackstone's Magistrates' Court Handbook 2026. Bartholomew Dalton and Caroline Liggins, Oxford University Press. © Oxford University Press 2026.
DOI: 10.1093/oso/9780198963943.003.0058

(d) an offence under section 75A of the Serious Crime Act 2015 (strangulation or suffocation).

Children (Abolition of Defence of Reasonable Punishment) (Wales) Act 2020 S 1

- Reasonable punishment has been abolished in Wales:
  (1) The common law defence of reasonable punishment is abolished in relation to corporal punishment of a child taking place in Wales
  (2) Accordingly, corporal punishment of a child taking place in Wales cannot be justified in any civil or criminal proceedings on the ground that it constituted reasonable punishment.
  (3) Nor can corporal punishment of a child taking place in Wales be justified in any civil or criminal proceedings on the ground that it constituted acceptable conduct for the purposes of any other rule of the common law.
  (4) For the purposes of this section, 'corporal punishment' means any battery carried out as a punishment.

- **Self-defence.** Because there must be an unlawful act, a person acting in self-defence cannot be guilty of an assault; and once the issue has been raised by the defence in evidence, the Crown must prove that the defendant was not acting in self-defence. Householders enjoy a wider definition of self-defence under the amended s 76 Criminal Justice and Immigration Act 2008. The 'householder' version of self-defence (was the act grossly disproportionate) applies to all lawful occupiers of a property and not just to the owner (*R v Day* [2015] EWCA Crim 1646). It applies against all trespassers whether or not an intruder (*R v Cheeseman* [2019] EWCA Crim 199) and regardless of whether the household has committed other criminal acts (*R v Gill* [2023] EWCA Crim 259).
- **Defence of property.**
- **Prevention of crime.**
- **Horseplay.** Consent to rough and undisciplined play where there is no intention to harm is a defence to a charge of assault including where, consent being absent, there is a genuine (however unreasonable) belief by a defendant that consent was present (*R v Jones and others* (1986) 83 Cr App R 375).

C17.1.2 *Sentencing*

Key points: Sentencing — Assaults on those providing a public service etc

SA 2022 s 68A

68A(1) This section applies where—
(a) a court is considering the seriousness of an offence listed in subsection (3), and
(b) the offence is not aggravated under section 67(2).

(2) If the offence was committed against a person providing a public service, performing a public duty or providing services to the public, the court—
(a) must treat that fact as an aggravating factor, and
(b) must state in open court that the offence is so aggravated.

(3) The offences referred to in subsection (1) are—
  (a) an offence of common assault or battery, except where section 1 of the Assaults on Emergency Workers (Offences) Act 2018 applies;
  (b) an offence under any of the following provisions of the Offences against the Person Act 1861—
    (i) section 16 (threats to kill);
    (ii) section 18 (wounding with intent to cause grievous bodily harm);
    (iii) section 20 (malicious wounding);
    (iv) section 47 (assault occasioning actual bodily harm);
  (c) an inchoate offence in relation to any of the preceding offences.

(4) In this section—
  (a) a reference to providing services to the public includes a reference to providing goods or facilities to the public;
  (b) a reference to the public includes a reference to a section of the public.

(5) Nothing in this section prevents a court from treating the fact that an offence was committed against a person providing a public service, performing a public duty or providing services to the public as an aggravating factor in relation to offences not listed in subsection (3).

C17.2 Assault occasioning actual bodily harm

Offences Against the Person Act 1861, s 47

47 Assault occasioning bodily harm

Whosoever shall be convicted . . . of any assault occasioning actual bodily harm shall be liable . . .

EW

Fine and/or 12 months'/5 years' imprisonment (7 years if racially aggravated)

C17.2.1 *Sentencing*

SCG **Assault occasioning actual bodily harm**

Offence against a person providing a public service is a mandatory aggravating factor (see **C17.1.2**). A person could be seen as particularly vulnerable because he was intoxicated even where he struck the first blow, if there is an excessive response (*R v Halane* [2014] EWCA Crim 477). Not every victim of domestic violence is to be treated as particularly vulnerable for the purpose of the guideline. Serious injury must be interpreted in the context of the particular offence. It means not on the margins and more substantial injury (*R v Thomas* [2014] EWCA Crim 1715). In *R v Maloney (James)* [2015] EWCA Crim 798 the Crown alleged the deliberate targeting of a vulnerable victim, acknowledging that this may involve an element of double counting, thus increasing both harm and culpability. The court found that there was not enough evidence that the defendant targeted the victim *because* she was vulnerable; rather, he was angry with her and she happened to be vulnerable. On the facts in *R v Wilson* [2019] EWCA Crim 468, there being two blows could not properly be described as a repeated assault.

C17.2.2 Key points

- Action or words causing the person to apprehend imminent unlawful force. A conditional threat amounts to an assault, as does a threat to do something in the future (how far into the future is a matter of debate: see *R v Constanza* [1997] 2 Cr App R 492). Words in themselves could suffice, as could a gesture (eg using fingers to imitate a gun being fired, or a slashing action across the throat). An extreme example can be found in *R v Ireland* [1998] AC 147, a case where the appellant made silent phone calls to the victim. Conditional actions—for example, 'get out of my house or I will hurt you'—will amount to an assault. The words may also indicate that no assault is going to happen, as in *Tuberville v Savage* (1669) 1 Mod Rep 3 ('if it were not assize time, I would not take such language from you'). Creating a danger can amount to an assault; for example if a prisoner knows that he has a needle secreted on him and dishonestly does not inform a police officer carrying out a search, he may be liable if the officer injures himself on that needle, such a risk being reasonably foreseeable (*DPP v Santana-Bermudez* [2003] EWHC 2908 (Admin)).
- A battery involves the use of actual force being applied to the victim.
- Harm, which must be more than merely transient or trifling, encompasses not only injury but also hurt and damage. The concept of bodily harm is wide-ranging, and includes the cutting off of someone's hair (*DPP v Smith* [2006] 2 Cr App R 1). Psychiatric injury, in a medically diagnosed form, can amount to bodily harm, but anything short of this, for example upset or distress, will not.
- *Mens rea* is intention or recklessness. Note that the *mens rea* relates to the act of assault or battery; there is no requirement to prove that harm was intended, or that the defendant was reckless as to whether or not harm would be caused.

See *Blackstone's Criminal Practice 2026* **B2.28**

C17.3 Assault with intent to resist arrest

Offences Against the Person Act 1861, s 38

38 Assault with intent to resist apprehension, etc

Whosoever shall assault any person with intent to resist or prevent the lawful apprehension or detainer of himself or of any other person for any offence, shall be guilty of an offence.

EW

12 months' imprisonment and/or fine/2 years' imprisonment

DO

C17.3.1 *Sentencing*

SCG Assault with intent to resist arrest

C17.3.2 Key points

- The arrest must be a lawful one, and the defendant's honest but mistaken belief in that regard does not afford a defence (*R v Lee* (2001) 165 JP 344).
- The prosecution do not need to prove that the defendant knew that the person was a police officer (*R v Brightling* [1991] Crim LR 364).

See *Blackstone's Criminal Practice 2026* **B2.22**

C17.4 Assaulting a police constable or resisting or obstructing a police constable

Police Act 1996, s 89(1)–(2)

89 Assaults on constables

(1) Any person who assaults a constable in the execution of his duty, or a person assisting a constable in the execution of his duty, shall be guilty of an offence . . .

(2) Any person who resists or wilfully obstructs a constable in the execution of his duty, or a person assisting a constable in the execution of his duty, shall be guilty of an offence . . .

SO

Assault: Fine and/or 6 months' imprisonment

Obstruct/resist: Level 3 fine and/or 1 month's imprisonment

C17.4.1 *Sentencing*

SCG **Assault on a police constable in execution of his duty**

Obstruct/resist a police constable in execution of duty

C17.4.2 Key points

- The constable must be acting lawfully (ie in execution of his duty).
- Self-defence may be raised as a defence to both assault and obstruction of a police officer, even one acting in the execution of their duty (*Wheeldon v CPS* [2018] EWHC 247 (Admin); *Oraki v DPP* [2018] EWHC 115 (Admin)). So in *Dixon v CPS* [2018] EWHC 3154 (Admin), where two officers unlawfully detained the defendant who was entitled to use reasonable force to resist but the court held that a third officer intervened lawfully

because he feared the defendant had a weapon, there was a defence if the defendant honestly believed the officer was assaulting him. However the force must be reasonable—a bite was not.

- The prosecution do not need to prove that the defendant knew that the person was a police officer (*R v Brightling* [1991] Crim LR 364).
- If officer A is not acting lawfully in arresting a suspect, officer B who in good faith seeks to assist officer A will not be acting lawfully (*Cumberbatch v CPS* [2009] EWHC 3353 (Admin)).
- If a suspect is accused of trying to impede the arrest of a third party, it must be shown that the arrest of that third party was lawful (*Riley v DPP* (1990) 91 Cr App R 14).
- Where the defendant interfered with the lawful detention by a police officer of another, an officer pushing the defendant away cannot
  - (i) legitimize an earlier obstruction by the defendant of an officer in execution of his duty; or
  - (ii) provide an indemnity against all further actions of the defendant including a continuing obstruction. This is a different scenario to that when the only issue is whether the officer was touching the person without any intention to arrest. In any event the officer's push was a lawful act in accordance with s 3 Criminal Law Act 1967 (*Metcalfe v CPS* [2015] EWHC 1091 (Admin)).
- For the lawfulness of a police officer entering premises to save life or limb, see *Baker v CPS* [2009] EWHC 299 (Admin). An officer may enter premises to prevent a potential breach of the peace (*Laporte v MPC* [2014] EWHC 3574 (QB)).
- For the situation where a police officer has had a licence to remain on property revoked, see *R (Fullard) v Woking Magistrates' Court* [2005] EWHC 2922 (Admin).
- An officer who had not yet established grounds for arrest was acting unlawfully in restraining a suspect (*Wood v DPP* [2008] EWHC 1056 (Admin)). It was unlawful to take hold of a woman to question her (*Collins v Wilcock* [1984] 1 WLR 1172), but not every interference with a citizen's liberty will be sufficient to take the officer outside the course of his duty. A police officer may take hold of a person's arm to attract his attention and calm him down (*Mepstead v DPP* (1996) 160 JP 175).
- While a police officer may touch someone to gain their attention, if they are told to desist, a further touching will take the officer outside the execution of their duty (*R (Shah) v Central Criminal Court* [2013] EWHC 1747 (Admin)). A police officer may not detain a person, beyond acceptable conduct by any member of the public, even for one second, without intending to exercise a power of arrest. This included the use of an implied threat of force if the person did not remain (*Walker v Commissioner of the Metropolitan Police* [2014] EWCA Civ 897). However, where an officer seeks to have the defendant stop but does not use or threaten violence the action is lawful notwithstanding that he may have had an unlawful intent to detain without an arrest. It is what is said and done and not what is intended that is critical (*Tester v DPP* 2015 EWHC 1353 (Admin)).

- The powers of the police to stop and search, and of entry under the Police and Criminal Evidence Act 1984, are interpreted strictly (see *R v Bristol* [2007] EWCA Crim 3214 and *B v DPP* [2008] EWHC 1655 (Admin)).
- A police officer who had a mere belief in the existence of a search warrant was not acting in the execution of their duty. But the existence of a warrant could be inferred by the court from other facts proved such as evidence that it was a planned raid by a specialist unit (*Sykes v CPS* [2013] EWHC 3600 (Admin)).
- An arrest is lawful if the factual grounds are explained. It is not necessary to identify the statute creating the offence (*McCann v CPS* [2015] EWHC 2461 (Admin)).

See *Blackstone's Criminal Practice 2026* **B2.50**

C17.5 Common assault/assault on emergency workers

Criminal Justice Act 1988

(1) Common assault and battery shall be . . . offences

Assaults on Emergency Workers (Offences) Act 2018

1 Common assault and battery

(1) The section applies to an offence of common assault, or battery, that is committed against an emergency worker acting in the exercise of functions as such a worker.
(3) For the purposes of subsection (1), the circumstances in which an offence is to be taken as committed against a person acting in the exercise of functions as an emergency worker include circumstances where the offence takes place at a time when the person is not at work but is carrying out functions which, if done in work time, would have been in the exercise of functions as an emergency worker.

Sentencing Act 2020, ss 67 and 68

67 Assaults on emergency workers

(1) This section applies where a court is considering the seriousness of an offence listed in subsection (3).
(2) If the offence was committed against an emergency worker acting in the exercise of functions as such a worker, the court—(a) must treat that fact as an aggravating factor, and
 (b) must state in open court that the offence is so aggravated.
(3) The offences referred to in subsection (1) are—
 (a) an offence under any of the following provisions of the Offences Against the Person Act 1861—
  (i) section 16 (threats to kill);
  (ii) section 18 (wounding with intent to cause grievous bodily harm) ;
  (iii) section 20 (malicious wounding);
  (iv) section 23 (administering poison etc);
  (v) section 28 (causing bodily injury by explosives);
  (vi) section 29 (using explosives etc with intent to do grievous bodily harm);
  (vii) section 47 (assault occasioning actual bodily harm);
  (aa) an offence under section 75A of the Serious Crime Act 2015 (strangulation or suffocation);
 (b) an offence under section 3 of the Sexual Offences Act 2003 (sexual assault);
 (c) manslaughter;

(d) kidnapping;
(e) an inchoate offence in relation to any of the preceding offences.

(4) For the purposes of subsection (2) the circumstances in which an offence is to be taken as committed against a person acting in the exercise of functions as an emergency worker includes circumstances where the offence takes place at a time when the person is not at work but is carrying out functions which, if done in work time, would have been in the exercise of functions as an emergency worker.

(5) In this section, 'emergency worker' has the meaning given by section 68.

(6) Nothing in this section prevents a court from treating the fact that an offence was committed against an emergency worker acting in the exercise of functions as such as an aggravating factor in relation to offences not listed in subsection(3).

68 Emergency workers for the purposes of section 67

(1) In section 67, 'emergency worker' means—
(a) a constable;
(b) a person (other than a constable) who has the powers of a constable or is otherwise employed for police purposes or is engaged to provide services for police purposes;
(c) a National Crime Agency officer;
(d) a prison officer;
(e) a person (other than a prison officer) employed or engaged to carry out functions in a custodial institution of a corresponding kind to those carried out by a prison officer;
(f) a prisoner custody officer, so far as relating to the exercise of escort functions;
(g) a custody officer, so far as relating to the exercise of escort functions;
(h) a person employed for the purposes of providing, or engaged to provide, fire services or fire and rescue services;
(i) a person employed for the purposes of providing, or engaged to provide, search services or rescue services (or both);
(j) a person employed for the purposes of providing, or engaged to provide—
(i) NHS health services, or
(ii) services in the support of the provision of NHS health services, and whose general activities in doing so involve face to face interaction with individuals receiving the services or with other members of the public.

(2) It is immaterial for the purposes of subsection (1) whether the employment or engagement is paid or unpaid.

(3) In this section—
'custodial institution' means any of the following—
(a) a prison;
(b) a young offender institution, secure training centre or secure college;
(c) a removal centre, a short-term holding facility or pre-departure accommodation, as defined by section 147 of the Immigration and Asylum Act 1999;
(d) services custody premises, as defined by section 300(7) of the Armed Forces Act 2006;

'custody officer' has the meaning given by section 12(3) of the Criminal Justice and Public Order Act 1994;

'escort functions'—
(a) in the case of a prisoner custody officer, means the functions specified in section 80(1) of the Criminal Justice Act 1991;
(b) in the case of a custody officer, means the functions specified in paragraph 1 of Schedule 1 to the Criminal Justice and Public Order Act 1994;

'NHS health services' means any kind of health services provided as part of the health service continued under section 1(1) of the National Health Service Act 2006 and under section 1(1) of the National Health Service (Wales) Act 2006;

'prisoner custody officer' has the meaning given by section 89(1) of the Criminal Justice Act 1991.

EW Assault on emergency workers and racially aggravated common assault

SO Common assault and battery

卌 Assault on emergency worker: Fine and/or 12 months'/2 years' imprisonment

Racially or religiously aggravated common assault and battery: Fine and/or 12 months'/2 years' imprisonment

Common assault and battery: Fine and/or 6 months' imprisonment

DO Racially or religiously aggravated common assault and battery

C17.5.1 *Sentencing*

SCG Common assault

Offence against a person providing a public service is a mandatory aggravating factor (see C17.1.2).

C17.5.2 Key points

- Common assault comprises both assault (where 'assault' means the intentional or reckless causing of another to apprehend immediate unlawful violence) and assault by beating (battery—the intentional or reckless inflicting of unlawful force) (*R (Ward) v Black Country Magistrates' Court* [2020] EWHC 680) but they are best treated as separate offences (*DPP v Taylor* [1992] QB 645 DC).
- The element of assault described as 'hostility' conveys that some non-hostile contact is an ordinary incident of life to which there is implied consent. A genuine belief that an assault is necessary to save a life or prevent a third party attack is a defence but a wish to do good is not. Forced feeding is an offence. (*R v B* [2013] EWCA Crim 3). Touching someone against their wishes whilst attempting to act in their "best interests", supporting their intoxicated partner home in this instance, amounts to an assault (*Marland v DPP* [2023] EWHC 1046 (Admin)).
- See A12.1.2 for time limits in prosecuting domestic abuse cases.
- Defences (see C17.1.1):
  - Consent: evidence of a lack of consent can be inferred from evidence in the case and need not come from the complainant (see *DPP v Shabbir* [2009] EWHC 2754 (Admin)).
  - Lawful correction or chastisement: this defence survives the implementation of s 58 Children Act 2004.
  - Self-defence.
  - Defence of property.
  - Prevention of crime.

- The expression 'in the execution of his functions' in s 1 of the Assaults on Emergency Workers (Offences) Act 2018 Act is not to be construed in the same way as 'in the execution of his duty' under s 89 Police Act 1996. It does not require that the emergency worker be acting lawfully (*Campbell v CPS* [2020] EWHC 3868 (Admin)). Proportionate and good faith actions to assist those in distress are likely to be within the concept of these 'functions' (*DPP v Ahmad* [2021] EWHC 2122 (Admin)).

See *Blackstone's Criminal Practice 2026* **B2.1** and **B2.45**

C17.6 Child neglect, etc

Children and Young Persons Act 1933, s 1(1)

1 Cruelty to persons under 16

(1) If any person who has attained the age of sixteen years and has responsibility for any child or young person under that age, wilfully assaults, ill-treats, (whether physically or mentally), neglects, abandons, or exposes him, or causes or procures him to be assaulted, ill-treated (whether physically or mentally), neglected, abandoned, or exposed, in a manner likely to cause him unnecessary suffering or injury to health (whether the suffering or injury is of a physical or a psychological nature), that person shall be guilty of an offence.

EW

Fine and/or 12 months'/14 years' imprisonment

DO

C17.6.1 *Sentencing*

SCG **Cruelty to a child—assault and ill treatment, abandonment, neglect, and failure to protect**

C17.6.2 Key points

- Section 1(2) to s 1(3) Children and Young Persons Act 1933 provides that:

Children and Young Persons Act 1933, sub-ss 1(2) to 1(3)

(2) For the purposes of this section—

(a) a parent or other person legally liable to maintain a child or young person, or the legal guardian of a child or young person, shall be deemed to have neglected him in a manner likely to cause injury to his health if he has failed to provide adequate food, clothing, medical aid, or lodging for him, or if, having been unable otherwise to provide such food, clothing, medical aid, or lodging, he has failed to take steps to procure it to be provided under the enactments applicable in that behalf;

(b) where it is proved that the death of an infant under three years of age was caused by suffocation (not being suffocation caused by disease or the presence of any foreign body in the throat or air passages of the infant) while the infant was in bed, or lying next to an adult in or on any kind of furniture or surface being used by the adult for the purpose of sleeping, with some other person who has attained the age of 16 years, that other person shall, if he was, when he went to bed, under the influence of drink or drugs, be deemed to have neglected the infant in a manner likely to cause injury to its health.

(2A) The reference in subsection (2)(b) to the infant being *"in bed"* with another ("the adult") includes a reference to the infant lying next to the adult in or on any kind of furniture or surface being used by the adult for the purpose of sleeping (and the reference to the time when the adult *"went to bed"* is to be read accordingly).

(2B) A drug is a prohibited drug for the purposes of subsection (2)(b) in relation to a person if the person's possession of the drug immediately before taking it constituted an offence under section 5(2) of the Misuse of Drugs Act 1971.

(3) a person may be convicted of an offence under this section:

(a) notwithstanding that actual suffering or injury to health, or the likelihood of actual suffering or injury to health, was obviated by the action of another person;

(b) notwithstanding the death of the child or young person in question.

R v Turbill and Broadway [2012] EWCA Crim 1422 confirms that offences requiring wilful neglect require more than carelessness (even gross carelessness) or negligence. The neglect must be wilful. The definition in *Shepherd* (1981) AC 394 applies to child neglect and to neglect under the Mental Capacity Act 2005.

See *Blackstone's Criminal Practice 2026* **B2.161**

C17.7 Controlling or coercive behaviour

Serious Crime Act 2015, s 76

Controlling or coercive behaviour in an intimate or family relationship

(1) A person (A) commits an offence if—

(a) A repeatedly or continuously engages in behaviour towards another person (B) that is controlling or coercive,

(b) at the time of the behaviour, A and B are personally connected (see subsection (6)),

(c) the behaviour has a serious effect on B, and

(d) A knows or ought to know that the behaviour will have a serious effect on B.

(3) But A does not commit an offence under this section if at the time of the behaviour in question—

(a) A has responsibility for B, for the purposes of Part 1 of the Children and Young Persons Act 1933 (see section 17 of that Act), and

(b) B is under 16.

(4) A's behaviour has a "serious effect" on B if—

(a) it causes B to fear, on at least two occasions, that violence will be used against B, or

(b) it causes B serious alarm or distress which has a substantial adverse effect on B's usual day-to-day activities.

(5) For the purposes of subsection (1)(d) A "ought to know" that which a reasonable person in possession of the same information would know.

(6) A and B are "personally connected" if any of the following applies—

(a) they are, or have been, married to each other;
(b) they are, or have been, civil partners of each other;
(c) they have agreed to marry one another (whether or not the agreement has been terminated);
(d) they have entered into a civil partnership agreement (whether or not the agreement has been terminated);
(e) they are, or have been, in an intimate personal relationship with each other;
(f) they each have, or there has been a time when they each have had, a parental relationship in relation to the same child (see subsection (6A));
(g) they are relatives.

(6A) For the purposes of subsection (6)(f) a person has a parental relationship in relation to a child if—

(a) the person is a parent of the child, or
(b) the person has parental responsibility for the child.

(7) In subsection (6) and (6A)—

"civil partnership agreement" has the meaning given by section 73 of the Civil Partnership Act 2004;
"child" means a person under the age of 18 years;
"parental responsibility" has the same meaning as in the Children Act 1989;
"relative" has the meaning given by section 63(1) of the Family Law Act 1996.

(8) In proceedings for an offence under this section it is a defence for A to show that—

(a) in engaging in the behaviour in question, A believed that he or she was acting in B's best interests, and
(b) the behaviour was in all the circumstances reasonable.

(9) A is to be taken to have shown the facts mentioned in subsection (8) if—

(a) sufficient evidence of the facts is adduced to raise an issue with respect to them, and
(b) the contrary is not proved beyond reasonable doubt.

(10) The defence in subsection (8) is not available to A in relation to behaviour that causes B to fear that violence will be used against B.

EW

Fine and/or 12 months'/5 years' imprisonment

C17.7.1 *Sentencing*

SCG **Controlling or coercive behaviour in an intimate or family relationship**

C17.7.2 Key points

The following definitions are included in the definitive guideline on domestic abuse:

- Controlling behaviour is a range of acts designed to make a person subordinate and/ or dependent by isolating them from sources of support, exploiting their resources and capabilities for personal gain, depriving them of the means needed for independence, resistance, and escape and/ or regulating their everyday behaviour.

- Coercive behaviour is an act or pattern of acts of assault, threats, humiliation (whether public or private) and intimidation or other abuse that is used to harm, punish, or frighten the victim. Abuse may take place through person to person contact, or through other methods, including but not limited to, telephone calls, text, email, social networking sites, or use of GPS tracking devices

The court should have regard to the entirety of the behaviour in question (*R v Chilvers* [2021] EWCA Crim 1311)

See *Blackstone's Criminal Practice 2026* **B2.191**

C17.8 **False imprisonment**

A common law offence—the unlawful and intentional or reckless restraint of a victim's freedom of movement from a particular place (*R v Rahman* (1985) 81 Cr App R 349).

IO

Life

DO

GC

C17.8.1 ***Sentencing***

SCG Kidnap/False Imprisonment

C17.8.2 Key points

- The requisite *mens rea* is intention or subjective recklessness.
- This is an offence of basic intent. Voluntary intoxication is not a defence.

See *Blackstone's Criminal Practice 2026* **B2.115**

C17.9 **Grievous bodily harm/unlawful wounding**

Offences Against the Person Act 1861, s 20

20 Inflicting bodily injury, with or without weapon

Whosoever shall unlawfully and maliciously wound or inflict any grievous bodily harm upon any other person, either with or without any weapon or instrument, shall be guilty of an offence.

EW

12 months' imprisonment and/or fine/5 years' imprisonment (7 years if racially or religiously aggravated)

DO

GC

C17.9.1 ***Sentencing***

SCG **Inflicting grievous bodily harm/Unlawful wounding**

Offence against a person providing a public service is a mandatory aggravating factor (see C17.1.2).

C17.9.2 Key points

Wounding requires the breaking of the continuity of the whole of the skin. Although this may include relatively minor injuries, charging standards indicate that this offence should not be used in such cases.

Harm can be inflicted without the need for an assault. Grievous bodily harm has no statutory definition but the harm must be really serious (*DPP v Smith* [1961] AC 290). It may include psychiatric injury but only if both causation and extent of the disorder is established by expert psychiatric evidence (*R v Ireland* [1998] AC 147).

To be malicious there must be intention or subjective recklessness to inflict some kind of bodily harm, but the harm foreseen need not be serious. (*R v Mowatt* [1968] 1 QB 421.)

This is a crime of basic intent.

C17.9.3 ***Defences***

For defences see C17.1.1.

See *Blackstone's Criminal Practice 2026* **B2.61**

C17.10 **Kidnapping**

Common law offence—the taking or carrying away of one person by another by force or fraud, without the consent of that person and without lawful excuse.

IO

Life

DO

GC

C17.10.1 *Sentencing*

SCG Kidnap/False Imprisonment

See *Blackstone's Criminal Practice 2026* **B2.121**

C17.11 Strangulation or suffocation

Serious Crime Act 2015, s 75A

75A Strangulation or suffocation

(1) A person ('A') commits an offence if—
 (a) A intentionally strangles another person ('B'), or
 (b) A does any other act to B that—
  (i) affects B's ability to breathe, and
  (ii) constitutes battery of B.
(2) It is a defence to an offence under this section for A to show that B consented to the strangulation or other act.
(3) But subsection (2) does not apply if—
 (a) B suffers serious harm as a result of the strangulation or other act, and
 (b) A either—
  (i) intended to cause B serious harm, or
  (ii) was reckless as to whether B would suffer serious harm.
(4) A is to be taken to have shown the fact mentioned in subsection (2) if—
 (a) sufficient evidence of the fact is adduced to raise an issue with respect to it, and
 (b) the contrary is not proved beyond reasonable doubt. . . .
(6) In this section 'serious harm' means—
 (a) grievous bodily harm, within the meaning of section 18 of the Offences Against the Person Act 1861,
 (b) wounding, within the meaning of that section, or
 (c) actual bodily harm, within the meaning of section 47 of that Act.

EW

Fine and/or 12 months'/5 years' imprisonment

DO

C17.11.1 *Sentencing*

SCG Strangulation or suffocation / Racially or religiously aggravated strangulation or suffocation

See *Blackstone's Criminal Practice 2026* **B2.194**

C17.12 Threats to kill

Offences Against the Person Act 1861, s 16

16 Threats to kill

A person who without lawful excuse makes to another a threat, intending that that other would fear it would be carried out, to kill that other or a third person shall be guilty of an offence.

EW

12 months' imprisonment and/or fine/10 years' imprisonment

DO

C17.12.1 *Sentencing*

SCG Threats to kill

Offence against a person providing a public service is a mandatory aggravating factor (see **C17.1.2**). Where offence is committed in a domestic context, also refer to the Overreaching principles: Domestic abuse guideline

See *Blackstone's Criminal Practice 2026* **B1.161**

C17.13 Wounding or inflicting grievous bodily harm with intent

Offences Against the Person Act 1861, s 18

Whosoever shall unlawfully and maliciously by any means whatsoever wound or cause any grievous bodily harm to any person, with intent, to do some grievous bodily harm to any person, or with intent to resist or prevent the lawful apprehension or detainer of any person, shall be guilty of [an offence].

IO

Life

DO

GC

C17.13.1 *Sentencing*

SCG **Causing grievous bodily harm with intent to do grievous bodily harm/Wounding with intent to do GBH**

Offence against a person providing a public service is a mandatory aggravating factor (see **C17.1.2**).

C17.13.2 Key points

For the definitions of wound and grievous bodily harm see **C17.9.2**.

Key points: Sentencing

A knee may be 'weapon equivalent' for the purposes of the guideline (*R v JDL* [2018] EWCA Crim 1766).

Key points: General defence

The defence of consent is limited by Domestic Abuse Act 2021 s 71 where serious harm is caused for the purposes of obtaining sexual gratification (see **C17.1.1**).

See *Blackstone's Criminal Practice 2026* **B2.82**

C18 **Weapons Offences**

C18.1 **Firearms—general**

C18.1.1 ***Definitions***

***Firearm*—defined by the Firearms Act 1968, s 57(1)**

57

(1) In this Act, the expression 'firearm' means—
  (a) a lethal barrelled weapon (see subsection (1B));
  (b) a prohibited weapon;
  (c) a relevant component part in relation to a lethal barrelled weapon or a prohibited weapon (see subsection (1D));
  (d) an accessory to a lethal barrelled weapon or a prohibited weapon where the accessory is designed or adapted to diminish the noise or flash caused by firing the weapon;

 and so much of section 1 of this Act as excludes any description of firearm from the category of firearms to which that section applies shall be construed as also excluding component parts of, and accessories to, firearms of that description.

(1A) . . .

(1B) In subsection (1)(a), 'lethal barrelled weapon' means a barrelled weapon of any description from which a shot, bullet or other missile, with kinetic energy of more than one joule at the muzzle of the weapon, can be discharged.

(1C) Subsection (1) is subject to section 57A (exception for airsoft guns).

(1D) For the purposes of subsection (1)(c), each of the following items is a relevant component part in relation to a lethal barrelled weapon or a prohibited weapon—
  (a) a barrel, chamber or cylinder,
  (b) a frame, body or receiver,
  (c) a breech block, bolt or other mechanism for containing the pressure of discharge at the rear of a chamber,

 but only where the item is capable of being used as a part of a lethal barrelled weapon or a prohibited weapon.

(2) In this Act, the expression 'ammunition' means ammunition for any firearm and includes grenades, bombs and other like missiles, whether capable of use with a firearm or not, and also includes prohibited ammunition.

(2A) In this Act 'self-loading' and 'pump-action' in relation to any weapon mean respectively that it is designed or adapted (otherwise than as mentioned in section 5(1)(a)) so that it is automatically re-loaded or that it is so designed or adapted that it is reloaded by the manual operation of the fore–end or forestock of the weapon.

(2B) In this Act 'revolver', in relation to a smooth-bore gun, means a gun containing a series of chambers which revolve when the gun is fired.

57A Exception for airsoft guns

(1) An 'airsoft gun' is not to be regarded as a firearm for the purposes of this Act.

(2) An 'airsoft gun' is a barrelled weapon of any description which—
  (a) is designed to discharge only a small plastic missile (whether or not it is also capable of discharging any other kind of missile), and
  (b) is not capable of discharging a missile (of any kind) with kinetic energy at the muzzle of the weapon that exceeds the permitted level.

(3) 'Small plastic missile' means a missile that—
  (a) is made wholly or partly from plastics,

Blackstone's Magistrates' Court Handbook 2026. Bartholomew Dalton and Caroline Liggins, Oxford University Press. © Oxford University Press 2026.
DOI: 10.1093/oso/9780198963943.003.0059

(b) is spherical, and
(c) does not exceed 8 millimetres in diameter.

(4) The permitted kinetic energy level is—
(a) in the case of a weapon which is capable of discharging two or more missiles successively without repeated pressure on the trigger, 1.3 joules;
(b) in any other case, 2.5 joules.

***Imitation firearm*—defined by the Firearms Act 1968, s 57(4)**

57(4)

'imitation firearm' means any thing which has the appearance of being a firearm (other than such a weapon as is mentioned in section 5(1)(b) of this Act) whether or not it is capable of discharging any shot, bullet or other missile; . . .

An item is an imitation firearm if it 'looked like' a firearm at the time of its use (*R v Morris and King* (1984) 149 JP 60).

An imitation firearm has to be a thing which was separate and distinct from the defendant; putting one's hand inside a jacket pocket and using the fingers to give the impression of a firearm was not enough (*R v Bentham* [2005] UKHL 18).

***Ammunition*—defined by the Firearms Act 1968, s 57(2)**

57(2)

In this Act, the expression 'ammunition' means ammunition for any firearm and includes grenades, bombs and other like missiles, whether capable of use with a firearm or not, and also includes prohibited ammunition.

S 58 Particular savings

[sets out closely defined exceptions from liability under s 57 including for 'antique firearms']

See *Blackstone's Criminal Practice 2026* **B12.8**

C18.1.2 *Mandatory minimum sentence (see D20)*

C18.1.3 *Possessing firearm or ammunition without firearm certificate*

Firearms Act 1968, s 1

1. Requirement of firearms certificate

(1) Subject to any exemption under this Act, it is an offence for a person—
(a) to have in his possession, or to purchase or acquire, a firearm to which this section applies without holding a firearm certificate in force at the time, or otherwise than as authorised by such a certificate;
(b) to have in his possession, or to purchase or acquire, any ammunition to which this section applies without holding a firearm certificate in force at the time, or

otherwise than as authorised by such a certificate, or in quantities in excess of those so authorised.

(2) It is an offence for a person to fail to comply with a condition subject to which a firearm certificate is held by him.

(3) This section applies to every firearm except—

(a) a shot gun within the meaning of this Act, that is to say a smooth-bore gun (not being an air gun) which—

(i) has a barrel not less than 24 inches in length and does not have any barrel with a bore exceeding 2 inches in diameter;

(ii) either has no magazine or has a non-detachable magazine incapable of holding more than two cartridges; and

(iii) is not a revolver gun; and

(b) an air weapon (that is to say, an air rifle, air gun or air pistol which does not fall within section 5(1) and which is not of a type declared by rules made by the Secretary of State under section 53 of this Act to be specially dangerous).

(3A) A gun which has been adapted to have such a magazine as is mentioned in sub-section (3)(a)(ii) above shall not be regarded as falling within that provision unless the magazine bears a mark approved by the Secretary of State for denoting that fact and that mark has been made, and the adaptation has been certified in writing as having been carried out in a manner approved by him, either by one of the two companies mentioned in section 58(1) of this Act or by such other person as may be approved by him for that purpose.

(4) This section applies to any ammunition for a firearm, except the following articles, namely:—

(a) cartridges containing five or more shot, none of which exceeds. 36 inch in diameter;

(b) ammunition for an air gun, air rifle or air pistol; and

(c) blank cartridges not more than one inch in diameter measured immediately in front of the rim or cannelure of the base of the cartridge.

EW

12 months and/or fine/on indictment either
(i) where the offence is committed in an aggravated form within the meaning of section 4(4) of this Act, 7 years or a fine; or both,
s 4 (4) A person who commits an offence under section 1 of this Act by having in his possession, or purchasing or acquiring, a shotgun which has been shortened contrary to subsection (1) above or a firearm which has been converted as mentioned in subsection (3) above (whether by a registered firearms dealer or not), without holding a firearm certificate authorising him to have it in his possession, or to purchase or acquire it, shall be treated for the purposes of provisions of this Act relating to the punishment of offences as committing that offence in an aggravated form; or
(ii) in any other case, 5 years and / or fine;

C18.1.4 *Sentencing*

SCG **Firearms—Possession without certificate**

C18.1.5 Key points

- Possession contrary to s 1 is established if the prosecution can prove the defendant knowingly had in his possession an article which was in fact a firearm (*R v Hussain* (1981) 72 Cr App R 143).
- Section 1(1) of the Firearms Act 1982 applies to any article which has the appearance of being a firearm to which s 1 Firearms Act 1968 applies and is readily convertible into such a firearm. In such cases it will be an offence under s 1 1968 Act to possess the article without a firearms certificate. It shall be a defence for the accused to show that he did not know and had no reason to suspect that the imitation firearm was so constructed or adapted as to be readily converted into a firearm to which s 1 1968 Act applies (s 1(5) Firearms Act 1982).

See *Blackstone's Criminal Practice 2026* **B12.36**

C18.1.6 *Offences relating to air weapons*

Firearms Act 1968, s 22(4), s 23

22(4)

Subject to section 23 below, it is an offence for a person under the age of eighteen to have with him an air weapon or ammunition for an air weapon.

23

(1) It is not an offence under section 22(4) of this Act for a person to have with him an air weapon or ammunition while he is under the supervision of a person of or over the age of twenty-one; but where a person has with him an air weapon on any premises in circumstances where he would be prohibited from having it with him but for this subsection, it is an offence for the person under whose supervision he is to allow him to use it for firing any missile beyond those premises.

(1A) In proceedings against a person for an offence under subsection (1) it shall be a defence for him to show that the only premises into or across which the missile was fired were premises the occupier of which had consented to the firing of the missile (whether specifically or by way of a general consent).

(2) It is not an offence under section 22(4) of this Act for a person to have with him an air weapon or ammunition at a time when—

- (a) being a member of a rifle club or miniature rifle club for the time being approved by the Secretary of State for the purposes of this section or section 15 of the Firearms (Amendment) Act 1988, he is engaged as such a member in connection with target shooting; or
- (b) he is using the weapon or ammunition at a shooting gallery where the only firearms used are either air weapons or miniature rifles not exceeding.23 inch calibre.

(3) It is not an offence under section 22(4) of this Act for a person of or over the age of fourteen to have with him an air weapon or ammunition on private premises with the consent of the occupier.

Firearms Act 1968, s 21A

21A Firing an air weapon beyond premises

(1) A person commits an offence if—

- (a) he has with him an air weapon on any premises; and

(b) he uses it for firing a missile beyond those premises.

(2) In proceedings against a person for an offence under this section it shall be a defence for him to show that the only premises into or across which the missile was fired were premises the occupier of which had consented to the firing of the missile (whether specifically or by way of a general consent).

SO Note other provisions of s 22 are either-way offences with heavier penalties available to the court

Level 3 fine

C18.1.6.1 **Key points**

- Some barrelled air or gas weapons are capable of being firearms within the meaning of s 57(1) Firearms Act 1968.
- Air weapons are not subject to the certification requirements of s 1 Firearms Act 1968 unless the device has been declared 'specially dangerous' under the Firearms (Dangerous Air Weapons) Rules 1969 or it falls within the definition of a prohibited weapon (see **C18.1.8**).

See *Blackstone's Criminal Practice 2026* **B12.54**

C18.1.7 *Possessing component parts of ammunition with intent to manufacture*

Firearms Act 1968, s 3A

3A Possessing component parts of ammunition with intent to manufacture

(1) A person commits an offence if—
 (a) the person has in their possession any component parts of ammunition (see subsection (2)),
 (b) the person intends to manufacture ammunition to which section 1 applies using those parts, and
 (c) were the person to do so—
  (i) possession of the ammunition by the person would constitute an offence under section 1, or
  (ii) the manufacture or possession of the ammunition by the person would constitute an offence under section 3.

(2) For the purposes of this section the component parts of ammunition are—
 (a) bullet;
 (b) cartridge case;
 (c) primer;
 (d) propellant.

EW

Fine and/or 12 months'/5 years' imprisonment

C18.1.8 *Possessing prohibited weapons or ammunition*

Firearms Act 1968, s 5

5 Weapons subject to general prohibition

(1) A person commits an offence if, without authority, he has in his possession, or purchases or acquires,

(a) any firearm which is so designed or adapted that two or more missiles can be successively discharged without repeated pressure on the trigger;

(ab) any self-loading or pump-action rifled gun other than one which is chambered for .22 rim-fire cartridges;

(aba) any firearm which either has a barrel less than 30 centimetres in length or is less than 60 centimetres in length overall, other than an air weapon, a muzzle-loading gun or a firearm designed as signalling apparatus;

(ac) any self-loading or pump-action smooth-bore gun which is not an air weapon or chambered for .22 rim-fire cartridges and either has a barrel less than 24 inches in length or is less than 40 inches in length overall;

(ad) any smooth-bore revolver gun other than one which is chambered for 9 mm. rim-fire cartridges or a muzzle-loading gun;

(ae) any rocket launcher, or any mortar, for projecting a stabilised missile, other than a launcher or mortar designed for line-throwing or pyrotechnic purposes or as signalling apparatus;

(af) any air rifle, air gun or air pistol which uses, or is designed or adapted for use with, a self-contained gas cartridge system;

(ag) any rifle with a chamber from which empty cartridge cases are extracted using—

(i) energy from propellant gas, or

(ii) energy imparted to a spring or other energy storage device by propellant gas, other than a rifle which is chambered for .22 rim-fire cartridges;

(b) any weapon of whatever description designed or adapted for the discharge of any noxious liquid, gas or other thing; and

(ba) any device (commonly known as a bump stock) which is designed or adapted so that—

(i) it is capable of forming part of or being added to a self-loading lethal barrelled weapon (as defined in section 57(1B) and (2A)), and

(ii) if it forms part of or is added to such a weapon, it increases the rate of fire of the weapon by using the recoil from the weapon to generate repeated pressure on the trigger; and

(c) any cartridge with a bullet designed to explode on or immediately before impact, any ammunition containing or designed or adapted to contain any such noxious thing as is mentioned in paragraph (b) above and, if capable of being used with a firearm of any description, any grenade, bomb (or other like missile), or rocket or shell designed to explode as aforesaid.

(1A) Subject to section 5A of this Act, a person commits an offence if, without the authority, he has in his possession, or purchases or acquires, or sells or transfers—

(a) any firearm which is disguised as another object;

(b) any rocket or ammunition not falling within paragraph (c) of subsection (1) of this section which consists in or incorporates a missile designed to explode on or immediately before impact and is for military use;

(ba) any device (commonly known as a bump stock) which is designed or adapted so that—

(i) it is capable of forming part of or being added to a selfloading lethal barrelled weapon (as defined in section 57(1B) and (2A)), and

(ii) if it forms part of or is added to such a weapon, it increases the rate of fire of the weapon by using the recoil from the weapon to generate repeated pressure on the trigger; and'

(c) any launcher or other projecting apparatus not falling within paragraph (ae) of that subsection which is designed to be used with any rocket or ammunition falling within paragraph (b) above or with ammunition which would fall within that paragraph but for its being ammunition falling within paragraph (c) of that subsection;

(d) any ammunition for military use which consists in or incorporates a missile designed so that a substance contained in the missile will ignite on or immediately before impact;

(e) any ammunition for military use which consists in or incorporates a missile designed, on account of its having a jacket and hard-core, to penetrate armour plating, armour screening or body armour;

(f) any ammunition which incorporates a missile designed or adapted to expand on impact;

(g) anything which is designed to be projected as a missile from any weapon and is designed to be, or has been, incorporated in—

(i) any ammunition falling within any of the preceding paragraphs; or

(ii) any ammunition which would fall within any of those paragraphs but for its being specified in subsection (1) of this section.

(2) The weapons and ammunition specified in subsections (1) and (1A) of this section (including, 'in the case of weapons, any devices falling within subsection (1)(ba) of this section and,'. in the case of ammunition, any missiles falling within subsection (1A)(g) of this section) are referred to in this Act as 'prohibited weapons' and 'prohibited ammunition' respectively.

(2A) A person commits an offence if without authority—

(a) he manufactures any weapon device or ammunition specified in subsection (1) of this section,

(b) he sells or transfers any prohibited weapon or prohibited ammunition,

(c) he has in his possession for sale or transfer any prohibited weapon or prohibited ammunition, or

(d) he purchases or acquires for sale or transfer any prohibited weapon or prohibited ammunition.

(3) In this section 'authority' means an authority given in writing by—

(a) the Secretary of State (in or as regards England and Wales),

(4) An authority shall be subject to conditions specified in it, including such as the Secretary of State or the Scottish Ministers (as appropriate), having regard to the circumstances of each particular case, think fit to impose for the purpose of securing that the prohibited weapon or ammunition to which the authority relates will not endanger the public safety or the peace.

(5) It is an offence for a person to whom an authority is given under this section to fail to comply with any condition of the authority.

. . .

(7) For the purposes of this section and section 5A of this Act—

(a) any rocket or ammunition which is designed to be capable of being used with a military weapon shall be taken to be for military use;

(b) references to a missile designed so that a substance contained in the missile will ignite on or immediately before impact include references to any missile containing a substance that ignites on exposure to air; and

(c) references to a missile's expanding on impact include references to its deforming in any predictable manner on or immediately after impact.

(8) For the purposes of subsection (1)(aba) and (ac) above, any detachable, folding, retractable or other movable butt-stock shall be disregarded in measuring the length of any firearm.

(9) Any reference in this section to a muzzle-loading gun is a reference to a gun which is designed to be loaded at the muzzle end of the barrel or chamber with a loose charge and a separate ball (or other missile).

IIII (unless mandatory minimum sentence (**D20**))—

Section 5(1)(a), (ab), (aba), (ac), (ad), (ae), (af) or (c)	Possessing ... prohibited weapons or ammunition.	On indictment	10 years or a fine, or both.
Section 5(1)(b)	Possessing. prohibited weapon designed for discharge of noxious liquid etc.	(a) Summary (b) On indictment	(a) 6 months or a fine or both. (b) 10 years or a fine or both.
Section 5(1)(a), (ab), (aba), (ac), (ad), (ae), (af), (ag), (ba), or (c), and Section 5(1A)(a)	Possessing . . . prohibited weapons or ammunition Possessing. . . firearm disguised as other object.	On indictment	10 years or a fine, or both.
Section 5(1A)(b), (c), (d), (e), (f), or (g)	Possessing. . . other prohibited weapons.	(a) Summary (b) On indictment	(a) 6 months or a fine or both. (b) 10 years or a fine, or both.
Section 5(2A)	Manufacturing or distributing, or possessing for distribution, prohibited weapons or ammunition	On indictment	Imprisonment for life.[GC]
Section 5(5) . . .	Non-compliance with condition of Defence Council authority.	Summary . . .	6 months or a fine of level 5; or both.

C18.1.8.1 *Allocation*

Where the statutory minimum sentence under s 311 Sentencing Act (SA) 2020 applies (see **D20**) the court must send for trial.

C18.1.8.2 *Sentencing*

SCG **Firearms—Possession of prohibited weapon/Firearms—Transfer and manufacture**

C18.1.8.3 Key points

- To prove possession contrary to s 5 the prosecution merely had to prove possession of the object and that it was a prohibited weapon. It did not have to prove that the defendant either knew, or could have known, that the object was a weapon prohibited by the 1968 Act (*R v Deyemi* [2007] EWCA 2060.

- Whether a person is in possession of a weapon is a question of fact and can be proprietary and/or custodial. It is not confined to physical possession and can be for a very short period of time (*Jenkins v DPP and another* [2020] EWHC 1307 (Admin)).
- Momentary handling of a firearm by the accused, followed by his immediate rejection of it, did not constitute possession of it within the meaning of s 5 (*R v T* [2011] EWCA Crim 1646).
- Where a defendant is found in possession of a 'container' in which there is a firearm, it is no defence for the defendant to state they did not know what was in the container. A car is capable of being a container (*R v Hassan* EWCA Crim 786).
- A person found in possession of a sawn-off shotgun inside a plastic bag is still in possession of the firearm even if he thought the bag contained a crowbar (*R v Waller* [1991] Crim LR 381).
- It was not a defence to possession of a CS gas canister contrary to s 5(1)(b) that the defendant did not know or could not reasonably have been expected to know that the canister contained CS gas (*R v Bradish* (1990) 90 Cr App R 271).

The offence under s 5(1)(b) is used to prosecute those in possession of CS gas.

See *Blackstone's Criminal Practice 2026* **B12.61**

C18.1.9 *Possession of firearm with intent to endanger life*

Firearms Act 1968, s 16

It is an offence for a person to have in his possession any firearm or ammunition with intent by means thereof to endanger life or cause serious injury to property, or to enable another person by means thereof to endanger life or cause serious injury to property, whether any injury to person or property has been caused or not.

IO

Life

DO

GC

C18.1.9.1 *Sentencing*

A mandatory minimum sentence applies in the case of certain prohibited weapons specified in s 311 SA 2020.

SCG **Firearms—Possession with intent to endanger life**

C18.1.9.2 Key points

- There is no requirement that the firearm or ammunition is prohibited under s 5 Firearms Act 1968 (*R v Salih* [2008] 1 WLR 2627).
- Section 16 does not extend to imitation firearms.
- The prosecution are not required to prove an immediate or unconditional intention to endanger life. The intention may last as long as the possession lasts and to possess a firearm ready for use if and when an occasion arises is an offence within s 16 (*R v Bentham* [1973] QB 357).
- It is possible to raise self-defence (*R v Georgiades* [1989] 1 WLR 759) but for the issue to be left to a jury there must be evidence of fear of imminent attack (*R v Stubbs* [2007] EWCA Crim 1714).

See *Blackstone's Criminal Practice 2026* B12.93

C18.1.10 *Possession of firearm with intent to cause fear of violence*

Firearms Act 1968, s 16A

It is an offence for a person to have in his possession any firearm or imitation firearm with intent—
(a) by means thereof to cause, or
(b) to enable another person by means thereof to cause, any person to believe that unlawful violence will be used against him or another person.

IO

10 years' imprisonment

DO

GC

C18.1.10.1 *Sentencing*

A mandatory minimum sentence applies in the case of certain prohibited weapons specified in s 311 SA 2020.

SCG **Firearms—Possession with intent to cause fear of violence**

C18.1.10.2 **Key points**

- For the meaning of firearm and imitation firearm see **C18.1.1**.
- The requirement that the violence must be 'unlawful' allows the defendant to raise the fact that he was acting in self-defence.
- As long as the defendant intends to cause a fear of unlawful violence, it does not matter that the victim is aware that the item is in fact an imitation firearm (*K v DPP* [2006] EWHC 2183 (Admin)).

See *Blackstone's Criminal Practice 2026* **B12.100**

C18.1.11 *Use of firearm to resist arrest*

Firearms Act 1968, s 17

(1) It is an offence for a person to make or attempt to make any use whatsoever of a firearm or imitation firearm with intent to resist or prevent the lawful arrest or detention of himself or another person.

(4) For purposes of this section, the definition of 'firearm' in section 57(1) of this Act shall apply without paragraphs (b) and (c) of that subsection, and 'imitation firearm' shall be construed accordingly.

Life

IO

DO

GC

C18.1.11.1 *Sentencing*

A mandatory minimum sentence applies in the case of certain prohibited weapons specified in s 311 SA 2020.

SCG **Firearms—Possession with intent - other offences**

See *Blackstone's Criminal Practice 2026* **B12.103**

C18.1.12 *Possessing firearm while committing an indictable offence*

Firearms Act 1968, s 17(2) and (4)

(2) If a person, at the time of his committing or being arrested for an offence specified in Schedule 1 to this Act, has in his possession a firearm or imitation firearm, he shall be guilty of an offence under this subsection unless he shows that he had it in his possession for a lawful object.

(4) For purposes of this section, the definition of 'firearm' in section 57(1) of this Act shall apply without paragraphs (b) and (c) of that subsection, and 'imitation firearm' shall be construed accordingly

IO

Life

DO

GC

C18.1.12.1 *Sentencing*

A mandatory minimum sentence applies in the case of certain prohibited weapons specified in s 311 SA 2020.

SCG **Firearms—Possession with intent—other offences**

C18.1.12.2 Key points

- For the definition of firearm and imitation firearm see **C18.1.1**.
- Possession for the purposes of s 17(2) is satisfied by custody and control of the firearm and does not require that the defendant has the firearm with him at the time of his arrest (*R v North* [2001] EWCA Crim 544).
- Sch 1 Firearms Act 1968 contains the following offences:
  (a) Offences under s 1 Criminal Damage Act 1971;
  (b) Offences under any of the following provisions of the Offences Against the Person Act 1861: ss 20 to 22 (inflicting bodily injury; garrotting; criminal use of stupefying drugs); s 30 (laying explosive to building etc); s 32 (endangering railway passengers by tampering with track); s 38 (assault with intent to commit felony or resist arrest); s 47 (criminal assaults);
  (c) Offences under Part I of the Child Abduction Act 1984 (abduction of children);
  (d) Theft, robbery, burglary, blackmail, and any offence under s 12(1) Theft Act 1968;
  (e) Offence under s 89(1) Police Act 1996 (assaulting constable in execution of his duty);
  (f) Offences under s 90(1) Criminal Justice Act 1991 (assaulting prisoner custody officer);
  (g) Offences under s 12(1) Criminal Justice and Public Order Act 1994 (assaulting secure training centre officer);

(h) Offences under Sch 11 para 4 Immigration and Asylum Act 1999 (assaulting a detainee custody officer);

(i) Offences under the Sexual Offences Act 2003: ss 1 (rape); s 2 (assault by penetration); s 4 (causing a person to engage in sexual activity involving penetration without consent); s 5 (rape of child under 13); s 6 (assault by penetration of child under 13); s 30 (sexual activity involving penetration with a person with a mental disorder impeding choice); and s 31 (causing or inciting a person with a mental disorder impeding choice to engage in sexual activity involving penetration);

(j) Aiding and abetting the commission of any such offence; and

(k) Attempting to commit any such offence.

- An offence specified in Sch 1 need not have been committed but the defendant must have been lawfully arrested for one of the offences specified (*R v Nelson* [2001] 1 QB 55).

See *Blackstone's Criminal Practice 2026* **B12.107**

C18.1.13 *Possession of firearm with intent to commit indictable offence*

Firearms Act 1968, s 18

(1) It is an offence for a person to have with him a firearm or imitation firearm with intent to commit an indictable offence, or to resist arrest or prevent the arrest of another, in either case while he has the firearm or imitation firearm with him.

(2) In proceedings for an offence under this section proof that the accused had a firearm or imitation firearm with him and intended to commit an offence, or to resist or prevent arrest, is evidence that he intended to have it with him while doing so.

IO

Life

DO

GC

C18.1.13.1 *Sentence*

A mandatory minimum sentence applies in the case of certain prohibited weapons specified in s 311 SA 2020.

SCG **Firearms—Possession with intent—other offences**

C18.1.13.2 Key points

- For the definition of firearm and imitation firearm see **C18.1.1**.
- In *R v Stoddart* [1998] 2 Cr App R 25 the Court of Appeal held that there are three elements to an offence under s 18:

(a) that the defendant had with him a firearm or imitation firearm;

(b) that he intended to have it with him; and
(c) that at the same time he had the intention to commit an indictable offence or to resist or prevent arrest.

The prosecution must prove that the firearm or imitation firearm was with the defendant as opposed to being under his control somewhere else. He may have the firearm with him if it is readily accessible to him at the time of the offence (*R v Pawlicki* [1992] 1 WLR 827).

See *Blackstone's Criminal Practice 2026* **B12.110**

C18.1.14 *Carrying firearm in public place*

Firearms Act 1968, s 19

19 Carrying a firearm in a public place

A person commits an offence if, without lawful authority or reasonable excuse (the proof whereof lies on him) he has with him in a public place—
(a) a loaded shot gun,
(b) an air weapon (whether loaded or not),
(c) any other firearm (whether loaded or not) together with ammunition suitable for use in that firearm, or
(d) an imitation firearm.

SO (but; indictable only if the firearm is a firearm specified in s 5(1)(a), (ab), (aba), (ac), (ad), (ae), (af), (ag), (ba), and s 5(1A)(a)) unless it is an air weapon

6 months' imprisonment and/or fine/7 years' imprisonment

C18.1.14.1 *Sentencing*

A mandatory minimum sentence applies in the case of certain prohibited weapons specified in s 311 SA 2020.

SCG Firearms—Carrying in a public place

C18.1.14.2 Key points

- It is not necessary to show that the defendant knew that a gun was loaded (*R v Harrison* [1996] Crim LR 200).
- An item is an imitation firearm if it 'looked like' a firearm at the time of its use (*R v Morris and King* (1984) 149 JP 60).

- A part of the body (eg fingers pointed under clothing) could not constitute an imitation firearm (*R v Bentham* [2005] UKHL 18).
- For the definition of firearm and imitation firearm see **C18.1.1**.
- Public place includes any highway and any other premises or place to which at the material time the public have or are permitted to have access, whether on payment or otherwise (s 57(4) Firearms Act 1968).

See *Blackstone's Criminal Practice 2026* **B12.113**

C18.1.15 *Trespassing with a firearm*

Firearms Act 1968, s 20

20 Trespassing with firearm

(1) A person commits an offence if, while he has a firearm or imitation firearm with him, he enters or is in any building or part of a building as a trespasser and without reasonable excuse (the proof whereof lies on him).
(2) A person commits an offence if, while he has a firearm or imitation firearm with him, he enters or is on any land as a trespasser and without reasonable excuse (the proof whereof lies on him).
(3) In subsection (2) of this section the expression "land" includes land covered with water.

SO s 20(1) but indictable only if the firearm is a firearm specified in section 5(1)(a), (ab), (aba), (ac), (ad), (ae), (af), (ag) or (ba) or section 5(1A)(a) of this Act, except summary only in the case of an imitation firearm or if the firearm is an air weapon)

SO s 20(2)

s 20(1): 6 months' imprisonment and/or fine/7 years; a mandatory minimum sentence applies in the case of certain prohibited weapons specified in s 311 SA 2020.

s 20(2): 3 months' imprisonment and/or level 4 fine

See *Blackstone's Criminal Practice 2026* **B13.88**

C18.1.16 *Possession of firearms by persons previously convicted of crime*

Firearms Act 1968, s 21

21 Possession of firearms by persons previously convicted of crime.

(1) A person who has been sentenced to custody for life or to preventive detention, or to imprisonment or to corrective training for a term of three years or more or to youth custody or detention in a young offender institution for such a term . . . shall not at any time have a firearm or ammunition in his possession.

(2) A person who has been sentenced . . . to imprisonment for a term of three months or more but less than three years or to youth custody or detention in a young offender institution for such a term, or who has been subject to a secure training order or a detention and training order, shall not at any time before the expiration of the period of five years from the date of his release have a firearm or ammunition in his possession.

EW

12 months' imprisonment and/or fine/5 years' imprisonment

C18.1.16.1 *Sentencing*

SCG Firearms—Possession by person prohibited

See *Blackstone's Criminal Practice 2026* B12.115

C18.2 Possession of bladed article or offensive weapon

Obligatory minimum sentences will apply to those committing second offences on or after 17 July 2015 (see D20). The difference between the two offences is that offences related to bladed articles do not require the article either to be inherently offensive nor to be carried with an offensive intent. The definition of a bladed etc article is objective (*R v Szewczyk* [2019] EWCA Crim 1811).

Criminal Justice Act 1988, s 139(1)–(5) and (7)

139 Offence of having article with blade or point in public place

(1) Subject to subsections (4) and (5) below, any person who has an article to which this section applies with him in a public place shall be guilty of an offence.

(2) Subject to subsection (3) below, this section applies to any article which has a blade or is sharply pointed except a folding pocketknife.

(3) This section applies to a folding pocketknife if the cutting edge of its blade exceeds 3 inches.

(4) It shall be a defence for a person charged with an offence under this section to prove that he had good reason or lawful authority for having the article with him in a public place.

(5) Without prejudice to the generality of subsection (4) above, it shall be a defence for a person charged with an offence under this section to prove that he had the article with him—
   (a) for use at work;
   (b) for religious reasons; or
   (c) as part of any national costume.

. . .

(7) In this section 'public place' includes any place to which at the material time the public have or are permitted access, whether on payment or otherwise.

Prevention of Crime Act 1953, s 1(1) and (4)

1 Prohibition of the carrying of offensive weapons without lawful authority or reasonable excuse

(1) Any person who without lawful authority or reasonable excuse, the proof whereof shall lie on him, has with him in any public place any offensive weapon shall be guilty of an offence . . .

(4) In this section 'public place' includes any highway and any other premises or place to which at the material time the public have or are permitted to have access whether on payment or otherwise and 'offensive weapon' means any article made or adapted for use for causing injury to the person, or intended by the person having it with him for such use by him or some other person.

Criminal Justice Act 1988, s 139A(1) and (2)

139A Offence of having article with blade or point (or offensive weapon) on school [educational] premises

(1) Any person who has an article to which section 139 of this Act applies with him on school premises or further education premises shall be guilty of an offence.

(2) Any person who has an offensive weapon within the meaning of section 1 of the Prevention of Crime Act 1953 with him on school premises or further education premises shall be guilty of an offence. It shall be a defence for a person charged with an offence under this section to prove that he had good reason or lawful authority for having the article with him in a public place.

EW

12 months' imprisonment and/or fine/4 years' imprisonment

Criminal Justice Act 1988, s 141

141 Possession of certain offensive weapons in private

(1A) Any person who possesses a weapon to which this section applies in private is guilty of an offence . . .

(1C) For the purposes of subsection (1A) as it has effect in relation to England and Wales, a person possesses a weapon to which this section applies in private if the person possesses the weapon in a place other than—
   (a) a public place,
   (b) school premises,
   (c) further education premises, or
   (d) a prison . . .

(7A) It is a defence for a person charged with an offence under subsection (1A) to show that the weapon in question is one of historical importance

(11ZA) It is a defence for a person charged with an offence under subsection (1A) to show that they possessed the weapon in question for educational purposes only

SO

6 months' imprisonment and/or a fine

These provisions apply to weapons specified in the Criminal Justice Act 1988 (Offensive Weapons) Order 1988 (SI 1988/2019) as amended. The Order also sets out a series of specific defences such as in relation to Sikh curved swords for use in a religious or ceremonial ceremony.

C18.2.1 *Sentencing*

SCG **Bladed articles and offensive weapons—possession**

Note: A separate guideline applies for children and young people and appears in the *Handbook* for youths in the criminal courts.

C18.2.2 Key points

Has with him

- The Crown must prove that the person had the item with him and that it falls within the definition in the section. Only then must the defence establish a defence to the civil standard.
- It is necessary to show that the person knew that he was in possession of the offensive weapon (*R v Cugullere* [1961] 2 All ER 343).
- A court should not approach the issue of 'good reason' (and thus 'reasonable excuse') wholly objectively, nor hold that an angry, intoxicated, or traumatized state of mind could not contribute to good reason. A fear of attack can constitute good reason, the defendant's state of mind was relevant, and 'good reason' should be allowed a natural meaning. In *R v Clancy* [2012] EWCA Crim 8 (a decision under s 139 Criminal Justice Act 1988) the distorted thinking of the defendant following a sexual assault had to be considered. Only if the view was wholly unreasonable in all the circumstances as perceived by her should a court dismiss the defence.
- While *Ohlson v Hylton* [1975] 1 WLR 724 confirms that an offence does not occur if a person lawfully in possession of an article, which is not offensive per se, suddenly uses it in the heat of an altercation, an offence does occur if a person leaves the scene to collect a weapon (*R v Tucker* [2016] EWCA Crim 13).

Public place

- A public place is defined by both statutes. A landing in a block of flats is a public place if it could be reached without hindrance (*Knox v Anderson* [1982] 76 Cr App R 156) but not if access was restricted by key, access code, or intercom (*Williams v DPP* [1992] 95 Crim App R 415). Unimpeded access does not necessarily make it a public place. Public access must be implied or tolerated (*Harriott v DPP* [2005] EWHC 965 (Admin)).

Offensive weapon

- Weapons held by the appellate courts to be offensive per se include: a bayonet, a stiletto, a handgun, a butterfly knife, and a flick knife. Items that are inherently dangerous but manufactured for a lawful purpose are not offensive per se (eg razor blades, baseball bats, kitchen knives). It is likely that items prohibited for sale in England and Wales or possession in a private place by virtue of the Criminal Justice Act 1988 (Offensive Weapons) Order 1988 (SI 1988/2019) are offensive per se.
- The definition of a zombie knife, which is included in Criminal Justice Act 1988 (Offensive Weapons) Order 1988 (SI 1988/2019), includes there being 'images or words (whether on the blade or handle) that suggest that it is to be used for the purpose of violence'. According to *Thompson v CPS* [2024] EWHC 470 (Admin) there will be a wide range of words that will meet the statutory definition and they can be either expressed or implied. A reference to a violent film (*Rambo* in this case) can be sufficient.
- A belt buckle that comprises a knuckleduster but has additional items to secure the belt closed is not necessarily offensive per se, rather the court must make findings of fact whether the buckle had been made (as a knuckleduster) for the purpose of causing injury, and had then been adapted by the belt manufacturer, or whether it had in fact been manufactured as a buckle for a belt as a fashion item (*R v Christof* [2015] EWHC 4096 (Admin)).

Bladed article

- A lock knife is not a folding knife, irrespective of the blade length (*Harris v DPP* [1993] 1 WLR 82).
- A blade capable of being locked, however weakly, was not a folding pocket-knife as it was not immediately foldable by simply applying pressure to the blade (*Sharma v DPP* [2018] EWHC 3330 (Admin)).
- A cut-throat razor, less than 3" in length, does not fall within the definition of a folding pocket knife as it is a razor and not a knife (*R v D* [2019] EWCA Crim 45).
- A screwdriver is not a bladed article (*R v Davis* [1998] Crim LR 564).
- A blade does not need to be sharp—a butter knife can be a bladed article (*Brooker v DPP* [2005] EWHC 1132 (Admin)).

Reasonable excuse / good reason

- 'Good reason' has been interpreted to mean the same as 'reasonable excuse' under the 1953 Act.
- The fact that a defendant's employment was only casual was not a relevant consideration to prevent it being a good reason (*Chalal v DPP* [2010] EWHC 439 (Admin)).
- While mere forgetfulness cannot amount to a reasonable excuse (or good reason) (*R v Glidewell* [1999] EWCA Crim 1221), the court must consider

all the circumstances in which the forgetfulness arose (*R v Jolie* [2003] EWCA Crim 1543).

- Fear of attack may amount to a reasonable excuse if the risk is imminent (*R v McAuley* [2009] EWCA Crim 2130).
- An innocent purpose for having a weapon, offensive per se, in a public place does not equate to a reasonable excuse. Rather the court is entitled to consider whether there is a necessity or immediate temporal connection between possession and the purpose for which it is carried (*Garry v CPS* [2019] EWHC 636 (Admin)).

Criminal Justice Act 1988, s 139A

- school premises extend to surrounding land, playing fields, and yards;
- the offence can be committed when the school is closed;
- private schools' premises fall within the Act.

See *Blackstone's Criminal Practice 2026* **B12.149; B12.182; B12.191**

C18.3 Aggravated possession of bladed articles and offensive weapons (threats)

Prevention of Crime Act 1953, s 1A

1A Offence of threatening with offensive weapon in public

(1) A person is guilty of an offence if that person—
  (a) has an offensive weapon with him or her in a public place,
  (b) unlawfully and intentionally threatens another person (A) with the weapon, and
  (c) does so in such a way that a reasonable person (B) who was exposed to the same threat as A would think there was an immediate risk of physical harm to B

(2) For the purposes of this section physical harm is serious if it amounts to grievous bodily harm for the purposes of the Offences against the Person Act 1861.]

(3) In this section 'public place' and 'offensive weapon' have the same meaning as in section 1.

. . .

(12) If on a person's trial for an offence under this section (whether on indictment or not) the person is found not guilty of that offence but it is proved that the person committed an offence under section 1, the person may be convicted of the offence under that section.

Criminal Justice Act 1988, s 139AA

139AA Offence of threatening with article with blade or point or offensive weapon

(1) A person is guilty of an offence if that person—
  (a) has an article to which this section applies with him or her in a public place or on school premises,
  (b) unlawfully and intentionally threatens another person *(A)* with the article, and
  (c) does so in such a way that a reasonable person (B) who was exposed to the same threat as A would think there was an immediate risk of physical harm to B

(1A) A person is guilty of an offence if that person—
(a) has an article to which this section applies with them on further education premises,
(b) unlawfully and intentionally threatens another person ('A') with the article, and
(c) does so in such a way that a reasonable person ('B') who was exposed to the same threat as A would think that there was an immediate risk of physical harm to B.

(2) In relation to a public place this section applies to an article to which section 139 applies.

(3) In relation to school premises this section applies to each of these—
(a) an article to which section 139 applies;
(b) an offensive weapon within the meaning of section 1 of the Prevention of Crime Act 1953.

(3A) In relation to further education premises this section applies to each of these—
(a) an article to which section 139 applies;
(b) an offensive weapon within the meaning of section 1 of the Prevention of Crime Act 1953.

(4) For the purposes of this section physical harm is serious if it amounts to grievous bodily harm for the purposes of the Offences against the Person Act 1861.

(5) In this section—
'public place' has the same meaning as in section 139; 'school premises' has the same meaning as in section 139A.

(12) If on a person's trial for an offence under this section (whether on indictment or not) the person is found not guilty of that offence but it is proved that the person committed an offence under section 139 or 139A, the person may be convicted of the offence under that section.

EW

12 months' imprisonment and/or fine/4 years' imprisonment *but* with a minimum obligatory sentence under s 312 SA 2020 unless there are exceptional circumstances. A 20 per cent reduction on that obligatory sentence is available for an early guilty plea, and there is no statutory reason why a sentence on an adult should not be suspended (*R v Uddin* [2012] EWCA Crim 751). See **D20**.

Offensive Weapons Act 2019, s 52

52 Offence of threatening with an offensive weapon etc in a private place

(1) A person ('A') commits an offence if—
(a) while A is in a private place, A unlawfully and intentionally threatens another person ('B') with an article or substance to which this subsection applies, and
(b) A does so in such a way that there is an immediate risk of serious physical harm to B.

(2) Subsection (1) applies to an article or substance if it is—
(a) an offensive weapon within the meaning of section 1 of the Prevention of Crime Act 1953,
(b) an article to which section 139 of the Criminal Justice Act 1988 (offence of having article with blade or point in public place) applies, or
(c) a corrosive substance.

(3) In the application of subsection (1) to an article within subsection (2)(a) or (b), 'private place' means a place other than—
  (a) a public place,
  (b) a place which is part of school premises, or
  (c) a place which is part of further education premises.
(4) In the application of subsection (1) to a corrosive substance, 'private place' means a place other than a public place.
(5) For the purposes of subsection (1) physical harm is serious if it amounts to grievous bodily harm for the purposes of the Offences against the Person Act 1861.
(8) In this section and section 53—
'corrosive substance' means a substance that is capable of burning human skin by corrosion; 'further education premises' means land used solely for the purposes of—
  (a) an institution within the further education sector (within the meaning of section 91 of the Further and Higher Education Act 1992), or
  (b) a 16 to 19 Academy (within the meaning of section 1B of the Academies Act 2010), excluding any land occupied solely as a dwelling by a person employed at the institution or the 16 to 19 Academy

EW

12 months' imprisonment and/or a fine/4 years' imprisonment

C18.3.1 *Sentencing*

Note: A separate guideline applies for children and young people and appears in the *Handbook* for youths in the criminal courts.

SCG **Bladed articles and offensive weapons—threats (doesn't apply to s 52 offence)**

C18.3.2 Key points

The defences available to the aggravated offences do not replicate those for the basic crimes

See *Blackstone's Criminal Practice 2026* **B12.179; B12.196; B12.200**

C18.4 Offences in relation to corrosive substances

See *Blackstone's Criminal Practice 2026* **B12.233**

C18.4.1 *Offence of having a corrosive substance in a public place*

Offensive Weapons Act 2019, s 6

(1) A person commits an offence if they have a corrosive substance with them in a public place.
(2) It is a defence for a person charged . . . with an offence under subsection (1) to prove that they had good reason or lawful authority for having the corrosive substance with them in a public place.

> (3) Without prejudice to the generality of subsection (2), it is a defence for a person charged . . . with an offence under subsection (1) to prove that they had the corrosive substance with them for use at work.

EW

12 months' imprisonment and/or fine/4 years' imprisonment but with a minimum obligatory sentence unless there are exceptional circumstances. A 20 per cent reduction on that obligatory sentence is available for an early guilty plea, and there is no statutory reason why a sentence on an adult should not be suspended. (*R v Uddin* [2012] EWCA Crim 751). See **D20**.

C18.4.2 Key points

- 'corrosive substance' means a substance which is capable of burning human skin by corrosion;
- 'public place', in relation to England and Wales or Northern Ireland, includes any place to which, at the time in question, the public have or are permitted access, whether on payment or otherwise; see **C18.2.2**.

Part D
Sentencing

D1 Alteration of Sentence

D1.1 Section 142 Magistrates' Courts Act 1980

Section 142 Magistrates' Courts Act 1980 gives the court power to reopen sentence. The procedure is set out in Crim PR 44.

There are no time restrictions, but a court must have regard to the principle of finality of sentence, meaning that in many cases it will not be proper to interfere (*R (Trigger) v Northampton Magistrates' Court* [2011] EWHC 149 (Admin)). For case law see A6.2. Section 142(1) provides:

Magistrates' Courts Act 1980, s 142(1)

142 Power of magistrates' court to re-open cases to rectify mistakes etc

(1) A magistrates' court may vary or rescind a sentence or other order imposed or made by it when dealing with an offender if it appears to the court to be in the interests of justice to do so, and it is hereby declared that this power extends to replacing a sentence or order which for any reason appears to be invalid by another which the court has power to impose or make.

See *Blackstone's Criminal Practice 2026* **D23.23**

Blackstone's Magistrates' Court Handbook 2026. Bartholomew Dalton and Caroline Liggins, Oxford University Press. © Oxford University Press 2026.
DOI: 10.1093/oso/9780198963943.003.0060

D2 Banning Orders (Football)

Banning orders are imposed under s 14A Football Spectators Act 1989.

D2.1 Criteria and effect

Banning orders must be imposed when an offender is convicted of a relevant offence, unless the court considers that there are particular circumstances relating to the offence or to the offender which would make it unjust in all the circumstances to do so.

The core requirements of such an order are to prohibit the offender from attending regulated football matches in England and Wales. When matches are being played abroad, the order will require the offender to report to a police station and surrender his passport (unless there are exceptional circumstances certified by the court as to why this should not be done). Other requirements can be imposed, for example not to go within a certain distance of a football ground.

The order must be for a period of between 3 and 5 years, or 6 and 10 years if a custodial sentence (including a sentence of detention) is imposed for the original offence. A banning order cannot be limited to matches between particular teams (*Commissioner of Police of the Metropolis v Thorpe* [2015] EWHC 3339 (Admin)).

In *Newman v Commissioner of Police of the Metropolis* [2009] EWHC 1642 (Admin), the court held that the police were entitled to rely upon compilation witness statements and compilation video footage, and had no duty to disclose the underlying material from which they were drawn. There is no statutory disclosure regime applicable to the making of banning orders and a court should apply normal principles of 'fairness'. Advocates seeking disclosure should be careful to specify the material that they wish to view and the reasons why. An application that amounts to nothing more than a 'fishing expedition' ought to be refused.

D2.2 Relevant offences

Relevant offences are listed in Sch 1 to the 1989 Act. For identified offences, the court will need to make a declaration of relevance (as to which see **D2.3**).

Football Spectators Act 1989, Sch 1

1. This Schedule applies to the following offences:
   (a) any offence under section 14J(1), 19(6), 20(10) or 21C(2) of this Act,
   (b) any offence under section 2 or 2A of the Sporting Events (Control of Alcohol etc) Act 1985 (alcohol, containers, and fireworks) committed by the accused at any football match to which this Schedule applies or while entering or trying to enter the ground,
   (c) any offence under section 4, 4A or 5 of the Public Order Act 1986 (fear or provocation of violence, or harassment, alarm, or distress) or any provision of Part III of that Act (racial hatred) committed during a period relevant to a football match to which this Schedule applies at any premises while the accused was at, or was entering or leaving or trying to enter or leave, the premises,

Blackstone's Magistrates' Court Handbook 2026. Bartholomew Dalton and Caroline Liggins, Oxford University Press.
DOI: 10.1093/oso/9780198963943.003.0061

(d) any offence involving the use or threat of violence by the accused towards another person committed during a period relevant to a football match to which this Schedule applies at any premises while the accused was at, or was entering or leaving or trying to enter or leave, the premises,
(e) any offence involving the use or threat of violence towards property committed during a period relevant to a football match to which this Schedule applies at any premises while the accused was at, or was entering or leaving or trying to enter or leave, the premises,
(f) any offence involving the use, carrying or possession of an offensive weapon or a firearm committed during a period relevant to a football match to which this Schedule applies at any premises while the accused was at, or was entering or leaving or trying to enter or leave the premises
(g) any offence under section 12 of the Licensing Act 1872 (persons found drunk in public places, etc) of being found drunk in a highway or other public place committed while the accused was on a journey to or from a football match to which this Schedule applies being an offence as respects which the court makes a declaration that the offence related to football matches,
(h) any offence under section 91(1) of the Criminal Justice Act 1967 (disorderly behaviour while drunk in a public place) committed in a highway or other public place while the accused was on a journey to or from a football match to which this Schedule applies being an offence as respects which the court makes a declaration that the offence related to football matches, . . .
(j) any offence under section 1 of the Sporting Events (Control of Alcohol etc) Act 1985 (alcohol on coaches or trains to or from sporting events) committed while the accused was on a journey to or from a football match to which this Schedule applies being an offence as respects which the court makes a declaration that the offence related to football matches,
(k) any offence under section 4, 4A or 5 of the Public Order Act 1986 (fear or provocation of violence, or harassment, alarm, or distress) or any provision of Part 3 or 3A of that Act (racial hatred) committed while the accused was on a journey to or from a football match to which this Schedule applies being an offence as respects which the court makes a declaration that the offence related to football matches,
(l) any offence under section 4 or 5 or 5A of the Road Traffic Act 1988 (driving etc when under the influence of drink or drugs or with an alcohol concentration above the prescribed limit or with a concentration of a specified controlled drug above the specified limit) committed while the accused was on a journey to or from a football match to which this Schedule applies being an offence as respects which the court makes a declaration that the offence related to football matches,
(m) any offence involving the use or threat of violence by the accused towards another person committed while one or each of them was on a journey to or from a football match to which this Schedule applies being an offence as respects which the court makes a declaration that the offence related to football matches,
(n) any offence involving the use or threat of violence towards property committed while the accused was on a journey to or from a football match to which this Schedule applies being an offence as respects which the court makes a declaration that the offence related to football matches,
(o) any offence involving the use, carrying or possession of an offensive weapon or a firearm committed while the accused was on a journey to or from a football match to which this Schedule applies being an offence as respects which the court makes a declaration that the offence related to football matches,
(p) any offence under the Football (Offences) Act 1991,

(q) any offence under section 4, 4A or 5 of the Public Order Act 1986 (fear or provocation of violence, or harassment, alarm, or distress)—
   (i) which does not fall within paragraph (c) or (k) above,
   (ii) which was committed during a period relevant to a football match to which this Schedule applies, and
   (iii) as respects which the court makes a declaration that the offence related to that match or to that match and any other football match which took place during that period,

(r) any offence involving the use or threat of violence by the accused towards another person—
   (i) which does not fall within paragraph (d) or (m) above,
   (ii) which was committed during a period relevant to a football match to which this Schedule applies, and
   (iii) as respects which the court makes a declaration that the offence related to that match or to that match and any other football match which took place during that period,

(s) any offence involving the use or threat of violence towards property—
   (i) which does not fall within paragraph (e) or (n) above,
   (ii) which was committed during a period relevant to a football match to which this Schedule applies, and
   (iii) as respects which the court makes a declaration that the offence related to that match or to that match and any other football match which took place during that period,

(t) any offence involving the use, carrying or possession of an offensive weapon or a firearm—
   (i) which does not fall within paragraph (f) or (o) above,
   (ii) which was committed during a period relevant to a football match to which this Schedule applies, and
   (iii) as respects which the court makes a declaration that the offence related to that match or to that match and any other football match which took place during that period.

(u) any offence under section 166 of the Criminal Justice and Public Order Act 1994 (sale of tickets by unauthorised persons) which relates to tickets for a football match.

(v) any offence under any provision of Part 3 or 3A of the Public Order Act 1986 (hatred by reference to race etc)—
   (i) which does not fall within paragraph (c) or (k), and
   (ii) as respects which the court makes a declaration that the offence related to a football match, to a football organisation or to a person whom the accused knew or believed to have a prescribed connection with a football organisation,

(w) any offence under section 31 of the Crime and Disorder Act 1998 (racially or religiously aggravated public order offences) as respects which the court makes a declaration that the offence related to a football match, to a football organisation or to a person whom the accused knew or believed to have a prescribed connection with a football organisation,

(x) any offence under section 1 of the Malicious Communications Act 1988 (offence of sending letter, electronic communication or article with intent to cause distress or anxiety)—
   (i) which does not fall within paragraph (d), (e), (m), (n), (r) or (s),
   (ii) as respects which the court has stated that the offence is aggravated by hostility of any of the types mentioned in section 66(1) of the Sentencing Code (racial hostility etc), and
   (iii) as respects which the court makes a declaration that the offence related to a football match, to a football organisation or to a person whom

the accused knew or believed to have a prescribed connection with a football organisation,

(y) any offence under section 127(1) of the Communications Act 2003 (improper use of public telecommunications network)—
  (i) which does not fall within paragraph (d), (e), (m), (n), (r) or (s),
  (ii) as respects which the court has stated that the offence is aggravated by hostility of any of the types mentioned in section 66(1) of the Sentencing Code (racial hostility etc), and
  (iii) as respects which the court makes a declaration that the offence related to a football match, to a football organisation or to a person whom the accused knew or believed to have a prescribed connection with a football organisation.

(z) any offence under section 4(3) or 5 of the Misuse of Drugs Act 1971 (supply or possession etc. of controlled substances) committed by the accused in relation to a Class A drug, as defined in section 2(1)(b) of that Act, at any football match to which this Schedule applies or while entering or trying to enter the ground.

With effect from a date to be appointed, para 1(c), (k), and (q) are amended by the Protection from Sex-based Harassment in Public Act 2023, s 3(1) so as to insert reference in each to the new offence under s 4B of the Public Order Act 1986.

D2.3 Declaration of relevance

The prosecution must give 5 days' notice that they intend to invite a court to make a declaration of relevance. That notice period may be waived by the defence; it can also be dispensed with by the court if the interests of justice do not require a longer notice period to be given. Note that the court can grant an adjournment to facilitate the 5-day notice period.

The declaration is that the offence related to that match, or to that match and any other football match which took place during that period.

Each of the following periods is 'relevant to' a football match to which Sch 1 applies:

- in the case of a match which takes place on the day on which it is advertised to take place, the period:
  - beginning 24 hours before whichever is the earlier of the start of the match and the time at which it was advertised to start, and
  - ending 24 hours after it ends;
- in the case of a match which does not take place on the day on which it was advertised to take place, the period:
  - beginning 24 hours before the time at which it was advertised to start on that day, and
  - ending 24 hours after that time. . . .

In *R v Arbery* [2008] EWCA Crim 702, the offenders were drinking in a public house following a football match, waiting for their train home, when violence broke out with rival supporters. A football banning order was quashed on appeal, as the court held that the offence arose out of a disagreement in the pub, completely unrelated to football.

In *R v Eliot* [2007] EWCA Crim 1002, the court gave a helpful insight into how the issue of 'relevance' might be approached:

> Did the offences committed in the present case relate to the match? Clearly, the presence of the applicants in London and indeed at Leicester Square related to the match. But it is not their presence, or their allegiance, which is the touchstone of the declaration; it is the relationship between the offence and the match. Here, the offences were sparked by the presence of a group of football supporters in London. The spark, however, had nothing to do with the match itself on the facts as found by the judge. The violence took place, not because of anything that had happened at the football match, or between supporters but because of disparaging remarks made to a lady who had nothing to do with the football match and remarks which had nothing to do with the football match. In those circumstances, we do not consider that, in this case, the statutory requirement was satisfied.

In *DPP v Beaumont* [2008] EWHC 523 (Admin), the court rejected an argument that there was a temporal limit to the making of a banning order. In that case the violence erupted more than one hour after the end of the match.

Reviewing the law in *R v Doyle* [2012] EWCA Crim 1869, the court sought to identify:

- a relevant offence (Sch 1—see **D2.2**). These offences must 'relate' to football matches, which is an issue of fact—one match will suffice. Merely being on a journey to a match is not enough. Groups of fans will more easily meet the test. It is not enough that the violence would not have occurred 'but for' the journey to the football match.
- In *R v Irving* [2013] EWCA Crim 1932, the court confirmed:
  - Where the particular offence in Sch 1 Football Spectators Act 1989 requires a declaration that the offence related to a particular football match, the failure to make such a declaration meant that no order could be made.
  - An offence could relate to a football match even though the defendant supported neither team and did not go to the game, as where there is an ambush of supporters.
  - Requirements attached to the order must be considered individually and be proportionate.

D2.4 Sentencing

In sentencing for breach of an order, the court should refer to the sentencing approach in step one of the guideline for breach of a criminal behaviour order to determine culpability and harm, and determine an appropriate sentence bearing in mind the maximum penalty for the offence.

D2.5 Appeals

An appeal lies to the Crown Court in respect to the making of a banning order or dismissal of prosecution application (Football Spectators Act 1989, s 14D).

See *Blackstone's Criminal Practice 2026* E21.3

D3 Breach of Post-Sentence Supervision

Under s 256AA Criminal Justice Act (CJA) 2003, if a person is sentenced to under 2 years in custody, they will be subject to supervision for a year from the date of their actual release 'for the purposes of rehabilitation'.

Similar arrangements are made for 'children' who are 18 on the date of their release from post-January 2015 sentences of detention and training, or detention, under s 249 SA 2022, extending their period of supervision in these cases.

D3.1 Breach of supervision requirements imposed under section 256AA

A new application for legal aid may be made under s 14(b) Legal Aid Sentencing and Punishment of Offenders Act 2012.

Criminal Justice Act 2003, s 256AC

(4) If it is proved to the satisfaction of the court that the person has failed without reasonable excuse to comply with a supervision requirement imposed under section 256AA, the court may—

  (a) order the person to be committed to prison for a period not exceeding 14 days (subject to subsection (7)),

  (b) order the person to pay a fine not exceeding level 3 on the standard scale, or

  (c) make an order (a 'supervision default order') imposing on the person—

    (i) an unpaid work requirement (as defined by paragraph 1 of Schedule 9 to the Sentencing Code), or

    (ii) a curfew requirement (as defined by paragraph 9 of that Schedule).

(5) Paragraph 10(3) of Schedule 9 to the Sentencing Code (obligation to impose electronic monitoring requirement) applies in relation to a supervision default order that imposes a curfew requirement as it applies in relation to a community order that imposes such a requirement.

(6) If the court deals with the person under subsection (4), it must revoke any supervision default order which is in force at that time in respect of that person.

(7) Where the person is under the age of 21—

  (a) an order under subsection (4)(a) in respect of the person must be for committal to a young offender institution instead of to prison,

(8) A person committed to prison or a young offender institution by an order under subsection (4)(a) is to be regarded as being in legal custody.

(9) A fine imposed under subsection (4)(b) is to be treated, for the purposes of any enactment, as being a sum adjudged to be paid by a conviction.

(10) In Schedule 19A (supervision default orders)—

  (a) Part 1 makes provision about requirements of supervision default orders, and

  (b) Part 2 makes provision about the breach, revocation and amendment of supervision default orders . . .

Blackstone's Magistrates' Court Handbook 2026. Bartholomew Dalton and Caroline Liggins, Oxford University Press.
DOI: 10.1093/oso/9780198963943.003.0062

D3.2 Remand on adjournment

If proceedings are adjourned the court has the power to remand in custody or on bail under ss 10(4) and 128 MCA 1980. Section 4(3) of the Bail Act 1976 does not apply and there is no statutory right to bail.

D3.3 Breach of a supervision default order

Breach of a supervision default order, without reasonable excuse, can be dealt with by using either:

- up to 14 days' custody;
- up to level 3 fine; or
- amended supervision default orders, taking account of what has already been done.

Supervision default orders are to be revoked if custody is later imposed (Sch 19A CJA 2003).

D4 Committal for Sentence

D4.1 Criteria

See also A4.

A magistrates' court may commit an offender for sentence for an either-way offence following a conviction (Sentencing Act (SA) 2020, s 14 or guilty plea s 18).

A magistrates' court will commit for sentence if the court is of the opinion:

- that the offence or the combination of the offence and one or more offences associated with it was so serious that greater punishment should be inflicted for the offence than the court has power to impose; or
- in the case of a violent or sexual offence, that a custodial sentence for a term longer than the court has power to impose is necessary to protect the public from serious harm from the offender.

Additional committal powers in relation to other offences are provided for under s 20 SA 2020. The powers of the Crown Court depend on the use of the correct section to commit the defendant.

Sentencing Act 2020, ss 14; 15; 18; 20

14 Committal for sentence on summary trial of offence triable either way: adults and corporations

(1) This section applies where—
  (a) on the summary trial of an offence triable either way a person aged 18 or over is convicted of the offence, and
  (b) the court is of the opinion that—
    (i) the offence, or
    (ii) the combination of the offence and one or more offences associated with it, was so serious that the Crown Court should have the power to deal with the offender in any way it could deal with the offender if the offender had been convicted on indictment.

This is subject to the provisions mentioned in subsection (4).

(2) The court may commit the offender in custody or on bail to the Crown Court for sentence in accordance with section 21(2).

(3) For powers of the court, where it commits a person under subsection (2), also to commit in respect of other offences, see section 20.

(4) For offences in relation to which this section does not apply see sections 17D and 33 of the Magistrates' Courts Act 1980 (exclusion in respect of certain offences where value involved is small).

(5) This section applies to a corporation as if—
  (a) the corporation were an individual aged 18 or over, and
  (b) in subsection (2) the words 'in custody or on bail' were omitted.

15 Committal for sentence of dangerous adult offenders

(1) This section applies where—
  (a) on the summary trial of a specified offence (see section 306) triable either way a person aged 18 or over is convicted of the offence, and (b) the court is of the opinion that an extended sentence of detention in a young offender

Blackstone's Magistrates' Court Handbook 2026. Bartholomew Dalton and Caroline Liggins, Oxford University Press. © Oxford University Press 2026.
DOI: 10.1093/oso/9780198963943.003.0063

institution or of imprisonment (see section 266 or 279) would be available in relation to the offence.

(2) The court must commit the offender in custody or on bail to the Crown Court for sentence in accordance with section 21(2).

(3) For powers of the court, where it commits a person under subsection (2) also to commit in respect of other offences, see section 20.

(4) In doing anything under or contemplated by this section, the court is not bound by any indication of sentence given in respect of the offence under section 20 of the Magistrates' Courts Act 1980 (procedure where summary trial appears more suitable).

(5) Nothing the court does under this section may be challenged or be the subject of any appeal in any court on the ground that it is inconsistent with an indication of sentence.

(6) Nothing in this section prevents the court from committing an offender convicted of a specified offence to the Crown Court for sentence under section 14 or 18 if the provisions of that section are satisfied.

18 Committal for sentence on indication of guilty plea to offence triable either way: adult offenders

(1) Where a magistrates' court—
  (a) has convicted an offender aged 18 or over of an offence triable either way following an indication of a guilty plea, and
  (b) has sent the offender to the Crown Court for trial for one or more related offences, it may commit the offender in custody or on bail to the Crown Court to be dealt with in respect of the offence in accordance with section 21(2).

(2) For offences in relation to which subsection (1) does not apply see section 17D of the Magistrates' Courts Act 1980 (cases where value involved is small).

(3) Where a magistrates' court—
  (a) convicts an offender aged 18 or over of an offence triable either way following an indication of a guilty plea, and
  (b) is still to determine to send, or whether to send, the offender to the Crown Court for trial under section 51 or 51A of the Crime and Disorder Act 1998, for one or more related offences, it must adjourn the proceedings relating to the offence until after it has made those determinations.

(4) Where the court—
  (a) commits the offender under subsection (1) to the Crown Court to be dealt with in respect of the offence, and
  (b) in its opinion also has power under section 14(2) or is required under section 15(2) to commit the offender to the Crown Court to be dealt with in respect of the offence, the court may make a statement of that opinion.

(5) For powers of the court, where it commits a person under subsection (1), also to commit in respect of other offences, see section 20.

(6) For the purposes of this section, a magistrates' court convicts a person of an offence triable either way following an indication of a guilty plea if—
  (a) the person appears or is brought before the court on an information charging the person with the offence, (b) the person or (where applicable) the person's representative indicates under—
    (i) section 17A or 17B of the Magistrates' Courts Act 1980 (indication of intention as to plea in case of offence triable either way), or
    (ii) section 20(7) of that Act (summary trial appears more suitable), that the person would plead guilty if the offence were to proceed to trial, and
  (c) proceeding as if—
    (i) section 9(1) of that Act were complied with, and
    (ii) the person pleaded guilty under it, the court convicts the person of the offence.

(7) For the purposes of this section—
  (a) 'related offence' means an offence which, in the opinion of the court, is related to the offence, and
  (b) one offence is related to another if, were they both to be prosecuted on indictment, the charges for them could be joined in the same indictment.

(8) In doing anything under or contemplated by this section, the court is not bound by any indication of sentence given in respect of the offence under section 20 of the Magistrates' Courts Act 1980 (procedure where summary trial appears more suitable).

(9) Nothing the court does under this section may be challenged or be the subject of any appeal in any court; and)

20 Committal in certain cases where offender committed in respect of another offence

(1) This section applies where a magistrates' court ('the committing court') commits an offender to the Crown Court under—
  (a) sections 14 to 19 (committal for sentence for offences triable either way),
  (b) paragraph 5(4) of Schedule 2 (further offence committed by offender given conditional discharge order),
  (c) paragraph 24(2) of Schedule 10 (committal to Crown Court where offender commits further offence while community order is in force),
  (d) paragraph 11(2) of Schedule 16 (committal to Crown Court where offender commits further offence during operational period of suspended sentence order),
  (e) section 43 of the Mental Health Act 1980 (power of magistrates' courts to commit for restriction order),
  (f) section 6(6) or 9(3) of the Bail Act 1976 (committal to Crown Court for offences of absconding by person released on bail or agreeing to indemnify sureties in criminal proceedings), or
  (g) the Vagrancy Act 1824 (incorrigible rogues), to be sentenced or otherwise dealt with in respect of an offence ('the relevant offence').

(2) Where—
  (a) the relevant offence is an indictable offence, and
  (b) the committing court has power to deal with the offender in respect of another offence, the committing court may also commit the offender to the Crown Court to be dealt with in respect of the other offence in accordance with section 23.

(3) It is immaterial for the purposes of subsection (2) whether the court which convicted the offender of the other offence was the committing court or another court.

(4) Where the relevant offence is a summary offence, the committing court may commit the offender to the Crown Court to be dealt with, in accordance with section 23, in respect of—
  (a) any other offence of which the committing court has convicted the offender which is punishable with—
    (i) imprisonment, or
    (ii) driving disqualification, or
  (b) any suspended sentence in respect of which it falls to the committing court to deal with the offender by virtue of paragraph 11(1) of Schedule 16.

(5) For the purposes of subsection (4)(a) an offence is punishable with driving disqualification if the committing court has a power or duty to order the offender to

be disqualified under section 34, 35 or 36 of the Road Traffic Offenders Act 1988 (disqualification for certain motoring offences) in respect of it.

(6) A committal to the Crown Court under this section is to be in custody or on bail as the case may require.

See *Blackstone's Criminal Practice 2026* **D23.29**

D5 Community Orders: Imposition and Breach

D5.1 Criteria for imposition

Note: A sentencing decision flow chart appears inside the back cover.

Sections 204 and 208 Sentencing Act (SA) 2020 (148 of the Criminal Justice Act (CJA) 2003 (as amended)) provides:

Sentencing Act, ss 204, 208

204 Exercise of power to impose community order: general considerations

(1) This section applies where a community order is available.
(2) The court must not make a community order unless it is of the opinion that—
  (a) the offence, or
  (b) the combination of the offence and one or more offences associated with it,
  was serious enough to warrant the making of such an order.
(3) In forming its opinion for the purposes of subsection (2), the court must take into account all the information that is available to it about the circumstances of the offence, or of it and the associated offence or offences, including any aggravating or mitigating factors.
(4) The pre-sentence report requirements (see section 30) apply to the court in relation to forming that opinion.
(5) The fact that, by virtue of subsection (2), the court may make a community order does not require it to do so.

208 Community order: exercise of power to impose particular requirements
Restrictions and obligations relating to imposing particular requirements

(2) The power to impose a particular community order requirement is subject to the provisions of the Part of Schedule 9 relating to requirements of that kind (see column 2 of the table in section 201).

Suitability of requirements

(3) The particular community order requirement or community order requirements imposed by the order must, in the opinion of the court, be the most suitable for the offender.

This is subject to subsection (10) . . .

(10) The order must include at least one community order requirement imposed for the purpose of punishment.
(11) Subsection (10) does not apply where—
  (a) the court also imposes a fine, or
  (b) there are exceptional circumstances relating to the offence or to the offender which—
    (i) would make it unjust in all the circumstances for the court to impose a requirement for the purpose of punishment in the particular case, and
    (ii) would make it unjust in all the circumstances for the court to impose a fine for the offence concerned.

Blackstone's Magistrates' Court Handbook 2026. Bartholomew Dalton and Caroline Liggins, Oxford University Press. © Oxford University Press 2026.
DOI: 10.1093/oso/9780198963943.003.0064

Because a court is not required to impose a community sentence in cases where the offence is serious enough to justify such a sentence, there is a wider discretion to impose financial penalties.

Section 202 SA 2020 (150A CJA 2003) restricts community orders for those aged 18 or above to offences that are punishable with imprisonment.

D5.2 Reports

The court must obtain a report unless the court is of the view that one is unnecessary. (See D25.)

D5.3 Sentencing guidelines

The Sentencing Council's definitive guideline on the imposition of community and custodial sentences provides that sentencers must consider all available disposals at the time of sentence; even where the threshold for a community sentence has been passed, a fine or discharge may be an appropriate penalty. In particular, a Band D fine may be an appropriate alternative to a community order.

The guideline provides that the seriousness of the offence should be the initial factor in determining which requirements to include in a community order. It establishes three sentencing ranges within the community order band based on offence seriousness (low, medium, and high), and identifies non-exhaustive examples of requirements that might be appropriate in each. These are set out in the table following. The examples focus on punishment in the community; other requirements of a rehabilitative nature may be more appropriate in some cases.

The particular requirements imposed within the range must be suitable for the individual offender and will be influenced by a wide range of factors, including the stated purpose(s) of the sentence, the risk of reoffending, the ability of the offender to comply, and the availability of the requirements in the local area. The court must ensure that the restriction on the offender's liberty is commensurate with the seriousness of the offence and that the requirements imposed are the most suitable for the offender.

Sentences should not necessarily escalate from one community order range to the next on each sentencing occasion. The decision as to the appropriate range of community order should be based upon the seriousness of the new offence(s) (which will take into account any previous convictions).

Low	Medium	High
Offences only just cross community order threshold, where the seriousness of the offence or the nature of the offender's record means that a discharge or fine is inappropriate	Offences that obviously fall within the community order band	Offences only just fall below the custody threshold or the custody threshold is crossed but a community order is more appropriate in the circumstances

Low	Medium	High
In general, only one requirement will be appropriate and the length may be curtailed if additional requirements are necessary		More intensive sentences which combine two or more requirements may be appropriate

Low	Medium	High
Suitable requirements might include:	Suitable requirements might include:	Suitable requirements might include:
• Any appropriate rehabilitative 40–80 hours' unpaid work • curfew requirement within the lowest range (eg up to 16 hours per day for a few weeks)** • exclusion requirement, for a few months • prohibited activity requirement	• Any appropriate rehabilitative • greater number of hours of unpaid work (eg 80–150 hours) • curfew requirement within the middle range (eg up to 16 hours per day for 2–3 months)** • exclusion requirement lasting in the region of 6 months • prohibited activity requirement	• Any appropriate rehabilitative 150–300 hours' unpaid work • curfew requirement up to 12 hours per day for 4–12 months** • exclusion order lasting in the region of 12 months

If order does not contain a punitive requirement, suggested fine levels are indicated below:		
BAND A FINE	BAND B FINE	BAND C FINE

**Note: Changes to the curfew requirements brought in by the Police, Crime, Sentencing and Courts Act 2022 are set out in the Requirements section in the Overarching Guideline: Imposition of community and custodial sentences, but are not reflected in the ranges above.

D5.4 Requirements

It is a matter for the court to decide which requirements amount to a punishment in each case. When imposing requirements on the offender as part of the community order, a court should balance the requirements, or combination of requirements, with the offender's personal circumstances, and avoid conflict with work, schooling, or religious beliefs.

The available requirements are:

- unpaid work (Sch 9 Part 1 SA 2020) of between 40 and 300 hours to be completed within 12 months;
- rehabilitation activity requirement (Sch 9 Part 2 SA 2020) (the court does not prescribe the activities to be included but will specify the maximum number of activity days the offender must complete); a rehabilitation requirement activity is not punitive and therefore on its own does not

comply with s 208 SA 2020 (*Att-Gen's Reference (R v Singh)* [2021] EWCA Crim 1426);

- a programme (Sch 9 Part 3 SA 2020) (the court must specify the initial length (*R v Price* [2013] EWCA Crim 1283));
- prohibited activity (Sch 9 Part 4 SA 2020);
- curfew (Sch 9 Part 5 SA 2020) of 2–20 hours in any 24 hours but not more than 112 hours in any period of 7 days beginning with the day of the week on which the requirement first takes effect for up to 2 years;
- exclusion, (Sch 9 Part 6 SA 2020) normally with electronic monitoring; such a requirement to exclude the offender from the UK is unlawful (*R (Dragoman) v Camberwell Green Magistrates' Court* [2012] EWHC 4105 (Admin)), maximum 2 years;

the exclusion may be continuous or during specified periods;

- residence (Sch 9 Part 7 SA 2020);
- foreign travel restriction (Sch 9 Part 8 SA 2020) for up to 12 months;
- mental health treatment (Sch 9 Part 9 SA 2020).

Drug testing requirement if the misuse of a drug or psychoactive substance—

(a) caused or contributed to the offence to which the order relates or an associated offence, or
(b) is likely to cause or contribute to the commission of further offences by the offender (Sch 9 Part 10A SA 2020);
    - drug rehabilitation (Sch 9 Part 10 SA 2020);
    - alcohol treatment (Sch 9 Part 11 SA 2020);
    - alcohol abstinence and monitoring (Sch 9 Part 12 SA 2020), if alcohol is an element of the offence or a factor contributing to it and the offender is not dependent on alcohol (s 207(1)(2) SA 2020);
    - electronic monitoring (Sch 9 Part 14 SA). This provision provides for both electronic compliance (s 207(4) SA 2020) and electronic whereabouts monitoring.

D5.5 Community order made after a remand in custody or on a qualifying curfew

Sentencing Act 2020, s 205

205 Community order: effect of remand in custody

(1) In determining the restrictions on liberty to be imposed by a community order in respect of an offence, the court may have regard to any period for which the offender has been remanded in custody in connection with—
    (a) the offence, or
    (b) any other offence the charge for which was founded on the same facts or evidence.

In *R v Hemmings* [2008] 1 Cr App R (S) 106, the court held:

> A sentence of a community order, and all the more so one coupled with requirements which have a real impact on the offender's liberty, is a form of punishment. It does not seem to us to be right that the appellant should receive a substantial further punishment in circumstances where he has already received what was in practice the maximum punishment by way of imprisonment which the law could have imposed. That reasoning seems to us to be in line with the reasoning in [earlier cases where] . . . the court took the course of imposing a conditional discharge.

In *R v Rakib* [2011] EWCA Crim 870, the court, considering *Hemmings*, held that time spent in custody was not a determinative factor, and the rehabilitative aims of sentencing (s 142(1) CJA 2003) may in some cases justify a community penalty even if the offender had served on remand the equivalent of the maximum custodial sentence.

Where the time spent on a qualifying curfew meant that there would be immediate release from the appropriate prison sentence, it was not improper to impose a community order with requirements to address the underlying cause of offending. The court would not have imposed a punitive unpaid work requirement in addition (*R v Pereira-Lee* [2016] EWCA Crim 1705).

D5.6 Breach of and offences while on a community order

D5.6.1 Key points

Breach of community orders imposed under the SA 2020 is dealt with in accordance with Sch 10 SA 2020. There is no power to remand a person alleged to be in breach on bail, save on a committal to the Crown Court. Bail Act issues cannot therefore arise. Proceedings for breach of an unpaid work requirement can be issued after the community order has expired: para 21(1)(2) Sch 10 SA 2020 as interpreted in *National Probation Service v Blackfriars Crown Court* [2019] EWHC 529 (Admin). It is otherwise if the requirement forms part of a suspended sentence order (*West Yorkshire Probation Board v Cruickshanks* [2010] EWHC 615 (Admin)).

A general defence of reasonable excuse is open to the defendant. The fact that a person is appealing against a community order does not give him a reasonable excuse not to comply (*West Midlands Probation Board v Sutton Coldfield Magistrates' Court* [2008] EWHC 15 (Admin)).

On breach of a community order due to the offender having failed to comply with the terms of the order, the court must act in one of the following ways:

- impose a fine of up to £2,500;
- impose more onerous requirements than the original order (having taken into account the offender's level of cooperation with the order) and let the order continue (including, on one occasion, lengthening the order by up to six months beyond its original date);
- if the order was made by the Crown Court, commit the offender for sentence;
- revoke the order and deal with the offender in any manner in which it could deal with him if he had just been convicted by the court of the offence

(having taken into account the offender's level of cooperation with the order).

It should be noted that, with respect to an offender aged 18 years or older, imprisonment for a term of up to 6 months can be imposed following a wilful and persistent failure to comply, even if the original offence is not in itself imprisonable.

A court must be 'satisfied' that a breach has occurred to the criminal standard of proof (*West Yorkshire Probation Board v Boulter* (2005) 169 JP 601).

If the breach has occurred due to the offender's ill-health, a court should not resentence (*R v Bishop* [2004] EWCA Crim 2956).

If a person breaches an order that does not already include an unpaid work requirement, and the court is minded to impose such a requirement, the minimum hours to be worked shall be 20 (Sch 10, para 13(4) SA 2020).

Putting an offender, subject to a community order, before the court for breach was an important tool available to the probation service to ensure that orders work effectively. Critical was whether there had been any reoffending; whether the risk had reduced and whether the probation service felt the order could usefully continue (*R v Aslam (Aqib)* [2016] EWCA Crim 845).

D5.6.2 *Sentencing*

The definitive Guideline on breach offences states the following.

Breach of community order by failing to comply with requirements

The court must take into account the extent to which the offender has complied with the requirements of the community order when imposing a penalty.

In assessing the level of compliance with the order the court should consider:

(i) the overall attitude and engagement with the order as well as the proportion of elements completed;
(ii) the impact of any completed or partially completed requirements on the offender's behaviour;
(iii) the proximity of breach to imposition of order; and
(iv) evidence of circumstances or offender characteristics, such as disability, mental health issues, or learning difficulties which have impeded the offender's compliance with the order.

Overall compliance with order	Penalty
Wilful and persistent non-compliance	Revoke the order and resentence imposing custodial sentence (even where the offence seriousness did not originally merit custody)
Low level of compliance	Revoke the order and resentence original offence **or** Add curfew requirement 20–30 days* **or** 30–50 hours' additional unpaid work/add additional requirement(s) **or** Band C fine

Overall compliance with order	Penalty
Medium level of compliance	Revoke the order and resentence original offence **or** Add curfew requirement 10–20 days* **or** 20–30 hours additional unpaid work/add additional requirement(s) **or** Band B fine
High level of compliance	Add curfew requirement 6–10 days* **or** 10–20 hours' additional unpaid work/add additional requirement(s) **or** Band A fine

* Curfew days do not have to be consecutive and may be distributed over particular periods, for example at weekends, as the court deems appropriate. The period of the curfew should not exceed the duration of the community order and cannot be for longer than 12 months. The court may extend the length of requirement(s) or the length of the order to allow time for the completion of requirement(s): simply extending the length of the order is not a standalone option for dealing with a breach.

Technical guidance

(a) If imposing more onerous requirements the length of the order may be extended up to six months even if that has the effect of extending the order beyond 3 years. The power to extend can only be exercised once.
(b) If imposing unpaid work as a more onerous requirement and an unpaid work requirement was not previously included, the minimum number of hours that can be imposed is 20.
(c) The maximum fine that can be imposed is £2,500.
(d) If resentencing, a suspended sentence MUST NOT be imposed as a more severe alternative to a community order. A suspended sentence may only be imposed if it is fully intended that the offender serve a custodial sentence in accordance with the Imposition of Community and Custodial Sentences guideline.
(e) Where the order was imposed by the Crown Court, magistrates should consider their sentencing powers in dealing with a breach. Where the judge imposing the order reserved any breach proceedings commit the breach for sentence.

D5.6.3 *Further offences whilst subject to a community order (Sch 10 paras 23, 24 SA 2020)*

If the offender has committed a further offence during the life of the community order and is convicted whilst that order is in force, the court has three options open to it in respect to the original order:

- do nothing, and sentence for the new offence; or
- if the order was made by the Crown Court, commit the offender for sentence; or
- revoke the order and/or deal with the offender in any manner in which it could deal with him if he had just been convicted by the court of the

offence (having taken into account the offender's level of cooperation with the order).

D5.6.4 *Sentencing*

The Definitive Guideline on breach offences states:

Powers of the court following a subsequent conviction

A conviction for a further offence does not constitute a breach of a community order. However, in such a situation, the court should consider the . . . guidance [in] the Offences Taken into Consideration and Totality guideline: (D23.1)

Offender convicted of an offence while serving a community order

The power to deal with the offender depends on his being convicted whilst the order is still in force; it does not arise where the order has expired, even if the additional offence was committed whilst it was still current.

If an offender, in respect of whom a community order made by a magistrates' court is in force, is convicted by a magistrates' court of an additional offence, the magistrates' court should ordinarily revoke the previous community order and sentence afresh for both the original and the additional offence.

Where an offender, in respect of whom a community order made by a Crown Court is in force, is convicted by a magistrates' court, the magistrates' court may, and ordinarily should, commit the offender to the Crown Court, in order to allow the Crown Court to resentence for the original offence. The magistrates' court may also commit the new offence to the Crown Court for sentence where there is power to do so.

The sentencing court should consider the overall seriousness of the offending behaviour taking into account the additional offence and the original offence. The court should consider whether the combination of associated offences is sufficiently serious to justify a custodial sentence.

If the court does not consider that custody is necessary, it should impose a single community order that reflects the overall totality of criminality. The court must take into account the extent to which the offender complied with the requirements of the previous order.

D5.6.5 *Approach to be taken by the court*

The Sentencing Council provided guidance in *Guideline: New Sentences: Criminal Justice Act 2003*, paras 1.1.44–1.1.47):

- When increasing the onerousness of requirements, the court must consider the impact on the offender's ability to comply and the possibility of precipitating a custodial sentence for further breach. For that reason, and particularly where the breach occurs towards the end of the sentence, the court should take account of compliance to date and may consider that extending the supervision or operational periods will be more sensible; in other cases it might choose to add punitive or rehabilitative requirements instead. In making these changes the court must be mindful of the legislative restrictions on the overall length of community sentences and on the supervision and operational periods allowed for each type of requirement.

- The court dealing with breach of a community sentence should have as its primary objective ensuring that the requirements of the sentence are finished, and this is important if the court is to have regard to the statutory purposes of sentencing. A court that imposes a custodial sentence for breach without giving adequate consideration to alternatives is in danger of imposing a sentence that is not commensurate with the seriousness of the original offence and is solely a punishment for breach. This risks undermining the purposes it has identified as being important. Nonetheless, courts will need to be vigilant to ensure that there is a realistic prospect of the purposes of the order being achieved.
- A court sentencing for breach must take account of the extent to which the offender has complied with the requirements of the community order, the reasons for breach, and the point at which the breach has occurred. Where a breach takes place towards the end of the operational period and the court is satisfied that the offender's appearance before the court is likely to be sufficient in itself to ensure future compliance, then given that it is not open to the court to make no order, an approach that the court might wish to adopt could be to resentence in a way that enables the original order to be completed properly—for example, a differently constructed community sentence that aims to secure compliance with the purposes of the original sentence. (Note the restriction on making no order has now been removed.)
- If the court decides to make the order more onerous, it must give careful consideration, with advice from the Probation Service, to the offender's ability to comply. A custodial sentence should be the last resort, where all reasonable efforts to ensure that an offender completes a community sentence have failed.

See *Blackstone's Criminal Practice 2026* E12

D6 Compensation Order

D6.1 Criteria

Sentencing Act 2020, ss 133–138

133 Compensation order

In this Code 'compensation order' means an order under this Chapter made in respect of an offender for an offence that requires the offender—

(a) to pay compensation for any personal injury, loss or damage resulting from—
  (i) the offence, or
  (ii) any other offence which is taken into consideration by the court in determining the sentence for the offence, or

(b) to make payments for—
  (i) funeral expenses, or
  (ii) bereavement, in respect of a death resulting from any such offence.

Making a compensation order

134 Compensation order: availability

(1) A compensation order is available to a court by or before which an offender is convicted of an offence.

This is subject to section 136 (road accidents).

(2) Where a compensation order is available, the court may make such an order whether or not it also deals with the offender for the offence in any other way.

135 Making a compensation order

(1) A compensation order must specify the amount to be paid under it.
(2) That amount must be the amount that the court considers appropriate, having regard to any evidence and any representations that are made by or on behalf of the offender or the prosecution.

But see also sections 136 to 139.

(3) In determining—
  (a) whether to make a compensation order against an offender, or
  (b) the amount to be paid under such an order, the court must have regard to the offender's means, so far as they appear or are known to the court.
(4) Where the court considers—
  (a) that it would be appropriate both to impose a fine and to make a compensation order, but
  (b) that the offender has insufficient means to pay both an appropriate fine and appropriate compensation, the court must give preference to compensation (though it may impose a fine as well).
(5) For modifications of this section where the court also makes an order under section 380 (power to order parent or guardian to pay fine, costs, compensation or surcharge), see section 140.
(6) For the effect of proceedings in relation to confiscation orders on the court's powers in relation to compensation orders, see the following provisions of the Proceeds of Crime Act 2002—
  (a) section 13(4) (where confiscation order has been made);
  (b) section 15 (where proceedings on a confiscation order have been postponed).

Blackstone's Magistrates' Court Handbook 2026. Bartholomew Dalton and Caroline Liggins, Oxford University Press.
DOI: 10.1093/oso/9780198963943.003.0065

Particular cases

136 Road accidents

(1) A compensation order may not be made in respect of funeral expenses or bereavement in respect of a death due to a road accident.

(2) A compensation order may be made in respect of injury, loss or damage due to a road accident only if it is in respect of—

(a) loss suffered by a person's dependants in consequence of the person's death,

(b) damage which is treated by section 137 as resulting from an offence under the Theft Act 1968 or Fraud Act 2006, or

(c) uninsured harm.

(3) In subsection (2), 'uninsured harm' means injury, loss or damage as respects which—

(a) the offender was uninsured in relation to the use of the vehicle in question, and

(b) compensation is not payable under any arrangements to which the Secretary of State is a party.

An offender is not uninsured in relation to the use of a vehicle for this purpose if that use of it is exempted from insurance by section 144 of the Road Traffic Act 1988.

(4) Where a compensation order is made in respect of injury, loss or damage due to a road accident, the amount to be paid may include an amount representing all or part of any loss of, or reduction in, preferential rates of insurance attributable to the accident.

(5) In this Chapter, 'road accident' means an accident arising out of the presence of a motor vehicle on a road.

137 Damage to property and clean-up costs resulting from certain offences

(1) Subsection (2) applies in the case of an offence under the Theft Act 1968 or Fraud Act 2006, where the property in question is recovered.

(2) Any damage to the property occurring while it was out of the owner's possession is to be treated for the purposes of section 133 as having resulted from the offence.

This applies regardless of how the damage was caused and who caused it.

(3) Section 29 of the Ancient Monuments and Archaeological Areas Act 1979 makes provision about the person in whose favour a compensation order relating to certain offences involving damage to monuments is to be made.
(4) Section 33B of the Environmental Protection Act 1990 (clean-up costs) provides for certain costs connected with certain offences relating to waste to be loss or damage resulting from those offences for the purposes of section 133.

138 Funeral expenses and bereavement: cases other than road accidents

(1) A compensation order in respect of funeral expenses may be made for the benefit of anyone who incurred the expenses.

(2) A compensation order in respect of bereavement may be made only for the benefit of a person for whose benefit a claim for damages for bereavement could be made under section 1A of the Fatal Accidents Act 1976.

(3) The amount to be paid in respect of bereavement under a compensation order must not exceed the amount for the time being specified in section 1A(3) of that Act.

(4) This section is subject to section 136(1) (compensation order not available in respect of bereavement or funeral expenses in respect of a death due to a road accident).

D6.2 **Principles**

A magistrates' court can order compensation for each offence without limit of amount, and may also award compensation in relation to offences taken into consideration. If there is a compensation order, a victim surcharge is not obligatory. The court must give reasons if it does not make a compensation order (s 55 Sentencing Act 2020).

The principles are set out in *R v York* [2018] EWCA Crim 2754:

1 an offender must give details of her means
2 a judge must enquire about, and make clear findings about the offender's means
3 the court must take into account an offender's means
4 an order should not be made unless it is realistic, in the sense the court is satisfied that the offender has or will have the means to pay within a reasonable time. In general, excessively long repayment periods should be avoided
5 a court should not make an order on the assumption that it will be paid by somebody else
6 it is wrong to fix an amount of compensation without regard to the instalments which are capable of being paid by the offender and the period over which they should be paid

In relation to motor vehicle damage, the maximum payable will generally be the excess not paid by the Motor Insurers Bureau (MIB) (£300 in untraced driver cases with significant personal injury; otherwise nil), save where it is in respect of a vehicle stolen or taken without consent and there is damage to that vehicle, or the claim is not covered by the MIB.

If the amount of compensation is not agreed, the prosecution must be in a position to call evidence. In cases where the loss is unclear or subject to complex argument, the best course of action is to leave the matter to the civil courts to resolve (*R v Horsham Justices, ex p Richards* [1985] 2 All ER 1114; *R v Bewick* [2007] EWCA Crim 3297). A court can, however, make a common-sense determination (eg £50 for a small broken window).

D6.3 **Assessment of means**

In determining whether to make a compensation order against any person, and in determining the amount to be paid by any person under such an order, the court shall have regard to his means so far as they appear or are known to the court. An order made in the absence of a means inquiry is at risk of being ruled unlawful (*R v Gray* [2011] EWCA Crim 225).

Where the court considers that the offender has insufficient means to meet all financial liabilities the order of priority is as follows

- compensation (D6)
- Victim surcharge (D34)
- fine (D17)
- Prosecution costs (D27)

Save where a sentence of custody impacts on the offender's ability to pay, there is nothing wrong in principle with imposing compensation in addition to a custodial penalty.

D6.4 Time for payment

Whilst payment within a year is often required, and the defendant's means are relevant to the amount of an order, the time for payment must be proportionate. A one-year period was inappropriate and was increased on the facts in *R v Campbell (Natalie)* [2015] EWCA Crim 1876.

D6.5 Suggested levels of compensation

The Magistrates' Court Sentencing Guidelines set out the following scales for the award of compensation:

Physical injury		
Type of injury	**Description**	**Starting point**
Graze	Depending on size	£75
Bruise	Depending on size	£100
Cut: no permanent scar	Depending on size and whether stitched	£100–300
Black eye		£125
Eye	Blurred or double vision lasting up to 6 weeks	£500
	Blurred or double vision lasting for 6–13 weeks	£1,000
	Blurred or double vision lasting for more than 13 weeks (recovery expected)	£1,500
Brain	Concussion lasting 1 week	£1,500
Nose	Undisplaced fracture of nasal bone	£1,000
	Displaced fracture requiring manipulation	£2,000
	Deviated nasal septum requiring septoplasty	£2,000
Loss of non-front tooth	Depending on cosmetic effect	£750 per tooth
Loss of front tooth	Depending on cosmetic effect	£1,500 per tooth
Facial scar	Minor disfigurement (permanent)	£1,000
Arm	Fractured humerus, radius, ulna (substantial recovery)	£1,500
Shoulder	Dislocated (substantial recovery)	£900

Physical injury		
Wrist	Dislocated/ fractured—including scaphoid fracture (substantial recovery)	£2,400
	Fractured—Colles type (substantial recovery)	£2,400
Sprained wrist, ankle	Disabling for up to 6 weeks	£500
	Disabling for 6–13 weeks	£800
	Disabling for more than 13 weeks	£2,500
Finger	Fractured finger other than index finger (substantial recovery)	£300
	Fractured index finger (substantial recovery)	£1,200
	Fractured thumb (substantial recovery)	£1,750
Leg	Fractured fibula (substantial recovery)	£1,000
	Fractured femur, tibia (substantial recovery)	£1,800
Abdomen	Injury requiring laparotomy	£1,800

Mental injury	
Description	**Starting point**
Temporary mental anxiety (including terror, shock, distress), not medically verified	£500
Disabling mental anxiety, lasting more than 6 weeks, medically verified	£1,000
Disability mental illness, lasting up to 28 weeks, confirmed by psychiatric diagnosis	£1,500

Physical and sexual abuse		
Type of abuse	**Description**	**Starting point**
Physical abuse of adult	Intermittent physical assaults resulting in accumulation of healed wounds, burns, or scalds, but with no appreciable disfigurement	£2,000
Physical abuse of child	Isolated or intermittent assault(s) resulting in weals, hair pulled from scalp, etc	£1,000
	Intermittent physical assaults resulting in accumulation of healed wounds, burns, or scalds, but with no appreciable disfigurement	£1,000

Physical and sexual abuse		
Sexual abuse of adult	Non-penetrative indecent physical acts over clothing	£1,000
	Non-penetrative indecent act(s) under clothing	£2,000
Sexual abuse of child (under 18)	Non-penetrative indecent physical act(s) over clothing Non-penetrative frequent assaults over clothing or non-penetrative indecent act under clothing	£1,000 £1,500 or £2,000
	Repetitive indecent acts under clothing	£3,300

See *Blackstone's Criminal Practice 2026* **E6**

D7 Confiscation: Proceeds of Crime Act 2002

D7.1 Criteria

A magistrates' court has no power to make a confiscation order. However, in some cases it will be appropriate to accept jurisdiction for an offence but find that the prosecution or court later consider that confiscation proceedings are appropriate (a common example is in relation to counterfeit goods). A magistrates' court may commit an offender to the Crown Court for the purposes of activating the confiscation regime under the Proceeds of Crime Act 2002, even where a discharge is considered the proper sentence (see *R v Varma* [2012] UKSC 42 and D14) or the offence is summary only (*R v Sumal & Sons (Properties) Limited* 2012 EWCA Crim 1840).

In the event that the prosecution wish to proceed with confiscation proceedings, the court *must* commit the offender to the Crown Court for sentence.

Proceeds of Crime Act 2002, s 70

70 Committal by magistrates' court

(1) This section applies if—
  (a) defendant is convicted of an offence by a magistrates' court, and
  (b) the prosecutor asks the court to commit the defendant to the Crown Court with a view to a confiscation order being considered under section 6.

(2) In such a case the magistrates' court—
  (a) must commit the defendant to the Crown Court in respect of the offence, and
  (b) may commit him to the Crown Court in respect of any other offence falling within subsection (3).

(3) An offence falls within this subsection if—
  (a) the defendant has been convicted of it by the magistrates' court or any other court, and
  (b) the magistrates' court has power to deal with him in respect of it.

(4) If a committal is made under this section in respect of an offence or offences—
  (a) section 6 applies accordingly, and
  (b) the committal operates as a committal of the defendant to be dealt with by the Crown Court in accordance with section 71.

(5) If a committal is made under this section in respect of an offence for which (apart from this section) the magistrates' court could have committed the defendant for sentence under section [14(2) of the Sentencing Code] (offences triable either way) or under section [s 16(2) of that Code] (committal of child or young person) the court must state whether it would have done so.

(6) A committal under this section may be in custody or on bail.

Particular note should be made of s 70(5), with the court being invited to confirm that it would not otherwise have committed for sentence. Later

Blackstone's Magistrates' Court Handbook 2026. Bartholomew Dalton and Caroline Liggins, Oxford University Press. © Oxford University Press 2026.
DOI: 10.1093/oso/9780198963943.003.0066

clarification cannot be relied upon and it is therefore essential that a full contemporaneous note is taken (*R v Blakeburn* [2007] EWCA Crim 1803).

The process of appeal against conviction is complex when a case is committed under these provisions. It seems that such an appeal should be lodged within 15 business days under the Criminal Procedure Rules Part 34(2)(b).

See *Blackstone's Criminal Practice 2026* E19

D8 Criminal Behaviour Orders

D8.1 Notice

Criminal Procedure rule 31.3(2) requires prosecutors to give notice as soon as practicable, on a prescribed form, of their intention to apply for a criminal behaviour order (CBO). A defence lawyer should not feel pressurized into dealing with what can be a complex area of law without adequate notice.

D8.2 Criteria

Criminal behaviour orders are made following conviction.

Sentencing Act 2020, Pt 11, ss 330, 331, and 334 (Anti-social Behaviour Crime and Policing Act 2014, Pt 2, ss 22 and 25)

330 Criminal behaviour order

In this Code 'criminal behaviour order' means an order which, for the purpose of preventing an offender from engaging in behaviour that is likely to cause harassment, alarm or distress to any person—

(a) prohibits the offender from doing anything described in the order;
(b) requires the offender to do anything described in the order.

331 Power to make criminal behaviour order

(1) This section applies where—
  (a) a person is convicted of an offence, and
  (b) the prosecution makes an application to the court for a criminal behaviour order to be made against the offender.
(2) The court may make a criminal behaviour order against the offender if it—
  (a) is satisfied that the offender has engaged in behaviour that caused or was likely to cause harassment, alarm or distress to any person, and
  (b) considers that making the order will help in preventing the offender from engaging in such behaviour.
(3) But the court may make a criminal behaviour order only if it—
  (a) does so in addition to dealing with the offender for the offence, and
  (b) does not make an order for absolute discharge under section 79 in respect of the offence.
(4) Prohibitions and requirements in a criminal behaviour order must, so far as practicable, be such as to avoid—
  (a) any interference with the times, if any, at which the offender normally works or attends school or any other educational establishment;
  (b) any conflict with the requirements of any other court order to which the offender may be subject . . .

334 Duration of order etc

(1) A criminal behaviour order takes effect on the day it is made, subject to subsection (2).
(2) If on the day a criminal behaviour order ('the new order') is made the offender is subject to another criminal behaviour order ('the previous order'), the new order may be made so as to take effect on the day on which the previous order ceases to have effect.
(3) A criminal behaviour order must specify the period ('the order period') for which it has effect.

Blackstone's Magistrates' Court Handbook 2026. Bartholomew Dalton and Caroline Liggins, Oxford University Press. © Oxford University Press 2026.
DOI: 10.1093/oso/9780198963943.003.0067

(4) In the case of a criminal behaviour order made before the offender has reached the age of 18, the order period must be a fixed period of—
   (a) not less than 1 year, and
   (b) not more than 3 years.
(5) In the case of a criminal behaviour order made after the offender has reached the age of 18, the order period must be—
   (a) a fixed period of not less than 2 years, or
   (b) an indefinite period (so that the order has effect until further order).
(6) A criminal behaviour order may specify periods for which particular prohibitions or requirements have effect.

D8.3 Relevant case law

DPP v Bulmer [2015] EWHC 2323 (Admin) confirms that there is no burden of proof as such. It is an evaluative exercise. However, such orders are not to be lightly imposed. The issue is not one of pure discretion. Whilst the availability of positive requirements is important their absence does not mean that an order cannot be made. A failure to comply with past orders is a relevant consideration but not of itself a reason for refusing an order— variation of the existing order or imposition of a new one may assist. Any requirement must be proportionate and tailored to the specific circumstances. The ordinary power to arrest may not be sufficient, without an order, for the police to prevent anti-social behaviour in advance.

The earlier case law in relation to anti-social behaviour orders (ASBOs) has been adopted for CBOs by *R v Khan* [2018] EWCA Crim 1472. CBOs can impose positive as well as negative obligations and can apply to members of the same household.

Evidence of post-complaint behaviour is admissible to show whether a person has acted in an anti-social manner (and whether an order is necessary) (*Birmingham City Council v Dixon* [2009] EWHC 761 (Admin)).

That conduct was likely to cause harassment, alarm, or distress does not require evidence that the conduct was actually witnessed as long as there were people in the vicinity (street drug dealing) who were likely to see it, and thereby be caused harassment, etc (*R v Hashi* [2014] EWCA Crim 2119).

Many of the principles established in the leading case, *R v Boness* [2005] EWCA Crim 2395, and other cases (notably *R v P (Shane Tony)* [2004] EWCA Crim 287, *R v McGrath* [2005] EWCA Crim 353, and *W v DPP* [2005] EWCA Civ 1333), continue to apply to CBOs.

- The requirement that a prohibition was necessary (helpful) to protect persons from further anti-social acts by the defendant means that the use of an ASBO to punish a defendant is unlawful.
- Each separate prohibition must be targeted at the individual and the specific form of anti-social behaviour it is intended to prevent. The order must be tailored to the defendant and not designed on a word processor for generic use. Therefore the court must ask itself when considering a specific

order, 'Is this order necessary (helpful) to protect persons in any place in England and Wales from further anti-social acts by the defendant?'

- Each prohibition must be precise and capable of being understood by the defendant. Therefore the court should ask itself before making an order: 'Are the terms of this order clear so that the defendant will know precisely what it is that he is prohibited from doing?' (So unfamiliar words like 'curtilage' and 'environs' should be avoided, as should vague ones like 'implement' or 'paraphernalia'.) For example, a prohibition should clearly delineate any exclusion zone by reference to a map and clearly identify those whom the defendant must not contact or associate with.
- The terms of the order must be proportionate in the sense that they must be commensurate with the risk to be guarded against. This is particularly important where an order may interfere with a Convention right protected by the Human Rights Act 1998, for example Articles 8, 10, and 11 ECHR.
- There is no requirement that the prohibited acts should by themselves give rise to harassment, alarm, or distress.
- An ASBO should not be used merely to increase the sentence of imprisonment which an offender is liable to receive.
- Different considerations may apply if the maximum sentence is only a fine, but the court must still go through all the steps to make sure that an ASBO is necessary (helpful).

Thus the fact that an order prohibits a defendant from committing a specified criminal offence does not automatically invalidate it, although in *R v Brain* [2020] EWCA Crim 457 the court considered that, as a matter of principle, prohibitions should not be imposed in relation to conduct which would constitute a criminal offence on its own merits. Under the previous law the court should not make such an order if the sentence which could be passed following conviction for the offence would be a sufficient deterrent. The Court of Appeal has indicated that prohibiting behaviour that is in any event a crime does not necessarily address the aim of an ASBO, which is to prevent anti-social behaviour. The better course is to make an anticipatory form of order, namely an order which prevents a defendant from doing an act preparatory to the commission of the offence, thereby helping to prevent the criminal offence from being committed in the first place. For example, an order might prevent a defendant from entering a shopping centre rather than stealing from shops; or possessing a can of spray paint rather than causing criminal damage.

If a court wishes to make an order prohibiting a group of youngsters from racing cars or motorbikes on an estate or driving at excessive speed then the order should not (normally) prohibit driving whilst disqualified. It should prohibit, for example, the offender whilst on the estate from taking part in, or encouraging, racing or driving at an excessive speed. It might also prevent the group from congregating with named others in a particular area of the estate.

In *R (Cooke) v DPP* [2008] EWHC 2703 (Admin), the court held that an order was not appropriate in relation to an offender who due to mental incapacity was not able to understand its terms, as such an order would fail to protect the public and could therefore not be said to be necessary to protect others. It is suggested that this will apply all the more forcefully under the CBO regime as an order cannot help to prevent antisocial behaviour where the defendant does not understand its terms or his obligations. This is confirmed by *Humphreys v CPS* [2019] EWHC 2794 which held that a finding of fact that the offender is incapable of understanding or complying with the terms of the order, so that the only effect of the order will be to criminalize behaviour over which he has no control, will indicate that the order will not be helpful and will not satisfy the second condition in s 22(4) Anti-social Behaviour Crime and Policing Act 2014. However, where a person's condition may mean that an order would generally be helpful, but that there might be occasions when, because of his condition, he is incapable of complying with the terms of the order, the question is whether the second condition is satisfied on the facts of the particular case.

A condition not to cause harassment, alarm, or distress was too imprecise; conditions had to be clear as to what behaviour the order was seeking to discourage (*Heron v Plymouth City Council* [2009] EWHC 3562 (Admin)).

D8.4 **Alternative orders**

The flexibility of CBOs has removed the need for orders such as those under the Licensed Premises (Exclusion of Certain Persons) Act 1980 when crimes involving violence occurred on licensed premises.

See *Blackstone's Criminal Practice 2026* **D25.16**

D9 Custodial Sentences

D9.1 Criteria

Note: A sentencing decision flow chart is available in Appendix 6.

The court must not pass a custodial sentence unless it is of the opinion that the offence, or the combination of the offence and one or more offences associated with it, was so serious that neither a fine alone nor a community sentence can be justified for the offence (s 230 Sentencing Act (SA) 2020).

The Sentencing Council's definitive guideline on the imposition of community and custodial sentences sets out four questions for consideration:

(1) Has the custody threshold been passed?
(2) Is it unavoidable that a sentence of imprisonment be imposed?
(3) What is the shortest term commensurate with the seriousness of the offence?
(4) Can the sentence be suspended?

It confirms that:

- The clear intention of the threshold test is to reserve prison as a punishment for the most serious offences.
- Passing the custody threshold does not mean that a custodial sentence should be deemed inevitable.
- For offenders on the cusp of custody, imprisonment should not be imposed where there would be an impact on dependants which would make a custodial sentence disproportionate to achieving the aims of sentencing.
- Sentencers should be clear that they would impose an immediate custodial sentence if the power to suspend were not available (see **D32**).

Nothing prevents the court from passing a custodial sentence on the offender if:

- he fails to express his willingness to comply with a requirement which is proposed by the court to be included in a community order and which requires an expression of such willingness; or
- he fails to comply with an order under s 230 (4) SA 2020 (s 161(2) Criminal Justice Act 2003) (pre-sentence drug testing *when in force*).

The custodial sentence must be for the shortest term (not exceeding the permitted maximum) that in the opinion of the court is commensurate with the seriousness of the offence, or the combination of the offence and one or more offences associated with it (s 231 SA 2020).

Blackstone's Magistrates' Court Handbook 2026. Bartholomew Dalton and Caroline Liggins, Oxford University Press. © Oxford University Press 2026.
DOI: 10.1093/oso/9780198963943.003.0068

D9.2 **Minima and maxima sentences**

Type of sentence	Age requirement	Notes
Detention in young offender institution	18–20 years	Minimum sentence of 21 days. Maximum 12 months for an either way offence. Subject always to the statutory maximum for the offences in question **s 263 SA 2020** See **D13**
Imprisonment	21 years+	Minimum 5 days save for detention imposed under ss 135 and 136 Magistrates' Courts Act (MCA) 1980. Maximum six months for a summary only offence. Maximum 12 months for an either way offence. Subject always to the statutory maximum for the offences in question; If at least two either way offences fall to be sentenced, the court has the power to impose a sentence up to 12 months in any aggregate combination and the aggregate sentence in respect of any summary offences, in addition to the either way offences, is not restricted to six months (R v Jex and others [2021] EWCA Crim 1708). These maxima may be consecutive to a sentence already imposed by another court; and do not restrict the activation consecutively of a suspended sentence (R v Palmer [2019] EWCA Crim 2231). **s 224 SA 2020 and s 133(1) and (2) MCA 2000**

D9.3 **Consequences of a maximum sentence**

If the court imposes a sentence of 12 months, the automatic deportation provisions in s 32 of UK Borders Act 2007 become effective and the court is able to recommend licence conditions that might be imposed on release from custody (s 228 SA 2020).

See *Blackstone's Criminal Practice 2026* E13

D10 Dangerous Offenders

D10.1 Criteria

Generally speaking, the dangerous offender provisions are of concern to the magistrates' court only when determining venue. The only sentence now available is an extended sentence, and this is available for those who commit a specified violent, sexual, or terrorist offence, where the court is of the opinion that 'there is a significant risk to members of the public of serious harm occasioned by the commission by him of further specified offences' (ss 254, 266, 280 Sentencing Act (SA) 2020. If new information becomes available during a summary trial, there is a residuary power to commit for sentence under these dangerous offender provisions (s 15 SA 2020).

D10.2 Specified offences

Specified offences are those listed in Sch 14 SA 2020 (Sch 15 CJA 2003).

See *Blackstone's Criminal Practice 2026* **E16.26**

Blackstone's Magistrates' Court Handbook 2026. Bartholomew Dalton and Caroline Liggins, Oxford University Press. © Oxford University Press 2026.
DOI: 10.1093/oso/9780198963943.003.0069

D11 Deferment of Sentence

D11.1 Criteria

The magistrates' court can defer sentence, on one occasion, for a maximum period of 6 months, to enable the court to assess the offender's capacity to change or carry out reparation to the victim. Such cases are simply adjourned, not on bail, so that there can be no question of a Bail Act offence (*R v Mizan* [2020] EWCA Crim 1553). A warrant can be issued (s 6(4) Sentencing Act (SA) 2020) if the offender fails to attend for sentence (the court also has the option of issuing a summons, and the court should be invited to try this option first). If the offender reoffends before the period of deferment has expired, he may be dealt with for the deferred matter.

The power to defer shall be exercisable only if:

- the offender consents;
- the offender undertakes to comply with any requirements as to his conduct during the period of the deferment that the court considers it appropriate to impose; and
- the court is satisfied, having regard to the nature of the offence and the character and circumstances of the offender, that it would be in the interests of justice to exercise the power.

D11.2 The legislative framework

Sections 3–13 SA 2020.

D11.3 Sentencing Council: deferred sentences—definitive guideline on new sentences (Criminal Justice Act 2003), paragraphs 1.2.6–1.2.9

A deferred sentence enables the court to review the conduct of the defendant before passing sentence, having first prescribed certain requirements. It also provides several opportunities for an offender to have some influence as to the sentence passed—

(a) it tests the commitment of the offender not to re-offend;
(b) it gives the offender an opportunity to do something where progress can be shown within a short period;
(c) it provides the offender with an opportunity to behave or refrain from behaving in a particular way that will be relevant to sentence.

The decision to defer sentence should be predominantly for a small group of cases at either the custody threshold or the community sentence threshold, where the sentencer feels that there would be particular value in giving the offender the opportunities listed because, if the offender complies with the requirements, a different sentence will be justified at the end of the deferment period.

Blackstone's Magistrates' Court Handbook 2026. Bartholomew Dalton and Caroline Liggins, Oxford University Press. © Oxford University Press 2026.
DOI: 10.1093/oso/9780198963943.003.0070

This could be a community sentence instead of a custodial sentence, or a fine or discharge instead of a community sentence. It may, rarely, enable a custodial sentence to be suspended rather than imposed immediately.

A court may impose any conditions during the period of deferment that it considers appropriate. These could be specific requirements as set out in the provisions for community sentences, or requirements that are drawn more widely. The requirements may include restorative justice requirements. These should be specific, measurable conditions so that the offender knows exactly what is required and the court can assess compliance; the restriction on liberty should be limited to ensure that the offender has a reasonable expectation of being able to comply whilst maintaining his or her social responsibilities.

Given the need for clarity in the mind of the offender and the possibility of sentence by another court, the court should give a clear indication (and make a written record) of the type of sentence it would be minded to impose if it had not decided to defer and ensure that the offender understands the consequences of failure to comply with the court's wishes during the deferral period.

See *Blackstone's Criminal Practice 2026* **D20.108**

D12 Deprivation Order

D12.1 Criteria

Orders of this kind should not be made without warning the defendant in advance and inviting representations, otherwise they are liable to be quashed on appeal (*R v Ball* [2002] EWCA Crim 2777). The court should not proceed without first ascertaining the value of the property, and should also ensure that an order made against just one offender does not result in an overly disproportionate sentence (*Ball*). Such an order will be invalid if the financial consequences and the value of the property have not been considered (*Trans Berckx BVBA v North Avon and Swindon Magistrates' Court* [2011] EWHC 2605 (Admin)).

The power can be used to deprive the defendant of their interest in property intended to be used for any offence, not just the particular offence before the court (*R v O'Farrell* [1988] Crim LR 387). Deprivation orders are intended only for straightforward cases involving unencumbered property (*R v Troth* [1980] Crim LR 249). In connection with child pornography the order should be proportionate in the particular circumstances (*R v Connelly* [2012] EWCA Crim 2049). An order may be made if, following proper procedures allowing the defendant and any relevant third party to give evidence, cash found at the home of a defendant convicted of drugs offences is identified as the proceeds of, or working capital for, drug dealing (*R v Rowan Jones* [2017] EWCA Crim 2192).

Sentencing Act 2020, ss 153–155

153 Deprivation order: availability

(1) A deprivation order relating to any property to which subsection (2) applies is available to the court by or before which an offender is convicted of an offence.

(2) This subsection applies to property which—
- (a) has been lawfully seized from the offender, or
- (b) was in the offender's possession or under the offender's control

when—
- (i) the offender was apprehended for the offence, or
- (ii) a summons in respect of it was issued, if subsection (3) or (5) applies.

(3) This subsection applies if the court is satisfied that the property—
- (a) has been used for the purpose of committing, or facilitating the commission of, any offence, or
- (b) was intended by the offender to be used for that purpose.

(4) For the purposes of subsection (3), facilitating the commission of an offence includes taking any steps after it has been committed for the purpose of—
- (a) disposing of any property to which the offence relates, or
- (b) avoiding apprehension or detection.

(5) This subsection applies if—
- (a) the offence mentioned in subsection (1), or
- (b) an offence which is taken into consideration by the court in determining the offender's sentence, consists of unlawful possession of the property.

Blackstone's Magistrates' Court Handbook 2026. Bartholomew Dalton and Caroline Liggins, Oxford University Press. © Oxford University Press 2026.
DOI: 10.1093/oso/9780198963943.003.0071

(6) Subsection (1) is subject to—
 (a) any restriction on forfeiture in any enactment contained in an Act passed on or after 29 July 1988,
 (b) section 33C(8) of the Environmental Protection Act 1990 (subsection (1) not to apply where section 33C of that Act provides for forfeiture of vehicles in connection with offence under that section), and
 (c) paragraph 7 of Schedule 5 to the Wireless Telegraphy Act 2006 (subsection (1) not to apply where person convicted of offence under Part 2, 3 or 5 of that Act).

154 Vehicle to be treated as used for purpose of certain offences

(1) This section applies where a person commits an offence listed in subsection (2) by—
 (a) driving, attempting to drive, or being in charge of, a vehicle,
 (b) failing to comply with a requirement made under section 7 or 7A of the Road Traffic Act 1988 (failure to provide specimen for analysis or laboratory test or to give permission for such a test) in the course of an investigation into whether the offender had committed an offence while driving, attempting to drive, or being in charge of, a vehicle, or
 (c) failing, as the driver of a vehicle, to comply with subsection (2) or (3) of section 170 of the Road Traffic Act 1988 (duty to stop and give information or report accident).
(2) Those offences are—
 (a) an offence under the Road Traffic Act 1988 which is punishable with imprisonment;
 (b) an offence of manslaughter;
 (c) an offence under section 35 of the Offences Against the Person Act 1861 (wanton and furious driving).
(3) The vehicle is to be regarded for the purposes of section 153 (and section 157(3)(b)) as used for the purpose of committing the offence (including where it is committed by aiding, abetting, counselling or procuring).

155 Exercise of power to make deprivation order

(1) In considering whether to make a deprivation order in respect of any property, a court must have regard to—
 (a) the value of the property, and
 (b) the likely financial and other effects on the offender of making the order (taken together with any other order that the court contemplates making).
(2) Where a deprivation order is available for an offence, the court may make such an order whether or not it deals with the offender in any other way for the offence . . .

See *Blackstone's Criminal Practice 2026* E8

D13 Detention in Young Offender Institution

D13.1 Criteria

The general requirements for the imposition of a custodial sentence (see **D9**) must be met. A minimum sentence of 21 days must be imposed.

A suspended sentence order (see **D32**) may be imposed.

D13.2 Breach of YOI licence

A new application for legal aid may be made under s 14(b) Legal Aid Sentencing and Punishment of Offenders Act 2012.

Section 256C Criminal Justice Act 2003 provides:

Criminal Justice Act 2003, s 256C

256C(4) Breach of supervision requirements imposed under s256B

(4) If it is proved to the satisfaction of the court that the offender has failed to comply with requirements under section 256B(6) (the supervision requirements), the court may—
  - (a) order the offender to be detained, in prison or such youth detention accommodation as the Secretary of State may determine, for such period, not exceeding 30 days, as the court may specify, or
  - (b) order the offender to pay a fine not exceeding level 3 on the standard scale.

If returned to custody the offender serves the whole of the period involved and the supervision period is reduced by the time served.

Blackstone's Magistrates' Court Handbook 2026. Bartholomew Dalton and Caroline Liggins, Oxford University Press.
DOI: 10.1093/oso/9780198963943.003.0072

D14 **Discharges: Conditional and Absolute**

D14.1 **Criteria**

A discharge can be imposed, under ss 79 and 80 Sentencing Act (SA) 2020 where it is inexpedient to inflict punishment having regard to the circumstances, including—

(a) the nature of the offence, and
(b) the character of the offender. A conditional discharge can be for up to three years. Only the orders mentioned in ss 79(4) and 80(7) SA 2020 can be made alongside a discharge, but a magistrates' court may commit an offender to the Crown Court for the purposes of activating the confiscation regime under the Proceeds of Crime Act 2002 even where a discharge is considered the proper sentence (*R v Varma* [2012] UKSC 42). Thus, ancillary orders may be made including disqualifications but a discharge may not be linked, for a single offence, with a fine, community order, or custodial sentence.

Sentencing Act 2020, ss 79(4) 80(7)

Nothing in these sections is to be taken to prevent a court, on discharging an offender absolutely/on making on order for conditional discharge in respect of an offence, from—

(a) imposing any disqualification on the offender,
(b) making any of the following orders in respect of the offence—
  (i) a compensation order (see section 133);
  (ii) an order under section 152 (deprivation orders);
  (iii) a restitution order (see section 147);
  (iv) an unlawful profit order under section 4 of the Prevention of Social Housing Fraud Act 2013,
(c) making an order under section 46 (criminal courts charge), or
(d) making an order for costs against the offender.

D14.2 **Limitations on the imposition of conditional discharges**

Where a person who has received a youth caution or a youth conditional caution is convicted of an offence committed within 2 years of the caution, the court by or before which he is so convicted:

- shall not impose a conditional discharge in respect of the offence unless it is of the opinion that there are exceptional circumstances relating to the offence or the offender which justify its doing so; and

Blackstone's Magistrates' Court Handbook 2026. Bartholomew Dalton and Caroline Liggins, Oxford University Press. © Oxford University Press 2026.
DOI: 10.1093/oso/9780198963943.003.0073

- where it does so, shall state in open court that it is of that opinion and why it is (ss 66ZB and 66ZF Crime and Disorder Act 1988).

A person convicted of breaching a Criminal Behaviour Order may not receive a conditional discharge (s 339(3) SA 2020 (s 30(3) Anti-social Behaviour Crime and Policing Act 2014)). The same rule applies to those who breach a Sexual Harm Prevention Order (s 103I(4) Sexual Offences Act 2003; a Sexual Risk Order (s 122H(4)); a Slavery and Trafficking Protection or Risk Order (s 30(4) Modern Slavery Act 2015); a stalking protection order (s 3 Stalking Protection Act 2019); a serious violence reduction order under s 342G SA 2020; a domestic abuse protection order (s 39(6) Domestic Abuse Act 2021); or a knife crime prevention order (s 29(4) Offensive Weapons Act 2019).

D14.3 Breach of a conditional discharge

Provision is made by Sch 2 SA 2020 that a person who commits an offence during the life of a conditional discharge may be resentenced for that original offence even if the period of discharge has expired at the date of sentence. Under s 402 SA 2020 the offender will be sentenced with reference to his or her age at the date of the previous offence, and can be sentenced in any way as if then convicted of the offence. If the conditional discharge was imposed by the Crown Court, the offender may be committed to that court for resentence.

There is no requirement to resentence, and a court could sentence for a new offence and leave the conditional discharge in place if it saw fit to do so.

See *Blackstone's Criminal Practice 2026* E3

D15 **Discounts for Early Plea**

The Sentencing Council has issued a guideline that is now the key point of reference. In relation to youths, *RB and others* [2020] EWCA Crim 643 confirms that any reduction for age should be taken into account before the discount is applied.

D15.1 **Criteria**

A court must discount a sentence in return for a guilty plea. A magistrates' court may impose a maximum sentence as an alternative to committing the case for sentence to the Crown Court. A full discount must be given even if the prosecution case is overwhelming. The amount of discount will depend upon the timing of the plea. A one-third reduction is only available, subject to exceptions, when a guilty plea is indicated at the first hearing whether the case proceeds in the magistrates' or Crown court. Thereafter the maximum is one-quarter, reducing to 10 per cent if the plea is entered at the time of trial. The discount is separate from any other reduction, for instance for remorse, which should be taken in to account before the discount for guilty plea is applied:

> The reduction has no impact on sentencing decisions in relation to ancillary orders, including disqualification.

Sentencing Guideline: Reduction in sentence for a guilty plea—first hearing on or after 1 June 2017

B. KEY PRINCIPLES . . .

Factors such as admissions at interview, co-operation with the investigation and demonstrations of remorse should not be taken into account in determining the level of reduction. Rather, they should be considered separately and prior to any guilty plea reduction, as potential mitigating factors.

D. DETERMINING THE LEVEL OF REDUCTION

The maximum level of reduction in sentence for a guilty plea is one-third.

D1. Plea indicated at the first stage of the proceedings

Where a guilty plea is indicated at the first stage of proceedings a reduction of one-third should be made (subject to the exceptions in section F). The first stage will normally be the first hearing at which a plea or indication of plea is sought and recorded by the court.

D2. Plea indicated after the first stage of proceedings—maximum one quarter—sliding scale of reduction thereafter

After the first stage of the proceedings the maximum level of reduction is one-quarter (subject to the exceptions in section F).

The reduction should be decreased from one-quarter to a maximum of one-tenth on the first day of trial having regard to the time when the guilty plea is first indicated to the court relative to the progress of the case and the trial date (subject to the exceptions in section F). The reduction should normally be decreased further, even to zero, if the guilty plea is entered during the course of the trial.

Blackstone's Magistrates' Court Handbook 2026. Bartholomew Dalton and Caroline Liggins, Oxford University Press. © Oxford University Press 2026.
DOI: 10.1093/oso/9780198963943.003.0074

For the purposes of this guideline a trial will be deemed to have started when pre-recorded cross-examination has begun.

Note: In cases where (in accordance with the Criminal Procedure Rules) a defendant is given the opportunity to enter a guilty plea without attending a court hearing, doing so within the required time limits will constitute a plea at the first stage of proceedings

E. APPLYING THE REDUCTION

E1. Imposing one type of sentence rather than another

The reduction in sentence for a guilty plea can be taken into account by imposing one type of sentence rather than another; for example:

by reducing a custodial sentence to a community sentence, or by reducing a community sentence to a fine.

Where a court has imposed one sentence rather than another to reflect the guilty plea there should normally be no further reduction on account of the guilty plea. Where, however, the less severe type of sentence is justified by other factors, the appropriate reduction for the plea should be applied in the normal way.

E2. More than one summary offence

When dealing with more than one summary offence, the aggregate sentence is limited to a maximum of six months. Allowing for a reduction for each guilty plea, consecutive sentences might result in the imposition of the maximum six-month sentence. Where this is the case, the court may make a modest additional reduction to the overall sentence to reflect the benefits derived from the guilty pleas.

E3. Keeping an either-way case in the magistrates' court to reflect a guilty plea

Reducing a custodial sentence to reflect a guilty plea may enable a magistrates' court to retain jurisdiction of an either way offence rather than committing the case for sentence to the Crown Court.

In such cases a magistrates' court should apply the appropriate reduction to the sentence for the offence(s) arrived at in accordance with any offence specific sentencing guideline and if the resulting sentence is then within its jurisdiction it should go on to sentence.

F. EXCEPTIONS

F1. Further information, assistance or advice necessary before indicating plea

Where the sentencing court is satisfied that there were particular circumstances which significantly reduced the defendant's ability to understand what was alleged or otherwise made it unreasonable to expect the defendant to indicate a guilty plea sooner than was done, a reduction of one-third should still be made.

In considering whether this exception applies, sentencers should distinguish between cases in which it is necessary to receive advice and/ or have sight of evidence in order to understand whether the defendant is in fact and law guilty of the offence(s) charged, and cases in which a defendant merely delays guilty plea(s) in order to assess the strength of the prosecution evidence and the prospects of conviction or acquittal.

F2. Newton hearings and special reasons hearings

In circumstances where an offender's version of events is rejected at a Newton hearing or special reasons hearing, the reduction which would have been available at the stage of proceedings the plea was indicated should normally be halved. Where witnesses are called during such a hearing, it may be appropriate further to decrease the reduction.

F3. Offender convicted of a lesser or different offence

If an offender is convicted of a lesser or different offence from that originally charged, and has earlier made an unequivocal indication of a guilty plea to this lesser or different offence to the prosecution and the court, the court should give the level of reduction that is appropriate to the stage in the proceedings at which this indication of plea (to the lesser or different offence) was made taking into account any other of these exceptions that apply. In the Crown Court where the offered plea is a permissible alternative on the indictment as charged, the offender will not be treated as having made an unequivocal indication unless the offender has entered that plea.

F4. Minimum sentence under section 51A of the Firearms Act 1968

There can be no reduction for a guilty plea if the effect of doing so would be to reduce the length of sentence below the required minimum term.

F5. Minimum sentences under sections 268C, 282C, 312, 313, 314 and 315 of the Sentencing Code for persons aged 18 or over

In circumstances where:

- an appropriate custodial sentence of at least 14 years falls to be imposed (under section 268C or 282C of the Sentencing Code) on a person aged 18 or over who has been convicted of a serious terrorism offence (as defined in section 306(2) of the Sentencing Code)
- an appropriate custodial sentence of at least six months falls to be imposed (under section 312 or 315 of the Sentencing Code) on a person aged 18 or over who has been convicted under sections 1 or 1A of the Prevention of Crime Act 1953; or sections 139, 139AA or 139A of the Criminal Justice Act 1988 (certain possession of knives or offensive weapon offences) or
- an appropriate custodial sentence falls to be imposed under section 313 (third class A drug trafficking offence) or section 314 (third domestic burglary) of the Sentencing Code.

the court may impose any sentence in accordance with this guideline which is not less than 80 per cent of the appropriate custodial period.

Section 73 of the Sentencing Code provides:

Sentencing Act 2020, s 73(1)–(2)

(1) This section applies where a court is determining what sentence to pass on an offender who has pleaded guilty to an offence in proceedings before that or another court.

(2) The court must take into account the following matters—

(a) the stage in the proceedings for the offence at which the offender indicated the intention to plead guilty, and

(b) the circumstances in which the indication was given.

D15.1.1 *Case law decisions*

To preserve discount defendants should be willing to indicate willingness to plead to lesser offences (*R v West* [2019] EWCA Crim 493). Guidance on the completion of BCM forms at sending is given in Appendix 1. Responsibility for completing the better case management (BCM) form falls on the parties and a failure to indicate plea will lose discount (*R v Yasin* [2019] EWCA Crim 1729). To obtain full credit the guilty indication must be unequivocal in the "Pleas (either way) or indicated pleas (indictable only) or alternatives offered" box on the BCM form, if there is to be a basis that fact should be recorded in the "Real issues in the case" box (*R v Dale* [2022] EWCA Crim 207). An indication that there is likely to be a guilty plea, on a basis, is not normally enough to earn a full discount (*R v Hodgin* 2020 EWCA Crim 1388; *R v Davis* [2019] EWCA Crim 553). However, a full discount was given when at a sending the defendant indicted that there would be a guilty plea with basis of plea to be uploaded by PTPH (*R v Whitty* [2022] EWCA Crim 1100). A 25 per cent discount was appropriate where the defence awaited medical evidence as to fitness to plead but had made no admissions about the evidence and had not raised that issue on the BCM form in the magistrates' court (*R v Clarke* [2018] EWCA Crim 1845). Yet in *R v Nolan* [2022] EWCA Crim 726 it was held that section F applied when a defendant, who has an established history of mental ill-health, and mental illness is a relevant feature of the case, enters a plea at the first opportunity after receipt of the forensic psychiatrist's report.

R v Joy [2014] EWCA Crim 2321 confirmed that the fact that on charge the defendant had said not guilty was not a relevant factor. Whilst the number of similar previous convictions goes to seriousness and so the sentence to be imposed, it cannot impact on the discount for guilty plea (*R v Darkwa* [2015] EWCA Crim 260).

In *R v Butt* [2017] EWCA Crim 352, where the defendant had seen initial details of the prosecution case and, at the police station, the CCTV, discount was lost when he delayed so that defence lawyers could view the CCTV. Not having seen the body worn video is not a reason to preserve the discount until it has been viewed (*R v Powlett* [2019] EWCA Crim 440). Admissions in interview but a not guilty indication on the BCM form at sending, will result in only a 25 per cent discount if the plea is entered at the plea and trial preparation hearing. It was not entered at the first opportunity. The admission may however add other mitigation such as remorse (*R v Price* [2018] EWCA Crim 1784). Credit levels may be maintained when the defence successfully negotiates down the value of the criminality from that originally alleged by the Crown (*R v Humphreys* [2019] EWCA Crim 2445).

A defendant is not entitled to full credit if they delay their guilty plea until after a legal ruling on the admissibility of the prosecution evidence, EncroChat messages in this instance, has gone against them (*R. v Richards* [2022] EWCA Crim 247).

The case law was reviewed in *R v Plaku* [2021] EWCA Crim 568.

D16 Disqualification from Driving

D16.1 Criteria

Disqualification (or in the fifth example, a revocation) may arise in one of five ways:

(1) Offence carrying obligatory disqualification (see **D16.4**).
(2) Offence carrying discretionary disqualification (see **D16.6**).
(3) As a result of accumulating 12 or more penalty points (see **D16.7**).
(4) As a result of conviction for any offence, or an offence where a vehicle was used for crime (ss 163 and 164 SA 2020 (see **D16.9**).
(5) As a result of a 'new driver' accumulating six penalty points (see **D16.10**)

Where disqualification is imposed the licence should be endorsed but not with any penalty points in respect of that offence or other offences perpetrated on the same occasion. The normal practice is to impose no separate penalty on the related crimes, but disqualify alone on the main crime (*R v Thomas* [2020] EWCA Crim 513). Section 44(1) Road Traffic Offenders Act (RTOA) 1988 (*R v Usaceva* [2015] EWCA Crim 166). Section 39 RTOA 1988 allows for applications to suspend a disqualification pending appeal.

D16.2 Interim disqualification

An interim disqualification can be imposed when the court commits an offender for sentence to the Crown Court, remits the case to another court, or defers or adjourns sentence (s 26 RTOA 1988). More than one interim disqualification may be imposed, but the total term must not exceed 6 months. An interim disqualification should not be imposed when the length of the disqualification will be extended because an immediate prison sentence will be imposed (*R v Needham and others* [2016] EWCA Crim 455 below).

See *Blackstone's Criminal Practice 2026* C7.29

D16.3 Disqualification with an immediate custodial sentence

A period of disqualification has to be extended by the time actually served in custody in accordance with ss 166–167 SA 2020 (ss 35A and 35B RTOA 1988). *R v Parkin* [2020] EWCA Crim 614 confirms that no account may be taken of release on home detention curfew.

Sentencing Act 2020, ss 166–167

166 Extension of disqualification where custodial sentence also imposed

(1) This section applies where a court—
   (a) imposes a custodial sentence on an offender for an offence, and
   (b) makes a driving disqualification order in respect of the offender for the same offence.

Blackstone's Magistrates' Court Handbook 2026. Bartholomew Dalton and Caroline Liggins, Oxford University Press.
DOI: 10.1093/oso/9780198963943.003.0075

(2) But this section does not apply where the custodial sentence is—
 (a) a suspended sentence, or
 (b) a life sentence in relation to which the court makes a whole life order under section 321(3).
(3) The disqualification period must be—
 (a) the discretionary disqualification period, and
 (b) the appropriate extension period.
(4) The discretionary disqualification period is the period which the court would, in the absence of this section, have specified in the driving disqualification order.
(5) The appropriate extension period for a sentence specified in column 2 is equal to the period calculated in accordance with column 3—

	Sentence	**Length of appropriate extension period**
1 . . .	a detention and training order under section 233 (offenders under 18: detention and training orders) . . .	half the term of the detention and training order . . .
8	any other case	half the custodial sentence imposed.

(6) Any period determined under subsection (5) which includes a fraction of a day must be rounded up to the nearest number of whole days . . .

167 Effect of custodial sentence in other cases

(1) This section applies where a court makes a driving disqualification order in respect of an offender for an offence, and—
 (a) it imposes a custodial sentence (other than a suspended sentence) on the offender for another offence, or
 (b) a custodial sentence previously imposed on the offender has not expired.
(2) In determining the disqualification period, the court must, so far as it is appropriate to do so, have regard to the diminished effect of disqualification as a distinct punishment if the person who is disqualified is also detained in pursuance of a custodial sentence.

But the court may not take into account for this purpose any custodial sentence that it imposes on the offender for the offence.

(3) In this section, 'custodial sentence' includes a pre-Code custodial sentence (see section 222(4)).

These provisions, when in the RTOA 1988, were given detailed consideration in *R v Needham and others* [2016] EWCA Crim 455 which offered the following staged guidance:

> Step 1—Does the court intend to impose a 'discretionary' disqualification under section 34 or section 35 for any offence?
>
> YES—go to step 2
>
> Step 2—Does the court intend to impose a custodial term for that same offence?
>
> YES—section 35A applies and the court must impose an extension period (see section 35A(4)(h) for that same offence and consider step 3.
>
> NO—section 35A does not apply at all—go on to consider section 35B and step 4

Step 3—Does the court intend to impose a custodial term for another offence (which is longer or consecutive) or is the defendant already serving a custodial sentence?

YES—then consider what increase ('uplift') in the period of 'discretionary disqualification' is required to comply with section 35B(2) and (3). In accordance with section 35B(4) ignore any custodial term imposed for an offence involving disqualification under section 35A.

Discretionary period + extension period + uplift = total period of disqualification

NO—no need to consider section 35B at all

Discretionary period + extension period = total period of disqualification

Step 4—Does the court intend to impose a custodial term for another offence or is the defendant already serving a custodial sentence?

YES—then consider what increase ('uplift') in the period of 'discretionary disqualification' is required to comply with section 35B(2) and (3).

Discretionary period + uplift = total period of disqualification

The total length of the disqualification should be reduced to allow for the time spent on remand, but the court cannot reduce the disqualification below the statutory minimum (*R v Gregory* [2017] EWCA Crim 2045; *R v Mascarenas.* [2018] EWCA Crim 1467; *R v Grant* [2023] EWCA Crim 1414).

D16.4 Obligatory disqualification

Where a person is convicted of an offence involving obligatory disqualification, the court must order him to be disqualified for such period not less than 12 months as the court thinks fit, unless the court for special reasons (see **D16.5**) thinks fit to order him to be disqualified for a shorter period or not to order him to be disqualified at all (s 34 RTOA 1988).

A person disqualified for dangerous driving must also be ordered to undertake an extended driving test.

A mandatory disqualification does not have the effect of removing any penalty points existing on the licence.

There are certain exceptions to the minimum 12-month period that are applicable to those sentenced *in the magistrates' court*, as set out in **D16.4.1–D16.4.5**.

D16.4.1 *Minimum 5 year disqualification*

A minimum 5 year disqualification shall be imposed in relation to offences under s 1 RTA 1988 (causing death by dangerous driving) or s 3A (causing death by careless driving when under the influence of drink or drugs) occurring on or after 28 June 2022, subject to s 34(3) RTOA 1988 (see **D16.4.2**).

D16.4.2 *Minimum 3 or 6 year disqualification*

A minimum 3 year disqualification follows where, within the 10 years immediately preceding the commission of the offence, a person has been convicted of any such offence, and is again convicted of an offence under any of the following provisions of the Road Traffic Act (RTA) 1988 (s 34 RTOA 1988), that is:

- s 3A (causing death by careless driving when under the influence of drink or drugs);
- s 4(1) (driving or attempting to drive while unfit);
- s 5(1)(a) (driving or attempting to drive with excess alcohol);
- s 7(6) (failing to provide a specimen) where that is an offence involving obligatory disqualification;
- s 7A(6) (failing to allow a specimen to be subjected to laboratory test) where that is an offence involving obligatory disqualification.

Where the offence within the 10 year period and occurring on or after 28 June 2022 is contrary to s 3A RTA 1988 (causing death by careless driving when under the influence of drink or drugs) then the minimum disqualification period is 6 years.

D16.4.3 *Minimum 2-year disqualification*

Under the 'totting-up' rules, a minimum 2-year disqualification follows in relation to a person on whom more than one disqualification for a fixed period of 56 days or more has been imposed within the 3 years immediately preceding the commission of the offence. Disqualifications for non-road traffic offences are not relevant to this 'totting-up' process.

A minimum 2-year disqualification shall be imposed in relation to offences under s 1A (causing a serious injury by dangerous driving) or s 3ZD (causing serious injury: disqualified driving).

D16.4.4 *Minimum 1-year disqualification*

A disqualification of 12 months is the starting point for an obligatory disqualification.

A minimum 1-year disqualification follows, under the 'totting-up' rules, in relation to a person on whom one disqualification for a fixed period of 56 days or more has been imposed within the 3 years immediately preceding the commission of the offence. Disqualifications for non-road traffic offences are not relevant to this 'totting-up' process.

D16.4.5 *Minimum 6 months' disqualification*

A minimum 6 months' disqualification follows where a person convicted of an offence under s 40A of the RTA 1988 (using vehicle in dangerous condition, etc) has, within the 3 years immediately preceding the commission of the offence, been convicted of any such offence.

D16.5 Special reasons

There is no statutory definition of 'special reasons', but it must not amount to a defence in law, must be directly connected with the offence in question (not the offender), and must be a mitigating or extenuating circumstance. The burden (civil standard) falls on the defendant. Good character, personal service to the community (eg being a doctor), financial hardship as a result of a disqualification, and the fact the offence was not particularly serious have all been held not to amount to special reasons.

It should be noted that under the guideline on discount for guilty plea, in circumstances where an offender's version of events is rejected at a special reasons hearing, the reduction which would have been available at the stage of proceedings the plea was indicated should normally be halved. Where witnesses are called during such a hearing, it may be appropriate further to decrease the reduction.

An ignorance of the terms of motor insurance cannot generally amount to special reasons (*Rennison v Knowler* [1947] 1 All ER 302), unless the person was misled or there is a particularly good reason for the ignorance (eg illness, confusion brought about by others).

If special reasons are found, the court has a discretion not to endorse points, and to reduce or not impose a mandatory period of disqualification. Note, however, that for an offence involving mandatory disqualification, where special reasons are found and the court does not disqualify, it must impose points, unless it finds special reasons also for not doing so.

Common special reasons are:

- spiked drinks or mistake as to item drunk;
- shortness of distance driven;
- medical or other emergencies.

In *Warring-Davies v DPP* [2009] EWHC 1172 (Admin), the court emphasized the need to find a causal link between any alleged medical condition and the driving in question.

In *DPP v Harrison* [2007] EWHC 556 (Admin), the court held it wrong to find special reasons where a drunken person drove 446 yards in order to find youths who had harassed him earlier.

In *DPP v Oram* [2005] EWHC 964 (Admin), the court held that special reasons would not be arguable to a drunk driver who relied upon shortness of distance driven alone.

Taylor v Rajan [1974] RTR 304 deals with the principles involved in 'emergency' cases:

> This is not the first case in which the court has had to consider whether driving in an emergency could justify a conclusion that there are special reasons for not disqualifying the driver. If a man, in the well-founded belief that he will not drive again, puts his car in the garage, goes into his house and has a certain amount to drink in the belief that he is not going to drive again, and if thereafter is an emergency which requires him in order to deal with it to take his car out despite his intention to leave it in the garage, then that is a situation which can in law amount to a special reason for not disqualifying a driver. On the other hand, Justices who are primarily concerned with dealing with this legislation should approach the exercise of the resulting discretion with great care. The mere fact that the facts disclose a special reason does not mean that the driver is to escape disqualification as a matter of course. There is a very serious burden upon the Justices, even when a special reason has been disclosed, to decide whether in their discretion they should decline to disqualify a particular case. The Justices should have very much in mind that if a man deliberately

> drives when he knows he has consumed a considerable quantity of drink, he presents a potential source of danger to the public which no private crisis can likely excuse. One of the most important matters which Justices have to consider in the exercise of this discretion is whether the emergency (and I call it such for want of a more convenient word) was sufficiently acute to justify the driver taking his car out. The Justices should only exercise a discretion in favour of the driver in clear and compelling circumstances . . . The Justices therefore must consider the whole of the circumstances. They must consider the nature and degree of the crisis or emergency which has caused the defendant to take the car out. They must consider with particular care whether there were alternative means of transport or methods of dealing with the crisis other than and alternative to the use by the defendant of his own car. They should have regard to the manner in which the defendant drove . . . and they should generally have regard to whether the defendant acted responsibly or otherwise . . . The matter must be considered objectively and the quality and gravity of the crisis must be assessed in that way. Last, but by no means least, if the alcohol content in the defendant's blood and body is very high, that is a powerful reason for saying that the discretion should not be exercised in his favour. Indeed, if the alcohol content exceeds 100 milligrammes per hundred millilitres of blood, the Justices should rarely, if ever, exercise this discretion in favour of the defendant driver. . . .

In *DPP v Heathcote* [2011] EWHC 2536 (Admin), it was held that in deciding whether an 'emergency' justified driving, the court should ask whether a sober, reasonable, and responsible friend would have advised the defendant to drive. Relevant factors included:

- amount drunk;
- threat to others;
- state of the roads;
- distance to be driven;
- nature of the emergency;
- what alternatives were available.

The court confirmed that the use of an emergency as a special reason was not limited to life and limb cases; but, on the facts, to chase the thieves of a relative's car was not acceptable.

Chatters v Burke [1986] 3 All ER 168 details the seven factors relevant to a 'shortness of distance driven' argument:

- distance;
- manner of driving;
- state of the vehicle;
- whether there was an intention to drive further;
- road and traffic conditions;
- possibility of danger to road users and pedestrians;
- reason for the driving.

In order to establish a spiked drinks defence, it will be necessary to prove that the drink was laced, that the defendant did not know it was laced, and that but for the lacing of the drink his alcohol level would not have exceeded the legal limit. It will normally be necessary to call expert evidence in relation to the last point. The higher the reading, the less likely it is that a defendant will be able to prove he had no knowledge. If a court is of the view that the defendant ought to have realized his drink was spiked, it will not find special reasons (*Pridige v Grant* [1985] RTR 196).

McCormick and Hitchins [1988] RTR 182 held that special reasons could be available not to endorse points, where the allegation was of failing to provide a specimen when in charge, if the court was satisfied there was no intention to drive and that the defendant could not have been a danger on the road.

See *Blackstone's Criminal Practice 2026* **C7.8** and **C7.54**

D16.6 Discretionary disqualification

Where an offence carries discretionary disqualification, the court must consider disqualification before it considers the imposition of penalty points. This is the case even if the offender would be liable to disqualification under the 'totting-up' provisions.

Practitioners will consider the tactical considerations of inviting a court to impose a discretionary disqualification as opposed to points that could trigger a totting-up disqualification. The benefit of a discretionary disqualification is that it can be for as short a period as the court directs; the negative side is that any previous points remain on the licence. If a totting-up disqualification were imposed, all the points would be removed but the defendant would face a minimum six-month period of disqualification. This applies only if the court is minded to impose a shorter period, as a defendant may prefer to tot up and clear his licence after a 6-month disqualification, rather than have, say, 4 months disqualified and still have the existing points hanging over him. If a court disqualifies then no additional penalty points are imposed. The period of disqualification can be for any period the court thinks proper.

See *Blackstone's Criminal Practice 2026* **C7.11**

D16.7 As a result of accumulating 12 or more penalty points

Under s 35 RTOA 1988 (see **D16.8**), if a driver has accumulated 12 or more points on his licence, the court must order him to be disqualified for not less than the minimum period, unless it is satisfied, having regard to all the circumstances, that there are grounds for disqualifying him for a shorter period or not to disqualify him. In calculating the points on the licence ('totting up'), the court will have regard to:

- the points to be imposed for the new offence, and
- any points on the licence for offences committed no longer than three years from the date of commission of the new offence (therefore, points run from the date of the old offence to the date of new offence) (s 29 RTOA 1988).

If there has been in the 3-year period a disqualification under the totting-up provisions, then points imposed prior to that disqualification would be disregarded.

The minimum period of disqualification is:

- 6 months if no previous disqualification;
- 12 months if one previous disqualification (for 56 days or more);
- 2 years if two or more previous disqualifications (for 56 days or more).

The previous disqualifications must have been imposed within 3 years of the date of the new offence to count.

D16.8 Mitigating circumstances

'Mitigating circumstances' may be argued in order to escape disqualification as a result of totting-up (see D16.7).

Section 35 RTOA 1988 provides:

> **Road Traffic Offenders Act 1988, s 35**
>
> **35 Disqualification for repeated offences**
>
> (1) Where—
>
> (a) a person is convicted of an offence to which this subsection applies, and
>
> (b) the penalty points to be taken into account on that occasion number twelve or more,
>
> the court must order him to be disqualified for not less than the minimum period unless the court is satisfied, having regard to all the circumstances, that there are grounds for mitigating the normal consequences of the conviction and thinks fit to order him to be disqualified for a shorter period or not to order him to be disqualified.
>
> (3) Where an offender is convicted on the same occasion of more than one offence to which subsection (1) above applies—
>
> (a) not more than one disqualification shall be imposed on him under subsection (1) above,
>
> (b) in determining the period of the disqualification the court must take into account all the offences, and
>
> (c) for the purposes of any appeal any disqualification imposed under subsection (1) above shall be treated as an order made on the conviction of each of the offences.
>
> (4) No account is to be taken under subsection (1) above of any of the following circumstances—
>
> (a) any circumstances that are alleged to make the offence or any of the offences not a serious one,
>
> (b) hardship, other than exceptional hardship, or
>
> (c) any circumstances which, within the three years immediately preceding the conviction, have been taken into account under that subsection in ordering the offender to be disqualified for a shorter period or not ordering him to be disqualified.

The burden of establishing mitigating circumstances is on the defendant; and those circumstances will generally need to be proved by way of evidence as opposed to submission. If hardship is argued as a mitigating circumstance it must be exceptional but hardship is not a prerequisite for finding mitigating circumstances in all the circumstances of a particular case (*R v Preston* [1986] RTR 136).

The Sentencing Council's guidance states:

When considering whether there are grounds to reduce or avoid a totting up disqualification the court should have regard to the following:

It is for the offender to prove to the civil standard of proof that such grounds exist. Other than very exceptionally, this will require evidence from the offender, and where such evidence is given, it must be sworn.

Where it is asserted that hardship would be caused, the court must be satisfied that it is not merely inconvenience, or hardship, but exceptional hardship for which the court must have evidence.

Almost every disqualification entails hardship for the person disqualified and their immediate family. This is part of the deterrent objective of the provisions combined with the preventative effect of the order not to drive.

If a motorist continues to offend after becoming aware of the risk to their licence of further penalty points, the court can take this circumstance into account.

Courts should be cautious before accepting assertions of exceptional hardship without evidence that alternatives (including alternative means of transport) for avoiding exceptional hardship are not viable.

Loss of employment will be an inevitable consequence of a driving ban for many people. Evidence that loss of employment would follow from disqualification is not in itself sufficient to demonstrate exceptional hardship; whether or not it does will depend on the circumstances of the offender and the consequences of that loss of employment on the offender and/or others. Useful information can be found in the Equal Treatment Bench Book (see in particular Chapter 11).

Where it finds that there are grounds for mitigating the 'normal consequences of the conviction', the court may consider whether this can be achieved by ordering a period of disqualification which is shorter than the statutory minimum or by ordering that the offender should not be disqualified at all.

See *Blackstone's Criminal Practice 2026* C7.27

D16.9 As a result of conviction for any offence, or an offence where a vehicle was used for crime

Section 163 SA 2020 gives a court the power to disqualify an offender from holding a driving licence following a conviction for any offence. There need be no nexus between driving and the offence in question, and nothing additional should be written into the statute over and above what is already present; this allows a court to use the provision whenever it feels it to be appropriate in all of the circumstances (*R v Sofekun* [2008] EWCA Crim 2035).

Section 164 SA 2020 gives courts a narrower power to disqualify where a motor vehicle was involved in the commission of the offence. In the magistrates' court the power is limited solely to the offences of assault:

Sentencing Act 2020, s 164 (3)

164 Driving disqualification order: availability where vehicle used for purposes of crime

(3) A driving disqualification order is available to the court by or before which an offender is convicted of an offence also where—

(a) the offence is—

(i) common assault, or

(ii) any other offence involving an assault (including an offence under Part 2 of the Serious Crime Act 2007 (encouraging or assisting) related to, or incitement to commit, an offence),

(b) the offence was committed on or after 1 July 1992, and

(c) the court is satisfied that the assault was committed by driving a motor vehicle.

See *Blackstone's Criminal Practice 2026* E21.14

D16.10 Road Traffic (New Drivers) Act 1995

Newly qualified drivers are subject to a 2-year probationary period. If at any time during that period the points to be endorsed on a driving licence amount to six or more, the licence will be automatically revoked. The relevant date is the date of offence not conviction, so revocation cannot be avoided by delaying court proceedings.

In appropriate cases, advocates may seek to invite courts to disqualify instead of endorse points, in order to try to avoid the draconian consequences of accumulating six or more penalty points.

See *Blackstone's Criminal Practice 2026* C7.45

D16.11 Disqualification in the offender's absence

Section 11(4) Magistrates' Courts Act 1980 provides that there can be no disqualification in absence except on the resumption of a hearing after adjournment. Disqualification should not be imposed in absence where there is evidence that the defendant has an acceptable reason for not attending or where there are reasons to believe it would be contrary to the interests of justice to do so.

D16.12 Return of driving licence

D16.12.1 *Overview*

Section 42 RTOA 1988 and Crim PR 29.2 provide for a disqualified driver to apply to the court for the return of his driving licence, prior to the expiry of the disqualification period. These proceedings may be funded at the magistrates' court by way of a means-tested representation order.

Period of disqualification	Minimum period of disqualification that must have elapsed before court can consider an application
Less than 4 years	2 years
4 years, but less than 10 years	One half of the disqualification period
10 years or more	5 years

If a disqualification is imposed by virtue of s 36(1) of the Act (disqualification until test is passed), there is no power to return a licence under s 43.

D16.12.2 *Criteria to be applied*

On any such application the court may, as it thinks proper having regard to:

- the character of the person disqualified and his conduct subsequent to the order;
- the nature of the offence; and
- any other circumstances of the case,

either by order remove the disqualification as from such date as may be specified in the order, or refuse the application.

D16.12.3 *Further application following refusal*

Where an application is refused, a further application shall not be entertained if made within three months after the date of the refusal.

See *Blackstone's Criminal Practice 2026* C7.43

D17 Fines

D17.1 Criteria

Maximum fine levels

For offences committed on or after 12 March 2015 there is no upper limit to the level of fine at Level 5 that may be imposed in a magistrates' court. The Legal Aid Sentencing and Punishment of Offenders Act 2012 (Fines on summary conviction) Regulations 2015 contain detailed exceptions to this rule. The Criminal Practice Direction 15.6 contains provisions requiring certain serious offences to be identified by the Crown so that an authorized district judge may be appointed to deal with the case.

Fine band starting points and ranges; fine levels

These appear inside the front cover of this edition.

The Magistrates' Court Sentencing Guideline contains the following guidance:

Approach to the assessment of fines—introduction

The amount of a fine must reflect the seriousness of the offence ([now s 125 Sentencing Act (SA) 2020] Criminal Justice Act ('CJA') 2003, s 164(2)).

The court must also take into account the financial circumstances of the offender; this applies whether it has the effect of increasing or reducing the fine [now ss 124 and 125 SA 2020] (CJA 2003, s 164(3) and 164(4)).

The aim is for the fine to have an equal impact on offenders with different financial circumstances; it should be a hardship but should not force the offender below a reasonable 'subsistence' level. Normally a fine should be of an amount that is capable of being paid within 12 months though there may be exceptions to this.

The guidance in this section aims to establish a clear, consistent and principled approach to the assessment of fines that will apply fairly in the majority of cases. However, it is impossible to anticipate every situation that may be encountered and in each case the court will need to exercise its judgement to ensure that the fine properly reflects the seriousness of the offence and takes into account the financial circumstances of the offender.

Definition of relevant weekly income

The seriousness of an offence determines the choice of fine band and the position of the offence within the range for that band. The offender's financial circumstances are taken into account by expressing that position as a proportion of the offender's relevant weekly income.

Where:

- an offender is in receipt of income from employment or is self-employed and
- that income is more than £120 per week after deduction of tax and national insurance (or equivalent where the offender is self-employed)—the actual income is the relevant weekly income.

Where:

- an offender's only source of income is state benefit (including where there is relatively low additional income as permitted by the benefit regulations), or

Blackstone's Magistrates' Court Handbook 2026. Bartholomew Dalton and Caroline Liggins, Oxford University Press. © Oxford University Press 2026.
DOI: 10.1093/oso/9780198963943.003.0076

- the offender is in receipt of income from employment or is self-employed but the amount of income after deduction of tax and national insurance is £120 per week or less,

the relevant weekly income is deemed to be £120.

Additional information about the basis for this approach is set out in Approach to offenders on low income.

In calculating relevant weekly income no account should be taken of tax credits, housing benefit, child benefit or similar.

No reliable information

Where an offender has failed to provide information, or the court is not satisfied that it has been given sufficient reliable information, it is entitled to make such determination as it thinks fit regarding the financial circumstances of the offender (now s 126 SA 2020] CJA 2003, s 164(5)). Any determination should be clearly stated on the court records for use in any subsequent variation or enforcement proceedings. In such cases, a record should also be made of the applicable fine band and the court's assessment of the position of the offence within that band based on the seriousness of the offence.

Where there is no information on which a determination can be made, the court should proceed on the basis of an assumed relevant weekly income of £440. This is derived from national median pre-tax earnings; * a gross figure is used as, in the absence of financial information from the offender, it is not possible to calculate appropriate deductions.

Where there is some information that tends to suggest a significantly lower or higher income than the recommended £440 default sum, the court should make a determination based on that information.

A court is empowered to remit a fine in whole or part if the offender subsequently provides information as to means (now s 127 SA 2020] CJA 2003, s 165(2)). The assessment of offence seriousness and, therefore, the appropriate fine band and the position of the offence within that band are not affected by the provision of this information.* (This figure is a projected estimate based upon the 2012–13 Survey of Personal Incomes using economic assumptions consistent with the Office for Budget Responsibility's March 2015 economic and fiscal outlook. The latest actual figure available is for 2012–13, when median pre-tax income was £404 per week.)

Assessment of financial circumstances

While the initial consideration for the assessment of a fine is the offender's relevant weekly income, the court is required to take account of the offender's financial circumstances including assets more broadly. Guidance on important parts of this assessment is set out below.

An offender's financial circumstances may have the effect of increasing or reducing the amount of the fine; however, they are not relevant to the assessment of offence seriousness. They should be considered separately from the selection of the appropriate fine band and the court's assessment of the position of the offence within the range for that band.

Out of the ordinary expenses

In deciding the proportions of relevant weekly income that are the starting points and ranges for each fine band, account has been taken of reasonable living expenses. Accordingly, no further allowance should normally be made for these. In addition, no allowance should normally be made where the offender has dependants.

Outgoings will be relevant to the amount of the fine only where the expenditure is out of the ordinary and substantially reduces the ability to pay a financial penalty so that the requirement to pay a fine based on the standard approach would lead to undue hardship.

Unusually low outgoings

Where the offender's living expenses are substantially lower than would normally be expected, it may be appropriate to adjust the amount of the fine to reflect this. This may apply, for example, where an offender does not make any financial contribution towards his or her living costs.

Savings

Where an offender has savings, these will not normally be relevant to the assessment of the amount of a fine although they may influence the decision on time to pay.

However, where an offender has little or no income but has substantial savings, the court may consider it appropriate to adjust the amount of the fine to reflect this.

Household has more than one source of income

Where the household of which the offender is a part has more than one source of income, the fine should normally be based on the income of the offender alone.

However, where the offender's part of the income is very small (or the offender is wholly dependent on the income of another), the court may have regard to the extent of the household's income and assets which will be available to meet any fine imposed on the offender (*R v Engen* [2004] EWCA Crim 1536 (CA)).

Potential earning capacity

Where there is reason to believe that an offender's potential earning capacity is greater than his or her current income, the court may wish to adjust the amount of the fine to reflect this (*R v Little* (unreported) 14 April 1976 (CA)). This may apply, for example, where an unemployed offender states an expectation to gain paid employment within a short time. The basis for the calculation of fine should be recorded in order to ensure that there is a clear record for use in variation or enforcement proceedings.

Variable income

The Sentencing Council has recently implemented guidance for cases involving offenders with variable income. In such cases, the court should take an average of four to six weeks' income to assess the relevant weekly income. However, if such approach fails to provide a fair reflection of the offender's means, the court should consider the offender's broader financial circumstances and exercise its judgment to ensure the fine reflects the seriousness of the offence and the financial circumstances of the offender.

Where an offender expresses their income in terms of an hourly rate, the court should make enquiries into the number of hours they typically work each week and apply the approach above.

High-income offenders

The court should ensure that any fine does not exceed the statutory maximum for the offence.

Approach to offenders on low income

[The paragraph explains how the low weekly figure of £120 is reached.]

Offence committed for 'commercial' purposes

Some offences are committed with the intention of gaining a significant commercial benefit. These often occur where, in order to carry out an activity lawfully, a person has to comply with certain processes which may be expensive. They include, for example, 'taxi-touting' (where unauthorised persons seek to operate as taxi drivers) and 'fly-tipping' (where the cost of lawful disposal is considerable).

In some of these cases, a fine based on the standard approach set out above may not reflect the level of financial gain achieved or sought through the offending. Accordingly:

a. where the offender has generated income or avoided expenditure to a level that can be calculated or estimated, the court may wish to consider that amount when determining the financial penalty;
b. where it is not possible to calculate or estimate that amount, the court may wish to draw on information from the enforcing authorities about the general costs of operating within the law.

Multiple offences

Where an offender is to be fined for two or more offences that arose out of the same incident, it will often be appropriate to impose on the most serious offence a fine which reflects the totality of the offending where this can be achieved within the maximum penalty for that offence. 'No separate penalty' should be imposed for the other offences.

Where compensation is being ordered, that will need to be attributed to the relevant offence as will any necessary ancillary orders.

Imposition of fines with custodial sentences

A fine and a custodial sentence may be imposed for the same offence although there will be few circumstances in which this is appropriate, particularly where the custodial sentence is to be served immediately. One example might be where an offender has profited financially from an offence but there is no obvious victim to whom compensation can be awarded. Combining these sentences is most likely to be appropriate only where the custodial sentence is short and/ or the offender clearly has, or will have, the means to pay.

Care must be taken to ensure that the overall sentence is proportionate to the seriousness of the offence and that better off offenders are not able to 'buy themselves out of custody'.

Payment

A fine is payable in full on the day on which it is imposed. The offender should always be asked for immediate payment when present in court and some payment on the day should be required wherever possible. Where that is not possible, the court may, in certain circumstances, require the offender to be detained (see section 82 of the Magistrates' Courts Act 1980 for restrictions on the power to impose imprisonment on default). More commonly, a court will allow payments to be made over a period set by the court:

a. if periodic payments are allowed, the fine should normally be payable within a maximum of 12 months.
b. compensation should normally be payable within 12 months. However, in exceptional circumstances it may be appropriate to allow it to be paid over a period of up to three years.

Where fine bands D, E and F apply, it may be appropriate for the fine to be of an amount that is larger than can be repaid within 12 months. In such cases, the fine should normally be payable within a maximum of 18 months (band D) or two years (bands E and F).

When allowing payment by instalments payments should be set at a realistic rate taking into account the offender's disposable income. The following approach may be useful:

Net weekly income	Suggested starting point for weekly payment
£60	£5
£120	£10
£200	£25
£300	£50
£400	£80

If the offender has dependants or larger than usual commitments, the weekly payment is likely to be decreased.

The payment terms must be included in any collection order made in respect of the amount imposed.

Collection orders

The Courts Act 2003 created a fines collection scheme which provides for greater administrative enforcement of fines.

[Collection orders are not available against youths (Sch 5 para 1 Courts Act 2003).]

Attachment of earnings orders/applications for benefit deductions

Unless it would be impracticable or inappropriate to do so, the court must make an attachment of earnings or (AEO) or application for benefit deductions (ABD) whenever:

- compensation is imposed (Courts Act 2003, schedule 5, paragraph 7A); or
- the court concludes that the offender is an existing defaulter and that the existing default(s) cannot be disregarded (Courts Act 2003, schedule 5, paragraph 8).

In other cases, the court may make an AEO or ABD with the offender's consent (Courts Act 2003, schedule 5, paragraph 9).

The court must make a collection order in every case in which a fine or compensation order is imposed unless this would be impracticable or inappropriate (Courts Act 2003, schedule 5, paragraph 12). The collection order must state:

- the amount of the sum due, including the amount of any fine, compensation order or other sum;
- whether the court considers the offender to be an existing defaulter;
- whether an AEO or ABD has been made and information about the effect of the order;
- if the court has not made an AEO or ABD, the payment terms
- if an AEO or ABD has been made, the reserve terms (in other words, the payment terms that will apply if the AEO or ABD fails). It will often be appropriate to set a reserve term of payment in full within 14 days.

The rate of payment for fines in bands D and E was approved in *R (Purnell) v South Western Magistrates' Court* [2013] EWHC 64 (Admin), which confirmed also that the responsibility to advise the court of other fines outstanding falls upon the offender. *R v Rance* [2012] EWCA Crim 2023 confirmed that it was for the defendant to provide the court with all relevant financial information, but that fines must have regard only to the means of the offender—there is no concept of a 'tainted gift'.

If the defendant fails to put all relevant information before the court, he cannot later complain that the court has failed to take account of financial circumstances as required by [s 124 SA 2020] s 164 CJA 2003.

R v Rance also held that whilst the court should have regard to any financial benefit from the crime, this is merely one consideration and does not mean that an equivalent or large proportion of the amount should be included in the fine.

D17.2 The detention alternative

Section 135 Magistrates' Courts Act 1980 provides:

Magistrates' Courts Act 1980, s 135

135 Detention of offender for one day in court-house or police station

(1) A magistrates' court that has power to commit to prison a person convicted of an offence, or would have that power but for section 82 or 88 above, may order him to be detained within the precincts of the courthouse or at any police station until such hour, not later than 8 o'clock in the evening of the day on which the order is made, as the court may direct, and, if it does so, shall not, where it has power to commit him to prison [or detention if aged 18–20 years], exercise that power.

(2) A court shall not make such an order under this section as will deprive the offender of a reasonable opportunity of returning to his abode on the day of the order.

D17.3 Enforcement of fines and confiscation orders

Separate representation orders should be obtained for these proceedings when appropriate

D17.3.1 *Principles*

The principles are set out in *R (Woolcock) v Secretary of State for Communities and Local Government and others* [2018] EWHC 17 (Admin), which was concerned with council tax enforcement, but the same principles apply to all fines and to the enforcement of confiscation orders (*R (Sanghera) v Birmingham Magistrates Court* [2017] EWHC 3323 (Admin)):

(i) The power to commit is coercive: it is intended to be used to extract payment of the debt from those who are able to pay, not to punish the debtor.

(ii) Because the liberty of the subject is at issue, even where the subject has been deliberately disobedient and/ or has ignored the enforcement process brought against him, it is vital that the magistrates conduct committal proceedings strictly in accordance with the applicable regulations and case law. If they do not, any committal will be unlawful.

. . .

(vi) Before making a committal order, the magistrates' court must conduct a means inquiry in the presence of the debtor. This inquiry is important in respect of a number of issues which the magistrates will or may need to consider, eg whether to make a committal order at all, the conditions upon which such an order may be postponed or suspended (eg the appropriate rate at which arrears should be paid), and whether to remit all or part of the debt.

(vii) The court must also consider, and determine, whether the failure to pay is the result of wilful refusal or culpable neglect, as any committal order (including a suspended order) can only be made if it is. Furthermore, even where the magistrates are satisfied that the failure to pay is the result of wilful refusal or culpable neglect, they will need to consider the degree of culpability, as that will be a factor that may be relevant to (e.g.) the period of imprisonment imposed.

. . .

(ix) Before making any committal order (including a suspended order), the magistrates' court must consider enforcement options to secure payment, other than imprisonment.

. . .

(xii) At the hearing for committal, the subject of the summons has the right to be legally represented. Usually, he will be represented by the duty solicitor. Magistrates should not proceed unless and until they have ascertained whether the subject wishes to be represented; and, if he does, that his representative has had a proper opportunity to take the subject's instructions and give him advice before the hearing commences.

(xiii) It is usual, although not obligatory, for magistrates to suspend at least a first committal order on condition that the subject makes regular instalment payments towards the arrears. However, they cannot make any unreasonable order for repayment. Therefore, each instalment to be paid must be reasonable in amount, given the assessment of means that has been conducted. Furthermore, the period for which instalments are to be paid must be reasonable. . . .; but, generally, where the period is two or three years, an order will be reasonable. Cases will be rare in which an instalment period of over three years will be appropriate. In no case has an instalment period of over five years been considered appropriate.

(xiv) Where instalments are made a condition of a suspended committal order, the appropriate course is for the magistrates' court to remit such part of the arrears as will reduce the total sum in respect of which the order is made to a sum which can be met by the instalments envisaged within the reasonable period as assessed by the court.

D17.3.2 *Available procedures*

The court may allow further time or further instalment payments.

Magistrates' Courts Act 1980, s 75

Power to dispense with immediate payment

(1) A magistrates' court by whose conviction or order a sum is adjudged to be paid may, instead of requiring immediate payment, allow time for payment, or order payment by instalments.

(2) Where a magistrates' court has allowed time for payment, the court may, on application by or on behalf of the person liable to make the payment, allow further time or order payment by instalments.

The court may, in appropriate circumstances, remit a fine.

Magistrates' Courts Act 1980, s 85

85 Power to remit fine

(1) Where a fine has been imposed on conviction of an offender by a magistrates' court, the court may at any time remit the whole or any part of the fine, but only if it thinks it just to do so having regard to a change of circumstances which has occurred—
  (a) where the court is considering whether to issue a warrant of commitment after the issue of such a warrant in respect of the fine has been postponed under subsection (2) of section 77 above, since the relevant time as defined in subsection (4) of that section; and
  (b) in any other case, since the date of the conviction

At a means enquiry, the powers of the court to impose imprisonment in default is set out in s 82 Magistrates' Courts Act 1980.

D17.3.3 *Powers in default*

Magistrates' Courts Act 1980, s 82

Restriction on power to impose imprisonment for default

(1) A magistrates' court shall not on the occasion of convicting an offender of an offence issue a warrant of commitment for a default in paying any sum adjudged to be paid by the conviction unless—
  (a) in the case of an offence punishable with imprisonment, he appears to the court to have sufficient means to pay the sum forthwith;
  (b) it appears to the court that he is unlikely to remain long enough at a place of abode in the United Kingdom to enable payment of the sum to be enforced by other methods; or
  (c) on the occasion of that conviction the court sentences him to immediate imprisonment, youth custody or detention in a detention centre for that or another offence or he is already serving a sentence of custody for life, or a term of imprisonment, youth custody, detention under section 9 of the Criminal Justice Act 1982 or detention in a detention centre.

(1A) A magistrates' court may not issue a warrant of commitment in reliance on subsection (1)(c) for a default in paying—
  (a) . . .
  (b) a surcharge ordered to be paid under section 42 of that (Sentencing) Code (victim surcharge)

. . .

(4) Where a magistrates' court is required . . . to inquire into a person's means, the court may not on the occasion of the inquiry or at any time thereafter issue a warrant of commitment for a default in paying any such sum unless—
  (a) in the case of an offence punishable with imprisonment, the offender appears to the court to have sufficient means to pay the sum forthwith; or
  (b) the court—
    (i) is satisfied that the default is due to the offender's wilful refusal or culpable neglect; and
    (ii) has considered or tried all other methods of enforcing payment of the sum and it appears to the court that they are inappropriate or unsuccessful.

(4A) The methods of enforcing payment mentioned in subsection (4)(b)(ii) above are—

(a) a warrant of distress under section 76 above;

(b) an application to the High Court or county court for enforcement under section 87 below;

(c) an order under section 88 below;

(d) an attachment of earnings order; and

(e) if the offender is under the age of 25, an order under section 17 of the Criminal Justice Act 1982 (attendance centre orders).

(4B) The cases in which the offender's default may be regarded for the purposes of subsection (4)(b)(i) as being attributable to his wilful refusal or culpable neglect include any case in which—

(a) he has refused, otherwise than on reasonable grounds, to consent to a work order proposed to be made under Schedule 6 to the Courts Act 2003 (discharge of fines by unpaid work), or

(b) he has without reasonable excuse failed to comply with such an order.

Under Sch 5 Courts Act 2003, where an offender is in receipt of Income Support, income-based Jobseeker's Allowance, income-related Employment and Support Allowance, Pension Credit or Universal Credit, the court can, with the offender's consent, order weekly direct deductions to be taken from the benefit to pay the fine. The deduction rate is £5 per week, but for Universal Credit only, the deduction can be up to £25 each week. If the benefit is contribution-based Jobseeker's Allowance or contribution-based Employment and Support Allowance, the deduction can be more. Consent is not required where there is a compensation order or there has been default on a collection order unless it would be impractical or inappropriate.

Procedures for fine enforcement appear in the Criminal Procedure Rules Part 30.

See *Blackstone's Criminal Practice 2026* E5.8

D18 Forfeiture Order

D18.1 Availability

Section 160 Sentencing Act (SA) 2020 contains a full list of the court's forfeiture powers. These include powers under the Knives Act 1997, the Obscene Publications Act 1959, and the Misuse of Drugs Act 1971.

Section 1 Prevention of Crime Act 1953 provides that, where any person is convicted of an offence under that section, the court may make an order for the forfeiture or disposal of any weapon in respect of which the offence was committed.

D18.2 Criteria under s 27 Misuse of Drugs Act 1971

Misuse of Drugs Act 1971, s 27

27 Forfeiture

(1) Subject to subsection (2) below, the court by or before which a person is convicted of an offence under this Act or an offence falling within subsection (3) below may order anything shown to the satisfaction of the court to relate to the offence, to be forfeited and either destroyed or dealt with in such other manner as the court may order.

(2) The court shall not order anything to be forfeited under this section, where a person claiming to be the owner of or otherwise interested in it applies to be heard by the court, unless an opportunity has been given to him to show cause why the order should not be made.

(3) An offence falls within this subsection if it is an offence which is specified in—
- (a) paragraph 1 of Schedule 2 to the Proceeds of Crime Act 2002 (drug trafficking offences), or
- (b) so far as it relates to that paragraph, paragraph 10 of that Schedule.

See also D12 on deprivation orders.

See *Blackstone's Criminal Practice 2026* E8.7

Blackstone's Magistrates' Court Handbook 2026. Bartholomew Dalton and Caroline Liggins, Oxford University Press. © Oxford University Press 2026.
DOI: 10.1093/oso/9780198963943.003.0077

D19 **Mental Health Disposals**

Mental health procedures are dealt with at **A20**.

D19.1 **Sentencing guidelines**

The Sentencing Council has issued a guideline on sentencing offenders with mental disorders, developmental disorders, or neurological impairments. The fact that an offender has an impairment or disorder should always be considered by the court but will not necessarily have an impact on sentencing. Culpability may be reduced if an offender was at the time of the offence suffering from an impairment or disorder.

> Courts may find the following questions a useful starting point. They are not exhaustive, and they are not a check list as the range of offenders, impairments and disorders is wide.
>
> - **At the time of the offence did the offender's impairment or disorder impair their ability:**
>
>   o to exercise appropriate judgement,
>
>   o to make rational choices,
>
>   o to understand the nature and consequences of their actions?
> - At the time of the offence, did the offender's impairment or disorder cause them to behave in a disinhibited way?
> - Are there other factors related to the offender's impairment or disorder which reduce culpability?
> - **Medication**. Where an offender was failing to take medication prescribed to them at the time of the offence, the court will need to consider the extent to which that failure was wilful or arose as a result of the offender's lack of insight into their impairment or disorder,
> - **'Self-medication'**. Where an offender made their impairment or disorder worse by 'self-medicating' with alcohol or non-prescribed or illicit drugs at the time of the offence, the court will need to consider the extent to which the offender was aware that would be the effect,
> - **Insight**. Courts need to be cautious before concluding that just because an offender has some insight into their impairment or disorder and/or insight into the importance of taking their medication, that insight automatically increases the culpability for the offence. Any insight, and its effect on culpability, is a matter of degree for the court to assess.

D19.2 **Guardianship and hospital orders**

Section 37 Mental Health Act 1983 provides:

> ### Mental Health Act 1983, s 37
>
> **37 Powers of court to order hospital admission or guardianship**
>
> (1) Where a person is convicted . . . by a magistrates' court of an offence punishable on summary conviction with imprisonment, and the conditions mentioned

Blackstone's Magistrates' Court Handbook 2026. Bartholomew Dalton and Caroline Liggins, Oxford University Press. © Oxford University Press 2026.
DOI: 10.1093/oso/9780198963943.003.0078

in subsection (2) below are satisfied, the court may by order authorise his admission to and detention in such hospital as may be specified in the order or, as the case may be, place him under the guardianship of a local social services authority or of such other person approved by a local social services authority as may be so specified.

(1A) . . .

(1B) . . .

(2) The conditions referred to in subsection (1) above are that—

(a) the court is satisfied, on the written or oral evidence of two registered medical practitioners, that the offender is suffering from mental disorder and that either—

(i) the mental disorder from which the offender is suffering is of a nature or degree which makes it appropriate for him to be detained in a hospital for medical treatment, and appropriate medical treatment is available for him; or

(ii) in the case of an offender who has attained the age of 16 years, the mental disorder is of a nature or degree which warrants his reception into guardianship under this Act; and

(b) the court is of the opinion, having regard to all the circumstances including the nature of the offence and the character and antecedents of the offender, and to the other available methods of dealing with him, that the most suitable method of disposing of the case is by means of an order under this section.

(3) Where a person is charged before a magistrates' court with any act or omission as an offence and the court would have power, on convicting him of that offence, to make an order under subsection (1) above in his case, then, if the court is satisfied that the accused did the act or made the omission charged, the court may, if it thinks fit, make such an order without convicting him.

(4) An order for the admission of an offender to a hospital (in this Act referred to as 'a hospital order') shall not be made under this section unless the court is satisfied on the written or oral evidence of the approved clinician who would have overall responsibility for his case or of some other person representing the managers of the hospital that arrangements have been made for his admission to that hospital, and for his admission to it within the period of 28 days beginning with the date of the making of such an order; and the court may, pending his admission within that period, give such directions as it thinks fit for his conveyance to and detention in a place of safety . . .

(8) Where an order is made under this section, the court shall not—

(a) pass sentence of imprisonment or impose a fine or make a community order (within the meaning given by section 200 of the Sentencing Code; or a youth rehabilitation order (within the meaning given by section 173 of that Code in respect of the offence,

(b) if the order under this section is a hospital order, make a referral order (within the meaning given by section 83 of that Code) in respect of the offence, or

(c) make in respect of the offender an order under section 376 of that Code (binding over of parent or guardian),

but the court may make any other order which it has power to make apart from this section; and for the purposes of this subsection 'sentence of imprisonment' includes any sentence or order for detention.

It is suggested that the wording of s 37(8) prevents the making, for instance, of a discharge (ss 79 and 80 SA 2020), a compensation order (s 134 SA 2020), and a disqualification from driving (s 34 Road Traffic Offenders Act 1988) as the court's powers in each case only arise on a conviction.

When disposing of a defendant who is already sectioned under the Mental Health Act 1983 and there is no imminent plan for discharge, the court should impose a medical disposal (e.g. an order under s 37) and avoid the risk of conflicting regimes that might occur if the defendant were sentenced to a sentence such as a conditional discharge or suspended sentence order (*R v Hawkridge* [2023] EWCA Crim 1288).

See *Blackstone's Criminal Practice 2026* E22

D19.3 Remand to hospital for reports and committal for sentence

Section 35 Mental Health Act 1983 provides:

Mental Health Act 1983, s 35

35 Remand to hospital for report on accused's mental condition

(1) Subject to the provisions of this section, the Crown Court or a magistrates' court may remand an accused person to a hospital specified by the court for a report on his mental condition.

(2) For the purposes of this section an accused person is—

(a) . . .

(b) in relation to a magistrates' court, any person who has been convicted by the court of an offence punishable on summary conviction with imprisonment and any person charged with such an offence if the court is satisfied that he did the act or made the omission charged or he has consented to the exercise by the court of the powers conferred by this section.

(3) Subject to subsection (4) below, the powers conferred by this section may be exercised if—

(a) the court is satisfied, on the written or oral evidence of a registered medical practitioner, that there is reason to suspect that the accused person is suffering from mental disorder; and

(b) the court is of the opinion that it would be impracticable for a report on his mental condition to be made if he were remanded on bail; but those powers shall not be exercised by the Crown Court in respect of a person who has been convicted before the court if the sentence for the offence of which he has been convicted is fixed by law.

(4) The court shall not remand an accused person to a hospital under this section unless satisfied, on the written or oral evidence of the approved clinician who would be responsible for making the report or of some other person representing the managers of the hospital, that arrangements have been made for his admission to that hospital and for his admission to it within the period of seven days beginning with the date of the remand; and if the court is so satisfied it may, pending his admission, give directions for his conveyance to and detention in a place of safety.

(5) Where a court has remanded an accused person under this section it may further remand him if it appears to the court, on the written or oral evidence of the approved clinician responsible for making the report, that a further remand is necessary for completing the assessment of the accused person's mental condition.

(6) The power of further remanding an accused person under this section may be exercised by the court without his being brought before the court if he is represented by an authorised person who is given an opportunity of being heard.

(7) An accused person shall not be remanded or further remanded under this section for more than 28 days at a time or for more than 12 weeks in all; and the court may at any time terminate the remand if it appears to the court that it is appropriate to do so.

Section 43 Mental Health Act 1983 provides:

Mental Health Act 1983, s 43

43 Power of magistrates' courts to commit for restriction order

(1) If in the case of a person of or over the age of 14 years who is convicted by a magistrates' court of an offence punishable on summary conviction with imprisonment—

(a) the conditions which under section 37(1) above are required to be satisfied for the making of a hospital order are satisfied in respect of the offender; but

(b) it appears to the court, having regard to the nature of the offence, the antecedents of the offender and the risk of his committing further offences if set at large, that if a hospital order is made a restriction order should also be made,

the court may, instead of making a hospital order or dealing with him in any other manner, commit him in custody to the Crown Court to be dealt with in respect of the offence.

(4) The powers of a magistrates' court under section 14 or 16 or 16A of the Sentencing Code (which enable such a court to commit an offender to the Crown Court where the court is of the opinion, or it appears to the court, as mentioned in the section in question) shall also be exercisable by a magistrates' court where it is of that opinion (or it so appears to it) unless a hospital order is made in the offender's case with a restriction order.

D20 Minimum Sentences

D20.1 Criteria

Burglary s 314 Sentencing Act (SA) 2020*+	• Latest offence committed on or after 1 December 1999. • Offender aged 18 or over at date of this offence. • Convicted of two previous domestic burglaries, both of which occurred after 1 December 1999, and had been convicted of the first burglary before he committed the second. Must have been sentenced to a penalty greater than a discharge. On the meaning of a dwelling **see C16.5.2** • Minimum 3-year sentence (discount of 20% permissible for guilty plea). • The case must be sent to the Crown Court.
Drug trafficking s 313 SA 2020*+	• Latest offence committed on or after 1 October 1997. • Offender aged 18 or over at date of this offence. • Convicted of two previous drug trafficking offences and had been convicted of the first offence before he committed the second but the dates of conviction are not relevant. Must have been sentenced to a penalty greater than a discharge. • 7-year sentence (discount of 20% permissible for guilty plea). • The case must be sent to the Crown Court.
Firearms s 311 SA 2020*	Minimum 5 years if 18 or over on the date of conviction, or 3 years if 16 or over but under 18 on that date (5) This section applies where (Sch 20 SA 2020)— 1 An offence under section 5(1)(a), (ab), (aba), (ac), (ad), (ae), (af), (ag), (ba) or (c) of the Firearms Act 1968 (offence of having in possession, purchasing or acquiring, weapon or ammunition) committed on or after 22 January 2004. 2 An offence under section 5(1A)(a) of the Firearms Act 1968 (offence of having in possession, purchasing or acquiring firearm disguised as another object) committed on or after 22 January 2004. 3 An offence under section 5(2A) of the Firearms Act 1968 (manufacture, sale or transfer of firearm or ammunition, or possession etc for sale or transfer) committed in respect of a relevant firearm or relevant ammunition. 4 (1) An offence under any of the provisions of the Firearms Act 1968 listed in sub-paragraph (2) committed on or after 6 April 2007 in respect of a relevant firearm or relevant ammunition. (2) Those provisions are section 16 (possession of firearm or ammunition with intent to injure); section 16A (possession of firearm with intent to cause fear orviolence);

Blackstone's Magistrates' Court Handbook 2026. Bartholomew Dalton and Caroline Liggins, Oxford University Press. © Oxford University Press 2026.
DOI: 10.1093/oso/9780198963943.003.0079

	section 17 (use of firearm to resist arrest); section 18 (carrying firearm with criminal intent); section 19 (carrying a firearm in a public place); section 20(1) (trespassing in a building with firearm). 5 An offence under section 28 of the Violent Crime Reduction Act 2006 (using someone to mind a weapon), where the dangerous weapon in respect of which the offence was committed was a relevant firearm
Aggravated possession of weapons Prevention of Crime Act 1953, s 1A; Criminal Justice Act (CJA) 1988, s 139AA) s 312 SA 2020*⁺	• Offence committed on or after 3 December 2012. • Minimum 6-month sentence (or 4 months DTO for those of 16 or 17 on the date of conviction with a 20% discount available for a guilty plea (which makes a DTO impossible) • A suspended sentence is available for those of 18 or over but will only rarely be appropriate (R. v Uddin [2022] EWCA Crim 751). The court must have regard to its duty under s 44 Children and Young Persons Act 1933 for those under 18
Second offence under any of s 1 Prevention of Crime Act 1953, s 139 and s 139A CJA 1988 or s 6 Offensive Weapons Act 2019 s 315 SA 2020*⁺	• Offence committed on or after 17 July 2015 (or on or after 6 April 2022 for s 6 offensive weapons Act 2019) • Already convicted when over 16 of any of these offences. • Minimum 6-month sentence or 4 months DTO for those of 16 or 17 on the date of conviction with a 20% discount available for a guilty plea (which makes a DTO impossible) • A suspended sentence is available for those of 18 or over but will only rarely be appropriate (R v Uddin [2022] EWCA Crim 751). The court must have regard to its duty under s 44 Children and Young Persons Act 1933 for those under 18

*unless there are exceptional circumstances which—

(a) relate to the offence or to the offender, and

(b) justify not doing so

⁺ The Exceptional circumstances test applies to all offences committed on or after 28 June 2022. The interests of justice test still applies to offences committed prior to 28 June 2022.

D20.2 Case law

The correct approach to minimum sentencing provision is to apply the relevant sentencing guidelines without reference to the applicable minimum sentencing provisions and to then increase the sentence to comply with the minimum sentence if necessary (*R v Woofe* [2019] EWCA Crim 2249.

See *Blackstone's Criminal Practice 2026* E18

D21 *Newton* Hearings

D21.1 The rule in *Newton*

The rule in *R v Newton* (1982) 77 Cr App R 13 indicates that an offender will be sentenced on the prosecution's version of the facts unless the defence make clear that they are pleading on an alternative basis. In that situation, the Crown must prove its version of the facts by admissible evidence to the criminal standard of proof.

The purpose of a *Newton* hearing is to establish the factual basis for sentence in a case where there is a factual dispute and that dispute is material to sentence. A material difference in relation to sentence is not restricted to whether or not a different category within the sentencing guidelines is going to be selected; a *Newton* can make a material difference within a range set out in a category (*R v Hewitt* [2020] EWCA Crim 1225). Once a *Newton* hearing takes place the defendant is at risk of findings conflicting with an earlier basis of plea (*Nicholls v DPP* [2013] EWHC 4365 (Admin)).

D21.2 Procedure

In the magistrates' and youth court it was not proper for the trial of one defendant and a *Newton* in relation to the other to take place at the same time. It meant that the inadmissible evidence of the defendant who had pleaded guilty was used at the trial of the co-defendant. (*KK v DPP* [2016] EWHC 1976 (Admin)).

D21.3 Criteria

R v Cairns [2013] EWCA Crim 467 confirmed that there is no obligation to hold a *Newton* hearing:

(a) if the difference between the two versions of fact is immaterial to sentence (in which event the defendant's version must be adopted: *R v Hall* (1984) 6 Cr App R (S) 321);
(b) where the defence version can be described as 'manifestly false' or 'wholly implausible': *R v Hawkins* (1985) Cr App R (S) 351; or
(c) where the matters put forward by the defendant do not contradict the prosecution case but constitute extraneous mitigation where the court is not bound to accept the truth of the matters put forward whether or not they are challenged by the prosecution: *R v Broderick* (1994) 15 Cr App R (S) 476.

Guidance in relation to the holding of *Newton* hearings was set down in *R v Underwood* [2004] EWCA Crim 2256:

(1) The starting point has to be the defendant's instructions. His advocate will appreciate whether any significant facts about the prosecution evidence are disputed and the factual basis on which the defendant intends to plead guilty. Responsibility for taking initiative and alerting the prosecutor to the disputed areas rests with the defence.

Blackstone's Magistrates' Court Handbook 2026. Bartholomew Dalton and Caroline Liggins, Oxford University Press. © Oxford University Press 2026.
DOI: 10.1093/oso/9780198963943.003.0080

(2) Where the Crown accepts the defendant's account of the disputed facts, the agreement should be written down and signed by both advocates. It should then be made available to the judge. If pleas have already been accepted and approved then it should be available before the sentencing hearing begins. If the agreed basis of plea is not signed by both advocates, the judge is entitled to ignore it. The Crown might reject the defendant's version. If so, the areas of dispute should be identified in writing, focusing the court's attention on the precise facts in dispute.
(3) The prosecution's position might be that they have no evidence to contradict the defence's assertions. In those circumstances, particularly if the facts relied on by the defendant arise from his personal knowledge and depend on his own account of the facts, the Crown should not normally agree the defendant's account unless supported by other material. The court should be notified at the outset in writing of the points in issue and the Crown's responses.
(4) After submissions, the judge will decide how to proceed. If not already decided, he would address the question of whether he should approve the Crown's acceptance of pleas. Then he would address the proposed basis of plea. It should be emphasized that whether or not the basis of plea is agreed, the judge is not bound by any such agreement and is entitled of his own motion to insist that any evidence relevant to the facts in dispute should be called before him, paying appropriate regard to any agreement reached by the advocates and any reasons which the Crown, in particular, might advance to justify him proceeding immediately to sentence. The judge is responsible for the sentencing decision and may order a *Newton* hearing to ascertain the truth about disputed facts.
(5) Relevant evidence should be called by prosecution and defence, particularly where the issue arises from facts which are within the exclusive knowledge of the defendant. If the defendant is willing to give evidence he should be called and, if not, subject to any explanation offered, the judge may draw such inference as he sees fit. The judge can reject the evidence called by the prosecution or by the defendant or his witnesses even if the Crown has not called contradictory evidence. The judge's conclusions should be explained in the judgment.

...

(7) Normally, matters of mitigation are not dealt with by way of a *Newton* hearing but it is always open to the court to allow a defendant to give evidence on matters of mitigation which are within his own knowledge. The judge is entitled to decline to hear evidence about disputed facts if the case advanced is, for good reason, to be regarded as absurd or obviously untenable.
(8) If the issues at the *Newton* hearing are wholly resolved in the defendant's favour, mitigation for guilty pleas should not be reduced. If the defendant is disbelieved or obliges the prosecution to call evidence from the victim, who is then subjected to cross-examination which, because it is entirely unfounded, causes unnecessary and inappropriate distress, or if the defendant conveys that he has no insight into the consequences of his offence, and no genuine remorse, the judge might reduce the discount for the guilty pleas.

The guideline on discount for guilty plea states that if the offender's version of events is rejected at a *Newton* hearing the reduction which would have been available at the stage the plea was indicated should normally be halved. Where witnesses are called during a hearing it may be appropriate further to decrease the reduction.

In *R v Abbas* [2017] EWCA Crim 251 it was confirmed that where an unrealistic basis of plea was put forward and a *Newton* listed, discount could be reduced even though the *Newton* was not pursued. A realistic basis should have been proposed.

See *Blackstone's Criminal Practice 2026* D20.8

D22 Notification Requirements

Notification requirements under the Sexual Offences Act 2003; the Stalking Protection Act 2019; Domestic Abuse Act 2021; and the Offensive Weapons Act 2019 are considered in this section.

D22.1 Sexual Offences Act 2003

Note that for children and young offenders reference should also be made to Chapter **J21**. In the *Handbook of Youths in the Criminal Courts*

Breach is dealt with at **C2.4**.

It is not a requirement that a court 'orders' a notification requirement, as this will follow automatically as a result of a qualifying conviction (ie those offences specified in Sch 3 to the Sexual Offences Act 2003).

An offender will be given a notice to sign and be provided with his own copy that sets down the requirements to be satisfied. For some offences, a specific sentence is required before the liability arises. In relation to offences under s 1 Indecency with Children Act 1978, the notification regime only applies if the child is under 16 and the court should if necessary make a determination on that issue (*R v George* [2018] EWCA Crim 417). In *R v Davison* [2008] EWCA Crim 2795, D was ordered to complete 220 hours of unpaid work within a 12-month period. D submitted that a community order which contains solely an unpaid work requirement to be completed within 12 months is not a community sentence of at least 12 months' duration, as it is open to the offender to complete the work within the 12-month period and on completion of the work the community order ceases. The court held: the length of a community order must be capable of being determined on the date it is made. In our judgment the period specified under section 177(5) of the Criminal Justice Act 2003 by a court when imposing a community order is the relevant period for the purpose of determining the duration of the order under paragraph 18(b)(ii)(c) of Schedule 3 to the Sexual Offences Act 2003 however long it in fact takes the offender to carry out the requirements under the order.

In the case *R v Holmes (Peter)* [2023] 4 WLR 1, D appealed against 11 of the convictions for gross indecency, arguing proof of 'gross indecency' required some form of intercrural contact, and that it has a specific legal meaning so the judge was wrong to direct the jury to just apply contemporary moral standards as to how they decide what acts are 'indecent' and what level of indecency was 'gross'. The appeal was dismissed—it is settled law that gross indecency does not require actual physical contact between persons. The term 'gross indecency' has an ordinary meaning which juries have been able to determine and apply without difficulty for many years. The boundaries of the offence had been set which were sufficiently certain to have regulated the behaviour of persons subject to the criminal law and s 1 of the Indecency with Children Act 1960; and D's own evidence at trial had shown that he knew what were proper boundaries for his behaviour and he had merely denied acting in the grossly indecent way alleged by the complainants.

Blackstone's Magistrates' Court Handbook 2026. Bartholomew Dalton and Caroline Liggins, Oxford University Press. © Oxford University Press 2026.
DOI: 10.1093/oso/9780198963943.003.0081

Penalty	Notification period for an adult (Sexual Offences Act 2003, s 82)
Conditional discharge	Period of discharge
A person sentenced otherwise than as mentioned elsewhere	5 years
Imprisonment for a term of 6 months or less	7 years
Imprisonment for a minimum term of 6 months but less than 30 months	10 years
A person sentenced to imprisonment for life or for 30 months or more	Indeterminate

Note: Where the registration is indeterminate there is a power to apply for removal once 15 years has been served and then every 8 years.

In R v Allon [2023] EWCA Crim 204, the defendant was convicted of an offence of distributing indecent photographs of a child contrary to s 1(1)(b) of the Protection of Children Act 1978. He was 17 at the time of the offence, but 20 at the time of conviction. The judge held that as he was over 18 at the time of conviction, he was caught by the notification requirements. As a result, the Crown Court issued a certificate under s 92 of the Sexual Offences Act 2003 that he was subject to the notification requirements under Part 2 of that Act. The Court of Appeal held that issuing a certificate was not a decision or order of the sentencing judge and is in itself incapable of being appealed (in these circumstances, a challenge by way of judicial review is likely to be the appropriate vehicle). However, the court had jurisdiction where a judge had erroneously ruled that the notification requirements should apply. In these circumstances, the Court of Appeal held it could reconstitute itself as a Divisional Court (with the permission of counsel: [30] and [32]), treat the application for leave to appeal as including an application for permission to apply for judicial review, and quash the issuance of a s 92 certificate.

See *Blackstone's Criminal Practice 2026* E23

D22.2 s 9 Stalking Protection Act 2019

While a person is subject to a stalking protection order, or interim order, and is not subject to the notification arrangements set out above in D22.1, they must within 3 days notify their names and address.

D22.3 s 41 Domestic Abuse Act 2021

While a person is subject to a domestic abuse protection order and is not subject to notification arrangements set out in D22.1 or D22.2, they must within 3 days notify their name and address.

D23 Offences Taken into Consideration (TICs) and the Totality Principle

D23.1 Criteria for TICs

In *R v Miles* [2006] EWCA Crim 256, the court made the following observations:

> [T]he sentence is intended to reflect a defendant's overall criminality. Offences cannot be taken into consideration without the express agreement of the offender. That is an essential prerequisite. The offender is pleading guilty to the offences. If they are to be taken into account (and the court is not obliged to take them into account) they have relevance to the overall criminality. When assessing the significance of TICs, as they are often called, of course the court is likely to attach weight to the demonstrable fact that the offender has assisted the police, particularly if they are enabled to clear up offences which might not otherwise be brought to justice. It is also true that cooperative behaviour of that kind will often provide its own very early indication of guilt, and usually means that no further proceedings at all need be started. They may also serve to demonstrate a genuine determination by the offender (and we deliberately use the colloquialism) to wipe the slate clean, so that when he emerges from whatever sentence is imposed on him, he can put his past completely behind him, without having worry or concern that offences may be revealed and that he is then returned to court. As in so many aspects of sentencing, of course, the way in which the court deals with offences to be taken into consideration depends on context. In some cases the offences taken into consideration will end up by adding nothing or nothing very much to the sentence which the court would otherwise impose. On the other hand, offences taken into consideration may aggravate the sentence and lead to a substantial increase in it. For example, the offences may show a pattern of criminal activity which suggests careful planning or deliberate rather than casual involvement in a crime. They may show an offence or offences committed on bail, after an earlier arrest. They may show a return to crime immediately after the offender has been before the court and given a chance that, by committing the crime, he has immediately rejected. There are many situations where similar issues may arise. One advantage to the defendant, of course, is that if once an offence is taken into consideration, there is no likely risk of any further prosecution for it. If, on the other hand, it is not, that risk remains. In short, offences taken into consideration are indeed taken into consideration. They are not ignored or expunged or disregarded.

The Sentencing Council has issued a definitive guideline in relation to TICs, which was intended to reflect the existing law. It confirms that, when sentencing an offender who requests offences to be taken into consideration, courts should pass a total sentence which reflects all the offending behaviour. The sentence must be just and proportionate, and must not exceed the statutory maximum for the conviction offence.

The court is likely to consider that the fact that the offender has assisted the police (particularly if the offences would not otherwise have been detected) and avoided the need for further proceedings demonstrates a genuine determination by the offender to wipe the slate clean.

Blackstone's Magistrates' Court Handbook 2026. Bartholomew Dalton and Caroline Liggins, Oxford University Press.
DOI: 10.1093/oso/9780198963943.003.0082

The sentence imposed on the offender should, in most circumstances, be increased to reflect the fact that other offences have been taken into consideration. The court should:

- determine the sentencing starting point for the conviction offence;
- consider aggravating and mitigating circumstances. The presence of TICs should generally be treated as an aggravating feature that justifies an upward adjustment from the starting point. Where there is a large number of TICs, it may be appropriate to move outside the category range, although this must be considered in the context of the case and subject to the principle of totality. The court is limited to the statutory maximum for the conviction offence;
- consider whether the frank admission of a number of offences is an indication of a defendant's remorse or determination and/ or demonstration of steps taken to address addiction or offending behaviour.

Any reduction for guilty plea should be applied to the total sentence, as should the totality principle.

Ancillary orders may take account of TICs to the limit allowed by the offences for which there is a conviction.

See *Blackstone's Criminal Practice 2026* **D20.52**

D23.2 **Totality principle**

The principle of totality comprises two elements:

(1) all courts, when sentencing for more than a single offence, should pass a total sentence which reflects all the offending behaviour before it and is just and proportionate. This is so whether the sentences are structured as concurrent or consecutive. Therefore, concurrent sentences will ordinarily be longer than a single sentence for a single offence.

(2) it is usually impossible to arrive at a just and proportionate sentence for multiple offending simply by adding together notional single sentences. It is necessary to address the offending behaviour, together with the factors personal to the offender as a whole.

D23.2.1 ***Concurrent/consecutive sentences***

There is no inflexible rule governing whether sentences should be structured as concurrent or consecutive components. The overriding principle is that the overall sentence must be just and proportionate.

'When offences arise out of the same set of facts or a series of offences of the same kind, concurrent sentences will ordinarily be appropriate. Consecutive sentences will be appropriate where there are offences of the same kind, but the overall criminality will not be sufficiently reflected by concurrent sentences. Typically, this consideration will apply where a defendant commits similar offences over a substantial period or on different days. It may even apply where the offending is spread out over the course of a single day. But consecutive sentences cannot be justified when each offence effectively formed part of a single course of conduct' (*R v Brown* [2020] EWCA Crim 1095).

D23.3 Specific applications—custodial sentences

For an existing determinate sentence, where determinate sentence is still to be passed:

Circumstance	Approach
Offender serving a determinate sentence (offence(s) committed before original sentence imposed)	Consider what the sentence length would have been if the court had dealt with the offences at the same time and ensure that the totality of the sentence is just and proportionate in all the circumstances. If it is not, an adjustment should be made to the sentence imposed for the latest offence.
Offender serving a determinate sentence (offence(s) committed after original sentence imposed)	Generally the sentence will be consecutive as it will have arisen out of an unrelated incident. The court must have regard to the totality of the offender's criminality when passing the second sentence, to ensure that the total sentence to be served is just and proportionate. Where a prisoner commits acts of violence in prison, any reduction for totality is likely to be minimal.
Offender serving a determinate sentence but released from custody	The new sentence should start on the day it is imposed: s 265 Criminal Justice Act 2003 prohibits a sentence of imprisonment running consecutively to a sentence from which a prisoner has been released. The sentence for the new offence will take into account the aggravating feature that it was committed on licence. However, it must be commensurate with the new offence and cannot be artificially inflated with a view to ensuring that the offender serves a period in custody additional to the recall period (which will be an unknown quantity in most cases) this is so even if the new sentence will, in consequence, add nothing to the period actually served.
Offender sentenced to a determinate term and subject to an existing suspended sentence order	Where an offender commits an additional offence during the operational period of a suspended sentence and the court orders the suspended sentence to be activated, the additional sentence will generally be consecutive to the activated suspended sentence, as it will arise out of unrelated facts.

D24 Penalty Points for Driving Offences

(See ss 28 *et seq* Road Traffic Offenders Act (RTOA) 1988)

D24.1 Criteria

Penalty points must be imposed for all offences that are subject to obligatory endorsement, unless the court finds special reasons for not imposing points (see s 44(2) RTOA 1988 and **D16.5**).

A person who acts as a secondary party to an offence carrying obligatory disqualification is liable to 10 penalty points.

If a person is found guilty, on one or more occasions, of more than one offence committed on the same occasion, the range of penalty points is taken as being whichever is the highest available for any one offence (eg a person convicted of speeding (3–6 points) and no insurance (6–8 points) is liable to receive up to 6 or 8 points respectively). A court does, however, have discretion to disapply this rule if reasons are given (s 28 Road Traffic Act 1988).

Where a court orders obligatory disqualification and there are further offences to be sentenced, it should not order points for the further offences.

See *Blackstone's Criminal Practice 2026* **C7.16**

Blackstone's Magistrates' Court Handbook 2026. Bartholomew Dalton and Caroline Liggins, Oxford University Press.
DOI: 10.1093/oso/9780198963943.003.0083

D25 Pre-Sentence Reports

D25.1 Criteria

In deciding whether to impose youth rehabilitation orders, community orders, and custodial sentences, a pre-sentence report requirement arises under s 30 Sentencing Act 2020.

> **Sentencing Act 2020, ss 30 and 31(Criminal Justice Act 2003, s 156)**
>
> 30(2) If the offender is aged 18 or over, the court must obtain and consider a presentence report before forming the opinion unless, in the circumstances of the case, it considers that it is unnecessary to obtain a pre-sentence report.
>
> (3) If the offender is aged under 18, the court must obtain and consider a presentence report before forming the opinion unless—
>
> (a) there exists a previous pre-sentence report obtained in respect of the offender, and
>
> (b) the court considers—
>
> (i) in the circumstances of the case, and
>
> (ii) having had regard to the information contained in that report or, if there is more than one, the most recent report, that it is unnecessary to obtain a pre-sentence report.
>
> 31(4) Where by any provision of this Code, the court is required to obtain a presentence report, it may accept a pre-sentence report given orally in open court.
>
> But this is subject to—
>
> (a) any rules made under subsection (1)(b), and
>
> (b) subsection (5).
>
> (5) A pre-sentence report must be in writing if it—
>
> (a) relates to an offender aged under 18, and
>
> (b) is required to be obtained and considered before the court forms an opinion mentioned in—
>
> (i) section 230(2) (seriousness threshold for discretionary custodial sentence),
>
> (ii) section 231(2) (determining term of custodial sentence), . . .

D25.2 Reports in anticipated guilty plea cases in the magistrates' court

The Law Society and Probation Service have agreed a protocol.

Pre-Sentence report before plea

The Defence Legal Representative shall:

1.1 Apply for the IDPC and receive instructions from the defendant on likely plea, as soon as is reasonably practicable.

1.2 Where the plea is likely to be guilty confirm with the defendant whether the prosecution case is accepted in full.

1.3 Where the prosecution case is accepted in full, consider whether

Blackstone's Magistrates' Court Handbook 2026. Bartholomew Dalton and Caroline Liggins, Oxford University Press. © Oxford University Press 2026.
DOI: 10.1093/oso/9780198963943.003.0084

1.3.1 the offence on the full prosecution version is likely to pass the threshold for a community sentence;

1.3.2 a pre-sentence report is likely to be necessary and if so ask the defendant if they would agree to comply with a PSR Before Plea, were this to be arranged.

1.4 Where the Defence Legal Representative is of the opinion to request a PSR before Plea, explain the PSR before Plea process to the defendant reminding them that arranging a PSR Before Plea provides no indication of any sentence and that

1.4.1 all sentencing options remain open including an immediate sentence of imprisonment,

1.4.2 the court will decide whether to consider the PSR before Plea, if one is available,

1.4.3 the court may proceed to sentence without a pre-sentence report if the court considers it unnecessary.

1.5 Where the defendant agrees to the request for a PSR Before Plea complete the applicable form and send it electronically to the Probation Service mailbox for the magistrates' court scheduled to hear the case, with an email including the URN and scheduled hearing date, entitled 'PSR Before Plea', by the very latest 3 working days before the scheduled hearing, copying in the court and CPS.

D25.3 Reports in anticipated guilty plea cases when sending cases to the Crown Court

D25.3.1 *Criminal Practice Direction 9.2*

Where a magistrates' court is considering committal for sentence or the defendant has indicated an intention to plead guilty in a matter which is to be sent to the Crown Court, the magistrates' court should request the preparation of a pre-sentence report for the Crown Court's use if the magistrates' court considers that:

(a) there is a realistic alternative to a custodial sentence; or
(b) the defendant may satisfy the criteria for classification as a dangerous offender; or
(c) there is some other appropriate reason for doing so.

D25.3.2 *In addition it will usually be appropriate to order a report where*

- the defendant is 17 and under;
- the defendant is under 21 and is a first-time offender or has not served a prison sentence (*R v Townsend* [2018] EWCA Crim 875).

D25.4 Sentencing Council General Guideline

Sentencing Council General Guidance states that whenever the court reaches the provisional view that:

- the custody threshold has been passed; and, if so
- the length of imprisonment which represents the shortest term commensurate with the seriousness of the offence;
- the court should obtain a pre-sentence report, whether verbal or written, unless the court considers a report to be unnecessary. Ideally a pre-sentence report should be completed on the same day to avoid adjourning the case.

See *Blackstone's Criminal Practice 2026* E2.23

D26 Prevention Orders

D26.1 Sexual harm prevention orders

Sentencing Act 2020, s 345

345 Sexual harm prevention order: availability on conviction

(1) Where a person is convicted of an offence listed in Schedule 3 or 5 to the Sexual Offences Act 2003 (sexual offences, and other offences, for the purposes of Part 2 of that Act), the court dealing with the offender in respect of the offence may make a sexual harm prevention order.

(2) Where an offence listed in Schedule 3 to that Act is listed subject to a condition that relates—

(a) to the way in which the offender is dealt with in respect of an offence so listed, or

(b) to the age of any person, that condition is to be disregarded in determining for the purposes of subsection (1) whether the offence is listed in that Schedule.

346 Exercise of power to make sexual harm prevention order

Where a sexual harm prevention order is available to a court, the court may make such an order only if satisfied that it is necessary to do so for the purpose of—

(a) protecting the public or any particular members of the public from sexual harm from the offender, or

(b) protecting children or vulnerable adults generally, or any particular children or vulnerable adults, from sexual harm from the offender outside the United Kingdom.

347 Sexual harm prevention orders: matters to be specified

(1) A sexual harm prevention order must specify—

(a) the prohibitions and requirements included in the order, and

(b) for each prohibition or requirement, the period for which it is to have effect (the "specified period"). See section 348 for further matters to be included in the case of a prohibition on travelling to any country outside the United Kingdom and section 348A for further matters to be included in the case of an electronic monitoring requirement,

(2) The specified period must be—

(a) a fixed period of not less than 5 years, or

(b) an indefinite period (so that the prohibition or requirement has effect until further order).

This is subject to section 348(1) (prohibition on foreign travel and section 348A(8) (electronic monitoring requirements).

(3) A sexual harm prevention order—

(a) may specify fixed periods for some of its prohibitions or requirements and an indefinite period for others;

(b) may specify different periods for different prohibitions or requirements.

348 Sexual harm prevention orders: prohibitions on foreign travel

(1) A prohibition on foreign travel contained in a sexual harm prevention order must be for a fixed period of not more than 5 years . . .

Blackstone's Magistrates' Court Handbook 2026. Bartholomew Dalton and Caroline Liggins, Oxford University Press.
DOI: 10.1093/oso/9780198963943.003.0085

D26.1.1 **Key points**

- Schedule 5 contains a wide range of non-sexual offences.
- A Sexual Harm Prevention Order may, under s 103A Sexual Offences Act 2003, be made when a defendant is, in the Crown Court, found unfit to plead or not guilty by reason of insanity. A Sexual Risk Order under s 122A Sexual Offences Act 2003 may be sought in the magistrates' court.
- Cases on the predecessor order would appear to remain valid.
- There is nothing in these provisions to indicate that a court must believe a defendant to be 'dangerous' (within the meaning of the sentencing regime) before it can make such an order (*R v Richards* [2006] EWCA Crim 2519).
- Notice of at least two working days of an application for a sexual harm prevention order should always be given under Part 31 of the Criminal Procedure Rules.
- According to *DPP v Charlesworth* [2022] EWHC 2835 (Admin) s 345(1) does not prevent the court from adjourning consideration of a Sexual Harm Prevention Order having sentenced the defendant. The decision has been heavily criticized as being made per *incuriam*.

R v Mayne [2021] EWCA Crim 737 states that where the court is looking at making a drastic order, in this instance a Sexual Risk Order prohibiting contact with any female under 16, the defendant should be present and legally represented so that the court can consider submissions about the wording and proportionality of the proposed order.

The order must be capable of being complied with without unreasonable difficulty, and free of the risk of unintended breach (*R v Hemsley* [2012] EWCA Crim 225). It must be clear and necessary, and avoid a total ban on the use of the internet, though it can require a history of use of the internet to be kept (*R v Smith* [2011] EWCA Crim 1772; *Mortimer* [2010] EWCA Crim 1303).

R v Smith confirms that if it is intended to allow access to children under 16 only with the consent of their parent/guardian, provision should be made for accidental or inadvertent contact. It was further held that following convictions for possession of child pornography, each order must be individually considered with two days' notice. There can be no standard clauses. Contact with children and supervisory requirements should only be prevented when there was a real risk that the offending would progress to contact offences—safety first is not enough. See also *R v Jackson* [2012] EWCA Crim 2602, confirming that to order that the police have access at all times to any computer is too great an invasion of privacy. In *R v Liu* [2021] EWCA Crim 1125 a provision prevented contact with any child under 18 was amended to only prevent contact with any male child under 18.

In *R v Christopher James* [2012] EWCA Crim 81, where a defendant was convicted of offences of making indecent photographs, it was not on the facts necessary, while controlling the use of the internet, to insert non-contact provisions with children as there was no identified risk, and a 10-year order substituted for lifetime control.

R v NC [2016] EWCA Crim 1448 identified the issues as:

(1) Is the making of the order necessary to protect the public from sexual harm through the commission of schedules offences?
(2) If the order is necessary, are the terms oppressive?
(3) Overall, are the terms proportionate?

R v Sokolowski and *R v Pickard* [2017] EWCA Crim 1903 sets out the following principles:

(i) it is essential that a written draft of the proposed SHPO is both served on the defendant and lodged with the court. The draft should set out the proposed terms, including the proposed duration of the order or, at the very least, flag the question of duration for consideration by the defendant and the court.
(ii) Before it is imposed, the court must be satisfied that an SHPO is necessary for the statutory purpose of protecting the public or any particular members of the public from sexual harm from the defendant. The court has to be satisfied that the prohibitions sought are necessary, and neither oppressive nor disproportionate.
(iii) Particular care must be taken when considering whether prohibitions on contact with children are really necessary; although such orders may be necessary to prevent the defendant from seeking out children for sexual purposes. Where a defendant is convicted of viewing child pornography, then an SHPO should only contain provisions preventing contact, or permitting only supervised contact, with children where there is a real risk that the offending will progress to contact offences. It is not enough for the prosecution to assert, or for the court to assume, that such provisions are necessary on the safety first principle, irrespective of how remote or fanciful the risk of such progression might be. Even when provisions are necessary, they must still be proportionate in their scope.
(iv) It is not normally a legitimate use of an SHPO to use it simply to extend the notification requirements prescribed by law. It does not follow that the duration of an SHPO must be the same as or no longer than the period of the notification requirements.
(v) An SHPO should not be made for an indefinite period, unless the court is satisfied of the need to do so.

Further consideration to modern circumstances was considered in *R v Parsons and Morgan* [2017] EWCA Crim 2163, *R v Davidoff* [2022] EWCA Crim 1253 and *R v Hawkins* [2022] EWCA Crim 1806.

See *Blackstone's Criminal Practice 2026* E21.21

D26.2 **Serious violence reduction orders**

SA 2020 s 342A

342A Power to make serious violence reduction order

342(2) Subject to subsection (6), the court may make a serious violence reduction order in respect of the offender if—
(a) the condition in subsection (3) or (4) is met, and
(b) the condition in subsection (5) is met.

(3) The condition in this subsection is that the court is satisfied on the balance of probabilities that—
   (a) a bladed article or offensive weapon was used by the offender in the commission of the offence, or
   (b) the offender had a bladed article or offensive weapon with them when the offence was committed.

(4) The condition in this subsection is that the court is satisfied on the balance of probabilities that—
   (a) a bladed article or offensive weapon was used by another person in the commission of the offence and the offender knew or ought to have known that this would be the case, or
   (b) another person who committed the offence had a bladed article or offensive weapon with them when the offence was committed and the offender knew or ought to have known that this would be the case.

(5) The condition in this subsection is that the court considers it necessary to make a serious violence reduction order in respect of the offender to—
   (a) protect the public in England and Wales from the risk of harm involving a bladed article or offensive weapon,
   (b) protect any particular members of the public in England and Wales (including the offender) from such risk, or
   (c) prevent the offender from committing an offence involving a bladed article or offensive weapon.

(6) The court may make a serious violence reduction order in respect of the offender only if it—
   (a) does so in addition to dealing with the offender for the offence, and
   (b) does not make an order for absolute discharge under section 79 in respect of the offence.

(7) For the purpose of deciding whether to make a serious violence reduction order the court may consider evidence led by the prosecution and evidence led by the offender.

(8) It does not matter whether the evidence would have been admissible in the proceedings in which the offender was convicted.

342B Meaning of 'serious violence reduction order'

(1) In this Chapter, 'serious violence reduction order' means an order made in respect of an offender that imposes on the offender—
   (a) the requirements specified in subsections (2) and (4), and
   (b) the requirements and prohibitions, if any, specified in regulations made by the Secretary of State for the purposes of this section.

(2) The offender must be required to notify the information in subsection 5(3) to the police within the period of 3 days beginning with the day on which the order takes effect.

(3) That information is—
   (a) the offender's name on the day that the notification is given and, where the offender uses one or more other names on that day, each of those names,
   (b) the offender's home address on that day, and
   (c) the address of any other premises at which, on that day, the offender regularly resides or stays.

(4) The offender must be required to notify the information mentioned in subsection (5) to the police within the period of 3 days beginning with the day on which the offender—
   (a) uses a name which has not been previously notified to the police in accordance with the order,
   (b) changes their home address, or

(c) decides to live for a period of one month or more at any premises the address of which has not been previously notified to the police in accordance with the order.

(5) That information is—

(a) in a case within subsection (4)(a), the name which has not previously been notified,

(b) in a case within subsection (4)(b), the new home address, and

(c) in a case within subsection (4)(c), the address of the premises at which the offender has decided to live.

(6) A serious violence reduction order must provide that the offender gives a notification of the kind mentioned in subsection (2) or (4) by—

(a) attending at a police station in a police area in which the offender lives, and

(b) giving an oral notification to a police officer, or to any person authorised for the purpose by the officer in charge of the station . . .

342D Duration of serious violence reduction orders

(1) A serious violence reduction order takes effect on the day it is made, subject to subsections (3) and (4).

(2) A serious violence reduction order must specify the period for which it has effect, which must be a fixed period of not less than 6 months and not more than 2 years.

(3) Subsection (4) applies in relation to a serious violence reduction order if—

(a) the offender has been remanded in or committed to custody by an order of a court, or

(b) a custodial sentence has been imposed on the offender or the offender is serving or otherwise subject to a such a sentence.

(4) The order may provide that it does not take effect until the offender is released from custody or ceases to be subject to a custodial sentence.

(5) Where a court makes a serious violence reduction order and the offender is already subject to such an order, the earlier order ceases to have effect . . .

D27 Prosecution Costs

D27.1 Criteria

Compensation (D6), victim surcharge (D34), and fines (D17) take priority over prosecution costs when the offender had insufficient means to meet all such liabilities.

The following principles may be derived from the Criminal Practice Direction Division X Part 3 and *R v Northallerton Magistrates' Court, ex p Dove* [2000] 1 Cr App R (S) 136:

(1) An order to pay costs to the prosecutor should never exceed the sum which, having regard to the defendant's means and any other financial order imposed upon him, the defendant was able to pay and which it was reasonable to order the defendant to pay.
(2) Such an order should never exceed the sum that the prosecutor had actually and reasonably incurred (or was liable to a third party to pay, for example when that third party commissions a report on behalf of the prosecution).
(3) The purpose of such an order was to compensate the prosecutor and not punish the defendant. Where the defendant had by his conduct put the prosecutor to avoidable expense he might, subject to his means, be ordered to pay some or all of that sum to the prosecutor. However, he was not to be punished for exercising his constitutional right to defend himself.
(4) While there was no requirement that any sum ordered by justices to be paid to a prosecutor by way of costs should stand in any arithmetical relationship to any fine imposed, the costs ordered to be paid should not in any ordinary way be grossly disproportionate to the fine. Justices should ordinarily begin by deciding on the appropriate fine to reflect the criminality of the defendant's offence, always bearing in mind his means and ability to pay, and then consider what, if any, costs he should be ordered to pay to the prosecutor. If, when the costs sought by the prosecutor were added to the proposed fine, the total exceeded the sum which in the light of the defendant's means and all other relevant circumstances the defendant could reasonably be ordered to pay, it was preferable to achieve an acceptable total by reducing the sum of costs which the defendant was ordered to pay rather than by reducing the fine.
(5) If the offender fails to disclose properly his means to the court, reasonable inferences can be drawn as to his means from evidence they had heard and all the circumstances of the case.

In determining the amount of costs to be paid by an offender, consideration should be given to any time that the offender has spent in custody on remand, if the court is to go on to impose any further punishment (eg a community order) (*R v Rakib* [2011] EWCA Crim 870).

In *R v Rennie-Nash; Whitehouse* [2024] EWCA Crim 987, it was confirmed that financial orders should not go on for protracted periods, but there is no ceiling of 1 year to pay. In some cases a longer period to pay may be appropriate (e.g. 2 years to pay the prosecution costs of a Crown Court trial).

Blackstone's Magistrates' Court Handbook 2026. Bartholomew Dalton and Caroline Liggins, Oxford University Press. © Oxford University Press 2026.
DOI: 10.1093/oso/9780198963943.003.0086

D27.2 Specific costs

The costs of housing an animal pending appeal cannot be classified as prosecution costs but the powers under s 41 Animal Welfare Act 2006 are wide enough to make such a provision (*R (Donovan) v Burnley CC* [2014] EWHC 742 (Admin)).

See C1.1.5 and *Blackstone's Criminal Practice 2026* D33.23

D28 Protection Orders

D28.1 Domestic abuse protection orders

Note: Domestic Abuse Protection Orders were being piloted in a selection of Police Force areas in 2024. They are not available widely and are different to Domestic Violence Protection Orders.

Domestic Abuse Act 2021

Domestic abuse protection orders otherwise than on application

s 31 (1) A court may make a domestic abuse protection order under this section in any of the cases set out below.

Criminal proceedings

(3) Where a person ('P') has been convicted of an offence, the court dealing with P for that offence may (as well as sentencing P or dealing with P in any other way) make a domestic abuse protection order against P.

(5) A court by or before which a person is acquitted of an offence may make a domestic abuse protection order against the person.

s 48 (4) A domestic abuse protection order may be made or varied in addition to an order discharging the person conditionally or absolutely . . .

Breaching a DAPO will carry a penalty up to 5 years' imprisonment, or fine, or both. The following issues are dealt with in A11:

- Conditions for making an order
- Matters to be considered before making an order
- Provision that may be made by orders

Blackstone's Magistrates' Court Handbook 2026. Bartholomew Dalton and Caroline Liggins, Oxford University Press. © Oxford University Press 2026.
DOI: 10.1093/oso/9780198963943.003.0087

D29 Racially and Religiously Aggravated Crimes; Sexual Orientation, Disability, or Transgender Identity; Sex or Gender

D29.1 Meaning of 'racially aggravated'

Crime and Disorder Act 1998, s 28

28 Meaning of racially or religiously aggravated

(1) An offence is racially or religiously aggravated for the purposes of sections 29 to 32 below if—
  - (a) at the time of committing the offence, or immediately before or after doing so, the offender demonstrates towards the victim of the offence hostility based on the victim's membership (or presumed membership) of a racial or religious group; or
  - (b) the offence is motivated (wholly or partly) by hostility towards members of a racial or religious group based on their membership of that group.

(2) In subsection (1)(a) above—
'membership', in relation to a racial or religious group, includes association with members of that group;
'presumed' means presumed by the offender.

(3) It is immaterial for the purposes of paragraph (a) or (b) of subsection (1) above whether or not the offender's hostility is also based, to any extent, on any other factor not mentioned in that paragraph.

(4) In this section 'racial group' means a group of persons defined by reference to race, colour, nationality (including citizenship) or ethnic or national origins.

(5) In this section 'religious group' means a group of persons defined by reference to religious belief or lack of religious belief.

According to *Cain v DPP* [2022] EWHC 1466 (Admin) the circumstances and context of any words used must be considered. The mere utterance of a word or term that is capable of being racially abusive is not necessarily decisive. The fact that the defendant belongs to the same racial group as the victim is an important part of the circumstances and context, but does not necessarily prevent the offence being proved.

D29.2 Specific racially aggravated offences

The Crime and Disorder Act 1988 (CDA 1998) provides for increased sentences for specific offences that are racially or religiously aggravated:

- ss 20 (**C17.9**), 39 (**C17.5**), and 47 (**C17.2**) Offences Against the Person Act 1861; s 75A Serious Crime Act 2015 (strangulation and suffocation) (**C17.11**) (s 29 CDA 1998)
- criminal damage (**C6.1B**) (s 30 CDA 1998)
- ss 4 (**C12.10**), 4A (**C12.6**), and 5 (**C12.5**) Public Order Act 1986; (s 31 CDA 1998) and
- harassment offences under the Protection from Harassment Act 1997 (s 2 (**C9.1**); s 4 (**C9.2**); s 2A (**C9.3.1**); s 4A (**C93.3**)) (s 32 CDA 1998).

Blackstone's Magistrates' Court Handbook 2026. Bartholomew Dalton and Caroline Liggins, Oxford University Press. © Oxford University Press 2026.
DOI: 10.1093/oso/9780198963943.003.0088

D29.3 Offences motivated by hostility based on sex or gender

PCSCA 2022

73 Offences motivated by hostility towards the sex or gender of the victim

(3) A court considering the seriousness of an offence arising from a relevant crime not included in subsection (4) must treat the fact that the offence is aggravated by hostility or prejudice towards sex or gender as an aggravating factor when determining a sentence.

(4) Subsection (3) does not apply to—
  (a) an offence under the law of England and Wales which is for the time being specified in Schedule 3 to the Sexual Offences Act 2003, other than the offence specified in paragraph 14 of that Schedule (fraudulent evasion of excise duty),
  (b) an offence under the law of England and Wales which is for the time being specified in Part 6 of the Domestic Abuse Act 2021, or
  (c) an offence under the law of England and Wales which is defined in section 1 of the Domestic Abuse Act 2021 as 'domestic abuse'.

D29.4 Criteria for other offences

Sentencing Act 2020, s 66 (ss 145 and 146 Criminal Justice Act 2003) provides:

66 Hostility

(1) This section applies where a court is considering the seriousness of an offence which is aggravated by—
  (a) racial hostility,
  (b) religious hostility,
  (c) hostility related to disability,
  (d) hostility related to sexual orientation, or
  (e) hostility related to transgender identity.
  This is subject to subsection (3).

(2) The court—
  (a) must treat the fact that the offence is aggravated by hostility of any of those types as an aggravating factor, and
  (b) must state in open court that the offence is so aggravated.

(3) So far as it relates to racial and religious hostility, this section does not apply in relation to an offence under sections 29 to 32 of the Crime and Disorder Act 1998 (racially or religiously aggravated offences).

(4) For the purposes of this section, an offence is aggravated by hostility of one of the kinds mentioned in subsection (1) if—
  (a) at the time of committing the offence, or immediately before or after doing so, the offender demonstrated towards the victim of the offence hostility based on—
    (i) the victim's membership (or presumed membership) of a racial group,
    (ii) the victim's membership (or presumed membership) of a religious group,
    (iii) a disability (or presumed disability) of the victim,
    (iv) the sexual orientation (or presumed sexual orientation) of the victim, or (as the case may be)
    (v) the victim being (or being presumed to be) transgender, or
  (b) the offence was motivated (wholly or partly) by—

(i) hostility towards members of a racial group based on their membership of that group,
(ii) hostility towards members of a religious group based on their membership of that group,
(iii) hostility towards persons who have a disability or a particular disability,
(iv) hostility towards persons who are of a particular sexual orientation, or (as the case may be)
(v) hostility towards persons who are transgender.

(5) For the purposes of paragraphs (a) and (b) of subsection (4), it is immaterial whether or not the offender's hostility is also based, to any extent, on any other factor not mentioned in that paragraph.

(6) In this section—
(a) references to a racial group are to a group of persons defined by reference to race, colour, nationality (including citizenship) or ethnic or national origins;
(b) references to a religious group are to a group of persons defined by reference to religious belief or lack of religious belief;
(c) 'membership' in relation to a racial or religious group, includes association with members of that group;
(d) 'disability' means any physical or mental impairment;
(e) references to being transgender include references to being transsexual, or undergoing, proposing to undergo or having undergone a process or part of a process of gender reassignment;
(f) 'presumed' means presumed by the offender.

Following the guidance given by the court in *R v Kelly and Donnelly* [2001] 2 Cr App R (S) 73, the court should follow a two-stage process, identifying first the sentence it would have passed if the offence had not been racially aggravated and then adding an appropriate uplift to reflect the racial element, so that the sentencing process is transparent and the public can see to what extent the racial element has been reflected. There is no fixed uplift, but in *Kelly and Donnelly*, an uplift of 50 per cent was applied.

When sentencing a judge may take account of matters relating to racial, etc aggravation where there had been no acquittal of the aggravated offence, such an allegation had not been deleted, and the issue had been addressed in evidence: *R v O'Leary* [2015] EWCA Crim 1306.

See *Blackstone's Criminal Practice 2026* **E2.11.**

D30 **Restraining Order**

D30.1 **Criteria**

Under the Sentencing Act (SA) 2020 a court may impose a restraining order following conviction and under the Protection from Harassment Act 1997, on acquittal (*R v Kapotra* [2011] EWCA Crim 1843 and *R v Brough* [2011] EWCA Crim 2802 confirm that an acquittal includes where the prosecution offer no evidence on a charge).

Sentencing Act 2020, ss 359–363 (Protection from Harassment Act 1997, s 5(2)–(6))

359 Restraining order

(1) In this Code 'restraining order' means an order made under section 360 against a person which prohibits the person from doing anything described in the order.
(2) A restraining order may have effect—
 (a) for a period specified in the order, or
 (b) until further order.

360 Restraining order: availability

(1) This section applies where a court is dealing with an offender for an offence.
(2) The court may make a restraining order under this section against the offender for the purpose of protecting the victim or victims of the offence, or any other person mentioned in the order, from conduct which—
 (a) amounts to harassment, or
 (b) will cause a fear of violence.
(3) But the court may make a restraining order under this section only if it does so in addition to dealing with the offender for the offence.

361 Procedure for varying or discharging restraining order

(1) Where a person is subject to a restraining order—
 (a) that person,
 (b) the prosecution, or
 (c) any other person mentioned in the order,
may apply to the court which made the order for it to be varied or discharged by a further order.
(2) Any person mentioned in the order is entitled to be heard on the hearing of an application under subsection (1).

362 Evidence in proceedings relating to restraining orders

(1) This section applies to—
 (a) proceedings under section 360 for the making of a restraining order;
 (b) proceedings under section 361 or 363(6) for the variation or discharge of a restraining order.
(2) In any such proceedings, both the prosecution and the defence may lead, as further evidence, any evidence that would be admissible in proceedings for an injunction under section 3 of the Protection from Harassment Act 1997 (civil remedy).

363 Offence of breaching restraining order

(1) It is an offence for a person who is subject to a restraining order without reasonable excuse to do anything prohibited by the restraining order.
(2) A person guilty of an offence under this section is liable—

Blackstone's Magistrates' Court Handbook 2026. Bartholomew Dalton and Caroline Liggins, Oxford University Press. © Oxford University Press 2026.
DOI: 10.1093/oso/9780198963943.003.0089

(a) on summary conviction, to imprisonment for a term not exceeding 6 months, or a fine, or both;
(b) on conviction on indictment, to imprisonment for a term not exceeding 5 years, or a fine, or both.

(3) Subsection (1) does not apply to conduct of a person on a particular occasion if the Secretary of State certifies that, in the opinion of the Secretary of State, anything done by that person on that occasion related to—
(a) national security,
(b) the economic well-being of the United Kingdom, or
(c) the prevention or detection of serious crime,
and was done on behalf of the Crown.

(4) A certificate under subsection (3) is conclusive evidence that subsection (1) does not apply to conduct of that person on that occasion.

(5) A document purporting to be a certificate under subsection (3) is to be received in evidence and, unless the contrary is proved, to be treated as being such a certificate.

(6) A court dealing with a person for an offence under this section may vary or discharge the restraining order by a further order.

364 Restraining orders: meaning of 'conduct' and 'harassment'

For the purposes of this Chapter—
'conduct' includes speech;
'harassment', in relation to a person, includes—
(a) alarming the person, or
(b) causing the person distress.

D30.2 Procedural requirements

When a prosecutor seeks a restraining order, Criminal Procedure Rules (Crim PR) Part 31.3 requires the following.

(6) Where paragraph (1)(c) applies (restraining order or domestic abuse protection order proposed), the prosecutor must—
(a) serve a draft order on the court officer and on the defendant as soon as practicable (without waiting for the verdict);
(b) in the draft order specify—
(i) those prohibitions which, if the defendant is convicted, the prosecutor proposes for the purpose of protecting a person from conduct which amounts to harassment or will cause fear of violence, or
(ii) those prohibitions which, if the defendant is acquitted, the prosecutor proposes as necessary to protect a person from harassment by the defendant.

D30.3 Key points on conviction

R v Herrington [2017] EWCA Crim 889, following *R v Brown* [2012] EWCA Crim 1152 but qualifying *R v Khellaf* [2016] EWCA Crim 1297, confirms that a restraining order should not be used to prevent an offender living with the adult victim of an assault who wishes, in a freely given decision, to live with him. Protection of any children should be left to the family court. In the definitive guideline on domestic abuse it is confirmed:

Orders can be made on the initiative of the court; the views of the victim should be sought, but their consent is not required.

The order may prohibit the offender from doing anything for the purpose of protecting the victim of the offence, or any other person mentioned in the order, from further conduct which amounts to harassment or will cause a fear of violence.

If the parties are to continue or resume a relationship, courts may consider a prohibition within the restraining order not to molest the victim (as opposed to a prohibition on contacting the victim).

The terms of the order must be proportionate and not violate the offender's human rights. However, a person can harass someone by publishing truthful things (eg that someone is gay), and an order may be made preventing publication of information that is the truth; such an order will not violate a person's right to freedom of expression under the European Convention (*R v Debnath* [2006] 2 Cr App R (S) 25).

An order should not be made simply because it is requested, even unopposed. There must be some evidential basis to show why the order is necessary. In *R v Hunter* [2024] EWCA Crim 857, there was no evidence linking the defendant, who had pleaded guilty to handling stolen goods, to the victim of the domestic burglary from whom the goods had been taken, and the order should not have been made.

Even though the defendant had been convicted of an offence against a neighbour under s 3 Sexual Offences Act 2003, an order excluding him from his home, where he cared for elderly parents, for five years, could not be justified. The order already prevented him from contacting the neighbour directly or indirectly. Neither the fact of knowing he was living next door nor anxiety from knowing there might be a sighting of him, made this part of the order necessary for the protection of the victim from conduct of the defendant which would cause fear of violence (see *R v M* [2012] EWCA Crim 1144).

An order must name the person it is seeking to protect (*R v Mann*, The Times, 11 April 2000), but there is no reason in principle why an order cannot be made to protect a group of individuals or a company (*R v Buxton* [2010] EWCA Crim 2023). A restraining order must be directed at particular victim(s). A criminal behaviour order should rather be used, for instance, to prevent unsupervised contact with children under 16 (*R v AD* [2019] EWCA Crim 1339).

D30.4 Restraining orders on acquittal

Section 5A of the Protection from Harassment Act 1997 provides:

Protection from Harassment Act 1997, s 5A(1), (2), and (5)

5A Restraining orders on acquittal

(1) A court before which a person ('the defendant') is acquitted of an offence may, if it considers it necessary to do so to protect a person from harassment by the defendant, make an order prohibiting the defendant from doing anything described in the order.

(2) Subsections (3) to (7) of section 5 apply to an order under this section as they apply to an order under that one.

(3) . . .

> (4) . . .
> (5) A person made subject to an order under this section has the same right of appeal against the order as if—
> (a) he had been convicted of the offence in question before the court which made the order, and
> (b) the order had been made under section 5.

In relation to restraining orders after acquittal, a new legal aid order may be sought from the court and the matter billed separately (as a CRM 7 non-standard claim).

D30.5 Key points on acquittal

The following points emerge from *R v Major* [2010] EWCA Crim 3016:

- it was not Parliament's intention that orders be made only when the facts are uncontested, nor that orders should be made only rarely;
- the civil standard of proof applies;
- there is no contradiction in making an order post-acquittal, as the standard of proof required for a conviction is higher than that for making a restraining order;
- the evidence did not have to establish on the balance of probabilities that there had been harassment; it was enough if the evidence established conduct which fell short of harassment but which might well, if repeated in the future, amount to harassment and so make an order necessary;
- the court should set out the factual basis for making an order.

In making an order on acquittal, the court must ensure that the defendant is not denied the opportunity to make submissions on the propriety and the terms of an order. See *R v Trott* [2011] EWCA Crim 2395, following *R v Kapotra* [2011] EWCA Crim 1843 (see also Crim PR Part 31). In *R v Khan* [2021] EWCA Crim 1526 the court held that the decision to proceed in the defendant's absence must be taken cautiously; in this instance the order made in absence after the defendant arrived 2 hours and 20 minutes late, but having communicated to the court that he was delayed, was quashed.

Where the court is considering making an order after no evidence is offered the defendant must be given the opportunity to consider the evidence in support and to adduce evidence against making the order; the court is also likely to need to hear oral evidence to resolve any relevant dispute of facts (*R v Baldwin* [2021] EWCA Crim 703). *R v McCarren* [2023] EWCA Crim 1233 provides further guidance on making a restraining order on acquittal. Even though the defendant consented to the order, the court should not have made the order as it was not necessary.

In *R v M J Smith* [2012] EWCA Crim 2566, the court quashed an order on acquittal following a finding that the defendant was not guilty by reason of insanity, as that meant there was no sufficient intent and it unnecessarily criminalized acts that were otherwise lawful; and held that the order was not for the benefit of a sufficiently identifiable group of persons.

The statute requires that the order be necessary and the word is not to be diluted (*R v Taylor (David)* [2017] EWCA Crim 2209 and *R v Jackson (John)* [2021] EWCA Crim 901).

D30.6 Unfitness to plead

A restraining order cannot be made against someone who has been found unfit to plead (and thus where there has been a finding of fact under s 37(3) Mental Health Act 1983) as that finding is neither a conviction nor an acquittal (*Chinegwundoh v R* [2015] EWCA Crim 109).

See *Blackstone's Criminal Practice 2026* E21.31

D31 Sentencing Guidelines

Sentencing Act 2020, s 59 (Coroners and Justice Act 2009, s 125)

59 Sentencing guidelines: general duty of court

(1) Every court—
- (a) must, in sentencing an offender, follow any sentencing guidelines which are relevant to the offender's case, and
- (b) must, in exercising any other function relating to the sentencing of offenders, follow any sentencing guidelines which are relevant to the exercise of the function,

unless the court is satisfied that it would be contrary to the interests of justice to do so.

D31.1 Process

Guidelines are structured in a series of steps, normally:

STEP ONE: determining the offence category

The court should determine the offence category with reference **only** to the factors identified in the published tables. In order to determine the category the court should assess **culpability** and **harm.**

STEP TWO: starting point and category range

Having determined the category at step one, the court should use the starting point to reach a sentence within the appropriate category range in the published table.

STEP THREE: consider any factors which indicate a reduction, such as assistance to the prosecution

STEP FOUR: reduction for guilty pleas (see D15)

The court should take account of any potential reduction for a guilty plea in accordance with s 73 SA 2020 (s 144 CJA 2003) and the *Guilty Plea* guideline.

STEP FIVE: totality principle (see D23.2)

If sentencing an offender for more than one offence, or where the offender is already serving a sentence, consider whether the total sentence is just and proportionate to the overall offending behaviour in accordance with the *Offences Taken into Consideration* and *Totality* guidelines.

Blackstone's Magistrates' Court Handbook 2026. Bartholomew Dalton and Caroline Liggins, Oxford University Press. © Oxford University Press 2026.
DOI: 10.1093/oso/9780198963943.003.0090

STEP SIX: compensation (see D6) and other ancillary orders

D31.2 General sentencing guideline and expanded explanations of aggravating and mitigating factors

The Sentencing Council has published general sentencing guidelines for offences with no individual guidelines and expanded definitions of aggravating and mitigating factors.

D31.3 Specific considerations

D31.3.1 *Failure to appear*

Although there is no statutory obligation for the court to treat offending whilst subject to a postal requisition as aggravated (cf s 64 SA 2020 in relation to offending on bail), there is no reasons why such an offence should be treated any differently to offending on bail (*AG's Reference (R v Shaw)* [2021] EWCA Crim 685).

D31.3.2 *Neurodiversity*

The Sentencing Council's guideline on *sentencing offenders with mental disorders, developmental disorders, or neurological impairments* should be considered when a court is sentencing mentally disordered offenders

SCG Sentencing offenders with mental disorders

D31.3.3 Prevalence

The issue of prevalence was considered in *R v Bondzie* [2016] EWCA Crim 552 which confirmed that a court will only be entitled to treat prevalence as an aggravating factor if satisfied:

(a) that the level of harm caused in a particular locality is significantly higher than that caused elsewhere (and thus already inherent in the guideline levels);
(b) that the circumstances can properly be described as exceptional; and
(c) that it is just and proportionate to increase sentence for such a factor in the particular case.

A court should be hesitant before aggravating a sentence by reason of prevalence. Thus only if the evidence, normally provided by a senior police officer, placed before the court demonstrates a level of harm which clearly exceeds the well understood consequences of [the relevant crime] by a significant margin should courts be prepared to reflect this in sentence. If judges do so, they must clearly state when sentencing that they are doing so.

D32 Suspended Sentences

See s 286 Sentencing Act (SA) 2020 (s 189 Criminal Justice Act).

D32.1 Principles for imposition

The Sentencing Council's definitive guideline on the imposition of community and custodial sentences confirms that 'a suspended sentence must not be imposed as a more severe form of community order. A suspended sentence is a custodial sentence. Sentencers should be clear that they would impose an immediate custodial sentence if the power to suspend were not available. If not, a non-custodial sentence should be imposed.'

The following factors should be weighed in considering whether it is possible to suspend the sentence:

Factors indicating that it would not be appropriate to suspend a custodial sentence	Factors indicating that it may be appropriate to suspend a custodial sentence
Offender presents a risk/ danger to the public	Realistic prospect of rehabilitation
Appropriate punishment can only be achieved by immediate custody	Strong personal mitigation
History of poor compliance with court orders	Immediate custody will result in significant harmful impact upon others

D32.2 Length of suspended sentences

A magistrates' court may suspend a sentence of not less than 14 days and not more than 6 months (s 277(2) SA 2020 (s 189 CJA 2003)). A custodial sentence that is suspended should be for the same term that would have applied if the sentence was to be served immediately. Where a person has served such time on remand that a custodial sentence would result in immediate release, it may not be appropriate to impose a suspended sentence order (*R v Waters and Young* [2008] EWCA Crim 2538).

The court may suspend the sentence for between 6 months and 2 years, and may add appropriate requirement(s) to be completed as part of the order. The time for which a sentence is suspended should reflect the length of the sentence. For sentences up to 12 months, it might normally be appropriate for a sentence to be suspended for 6 months.

D32.3 Requirements

Section 287 SA 2020 provides for requirements that may be imposed as part of a suspended sentence. They appear at D5.4 and are listed in Sch 9 SA 2020.

Blackstone's Magistrates' Court Handbook 2026. Bartholomew Dalton and Caroline Liggins, Oxford University Press. © Oxford University Press 2026.
DOI: 10.1093/oso/9780198963943.003.0091

D32.4 Breach of suspended sentence order

D32.4.1 *Principles*

See Sch 16 SA 2020 (Sch 12 to the CJA 2003).

An order will be breached if the offender does not comply with any community requirement during the period of suspension, or is convicted of a further offence during the operational period. A conditional discharge is not a conviction for this purpose. Following conviction for a new offence, a magistrates' court has no jurisdiction to deal with breach of a suspended sentence order imposed by the Crown Court; it must either commit the offender for sentence upon conviction for the new offence, or notify the Crown Court of the breach so that that court can take action if it so wishes. A Crown Court order will specify whether or not any breach of its requirements should result in a return to the Crown Court or be left to the magistrates' court (it is the norm for a Crown Court to order any breach be reserved to itself).

There will generally be some reduction of the term of the suspended sentence if there has been substantial compliance with an unpaid work requirement, although there will sometimes be a case in which it is nevertheless appropriate in all the circumstances to activate the suspended sentence in full (*R v McDonagh* [2017] EWCA Crim 2193).

A suspended sentence is a single sentence which, if activated, cannot be activated a second time in respect of a constituent element of the original sentence (*R v Bostan* [2018] EWCA Crim 494)

D32.4.2 *Powers*

Upon a breach being proved the court has the following options open to it:

- order the sentence to take effect (ie send the offender to prison); or
- order the sentence to take effect but with a reduced term of imprisonment; or with an extended operational period; or
- impose more onerous community requirements or extend the supervision or operational period; or
- impose a fine of up to £2,500.
- if no requirements extend operational period.

Note: The court must order one of the first two options unless it would be unjust to do so in all the circumstances. A court must give reasons for so ordering.

D32.4.3 *Sentencing guideline*

D32.4.3.1 *Conviction for further offence committed during operational period of order*

The court must activate the custodial sentence unless it would be unjust in all the circumstances to do so. The predominant factor in determining whether activation is unjust relates to the level of compliance with the suspended sentence order and the facts/nature of any new offence. These factors are already provided for in the penalties below, which are determined by the nature of the new offence and level of compliance but permit a reduction to the custodial term for relevant completed or partially completed requirements where appropriate.

The facts/nature of the new offence is the primary consideration in assessing the action to be taken on the breach.

Where the breach is in the second or third category below, the prior level of compliance is also relevant. In assessing the level of compliance with the order the court should consider:

(i) the overall attitude and engagement with the order as well as the proportion of elements completed;
(ii) the impact of any completed or partially completed requirements on the offender's behaviour;
(iii) the proximity of breach to imposition of order; and
(iv) evidence of circumstances or offender characteristics, such as disability, mental health issues, or learning difficulties which have impeded offender's compliance with the order.

Breach involves	**Penalty**
Multiple and/ or more serious new offence(s) committed	Full activation of original custodial term
New offence similar in type and gravity to offence for which suspended sentence order imposed and: (a) No/ low level of compliance with suspended sentence order **or** (b) Medium or high level of compliance with suspended sentence order	(a) Full activation of original custodial term (b) Activate sentence but apply appropriate reduction* to original custodial term taking into consideration any unpaid work or curfew requirements completed
New offence less serious than original offence but requires a custodial sentence and: (a) No/ low level of compliance with suspended sentence order or (b) Medium or high level of compliance with suspended sentence order	(a) Full activation of original custodial term (b) Activate sentence but apply appropriate reduction* to original custodial term taking into consideration any unpaid work or curfew requirements completed
New offence does not require custodial sentence	Activate sentence but apply reduction* to original custodial term taking into consideration any unpaid work or curfew requirements completed **or** Impose more onerous requirement(s) and/ or extend supervision period and/ or extend operational period and/ or impose fine

* It is for the court dealing with the breach to identify the appropriate proportionate reduction depending on the extent of any compliance with the requirements specified.

32.4.3.2 *Unjust in all the circumstances*

The court dealing with the breach should remember that the court imposing the original sentence determined that a custodial sentence was appropriate in the original case.

In determining if there are other factors which would cause activation to be unjust, the court may consider all factors including:

- any strong personal mitigation;
- whether there is a realistic prospect of rehabilitation;
- whether immediate custody will result in significant impact on others.

Only new and exceptional factors/ circumstances not present at the time the suspended sentence order was imposed should be taken into account. In cases where the court considers that it would be unjust to order the custodial sentence to take effect, it must state its reasons and it must deal with the offender in one of the following ways:

(a) impose a fine not exceeding £2,500; or
(b) extend the operational period (to a maximum of 2 years from date of original sentence); or
(c) if the SSO imposes community requirements, do one or more of the following:
   (i) impose more onerous community requirements;
   (ii) extend the supervision period (to a maximum of 2 years from date of original sentence);
   (iii) extend the operational period (to a maximum of 2 years from date of original sentence).

See *Blackstone's Criminal Practice 2026* E14

D33 Time on Remand or Qualifying Curfew

D33.1 Criteria

Section 240ZA Criminal Justice Act (CJA) 2003 provides that any immediate custodial sentence shall be reduced automatically by any time spent on remand in custody. Under this section time spent on remand in relation to a new offence cannot count if it coincides with a recall. There would have to be an excessive delay to reduce an otherwise appropriate sentence (*R v Phillips (Nathan)* [2015] EWCA Crim 427).

Section 325 Sentencing Act (SA) 2020 (240A CJA 2003) requires the sentencing court to direct that time spent on bail under an electronically monitored curfew should be credited against an immediate custodial sentence in a similar way. A person will receive credit at the rate of a half a day for every day spent subject to a qualifying electronically monitored curfew (ie a curfew of nine hours a day or more). The section sets out the procedure as follows:

Sentencing Act 2020, s 325 (Criminal Justice Act 2003, s 240A)

325 Time on bail under certain conditions: declaration by court

(3) The credit period is calculated by taking the following steps.

Step 1

Add—

(a) the day on which the offender's bail was first subject to the relevant conditions (and for this purpose a condition is not prevented from being a relevant condition by the fact that it does not apply for the whole of the day in question), and

(b) the number of other days on which the offender's bail was subject to those conditions (but exclude the last of those days if the offender spends the last part of it in custody).

Step 2

Deduct the number of days on which the offender, whilst on bail subject to the relevant conditions, was also—

(a) subject to any requirement imposed for the purpose of securing the electronic monitoring of the offender's compliance with a curfew requirement, or

(b) on temporary release under rules made under section 47 of the Prison Act 1952.

Step 3

From the remainder, deduct the number of days during that remainder on which the offender has broken either or both of the relevant conditions.

Step 4

Divide the result by 2.

Step 5

If necessary, round up to the nearest whole number.

Blackstone's Magistrates' Court Handbook 2026. Bartholomew Dalton and Caroline Liggins, Oxford University Press. © Oxford University Press 2026.
DOI: 10.1093/oso/9780198963943.003.0092

Criminal Justice Act 2003, s 240ZA

(5) A day of the credit period counts as time served—
  (a) in relation to only one sentence, and
  (b) only once in relation to that sentence.
(6) A day of the credit period is not to count as time served as part of any automatic release period served by the offender (see section 255B(1)).

If there is a dispute as to the time to be allowed, the burden to the criminal standard is on the Crown but the strict rules of evidence do not apply (*R v Hoggard* [2013] EWCA Crim 1024). The matter was further examined in *R v Marshall and others* [2015] EWCA Crim 1999, which emphasized that approved wording should be used so that any error could be corrected administratively under s 142 Magistrates' Courts Act 1980 (**A6.2.1**):

> The defendant will receive full credit for half the time spent under curfew if the curfew qualified under the provisions of section [240A]. On the information before me the total period is . . . days (subject to the deduct of . . . days that I have directed under the Step(s) 2 and/ or 3 making a total of . . . days), but if this period is mistaken, this court will order an amendment of the record for the correct period to be recorded.

D34 Victim Surcharge Order

D34.1 Criteria

In any case relating to an offence committed on or after 1 October 2012, the court must impose a surcharge order in accordance with the following tables (s 42 Sentencing Act (SA) 2020 (s 161A Criminal Justice Act 2003)). The amounts increase depending on the date of the offence. The higher figures do not apply where a court deals with a person for:

(a) a single offence committed before the date shown or
(b) more than one offence, at least one of which was committed before the date shown.

If any one offence was committed as a child then the youth court figures apply.

The charge may be ignored or reduced if the offender would not be able to pay both the surcharge and compensation. If the offender would not be able to pay both a surcharge and a fine, the surcharge takes precedence and the fine should be reduced.

Blackstone's Magistrates' Court Handbook 2026. Bartholomew Dalton and Caroline Liggins, Oxford University Press. © Oxford University Press 2026.
DOI: 10.1093/oso/9780198963943.003.0093

D34.2 The charges

Sentence	Adult		Offenders under 18 at the date of the offence		Company	
	An offence before 16.6.22	All offences on or after 16.6.22	An offence before 16.6.22	All offences on or after 16.6.22	An offence before 16.6.22	All offences on or after 16.6.22
Conditional discharge	£22	£26	£17	£20	£22	£26
Fine	10% of fine (rounded to nearest pound) range £34 to £190	40% of fine (rounded to nearest pound) with max of £2,000	£22	£26	10% in range £34 to £190	40% of fine (rounded to nearest pound) with max of £2,000
YRO/ Referral order			£22	£26		
Community order	£95	£114	£22	£26		
Suspended or immediate custodial sentence	£128 if 6 months or less, £156 if over 6 months	£154 if 6 months or less, £187 if over 6 months	£34 for all custodial sentences	£41 for all custodial sentences		

R v Abbott [2020] EWCA Crim 516 confirms the following principles:

(i) The surcharge is calculated by reference to the totality of the fines or periods of imprisonment imposed.

(ii) In a case involving a fine and a period of imprisonment, the surcharge is the higher of the amount corresponding to the aggregate fine and the amount corresponding to the aggregate period of imprisonment. The same principles apply to any other available combination of orders, and the position is the same whether there is a mixed disposal in relation to a single offence, or different disposals in relation to different offences.

(iii) A second surcharge is not payable on sentence for breach of an order. Liability stems from conviction and the 'notional' existence of a 'victim'.

TICs are not relevant to the calculation of the surcharge (*R v Bailey; R v Kirk; R v Tote* [2013] EWCA Crim 1551).

See *Blackstone's Criminal Practice 2026* E19.67

Appendices

1 Preparation for Effective Trial
2 Extracts from the Criminal Procedure Rules
3 Rehabilitation Periods
4 2026 Supplement to Handbook of Youths in the Criminal Courts (Third Edition)
5 Fine Bands
6 Sentencing Decision Flow Chart

Appendix 1

Preparation for Effective Trial

These notes are prepared by reference to questions for the defence raised by the current Preparation for trial forms in the Magistrates' Court and when a case is sent to the Crown Court for trial.

1.1 Preparation for trial in a magistrates' court: relevant questions

6 Advice on plea and absence / 7 Partial or different guilty plea

The current law on discount for guilty plea is summarized at D15.

The law on trials in the absence of a defendant is at A2.2.6.

The law on disclosure of the initial details of the prosecution case is set out in Rule 8 of the Criminal Procedure Rules.

> **8.3.** Initial details of the prosecution case must include—
>
> (a) where, immediately before the first hearing in the magistrates' court, the defendant was in police custody for the offence charged—
>
> (i) a summary of the circumstances of the offence, and
>
> (ii) the defendant's criminal record, if any; or
>
> (b) where paragraph (a) does not apply—
>
> (i) a summary of the circumstances of the offence,
>
> (ii) any account given by the defendant in interview, whether contained in that summary or in another document,
>
> (iii) any written witness statement or exhibit that the prosecutor then has available and considers material to plea, or to the allocation of the case for trial, or to sentence,
>
> (iv) the defendant's criminal record, if any, and
>
> (v) any available statement of the effect of the offence on a victim, a victim's family or others.
>
> **8.4.** Use of initial details
>
> (1) This rule applies where—
>
> (a) the prosecutor wants to introduce information contained in a document listed in rule 8.3; and
>
> (b) the prosecutor has not—
>
> (i) served that document on the defendant, or
>
> (ii) made that information available to the defendant.
>
> (2) The court must not allow the prosecutor to introduce that information unless the court first allows the defendant sufficient time to consider it.

The Law Society has given guidance on entering a plea when there is insufficient disclosure fully to advise:

> **4 Meeting your professional obligation**
>
> If your client is unsure about how to plead to the charge/ s but you require further information in order to meet your professional obligations in providing adequate advice, you should make both the court and your client aware of any problems this may present.

4.1 Providing advice

You should advise your client about the sentencing discount they will be entitled to if they plead guilty at the first opportunity.

If you advise the client to enter a not guilty plea, or to enter no plea, to protect his or her position due to the lack of information, you should ask the court to make a note of the circumstances and the reasons for pleading so.

To help your client retain the maximum credit for any subsequent guilty plea, you should both:

advise your client about the situation

inform the court of the predicament you face due to the lack of disclosure.

There is a risk that any admission of a lesser offence may be used in evidence to prove ingredients of the greater. However, consideration should be given to *R v Newell* [2012] EWCA Crim 650:

> Whilst an answer by a lawyer on a case management form may be admissible as hearsay under the agency rule, a discretion should be exercised to exclude the answer from evidence under section 78 of the Police and Criminal Evidence Act 1984, provided that the case is conducted in accordance with the letter and spirit of the Criminal Procedure Rules. It would be otherwise if there was an ambush.

The *Newton* principles in relation to a basis of plea appear at **D21**.

8 Case management information

Facts agreed in section 8.2 may be used in evidence by the Crown and the defendant can be cross-examined on them. Great care should be taken before admissions are made, and specific authority obtained from the client.

There was again a risk that other responses in sections 8.1 and 8.3 might also be used by the Crown in evidence, but that risk has been largely removed by the decision in *R v Newell* (above). However, the material can amount to admissible hearsay if the defence have obtained an unfair advantage and a properly constituted hearsay application is made (*Valiati v DPP* [2018] EWHC 2908 (Admin) and *Randell v DPP* [2018] EWHC 1048 (Admin)). See **A10.13**.

The tape summary should not be agreed unless the solicitor was present or the tape has been played. Obtaining a copy of the tape or disc of interview is often problematic. The court has a jurisdiction to order production to the defence under PACE Code E paragraph 3.21.

3.21 The suspect shall be handed a notice which explains:

- how the audio recording will be used;
- the arrangements for access to it;
- that if they are charged or informed they will be prosecuted, a copy of the audio recording will be supplied as soon as practicable or as otherwise agreed between the suspect and the police or on the order of a court.

Information about the defendant's previous convictions held by a solicitor is confidential and must not be disclosed to the client's detriment, but great care must be taken not to mislead the court. It is for the Crown to prove to the criminal standard the existence of previous convictions if they are not agreed.

Note that a Streamlined Forensic Report (SFR) may provide no detail of how the findings have been arrived at or the conditions under which the tests were commissioned. Individuals who are not scientific experts can also produce them: for example, a DNA match report could have been generated and reported automatically as part of an administration process. Test results may not have been generated using accredited procedures. In combination, this can mean that it may not be easy for the defence to discover whether the evidence is robust or identify if they should challenge it. A Form SFR1 is inadmissible hearsay (*Hunt v CPS* [2018] EWHC 3341 (Admin)).

8.2 **Admissions**

These are formal admissions that will be admitted at trial and on which a defendant can be cross-examined.

8.3 **Issues of fact or law**

Objection should be taken to inadmissible evidence to avoid issues arising, for instance, over implied consent to the admission of that evidence. However, in *R v Smith* (Alec) 2020 EWCA Crim 777 the Court emphasised the need for the Crown to comply with the notice provisions of the Criminal Procedure Rules. The areas in dispute should be identified. A defendant is entitled to put the Crown to proof. The form should indicate that the defence put the Crown to proof and do not raise any positive defence. The absence of a defence may be used in cross-examination should the defendant later raise a specific issue. The law is set out in *R v Rochford* [2010] EWCA Crim 1928. The words in square brackets are so marked because defence statements are not obligatory in the magistrates' court:

> What is the duty of the lawyer if the defendant has no positive case to advance at trial but declines to plead guilty? That is a realistic (if rare) practical possibility. It may occur in at least two situations. It might happen that a defendant within the cloak of privilege confides in his lawyer that he is in fact guilty of the offence charged but refuses to plead guilty. He cannot be prevented from taking that course and his instructions to his lawyer are covered by privilege. He is entitled in those circumstances to sit through the trial and to see whether the Crown can prove the case or not. What he is not entitled to do is to conduct the trial by the putting in issue of specific matters and advancing either evidence or argument towards them without giving notice [in his defence statement] that he is going to do it. A less extreme but equally possible example is the defendant who refuses to give instructions either at all or on specific points. That too can occur. In neither of those situations can it possibly be the obligation of the defendant to put in [to his defence statement] an admission of guilt or a refusal to give instructions. What are the lawyers to do? It seems to us that we can give an answer only in general terms because it would be unhelpful for us to attempt the impossible task of foreseeing every factual scenario that might occur in future. They will have to be dealt with as they arise, case by case. But in general terms our answer is this. The defence [statement] must say that the defendant does not admit the offence or the relevant part of it as the case may be, and calls for the Crown to prove it. But it must also say that he advances no positive

> case because if he is going to advance a positive case [that must appear in the defence statement and] notice of it must be given.

In its guidance on the Criminal Procedure Rules, the Law Society states:

> Your client is entitled to put the prosecution to proof and you are not required by the CPR to cease acting simply because you are unable to assist the court further. However, you will note the consequent limitation on your client's ability to raise any positive case at his trial.

8.5 Defence statements

These are not obligatory in the magistrates' court but will be required if there are disclosure issues, and such issues cannot be raised without one. A defence statement cannot be filed without the defendant's consent. *R v Rochford* (above) has made clear that compliance with the requirement for a defence statement cannot require a breach of privilege.

9 Application for directions

Check that you will be able to comply with the standard time limits, or apply to vary them. Consider particularly issues around disclosure, if this was served prior to the first hearing and it is intended to serve a defence statement, expert evidence, CCTV, and tapes.

Consideration should also be given to the needs of the defendant for an interpreter or for translation of essential documents as well as any special measures required for the defendant or defence witnesses (A27).

10 Prosecution witnesses

Appropriate assistance should be given in identifying the relevant witnesses and witnesses whose evidence can be read, but this should always be checked with the client. Nothing that is said, including by the court, can make hearsay evidence admissible upon the completion of the form. Either there must be agreement under section 10 of the CJA 1967, or there must be compliance with section 9 of the CJA 1967 or section 114(1)(d) of the CJA 2003. The latter is likely to be used unless the defence identifies the grounds on which the witness is required to attend. (See A10.10 and A17.3.)

The form seeks to identify the time needed to examine and cross-examine each witness. Generous estimates should be given particularly if time is needed to establish a picture to enable effective cross-examination. However, whilst courts will seek to set (*Drinkwater v Solihull MC* [2012] EWHC 765 (Admin)) and enforce a timetable, the resulting trial must be fair. In *R v Jisl* [2004] EWCA Crim 296 the court said:

> The starting point is simple. Justice must be done. The judge should consider whether to direct a timetable to cover pre-trial steps, and eventually the conduct of the trial itself, not rigid, nor immutable, and fully recognising that during the trial at any rate the unexpected must be treated as normal, and making due allowance for it in the interests of justice. To enable the trial judge to manage the case in a way which is fair to every participant, pre-trial, the potential problems as well as the possible areas for time saving, should be canvassed. In short, a sensible informed discussion about the future management of the case and the most convenient way to present the evidence, whether disputed or not, and where appropriate, with admissions by one or other or both *sides*, should enable the judge to make a fully informed analysis of the future timetable, and the proper conduct of the trial. The objective is not haste and rush, but greater efficiency and better use of limited resources by closer identification of and focus on critical rather than peripheral issues.

In principle, the trial judge should exercise firm control over the timetable, where necessary, making clear in advance and throughout the trial that the timetable will be subject to appropriate constraints, with such necessary even-handedness and flexibility as the interests of the justice require as the case unfolds (*R v Chabban* [2003] EWCA Crim 1012).

11 Expected defence witnesses

An estimate of the number of defence witnesses and details of known witnesses can be given, though there is no obligation to do so and it is unlikely that they have been proofed at this stage. The defence comply with their obligations to notify the details of witnesses if they do so once there is an intention to call them (see **A10.9**). Evidence of general reputation is admissible from character witnesses and particularly when the defendant's credibility was central to the defence. A good character direction was insufficient (*R v Grimes* [2017] NICA 19).

1.2 Case management questionnaire where a case is sent to the Crown Court for trial

The key question is concisely to identify the **real issues** in the case. To receive the full discount for guilty plea a clear plea must be indicated. Issues around a basis of plea should be entered in the real issues section (*R v Dale* 2022 EWCA Crim 207)(See **D15**). There will be cases falling within the exception in paragraph F1 of the Guideline as the case for the prosecution is not yet clear. However, admissions as to any facts that are not in dispute are encouraged, even if other issues remain. The Crown may be put to proof but the client should understand the implications on any later discount. Responsibility for the completion of the BCM form and for any indication as to plea clearly rests with the parties and their legal representatives (*R v Ahmed Yasin* [2019] EWCA Crim 1729). A failure to indicate a willingness to plead to a s 47 offence (and so admitting the fact of assault) when charged only with s 18 and s 20 will result in a loss of discount (*R v Bannerjee* [2020] EWCA Crim 909).

Appendix 2

Extracts from the Criminal Procedure Rules

Extracts from the following rules are reproduced in this appendix:

- Rule 1 (the overriding objective); and
- Rule 3 (case management).

Part 1 The overriding objective

The overriding objective

1.1— (1) The overriding objective of this procedural code is that criminal cases be dealt with justly.

(2) Dealing with a criminal case justly includes—

(a) acquitting the innocent and convicting the guilty;

(b) treating all participants with politeness and respect;

(c) dealing with the prosecution and the defence fairly;

(d) recognising the rights of a defendant, particularly those under Article 6 of the European Convention on Human Rights;

(e) respecting the interests of witnesses, victims and jurors and keeping them informed of the progress of the case;

(f) dealing with the case efficiently and expeditiously;

(g) ensuring that appropriate information is available to the court when bail and sentence are considered; and

(h) dealing with the case in ways that take into account—

(i) the gravity of the offence alleged,

(ii) the complexity of what is in issue,

(iii) the severity of the consequences for the defendant and others affected, and

(iv) the needs of other cases.

The duty of the participants in a criminal case

1.2— (1) Each participant, in the conduct of each case, must—

(a) prepare and conduct the case in accordance with the overriding objective;

(b) comply with these Rules, practice directions and directions made by the court; and

(c) at once inform the court and all parties of any significant failure (whether or not that participant is responsible for that failure) to take any procedural step required by these Rules, any practice direction or any direction of the court. A failure is significant if it might hinder the court in furthering the overriding objective.

(2) Anyone involved in any way with a criminal case is a participant in its conduct for the purposes of this rule.

The application by the court of the overriding objective

1.3 The court must further the overriding objective in particular when—

(a) exercising any power given to it by legislation (including these Rules);

(b) applying any practice direction; or

(c) interpreting any rule or practice direction.

Part 3 Case management

The duty of the court

3.2—(1) The court must further the overriding objective by actively managing the case.

(2) Active case management includes—

(a) the early identification of the real issues;

(b) the early identification of the needs of witnesses;

(c) achieving certainty as to what must be done, by whom, and when, in particular by the early setting of a timetable for the progress of the case;

(d) monitoring the progress of the case and compliance with directions;

(e) ensuring that evidence, whether disputed or not, is presented in the shortest and clearest way;

(f) discouraging delay, dealing with as many aspects of the case as possible on the same occasion, and avoiding unnecessary hearings;

(g) encouraging the participants to co-operate in the progression of the case; and

(h) making use of technology.

(3) The court must actively manage the case by giving any direction appropriate to the needs of that case as early as possible.

(4) Where appropriate live links are available, making use of technology for the purposes of this rule includes giving a live link direction for a person's participation—

(a) under a power to which rule 3.35 applies (Live link direction: exercise of court's powers); and

(b) whether an application for such a direction is made or not.

Appendix 3

Rehabilitation Periods

A Disclosure periods for particular sentences

The rehabilitation 'period' for a sentence relevant to magistrates' court sentencing is the period listed in the following table, as per s 5(2) Rehabilitation of Offenders Act 1974 as amended by the PCSCA 2022:

Sentence	End of rehabilitation period for adult offenders	End of rehabilitation period for offenders under 18 at date of conviction
A custodial sentence of I year or less	The end of the period of 12 months beginning with the day on which the sentence (including any licence period) is completed	The end of the period of 6 months beginning with the day on which the sentence (including any licence period) is completed
A fine	The end of the period of 12 months beginning with the date of the conviction in respect of which the sentence is imposed	The end of the period of 6 months beginning with the date of the conviction in respect of which the sentence is imposed
A compensation order	The date on which the payment is made in full	The date on which the payment is made in full
A relevant order as defined below.	The day provided for by or under the order or 24 months	The day provided for by or under the order or 24 months
Conditional caution	The day 3 months from the date of imposition	The day 3 months from the date of imposition
Absolute discharges and other alternatives to prosecution including cautions	Immediately rehabilitated	Immediately rehabilitated

Rehabilitation of Offenders Act 1974, s 5(2A) to (4) and (8)

(2A) Subsection (2B) applies where provision is made by or under a relevant order for the order to have effect—

(a) until further order,

(b) until the occurrence of a specified event, or

(c) otherwise for an indefinite period.

(2B) The rehabilitation period for the order is the period—

(a) beginning with the date of the conviction in respect of which the order is imposed, and

(b) ending when the order ceases to have effect.]

(3) The rehabilitation period for a relevant order which is not otherwise dealt with in the [above] Table or under subsections (2A) and (2B) is the period of 24 months beginning with the date of conviction.

(4) There is no rehabilitation period for—
 (a) an order discharging a person absolutely for an offence, or
 (b) any other sentence in respect of a conviction where the sentence is not dealt with in the [above] Table or under any of subsections (2A) to (3),
 and, in such cases, references in this Act to any rehabilitation period are to be read as if the period of time were nil.

...

(8) In this section—

...

"relevant order" means—
(za) a community or youth rehabilitation order,
(a) an order discharging a person conditionally for an offence,
(b) an order binding a person over to keep the peace or be of good behaviour,
(c) an order under section 1(2A) of the Street Offences Act 1959,
(d) a hospital order under Part 3 of the Mental Health Act 1983 (with or without a restriction order),
(e) a referral order under Chapter 1 of Part 6 of the Sentencing Code,
(f) an earlier statutory order, or
(g) any order which—
 (i) imposes a disqualification, disability, prohibition, penalty, requirement or restriction, or
 (ii) is otherwise intended to regulate the behaviour of the person convicted,
 and is not otherwise dealt with in the [above] Table,

but does not include a reparation order under section 73 of the Powers of Criminal Courts (Sentencing) Act 2000 or Chapter 2 of Part 6 of the Sentencing Code,

Note: Endorsements on driving licences are excluded from rehabilitation.

B Disclosure and Barring Service (DBS) checks

The types of DBS check are:

- a basic check which shows unspent convictions and conditional cautions
- a standard check which shows any spent and unspent convictions, cautions, reprimands, and final warnings
- an enhanced check which shows the same as a standard check plus any information held by local police that is considered relevant to the role
- an enhanced check with barred lists which shows the same as an enhanced check plus whether someone is on the list of people barred from doing the role.

Appendix 4

2026 Supplement to Handbook of Youths in the Criminal Courts (Third Edition)

By Gareth Branston

E1 Offences Guidelines – Introduction

In May 2025, following consultation, the Sentencing Council confirmed that it would change references in all guidelines concerned with sentencing defendants aged under 18 to use the term 'children' rather than 'children and young people'. However, the Council noted that the draft legislation then before Parliament used various different terms to describe offenders under the age of 18, and therefore decided to defer making the proposed changes until it was clear what language would be used in forthcoming legislation.

When it happens, this change will affect the Overarching Principles guideline and all three offence-specific guidelines directed at defendants aged under 18, which, it is anticipated, will become:

- 'Bladed Articles and Offensive Weapons (Having in Public/Education Premises and Threats) – Sentencing Children'
- 'Robbery – Sentencing Children'
- 'Sexual Offences- Sentencing Children

H2 Allocation and Sending Proceedings

H2.4 'Grave Crimes'

H2.4.1 Plea before venue

A failure to follow the plea before venue procedure under the MCA 1980, s. 24A does not affect the jurisdiction of the youth court to try indictable offences: *R (BH) v Norwich Youth Court* [2023] EWHC 25 (Admin).

H2.9 Youth charged jointly with an adult

H2.9.4 Interests of justice

The Sentencing Council has amended para. 2.12 of the *Sentencing Children and Young People - Overarching Principles* definitive guideline to add a seventh factor to consider when deciding whether it is in the interests of justice to send a child or young person to the Crown Court with an adult co-defendant rather than having their trial in the youth court:

> the likely waiting time in trying the youth in the Crown Court as compared to the youth court.

This replicates and replaces the guidance given by William Davis J, then Judicial Lead for Youth Justice, in July 2020.

H4 Bail Refused

H4.3 Conditions on remand to local authority accommodation

The imposition of an electronically-monitored curfew as a condition attached to a remand to local authority accommodation does not count towards time served on a subsequent custodial sentence, even if the curfew is for nine hours or more. A sentencing court should, however, always have regard to any such curfew in determining the length of a custodial sentence: *R v Shotayo* [2024] EWCA Crim 596; *R v ADE* [2024] EWCA Crim 350.

H11 Reporting Restrictions in Other Criminal Courts

H11.2 Judicial guidance

The court may vary or remove a s. 45 reporting restriction by means of an exception direction if satisfied it is necessary and in the interests of justice so to do (s.45(4)) or if satisfied that the reporting restriction imposes a substantial and unreasonable restriction on the reporting of proceedings and it is in the public interest to remove or relax the restriction (s.45(5)).

The relevant principles are summarized in *R v KL* [2021] EWCA Crim 200; [2021] 2 Cr.App.R.4. The removal of a reporting restriction for a child or young person should be rare because very great weight must be given by the court to their welfare. However, this will not always trump other considerations, particularly open justice. The decision for a trial judge is case specific.

Any party seeking an excepting direction should make their application as soon as reasonably practicable: BSW v The Crown Court at Birmingham [2024] EWHC 3308 (Admin). Fairness requires the court to afford sufficient time to the offender and the youth offending team/youth justice service to address any application. The court will need to consider the impact of lifting a reporting restriction not only on the child or young person but also on parents, siblings and other members of the family. The court should consider whether there will be a negative impact on the prospects of rehabilitation for the young defendant.

I2 Effective Participation

I2.1 Introduction

The Court of Appeal in *R v ZA* [2023] EWCA Crim 596 emphasized that sentencing children in the Crown Court requires an entirely different approach to that used when sentencing adults. The Court proposed the following checklist:

(1) Court listing should ensure that there is sufficient time for the judge, even if that judge heard the trial and knows the case well, to read and consider all reports and to prepare sentencing remarks in age-appropriate language.
(2) Consideration should be given to listing separately, and as a priority, the sentence of any child(ren) or young person(s) jointly convicted with adult co-defendants.
(3) The courtroom should be set up and arranged to ensure that the child or young

person to be sentenced is treated appropriately, namely as a vulnerable defendant entitled to proper support. So far as possible the judge should be seated on a level with the child or young person, and the latter should be able to sit near to counsel, with parental or other support seated next to them (see further below).

(4) Counsel must expect to submit full sentencing notes identifying all relevant Sentencing Council Guidelines, in particular any youth-specific guideline(s), addressing material considerations in an individualistic way for each defendant separately (if more than one young defendant is to be sentenced). Where an individualistic approach is mandated, as it is for a child or young person, a note which addresses all defendants compendiously risks missing important distinctions. These notes should be uploaded well in advance of the sentencing hearing.

(5) The contents of the Youth Justice Service pre-sentence report and any medical/psychiatric/psychological reports will be key. Courts should consider these reports bearing in mind the general principles at section 1 of the overarching youth guideline, together with any youth-specific offence guideline, carefully working through each.

(6) In general it will not be helpful to go straight to paragraph 6.46 of the overarching youth guideline without having first directed the court to general principles canvassed earlier in that guideline, as well as to any youth-specific guideline. The stepped approach in the overarching youth guideline and any youth-specific offence guideline should be followed. Working through the guideline(s) in this way will enable the court to arrive at the most appropriate sentence for the particular child or young person, bearing in mind their individual circumstances together with the dual aims of youth sentencing.

(7) If the court considers that the offence(s) is(are) so serious as to pass the custody threshold, the court must consider whether a YRO with intensive supervision and surveillance (ISS) can be imposed instead. If it cannot, then the court must explain why.

J5 Detention and Training Order

J5.2 Custody threshold

J5.2.3 Consecutive orders

The court may order a DTO to run consecutively to a sentence of long-term detention or to a special sentence of detention for terrorist offenders of particular concern, as long as the offender is already subject to such a sentence and has not already been released on licence. The court may not impose a DTO consecutive to such a sentence of detention on the same occasion: *R v Kovalkov* [2023] EWCA Crim 1509; [2024] 1 Cr.App.R.(S) 47.

J5.6 Placement and release from detention

Section 241(5) of the SC places no restriction or limitation on the power of the youth court to order late release from a DTO, other than the requirements that the order has to be made on an application by the Secretary of State for that purpose and that the order has to delay release by either one month or two months. The youth court therefore has an unfettered discretion to make an order for late release, which is not restricted to cases of exceptionally poor progress in custody. Nor does non-statutory guidance issued by the Youth Justice Board place any fetter on the youth court's discretion: *R (X) v Ealing Youth Court* [2020] EWHC 800 (Admin).

K1 Routes to Trial on Indictment

K1.1 Remittal for trial

Section 46ZA(3) of the Senior Courts Act 1981 applies only to an offence that is triable either way. This distinction is irrelevant to a defendant under 18 as the youth court (unlike the adult magistrates' court) is able to try indictable-only offences. It may be sensible to read s.46ZA(3)(a) more widely in relation to defendants under 18 so that, in relation to all offences, the Crown Court may not exercise its power to remit for trial unless the person appears in court or consents to the power of remittal being exercised in their absence.

K4 Sentences Available to Crown Court

K4.2 Long-term detention under section 250

K4.2.10 Interaction with detention and training order

The court may order a sentence of long-term detention to run consecutively to a DTO as long as the offender is already subject to such a sentence. The court may not impose a sentence of long-term detention consecutive to a DTO on the same occasion: *R v Kovalkov* [2023] EWCA Crim 1509; [2024] 1 Cr.App.R.(S) 47.

K5 Appeal Cases

K5.3 Powers on appeal

Section 48(4) of the Senior Courts Act 1981 allows the Crown Court to order a more severe punishment on appeal but the power is limited to any punishment that the magistrates' court might have awarded. This limitation means that, where an appellant would satisfy the compulsory referral order conditions, the Crown Court on appeal is limited to a discharge, referral order or detention and training order.

L6 Sentence

L6.6 Sentencing an adult for offences committed as a child

In *R v Ahmed*; *R v Stansfield*; *R v Priestley*; *R v RW*; *R v Hodgkinson* [2023] EWCA Crim 281, the Court of Appeal set out the correct approach to take when sentencing adults for offences committed as children:

(i) Whatever may be the offender's age at the time of conviction and sentence, the Children guideline is relevant and must be followed unless the court is satisfied that it would be contrary to the interests of justice to do so.

(ii) The court must have regard to (though is not necessarily restricted by: see (v) below) the maximum sentence which was available in the case of the offender at or shortly after the time of his offending. Depending on the nature of the offending and the age of the offender, that maximum may be (a) the same as would have applied to an adult offender; (b) limited by statutory provisions setting a different maximum for an offender who had not attained a particular age; or (c) limited by statutory provisions restricting the availability of different types or lengths of custodial sentence according to the age of the offender.

(iii) the court must take as its starting point the sentence which it considers was likely to have been imposed if the child offender had been sentenced shortly after the offence.

(iv) If in all the circumstances of the case the child offender could not in law have been sentenced (at the time of his offending) to any form of custody, then no custodial sentence may be imposed.

(v) Where some form of custody was available, the court is not necessarily bound by the maximum applicable to the child offender. The court should, however, only exceed that maximum where there is good reason to do so. In this regard, the mere fact that the offender has now attained adulthood is not in itself a good reason. We would add that we find it very difficult to think of circumstances in which a good reason could properly be found …

(vi) The starting point taken in accordance with (iii) above will not necessarily be the end point. Subsequent events may enable the court to be sure that the culpability of the child offender was higher, or lower, than would likely have been apparent at the time of the offending. They may show that an offence was not, as it might have seemed at the time, an isolated lapse by a child, but rather a part of a continuing course of conduct. The passage of time may enable the court to be sure that the harm caused by the offending was greater than would likely have been apparent at that time. Because the court is sentencing an adult, it must have regard to the purposes of sentencing set out in section 57 of the Sentencing Code. In each case, the issue for the court to resolve will be whether there is good reason to impose on the adult a sentence more severe than he would have been likely to have received if he had been sentenced soon after the offence as a child.

Any court sentencing an adult for an offence committed as a child should also be referred to *R v Smith* [2024] EWCA Crim 1883.

Appendices

Appendix Y1

In May 2025, following consultation, the Sentencing Council confirmed that it would change references in all guidelines concerned with sentencing defendants aged under 18 to use the term 'children' rather than 'children and young people'. However, the Council noted that the draft legislation then before Parliament used various different terms to describe offenders under the age of 18, and therefore decided to defer making the proposed changes until it was clear what language would be used in forthcoming legislation.

When it happens, this change will affect the Overarching Principles guideline and all three offence-specific guidelines directed at defendants aged under 18.

The definitive guideline is anticipated to become '*Sentencing Children: Overarching Principles*'.

Appendix 5

Fine Bands

For the purpose of the offence guidelines, a fine is usually based on one of three bands (A, B or C). The selection of the relevant fine band, and the position of the individual offence within that band, is determined by the seriousness of the offence. In some cases fine bands D – F may be used even where the community or custody threshold have been passed.

Fine band	Starting point	Range
A	50% of relevant weekly income	25–75% of relevant weekly income
B	100% of relevant weekly income	75–125% of relevant weekly income
C	150% of relevant weekly income	125–175% of relevant weekly income
D	250% of relevant weekly income	200–300% of relevant weekly income
E	400% of relevant weekly income	300–500% of relevant weekly income
F	600% of relevant weekly income	500–700% of relevant weekly income

Maximum fines

A fine must not exceed the statutory limit. Where this is expressed in terms of a 'level', the maxima are:

1	£200
2	£500
3	£1000
4	£2500
5	Unlimited

Victim surcharges

Sentence	Adult/Company		Child	
	All before 16.6.22	All on or after 16.6.22	All on or before 16.6.22	All on or after 16.6.22
Conditional discharge	£22	£26	£17	£20
Fine	10% in range £34 to £190	40% to a maximum of £2000	£22	£26
YRO/Referral order	NA	NA	£22	£26
Community order	£95	£114	£22	£26
Suspended or immediate custodial sentence up to and including 6 months	£128	£154	£34	£41
Suspended or immediate custodial sentence of over 6 months	£156	£187	£34	£41

Sentencing Decision Flow Chart

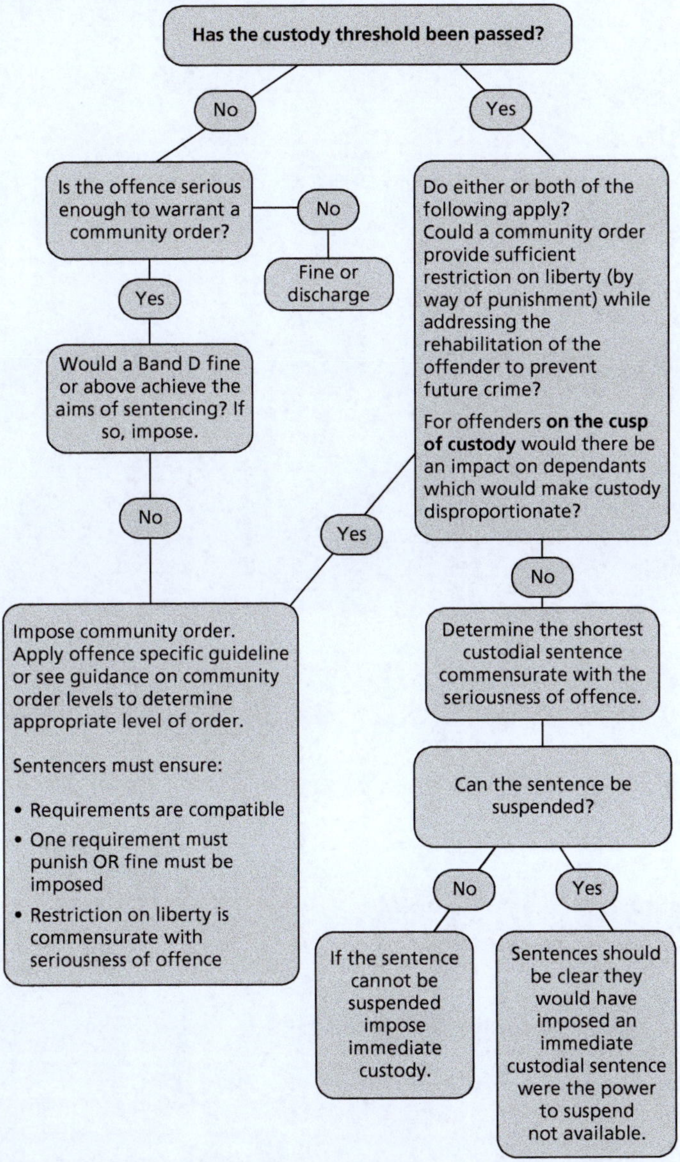

Figure 2 Sentencing decision flow chart

Index

Boxes are indicated by *b* following the page number